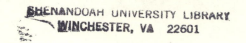

Beyond Mass Production

BEYOND MASS PRODUCTION

The Japanese System and Its Transfer to the U.S.

MARTIN KENNEY
RICHARD FLORIDA

New York   Oxford
OXFORD UNIVERSITY PRESS
1993

Oxford University Press

Oxford   New York   Toronto
Delhi   Bombay   Calcutta   Madras   Karachi
Kuala Lumpur   Singapore   Hong Kong   Tokyo
Nairobi   Dar es Salaam   Cape Town
Melbourne   Auckland   Madrid

and associated companies in
Berlin   Ibadan

Library of Congress Cataloging-in-Publication Data
Kenney, Martin.
Beyond mass production : the Japanese system and
its transfer to the U.S. /
Martin Kenney and Richard Florida.
p.   cm.   Includes bibliographical references and index.
ISBN 0-19-507110-7
1. Japan—Manufactures.   2. Industrial organization—Japan.
3. Industrial management—Japan.   4. Technology transfer—Japan.
5. Technology transfer—United States.   6. Investments, Japanese—United States.
I. Florida, Richard L.   II. Title.
HD9736.J32K46   1993   338.6′0952—dc20   91-36520

Printed in the United States of America
on acid-free paper

Acknowledgments

This is the authors' second book together. In both volumes, we have tried to develop new concepts and understanding of the new industrial revolution that is going on all around us. Our first book explored the U.S. response to this new industrial revolution. This one chronicles the rise of an entire model of production and industrial organization in Japan and the transfer and diffusion of that model to the United States. We are equally responsible for this work. The order of the names reflects our long-standing policy of rotating lead authorship.

We began the set of projects that led to *Beyond Mass Production* in 1986 as a study of the Honda automobile assembly complex in and around central Ohio. That small study soon mushroomed into a major research undertaking on the origins and development of the Japanese production system and its transfer to the United States in the manufacturing sectors of automobile assembly, automotive parts, steel, rubber and tires, electronics, and more. In the course of this research we visited dozens of plants; we interviewed hundreds of managers, executives, union officials, workers, and government representatives; we collaborated with various scholars, and we benefitted from the able assistance of dozens of graduate students and staff members. In any undertaking of this size and scope, significant debts are accumulated.

We would like to thank the Ohio Board of Regents, the U.S. Department of Agriculture's Economic Research Service, and the National Science Foundation (NSF) Division of Geography and Regional Science for providing the funds that made this research possible. David McGranahan of the Agriculture Department and Thomas Baerwald of NSF merit a special note of thanks for their comments and personal attention. Generous and patient funders are a precious asset indeed. Of course, the findings and conclusions presented here are entirely our own.

We both owe a major debt of gratitude to the Ritsumeikan Automotive Research Group of Akio Kida, Katsuji Tsuji, Bunji Murakami, Katsuo Nakagawa, and Terje Gronning for their collaboration on a series of interviews and case studies of automotive assembly transplants during the summer of 1990. Their help, criticisms, and counsel have made the chapters on automobile assembly, automotive parts, and the tensions and contradictions of the transplants immeasurably stronger.

We thank an extremely capable and stimulating group of students from Carnegie Mellon University, The University of California, Davis, and The Ohio State University, for their helpful comments, criticisms, and assistance: James Curry, W. Richard Goe, James Gordon, Andrew Mair, Maria Theresa Paterno, Dawn Rice, and Donald Smith. Without their assistance, this project would not have become a reality.

In addition, we owe an intellectual debt to the following individuals who have commented on the whole or specific parts of this work, and in doing so have helped us sharpen our analysis and arguments: Nicole Biggart, Harvey Brooks, Gordon Clark, Wesley Cohen, Robert Cole, Marshall Feldman, Akihisa Fujita, Norman Glickman, Gary Hamilton, Ken-ichi Imai, Kozo Inoue, Raymond Jussaume, Tetsuro Kato, Linda Lobao, Ruth Milkman, Richard Nelson, Hikari Nohara, Ikujiro Nonaka, Charles Perrow, John Singleton, Dale Squires, Shoko Tanaka, Tsuyoshi Tsuru, Richard Walker, and Seiichiro Yonekura. Thanks are also due Herb Addison, Mary Sutherland, and Dolores Oetting of Oxford University Press for their attention, assistance, and support.

Special gratitude must be extended to the hundreds of Japanese and American executives, managers, engineers, and workers in the automobile, automobile parts, rubber, steel, biotechnology, chemical, electronics, and software industries who answered our questions in interviews of one, two, and sometimes three or more hours in length. We also must thank the dozens of union officials, state, county and local officials, and community leaders who also participated in our interviews. And we thank the hundreds of individuals who took valuable time from their schedules to fill out our survey questionnaires. It is hoped that the information and analysis presented in this book adequately reflect and justify their time and energy.

Martin Kenney would like to thank the California Policy Seminar for the funding that made the research on the Japanese electronics industry possible. He would also like to thank the Institute of Business Research of Hitotsubashi University for kindly providing the funding and support that made the research on the Japanese software industry possible.

Richard Florida would like to thank the Center for Economic Development at Carnegie Mellon for helping to fund the research on Japanese involvement in the U.S. steel industry. He acknowledges Ben Fisher of Carnegie Mellon University, and Charles Butler of the Japan Steel Information Center for their help with various aspects on the steel industry portion of the study. He would also like to thank his colleagues at Carnegie Mellon's H. John Heinz III School of Public Policy and Management and the Department of Engineering and Public Policy, especially Al Blumstein, Robert Gleeson, Granger Morgan, and Joel Tarr, for providing a stimulating environment in which to work. He acknowledges the extremely capable present and former students at Carnegie Mellon and Ohio State who have contributed to this research effort over the years. Special debts of gratitude are owed Karen Dunkleberger for typing most of the tables and Mary Joyce Airgood for transcribing hundreds of pages of interview tapes. He would like to thank Akio Kida personally for an enlightening nine-month collaboration in 1990–91 including joint research trips to a dozen or more transplant factories. Most of all, his deepest thanks go to his wife, Joyce Florida, for her intellectual companionship and support.

Finally, we both acknowledge the many and often neglected contributions made by our friends and families.

Contents

Beyond Mass Production

Nature builds no machines, no locomotives, railways, electric tele-
graphs, self-acting mules, etc. These are the products of human
industry. . . . They are organs of the human brain, created by the
human hand; the power of knowledge, objectified. The development of fixed capital indicates to what degree general social knowledge has become a direct force of production.

Karl Marx, *The Grundrisse,*
p. 706.

A company will get nowhere if all the thinking is left to management. Everybody in the company must contribute and for the lower
level employees their contribution must be more than just manual
labor. We insist that all our employees contribute their minds.

Akio Morita, former Chairman of Sony,
Made in Japan
(New York, Penguin, 1986), p. 165.

1

Introduction

Two steel mills sit barely an hour apart in the heart of America's industrial rustbelt. The first is a sprawling, old, rusted mass of buildings, pipes, wires, dirt, and sheds. Inside, thousands of workers covered in sweat and grime toil over aging steel furnaces, turning molten metal into steel slabs. There is a distinct hierarchy here; each worker does his or her own job with its own rate of pay, which is codified into a legalistic system of literally hundreds of separate job classifications. Managers and supervisors in shirts and ties stand watch over the workers, who perform the actual physical labor. Strewn everywhere across the muddied dirt floor are old wires, chemical containers, tools, and all sorts of debris. The noise level is so deafening that some of the workers wear protective ear coverings. The steel moves slowly by overhead crane, or at times on aging trucks, across the huge complex to be processed into steel sheets and coils. Outside, rusted steel slabs and coils are piled everywhere; beside them rest broken-down machines, trucks, and industrial vehicles.

The second mill is a gleaming white building reminiscent of the futuristic industrial parks of Silicon Valley. Inside are brightly colored machines, day-glo–colored guardrails, and a brightly polished concrete floor. Gleaming sheets of steel zip through the machinery, like sheets of paper through a paper mill. At the center of the process stands a large glass-enclosed booth housing computers, digital readouts, and electronic gauges and controls. Workers, managers, and engineers in the same dark uniforms oversee the process, but do not actually handle the steel. The workers themselves monitor, modify, and program the computers that guide the steelmaking process. Some even carry mobile computer packs so they can control the process from anywhere within the plant. They do so with assistance from, but not the interference of, managers and engineers. These workers, engineers, and supervisors are constantly discussing new ways to improve the process and make it more efficient. Strikingly, there are no time clocks or time cards in this factory; everyone here draws a monthly salary. This steel mill produces cold-rolled steel in less than an hour from start to finish; it used to take as long as 12 days for the same process.

The first factory is owned and operated by a U.S. business, and the other is a joint venture between a Japanese steel company and an American one. This book attempts to explain how such a contrast could exist. It provides a theoretical and historical analysis of the Japanese production system and examines the transfer of that system to the United States. We argue that Japan is at the center of an epoch-making new model of technology, work, and production organization that is now being transferred to the United States and elsewhere around the globe. The key to the new model lies in organizational forms and practices—work teams, rotation, and workers' involvement—which when taken together effectively function to harness the intelligence as well as the physical labor of workers. We see this new model as involving a synthesis of innovation and production and thus refer to it as "innovation-mediated production." This revolutionary method of organizing production integrates the knowledge and intelligence of a far wider spectrum of workers, from R&D (research and development) scientists and engineers who create new technologies and product ideas to shop-floor workers who turn those innovations into products. It blurs the boundaries between innovation and production, emphasizes continuous improvement in manufacturing processes, and, most significantly, results in a powerful synthesis of intellectual and physical labor. This is a major advance over traditional fordist mass production, which was based simply on squeezing physical labor out of workers. By applying intelligence to mass production, this new model has transformed forever the way work is done, even in the United States—the home of the old Taylor–Ford model of scientific management and assembly-line mass production.

Japanese Transplants in the United States

Over the past two or three decades, entire segments of American mass-production industry declined; cities and entire regions bore the brunt of devastating deindustrialization, and millions of workers lost their livelihoods and homes. For most students of economic change, the prognosis was bleak—the United States would face long-term deindustrialization, and rustbelt industry would become a relic of the past. But in the very face of all of this, a startling turnaround emerged. Armed with a new model of production organization, Japan's leading industrial corporations are transplanting a modern manufacturing infrastructure into the U.S. industrial heartland—right beside the one abandoned by American companies.[1]

During the 1980s and continuing into the 1990s, 1,275 Japanese "transplants" established manufacturing operations in the United States.[2] There are now 8 Japanese automotive assembly transplants (3 more are in Canada near the U.S. border), more than 320 Japanese-owned or Japanese-American joint venture automotive suppliers in the United States, 72 Japanese-owned or Japanese-American joint ventures in steel (roughly a dozen larger integrated steel mills, mini-mills or steel coating lines, the remainder being smaller steel processors and steel service centers), and 21 Japanese-owned rubber and tire plants.[3] A large share of these transplants are in heavy industry—the industry that experienced widespread deindustrialization, decapitalization, and disinvestment under U.S. fordism.[4] Since 1987, for example, some 32 Big Three auto plants have closed.[5] Figure 1.1 shows the heavy concentration of automobile assembly, automobile parts, steel, and rubber and tire transplants in and around the industrial heartland—in a region we term the "transplant corridor."[6]

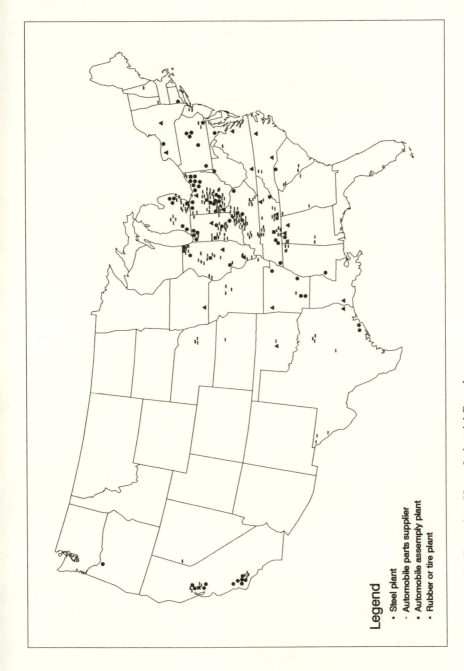

Legend

- Steel plant
- Automobile parts supplier
- Automobile assembly plant
- Rubber or tire plant

FIGURE 1.1. The Transplant Heavy Industrial Complex.
Source: Authors' database.

The automobile industry has been the catalyst for the wave of Japanese investment in American heavy industry. Automotive transplants include a large Honda
assembly and manufacturing complex in central Ohio; Nissan's plant in Smyrna,
Tennessee; the NUMMI joint venture between General Motors (GM) and Toyota
in Fremont, California; a large Toyota assembly complex in Georgetown, Kentucky; a Mazda assembly plant on the grounds of an old engine and transmission
foundry outside Detroit; Diamond Star, which began as a joint venture between
Mitsubishi and Chrysler plant in Illinois, but which is now wholly owned by Mitsubishi; SIA, a joint venture between Subaru-Isuzu in Indiana; and a new Ford-
Nissan joint venture in northeastern Ohio. These transplant assembly plants have
been complemented by hundreds of transplant parts suppliers who have chosen to
locate in close proximity to them.

Japanese steelmakers have followed automakers to the United States, in large
part to tap the growing demand for high-quality steel generated by the automotive
transplants. Japanese involvement in the American Steel industry has come in
three forms: joint ventures with U.S. corporations in large integrated production
facilities, new galvanizing and coating lines that serve the automotive transplants
(galvanizing is a technology that Japanese steelmakers have refined far beyond U.S.
firms), and solely owned steel-processing facilities and steel service centers. Japan's
major steel corporations—Nippon Steel, NKK, Kobe Steel, Kawasaki Steel, and
Sumitomo Metal—all operate U.S. plants. NKK is working to revitalize old
National Steel mills near Detroit, Chicago, and St. Louis. Kobe Steel has brought
new technology and new production organization to an old U.S. Steel plant in
Lorain, Ohio. Kawasaki Steel is working with Armco to refurbish two of Armco's
old Midwestern steel mills. Nippon Steel, Sumitomo Metal, and Nisshin Steel are
bringing to America state-of-the-art steel galvanizing lines that coat and prepare
steel for automotive and other uses.

Japanese corporations have also invested heavily in American rubber and tire
production, mainly through direct buy-outs and acquisitions of U.S. companies. In
1983, Bridgestone, Japan's largest rubber and tire producer, purchased a Firestone
plant in Tennessee, and in 1988 it purchased all of Firestone Corp. for $2.6 billion.
In 1986, Sumitomo Rubber bought Dunlop's entire U.S. tire operations for $350
million and has since spent more than $200 million turning them into state-of-the-
art factories. Yokohama Rubber has recently purchased Mohawk Rubber. Toyo
Tire is involved in a joint venture with both Yokohama and German tiremaker,
Continental. Today, four of Japan's five major rubber and tire companies have U.S.
factories.

Japanese manufacturing investment in the United States is not simply confined
to mature "sunset" industries; Japanese multinationals are also rapidly extending
their investments into U.S. high technology. This has come in various forms: direct
investment in electronics factories; alliances, mergers, and acquisitions of existing
U.S. high-technology firms; and financial investments in U.S. venture capital
funds. Nearly all major Japanese electronics companies operate television, semiconductor, telecommunications, and computer manufacturing facilities in the
United States. A growing number of them are building new product-development
centers and advanced R&D labs in the United States to bolster their technological
capability and to support U.S.-based manufacturing activities.

Large Japanese firms in both high-technology and traditional industries have pursued an aggressive policy of alliance building with fledgling U.S. startups. Japanese multinationals are pumping capital into U.S. microelectronic, software, biotechnology, and superconductor firms in return for privileged access to the cutting-edge technology these American companies develop. Japanese companies in traditional heavy industries, such as steel, view these technologies as part of an effort to create a "new iron age" that will use high-technology microelectronics and software to transform steelmaking into a revolutionary continuous process.[7] Between 1983 and 1989, Japanese corporations invested more than $882 million in 217 U.S. enterpreneurial startup companies and another $224 million in American venture capital funds directly.[8] For example, Steven Jobs' company, Next, sold 16 percent of its shares to the Canon Corporation of Japan for $100 million.

Transfer of the Japanese System

The phenomenon of Japanese industrial transplants in the United States raises two basic issues: the first concerns the process of organizational transfer or transplant itself, and the second revolves around the deeper question of the generalizability of the Japanese production system and the new model of innovation-mediated production that it reflects.

Ever since the 1950s, there has been a persistent tendency among scholars to explain Japanese industrial and production organization as the product of unique social and cultural attributes. Early theories explained the Japanese production system in terms of cultural stereotypes such as homogeneity, obedience, groupism, paternalism, and Japan, Inc.[9] These were seen to promote a close alignment among individuals and groups or organizations. In a now classic formulation, the British sociologist Ronald Dore contrasted the Japanese system of "welfare corporatism" with the Anglo-American model of "market individualism."[10] In the late 1970s, the management literature advanced the argument that the Japanese system was little more than a set of techniques that could be copied by traditional U.S. firms.[11] More recent work in the neo-Marxist tradition conceptualizes the Japanese model in terms of the "hegemonic despotism" of Japanese firms and the super-exploitation of Japanese workers.[12] Mike Parker and Jane Slaughter advance the concept of "management-by-stress," arguing that the key to the Japanese model lies in a fast work pace and the self-discipline imposed by work teams.[13] Interestingly, while both the culturalist and neo-Marxist perspectives see the Japanese model as a product of unique social and cultural climate and/or economic factors, and thus imply that it cannot be transferred to other nations, the managerialist perspective reduces it to a simple set of "cookbook" techniques that can be replicated in piecemeal fashion.

More recent formulations see the Japanese system as comprising a unique model. Kurt Hoffman and Raphael Kaplinsky advance the concept of "systemofacture" to describe the restructuring of the labor process and supplier relations in the Japanese manufacturing industry.[14] Several scholars associated with the MIT International Motor Vehicle Program suggest that Japanese organizational practices constitute a new model of "lean production" toward which companies all over the world are converging. The defining features of so-called lean production include efficient use of resources, low inventories, and just-in-time production and delivery practices.[15] Of course the Japanese production system is efficient. The real question is why—what underlying organizational, institutional, and behavioral factors make it efficient. This is the question this book tries to answer.

In examining the transfer of the Japanese system to the United States, we confront questions similar to those advanced by the Italian social theorist, Antonio Gramsci, in his classic essay "Americanism and Fordism."[16] Gramsci was concerned with the impact of American production methods and American culture on Europe in the period immediately following World War I. Gramsci posed this question: Were the changes occurring at the point of production the beginnings of a new historical epoch? From this, two additional questions followed. First, could the then new model of U.S. fordism be transferred to Europe? And second, to what extent was the fordist model bound up with a set of social and cultural practices Gramsci referred to as "Americanism"? Gramsci answered that the new model of fordism was the most advanced system of production organization of its time and that as such it would surely diffuse to Europe over time. He further argued that there was not a necessary or determinant relationship between fordism and American culture. Fordism represented certain organizational practices constructed at the factory level; these practices were not dependent upon Americanism and thus would eventually be transferred to Europe.

The findings of our research—based upon site visits to dozens of firms, personal interviews with hundreds of company officials and factory workers, and detailed survey research—provide ample evidence that in the old fordist industries the Japanese transplants are successfully transferring the basic elements of the Japanese production system to the United States. The Japanese system, along with the underlying model of innovation-mediated production upon which it is based—like the fordist mass-production model before it—consists of organizational practices whose fundamental "genetic code" can be successfully inserted into another society and can then begin to successfully reproduce in the new environment. In this sense, the system is independent of Japanese culture and society.

This transfer is neither natural nor automatic, but rather is the result of the concerted actions and strategies undertaken by large Japanese corporations to implant their new model of production organization in a nonsupportive U.S. environment with its long legacy of fordist practices. Where the Japanese companies did not actively try to implement the innovation-mediated production system such as in electronics, the existing situation is far closer to that of their U.S. competitors. Generally speaking, we advance the argument that the Japanese system of production organization is a set of interactive organizational practices that are transferable to foreign environments.[17]

Beyond Fordism?

This brings us to an even more fundamental issue—the extent to which the Japanese model can play a role as a general model for industrial organization and as such function as a successor model to fordism. Our research informs a view that differs and goes beyond contemporary theories of Japanese production and industrial organization.[18] The underlying conceptual premise of this book is that Japan is at the cusp of a new model of production organization that mobilizes workers' intelligence as well as physical skill. This new mode of production organization extends across all facets of the innovation-production spectrum, harnessing the intelligence and knowledge of both R&D scientists and engineers and factory workers. It is organized through the use of teams and other organizational techniques that explicitly harness workers' knowledge at the point of production. As such, the new model has transformed ordinary workers' knowledge and intelligence into a source of value, created new methods of work, and established a very efficient system for turning the potential value embodied in innovations into mass-produced commodities that are the source of tremendous profit and capital accumulation. This system of innovation-mediated production harnesses the worker more totally and completely than did previous institutional and organizational arrangements.

We thus see this new model as a fundamental supercession and potential successor to mass-production fordism. Indeed, its rise is in many respects more sweeping than the growth of fordist mass production during the industrial revolution of the late nineteenth century, when the rise of the factory system, scientific management, and the moving assembly line enabled industrial capitalists to more efficiently harness physical labor from huge masses of relatively unskilled shop-floor workers.[19] This theoretical premise allows us to tackle the question of the transfer of the Japanese production system in terms of the broader question of the generalizability of innovation-mediated production as a successor to fordist production organization.

This leads to a related question: Is Japan postfordist?[20] There are really two answers—depending upon how the term "postfordist" is interpreted. The answer is yes, if postfordist is simply used to refer to a new model that comes "after" fordism. It is no, however, if postfordist is used strictly to imply a direct progression from and a strong genealogical link to fordism.

Clearly, Japanese industry benefitted from contact with and learning from U.S. fordism. It is well known that U.S. quality-control experts such as Deming and Juran were accepted, even hailed, in Japan. Further, as even popular books such as David Halberstam's *The Reckoning*[21] have made widely known, Japanese managers and others visited U.S. factories en masse and returned to Japan with a variety of ideas. Certainly some of the technical aspects of production in Japanese factories were fordist—for example, the moving assembly line and the implementation of statistical quality-control techniques among other things. But, the organizational context into which these seeds were planted was sufficiently different from that of U.S. or even Western European production organization. Facing deep industrial conflicts and a unique constellation of management-labor relations, Japanese industry embarked on an evolutionary path that was markedly different from Western fordism quite early on. The social relations of production were based on social contract between capital and labor that differed markedly from those in Western countries. For these reasons, it is difficult to consider the organization of work and production in immediate postwar Japan as fordist.

It is important to point out here that we are principally concerned with developing an objective theory of the Japanese production system and of the new stage of capitalism which it reflects. We do not consider the normative question of whether this model is "better" or "worse" than fordism or other Western economic arrangements. However, it is clear that the Japanese production system and the Japanese transplants in the U.S. are beset by various tensions and contradictions. Japanese scholars and critics of the Japanese industrial system have long noted the problematic features of the Japanese production system. Long hours and high stress are defining features of Japanese manufacturing. Workers in Japanese industry average more than 2,000 working hours annually, roughly 200 to 500 hours more than their counterparts in the United States and Europe.[23] Life on the Japanese assembly line is stressful, difficult, and at times even unhealthy.[24] A 1986 survey by the All Toyota Union found that approximately 124,000 of its 200,000 members suffer from chronic fatigue.[25] In Japan, a major social issue is *karoshi,* or death from overwork.[26]

As many have noted, the positive aspects of the Japanese production system—high wages, secure employment, and long-term tenure—accrue mainly to male, permanent employees of large companies who comprise roughly one-third of the labor force. Fundamentally linked with this "core" of the Japanese labor force is an extensive periphery of lower-paid, part-time, and temporary workers, especially women, who work for suppliers, subcontractors, and small firms and who do not benefit from the conditions afforded core workers. Both Japan and Japanese industry continue to suffer from serious problems of racism, sexism, conformity, and exploitation. Of course, some aspects of workers' standards of living, especially housing, are lower than in the advanced Western industrialized nations.

Theories of Industrial Change and Restructuring

In this book we consider the Japanese production system and its transfer to the United States in light of the more general debate over new models of production and industrial organization. Our conceptualization builds from and goes beyond a variety of contemporary theories of industrial and technological change, organizational transformation, and political-economic restructuring. Over the past decade or so there has been an outpouring of theory and speculation over the issue of what comes next: What are the new technological, social, and organizational forms that might replace fordist mass production? Theorists have advanced various alternative models of the next stage of capitalism. While the debate has taken different forms in different places, the core issues are strikingly similar. There is broad concern for the rise of new organizational forms, much of which has been stimulated by the decline and transformation of twentieth-century fordist industrial capitalism. Moreover, there is a general awareness of and concern for the rise of new technologies as reflected in the outpouring of writing on high-technology industry, postindustrialism, the information economy, and postfordism.

Long-Wave Theories

The first of these theories is the renewed interest in the long-wave perspectives that grew up almost simultaneously within the Marxian, Schumpeterian, and mainstream traditions in the mid- to late 1970s. The long-wave perspective basically contends that capitalism can be divided into a series of stages or historical periods that differ on the basis of underlying technological conditions, organizational forms, and so on.[27] This includes the work of Ernst Mandel on the Continent,[28] Christopher Freeman and the Science Policy Research Unit of Sussex University (SPRU) school in Great Britain,[29] and the "social structure of accumulation" perspective in the United States.[30] Adherents of the SPRU school—most notably Christopher Freeman and Carlotta Perez—emphasize the relationship between technology and social structure, conceptualizing this in terms of "techno-economic paradigms."[31] These authors suggest that the existing mode of technological-economic organization is in the throes of decline and change because existing institutional and organizational forms are ill-suited to support new technologies. They in turn suggest that advanced industrial societies are entering a new techno-economic paradigm based upon information technologies. Following Schumpeter, both Freeman and Perez place great emphasis on technology effects and the adaptive responses in social and economic structures.

Postindustrialism

As early as the 1960s, sociologists in the United States, Europe, and Japan began to argue that the United States was moving from an industrial society to one based on postindustrial information and service industries. According to this view, capitalism was evolving toward a postindustrial white-collar world where manufacturing would be replaced by automation. In Daniel Bell's conceptualization, the industrial working class would shrink and be replaced by a growing white-collar meritocracy.[32] In contemporary versions of the postindustrial thesis, Fred Block and Larry Hirschhorn contend that services and automated manufacturing are coming to replace older manufacturing industries.[33]

The postindustrial position has important weaknesses. First, there is no sustained analysis of what exactly constitutes a "service."[34] Indeed, not all services are created equal and not all services are services. According to the postindustrialists, only sweaty, physical labor in traditional heavy industries qualifies as industrial activity. This is a very narrow definition. Is the woman who cooks hamburgers at McDonald's a service worker? She is performing an activity that physically transforms meat from an uncooked to a cooked state. There are some rather basic similarities between her work and that of a steelworker who transforms iron ore into steel. Is a software programmer a service worker? The programmer produces a product that actually performs work—it totals numbers, runs machine tools, etc. How different is this software worker from a machinist who, by using his physical strength and knowledge of metal, essentially instructs a machine tool in metal cuts?[35]

The entire postindustrial position rests on the belief that the demise of the steel, automobile, and other heavy industries in the United States is co-terminus with the rise of a new postindustrial order. Yet the United States continues to have a manufacturing base. According to recent empirical studies, manufacturing continues to comprise roughly the same share of the American economy as it did in earlier times.[36] A semiconductor fabrication facility and a biotechnology fermentation plant are both industrial facilities; they are not postindustrial at all. Both cost money to build, employ operators, and actually produce things. According to Michael Cusumano, software production in Japan can and does take place in factories that on many dimensions are comparable to Japanese automobile factories.[37] Moreover, Japan and Germany, two of the most vibrant economies on earth, have strong manufacturing bases: How do they fit with the postindustrial thesis?

Indeed, recent research has found that so-called postindustrial technologies such as software and computerized automation are inextricably bound to manufacturing and actual factory production. According to recent research, computer automation is most successful in environments where workers are integrated into the production process and where continuous learning can occur.[38] In other words, effectiveness stems from an organizational context and concrete social relationships that can optimize the use of new technology, not from technology that simply displaces workers. These social relationships are critical for implementing higher and higher levels of technology.[39] And as we shall demonstrate, to be truly effective in the new environment, the factory is more—not less—important. Indeed, the laboratory and factory must be linked in a continuum of innovation and production.[40] In short, postindustrialists understand that intellectual activity will become ever more important, but they make the mistake of assuming that industrial production will disappear.

Flexible Specialization

Flexible specialization was originally put forward by the Italian economist Becattini and his students in Italy and later brought to the United States by Michael Piore and Charles Sabel.[41] Piore and Sabel basically argue that there is an historical tension between two basic modes of production organization: mass production and craft production. In their politically contingent model of development, which they call the "branching tree model," struggles among political groups (though not necessarily classes) determine which of these forms will predominate in a given historical epoch. Using this general theoretical framework, they contend that the past century or so of industrial history saw the political ascension of mass-production organization over craft production. However, the current period of decline of mass production opens up a renewed era of indeterminacy and choice, when a new form of craft production or flexible specialization becomes politically possible. The ideal-typical model of flexible specialization is the tightly networked firms of northern Italy, which are characterized by high degrees of cooperation and knowledge sharing, joint development, and joint involvement in production. They further argue that the seeds of this new form of production are already in place in many of the advanced industrial countries that have and continue to experiment with cooperative networks of small industrial firms. The flexible specialization model has been subject to stinging critiques on various theoretical and empirical grounds as scholars have questioned its underlying theoretical framework, the conceptual validity of the flexible specialization model, and whether this is a transitory phenomenon or simply a misreading of current trends.[42]

Still, both this and other works have stimulated an outpouring of research on the changing social division of labor in capitalism that integrates a wide range of disciplines and perspectives including the transaction-cost approach to economic organization pioneered by Oliver Williamson,[43] the "social embeddedness" theory of Mark Granovetter,[44] and Charles Sabel's[45] recent arguments regarding the role of trust in economic development. Interestingly, this work has influenced an intense debate over what are the most effective mechanisms for organizing the division of labor, including research on new forms of corporate organization[46] and inter-firm production networks.[47] These and other approaches share a common point of departure, for they contend that the future of capitalism can be best understood by looking at changes in the organization of the division of labor.

This theoretical and empirical preoccupation with the social division of labor inside and outside the firm and related organizational forms diverts attention from the more fundamental matter at hand: the restructuring that is going on at the point of production. To place the matter in perspective: It is akin to elevating the theory of industrial bureaucracy or the multidivisional, vertically integrated corporation[48] to the level of a theory of twentieth-century fordist industrial capitalism. Simply put, the debate over networks and flexible specialization as it is currently taking place revolves around important but nonetheless second-order phenomenon.

Regulation Theory

Perhaps the most significant current body of theory and research aimed at explicating the development of capitalist economies is the "regulation school" of political economy.[49] Going beyond the long-wave approach, but still operating within a world historical context, adherents of the regulation school focus on relationships between the technological base of production and consumption (or demand), which in their vocabulary constitute an abstract "regime of accumulation," and the concrete institutional fabric of society, which they refer to as the "mode of regulation." This perspective represents a melding of insights of Schumpeter and Keynes within a basic Marxian perspective that emphasizes the primacy of the forces and relations of production in outlining the parameters of social and economic structure.

There are a number of views from within regulation theory that focus on future pathways of industrialization. Perhaps the most common is that of neo-fordism.[50] As its name implies, the neo-fordist position suggests that the current period is not a break with the older model of fordism, but simply represents an extension and advance of that model. A variant of this, to which we will return later, is the "toyotism" model of Knuth Dohse and his colleagues.[51] The toyotism model suggests that Japanese capitalism has established a more efficient way of organizing production based upon the regrouping of tasks and a very fast workpace. Toyotism thus extends but does not break with fordist principles for the organization of mass production.[52]

A number of regulation theorists suggest that a new model of industrial organization is developing as a clear-cut break with fordism. Annemieke Roobeek suggests that the rise of new information technologies will increasingly disrupt fordist organization, thus resulting in the rise of a new postfordist order.[53] Although her analysis is somewhat vague, it suggests that microelectronics, biotechnology, and new materials technology are bringing about both increased productivity and the "de-materialization" of production, as for example, fiber optics replace copper wires and genetically engineered products replace traditional chemicals. This in turn requires new social institutions and organizational forms that are different from those of fordism. Benjamin Coriat argues that we are witnessing a melding of traditional mass production, automated robotics technologies, and flexibility.[54] Coriat's basic argument is that automated technologies—for example, numerically controlled machine tools, flexible manufacturing systems, and robotics—are fundamentally transforming industrial production, leading to a new model of "flexible mass production."

Our conceptualization builds from regulation theory and from elements of the other theories outlined above, as well as from detailed research and observation in actual factories and laboratories, to outline the contours of a new model of production organization that is emerging as a successor to mass-production fordism.

Innovation-Mediated Production: A New Model

The salient features of a new model of production organization are now visible across the landscape of global capitalism. They are increasingly evident in the sweeping transformation of production, innovation, and organization in the factory, in the R&D laboratory and in relations among and between firms. What we are witnessing is a fundamental realignment of the forces and relations of production that is opening up new possibilities for value creation, productivity improvement, capital accumulation, and economic growth.[55] This is in keeping with the nature of industrial progress to the present—the rise of textiles, steel, and automobile production technology as defining features of previous industrial epochs.

In our view, there are five basic dimensions to the new model: (1) a transition from physical skill and manual labor to intellectual capabilities or mental labor, (2) the increasing importance of social or collective intelligence as opposed to individual knowledge and skill, (3) an acceleration of the pace of technological innovation, (4) the increasing importance of continuous process improvement on the factory floor and constant revolutions in production, and (5) the blurring of the lines between the R&D lab and the factory. This new model can be conceptualized as one of *innovation-mediated production*—a concept we advance to refer to the integration of innovation and production, of intellectual and physical labor.

Innovation-mediated production should not be considered synonomous with the Japanese model. Just as the previous model of mass-production fordism could be seen as distinct from the United States, the new model of innovation-mediated production is distinct from Japan. And just as different regions, different firms, and different nations developed their own specific variants of fordism, so too it should be possible with innovation-mediated production. Simply put, innovation-mediated production is neither specific to Japan per se nor only possible in the Japanese context; rather, as Chapters 2 and 3 will show, historical conditions, struggles, conflicts, and structures specific to Japan caused it to crystalize there and become dominant.[56] However, we argue that Japan, like the United States before it, has gone the furthest toward generalizing the new model across the broad spectrum of its industrial structure and broader political economy. Japan—more than any other nation—has been able to institutionalize and generalize the new model at the very core of its industrial structure. The Japanese expression of innovation-mediated production thus comprises both the traditional heavy industries of automobile, steel, and rubber and the new high-technology industrial sectors of electronics and biotechnology.

The cornerstone of innovation-mediated production lies in the harnessing of workers' intelligence and knowledge of production. Here we conceptualize knowledge as a form of human creative capability and value-creating activity. This includes, for example, the knowledge embodied in software programs that image the labor process and "run" machines and the ability of shop-floor workers to modify and improve the production process. Our conceptualization of social or collective knowledge thus extends to both the abstract scientific and technical knowledge of R&D workers, which is embodied in innovations and salable commodities, and the knowledge of shop-floor workers, which provides a crucial source of shop-floor product and process improvements. This overcomes the traditional (and largely artificial) distinctions among science, technology, and factory production, and the related distinction between mental and manual labor.[57] In our view, these are different faces of the same general process of human creativity and value creation. In a word, value is created both on the factory floor and in the R&D laboratory. Innovation-mediated production integrates the knowledge and intelligence of all workers, from R&D scientists and engineers who create new technologies and product ideas, to shop-floor workers who turn those innovations into marketable products. It is thus a major advance over traditional mass production, which was based simply on pumping physical work out of workers and pumping plans and specifications out of researchers and engineers.

The new technologies and productive forces are increasingly digitized and cybernetic—that is, they are run by computer programs that encapsulate abstract intelligence. This contrasts with the practical or mechanical methods of fordist mass production that both promoted and were based upon de-skilling and an attendant separation of intellectual from manual labor both on the shop floor and between the factory and R&D laboratory. The new forces of production thus provide an additional impetus for the synthesis of intellectual and manual labor, as abstract mathematical reasoning is increasingly required of workers. Among all workers, narrow skills must be accompanied by broad knowledge and an ability to understand and think abstractly and to continually grasp new concepts.

At the organizational level, the new model revolves around the blurring of the lines between "production" and "innovation." We refer to this reorganization as the *new shop floor*—by which is meant the easing of the distinctions between the factory floor and the R&D lab, as innovation becomes more continuous and the factory itself becomes a laboratory-like setting. The underlying organizational feature is the self-managing work team that enhances the *functional integration* of tasks. The new shop floor thus integrates formerly distinct types of work—for example, R&D and factory production, thus making the production process ever more social. In doing so, the organizational forms of the new shop floor mobilize and harness the collective intelligence of workers as a source of continuous improvement in products and processes, of increased productivity, and of value creation.

At the technological level, the new model is characterized by an increasing pace of innovation. Here, one need only note the incredible pace of progress in semiconductor electronics and computers where new products and technologies are revolutionized in a period of three or four years. This is a product partly of the wide open technological opportunity for upgrading and improving these technologies and partly of the intense capitalist competition in these sectors. In one of the most insightful examinations of contemporary capitalism, Tessa Morris-Suzuki advances the concept of "perpetual innovation" to explain the rapid and continuous nature of technological change that follows the shift from older mass-production industries to new information-intensive, microelectronic technologies and industries.[58]

Innovation-mediated production is distinguished by an emphasis on incremental improvement innovation as well as radical new breakthrough technology.[59] What matters is not only the ability to invent new products and technologies but also the ability constantly to upgrade and improve those products and manufacture them as efficiently as possible. Small, incremental improvements in products and processes accumulate into major advances. In industry after industry, Japanese firms, for example, have overtaken very advanced technological competitors by constantly upgrading and improving the features of the products that they offer. A salient example of this is the nearly constant new product releases of laptop computers with new and improved features: screens, hard drives, processors—all in smaller yet more powerful packages.

The output of innovation-mediated production—its products—are incredibly diverse. This is in sharp contrast to the highly standardized mass products of fordism. Products are constantly improved, customized, and revolutionized to tap into and indeed to open up new market spaces. This revolutionizing process provides an incredible mechanism for realizing the value and super-profits created by the process of innovation-mediated production. This in turn requires constant revolutions in the production process itself.

Of crucial importance here is the role of *continuous process improvement* on the factory floor. At bottom, all product improvements require process improvements. Furthermore, manufacturing and the point of production on the factory floor are the crucial sites for process improvements. There have no doubt been major process breakthroughs such as Ford's moving assembly line[60] or Taiichi Ohno's *kanban* system.[61] But even these provide only a short respite from competitors. To survive in capitalism it is necessary to adapt, refine, and improve manufacturing processes, while also developing new products. The factory itself and its workers are the arena for accomplishing continuous process improvement. Japanese firms see workers' involvement in continuous process improvement as the key to their productivity, and even have a word for it—*kaizen.* As a result, the production process under innovation-mediated production is dynamic and continuously becomes more efficient.

The ability to diffuse and integrate innovations throughout the industrial structure is another important element of the new model. In Japan, for example, both technological and organizational innovations diffuse readily through the industrial structure. Innovations in electronics and other advanced technology areas are quickly adopted in new industrial systems and processes, office products, and consumer goods. Moreover, there is a high level of organizational congruence and integration across the industrial structure—the transcendance of traditional industrial boundaries.

In short, under innovation-mediated production, the organization of production and the labor process are oriented toward harnessing the intellectual capabilities of workers. This is not to imply that the extraction of physical or manual labor at the point of production is no longer important; it simply suggests that intelligence and knowledge are more explicitly integrated into the production process. Simply put, what lies at the bottom of the new industrial revolution is a synthesis of intellectual and manual labor designed to mobilize and harness the knowledge and intellectual capabilities (in addition to the physical labor) of the entire strata of workers from the R&D lab to the factory floor. Far from being romantic or naive, this view recognizes quite explicitly that the new industrial revolution exploits the worker more completely and totally than before.

Outline of the Text

This book explores the emergence of innovation-mediated production in Japan and the diffusion of that model to the United States. Many scholars have chronicled the decline of the old system of mass production, and an increasing number have begun to identify various dimensions of the new order. Yet we still lack anything approaching a unified theory of this new stage of capitalism. Through an exploration of the development of Japanese industry in both the traditional heavy industries and the new high-technology sectors of microelectronics and biotechnology, Part I of the text develops the theoretical structure with which to understand the rise of innovation-mediated production in Japan.

Chapter 2 develops the main theoretical structure of the book, outlining the transition from fordism to innovation-mediated production in Japan. This chapter provides a theorized history of the Japanese model in light of changing economic conditions, state policy, and evolving conflicts between labor and capital. It focuses on the establishment of the unique Japanese "social contract" or "class accord" among capital, labor, and the state in the immediate postwar years that institutionalized many of the basic elements of the Japanese production system and laid the foundation and the constraints within which Japanese capitalism would develop.

Chapter 3 continues this historically grounded theoretical excursus by exploring the further development of innovation-mediated production in Japanese high-technology industry. It documents the ability of the Japanese model to incubate and foster high-technology industry within large, powerful corporations. This chapter also focuses on the role of knowledge-intensive production in Japanese high technology, the integration of innovation and production activities, and the development of industrial galaxies of small and medium-sized firms around large industrial corporations.

Part II turns to the transfer and diffusion of the Japanese expression of innovation-mediated production to the United States, exploring the issue of its generalizability. This section of the book confronts a series of basic conceptual questions of organizational theory and of the general relationship between organizations and culture. To answer these questions, we examine the transfer of the Japanese expression of innovation-mediated production to the United States in a series of key industrial sectors—automobiles, automotive parts, steel, rubber, and electronics.

Chapter 4 begins the empirical analysis of the Japanese transplants, exploring the Japanese automotive transplants—the linchpin of the Japanese heavy industrial transplant complex. It outlines the nature and extent of investment and the different strategies pursued by various auto assemblers. It focuses upon the transfer of the basic features of Japanese production and work organization: work teams, job rotation, long-term employment guarantees, *kaizen*, and quality-control circles among others. This provides evidence of the successful transfer of Japanese production organization to the United States. These data are used to counter the prevailing culturalist interpretation of Japan, suggesting instead that the Japanese model consists of a set of basic organizational practices that can be implanted in other societies.

Chapter 5 deepens our analysis by examining the relocation of Japanese automotive parts suppliers to the United States. This entails an examination of the transfer of work and production organization in these suppliers and of the transfer of Japanese subcontracting relations to the United States. The supplier transplants are far more numerous than the automobile assemblers and thus are planting the "seeds" of the Japanese model more widely across the United States. The basic finding is that the transplants have re-created a Japanese-style just-in-time subcontracting system in the United States. This further confirms the thesis that the Japanese production system is transferable.

Chapter 6 explores Japanese investment in the American steel industry. Ever since the early 1980s, Japanese steel manufacturers have made major investments in U.S. production. The steel investments are thus a major and vital cog in the Japanese heavy industrial manufacturing complex that is emerging in the United States. We also explore the transfer of Japanese production organization in the steel industry. Our findings here suggest that Japanese firms have had considerable success in transferring the Japanese model to U.S. transplant facilities. The basic conclusion of the chapter is that Japanese investment is resulting in both the successful transfer of the Japanese production system and a creeping takeover of the American steel industry.

Chapter 7 explores Japanese investment in the rubber, tires, and related industries, and the process of transferring the Japanese model in these industries. It documents the emergence of an integrated transplant industrial complex of automobile assembly, automotive parts, steel, rubber, and other basic industries. It explores the impact of this complex on jobs and employment and examines its underlying geographic and locational logic. This chapter also examines the question of whether Japanese firms are simply opening low-end branch plants or whether they are bringing higher-end, higher value activities to the United States; in particular, the chapter looks at domestic sourcing of key components and the establishment of product development and R&D facilities. In doing so, it contrasts Japanese-sponsored "reindustrialization" with the long legacy of deindustrialization and disinvestment under U.S. fordism. Finally, it provides a critical look at the current array of economic development policies being used to recruit transplant producers and new industry, suggesting a new model for policy intervention.

Chapter 8 focuses on Japanese investment in consumer and high-technology electronics—televisions, semiconductors, computers, and telecommunications. It examines trends in Japanese direct investment in plant and equipment via new investment and the purchase of U.S. facilities. This chapter explores the process of transferring both work and production organization and Japanese supplier relations in these sectors. The basic conclusion of this chapter is that the process of transfer has occurred differently in the electronics sector. Basically, the electronics transplants show greater evidence of "fitting in" to the American environment.

Chapter 9 looks at the tensions and contradictions of the transplants. It explores problems of injury, fast work pace, racial discrimination, and labor-management relations. But most importantly, it focuses on the new model of corporate control that the transplants and the Japanese model more generally use to motivate, indoctrinate, and control workers. Here we explore the origin, impact, and ramifications of corporate hegemony. This powerful system of corporate motivation and control, which is required to harness workers' energy and necessary for the very functioning of the new model of production, can create serious problems.

The concluding chapter reflects on the epochal changes in production and industrial organization that are sweeping the globe. We reexamine the general issue of the transfer of production systems in light of the dynamics of international economic competition and the requirements of capital accumulation. The actual and potential limits to transfer and diffusion of production systems—for example, the particular constellation of class forces, the ingrained legacy of past organizational practices, the nature of industrial unrest and class struggle, internal contradictions, etc.—are revisited. From there we turn to the question of a potential new international division of labor organized around and based upon the new model. Finally, we speculate on the potential emergence of a broader model of social and economic reproduction or mode of social organization in Japan that would establish the conditions for long-term, self-reinforcing growth. In doing so, we set out some basic propositions, concepts, and theoretical insights which, we believe, can help reframe the debate over the sea-change in production and industrial organization now occurring in the advanced industrial economies.

I

ORIGINS AND DEVELOPMENT OF THE SYSTEM

2

Beyond Fordism

An employee today is no longer a slave to machinery who is expected to repeat simple mechanical operations like Charlie Chaplin in the film *Modern Times*. He is no longer a beast of burden who works under the carrot-and-stick rule and sells his labor. After all, manual labor can be taken over by a machine or computer. Modern industry has to be brain intensive and so does the employee. Neither machinery nor animals can carry out brain intensive tasks.

Akio Morita, former chairman of Sony.[1]

There is little doubt that Japan has become a major force in the international economy, one that increasingly threatens and may have indeed already surpassed the technological and industrial hegemony of the United States. The postwar Japanese economic miracle remains unparalleled among the advanced industrial nations. Today, Japanese corporations number among the world's most important in sectors such as steel, automobiles, rubber and tires, consumer electronics, semiconductors and a growing array of high-technology industries.[2] The Japanese industrial system has proven to be clearly superior in "sunset" industries such as steel, textiles, and ship-building and in "mature" industries such as automobiles, consumer electronics, and machine tools; and it is proving itself to be a potent competitor in high-technology "sunrise" sectors such as semiconductors, telecommunications, computers, biotechnology, and more recently software and superconductivity. Japanese manufacturing companies like Toyota, Nissan, Honda, Nippon Steel, NKK, Bridgestone, Asahi Glass, NTT, Sony, Toshiba, Mitsubishi, Fujitsu, NEC, and Hitachi as well as the trading companies Mitsui, Mitsubishi, Marubeni, C. Itoh, Nissho Iwai, Sumitomo, and others number among the world's largest and most significant companies. Despite the tremendous growth and dynamism of the Japanese political economy, there is a noticeable lack of integrative theoretical work on the underlying dynamics of Japanese capitalism.

This chapter outlines such a theory by exploring the origins, historical determinants, and evolution of innovation-mediated production in Japan. The basic contours of the argument are as follows. The rise of innovation-mediated production in Japan was tied in large measure to the specific constellation of political and economic forces acting on Japan in the immediate postwar years. During this crucial period, intense industrial unrest at the point of production, popular struggle, and class conflict unleashed a set of forces that altered the balance of class power or "class accord," produced a distinct pattern of capital-labor accommodation, and resulted in a dramatic restructuring of work and production organization. These forces set Japan on an evolutionary trajectory that was qualitatively different from that of mass-production fordism in the United States and Western Europe.

We pose our argument in light of what we consider to be the leading explanations or models of the Japanese political economy. The first of these is the "statist" approach associated with Chalmers Johnson.[3] This view essentially portrays Japanese development in terms of the actions of a highly centralized "developmental state." In its cruder manifestations, this view translated into the "Japan, Inc." characterization of Japanese capitalism.[4] The "strong state" thesis not only overestimates the capacities of the Japanese state but poses it as uniquely equipped among advanced industrial states—as standing in a distinctively autonomous position vis-à-vis the domestic economy. The fact remains, however, that according to aggregate measures the Japanese state is among the smallest in the advanced capitalist world. Indeed, MITI's budget represents just 1.1% of Japan's total national budget. Also, the Japanese state has repeatedly been thwarted when it backed initiatives against the perceived interests of companies or industries. Indeed, T.J. Pempel has argued that: "Japanese policymaking today involves far more complexity and less coherence than it displayed two decades ago. If there was ever much reason to give credence to the notion of Japan, Inc., there is no reason to do so in the 1980s."[5] While the organizational and directive roles of the Japanese state have certainly played an important role in specific industrial sectors, the critical determinants of Japanese economic growth and development are the organization of production and the labor process (including both the R&D laboratory and the factory)—that is, the spot where economic value is created.

A second view, put forward by Knuth Dohse and his colleagues in Germany, is the thesis that Japan is essentially a more advanced and exploitative version of fordism—or "toyotism"—which pumps more surplus out of workers and eliminates the obstacles of recalcitrant unions and labor legislation that protect workers from management prerogatives.[6] As Dohse and his colleagues put it: "'Toyotism' is simply the practice of the organizational principles of fordism under conditions in which management prerogatives are largely unlimited."[7] According to this model, sweeping rationalization of production and the super-exploitation of labor are the cornerstones of Japanese industrial progress and stem directly from the relative disorganization and powerlessness of the Japanese working class. This view is similar to that of Michael Burawoy[8] who describes Japanese production in terms of the "despotic factory regimes" of early capitalism. Burawoy sees the Japanese factory system as one of "hegemonic despotism" suggesting that it is designed to build worker dependence and submission by extending the reach of the company more completely over the worker. A more recent version of this argument is the "management-by-stress" thesis advanced by Mike Parker and Jane Slaughter, who contend that the Japanese system is simply a faster and more exploitative form of fordism—a "hyper-fordism" of sorts—characterized by an intense work pace and the internal discipline imposed by work teams.[9]

These scholars working in the labor-process tradition view the Japanese system in terms of labor control, arguing that Japanese organizational structures allow management to extract greater surplus from workers by increasing the pace of work, devolving managerial responsibilities to the shop floor, and creating an enforced sense of loyalty that stems from fear of job loss. Both Dohse and his colleagues and Burawoy rely primarily upon Satoshi Kamata's important book *Japan in the Passing Lane,* which depicts life on the Toyota assembly line in the early 1970s.[10] Kamata, a reporter, who worked undercover as a temporary worker in a Toyota plant, describes the extremely fast work pace in frightening detail. Clearly, Japanese factories are not a workers' paradise. There can be little doubt that assembly-line work, especially during the labor shortages in the early 1970s, was quite brutal. As both Kamata and Ichiyo Muto have shown,[11] work in large Japanese factories is constantly being rationalized, and understaffing is endemic.

Nevertheless, whether the Japanese assembly line was or is more brutal than, for example, the GM Lordstown plant that Stanley Aronowitz describes in *False Promises*[12] is open to debate. Japanese manufacturing wages are not only increasing but are currently comparable to U.S. wages in manufacturing—a fact that hardly seems likely if management power is completely unchecked. Moreover, it seems clear that an inefficient system of industrial organization that both wastes human labor power and poorly integrates workers into production (such as U.S. fordism) is not necessarily less onerous than one that effectively harnesses and integrates labor.

Moreover, Dohse and Burawoy's narrow focus on super-exploitation misses the critical organizational innovations that have propelled Japanese industry to the forefront of global capitalism and have led to dramatic increases in living standards for Japanese workers. The toyotism view neglects the crucial extension of the model to incorporate intellectual capabilities as well as physical labor. It also gives scant attention to the structural-historical forces that have shaped the developmental trajectory of that model. For us, the social and organizational context of Japanese production far outweighs issues related to labor costs or comparative levels of exploitation. The social organization of Japanese production is not simply a better or more advanced version of fordism; it is a distinct alternative to it.

A popular view associated with the MIT International Motor Vehicle Program is that of "lean production."[13] The concept of lean production, or what James Womack refers to as "Ohnoism," is used to capture the efficiency of the Japanese automobile industry based upon low inventories, just-in-time production inside the factory, rapid product development, efficient staffing, and just-in-time supply.[14] This view further suggests that other automobile producers in the United States and Europe are converging toward lean production. This view provides an accurate surface-level description of the operation of Japanese automobile factories, but it neglects the crucial role of intellectual labor at the point of production. Moreover, it fails to specify the underlying forces and relations—the historical trajectory, the balance of class forces, and the structural, organizational, and institutional patterns—that underpin the new model of production organization in Japan and give it motion. In doing so, adherents of the lean production concept provide a static, ahistorical view of the simple forms of the Japanese system, which are seen as capable of simply being picked up and adopted by Western producers in piecemeal fashion. Thus, their analysis remains superficial, unable to penetrate and explicate how the Japanese production system developed to its current level.

A third view is essentially an application of Michael Piore and Charles Sabel's concept of "flexible specialization" to Japan.[15] Building upon the general model of small-firm flexible networks, David Friedman views Japan as a "hybrid economy" characterized by complex linkages and mutual adjustment between large and small firms. According to Friedman, neither the state nor powerful industrial sectors were able to impose fordist solutions on postwar Japan. Based upon a case study of the machine tool industry, Friedman suggests that large firms were forced to decentralize production because of a combination of market forces, labor practices, and public policies; hence, small flexible companies came to be an integral component of Japan's industrial structure.[16] Posing his hybrid economy model as an alternative to traditional dualist theory, Friedman further argues that large firms eventually became dependent upon the flexibility and specialized skills possessed by small firms. Drawing from Friedman's work, Sabel, in a more recent paper, goes so far as to claim that Japanese industry more generally is converging toward the flexible specialization model.[17]

There are numerous empirical and theoretical problems with this view. Friedman completely ignores the role of large firms in structuring production relationships and actually creating new spin-off companies. He neglects the fact that a number of the major players in the Japanese machine tool industry are spin-outs from giant corporations such as Fujitsu, Toshiba, and Hitachi. As shown by our own research and careful studies by others, production networks in Japan are oriented around and frequently structured directly by large firms that function as "hubs" for the network. In Sakaki City these small machine tool companies survive and prosper in the smaller niches the large firms such as Yamazaki Mazak, Fanuc, and Okuma do not find lucrative—they are not an alternative to, but rather a part of the Japanese industrial structure.[18] There is little evidence to suggest that Japan—not to mention the advanced industrial world—is evolving in the direction of flexible specialization *a la* the Italian model. In fact, the available evidence indicates that it is much more likely that what we are witnessing is convergence toward the Japanese industrial system and the model of innovation-mediated production. And, as Chapter 1 has pointed out, there is accumulating evidence that questions the very concept of flexible specialization. Flexibility in the Piore and Sabel formulation is a catch-all concept—open, indeterminate, and unspecified; worse yet, it often changes meaning to fit new situations.[19]

An alternative view that we find more accurate—and from which we draw—emphasizes the concrete organizational context of Japanese production. In recent work, Haruo Shimada, Masahiko Aoki, and Kazuo Koike elucidate the unique features of Japanese production and industrial organization. Their research suggests that the introduction of new forms of work organization have helped facilitate the learning curve economies, product and process innovation, and productivity increases that underpin Japan's growth. This work evidences a shift away from the previous concern for cultural influences toward a focus on the Japanese model as a distinctive set of organizational practices that are the source of production advantages and economic efficiencies. For Haruo Shimada, Japan's unique systems of wage determination and tenure security enable Japanese corporations to internalize productivity gains associated with human resources improvements.[20] Masahiko Aoki views the Japanese system in terms of transaction costs and information economies.[21] He suggests that team-based models of work organization reduce transactional friction, increase information sharing, and enhance worker skills (or "human capital"), creating powerful production efficiencies. Kazuo Koike highlights the importance of Japanese work organization, which contributes to the multiskilling of workers and shapes a considerable degree of organizational "learning-by-doing." Multiskilling increases the interchangeability of workers, allows them to develop a comprehensive view of the production process, and enables workers to participate in design and redesign of tasks.[22] Others see the overlapping relationships among various elements of Japanese organizations (e.g., R&D, product development, and manufacturing) as a source of considerable advantage in turning innovations into commercial products.[23]

A number of theorists have begun to identify kernels of the broader political-economic context of the Japanese industrial system. For Andrew Sayer, the emergence of new forms of work organization are reflected and reinforced by the rise of new forms of industrial organization, in particular by the tightly integrated just-in-time system of producer-supplier relations.[24] Others are beginning to see the potential for Japan to move beyond fordism. As we have already seen, Benjamin Coriat argues that a hybrid model of "flexible mass production" is emerging in Japan.[25] Stephen Wood concludes that the Japanese labor process integrates the "tacit knowledge" of workers to overcome the limits of "taylorist" industrial organization.[26] This point is echoed by the French regulation theorist Alain Lipietz, who suggests that "Japanese capitalism did not simply catch up with the USA; it overtook it by discovering a new postfordist way of translating the skill of its producers, both manual and intellectual, into productivity."[27] Extending Marx's discussion of handicraft production, simple manufacture, and machine-based production or "machinofacture," Kurt Hoffman and Raphael Kaplinsky believe "systemofacture" accurately captures the changing nature of the Japanese production system. In their view, the restructuring of technological change and social relations in Japan is of epochal significance.[28] They suggest that systemofacture rests on three related pillars: flexibility in the labor process, the increasing use of new microelectronics technologies in production, and new forms of interfirm cooperation.

Finally, it is important to note that our view is influenced by the detailed historical scholarship of Andrew Gordon, who suggests that Japanese organizational forms emerged from a long historical process of labor-management conflict and the responses of capital, the Japanese state, and U.S. Occupation forces to evolving class struggle.[29] For Gordon, the emergence of permanent employment was in part a response to workers' "anti-firing" struggles in the 1920s and 1930s,[30] and team-based work organization was partly the result of workers' struggles around "production control" of the late 1940s.

Industrial Unrest, Accommodation, and the Japanese System

The rise of an alternative form of production and industrial organization in Japan was not implemented by managerial fiat or unbridled state power but was the outcome of bitter postwar class struggles. As in other advanced industrial countries, neither capital nor labor was able to impose its will entirely on the other—a relatively stable series of "trench lines" being the result.[31] In Japan, these lines of accommodation were reflected in the rise of a new system of industrial relations that revolved around guaranteed long-term employment, a seniority-based wage system, and enterprise unionism for the core of the labor force. These features then became the foundations from which the postwar economy evolved.

Both the class accommodation or "accord" and the corresponding institutional structure that arose in postwar Japan were shaped by earlier periods of class formation and struggle. In the prewar era, early attempts at unionization were defeated by the combination of business and government. However, the early struggles framed a number of issues—including tenure guarantees, the method for determining wages, the relative status and wages of blue- and white-collar workers, and the role of shop-floor workers in enterprise decision making—that would be resurrected in the industrial struggles of the immediate postwar period.[32]

As Japanese defeat in World War II became certain, concern over labor unrest arose among both business and political leaders.[33] The Japanese surrender in August 1945 discredited the ruling class and unleashed widespread working-class discontent. Allied Occupation forces were intent upon rendering Asia safe for U.S. capital and entered Japan with the initial agenda of making Japan an agricultural nation. General Headquarters ordered the Japanese government to disband the secret police, purge top leaders in government and industry, release political prisoners (including Communists), and allow the organizing of trade unions.[34] These policies created an environment conducive to trade-union organizing and other progressive political activity.[35]

Initial labor unrest broke out among captured Chinese Communist soldiers who had been forced into coal mining in Hokkaido and quickly spread to other mines and factories. Japanese workers developed a radical form of industrial struggle referred to as "production control" where workers occupied factories, ousted top management, and continued to produce and sell the output using stocks that management had hoarded. In many production-control struggles, shop-floor workers and line managers cooperated to keep plants running. In one case, workers in a fertilizer company organized barter arrangements with workers in other companies to secure inputs and even developed networks of reciprocal agreements with radicalized agricultural cooperatives to obtain food. In fact, when company officials and the Ministry of Transportation attempted to block shipments, the railway worker's union overrode the objections of government officials and made the shipments. The radical potential of these actions can hardly be overestimated, though often they were not yet explicitly political.[36] These struggles essentially established the roots of the Japanese system of team-based work organization.

During the immediate postwar period, the initial goals of union organizers were for enterprise-wide, all-inclusive unions (i.e., white- and blue-collar workers) rather than industrial unions. One of the goals was to transform these unions into factory Soviets.[37] It was the emphasis on enterprise unions that allowed the Communist-led Sanbetsu (All Japan Congress of Industrial Unions) to grow to 1,600,000 members in only one year.[38] Unions were able to secure contracts that included provisions for worker-management councils, temporarily obtaining a significant role in enterprise decision making. Labor organizations also fought for wages that had a "need" component—a radical demand that has some resemblance to the axiom "from each according to his ability, to each according to his need."[39] Under this scheme, a worker's pay would reflect nonwork performance variables such as the size and age of his family. Largely because of postwar labor struggles, the number of unions grew from zero in 1945 to 34,688 by 1949, while union membership increased to 6.7 million in 1949. By 1949, more than half the work force was organized.[40] Clearly, then, the Japanese model of production organization has been shaped both by explicit class struggle and implicit, ongoing industrial unrest. In his important work on the history of Japanese labor relations, Andrew Gordon made explicit note of the intricate balance of power that runs through twentieth-century Japanese industrial relations:

> Subtle tensions between workers and managers were as important as open disputes in reshaping the labor relationship. The fear of a strike or . . . the desire to satisfy workers' expectations before they were expressed as demands or even requests could be as important as a strike in stimulating new policy. Policies that appear at first glance to have been unilateral management innovations often emerged against such a background.[41]

In effect, many of the characteristics now interpreted as indicating capital's control of labor were initially labor demands. Like the postwar accords of the United States and Western European countries, only later were these demands integrated into the logic of capitalist accumulation. The lack of understanding of the historical legacy of the struggles of Japanese workers allows both Japan boosters and critics to ignore the role played by workers in creating the institutional basis of postwar Japan and advance an overly simplistic top-down view of the emergence of the Japanese production system.

Capitalist responses were framed on this newly created terrain of conflict. In the context of the Cold War in the United States, the "hot war" in Korea, and the McCarthyite "witch hunts" of the late 1940s, U.S. Occupation policy shifted dramatically. The late 1940s and early 1950s saw elements of both U.S. and Japanese business become increasingly concerned over the issue of labor militancy. Worker organizations were seen as posing a serious threat to management prerogatives over investment, staffing, and other important components of enterprise decision making; and business was particularly concerned with reasserting control over wage determination and work rules.[42] The U.S. government saw Japanese unions as a springboard for communism.

The business counteroffensive was massive. The combination of management—organized under the Federation of Employers *(Nikkeiren)*—and the state defeated the unions in a series of major strikes during 1949–50.[43] An important management weapon was the creation of new conservative "enterprise" unions as an alternative to more militant labor organizations, a process that finally resulted in targeted dismissals of thousands of radical union leaders and workers. Labor thus lost much of its radical orientation; and even in the companies where old unions survived, management gained an upper hand in the workplace.[44] The share of Japanese workers represented by unions declined sharply in the 1950s to roughly one-third of the work force.[45]

The undermining of radical forces made it easier to integrate many worker gains into the evolving framework of capitalist accumulation. Still, management was unable to reestablish the prewar terrain and rules of the game. Further, to gain support, enterprise unions had to deliver on demands raised in previous worker struggles. First among these was the demand for employment or tenure security (in contrast to fordist job security).[46] Ironically, enterprise unionism made this demand important to the very survival of the union movement itself since dismissal of workers meant automatic union shrinkage with little prospect of replacing lost membership. As a consequence, even the most conservative unions were compelled to support long-term employment.

In addition, elements of Japanese capital were not necessarily antagonistic to the demand for employment security. As Koji Taira has pointed out, high labor turnover and chronic labor shortage had been recurring problems for Japanese capitalists who were trying to expand their businesses and to develop a modern Japanese economy during the first half of the twentieth century.[47] These problems were acute in the 1920s and 1930s, and became even more pressing in the 1950s as the Japanese economy boomed and experienced labor shortages. Management was similarly aware that significant investments in training were necessary to prepare the still largely agricultural work force for economic revitalization based upon some form of industrial mass production. The emergence of enterprise unionism made management more vulnerable to worker prerogatives to withhold labor power and thus more amenable to tenure guarantees. Since enterprise unionism confined strikes to individual enterprises rather than entire industries, work stoppages threatened to irrevocably damage market share and profits. This "dependence" of management on labor was reinforced by postwar labor market shortages and the emergence of a just-in-time production system that is immediately immobilized by work stoppages or even production slowdowns.

As a result, guaranteed employment for male workers in core firms became a fundamental feature of postwar Japan, with dismissal of workers falling largely outside routine management prerogatives.[48] Indeed, layoffs and firings have provoked the longest and most bitter strikes in postwar Japan, including the 113-day Miike coal strike of 1960; the 173-day Japan Steel strike of 1953; and the bitter 1953 Nissan Motors strike.[49] In the immediate postwar period, Andrew Gordon found that roughly 50 percent of strikes over one month in length were related to layoffs or dismissals.[50] The unwritten terms of the Japanese accord implied that layoffs could only occur after alternative measures such as wage freezes, progressively indexed wage cuts, and early retirement had been implemented, and then only if the economic health of the company was truly in jeopardy.[51] This point is clearly reflected in remarks by Osamu Nobuto, a Mazda executive who headed Mazda's U.S. automobile plant:

Even in Japan, the idea of lifetime employment is a moral obligation between the employer and the employee, requiring commitments on both their parts. There is nothing formal. We believe job security is a desirable goal to work toward. However, it can only truly be achieved by building a healthy, successful company. . . .

Our basic principle is to give job security the highest priority and to rotate workers between a variety of jobs within their team, in keeping with our teamwork philosophy.[52]

To some extent, however, the terms of the Japanese accord are codified by the state. Japanese labor law makes dismissal justifiable only as a measure of last resort; the provision of bonuses or wage increases after dismissal is considered proof that dismissals were not warranted.[53] In reaction to the oil crisis-related recession in the early 1970s, legislation (e.g., the Employment Insurance Act of 1974) was passed that provided government assistance for the retention of employees in seriously threatened companies or industries. The seriousness with which Japanese workers and Japanese society view the labor-management accord is underscored in a recent *Wall Street Journal* article that discusses the problems foreign companies in Japan are having with their Japanese workers.[54] Of the outstanding official labor complaints under arbitration in Japan, 10 percent are against foreign firms, even though they employ less than 1 percent of the work force. For example, when a foreign company terminated its Japanese employees without notifying its workers in advance, it resulted in Japanese worker claims of $11 million in severance and retirement bonuses and one month's salary in lieu of the required one-month termination notice. In another case, when American Express closed down a regional office and fired its workers, it was required to reinstate the employees and give back pay because it had not "exerted enough effort to find jobs for the dismissed employees." Japanese working for foreign firms are far more prone to strike because of the perceived lack of commitment by foreign companies to the long-term employment system.

The intense labor upheavals and class accord of the postwar era also resulted in a second basic feature of the Japanese political economy—a unique remuneration scheme centered around a tripartite wage comprised of seniority, base, and merit components. Workers initially sought to reduce management's arbitrary control over wage determination by demanding a wage system comprised mainly of base and seniority components (in other words, a "need"-based system). Management counterposed a wage system emphasizing a relatively large "merit" component. All three components ultimately became part of the system for determining wages.[55] The Japanese system of wage determination differs in fundamental respects from the job-specific, productivity-indexed system of U.S. fordism.[56] The seniority component provides significant incentives for workers to remain with the company. The system of semiannual bonuses hinges individual remuneration to corporate performance and creates increased incentives for greater work effort, while the merit-based component spurs individual effort.[57]

Japanese labor's defeat of the late 1940s and the early 1950s was not the end of the Japanese struggle over improved living conditions. In 1954, Japanese labor developed the *shunto* as a strategy to increase their leverage in management-labor bargaining. The basic strategy was to gain bargaining leverage with the largest and most successful companies in a unified spring offensive and then use these settlements for the leading firms and industries to set a basic "bargaining pattern" for the Japanese economy. Between 1955 and 1965, the *shunto* focused on the steel and private railway sectors, but between 1965 and 1975 the focus shifted to the four major metalworkers' unions.[58] In effect, during this entire period there was a stable hierarchical set of relationship between labor and management based upon shunto bargaining. In fact, as Tsuneo Ono argues, a number of other prices became directly linked to the outcome of the *shunto* such as public workers' salaries, price supports for rice, and the annual revision of health fees.[59]

By the early to mid-1970s, this steady pattern of modest wage increases began to erode profits as wage increases began to exceed productivity gains, setting a classic "profit squeeze" in motion. In 1972, labor succeeded in achieving a 14.9 percent wage increase. According to Ikuo Kume, this was largely "because individual employers feared that hostile labor relations, coupled with the conditions of a tight labor market and intense interfirm competition, might lead to disturbances" that would hurt the individual firm.[60] In 1974, labor won a 32.9 percent nominal wage increase, which translated into a 4.5 percent increase in labor's relative share of corporate profit.[61]

The oil crisis of the 1970s put additional pressure on Japanese business and in turn on Japanese management-labor relations. The oil crisis crystallized, but did not necesarily cause, a number of evolving tensions in the Japanese political economy. The main point of tensions involved new strains in labor-management relations and increasing environmental problems and a budding environmental movement that questioned the implicit policy of "growth at all costs."[62]

The Japanese state and business responded rapidly and massively to these multiple crises. First, a massive industry-led conservation drive was launched to cut energy consumption. This was accompanied by an enormous antipollution effort that substantially cut pollution levels. Second, Japanese industry began to reorient from its heavy and chemical industries toward higher-value skill and knowledge-intensive products. Naturally, this process was gradual, but there was a noticeable change in direction.

Third, both business and government attempted to reorient the framework of the postwar labor-management relation. During 1974–75, there was a large-scale layoff of workers. Essentially, the government-business alliance was able to deal a broad and serious defeat to labor, including measures to root out militant unionism and break up interindustry solidarity. By breaking inter-industry solidarity, management could force unions in the weaker industries to take lower wage increases.

This resulted in a new general pattern—where salaries are set on an industry-by-industry basis.[63] In fact, Solomon Levine and Koji Taira argue that the nature of the *shunto* has changed and now focuses more on "broader-front bargaining over working conditions and economic policy at the enterprise, industry and national levels."[64] As Toshio Kurokawa explains, the *shunto* strategy had considerable success in compensating for the weakness of the enterprise union system and securing wage increases.[65]

Over time, economic success combined with management's constant efforts to co-opt union leadership (or remove radical union leaders) led to a situation where Japanese unions became more or less complicit partners in Japanese capitalism. One Japanese manager we interviewed described the union as having become a "kind of shock absorber for employee frustrations about the company. . . . Conflict [between the company and union] is a kind of drama which is necessary to make employees believe the union is their representative."[66] All in all, unions were largely successful in their goal of securing incomes for Japanese workers roughly comparable to that of workers in other advanced industrial societies, but far less successful on issues such as work hours. In Japan, legal holidays have increased and Saturdays are no longer workdays in many larger firms. Workers are still required to work massive amounts of overtime, thus weakening the trend toward more leisure time.[67] However, based largely on union efforts, the average number of annual hours worked per employee declined steadily from 2,432 in 1960 to 2,088 in 1989.[68]

The Accord and the Unevenness of the Japanese Political Economy

The postwar accord in Japan set the contours for Japanese political economic structure, the balance of class power, and its expression in socioeconomic inequality. The Japanese political economy—like that of the United States and Western Europe—is characterized by uneven social relations and in particular by segmented labor markets. Workers and managers in large corporations comprise the privileged core of the Japanese economy. This core labor force includes roughly one-third of all workers and they participate fully in the Japanese accord. Surrounding the core is a continuous gradient of workers employed by suppliers or subcontractors of large companies and a sizable group of part-time and temporary workers, especially women, who comprise the periphery of the Japanese economy. There is little mobility between the various segments, or tiers, of the Japanese labor market; secondary peripheral workers are always kept outside the inner circle, or regular permanent employees, of large corporations. Norma Chalmers estimates that over 98 percent of small firms are involved in some type of subcontracting.[69]

Promotion and tenure patterns differ among the various segments of the work force. Managers and workers in large companies enjoy secure tenure and relatively high wages. Kazuo Koike argues that blue-collar employees in the core companies have been "white-collarized" in terms of wages, employment tenure, and relationship to the enterprise.[70] For university graduates on a management track, attrition is very low and promotion is relatively standardized. Only after the first decade of employment does promotion become more individually based. However, there is a relatively high attrition rate for workers joining directly after high school.[71] Attrition also varies by industrial sector. Separation rates in steel mills are 20 percent per annum for males in their twenties.[72] Finally, tenure is less secure on the periphery of the Japanese labor market where temporary workers, often female, face low-wage employment and high rates of separation.

The periphery of the Japanese labor market is very important both in terms of its size and centrality to the Japanese economy. Table 2.1 summarizes relatively recent data on the distribution of employment, annual wages, and value-added by firm size.[73] According to these data, companies with fewer than 100 employees accounted for 34 percent of total employment, and those with under 500 workers accounted for 61.5 percent of all employment in Japan.[74] Generally speaking, wages run along a company size gradient with the smallest firms (20–29 employees) paying roughly half as much as the largest ones (5,000-plus workers). According to Yasuo Kuwahara, as of 1987, only 16 percent of workers in firms of fewer than 300 employees belonged to a union.[75]

The periphery of the Japanese labor market is also much more woven into the production process. In some industries, subcontractors may work in the same factory as permanent core employees. Shigeyoshi Tokunaga reports that in newer steel mills up to half of some functions are performed by subcontractors.[76] For example, at Nippon Steel's Kimitsu works there are 30 subcontractors with between 10 and 1,200 employees. One of these subcontractors has 500 direct employees, and it has seven subcontractors with between 6 and 20 employees. One of these seven has four sub-sub-subcontractors with between 2 and 7 employees. Workers for subcontractors at times work alongside the regular permanent employees in the parent firm's plant. The working conditions, wage rates, and rules vary from firm to firm. As Norma Chalmers observes, "Relations between management and labor are specific to each firm; for example, collective bargaining and work rules must be negotiated firm by firm."[77]

The enterprise union system operates against worker solidarity by separating the interests of contractor and subcontractor workers even when they are in the same factory. In other industries, such as automobiles and electronics, there are far fewer subcontractor employees in the assembler's factory, but there are varying

TABLE 2.1.   Employment, Wages, and Share of Value-Added by Firm Size

Employment Level by Firm	Percent of Employees	Average Annual Cash Earnings (thousand yen)	Cumulative Gross Value-Added (%)
20–29	11.4	Y2,628	6.7
30–49	8.9	2,745	12.1
50–99	13.8	2,763	21.0
100–199	13.1	2,923	30.4
200–299	6.9	3,084	35.7
300–499	7.4	3,452	42.8
500–999	8.4	3,680	52.2
1,000–4,999	14.0	4,307	72.5
Over 5,000	16.2	4,838	100.0
Total	100.0	3,469	100.0

Source: Ministry of International Trade and Industry, *Census of Manufacturers 1985* as summarized in "The Changing Nature of Japanese Manufacturing," *JEI Report* No. 23A, (17 June, 1988).
Note: Percentages may not total 100 due to rounding.

numbers of temporary employees. These industries, however, take advantage of lower-paid employees working for subcontractors and subsidiaries that deliver just-in-time (JIT) to the assembler from factories and small workplaces in close proximity to the main plant.

The periphery of the labor market is the location of many of the Japanese system's tensions and contradictions. Small firms have a greater tendency to employ minority workers, notably Koreans and the *burakumin* (a formerly segregated group that undertook so-called "unclean" activities such as tanning animal hides). Small firms also employ a disproportionate share of older workers, many of whom in keeping with traditional practice were retired from the large firms at age 55. Since pension benefits are marginal and the average life expectancy for Japanese males is 78 years, retirees must seek new employment. These older workers are also compelled to work at significantly lower pay than workers in core firms.[78]

There is some debate regarding the true magnitude of the wage and salary differentials between workers in large and small firms and whether these have narrowed. In a 1989 report for the OECD, (Organization for Economic Cooperation and Development), Ronald Dore and colleagues observed that employment guarantees are being extended to male permanent employees in smaller companies.[79] Thus, the differences between "core" and "peripheral" firms may be narrowing somewhat.

The Japanese labor market is characterized by significant gender-based segmentation and discrimination. For example, women are prohibited from working in automotive assembly plants by a law that makes it illegal for Japanese women to work the night shift; Japanese automotive firms require all employees to rotate their shift assignments. Women receive significantly lower wages than do males across every category of company size and industrial branch. The exact size of this differential is age-dependent. For example, in the 16–20 age group, the differential is approximately 15 percent. The differential increases radically with age until approximately age 35 where it levels off at approximately 50 percent of male wages.[80] Women's position in the labor market is made more problematic because Japanese women are highly concentrated in part-time and temporary jobs that are quite vulnerable to layoffs. Between 1960 and 1986, the share of all women employees working part-time increased from 8.9 to 22.7 percent.[81] However, women in the labor force are often members of dual-worker households; this reduces incentives for labor organization and collective action by women workers as personal ties cut across workplace relationships.[82] While gender-based segmentation has thus far not been a source of major industrial unrest or political struggle, it remains to be seen whether future economic downturns (or conversely the extremely tight labor markets of the late 1980s) might erode the structure of the Japanese labor market.

The Japanese labor market has a tripartite union structure. The best known type of unions are "enterprise" unions. They encompass all the regular employees, including many white-collar workers, within a single enterprise. "Plural" unions describe those cases where worker-organized and company-sponsored unions coexist within the same enterprise. The last category includes the "new" unions that

organize workers in small companies and operate across enterprises.[83] This varie-
gated union structure both overlaps and cuts across existing patterns of labor market segmentation, evidencing the evolving nature of worker organization, class
formation, and conflict in Japan.[84]

Divisions among workers are integral components of the labor market and production in the Japanese political economy. Small firm/large firm relations and patterns of gender-based divisions provide clear evidence of structurally unequal
access to jobs and benefits. These relationships are important supports for the
"core" of the Japanese economy and help to create the institutional topography
upon which the Japanese organization of production rests.

The Organization of Work and Production: The Core of the System

The postwar Japanese accord and the balance of class forces it produced also created the context within which the new model of organization at the point of production could emerge. As we have already seen, the production-control struggles of
the immediate postwar era established the precedent for work teams, rotation,
worker input, and other key aspects of the Japanese industrial system. The labor,
capital, and resource shortages of the postwar period accelerated these experiments
in the organization of work. Basically, the Japanese accord and the particular type
of capital-labor accommodation it produced established a social context that would
propel the Japanese system on an alternative evolutionary trajectory from fordism.
Long-term employment, which is a fundamental aspect of the postwar capital-labor
compact, enabled Japanese management to overcome many of the organizational
rigidities endemic to fordism, as tenure guarantees reduced incentives for workers
to resist automation or work redesign. Conversely, the seniority system and the
lump sum "golden handshake," which is often equivalent to four years of salary,
ensured that workers would remain committed to the company—willing to sacrifice for its economic success. Given this context, skill-sharing occurred more
readily, and rotation could be used both to upgrade skills and increase interaction
among workers.[85] Long-term employment made it possible for large corporations
to make sizable investments in skill upgrading and training with little fear of
employee turnover and the loss of investment.

The team-based organization of work, which workers' production-control
struggles had set in motion, was quickly seen by management as a way to reduce
costs and increase productivity. With teams, work roles overlap and tasks can be
assigned to groups of workers and then reallocated internally by team members.[86]
This obviates the need to further subdivide tasks in order to increase productivity,
a process that exemplified both fordism's method of increasing productivity and its
institutional rigidities. The productivity increases associated with team-based production organization have been amply documented.[87] Through the use of teams,
the pace of production can be changed by adding or removing workers, and management and team members can experiment with different configurations for completing specified tasks. Teams also provide an internal source of motivation and of

discipline for workers. Teams perform routine quality control, thereby undertaking much of the work that is performed by the quality-control departments of fordist manufacturing. Teams are the basic mechanism for achieving the *functional integration* of tasks, which stands at the heart of the Japanese model.

Team-based organization of work also resulted in the combination of task and resulting production efficiencies. Japanese workers are multiskilled and perform more than one job. Workers also do most direct quality-control activity and preventive maintenance on their machines, resulting in significantly lower rates of downtime. According to James Harbour's data on the automobile industry, U.S. machines were inoperative 50 percent of the time, while in Japan similar machines were down only 15 percent of the time.[88] Higher rates of capital utilization enable Japanese firms to make smaller capital investments and to amortize them more quickly. In contrast to American mass production where work arrives on a conveyor belt, Japanese workers often move with the production line. For example, there are reports that one Toyota worker performed 35 different production processes and walked 6 miles in one day.[89] Team organization and increased worker input not only increase productivity but also reduce certain aspects of worker alienation, which resulted in high rates of sabotage and absenteeism under fordism.[90]

The implementation of just-in-time inventory procedures inside the plant, new assembly-line configurations, and other elements of the technical organization of production also stemmed from the upheavals and changes of the immediate postwar period. A major architect of these postwar changes was Taiichi Ohno of Toyota Motors, who is associated with Japan's now famous *kanban,* or card system, for controlling production flows.[91] The *kanban* system replaces the top-down coordination of fordism with mutual adjustment among contiguous work groups. Under this system, neighboring work units use cards (referred to as "*kanbans*") to order supplies, deliver processed materials, and synchronize production activities. Constant communication reduces planning and supervision costs and creates another location of shared knowledge and work-based learning.

As early as 1947, Ohno, who was then head of Toyota's No. 2 Manufacturing Machinery Plant, began to experiment with new ways to organize machines on the assembly line. Ohno and his group started to rearrange machines, reorganize the lines, and develop new ways of organizing production. The basic idea was to create configurations where one worker could tend multiple machines. In most factories of the period, in Japan as well as in America, the machinery was set up in separate sections. In other words, at one place there would be a dedicated section of 50 to 100 lathes, then 50 or 100 drills, and so on. Parts would move sequentially from the lathe section to the drilling section and on down the line. Complicating this was the functional specialization of tasks—lathe operators only operated lathes, drill operators only operated drills. It was in such a context that Ohno began his crucial efforts to reorganize production. In his own words:

> Even though the economy was now booming, we were far from mass production. There were still too many models, and we were still producing them in limited numbers. At that time I was head of the machinery plant at the main factory. I started a small experiment: instead of the old system, where each section produced

a great deal and sent it on to the next process, I tried arranging the different types of machines in a line, so that each unit could be produced in an unbroken chain, thereby creating a "flow" of production. In 1947, I tried arranging the machines in an L-shaped or parallel formations, so that each operator could handle two machines. From 1949 to 1950, we began experimenting with U-shaped or square formations, so that each operator could manage three or even four machines along the manufacturing lines.[92]

Ohno then began to experiment with "time-equalized production" to regulate production flows so that parts would be supplied "just-in-time," or only when needed. But it was not only technical problems and obstacles Ohno confronted. He also ran up against the existing organization of production, which itself comprised an obstacle to his new technical configuration of the assembly line. He continues:

Of course resistance within the factory ran high. It was not that the volume of work or the working hours had increased. The skilled workers of that time, for better or worse, were full of artisan's pride. They were reluctant to accept a new system in which the machines were rearranged. Under the new system rather than operating a machine, they would have to manage a processing chain. Moreover they would be required to do several different jobs—to not just operate a lathe but also a milling machine or a drill press. . . . Production flow, which I instituted by rearranging the machines in the machinery factory, helped eliminate wasteful, defective parts, and at the same time meant doubled or even tripled productivity, because one worker could handle one, two, or several machines. . . . [I]n the United States it would have been difficult to introduce a system where a single operator manages several different kinds of machines. The reason why it is possible in Japan is, for one, that we do not have Western-style craft unions, and so the transition from single-skilled to multi-skilled workers went relatively smoothly, the only resistance being "artisan's pride." This does not mean that the position of Japan's company unions is weaker than that of the Western trade unions. It is mostly a difference of history.[93]

Ohno's comments not only shed important light on the postwar experiments carried out in the organization of production but they also reflect on the crucial point that the organizational context and social relations of the Japanese workplace were never deeply fordist—certainly not in comparison to the United States or the Western European nations.

Today, "just-in-time" is a distinguishing feature of Japanese production. Based on Ohno's work and constant experimentation in myriad other firms, Japanese assembly lines are more adaptable than traditional assembly lines. They can be rapidly reconfigured to shift between different products such as various models of automobiles or between cars and light trucks. These arrangements facilitate rapid shifts between different products within a product family. Under this type of setup, lines can be readily converted to different products and workers can perform a number of tasks on different machines simultaneously. In some industries, U-shaped or modular systems have replaced traditional assembly lines. Workers thus perform a number of tasks on different machines simultaneously while individual machines "mind" themselves. Multiskilling is absolutely essential for this strategy to be successful. Workers thus obtain a broad view of the production process, develop multiple skills or become "polyvalent," and are more fully integrated with the interests of the company and thus into the logic of capital accumulation.

Harnessing Knowledge at the Point of Production

Perhaps the key element of the Japanese industrial system lies in its ability to harness workers' knowledge as a source of value directly at the point of production. This occurs through many mechanisms, from team-based quality circle efforts and workplace suggestion systems and the everyday involvement of workers in *kaizen,* or continuous improvement activities. There is now a sizable literature that recognizes the importance of shop-floor participation, information transfer, and learning-by-doing in Japanese industry.[94] Such mechanisms allow employees to accumulate increasing knowledge of the labor process and, in effect, create a more "social" worker. According to a 1984 report by the Ministry of Labor, two-thirds of all Japanese establishments with more than 100 employees used suggestion systems, while 60 percent involved workers in small-group "kaizen-like" activities; and roughly 70 percent made use of labor-management consultation systems designed to provide worker input into enterprise-level decision making.[95]

Team-based organization of work provides the concrete organizational mechanism for tapping workers' intelligence and knowledge. For critics like Parker, Dohse, and others, the team is a vehicle for pumping more effort out of workers. However, this captures only part of what teams do.[96] For example, Haruo Shimada advances the concept of "humanware" to describe Japan's smart production workers; Masahiko Aoki and Kazuo Koike use the notion of "learning-by-doing" to convey the combination of intelligence and production.

Teams are the basic mechanism for moving decision making down to the shop floor and for tapping the intelligence of factory workers. The team is the mechanism through which workers solve production problems and innovate for management. It becomes the source for solving production problems as workers use their own intelligence and knowledge to devise cooperative strategies to overcome such bottlenecks. The team is a simultaneous source of motivation, discipline, and social control for team members, driving them to work harder and more collectively. In this way, workers are encouraged, stimulated, and provided incentives to offer up their ideas and continuously improve the production process.

The self-managing work team of contemporary Japanese capitalism devolves a variety of managerial responsibilities to the shop-floor. It thus facilitates the functional integration of tasks and in turn overcomes the fine-grained functionally specialized division of labor of fordist production organization. The team makes the extraction of intellectual (and manual) labor a quintessentially social, intersubjective, and collective process. In addition, teams are a mechanism for socializing and training new workers. After rigorous basic training, new employees are inserted into work teams where knowledge and skills are passed intergenerationally.

Perhaps most importantly, teams tap the collective knowledge of a group. Teams comprise the microorganizational solution to the problem of extracting both knowledge and physical labor from workers. This is an inherently social way of creating value and achieving productivity improvements. Workers are thus made to "voluntarily" mobilize their own intellectual labor.

Transfer or rotation of workers enhances the process of knowledge acquisition and diffusion. Rotation within teams allows workers to familiarize themselves with various aspects of the work process, thus creating a powerful learning dynamic and enhancing the problem-solving capabilities of both individual workers and teams.[97] Workers are also rotated frequently from task to task to reduce the rate of repetitive-motion injury. In ergonomics terms, rotation allows a more total usage of the human body. No single part is overstressed; rather, each part of the body is stressed more evenly. Rotation also extends to the entire plant.[98] Workers are able sequentially to master the complexities of different tasks and to grasp the interconnectedness among them. By breaking down the communication barriers that exist among work groups, rotation enhances the flow of information among workers and across functional units.[99] Rotation generates a storehouse of knowledge that can be applied to a variety of work situations and enhances problem-solving capabilities at the enterprise level.

Other formal and informal mechanisms exist for tapping the knowledge and intelligence of workers. Such mechanisms include suggestion systems, quality circles, and *kaizen*, or continuous-process improvement activities. The impetus for these organizational forms and mechanisms also dates back to the crucial postwar period of restructuring when Japanese businesses sought to devise new mechanisms to co-opt unrest and gain workers' insights into problems at the point of production.

Japanese quality-control efforts began in 1949 in response to demands by the U.S. government, which wanted high-quality products for American military forces in Korea, and the recognition by Japanese industry of the importance of quality. In the early 1950s, W. E. Deming and Joseph Juran visited Japan to begin training Japanese in statistical quality-control techniques. In 1955, the Japan Productivity Center (JPC) was formed to encourage labor-management cooperation. The JPC secured the cooperation of conservative union leaders and pragmatic managers in its efforts to increase productivity.[100] Takashi Kawashita argues that "the concept of labor-management collaboration won the production managers over, that is the managers who were leading (quality control) movements in their everyday lives under the double pressure from the unions and top managers."[101]

In the 1960s, a strategy was developed to involve all workers in the quality-control process.[102] Quality activity was devolved to the work teams themselves, reinforcing the trend toward shop-floor problem solving. This was a fundamental step beyond the fordist concept of quality control and led in the direction of increasing training and reliance upon workers for production-process improvements. Teams were able to detect and remedy most problems much more quickly than designated inspectors, thereby saving considerable rework and scrappage.[103] This in turn demanded more skills and greater training, creating upward skill pressures for the work force. These developments freed quality-control personnel for more sophisticated activities. They also enabled companies to form special quality circles with different combinations of workers to address more serious quality problems, and to devise both product and process improvements to solve these problems. Nonaka and Yonekura[104] document the evolution of traditional "quality control circles" to "voluntary control circles" (or JK groups) in a Nippon Steel plant. These voluntary control groups were comprised of both line workers and engineers who not only performed quality inspection but were able to recommend technological and process improvements. This made the technical configuration of production and the line itself more dynamic and reinforced the trend toward a shop floor of ongoing learning and continuous improvement. In short, the quality-circle movement reinforced and resonated with both changes in the technical configuration of production, and it was supported by the labor-management accord of the immediate postwar period.

Suggestion systems are a more or less formal mechanism for harnessing workers' knowledge. Michael Cusumano points out that Toyota's suggestion program yielded nearly 33 suggestions per worker in 1982.[105] While suggestions are not mandatory for Toyota personnel, workers who do not contribute are criticized and may receive smaller bonuses.[106] Certainly, in some cases the number of suggestions per worker is inflated by workers providing trivial suggestions merely to appease management.

The crux of worker involvement in improvement and innovative activity comes in the form of less formal *kaizen,* or continuous-improvement activities. The roots of *kaizen* also lie in the immediate postwar restructuring period. Various Japanese scholars point out that Japanese capitalists initiated *kaizen* activities in their plants as a strategy to collect information on problems that might be causing worker dissatisfaction in order to staunch the demands of radical unionists.[107] *Kaizen* activities gradually evolved into a more formal mechanism for harnessing workers' ideas on how to improve the production process.

Kaizen is important not only to assembly-type operations but also in continuous-process industries such as chemicals. In the chemical industry, operators can contribute important process improvements, especially when a new plant or procedure is initially placed on-line. Team work is also important in the chemical industry in an effort to prevent accidents, which in continuous-flow industries can result in enormous damage or material wastage. In chemical plants, *kaizen* is very important for equipment control and facility maintenance to ensure against untoward events. The former plant manager of a chemical plant distinguished between "big *kaizen,*" done by engineers, and "small *kaizen,*" which occurs on the shop floor.

> Big kaizen usually can be done by engineer or high-level person. But another *kaizen* can be done by the operator, because the operator knows everything to operate the machine. And, if he is a good idea man, he will make a good suggestion too. If he is a very good idea man, we have a strong possibility we will get a good suggestion. . . . In the chemical industry, of course, in the beginning [when setting up production] we need to make small *kaizen,* improving step-by-step.[108]

The idea expressed years ago by Joe Hill of "manager's brains" being under "worker's hats" is dynamically implemented via the social organization of Japanese production. Japanese companies treat all permanent employees as smart workers.

The Management of Knowledge

The harnessing of knowledge and intelligence is also reflected in Japanese management practices. Japanese managers and engineers are in constant contact with the shop floor. Using the concept of "management-by-walking around," engineers spend a great deal of time on the factory floor, talking to shop-floor workers and devising on-the-spot solutions to problems. Both low-level and middle-level managers are often recruited directly from the ranks of shop-floor workers. Even high-level Japanese managers spend the early part of their careers in shop-floor positions and all were members of the enterprise union. Often these managers also served as union officials. Thus the social distance between managers and workers is not as great as in fordism.

Knowledge acquisition and information sharing are also encouraged by the open access to information policies of many Japanese corporations. According to Rodney Clark, printed documents constantly circulate within Japanese firms, even to persons only marginally affected.[109] While the general directions of a company are set by top management, specific programs usually are developed interactively at the middle levels. Proposals for new products or process improvements can surface anywhere in the organization. However, new decisions require participation from all affected parties. This consensus-seeking process *(nemawashi)* reduces problems associated with lack of commitment or outright sabotage at later stages. Additionally, decisions can be presented as collective until it becomes worthwhile to claim them, thus reducing the fear of failure. Consensus decision making provides an environment where ideas can surface, ensures thorough dissemination of information, and mitigates problems associated with lack of commitment to new decisions.[110] The evolution that this concept has undergone in the electronic age is illustrated by the remarks made by the president of Kao Soap, a Japanese consumer products company comparable to Procter & Gamble.

> One of our most important management jobs is to make all of our employees willing to cooperate fully, and to make them want to continually improve themselves. To achieve this, it is neccesary for us to provide all kinds of information *equally to everyone* [emphasis in original]. . . . Every employee has the right of access to *all* [emphasis in original] computerized information within the company.[111]

Japanese companies are thus able to use computers more completely and without the tight security that permeates the fordist firm. The computer can be used as a medium for circulating information more widely, thus adding more people to the loop. In the United States, computerization reinforces hierarchy and is used as a mechanism for top-down communication. The traditional U.S. firm, for example, has developed hierarchies of information access, levels of classification, and increased security. Security, which is an overhead cost, weighs down the company, and the lack of access interferes with speedy response to change.

The management structure of Japanese companies is more adaptable than that under fordism.[112] Managers are usually not specialists in accounting, finance, or marketing but are generalists who transfer among posts. Management rotation results in flexibility and learning-by-doing similar to that experienced on the shop floor. This blurs distinctions between separate departments, between line and staff, and between management and workers. The Japanese corporation has a flexible managerial hierarchy, similar in certain respects to the concept of a "matrix organization"[113] but not organized like a matrix. Management positions overlap with one another, and titles do not unequivocally indicate authority. Some management slots are always open, and nominal subordinates discharge tasks. Conversely, titles denote status relative to rank, but not necessarily function or scope of responsibility. A title can mean nothing more than seniority in a particular unit.[114] Combined with rotation, this means that job advancement is not necessarily blocked by one's immediate superior, and that superior need not be concerned about being displaced by a subordinate. Japanese corporate organization facilitates knowledge sharing and ameliorates some of the negative aspects of the low-key but intense internal competition for promotion. An illustration of Japanese versus traditional fordist corporate organization is provided in a quote from a Japanese manager at Mitsubishi Electric, USA:

> The volume of written materials describing work processes in the U.S. and Japan are comparable, but the actual meaning and intentions are totally apart. In America the contents of these descriptions have a direct bearing on contracts and workers' performance within the sphere specified. Work descriptions in Japan are merely a framework, with everyone crossing boundaries in performing their work.[115]

On the negative side, consensus decision making can lead to a corporate "group think," mitigating against the development of new ideas. This can help explain the Japanese inability until recently to pioneer radically discontinuous change. Some Japanese companies are attempting to overcome the group-think problem by hiring mid-career researchers. For example, Canon Corporation hires groups of mid-career researchers so that they can form a nucleus of resistance to "group-think." As a group, they are not immediately integrated into the corporate culture, but rather are seen as a focus for change.[116] The Japanese approach to management can be characterized as one of many "little brains" that share information and coordinate objectives as opposed to the one "big brain" directing many "appendages" as in fordism.[117]

Japanese organization contrasts sharply with traditional corporate organization characterized by extreme functional specialization and highly compartmentalized information flows. Long-term employment and extremely low rates of labor mobility ensure that shared knowledge remains internal to the enterprise and that leakage is minimal. This provides firms with large collective memories and a perseverance in executing their long-term strategies. The Japanese remuneration schedule sets up sizable disincentives to careerism based upon information hoarding. Since bonuses hinge on overall corporate performance and wage increases take into account group performance, ability to share information, and the development of multiple skills, there are very strong incentives for interaction and cooperation.

The Japanese company is an information-laden organization with problem-solving and regenerative capabilities that far exceed its fordist counterparts. Knowledge and information flow back and forth, rather than travelling through the formalized mechanisms of a bureaucratic pyramid. The knowledge-based nature of Japanese production has led Aoki to characterize Japanese factories as "information systems" as opposed to production systems.[118]

Finally, as is now widely known, Japanese management has considerable autonomy from outside stockholders. This weakness of shareholders is reinforced by the *keiretsu* system of corporate ownership where large blocks of shares are held by firms within the corporate group. In 1974, the share of cross-ownership within established corporate groupings ranged from about 30 percent in the cases of Mitsubishi (30.6%) and Sumitomo (27.9%) to slightly less than 20 percent for Mitsui (17.4%), Fuyo (17.4%), and Dai Ichi Kangyo (16.0%). By the early 1980s, joint stock ownership within major corporate groups accounted for nearly one-third of the assets of nonfinancial corporations. Highly concentrated stock ownership minimizes the possibilities for serious disagreements between blocks of stockholders (or for hostile takeovers) and allows corporate decision making to be left almost exclusively with management. It should also be noted that many competitive decisions are not affected by the *keiretsu* grouping. Some of the most important Japanese firms are only marginally affiliated with these enterprise groups: Nippon Steel, Hitachi, Toyota, Nissan, Honda, Kyocera, and Sony Corp.[119] However, each of these large firms does have a supplier *keiretsu*. In cases of extreme mismanagement, however, the stockholders (i.e., the other institutional holders represented by the lead bank) have removed the top-level executives of a firm and replaced them with dispatched managers from the bank.[120]

This aspect of the Japanese system also stems from the immediate postwar period. A major element of postwar restructuring of the Japanese political economy was the American-led effort to break up the old *zaibatsu* system in which a few families controlled vast segments of the economy. Eventually, the *zaibatsu* were reformed as *keiretsu;* however, in these new groupings the power of independent shareholders was lessened and that of management strengthened. This essentially freed many firms from being influenced by individual shareholders.[121] In some real sense, then, the postwar reforms of the American New Dealers created a "managerial" capitalism in Japan.[122]

Production Networks

The final structural element of the Japanese system is the well-developed production complexes of end-users and suppliers that blur the boundaries of the corporation and function as a mechanism for harnessing the knowledge and intelligence of a broad complex of end-users and suppliers. Large Japanese manufacturing firms organize supplier transactions through multilayered supplier complexes rather than internalizing them through vertical integration. In the automobile industry, for example, suppliers provide as much as 70 percent of the components that go into a vehicle or consumer electronics product.[123] In contrast, U.S. automakers rely on suppliers for 30 to 50 percent of inputs.[124]

The Japanese supplier system is organized according to a pyramidal structure. Under this system, rings of first-tier, second-tier, third-tier, and up to ten tiers of suppliers surround a central hub company.[125] The core company (i.e., the final assembler) plays a key role in this system by helping to structure linkage and coordinate flows within the network of producers.[126] First-tier suppliers are next in importance, playing a role as coordinators organizing flows of supplies between lower-level suppliers and the assembler. First-tier suppliers are located close to assemblers, interact constantly with them, and are frequently at least partly owned by them.[127] Overall, between 1966 and 1981, the percentage of manufacturing workers employed by subcontractors increased from 53 to 66 percent.[128]

The structure of Japanese production networks is perhaps best illustrated by the Toyota City production complex where until recently nearly all 3 million Toyota automobiles were produced. In 1980, Toyota controlled 10 important subsidiaries and 220 primary subcontractors—80 percent of which had plants within the production complex. Subsidiary companies were quite large, averaging about 6,500 employees. Indeed, Nippondenso—Toyota's electrical products supplier— employs 30,000 workers worldwide.[129] According to Michael Cusumano, Toyota's 10 subsidiaries and 220 primary subcontractors were served by 5,000 secondary subcontractors and approximately 30,000 tertiary subcontractors.[130]

However, Japanese suppliers and subcontractors are not exclusively tied to a single customer. Many supply more than one customer. This provides the supplier greater security and stability.[131] Generally speaking, larger and more profitable subsidaries have greater independence from core corporations. Nippondenso, an electrical company that was a spin-off of Toyota in the early postwar period, is still 23 percent owned by Toyota, but now does more than 40 percent of its business with other firms, and it supplies parts to some of Toyota's competitors such as Honda, Ford, and General Motors. While Japan critics and some scholars believe that Japanese supplier pyramids are monolithic, we accept, and our interviews confirm, Ken-ichi Imai's contention that firms apparently in one enterprise group may not be completely controlled by the group leader and may supply some of the leader's competitors.[132]

There is now a fairly extensive literature on Japanese production networks and the "just-in-time" (JIT) supplier system.[133] This system is noted for its close geographic proximity of producers, long-term relationships, and tight interorganizational linkages characterized by personnel sharing, joint participation in product development, and regular communication and interaction. With JIT production complexes, coordination is achieved through shared information, continuous interaction, and by having suppliers and subcontractors locate in close proximity to final assembly facilities. End-users often have sizable financial holdings in their suppliers and subcontractors. This interfirm coordination differs markedly from the geographically dispersed "just-in-case" (JIC) production system[134] of fordism where different elements of the production process were located in different areas of the world without consideration for productive efficiency.[135] Japanese produc-

tion networks operate as mechanisms for harnessing the intelligence and knowledge spread throughout a broad complex of end-users and suppliers.

The JIT supply system is reinforced by a well-articulated distribution and deal-
ership system. Toyota car dealers, for example, have the capacity to transmit computer orders directly to the factory, virtually eliminating the need for inventory
stockpiling. Distributors provide an important source of information on product
quality and markets and function as intelligence-gathering mechanisms.[136] As
George Fields observes, the Japanese distribution system resembles an upside-
down pyramid similar to that of the Japanese production system.[137]

At a superficial level, the Japanese system can be thought of as occupying a middle ground in terms of Oliver Williamson's theory of markets and hierarchies.[138] For
Williamson, hierarchies economize on transaction costs and thus offer an efficient
organizational solution to the coordination problems of market exchanges. But
whereas Williamson presents the markets and hierarchies dichotomy as a more or
less exclusive trade-off, others suggest that "hybrid organizational forms" may in
fact be more effective in dealing with a range of production, control, coordination,
and exchange problems.[139]

Aoki refers to the Japanese system as one of "quasi-disintegration" that offers
the combined benefits of integration and disintegration, combining a variety of
types and sizes of firms in an integrated network.[140] Japanese production networks
provide a novel solution to the coordination dilemma that affects pure markets and
bureaucratic hierarchies. Whereas market relations provide *ex poste* information
on a firm's costs of production,[141] active ongoing relationships provide up-to-date
information on a range of production activities.[142] The existence of the network
allows the assembler to delegate many production and coordination responsibilities
to suppliers. In effect, the assembler depends upon each tier to coordinate the tier
below it and deliver a defect-free part to the next link in the chain. Jon Sigurdson
characterizes the multilayered relationships of JIT complexes as comprising the
"ultrastructure" of the Japanese economy.[143] JIT complexes replace the simple vertical integration of traditional U.S. manufacturing corporations with a network of
quasi-market, semi-integrated relationships.

Japanese production networks are the corollary to the highly developed internal
relationships of the firm. JIT relations are highly contingent upon stability, since
work stoppage can seriously disrupt production schedules. Quality parts are
required to eliminate inspections of subcontractor deliveries and to keep production running smoothly. This makes Japanese industry highly vulnerable to strikes
or sabotage not only at the assembly firm but throughout the production chain.
Thus, the pressure is constantly upon subsidiary firms to become more efficient and
to ensure labor peace.

Both the literature and the conventional wisdom on Japanese production networks focus almost exclusively on the cooperative, more or less harmonious aspects
of Japanese supplier relations. This is reflected in Ronald Dore's much-cited concept of "relational subcontracting."[144] The idea is that the Japanese production system is embedded in a set of supportive sociological relationships that help structure
economic behavior. The content of Japanese subcontracting relations is vague in
terms of formal contracts and is achieved by a long legacy of social relationships

that create mutual understanding. This is roughly in line with Mark Granovetter's concept of the "embeddedness" of organizational systems.[145]

However, the Japanese subcontracting system also allows large parent firms to reduce both costs and risk by developing a hierarchy of production. In a recent study of the spatial structure of Japanese manufacturing, Koji Matsuhashi and Koichi Togashi conclude that

> Subcontracting is based on disparities in such indices as wages according to the size of the firm. By forming a subcontracting system, the parent company reduces costs and risks. Behind the technological linkage and inter-firm relations, however, close ties are established through the social relations and regional disparities that form the hierarchical organization of the labor force. Subcontracting is an element of the structural characteristics of intensive accumulation of Japanese capitalism.[146]

Moreover, coercion also plays an important role in Japanese production networks. Often, large hub companies apply pressure and coerce their suppliers to innovate, cut prices, and share proprietary data, information, and technology with one another for the benefit of the entire complex—that is, the core firm. The remarks of one Japanese subcontractor reflect the role of power, dominance, and coercion in the Japanese supplier system.

> This is how they do it: The parent gives you a nice fat order. You fill it. He gives you another, bigger order. You fill most of it. A guy from the main bank comes around and says, "You know, if you added an extra wing on the factory, you could handle a lot more work. For a solid young firm like yours, I'm sure we could arrange a loan at practically no interest." . . . While you're considering the idea, the parent offers you another order. "Can you handle it or not?" they ask. "If you can't, just say so and we'll use somebody else." That's it. Once he passes you by, it's over. You may never see a decent order again. . . . A year or two later, they pull the same routine. . . . Pretty soon you've got orders coming in nice and steady, but a third of your company is owned by your clients. They tell you to put one of their people on your board, so you put him on the board. . . . When they tell you to cut prices, you damn well better find a way to cut them. That's what really hurts. For instance, you get an order from the parent and start up production. A few weeks later one of the parent's managers comes to inspect your plant. He says you've got to lower costs 10%. . . . A few weeks later he comes back. "Another 5%," he says. . . . Then he comes back again . . ." Good job," he says, "but not good enough. We need another 5%."You tell him you're up against the wall. . . . He thinks awhile. "Okay, I can see you're pretty tight. Maybe we shouldn't push too hard. But this factory would run more smoothly if you got some new machinery." . . . He wants you to buy some new piece of machinery, probably from a *keiretsu* company, to increase production. You tell him you can't afford it. "Take out a loan," he says. "I'll call the bank and make sure your credit is good."[147]

Overall, JIT production confers some unique advantages to Japanese industry. As workers in subsidiaries generally receive lower wages than those in core firms, overall costs of production are reduced.[148] However, the use of subcontractors to absorb business cycle downturns does not appear to be as widespread as previously.[149] In fact, risk sharing between core companies and their primary subcontractors has become the norm, as core companies recognize the importance of stable, long-term relationships. Further, important suppliers invest heavily in training to build their own firm-specific knowledge, thereby making them more valuable to their assembler and thus strengthening their bargaining power. This also allows a loosening of their dependence on a single assembler.

A fundamental and not widely recognized element of the JIT system lies in its ability to harness the collective knowledge and innovatory capability of a broad corporate complex. The JIT system creates additional conduits for knowledge sharing and innovation. JIT production complexes are characterized by multidirectional flows of information.[150] Suppliers and subcontractors are typically linked in corporate federations such as the Toyota Subcontractors Discussion Group.[151] The core companies take an active hand in helping suppliers cope with problems and typically dispatch personnel to help solve them. It is quite common for engineers from suppliers to be intensively involved in new product planning.[152] More unusually, employees may be transferred among companies in the JIT complex—a process that typically occurs late in an employee's career cycle, when retiring executives of corporate parents are absorbed by smaller subsidiaries.[153]

Essentially, the large firm orchestrates an intense cross-flow of knowledge and information through its supplier complex. In doing so, it harnesses the knowledge and intelligence that is spread throughout the system of suppliers. The system enhances innovation and dynamic efficiency by involving suppliers and subcontractors in the design and development of new products, thereby spreading the costs and risks of new product development. This decentralized system allows suppliers to build up specialized knowledge and expertise in particular areas, which can be an important source of innovation. The core firm can support two or three suppliers who compete for contracts and thus have great incentive to make product and process innovations. Mari Sako refers to this aspect of the Japanese system as one of "competitive cooperation."[154]

Parent corporations sometimes learn from innovations made by their subsidiaries. In fact, Toyota modeled its first quality-control program after the one developed by its electrical and electronic components subsidiary, Nippondenso.[155] Also, suppliers in the same network share information, thus ensuring rapid diffusion of new techniques. Close corporate and contractual relationships facilitate this environment of information transfer and cross-fertilization. Diffusion occurs rapidly because of the close relationships within the network.

Finally, the core or hub firm is also able to launch new products and product lines through "sponsored spin-offs." Under this system, R&D scientists work on projects and gestate them to the point where they develop into actual products and product lines. As they grow, they can be transformed into self-standing enterprises in their parent's supplier galaxy and allowed to grow into new firms. As Chapter 3 will show, this is especially important in high-technology industries.

A Context for Change

As we have seen, the rise of a new model of production organization in Japan did not emerge in a vacuum but was nurtured in an evolving constellation of social and historical forces that were different from those of fordism in its U.S. or Western European variants. Of fundamental importance were the tremendous social upheavals, industrial unrest, and labor militance of the immediate postwar era. Like Western Europe and the United States, postwar Japan went through a prolonged period of domestic institution-building that came to be reflected in its unique "class accord" between capital and labor. An important consequence of this accord was the establishment of a system of tenure guarantees, or so-called lifetime employment, for workers in large manufacturing companies. In return, these workers gave up more radical demands for "production control," ceding management significant control over the organization of production. Institutionalization of long-term employment ultimately helped create a pattern of labor force stability. This gave companies tremendous incentives to invest in workers since it was uncommon for workers to leave a company. As a result, firms were able to create large stocks of knowledge within their work force, transforming Japanese companies into "learning organizations." The capital-labor accord allowed Japanese firms to experiment with new means and methods for organizing work and production— some of which were directly influenced by postwar workers' production-control struggles. The basic elements of these new forms are clear—work teams, job rotation, etc. And as we have seen, it is these forms that underpin the sweeping metamorphosis of the factory—the transformation of shop-floor workers into smart workers.

Simply put, the institutional matrix of postwar Japan opened up a series of important pathways outside and eventually beyond fordism. Evolving within those pathways, large Japanese corporations were able to avoid many of the institutional rigidities that plagued American and European fordism. If this was important in traditional heavy manufacturing industries, it would prove crucial in shaping Japan's approach to the high-technology age—setting the institutional context for its high-technology industrial organization. In the next chapter we describe the structural advantages Japanese industry has in superseding the old fordist economies and moving to a new, more advanced stage of capitalism.

3

High-Technology Capitalism in Japan

Japan is expected to become the first nation to complete the transformation into an information society. Japan will play the same role as that played by England in the Industrial Revolution.

NATIONAL INSTITUTE FOR RESEARCH ADVANCEMENT.[1]

One thing clear at Honda is that robotics is not the replacement of human work, nor is it going to be. Robotics is not a way to replace a human job—it is used where the human would suffer or where he is not suitable for the job. Our application of robotics is primarily for eliminating the dirty, dangerous work for humans, or eliminating errors caused by monotonous boredom if done by humans. Ideally, people must do jobs best done by humans. And these are the more creative or productive ones, ones which humans alone can do.

KIYOSHI KAWASHIMA, then president of Honda Motor Co. Ltd.[2]

It would have been one thing if the Japanese model's success had been limited to the old heavy industrial sectors of fordism—automobiles, steel, tires and rubber, and electrical equipment. But it was not. The true advance of the Japanese production system *can* and *must* be seen in the emergence of this new model of innovation-mediated production to exploit the opportunities presented by the new high-technology fields of the late twentieth century.

Both Marx and Schumpeter, as well as observers ranging from Kondratieff and Gerschenkron, to Mandel, Aglietta and Freeman, identify major technological shifts and the rise of new technological sectors as setting the contours for new rounds of innovation, productivity, capital accumulation, and economic growth.[3] Previous industrial revolutions have indeed been spurred by the rise of new technologies and industrial sectors—textiles, steel, and automobiles.[4] The key to understanding the new industrial high-technology industrial revolution—and Japan's role in it—lies in understanding the new high-technology sectors of semiconductors, computers, telecommunications, software, and biotechnology. According to recent data, the global market for computers and software alone is roughly $200 billion.[5] Electronics, broadly defined, already comprises the largest share of employment and of value-added of any industrial sector in Japan with 1.8 million employees, 16.8 percent of total, and 16.4 percent of all value-added. This compares to slightly less that one million workers in the motor vehicle and transportation equipment industry and less than 400,000 in steel.[6] Moreover, the new high technology sectors are setting in motion the all-important creative destruction effects that are key to transforming through automation the old mass-production industries like automobiles and steel. As these new high-technology sectors define the terrain of global competition in the twenty-first century, dominance in these areas is very likely to be coterminous with dominance in the world economy.

In the past decade, Japan has emerged as a global powerhouse in high technology. Table 3.1 charts the evolution of Japan's technological capability in industries ranging from automobiles and steel to semiconductor memory devices and super-computers. By 1989, the top four global producers of integrated circuits were Japanese.[7] The integrated circuit was invented in the United States, and up until the early 1980s American industry was clearly the world leader in design and manufacture of these crucial products for the microelectronics revolution.[8] Japan is the world's leading producer of semiconductors (see Fig. 3.1); Japanese dominance is particularly great in the area of dynamic random access memory (DRAM) chips, which are a highly standardized product requiring enormous capital investment. In 1990, Japanese firms held 8 of the top 12 global positions in the 1-megabit DRAM area.[9] Japanese success in computers and telecommunications is even more astounding. As late as 1975, Japanese firms were not even "players" in these areas. In 1984, the United States still controlled the top five spots in global sales of computers. In 1989, the United States controlled only three of the top five; and, in 1990, the runner-up spot was taken by Fujitsu as Digital Equipment Corporation (DEC) dropped to third.[10] According to recent estimates, Japan's share of the world market for computers and data-processing equipment will exceed that of the United States by 1992 (see Fig. 3.2). Remarkably, NEC, though much smaller than IBM or AT&T, has grown to be the world's largest integrated circuit producer, fifth in telecommunications equipment, and fourth in computers.[11] No other company in the

TABLE 3.1.   Level of Japanese vs. U.S. Technology

Product	Japan Behind	Even	Japan Ahead
Ships	—*	—	1955
Steel	1958	1960	1965
Videotape recorders	1956	1965	1975
Televisions	1965	1970	1975
Automobiles (compacts)	1972	1978	1982
Industrial robots	1974	1978	1982
Memory devices	1978	1982	1985
Supercomputers	1980	1990	1995
Telecommunications	1985	1990	?

Source: Adapted from Steven Vogel, *Japanese High Technology, Politics, and Power* (Berkeley: BRIE, 1989).
Note: Years listed denote estimates of when Japanese manufacturers (1) last clearly lagged, (2) were closest to even, and (3) first clearly surpassed U.S. manufacturers in their ability to produce the best product at the lowest cost.

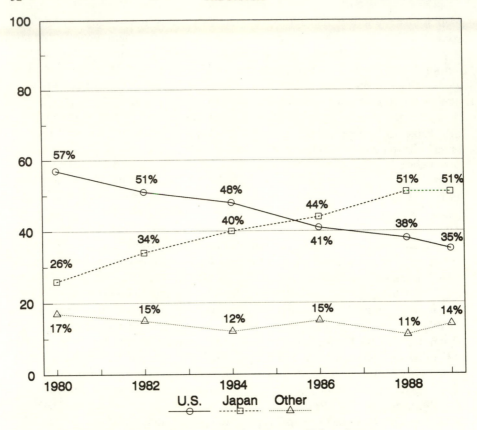

FIGURE 3.1. Worldwide Market Share of Semiconductors: U.S. vs Japan.
Source: Dataquest, 1991.

United States or Europe, not even IBM, is this diversified across the spectrum of information technology fields.

Japan's success is not simply confined to standardized, lower-value, manufacturing-intensive areas of high technology as many in the United States contend. Over the past five years Japan has extended its capability in high-end, highly innovative technology. Japanese companies are the unquestioned world leaders in high-resolution, flat-panel display technology used in laptop computers and potentially in high-definition television. In early 1991, Sony introduced a 17 pound portable UNIX workstation priced under $10,000. Sony also produces Macintosh Notebook and laptop computers for Apple. In October 1990, Cray Computer Corp. announced that it would use gallium arsenide chips made by Fujitsu Ltd. in its next-generation, Cray-3 supercomputer.[12] In late 1990, Hitachi announced development of a "neural network" computer that operated 10 times faster than the fastest supercomputer and it expected to have this new computer on the market in two years. Hitachi has also developed a software program for the computer that not only can

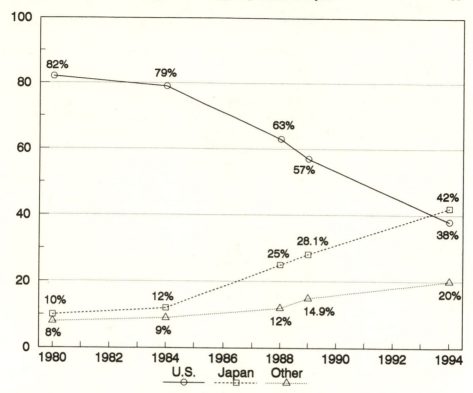

FIGURE 3.2. Worldwide Market Share of Data-Processing Equipment: U.S.-vs. Japan.
Source: Adapted from Andrew Grove, "The Future of the Computer Industry." *California Management Review* 33, no. 1 (1990), p. 155.

predict the price of a given stock within 10 seconds but can also do advanced pattern analysis. This stock prediction software program may provide an important advantage in stock arbitrage—an area where the United States still leads Japan.[13] Japanese firms have assumed the lead in the global race to superconductivity.[14] The extent of Japan's rise in these high-technology fields is astounding even when viewed in light of its previous success in automobile and steel.

In this chapter we explore the movement of Japan's industrial structure into the high-technology age. We argue that Japan's production system provides a powerful institutional context and organizational model for adapting to the high-technology age. This earlier transformation established the organizational context that is uniquely equipped to cope with the current round of restructuring based upon new, information-intensive technologies. It provides the "social space" needed to integrate research and innovation with basic manufacturing processes. Emerging within this broader institutional context, Japanese high-technology industry is defined by innovation-mediated production—the synthesis of innovation and production—and both intellectual and manual labor. Japan has not only applied its model to the new technologies, but it has used them to transform production in traditional fordist industries to create a powerfully diversified and integrated industrial structure.[15]

We advance the term of *fujitsuism* to refer to the application of innovation-mediated production in Japanese high-technology industry. Fujitsuism is distinguished by the blurring of the lines between the R&D lab and the broader synthesis of intellectual and manual labor. The term "fujitsuism" is taken from the name of one of Japan's most important information-based companies, Fujitsu Ltd.[16] In 1979, Fujitsu replaced IBM-Japan as Japan's largest computer company. With its purchase of the United Kingdom's ICL in 1990, it replaced DEC as the second largest computer firm in the world.[17] Its spin-off, FANUC, is currently the world's largest manufacturer of industrial robots. At one FANUC factory, unmanned robots work unattended at night in darkened factories producing parts of other robots.[18] In Japan, firms are moving toward accomplishing the "lights out" factory.

The rise of Japanese high technology should not be mistaken as part of some putative move to a "postindustrial" society but rather as a refutation of this theory.[19] As Chapter 1 has shown, the postindustrialists fail to understand that the material underpinnings of the information industries are produced in factories. Industrial production remains a vital part of Japan's response to the new high-technology age—a wellspring of its industrial and technological success. Similarly, the Japanese system also refutes the theory of "disorganized capitalism" advocated by Scott Lash and John Urry, among others.[20] As this chapter and the previous one show, the Japanese model is a highly organized capitalist system. If U.S. and European capital appear "disorganized" (and retreating), it is because they are being defeated by Japanese competition. A powerful discussion of Japan's movement into the high-technology age, one that provides important insights on the current developments in the global economy, is that of Tessa Morris-Suzuki. Based on her studies of the Japanese economy she argues that the current robotization of production is shifting value and the competitive struggle to constant innovation, or what she terms as the "perpetual innovation" economy. This formulation captures an important element of the move to knowledge-intensive production.[21]

Underlying our argument about Japan's entry into the high-technology age is a deeper argument about the transformation of work and production that is occurring as a result of this new industrial revolution. At the bottom of this lies the increasing informatization and digitization of production. Digitization is a fundamental underlying trend in the global economy, and Japanese firms are leaders in digital-based industries. This shift toward digitally based and information-intensive industries is not replacing factory production; rather, it is changing the focus toward the integration of workers' mental faculties and abstract intelligence in production. Under past forms of industrial production, including mass-production fordism, much of work was physical. Indeed, much of the conception was actually embodied in "skill" and the physical execution of work. The emergence of digitization increases the importance of abstract intelligence in production and thus requires that workers actively undertake what were previously thought of as intellectual activities. In this new environment, workers are no longer covered with grease and sweat, because the factory increasingly resembles a laboratory for experimentation and technical advance. The factory itself increasingly resembles a clean-room facility as the entropy that dust particles represent is removed from the production process.

An R&D-Intensive Production System

It is frequently thought that the success of Japan's industrial system is limited to lower-level, manufacturing-intensive products in both low- and high-technology industries alike. This assumption, however, is patently false. Indeed, R&D is not new to Japanese firms. Major Japanese companies have been investing significantly in R&D since before World War II. As James Bartholomew's historical research indicates, Japanese firms founded R&D units as far back as the early 1900s—virtually on the heels of U.S. firms.[22] In 1918, for example, Hitachi Corporation founded its research division.[23] NEC established R&D in the same period, adopting the U.S. model of independent R&D laboratories. In 1927 Yasujiro Niwa, an electrical engineer, left the Ministry of Communications' Electrotechnical Laboratory to head NEC's research and quickly moved to establish R&D at the factory level where it would be linked directly to factory production.[24] Japan's R&D thrusts accelerated during World War II. However, Japan still remained far behind the United States and Germany in many areas, suffering from an insufficient number of trained personnel and an underdeveloped technological infrastructure. In the aftermath of defeat in World War II, Japan's R&D infrastructure was decimated.

Japanese companies began to rebuild their R&D capacity by the early to mid-1950s. Initially, much of this was directed at imitation, reverse engineering, and process development. For example, Sony secured access to the transistor developed at AT&T's Bell Laboratories and developed a transistor radio that proved an enormous commercial success.[25] NEC began a serious telecommunications and computer research effort in the late 1950s and made significant advances in computerization, telecommunications switches and cables, optical fibers, and semiconductors independent of U.S. or Western European companies.[26]

The 1973–75 "oil crisis" marked an historic turning point in the development of Japan's indigenous R&D capability. The oil crisis confronted the Japanese economy with its most severe economic dislocation of the postwar period. Japanese capital, with backing from the state, concluded that knowledge-intensive industries were the key to continued growth. Double-digit inflation, layoffs at some firms, and a severe profit squeeze forced Japanese capitalists to accelerate their search for alternatives to traditional heavy industry. Japanese industry with backing from the state was already preparing to move beyond the low-quality, labor-intensive products such as textiles and transistor radios. In 1973, the Ministry of International Trade and Industry (MITI) released its "Vision of the 1970s" report, which concluded that it would be necessary to "shift away from Japan's heavy industry orientation to new knowledge-intensive industrial sectors."[27] The Japanese press picked up the theme and the media was filled with articles hailing the coming "information society." The strategy was to undertake a long-term shift to technology-intensive products that would not be as vulnerable to rising energy and raw-material costs.

Japanese firms have massively increased R&D spending in the move to reorient from commodity production toward knowledge-intensive products. As Figure 3.3 shows, Japan's R&D expenditures have skyrocketed over the past two decades, more than tripling in real dollars. Since 1965, the proportion of the Japanese labor force engaged in R&D also tripled, increasing from 2.5 percent to 6.2 percent of the work force. In the past few years, R&D spending has grown at a 15 percent annual rate.[28] Research investment is not limited to large firms; innumerable small firms are also investing in R&D.[29]

Figure 3.4 charts the growth in corporate R&D facilities per year for the entire

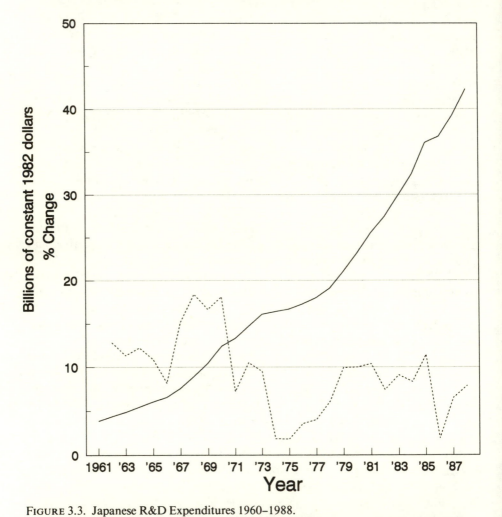

FIGURE 3.3. Japanese R&D Expenditures 1960–1988.
Note: Conversions of Japanese yen to U.S. dollars are calculated with the Organization for Economic Development and Cooperation purchasing power parity exchange rates.
Constant 1982 dollars are based on U.S. Department of Commerce GNP implicit price dollars.
Source: National Science Foundation, *International Science and Technology Data Update* (Washington, D.C., 1988), p. 5.

postwar period. As this graph indicates, there have been two boom periods. The first was from 1960 to 1965 when many large firms, especially those in the chemical and pharmaceutical industry, built R&D facilities. This tapered off during the 1970s as

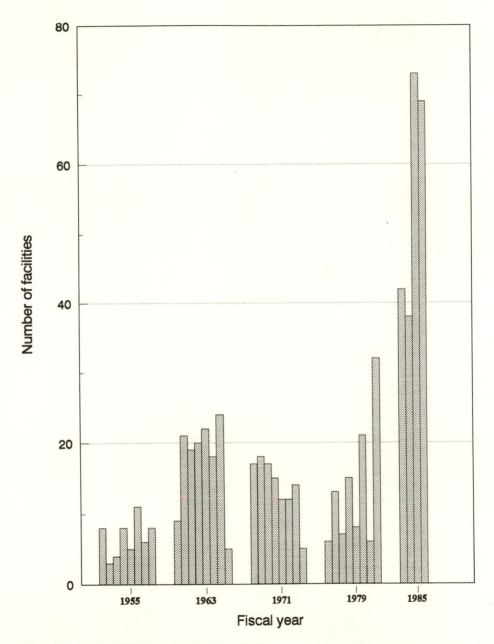

FIGURE 3.4. Growth in Japanese R&D Institutions.
Source: Ken-ichi Imai, "Japanese Pattern of Innovation and Its Commercialization Process." Paper presented at Conference on Economic Growth and the Commercialization of New Technologies, Stanford University (11–12 September 1992), p. 21B.

many of these companies faced economic difficulty. However, the 1980s saw a second boom in the establishment of new R&D facilities as companies moved to upgrade their technological capabilities in the face of two-sided competition from R&D-intensive competitors like the United States and the increasing challenge of the newly industrializing countries (NICs) of Asia in standardized technologies and mature industries.[30]

Japan's R&D expenditures are comparable to any technologically advanced industrial nation. While Japan spends roughly the same share of gross national product (GNP) on R&D as the United States, the share of GNP invested in commercial R&D is a full percentage point higher. More than two-thirds of Japanese R&D is funded by industry—the highest share of industry-financed R&D of any advanced industrial nation. In fact, Japan focuses nearly all of its R&D on commercial products and technologies. However, the comparative R&D statistics, if anything, understate the level of resources Japanese industry devotes to R&D. In the United States, for example, it is typical for large corporations to count all engineering expenses as R&D. A former high-ranking executive of Westinghouse who was closely involved with Westinghouse's joint ventures with Mitsubishi (a company similar in size and product areas to Westinghouse) told us that it was his belief that Mitsubishi Electric conducted far more basic R&D in the 1960s and 1970s than did Westinghouse.[31]

While Japan does basic research, it expends enormous sums on product development aimed at improving and readying products and processes for actual production and commercialization. According to recent estimates, nearly nine-tenths of Japan's total R&D effort is devoted to product development.[32] A large share of Japanese researchers are actually product development engineers—a striking contrast to the United States where researchers with doctorate degrees are more common.

The scholarly literature examining the role of the Japanese state in R&D is vast.[33] Generally speaking, this literature extends the "developmental state" perspective associated with Chalmers Johnson to the domain of R&D and innovative activity, seeing the state as the axis of the Japanese innovation system. The Japanese government has clearly played an important role in conducting, sponsoring, and encouraging R&D. Yet all indicators suggest that the Japanese state funds far less R&D than any other major capitalist economy, as measured on either a per capita or per unit of output basis. Our position is not that the state did not have an impact. Rather, the key to Japan's industrial and technological success lies in the dynamism of Japanese firms and the rapidity with which they embody R&D in actual products. The problem with the "statist" approach of Marie Anchordoguy or Malcolm Brock is their near-total focus on government policy-making to the exclusion of the corporate sector. Martin Fransman is more careful in arguing that the state plays a crucial role in helping corporations mobilize their internal research resources. The success of any industrial policy in capitalist economies depends on the ability of corporations to produce and compete in the world marketplace. The best evidence that government industrial policy cannot save industries with weak corporations is the utter failure of European "national champions" in computers and semiconductors to compete effectively in the world marketplace. The statist perspective ignores the fact that all production, as well as the vast bulk of Japanese R&D, takes place within the firm. Contrary to what so many observers imply, the state cannot create success for companies unwilling or unable to mobilize the internal resources to take advantage of the markets that new knowledge can create.

Japanese companies are broadening and deepening their R&D efforts as they accelerate their push into high-technology fields. In 1989, for example, Japan's top ten electronics companies spent $18 billion on R&D. This matches the total of the top 100 electronics companies in the United States. Even second-tier Japanese manufacturers of copiers and consumer electronics products, which have not been regarded as technological leaders, are investing in the range of $300 million to $400 million a year each on R&D.[34] All of these companies are coupling R&D investments with even more massive capital spending, which aims to deploy the state-of-the-art plant equipment required to embody these new technologies in actual products. Japanese managers and executives we have interviewed believe that R&D expenditures and personnel must increase in the future. This is true in high-technology industries where R&D spending is seen as a way to move ahead of U.S. and European competition. In mature industries like steel and textiles, R&D is needed to move into new growth areas.[35]

A classic example is the new biotechnologies. Companies in industries ranging from pharmaceuticals and chemicals to electronics, textiles and even steel began biotechnology research in the 1970s and 1980s to diversify into these new areas. Initial targets were quite modest as companies conducted exploratory research and looked for a niche to occupy. Major Japanese electronics firms hired biologists to conduct research into the ways in which the new developments in biology could be helpful to electronics and, simultaneously, how electronics could be used in biology. At NEC, for example, two target research areas emerged. First, NEC launched a short-term project to develop biosensors that use biological materials sensitive to certain changes in the environment. These biologically active materials emit electrical impulses that can serve as signals for controlling waste treatment or food processing. A second project aimed to develop methods of using the ability of biological structures to store information. These "biocomputers" were first touted by U.S. firms but were abandoned because there was little prospect of success in the medium term. Dr. Daizaburo Shinoda, then vice president of NEC's research operations and now executive vice president of NEC's basic research facility in Princeton, New Jersey, described the long-term nature of this effort: "The stockholders will not receive a quick return on investment [from this project]."[36] And yet, at some later date this research may provide important competitive advantages.

In the early 1980s, Japanese steel firms faced massive overcapacity. In response they began to rationalize production and to use their massive internal corporate resources to diversify into new businesses such as software, new materials, robotics, computers, and biotechnology. In the period from 1982 to 1986, Nippon Kokan Kogyo (NKK) increased R&D expenditures from 24 billion to 30 billion yen, from 1.35 to 2.08 percent of sales. In this period, NKK began investing in electronics, new materials, and biotechnology research. In biotechnology, the first research target was to use biological processes to develop a marketable product using indole—a by-product of the coal tar generated in steelmaking—as a feedstock. NKK aimed to connect its traditional expertise in coal tar chemistry with the expertise of its newly hired biotechnologists. The project had a ten-year time horizon. If it would somehow prove unsuccessful or be discontinued, the company would still benefit as the researchers would simply be transferred to other areas. Thus, even in a worst-case scenario, hard-earned learning and expertise can be capitalized upon and redeployed to other areas.[37]

Synthetic fibers and textiles are yet another illustrative area. In the 1970s and 1980s, the synthetic fiber industry, which was built on the basis of rayon and nylon, was negatively impacted by the movement to higher-quality natural fibers. Japanese firms responded by increasing R&D in an effort to find new "high-quality" synthetic fibers. In the late 1980s, a number of new polyester fibers were developed that could be sold to the Japanese and, more recently, Italian fashion industry for premium prices. Further, this research developed products such as super-absorbent towels and special lint-free eyeglass lens cloth.[38] Successful R&D has allowed Japanese firms wallowing in what were apparently stagnant markets to begin selling new high value-added products. These successes have convinced other firms in declining or stagnant industries to bolster R&D in the hope that they also can develop the "seeds" of new businesses.

Japanese companies are developing their R&D capacities in other areas and on other fronts as well. A growing number of firms are placing their R&D scientists in American university laboratories. A large number are engaging in joint research projects with both large and small American companies. Some are opening R&D labs in the United States, especially in Silicon Valley, to learn more about the U.S. R&D system. Others are making investments in American venture capital funds in order to gain accelerated access to new breakthroughs achieved in the United States. A few are investing in American universities to endow professorships, to join industrial liaison programs, and increasingly to build new laboratories on American university campuses.

Japanese firms are committed to globalization of their R&D facilities. Thus, there has been a rapid rise in the number of new laboratories and development facilities. The greatest investments in overseas R&D have quite naturally been taken by the gigantic automobile and electronics corporations and some of the software firms trying to secure access to U.S. programming skills. However, more recently Japanese pharmaceutical, consumer product, food processing, and cosmetic firms have also begun investing in laboratories to exploit U.S. biotechnology expertise. In a recent survey we conducted of all of the firms in the Japanese biotechnology industry association, 8 of 25 responding firms had overseas R&D facilities.[39]

Organization of the R&D Lab

The differences between the traditional Western and Japanese approaches to the organization of R&D are striking and reflect the differences between fordism and innovation-mediated models of production. In the traditional U.S. firm, there was a fundamental distinction drawn between R&D personnel and factory workers. College-trained scientists and engineers were considered the white-collar or managerial class. The R&D laboratory was separated from the factory and conceived of its role as creating innovations that would be implemented by others. The factory was not the site for creative work, but rather was where second-rate engineers were sent. As Harry Braverman pointed out, conception and execution were strictly separated.[40] Brains—like power—were to be centralized up the corporate ladder where they could be controlled and channelled. Only in the smaller entrepreneurial firms of California's Silicon Valley and Massachusetts's Route 128 would a special category of knowledge workers be freed from the stifling grip of corporate management.[41]

In Japan, the model of innovation-mediated production—with its emphasis on team work, collective effort, and the integration of intellectual and manual labor—enabled R&D scientists and engineers to be integrated with factory workers. R&D workers were not distinctly separated into the artificial categories of science and engineering favored by Western industry. In effect, no rigid caste system emerged to separate the R&D laboratory from the factory.

Teams are a cornerstone of Japanese R&D organization. Multidisciplinary research teams replace the strict specialization of traditional U.S. corporations. R&D workers are part of teams of between 5 and 15 scientists and engineers, and massive amounts of cross-learning and cross-training is used. These teams are typically "self-organizing"; often members are not assigned but rather volunteer and they typically form the core of larger multifunctional teams that will take new products from the idea stage through actual production. The emphasis is on collective rather than individual effort. Teams are formed to cope with actual problems and members added as needed. R&D scientists and engineers are also encouraged to use company time and equipment to work on their own ideas or "unofficial projects." This allows individual scientists and small groups to take initiative and begin work on new ideas without having to face the scrutiny of management review. If they prove successful, these unofficial projects can slowly turn into official projects with real budgets, larger staffs, and management backing; if not, they can be scuttled at very little cost. Taiyu Kobayashi, the former president of Fujitsu, highlights the advantage that flows from a team orientation to R&D:

> I believe the strength of Fujitsu lies in our group approach to research. . . . [F]rom what I have heard, it appears that individual abilities are given extremely high evaluation in the U.S. . . . I'm often told by my friends in competing companies, "You don't seem to have anybody with talent, but you sure get the job done!" Sort of a welcome insult, I suppose. . . . We place more value on cooperative development in which everyone has a sense of participation.[42]

The process of team-building and project formation thus bears at least some similarity to the process of entrepreneurial team formation in U.S. high-technology regions, such as Silicon Valley. In the Japanese model, teams are formed inside the company as opposed to the Silicon Valley model which creates teams in the form of new companies. The Japanese firm can therefore internalize the benefits of R&D efforts over a much longer period.

The Japanese system does suffer from some problems and weaknesses. The most salient of these is a kind of "group-think," a collectivist team orientation that mutes the expression of new ideas. Overwork and burnout are both vexing problems. According to Japanese sources, *karoshi*—death from overwork—is prevalent among R&D scientists and engineers who often become completely engrossed in their work and pressured by the team ethos. A similar burnout and stress-related illnesses are prevalent in the high-technology communities of Silicon Valley and Route 128.[43] Japanese firms are trying to deal with these problems by encouraging R&D workers to take relatively long amounts of time off to recharge themselves by going on company-sponsored sabbaticals and vacations.

Some Japanese companies are actively trying to create highly interactive, high-motivation skunk-works environments found in Silicon Valley and Route 128 start-ups. The development of Sony's new engineering workstation is a case in point. When Sony decided to develop this new product, it organized a team of 11 engineers and set them off in their own space with instructions to develop a new product within a year. The team developed a high level of internal motivation and members worked extraordinarily long hours to achieve their goal. Working in this high-motivation, high-effort environment, the team took less than a year to develop a working prototype; and Sony was able to start producing workstations barely two years after the project's inception.[44]

As we will show later in this chapter, a number of companies are developing spin-off businesses to develop software capability. In doing so, Japanese corporations try to replicate both the high-motivation environments and the rapid development cycle-times of U.S. start-ups. Because employees stay with the company for their entire career, Japanese firms can do so without incurring the high costs of disruption and turnover caused by hyper-mobile U.S. "think-workers." In effect, Japanese corporations are able to use their internal labor markets to perform a function similar to that performed by the external labor markets and process of entrepreneurial firm formation in Silicon Valley and along Route 128.

The recruitment and personnel practices of Japanese R&D laboratories differ fundamentally from those of the fordist laboratory. The majority of Japanese R&D personnel are recruited directly from undergraduate or master's degree science and engineering programs. New engineering recruits come from a variety of academic disciplines and departments. Japanese industry pays far less attention to a recruit's formal academic training and discipline and simply assigns that individual to an interdisciplinary team. Frequently, these assignments are not directly related to the recruit's background or academic training. The result is that engineers from different disciplines work together and learn from each other. This makes Japanese R&D laboratories very effective at combining and using interdisciplinary teams, but less effective at the types of technological innovation that require highly specialized researchers.

Japanese R&D benefits from long-term employment and low turnover. In fact, a recent study found that nearly three-quarters of Japanese engineers had only one employer during their entire career[45]—a far cry from the U.S. pattern of "hyper-mobility."[46] The firm therefore retains its "human" capital investments in R&D. Further, long-term employment coupled with the inability to shed workers easily provides a powerful impetus to innovation. Because increased competition is always threatening an overproduction crisis and concomitant layoffs, firms must always find new business opportunities. And, of course, there are always personnel available to be detailed to explore the new opportunities. Any business opportunity (no matter how small) will immediately have firms from a variety of industries exploring it from the perspective of their particular expertise. Each firm tries to establish a niche and then expand it. The result is that an infrastructure or community of firms is rapidly developed. If the new area expands (and, of course, crowds of entrants assist that expansion) each firm gears up production, reinvests profits, and attempts to expand its niche. Other firms are attracted and attempt to find opportunities and to supply inputs. Thus, the constraint of not being able to shed workers easily leads to a powerful economic stimulus to expand and continuously compete in any new technological and commercial openings.

Connecting the R&D Lab and the Factory

A key and defining element of the Japanese approach to innovation-mediated production is the tight linkage and integration between the R&D laboratory and the factory. This is a major advance over the fordist assembly line model of innovation where these activities were kept functionally separate. In Japan, R&D takes place at various types of institutions and facilities. First, most of the large companies have central R&D labs where both development and high-end basic research takes place. In addition, all have product development centers that are closely linked to actual factories.[47] The product development centers focus on developing new products and processes. Additionally, most factories have their own product development engineering staff whose main job is to upgrade the products and manufacturing processes used in the plant. Finally, work groups in the factory are involved in smaller scale, incremental product and process improvement on a continuous basis.

The ability to move a product quickly from R&D to factory production is being recognized as ever-more crucial to industrial success. At bottom, this transfer process is one of communication and interaction. The authors of a recent study of product development in the automobile industry in the United States, Japan, and Europe concluded that "notwithstanding the popular argument that electronic telecommunications media will substitute for face-to-face contact, interpersonal communication will continue to be critical to new product success."[48] In a survey of the relations between the production engineering department and other functional departments (e.g., R&D, manufacturing, marketing, etc.) of Japanese companies, Koji Okubayashi found that the most important single relationship was with production—with more than 85 percent of respondents identifying this as a key linkage. The next most important relationship was with R&D, which roughly 60 percent considered to be important. All of the other functional departments were less important.[49] This is reinforced by Eleanor Westney and Kiyonori Sakakibara's findings that Japanese engineers in both central and divisional laboratories communicated more frequently with manufacturing than did their American counterparts.[50] Interestingly, they found that the engineers in the central labs communicated far less frequently with sales and marketing than either their counterpart engineers in the development labs or their U.S. counterparts. However, the Japanese development laboratory engineers communicated much more frequently with sales and marketing than did the American engineers. Japanese corporations see R&D as an integral part of the corporation, not a separate activity. Further, since engineers know that later in their careers they will eventually move to manufacturing positions, it is incumbent upon them to develop good relations with the manufacturing units.

Japanese corporations use teams and functional integration to blur the boundaries between the R&D laboratory and the factory. Under this approach, teams develop links to and connections across the innovation-production spectrum. Overlapping membership allows R&D workers to work alongside product development engineers and even factory workers, thus blurring the boundaries separating them. Rather than having a strict purpose and fixed membership, teams continually adjust their goals and continuously add or remove members whose skills and expertise are needed to move forward.[51] This creates an interplay and synthesis of various types of knowledge in an explicitly social context.

This is best illustrated by providing a stylized account of R&D process for a new product. In Japan, when a product development project is approved, research and project engineers are joined by a small number of manufacturing engineers, industrial designers, and so forth. As product engineering and planning advances, more manufacturing engineers are added in order to focus on component design, machine setup, and assembly. Tool engineers are then integrated into the project team to develop special instruments and machinery necessary for manufacturing. At this stage, plant managers and representatives of suppliers become team members. Although previous members drop off as various stages are completed, some representatives of each group remain with the project until early production runs are accomplished.

This process of team-based functional integration facilitates knowledge-sharing and learning-by-doing in yet another aspect of the production process, one that feeds back into the most basic aspects of research and product planning.[52] This replaces the "not-invented-here" syndrome of fordist R&D with a powerful form of collaborative problem solving and organizational learning. Having "hands-on" personnel involved at early stages ensures that the design staff does not develop plans that are too difficult to implement. This process ensures that important new innovations are rapidly translated into new products and processes. These organizational innovations overcome the information blockages and other rigidities that characterize U.S. R&D and create powerful "learning-by-doing" effects similar to those on the shop floor.[53] Recent comparative studies of innovation in Japanese and U.S. corporations conclude that Japanese corporations convert new innovations, especially those coming from outside sources, into products more quickly than their American counterparts, compressing the time it takes to move innovations from R&D to manufacturing.[54]

This model of functional integration is a radical departure from the fordist assembly-line model of innovation that was distinguished by a highly specialized division of labor within various R&D activities, between R&D and manufacturing, and among firms and their suppliers. In fordist firms, this entire spectrum was split into self-contained and isolated segments; scientists and engineers typically operate along strict disciplinary lines and are compartmentalized in separate departments. It thus became difficult and at times virtually impossible to translate knowledge into commercial innovations or to translate innovations into mass-produced commodities.

This process of functional integration is reinforced and bolstered by the career cycle of Japanese R&D scientists and engineers. Transfer from R&D to manufacturing facilities is common. Japanese researchers spend the first decade or so of their career engaged in long-term research at central laboratories and then are deployed to manufacturing sites where they function as "carriers" of particular projects and technical knowledge.[55] In their comparative study of the organization of R&D in both U.S. and Japanese firms, Westney and Sakakibara concluded that

> In all three Japanese firms, one or more of the engineers involved with the project at the central lab will move with project to the division on permanent assignment. . . . Research managers at all three companies stressed . . . that the constant flow of people from the center to the divisions (transfer with a project is not the only occasion of such transfers) as the key factor in smooth technology transfer.[56]

At NEC, for example, approximately 50 percent of all research personnel are transferred to operating divisions during their first decade of service, and after 20 years 80 percent are transferred.[57] At Fujitsu, the typical researcher spends under ten years at the Central Research Institute before being transferred to an applied research facility at a factory site. The next transfer is often to production engineering inside an actual factory. Rotation is used both within research centers and between research facilities and operating divisions. This not only constantly reinforces the linkage between manufacturing and R&D, but also provides a method for continually refreshing R&D with new personnel.[58]

The Factory as a Center for Innovation

At the core of innovation-mediated production in Japan stands the transformation of the factory itself. Not only are the lines between the factory and the lab blurring, but the factory is itself becoming a laboratory setting. In a recent, prescient article, Robert Cole suggests that the Japanese factory in Japan has become a "school" in which learning constantly takes place.[59] But learning is not sufficient—it is the application of that learning that is crucial and that occurs through innovation. In this way the factory becomes a "living" technological system constantly evolving—in other words, a "laboratory."

The factory is no longer a place of dirty floors and smoking machines, but rather an environment of ongoing experimentation and continuous innovation. The shop floor is the place where new ideas and concepts are tested and actualized. The factory as a laboratory is a source of constant and continuous improvement in both products and processes, creating a powerful new source of innovation, productivity,

value generation, and capital accumulation. The new worker for this environment must be trained and managed more like a researcher than as a traditional factory worker.

Let us reflect upon the features of the laboratory. First, the laboratory is an environment created to exclude entropy or transient events—i.e., anything that would
interrupt an experiment. At the most basic level, this simply means keeping the
factory clean and tidy—a feature that decreases the probability of undesired materials entering the work-in-process or the probability that transient events will disrupt the process. As the engineering tolerances on products decrease, more and
more products are being assembled in clean environments. Yamazaki Mazak, for
example, assembles certain parts of its machine tools in a class 10,000 clean room.[60]
In yet another example, the drums for Canon's copy machines are also produced
in class 10,000 clean rooms.[61] This is also important in less technology-intensive
operations. A Japanese plant manager spelled out the importance of a clean factory
to the manufacture of "toner" for photocopiers and printers, a standard product:

> Toner is a black powder. If I had done nothing the factory would be very much
> contaminated, also the office would be contaminated by toner. Everything would
> be very dark and dirty; and we would lose control. So, my basic philosophy was
> clean up the factory—keep the factory clean.[62]

Surprises, glitches, or unplanned events will disrupt operations and slow down production. Similarly, waste and inefficiency must be continuously eliminated.

Second, experiments are exhaustively documented to ensure reproducibility,
which is crucial to any scientific activity. In another similarity to a laboratory, Japanese factories keep extensive documentation of procedures, results, and flaws in
the production process. Third, modern manufacturing requires that production
processes change continuously to produce new-generation products. The factory
must become a center for continuous improvement to ready these new processes.
In other words, the factory itself must become a center for dynamic change. For this
to occur, constant ongoing application of intelligence is required. The manager of
a Yamazaki Mazak plant put it succinctly:

> Getting the system to run and to make constant changes to it requires that produc-
> tion people have to work very closely with software people. Each has to do the oth-
> er's job to understand each other. In writing the software, all different cases have to
> be examined. They have to consider the kinds of work pieces they produce today
> as well as those they would make in the future. Besides, they have to consider the
> kinds of problems they may run into.[63]

Two examples illustrate the factory as laboratory concept. The first involves the
semiconductor industry. The United States, as is widely acknowledged, both
invented and developed the first systems for mass-producing semiconductors. The
U.S. approach—pioneered by corporations like Fairchild, Motorola, Texas Instruments, National Semiconductor, Intel, and more recent Silicon Valley start-ups
such as LSI Logic, Cypress Semiconductor, and others—was and still is to develop

important new semiconductor breakthroughs in controlled laboratory settings. Under this process, the intelligence of scientists and engineers is applied up front and encapsulated in new technologies. These and other engineers then design the basic manufacturing process also in a controlled laboratory or small pilot-plant setting. After this, the new technology and machines are moved to the factory, then other engineers set up the machines and turn them over to the operators with little interaction or input. Workers in the factory carry out their production tasks but contribute little if anything to upgrading or improving this new technology or its production process. In formal language the process of innovation is dynamic. But once the machinery is installed and the production processes and the engineers have fine-tuned them, there are supposed to be no more changes. Thus, production is static.

In Japanese corporations, however, the process is strikingly different. While engineers and scientists take the lead in design, factory workers and technicians are constantly consulted on the actual ability to produce with the new technology. Once the technology is designed and implemented, factory workers make continuous suggestions on how to upgrade and improve both the quality of the technology and the manufacturing process. This leads to continuous improvement in product quality and functionality and continuous improvement in the processes used to make these products. This continuous involvement and interaction contributes to the rapid development and introduction of new, more advanced product generations. Here, production has become constantly changing and dynamic.

The second example is from the steel industry, where the combination of new microelectronic technologies and, more importantly, the new shop-floor organization are exerting powerful creative destruction effects. This example concerns the process of cold-rolling whereby thick steel coils are turned into thinner sheet steel for application in automobiles, office furniture, refrigerators, washing machines, and other home appliances. In the United States and most of Europe cold-rolling was traditionally a batch process. Huge steel coils would be carried one step at a time, first to a machine that scraped rust and oxidation from their surface, then to another that bathed them in a chemical solution for further cleaning, to another that dried them off, to still another that pressed them to a desired thickness, and then to final cutting and preparation. Such a process would typically take about a week to complete. Nippon Steel has turned the cold-rolling of steel into a continuous process that takes less than one hour from start to finish. It achieved this by unleashing the collective intelligence of its workers. The company mobilized both factory workers and R&D workers to combine the various batch processes one at a time. Workers began by combining the entry and scraping processes; then they connected the chemical cleaning and drying process. With the help of computer specialists they added computer controls. The two processes were then connected together. Now this is a highly automated process, controlled by advanced computer technology that the shop-floor workers monitor, modify, and program on their own with the full support of management and engineers.

Since 1990 Nippon Steel has been working with Inland Steel at their joint-venture plant in Indiana to connect this continuous cold-rolling process to another process, called electro-galvanizing, which applies a zinc, nickel, or aluminum coating to steel, making it corrosion resistant for use in automobile body parts (see Chapter 6). The executives and workers we interviewed at the I/N Tek plant indicated that such innovations were not achieved in an R&D center; rather, the factory itself had become a laboratory setting for innovation and continuous improvement. In the words of one executive:

> The key is to use [the workers'] brains. Those are your resources, your technicians, your labs, but they're out there on the operating floor. . . . Constant improvement means constant change. You can't get constant improvement if you've got the status quo. How do you get constant change? You get it by doing things you've never done before. Isn't that what they do in a lab? Try to figure out things they never did before.[64]

These two examples illustrate the way that continuous improvements can come from workers' intelligence. These cumulative product and process innovations can eventually outdistance and at times replace laboratory breakthroughs. The factory floor itself has become a critical arena for innovation. The concepts, drawings, and blueprints must be actualized in the physical world to create products. For this to occur successfully, smart workers must be involved.

In the factory as laboratory, the distinction between intellectual and physical labor that Marx indicated and Harry Braverman raised to the fundamental contradiction of modern capitalism is at some fundamental level mitigated. Contrary to what U.S. managers believed, the new world of manufacturing will not be an environment of smart machines and automaton-like workers. In fact, this mode of organizing production will surely fail.

Marx recognized that the first Industrial Revolution rested upon a fundamental transformation of work when it transferred the tool from the human's hand to the machine.[65] The worker was in the process of becoming a machine "minder." For management, this meant that workers need only make sure the machines operated properly. With the rise of fordism, the organization of production was explicitly organized around a separation of mental and manual labor. According to Harry Braverman, management tried to take power away from workers by "de-skilling" them.[66] The basic idea was to separate the conception of tasks from their execution. As Joseph Schumpeter noted, in postwar U.S. and Western European industry, innovation—the process of turning rough technological ideas into commodities—was placed in specialized R&D labs.[67] In the fordist division of labor then, intellectual tasks became formally the responsibility of scientists and engineers who worked in R&D labs, while manual labor took place in factories. The entire division of labor was codified in an extensive system of written job classifications and work rules.

The fordist management strata simply assumed that everything would run smoothly as long as these job description and work rules were followed. However, this system did not necessarily result in the most efficient production organization. This could be most clearly seen when workers would "work to rule"—stop applying their intelligence in production—and bring the production process to a halt. Indeed, the separation of mental and manual labor under fordism did not come about because shop-floor workers were unable to unify their manual and mental labor; rather, the organization of production and its class relationships imposed this separation. As Herbert Marcuse recognized fairly early on and David Noble later documented, the "gap" between engineers and factory workers was "maintained more by the division of power than by the division of work."[68]

As the previous chapter has shown, Japanese corporations approached the organization of production differently. It was presumed that the machine "minders" actually had minds that could be tapped to improve the production process. In addition, it was recognized very early on that ignoring suggestions leads to demoralization and decreased commitment. The Japanese *kaizen* approach is predicated upon the concept that the factory should be a location for continuous innovation where unplanned events can be coped with and processes actively implemented and improved. This crucial point was reflected in an interview with a Japanese executive.

> The operator must understand the importance of and responsibilities of his area . . . and also must find something to improve in procedures. . . . Improvement is very important because the engineer designs the whole manufacturing procedure, but they do not design in such detail. Thus, the actual manufacturing activity is very confusing, many things happen. So we need to improve the procedure during manufacturing itself.[69]

He then gave a detailed illustration of how the actual real world of manufacturing differs from the engineer's designs and how workers must overcome these real-world obstacles.

What these comments reflect is the integration of conception and execution. In reality, these two different realms can never be fully separated; indeed each has aspects of the other embedded within it. For example, the engineer makes drawings—a physical activity; the shop-floor worker must think to operate. Yet, designs or engineering plans are an abstraction and therefore do not map one-to-one onto the real physical world. Thus, human beings, operating in the real physical world of manufacturing (of reshaping physical matter), are required to reconcile and bring together the two realms. The Japanese model recognizes the fundamental fact that this reconciliation is dynamic and must go on continuously.[70]

In the factory as laboratory, knowledge is socially and/or collectively created. Thus, the intellectual capabilities of various types of workers are integrated and explicitly harnessed in the process of turning knowledge into commodities and new productive forces. This implies overcoming the institutionally imposed divisions separating various strata of workers: R&D scientists who create innovations; engineers who develop them and turn them into commercial products; and shop-floor workers who produce them. Integration of functions is required so all the relevant actors can interact, exchange thoughts, and create new ideas as a unified "social brain" or "group mind" and then translate and embody those ideas in new products and production processes. In this sense, the process of innovation and production becomes more explicitly social or intersubjective.

The team is the concrete organizational mechanism for harnessing intelligence.

In high-technology industries, the team is used to harness the collective intelligence of scientists, engineers, and factory workers and turn it into commodities—a new microelectronic product, a new computer, a new software program, a new ceramic material, etc. It makes the extraction of intellectual (and manual) labor a quintessentially social, intersubjective, and collective process that blurs the distinctions among scientists, engineers, and factory workers.

Redefining Industrial Boundaries

Japan's approach to the high-technology age is also distinguished by an integration across what have been considered different high-technology sectors and between high-technology and basic industries. In effect, what is occurring is the redefinition and transcendance of the traditional industrial boundaries of the United States and Europe. In Japan, the same companies that make semiconductors also make personal computers, supercomputers, telecommunications, electronic instruments, and industrial robots as well as mass-market consumer electronics goods that provide ready outlets for microelectronic components.[71] So, for example, Canon Inc., originally a camera maker, now produces copiers, laser printers, semiconductor production equipment, calculators, word processors, facsimile machines, electronic typewriters, micromotors, and video cameras. The new microelectronics technologies have become a source of powerful corporate growth in the basic manufacturing industries such as automobiles and steel. The new model of innovation-mediated production thus applies increasingly to large segments of the Japanese industrial structure.

Large diversified Japanese electronics corporations—Fujitsu, Hitachi, Matsushita, Mitsubishi Electric, NEC, and Toshiba—are major players across a variety of high-technology sectors—computers, semiconductors, and advanced manufacturing—as well as being major consumer electronics companies. These six firms account for more than two-thirds of the Japanese market for a variety of semiconductors and integrated circuit products, 58 percent of the market for general-purpose computers, 48 percent of the personal computer market, and 43 percent of the office computer market, along with 60 percent of the market for computerized machine tools and 40 percent of the industrial robotics market. However, these companies cannot rest as they are constantly being challenged by competitors such as Sony and Canon.

These integrated firms contrast with the more segmented and fragmented organization of U.S. high technology. In America, the computer, semiconductor, telecommunications, and consumer electronics industries evolved as separate and distinct industrial sectors. This separation occurred because AT&T was a regulated monopoly that manufactured its equipment through its Western Electric subsidiary. In the 1950s, AT&T was prohibited by the U.S. Department of Justice from producing semiconductors for commercial sale. IBM, of course, controlled the computer industry but avoided the communication industry. While IBM is the world's largest producer of semiconductors nearly all of these are for its internal use.

To service other companies and users a separate group of so-called merchant producers developed.

The evolutionary pattern in Japan was quite different. The same firms that manufactured telecommunications equipment also produced computer equipment. This was because Nippon Telephone and Telegraph (NTT), in contrast to the private AT&T, was a government-regulated monopoly that did not produce any equipment. NTT developed a family of suppliers-most notably NEC, Fujitsu, Oki Electric, and Hitachi.[72] These companies would become the critical players in Japanese computer, semiconductor, and telecommunications production. They would later be joined by Toshiba, Mitsubishi Electric, Matsushita, and Sony from the consumer electronics and electrical equipment industries.

Japanese electronics firms benefit from integration, since they are able to supply semiconductors to their own computer and telecommunications divisions. Moreover, these companies have larger, powerful consumer electronics divisions that provide an even larger internal market for their high-technology products from semiconductors to new display technology. This is illustrated figure 3.5, which shows the source of final demand or end-use for semiconductors in Japan and the United States. Notice that nearly half of U.S. demand is for government (defense) and computers; there is very little consumer electronics demand. In contrast, Japan has huge demand from the consumer market and very little from defense. The result is that its electronics industry is powerfully attuned to the commercial market.

Such integration and scope gives Japanese high-technology companies important advantages in both technological innovation and downstream manufacturing. The integration of high-technology and consumer products within the same company makes it easier for new technical developments to diffuse into mass-market goods, and for the income from sales of mass-market goods to fuel additional innovations.[73] The end result is tremendous synergy in the development and implementation of technological innovations.

Moreover, there are close linkages and integration between high-technology sectors and mature basic industries. A number of key high-technology and heavy manufacturing companies share membership in broader *keiretsu* groupings that enhance linkages and accelerate technology transfer. So, for example, Sumitomo Electric Industry and NEC have cooperated in developing fiber optic cable and equipment. Also, Japanese high-technology companies are suppliers to basic industries, providing the technologies and processes that are spurring the transformation of those industries.

Japanese companies are now pacesetters in new mechatronics fields such as flexible manufacturing systems, industrial robots, computer vision systems, and new semiconductor fabrication techniques.[74] By 1989, Japanese corporations had deployed 219,667 industrial robots in manufacturing compared to 36,977 for the United States and 22,395 for Germany; no other country had deployed more than 10,000 industrial robots. In another important new field, namely phototonics, the combination of lasers and manufacturing technologies, a recent National Research Council report concluded that the United States has been reduced to an

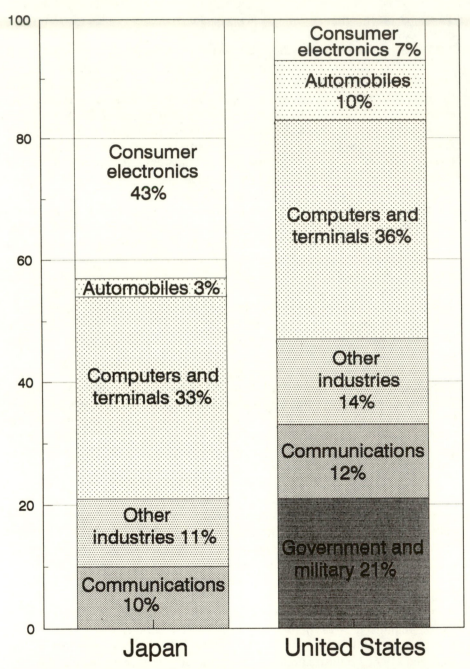

FIGURE 3.5. Final Demand for Semiconductors in Japan and the United States.
Source: Dempa Publication Inc., *Japan Electronics Almanac 1990*. (Tokyo: Dempa
Publications Inc., 1991.) p. 316.

"observer."[75] The Japanese steel industry is perhaps the best example of how new technologies are being used to promote "creative destruction" in traditional industries. Japanese steel executives are using new technologies to move into what they refer to as the "new iron age" in which steel will be a highly automated, computerized continuous process industry.[76]

Henry Ergas has advanced the conceptualization of "shifting" versus "deepening" models as a theory of comparative technological development.[77] Ergas's conceptualization provides insight into the integration of high technology and traditional industries in Japan. Countries like the United States develop by shifting toward new technological frontiers, while others like Germany evolve via intensive specialization in mature sectors. In Japan, however, there has developed an integration of shifting and deepening. As a result, technologies not only diffuse rapidly and help to rejuvenate mature sectors but large enterprises are able quickly to penetrate emerging areas that have relevance to their core production fields either through invention, successful imitation, or knowledge acquisition. As a result, the entire industrial structure is pushed toward new technological frontiers, as the new technologies deepen and strengthen the old industries allowing them to remain competitive.

The roots of such integration lie in the new model of innovation-mediated production itself. The Japanese capital-labor relation and organization of work at the point of production provide the context within which these powerful creative destruction effects take place. For example, when Nippon Steel automated its facilities, blue-collar workers were transferred to jobs as computer operators and some were even trained as computer programmers. In 1983, some 49 percent of the computer planner/programmers and 98 percent of the computer operators at Nippon Steel's Yawata facility were former blue-collar workers.[78] The already existing framework of Japanese industrial organization provided the context in which shop-floor workers were transformed into knowledge workers rather than simply being displaced.

Japan has seen rapid diffusion of automated production technology in its factories. Research by Ramchandran Jaikumar and others indicates that Japan is rapidly moving to a new version of the "factory of the future" by adopting flexible manufacturing systems and self-contained cells of machine tools. These new technologies are highly computerized, digitally based, and information-intensive—and they are operated by a new strata of smart workers.[79] The number of flexible manufacturing systems used in Japan is more than double that of the United States. Further, Japanese systems have significantly higher levels of capacity utilization. The two-shift utilization rate of flexible manufacturing systems in Japan was 84 percent versus 52 percent for the United States. On the third shift, some of the Japanese systems were being operated unattended for a total daily utilization rate of 92 percent.

In Japan, the introduction of advanced manufacturing technology such as flexible manufacturing systems (FMS) is tied to and enhanced by the organization of production. Because of long-term employment, workers need not fear displacement, and management will invest in training and skill upgrading. Multidisciplinary and cross-functional project teams are able to tailor FMS technology to a wide variety of production environments. Managers concentrate on upgrading and harnessing workers' technical skills and intellectual capabilities in ways that could create an effective organizational context for the constantly changing technology being introduced into the workplace. Jaikumar describes how the introduction of FMS technology in Japan has resulted in a drastic redefinition of management functions.

> Executives [in Japan] were largely absent from day-to-day operations. Instead of concerning themselves with internal operations, they focused their attention on how to meet competitive pressures on product performance. In the United States on the other hand, managers spend so much time on routine problems . . . that they virtually have no time left over to plan for long-term process improvement. . . . The prime task of management once the system has been made reliable is not to categorize tasks or regiment workers but to create the fixed assets—the systems and software—needed to make products. Thus the new role of management is to create and nurture the project teams whose intellectual capabilities produce competitive advantage. What gets managed is intellectual capital not equipment.[80]

A recent detailed empirical exploration of the relationship among product development, factory automation, and workers' skills suggests that the impact of automation in Japanese factories emphasizes new knowledge-based capabilities and deemphasizes traditional practically informed blue-collar skills. According to the study by Koji Okubayashi, 39 percent of respondents stated that automation led to "skills becoming useless, but more knowledge required"; another 40 percent reported that "all of the jobs [were] polarized into the simple and the complex"; for 16 percent "the contents of all the jobs [became] complex and especially new knowledge [was] required"; and for 4 percent both the skills and knowledge required became more important. According to Okubayashi, automated technologies in Japan are designed to optimize not obviate the capabilities of shop-floor workers:

> The fundamental philosophy of production engineers to choose [among] alternatives in designing hard systems is found from [sic] their idea about design principles. They realize that they should take account of the needs of rank and file workers who in practice operate the machines designed by them as well as of the technical characteristics of machines and apparatus. Our data confirms that Japanese production engineers usually give much consideration in designing systems to human aspects of the production systems as well as to their technological aspects.[81]

Effectively speaking, Okubayashi's findings suggest a sweeping transformation of work and the labor process—where traditional categories and conceptions of work are being de-skilled, while at the same time the labor process requires greater levels of intelligence and abstract knowledge on the part of traditional shop-floor workers.

In contrast to the U.S. experience, the implementation of industrial automation in Japan involves the creation of new work environments and the cultivation of workers' intellectual capabilities as well as the de-emphasis of traditional skills. The shift to highly automated manufacture reinforces the shift toward knowledge workers on the shop floor whose primary responsibility is to monitor and oversee advanced electronic technology. This involves a shift in management focus from the simple or coercive management of workers and hardware to the cultivation and deployment of smart workers or what Haruo Shimada refers to as "humanware."[82] Japanese corporations have thus far chosen not to implement an entirely computer-integrated factory, preferring to have workers and managers experiment with new manufacturing technology. The shift to the factory of the future in Japan is supported by a growing cadre of intelligent workers in both high technology and basic industry.

Innovation Complexes and Sponsored Spin-offs

Japan's high-technology industries have adopted the highly structured just-in-time linkages between parents and their subsidiaries, suppliers and subcontractors, that were developed in other industries. Research by Ken-ichi Imai indicates that 90 percent of the parts used in Fuji-Xerox products, 70 percent of the parts used in NEC and Epson products, and 65 percent of the parts used in Canon products are actually made by outside suppliers and subcontractors.[83] Hitachi, for example, has an immediate industrial galaxy of more than 700 suppliers, many of which it partly owns; other large firms have similar galaxies.

Table 3.2 sheds additional light on this process, showing the number of parent plants to various types of subsidiaries: majority-owned or affiliated subsidiaries, partly owned subsidiaries, and loosely affiliated subsidiaries for the six major high-tech electronics companies. Note the high degrees of parent ownership among these subsidiaries, which often function as major suppliers to parent company plants. As data are limited to major subsidiaries and affiliates, it is only a partial picture of the dense networks of secondary and tertiary suppliers in high-technology electronics.

TABLE 3.2.   Parent-Subsidiary Linkages in Japanese Electronics

	Parent Co. Plants	Majority Owned Subsidiary Plants	Partly Owned Subsidiaries	Loosely Related Subsidiaries	Total Subsidiaries	Parent-Sub Ratio
Fujitsu	16	46	34	80	160	10.0
Hitachi	37	46	530	153	729	19.7
Matsushita	38	82	270	111	463	12.2
Mitsubishi	32	24	109	71	204	12.2
NEC	7	88 *	34	64	186	26.6
Toshiba	26	32	182	192	412	15.9
Total	156	318	1,159	671	2,154	—
Mean	26	53	193	112	359	13.8

Source: Authors' compilation from Dodwell Marketing Consultants, *Key Players in the Japanese Electronics Industry.* (Tokyo: Dodwell Marketing Consultants, August 1985).
*Includes 44 wholly owned subsidiary NEC plants.

This system has resulted in the development of extremely strong and powerful supplier and input firms and industries in Japan. The Japanese semiconductor equipment supplier industry is the strongest in the world (see Fig. 3.6). In 1980, for example, the United States supplied 75 percent of the market for semiconductor equipment, while Japan had just an 18 percent share. By 1990, Japanese companies supplied over half of the $9 billion market for semiconductor manufacturing equipment and the $5.8 billion market for processing equipment. Japanese companies such as Nikon, Canon, Hitachi, Tokyo Electron, Kokusai Electric, and others are the world leaders in wafer steppers, wafer fabrication equipment, microlithography equipment, and diffusion furnaces. These firms not only serve their Japanese producers, but increasingly provide state-of-the-art equipment and supplies to U.S. customers. As Chapter 8 will show, these input and supplier firms have begun to open subsidiaries in the United States to serve both Japanese and American customers.[84] In a recent report on the global semiconductor equipment industry, the Japan Economic Institute concluded that:

> Japanese SME [semiconductor manufacturing equipment] suppliers readily admit that their working relationships with chip producers—which provide help with product planning and equipment testing in addition to financial and technical development support—are a major competitive advantage. In fact, they rank close customer involvement as their biggest strength.[85]

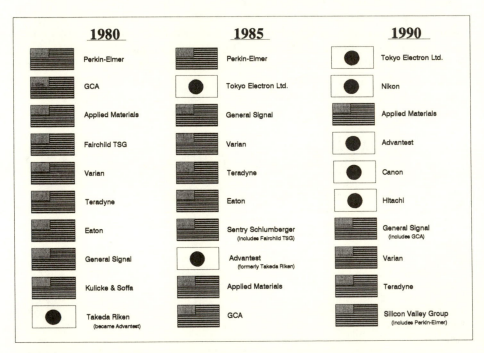

FIGURE 3.6. Top Ten Semiconductor Equipment Manufacturers.
Source: VLSI Research, Inc., 1991.

This stands in sharp contrast to the relations between U.S. semiconductor equipment makers and chip producers. Indeed, a survey of U.S. semiconductor equipment producers done by the U.S. General Accounting Office indicates that a major problem facing the American semiconductor equipment industry stems from poor relations on the part of end-users. According to the study, 25 of 31 suppliers stated that semiconductor manufacturers provide little support, 23 suppliers said that manufacturers did not involve them in design, 21 indicated that relationships were based purely on short-term considerations, and 15 considered their relationships with manufacturers too adversarial.[86]

This structure of Japanese high-technology production networks provides a powerful source of innovation. As Eric von Hippel has shown, the interaction between input firms and end-users is extremely important in developing innovations in all industries, especially high-technology sectors like semiconductors.[87] In Japan, R&D is far more decentralized as all of the suppliers know R&D is vital not only to growth but also to survival. Thus, the supplier network becomes another source of continuous improvement.

Japanese supplier networks also function as conduits for a rapid and continuous flow of information and technology transfer. The importance of this information exchange is reflected in the fact that at Honda's new R&D lab at Tochigi, for example, adjacent land is set aside for suppliers to build their own R&D facilities.[88] This collaborative aspect shifts the risk of innovation from individual firms to a network of firms, making innovation more attractive and more feasible. An example of this is provided by Ikujiro Nonaka who quotes a project leader at Hiroshima Aluminum on the interaction with Mazda regarding the design of a new car model:

> With this car, we had a designer from Mazda come in from the early first stages. Usually corporate secrets are not allowed outside, but in this case we worked closely together from the start. Until now, we would receive plans and work from those; this time, however, the design people and the manufacturing people formed a team and worked together. One question that comes up is why Mazda's people would go so far as to want to do something like this. There's a big gap between planning and manufacturing, and because this method covers that gap, I think it was very good. We can't understand things like the origins of the shapes we work with just from drawings. Oh, the shapes come out clearly, but the reasons behind them are not communicated just from the prints.[89]

When such a system operates properly it can generate powerful technological synergies between companies—combining the benefits of scale with the advantages of smaller size and flat management hierarchies and much faster information flow.

The supplier network also provides a unique vehicle for turning innovations into products through "sponsored spin-offs." A classic example of this is Fanuc, a Fujitsu spin-off, which currently ranks among the world's leading producers of industrial robots. Sponsored spin-offs are based on the concept of "growth through connection." Spin-off companies begin life within the corporate parent until they are large enough to leave. The parent provides financing, retains significant ownership, and ensures a permanent relationship with the new company. As we will see, many of Japan's leading electronics hardware companies like NEC, Toshiba, and Fujitsu are also spinning off their software operations because these firms are hardware-oriented and therefore cannot adequately manage software employees. As time progresses, the spin-off is gradually weaned until it becomes a free-standing member of the parent's industrial network. Spin-offs can grow large enough to seek out new business on their own, loosening their ties to the original parent. Nippondenso, a Toyota spin-off, has grown into Japan's leading manufacturer of automotive lighting and electrical systems and in the process has become a major supplier to other Japanese automobile companies.[90] A few spin-offs ultimately grow larger than their parents. Today, for example, Fujitsu is significantly larger than its parent, Fuji Electric. Such growth is itself beneficial, since it allows the fruits of innovation to diffuse through the economy as new connections are formed with other firms.

This system enables new technologies or products to be turned into subsidiaries. The sponsored spin-offs create a corporate family and encourage member firms to launch joint projects, transfer mutually useful information, and cross-fertilize one another. Japanese corporations use this spin-off process to avoid the diseconomies of scale associated with massive corporate bureaucracies and develop portfolios of satellite organizations suitable to a variety of types and stages of economic activity.[91]

Nippon Steel, for example, has spun out its information-processing activities into a new company called Enicom. Initially, Enicom will be staffed by Nippon Steel employees, but it has already begun hiring its own employees and over time will have ever fewer workers from Nippon Steel. During its start-up period, Enicom will be guaranteed Nippon Steel's business, but over time it is expected to develop new customers. This strategy has numerous advantages. It allows Nippon Steel to eliminate levels of bureaucracy and management, and it exposes the company's data-processing arm to the rigors of the market. As an independent company, Enicom can develop its own marketplace presence and network of subcontractors. The new company also creates a new career path for software and data-processing employees. The new firm makes it possible for software specialists to attain top executive positions, which were closed to them at Nippon Steel—where such posts are reserved for "steel men." Moreover, software production and information processing are activities that require skills which are rather different from steel-making. Enicom employees can be trained and transferred internally without going through the general training of Nippon Steel's regular steel division employees.[92]

These structured and integrated relationships may be a more effective way of organizing technological change than U.S. innovation complexes, which are characterized by high rates of employee turnover, new enterprise formation, and disruption of ongoing R&D efforts.[93] Restructuring in Japan replaces the strict dichotomy of vertical integration versus market relationships with new "network forms" characterized by organizational fuzziness, institutional overlap, and quasi-integrated/semi-market relationships.

Software in the Era of Innovation-Mediated Production

Software is perhaps the most important and intriguing of all high-technology sectors. Already it is estimated that the global market for software will approach $200 billion. Software is central to the entire digitization revolution and is embodied in any product that uses electronics to perform functions. It is critical to computing, to automated production, and increasingly to consumer products. As an example of software's growing importance, software and services at IBM have grown from less than 20 percent of total revenues in 1983 to 30 percent by 1986 and there is no reason to believe that this trend will not continue given declining hardware prices. Microsoft, the premier personal computer software maker, had revenues in 1990 in excess of $1 billion. The U.S. Office of Technology Assessment recently concluded that "computer manufacturers find themselves spending the majority of their R&D dollars on software."[94] Thus, the firms or nations that control software production will have a major source of competitive strength.

Software has long been considered a bastion of U.S. competitive strength. As late as 1987, Japanese software revenues were only 5 percent to 7 percent of global sales of $21 billion.[95] However, Michael Cusumano's recent book on Japan's software factories suggests that Japan has made important strides in the routinization and standardization of software development and production in so-called software factories, resulting in the production of reliable, high-quality software products.[96] It is our contention that the application of innovation-mediated production in the Japanese software industry goes far beyond the production of standardized products to the development of new sources of creativity and value.

We focus here on a crucial dimension of the software industry—"operating software," which includes both stand alone software packages and software which is embedded within electronic products. The many facets of software production in advanced industrial society make it difficult to grasp the software industry in its entirety. We omit from our definition "culture" products such as musical recordings and films. However, it is important to note that Japanese consumer electronics firms have purchased CBS Records and MCA among others to provide access to "programs" that can be considered the software of the consumer electronics industry.[97]

The Japanese commercial software industry can be divided into two parts: the internal software divisions of large firms along with their corporate subsidiaries and subcontractors, and a smaller group of independent software houses. Historically, the Japanese software industry has mainly focused on large systems software (i.e., mainframe software) in contrast to the personal computer orientation of important sectors of the software industry in the United States. Just 16 large diversified corporations—including electric industry giants Fujitsu, Hitachi, NEC, and Toshiba—account for three-quarters of all systems software production and introduces more than one-half of all applications packages. However, Fujitsu FIP, a Fujitsu software subsidiary, has 40 subcontractors, the largest of which has 400 people and the smallest has 20. Beneath this is another layer of "sub-subcontractors." Finally, there are still other contractors outside the group.[98]

A number of software establishments or so-called systems houses are actually spin-offs from these large companies' software factories; many others have close subcontracting relationships with them. The closest spin-offs are actually sponsored spin-offs from the big companies. All of the major electronics firms have a number of these. NEC, for example, has 33 software-related subsidiaries, Toshiba has 30, and Hitachi has 25. Additionally, NEC has close links with 80 major outside systems houses, while Toshiba has links with 40.[99] Because of the shortage of software engineers there is a constant effort by the large electronic firms to bring more software firms into their orbit. So, for example, Fujitsu Business Systems Corporation, a software producer, used to be an independent, company, but now has been absorbed by the Fujitsu group.[100] On the other hand, the software houses—even those which are dependent on another company—are attempting to increase their expertise levels with the aim of achieving a degree of independence. A Japanese External Trade Organization (JETRO) study indicates that only 350 software companies are engaged in actual software development and manufacturing; the remaining 2,500 or so perform simple data-entry and information-processing functions.[101]

The Japanese software industry has a different history and developmental trajectory from that of the United States. Japanese computer firms initially provided free or highly discounted customized software to purchasers of their hardware. This was done in large measure to compete against IBM. Further, Japanese customers were secretive regarding their internal operations and built their own captive internal software departments. In Japan, there was no market space for an independent software industry to develop.[102]

Much attention has been focused on Japan's so-called software factories.[103] The major hardware companies to open software factories were Hitachi, NEC, and Toshiba. Fujitsu, the company with most software personnel in Japan, chose not to call its software facilities factories; however, they do share characteristics with the factories.[104] The software factories can be quite large. For example, the Toshiba Fuchu Software Factory employs approximately 2,300 persons.[105] The actual production process is, as in the factory, broken down into team activities. Additionally, software production teams have also implemented quality-control techniques. Yukio Mizuno, senior vice president of NEC, describes the advantages that stem from the team approach to software development.

> Team members working together are, in their collective wisdom, far more effective than individuals working alone. . . . In problem solving, for example, a team can find defects overlooked by individual members in their own work. And team members' full understanding of each others' work keeps the same problem from cropping up again. Also, the exchange of information at team meetings keeps all members up to date on various problems. Clearly these practices contribute a great deal to overall team capability. At Nippon Electric, we call these SWQC, or software quality control activities.[106]

In general, this approach has reduced defects appreciably resulting in bug-free software. Mizuno indicates that NEC's quality activities reduced defect rates appreciably. Toshiba is credited with being able to produce software code with an error rate that is one-tenth of the typical U.S. error rates.[107]

Japanese firms developed the software factory approach to produce large-scale mainframe programs for large customers in service and manufacturing industry, for example, the banking industry's third-generation on-line systems. As we have already seen, Japanese hardware producers do not sell such programs off-the-shelf but customize software programs for their customers. The factory approach provides a way to reuse parts or modules and yet provide the customer with a customized product. This is accomplished by organizing production on a large scale and combining and recombining standard bits of software code. However, there is a downside to the factory approach. The president of a respected independent software maker called the factories "software prisons" because the factory atmosphere stifles the creativity of engineers and software developers.[108]

The second, and less understood, aspect of the software factory system is the creation of an external division of labor and a subcontractor system. The president of a software spin-off of a major Japanese electronics firm indicated that there are two types of subcontractors. The first and most prevalent are those who perform routine functions such as coding. There are also specialist firms that write highly sophisticated software and are often paid high premiums for their work.[109] The development of the subcontracting system has been stimulated by an acute labor shortage: Japan currently has a shortage of software engineers, this shortage of engineers is expected to grow to 965,000 by the year 2000.[110] As Table 3.3 indicates, even with such a serious shortage, most Japanese firms are still choosing to recruit software engineers in the same manner as other personnel. Not surprisingly, these companies drew on their own successes in hardware production to develop methods of decreasing costs and saving labor power in software. The shortage of personnel within the firms led to a massive amount of subcontracting of the more routine aspects of software production to outside firms. For example, NRI&NCC, a Nomura Securities spin-off, has developed a network of 70 subcontractors with over 1,600 employees, many of which do no more than coding.[111] Figure 3.7 is a chart from a major Japanese firm's software subsidiary that shows how aspects of a software development project can be routinized and then parts of the process can be contracted out to smaller firms with lower labor costs.[112] The project itself is divided into smaller parts or modules and different firms are contracted for completion of modules. This permits the firm to benefit from the lower wages and less overhead prevalent in subcontractors.

TABLE 3.3. Recruitment of Software Engineers

	Software Engineers	Senior Programmers	Novices and Junior Programmers
Division of in-house capable staff	29.1	21.1	5.7
New in-house staff	22.9	36.2	17.6
New graduates	19.5	20.4	71.8
Employment of experienced staff	28.5	22.3	4.9
Total	100.0	100.0	100.0

Source: Japan External Trade Organization, "Your Market in Japan: Software." no. 36, (Tokyo: Japan External Trade Organization, 1985).

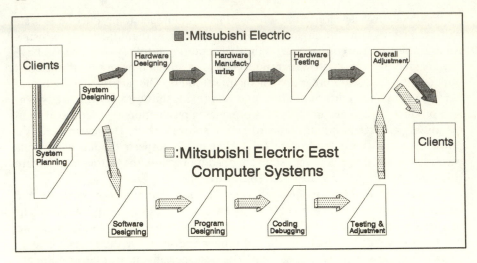

FIGURE 3.7. Software System Production Process.
Source: Mitsubishi Electric East Computer Systems, 1988.

Further, many of the largest independent software houses are little more than "body shops" that provide programmers who actually work in the same buildings with corporate staff—a process remarkably similar to the use of subcontractors in more traditional industries. For example, CSK Corporation, the largest independent software firm in Japan, dispatched over half of its 4,200 employees to other companies in 1986.[113] These contract workers are paid on a monthly basis and may remain guest workers for years at a time.[114] This system of "permanent temporaries" has generated much resentment and frustration on the part of the temporary workers especially given the closed promotion system of the Japanese firm. In 1986, the Law for Labor-Dispatching Businesses was passed making this form of labor dispatch much more difficult and encouraging these firms to do more in-house work.[115]

Actually defining software subsidiaries of Japanese electronic companies is difficult. There are what might be described as pure software subsidiaries and those that do systems development and engineering. The systems development and engineering subsidiaries frequently develop hardware as well as software. For example, a systems subsidiary might produce medical devices containing software components embodied in the operating systems and integrated circuits. Because these firms unite software and hardware development activities, they are not counted as software firms, yet they are an important source of embedded software.[116]

There is constant interaction between the major software subsidiaries and hardware firms. Usually a software subsidiary of a major electronics firm works for certain divisions of the parent company. Mitsubishi Computer Systems Corporation (MCSC), for example, works for two divisions of Mitsubishi Electric, the heavy equipment division and the information division. MCSC's three buildings are less than a ten-minute walk from a huge Mitsubishi Electric factory site that has another 1,000 software-related employees on site. The connections are so close that one of the MCSC buildings is on a local area network with the Mitsubishi Electric plant. The strength of the linkage is illustrated by the fact that the wage reference for MCSC is Mitsubishi Electric rather than the software subsidiaries of other large electrical firms.[117] At MCSC's facilities, there are rooms of terminals that are exclusively used by its subcontractors. The division of labor between and among companies is a complex organizational task. To organize a project with work for ten people, for example, a core company might recruit a team with three people from one company, three from another company, and four more from yet another company. These personnel would work under the direction of the core company until the project is completed, at which point they would return to their original employers.

Three fundamental tendencies operate in the computer industry that, when taken together, are working to transform the software industry as we know it. The first tendency is toward ever-smaller and less expensive computers and attendant standardization of components. The second tendency is toward open nonproprietary systems that provide interconnectability among different computer brands and machine sizes. The third trend is the increasing share of software in overall information-industry revenues. These developments pose special opportunities and unique problems for Japanese firms. The first advantage is that customers will increasingly free themselves from being captives of particular hardware suppliers, notably IBM and DEC. The cost, of course, is that Japanese customers might also be freed of the heretofore nearly unbreakable control of their hardware suppliers. Second, the rapid movement away from mainframes and minicomputers to powerful personal computers linked through networks provides opportunities for small entrepreneurial Japanese firms to fill new market niches.

Personal computer (PC) software is very different from mainframe and minicomputer software because of its small size in terms of lines of code. PC software has traditionally been created by small groups led by one or two brilliant programmers.[118] This type of programming seems to be more difficult for Japanese firms to manage. Indeed, the most successful Japanese firms in PC software are small entrepreneurial start-ups such as "Justsystem," which has created an enormously successful Japanese word-processing program.[119]

The personal computer industry in Japan is different from that in the United States. To understand the situation, it is important to consider the context in which PC growth has occurred. The main objective of the major Japanese computer makers—Fujitsu, NEC, IBM Japan, Toshiba, and Hitachi—has until recently been to sell their mainframes and minicomputers, personal computers were considered to be of little importance. However, as consumers increasingly demanded PCs, these manufacturers had to provide them, otherwise their customers would go to other vendors. Because there was no single firm or product that functioned like the IBM PC to standardize manufacturing, each Japanese company essentially developed an operating system for their particular personal computer, which would operate with the rest of their computer line.[120] Further, these companies bundled software with the PC, thus ensuring that there would be no market for independent software writers. Thus, the Japanese personal computer industry evolved differently from the rest of world, which adopted the IBM MS-DOS/Intel and the Apple/Motorola systems and microprocessors as standards. While Japan accepted MS-DOS, Japanese MS-DOS is incompatible with IBM PC MS-DOS, which is the standard in the United States.

In 1982, NEC developed its 9800 series personal computers. These were the first Japanese personal computers that did not have software bundled with them, creating the possibility for an independent software sector. Software writers and hobbyists quickly rallied around the NEC 9800 series, making it a de facto standard. This has a resemblance to the manner in which large camps of software writers and hobbyists rallied around the Apple II, Apple Macintosh, and IBM MS-DOS machines, which made them de facto standards.[121] Like the Macintosh, the NEC 9800 series was not an open standard. This provided NEC with a monopoly that has kept the price for comparable machines in Japan more than double those in the United States. By 1988, NEC controlled nearly 60 percent of the personal computer market; the remainder was the captive market of the other computer firms.[122] It was only in 1989 that Epson began offering a clone. All of the other major firms (Fujitsu, IBM Japan, Matsushita, Sharp, and Hitachi) have decided to remain in the PC business with unique machine architectures.

As a result, the Japanese PC software business is confronted by a huge problem of incompatibility—to tap the market each program must be rewritten for each company's different PC architecture. This is a time-consuming and expensive process.[123] For example, to translate Lotus 1–2–3 from the NEC system to Fujitsu took seven programmers six months; translation from NEC to the IBM55 system took yet another month. In each case, the Japanese language systems of the computers were quite different. The result is a segmented market that has had difficulty reaching critical mass; this has made it difficult for smaller software and add-on firms to be successful. As a result, both the Japanese PC market and PC software market remain less dynamic than in the United States.

However, one should not conclude that Japanese firms cannot develop software for personal computers. Japanese programmers are already world-class in the development of game software. Nintendo is a case in point. Its game software programs such as Super Mario Brothers and Dragonquest are both innovative and commercially successful. This is both a cause and effect of Nintendo's success in designing and producing inexpensive high-quality game hardware. Nintendo and its licensees virtually control the global computer game market. In 1988, Nintendo's U.S. sales of $1.7 billion comprised roughly 80 percent of the entire market; it was estimated that Nintendo machines were in 10 percent of U.S. households that have a TV. Nintendo achieved its control by designing a high-quality, low-cost computer system that would only operate with game cartridges containing proprietary chips.[124] Nintendo's hardware patents provided the leverage needed to control software writers, thus ensuring quality and allowing the extraction of monopoly rents.[125]

Nintendo's next objective is to use its computer serve as a home terminal. In Japan, Nintendo terminals are used as home terminals for stock trading.[126] Already, Fidelity Investments has signed up to operate over the Nintendo Network. If Nintendo's long-term plans are successful it will be in a position to capture the home computer communications market.[127] Japanese game software companies are confident of their abilities and have begun expanding their programming operations in the United States.[128]

Further, the U.S. lead in software is deceptive because so much software is embedded in products. There are enormous amounts of "embedded" software in hardware that is exported from Japan, in products ranging from computers to audiovisual equipment. Japanese success in hardware products may well provide the springboard for future growth in software. In addition, Japanese companies provide a large number of the high-technology peripherals used by American software companies. For example, the Saitama Prefecture-based Wacom Co. supplies electronic pens and digitizers for use in Microsoft's Pen-window operating system and Go Inc.'s pen-based notebook computers.[129]

A new global division of labor might well emerge where Japan retains its software market and expands to other Asian markets with which it shares common calligraphy systems, while the United States maintains strength in the West. In the medium run, it is also likely that the United States will continue to produce the most creative new package software programs for stand alone personal computers, but that Japan will lead in embedding software in advanced electronics products from new notebook computers, high definition television, and smart home appliances to highly automated industrial processes. In fact, as computers and entertainment electronics continue to converge and perhaps eventually fuse in new products such as multi-media computers or high definition television (HDTV) it is likely that Japanese companies' advantage in certain kinds of software will increase. Japanese companies such as Sony and Sega are already adept at such embedded software and user friendly software that comes as a part of products. It is very likely that Japan would accrue significant advantage from this division of labor. Even the most creative software programs have a "public goods" quality about them—that is, they are easily bought and sold much like commodities on a market; oftentimes they are simply copied. In fact, Japan's leading companies and software development firms are increasing their investments in and alliances with U.S. software firms. In late 1990, for example, Hitachi Software Engineering Co. Ltd. purchased a half interest in Information and Graphics Systems Inc. In 1990 and 1991, ASCII Corp., a leading Japanese independent software firm, took a 5 percent share in Informix, Inc. of Menlo Park, California, a top-supplier of UNIX-formatted relational databases; made a $5 million investment in Nex-Gen Microsystems Inc., which is developing new microprocessors to compete with Intel; and set up Hyper Desk Corp., an operating system development company that it purchased from Data General.[130]

However, the capacity to embed software in products and processes requires both significant investment and sizable firm-specific capabilities that are difficult, and in many cases impossible, to duplicate. Such a scenario—if it comes to pass— would in effect mirror Japan's developmental trajectory in other sectors of both traditional and high-technology industry—hardware would be the bridge to software.

Simply put, in contrast to the conventional wisdom, innovative technologies such as software need not necessarily stand outside the broader industrial structure and production system. In Japan, the model of innovation-mediated production is being successfully applied in an industry that by all accounts is radically different from both traditional manufacturing and even conventional high-technology industry. In the Japanese software industry we find team-based organization of work, rotation, "modular production," quality-control circles, even *kaizen,* or continuous improvement activity. The system is knit together in a set of well-articulated production networks linking together core electronics firms, subsidiaries, subcontractors, and even highly innovative independent firms and spin-outs in powerful communities. Most of all, the Japanese software industry is powerfully integrated with the remainder of its industrial structure ensuring that its full transformative effects can be realized.

Of course, a crucial aspect of the long-term staying power of any model of production organization lies in its ability to diffuse and be adopted across the landscape of global capitalism. Fordism, for example, diffused across the globe, moving from the United States to Europe and beyond. In the next part of this book we explore the ability of the Japanese expression of innovation-mediated production to spread outside Japan and take root in the United States—the home of mass-production fordism.

II

TRANSFER AND DIFFUSION

Dominant or hegemonic models of production organization tend to arise in one country, in one set of industries. This has already occurred in Japan, where the new model of innovation-mediated production has encompassed not only traditional heavy industries such as automobiles and steel but also new high-technology sectors. But the true test of dominance—indeed, of the model's hegemonic possibilities—lies in its ability to be transferred to other countries.

In this section of the book we explore the transfer and cross-national diffusion of the Japanese expression of innovation-mediated production. Drawing from the conceptual discussion of the first three chapters, we start from the hypothesis that the Japanese system of production organization is a set of organizational forms operating both inside the factory and extending outside its bounds to include suppliers. These new forms are not so culturally embedded as to make them untransferable to other nations and environments. This does not deny that some features of the Japanese production system were nurtured and supported by Japanese society and culture, but it does argue that once these features were created, refined, and formalized they became transferable as organizational forms or as an integrated "socio-technical system."

Japanese corporations have a long history of investing abroad. Japanese firms began investing in the United States in the late nineteenth and early twentieth centuries.[1] Still, the great bulk of Japanese foreign direct investment in the United States and elsewhere tended to be simple assembly operations that put together products from parts imported from Japan. Quite early in the post–World War II period, Japanese automotive companies established simple assembly operations in Australia and elsewhere in Asia to assemble cars from "knocked-down" kits made in Japanese factories.[2] In America, Japanese corporations have operated television and consumer electronics assembly facilities for roughly 20 years. These plants were mainly branch plant operations and their work and production organization was thoroughly modified to fit the U.S. environment.

Our exploration of the outward transfer and diffusion of the Japanese expression of innovation-mediated production focuses on movement of the model from Japan to the United States. The United States was the birthplace and, to a great extent, remains the home of the previous dominant model of production organization—mass-production fordism.[3] Thus, one might expect difficulty in transferring the Japanese model of production organization. Special difficulty might also be expected in transferring the Japanese system to the old core industries of fordism with their ingrained structures and organizational practices. The ongoing efforts by Japanese firms to implant their new model of production organization in the United States in the core fordist industries provides a unique case study of the long-run potential for transfer and diffusion to other advanced industrial societies.

The 1980s witnessed a dramatic increase in Japanese manufacturing investment in the United States (Table II.1). According to the U.S. Department of Commerce, between 1980 and 1989 the number of Japanese manufacturing facilities in the United States increased more than fivefold from 240 to 1,275 plants; the number of American workers employed by Japanese transplants increased from 52,339 to 304,244. This investment is strikingly concentrated in the core fordist industrial sectors of automobile production, steel, and rubber and tires along with consumer and high-technology electronics. According to a comprehensive 1990 report by the U.S. International Trade Administration, the top five U.S. industrial sectors receiving Japanese direct investment were computers and office machinery; electronics; primary metals and steel; automobiles and transportation equipment; and rubber and plastics, which together accounted for 50 percent of all transplant investment and more than 70 percent of all transplant employment (Table II.2).[4] This part of the book explores the transfer of the Japanese production system in these crucial sectors.

In the following chapters we return to Gramsci's two related questions. First, could the then new model of U.S. fordism be transferred abroad to Europe? And second, to what extent was this new model bound up with the set of sociocultural practices referred to as "Americanism"?[5] On the first question, Gramsci suggested that the new model of fordism was the most advanced and, indeed, "ultra-modern" (not postmodern) model of production organization of its time, and that as such not only was that model transferable—it would naturally diffuse to Europe and elsewhere.

TABLE II.1.   Japanese Direct Investment
in U.S. Manufacturing, 1980–1989

Year	Number of Plants	Total Employment
1980	240	52,399
1981	277	57,856
1982	308	68,532
1983	346	77,094
1984	387	97,507
1985	462	112,883
1986	606	142,594
1987	850	185,241
1988	1,131	259,616
1989	1,275	304,244

Source: Data for the period 1980–1988 are from U.S. Department of Commerce, International Trade Administration, *Japanese Direct Investment in U.S. Manufacturing* (Washington, D.C., October 1990).

TABLE II.2.   Japanese Direct Manufacturing Investment, by Leading Sector
(top five sectors by employment)

Industrial Sector	Number of Plants	Employment (1989)
Computers, Industrial/Commercial Machinery	189	56,421
Electronics	191	56,084
Primary Metals and Steel	70	41,280
Automobile and Transportation Equipment	68	33,591
Rubber and Plastics	102	30,188
Top Five Sectors (subtotal)	620	217,564
Total	1,275	303,244
Share of Total	48.6%	71.7%

Source: U.S. Department of Commerce, International Trade Administration, *Japanese Direct Investment in U.S. Manufacturing* (Washington, D.C., October 1990).
Note: These data are for SIC codes 35, 36, 33, 37, and 30, respectively.

On the second question, Gramsci argued that there was not a necessary or determinant relationship between fordism and Americanism. Gramsci suggested, in turn, that the two could—and should—be analytically disengaged from one another. For Gramsci, fordism was a set of organizational conditions and practices that operate at the level of the factory, a way of producing value. These organizational forms required supportive elements (e.g., relatively high wages and new forms of worker behavior), but these modes of organizing production were specific to the factory. Indeed, for Gramsci hegemony was constructed at the factory level and then moved outward into society. Americanism—and American culture (Gramsci used the example of the Rotary Club)—was a broader ideological construction that was neither central to the progress of fordism nor a new model of social life or civilization that could propel the economy forward. For Gramsci, Americanism was seen to be a hindrance or fetter to the eventual material progress of fordism. Thus, wholly new forms of social organization—based on the fordist model (building from the factory outward)—were necessary to allow fordism to emerge fully developed. Gramsci went on to say that European, especially French, opposition to fordism and/or Americanism was a response of the backward and marginal forces in society who believed they might lose their economic position with the advance of new methods of production organization and the new competitors they brought forward—a particularly ironic observation given former French Prime Minister Edith Cresson's antagonistic position regarding Japanese investment in Europe.

Perspectives on the Transfer of the Japanese System

Reflecting conventional wisdom, most scholarly analyses have been pessimistic about the ability to transfer the Japanese model to the United States or anywhere else for that matter. It is usually argued that the Japanese model is a product of Japan's homogeneous, group-oriented society; hence, it should be difficult if not impossible to transfer this system outside Japan. Most Americans believe that the success of Japan's automobile industry rests upon a "collectivist" orientation among Japanese, something entirely different from the "individualistic" orientation of the Western democracies. Some go so far as to suggest that the success of the Japanese production system rests on the availability of docile, obedient workers who could not be found in Europe or North America. Others go further still. Arndt Sorge and Wolfgang Streeck argue that "all attempts to transfer model institutions of industrial relations from one country to another have failed."[6]

In a seminal contribution, James Abegglen advanced a powerful cultural model of Japanese industrial organization and development that has influenced thinking to this day.[7] Documenting the enormous differences between the Japanese and Anglo-European models of industrial organization, Abegglen suggested that such differences were the product of Japanese cultural factors such as the high degrees of homogeneity, familism, and loyalty. For Abegglen, the organizational characteristics of the Japanese system—for example, team-based work organization, long-term tenure, etc.—were a reflection of a general pattern of close alignment between persons and groups.

Many early conceptualizations of Japanese industrial development and production organization were influenced by the broader modernization theory of development.[8] Basically, modernization theory saw development as a long march toward the advanced industrial models of the United States and Western Europe. Japan was thus posed as a backward nation whose development process would eventually be characterized by catch up with and convergence to the West. Writing in the early 1970s, Marsh and Mannari used the broad perspective of modernization theory to argue against those who saw Japanese industrial organization as a by-product of Japanese culture.[9] For Marsh and Mannari, formerly unique aspects of the Japanese system—high levels of company loyalty for example—were seen to be diminishing, as Japanese firms and Japanese society converged toward Western economies and societies.

Only a few challenged the modernization perspective. Perhaps the most insightful analysis was put forward by Koji Taira, who argued that the emergence of permanent employment was not the result of Japanese paternalism but a concrete and historically specific organizational response by Japanese industrialists to cope with high rates of labor mobility and exert more effective control over the labor force.[10]

Still, most of those who broke with the modernization theory continued to see Japanese development in more or less cultural terms. In a series of very important works written in the early 1970s, Ronald Dore contrasted the Japanese model of "welfare corporatism" with the Anglo-American model of "market individualism."[11] However, Dore noted that the Japanese model appeared more advanced than the British one and that over time there would likely be reverse convergence toward it. Dore further argued that any attempt to transfer bits and pieces of the model would fail as they are interrelated organizational forms that comprise an integrated system. Robert Cole argued that Japan's unique cultural legacy informed the emergence of unique organizational solutions to general development problems.[12] However, Cole's position changed substantially by the late 1980s as his research on quality-control circles led him to the belief that aspects of the Japanese system could be transferred.[13] Still, even very recent conceptualizations continue to see the Japanese model as culturally-bound and hence difficult to transfer abroad.[14]

But these were not the only scholars or scholarly traditions that were pessimistic about the potential transfer of Japanese industrial organization. Indeed, such pessimism permeated the core of the entire field of organization studies. Basically, the broad body of work on organizational theory suggested that organizations were deterministically connected to the environments in which they functioned. While some argued for a tight environmental determinism, others suggested that organizations gradually take on characteristics of the environment and of organizations with which they interact. Theorists such as Paul DiMaggio and Walter Powell argued that organizations are "isomorphic" vis-à-vis their environments.[15] Other institutionalists suggested that organizations conform to prevailing social and cultural conditions.[16] The population ecology school of organization theory borrowed a Darwinian-type model of adaptation and "survival of the fittest," arguing that under the process of organizational evolution, "fit" organizations survive while others die off.[17] In his influential writings on the sociology of "embedded" relations, Mark Granovetter suggested that organizations are derivative of the social matrix in which they reside.[18] The overwhelming conclusion of this work was that organizational forms, in particular Japanese organizational forms—were not amenable to outside transfer and diffusion.

Interestingly, scholars who had studied the postwar American experience came to an entirely different set of conclusions. In his seminal 1979 book on the U.S. fordist model of industrial organization, Michel Aglietta identified the emergence of a basic model of mass production fordism in the United States.[19] The French theorist Alain Lipietz then extended Aglietta's work to explore the diffusion of fordist production organization to the advanced industrial countries and to a segment of the developing world, coining the phrase "global fordism."[20] This work suggested that some forms of industrial organization are both amenable to outside transfer and diffusion, and that they become an international standard for imitation and replication in other countries.

Strikingly, only a very few scholars after Gramsci were able to lend any theoretical insight into this process of organizational transfer and diffusion. In his classic studies of innovation in capitalism, Joseph Schumpeter differentiated between "creative" responses, which alter social and economic situations, and the more typical "adaptive" response of firms and economic organizations.[21] The resource dependency theory of Pfeffer and Salancik allowed that, while organizations tend to adapt to their environments, they will at times alter the environment to suit their needs.[22] Karl Weick went further and argued that the ability of organizations to influence, construct, or "enact" their environment is a function of organizational size.[23] Ruth Young, in a devastating and still unanswered critique of population ecology, suggested that organizations "can change their environments and alter their resources, sometimes in dramatic ways. Organizations can expand resources by importing them, inventing them or substituting them. They can change the environment in its entirety."[24] From this work there came the alternative perspective that certain types organizations possess resources that they can use to alter the environment, and that organizations can indeed be successfully transferred from one environment to another.

Early Studies of Japanese Investment in the United States

The rapid increase in Japanese foreign direct investment during the 1970s and 1980s provided the first real opportunity to examine questions related to the generalizability of the Japanese model and its relationship to the broader context of Japanese culture and society. In a review of research on the organizational characteristics and outside transfer of Japanese business practices, Dexter Dunphy concluded that

> The increasing success of Japanese overseas operations raised the issue whether distinctive Japanese business practices were exportable. Exportability represented a critical test for cultural determinism because if Japanese practices were a response to Japan's unique cultural tradition and environment, these should not be easily exportable to different cultures.[25]

The empirical evidence regarding transfer of Japanese organization is mixed. In an early assessment, Yoshino suggested that the absence of Japanese sociocultural conditions in other countries comprises a serious obstacle to outside transfer.[26] Yoshihara argued that Japanese practices would not transfer because they were designed for a culturally homogeneous workforce.[27] Writing in 1979, Robert Cole was guardedly optimistic, regarding the transferability of quality-control circles even though they had emanated from Japanese cultural and institutional conditions.[28] That same year, Ronald Dore, commenting on the outside transfer of Japanese practices to Europe, suggested that Japanese firms abroad tended to adapt their practices to the country in which they were inserted.[29] In the early 1980s, Ishida argued that there was a differential pattern of transfer, suggesting that aspects of the Japanese system that "benefit" employees—for example, employment security and participation in management—tend to transfer more easily, while those requiring significant "adaptation"—for example, a collective orientation or long-term loyalty to one employer—cannot be transferred easily.[30]

There is now a small body of literature on the transfer of Japanese practices to Japanese firms in Europe, especially the United Kingdom. Writing in 1983, Michael White and Malcolm Trevor concluded that Japanese organizational traits had not been transferred to Japanese firms operating in the U.K.[31] However, more recent work on the transfer of Japanese forms to the United Kingdom found that the crucial aspects of the Japanese management system were successfully transferred.[32] For example, a recent study of Nissan in the United Kingdom documented the emergence a Japanese-style automobile production complex of a main assembly plant and supplier firms.[33]

Research on the transfer of Japanese organization to the United States is also sparse. Early research by Pascale and his collaborators on Japanese banks in the United States argued that there were few differences in the management and organization of Japanese-owned and American-owned financial institutions operating in the United States.[34] However, more recent research on manufacturing firms has come to different conclusions. In a 1980 study, Kagono and his collaborators found significant differences between Japanese firms in the United States and their American-owned counterparts.[35] For example, case studies of the NUMMI plant in Fremont, California, provided evidence of successful transfer of Japanese organization and management.[36] Other studies documented the emergence of a large complex of Japanese automotive assemblers and suppliers in the midwestern United States.[37] A broader study of a sample of Japanese transplants in the consumer electronics, semiconductor, and automobile industries by a group of Japanese social scientists concluded that automotive plants have been most successful in transferring Japanese practices, while consumer electronics firms have tended to adapt or conform to the U.S. environment, with semiconductor firms occupying a middle position.[38] Finally, a recent book based upon interviews with workers at Mazda's Michigan plant provided evidence of adaptation problems including high rates of injury, worker discontent, and labor-management conflict.[39] These studies, while invaluable, suffer from small sample sizes, reliance upon case-specific data from which it is hard to generalize, and a narrow conceptual focus on managerial practices. This may provide a partial explanation of the contradictory and tentative nature of their results.

In the following chapters, we look in detail at the transfer and diffusion of the Japanese expression of innovation-mediated production to the United States in both the traditionally fordist industries of automobile assembly; automobile parts; steel; rubber and tires; and both high-technology and consumer electronics. After this, in Chapter 9, we turn to the obstacles and tensions that have been confronted during the transfer process.

4

Proving Ground: Japanese Automobile Assembly in the United States

> The key to sucess of Toyota Motor Manufacturing USA, Inc., will depend upon the support and contribution of our human resources in implementing the Toyota Production System. . . . The very basis of the Production System is respect and dignity of team members through effective utilization of their time—allowing team members to use their ingenuity and to participate in the design of their jobs.
>
> TOYOTA, MOTOR MANUFACTURING USA, INC. TEAM MEMBER HANDBOOK[1]

> The idea is to work smarter, not harder.
>
> JOEL SMITH, ORIGINAL UAW REPRESENATIVE TO NUMMI.[2]

Ever since 1980, Japan's major automobile companies have set up a dozen major automobile assembly plants in North America—nine of these are in the United States; another three are in Canada. The transplants produce an estimated 2.4 million cars annually in the United States, roughly 20 percent of total U.S. production. Total investment in U.S. production already exceeds $8.9 billion and continues to increase. The U.S. transplants employ more than 30,000 American workers, and Honda, the largest employer, currently employs an excess of 9,000 workers in the United States and this number was expected to increase to 11,000. The vast bulk of these workers are at Honda's central Ohio assembly complex. Employment is also increasing at Toyota and Nissan as they complete major expansions. (See Table 4.1.)

Beginning in the 1960s, and certainly by the 1970s, Japanese automotive companies saw the need to expand into the U.S. market. These efforts intensified after the economic crisis engendered by the 1974–75 oil shortage and Japanese producers saturated the Japanese and Asian markets. Initial Japanese entry into the American market came in the form of exports of small economy cars designed for the first-time car buyer and for the fuel-conscious automobile market of the 1970s.[3] Despite initial setbacks stemming from the fact that Japanese automobiles were underpowered and not well equipped for the U.S. market, Japanese autos by the end of the 1970s had captured a substantial market share in the United States.[4]

The continuing market share erosion experienced by American automakers combined with an overall trade deficit led to calls for protectionism from U.S. car-

95

TABLE 4.1.   Japanese Automobile Assembly Plants in the United States

Japanese Company	Location	Start Date	Projected Capacity	Employment at Full Capacity	Investment* (millions)
Honda	Marysville, OH	1982	500,000	8,000	2,000
Nissan	Smyrna, TN	1983	450,000	5,100	1,700
NUMMI	Fremont, CA	1984	300,000	3,400	500
Mazda	Flat Rock, MI	1987	240,000	3,400	750
Toyota	Georgetown, KY	1988	400,000	5,000	2,000
Diamond-Star	Normal, IL	1988	240,000	2,900	700
Subaru-Isuzu (SIA)	Lafayette, IN	1989	120,000	1,700	600
Ford-Nissan	Avon Lake, OH	1992	130,000	1,300	700
Total			2,380,000	30,800	8,950

Source: Compiled by authors, from the most current data available, from the Japanese Automobile Manufacturers Association, Japan Economic Institute, U.S. International Trade Commission, and the companies themselves.
*Investments are in millions of U.S. dollars.

makers, automotive parts suppliers, and other segments of domestic industry, as well as from American labor unions. These interests sought to insulate U.S. manufacturers from further encroachment. This pressure for protectionism rose throughout the 1970s, and in 1981 with the Big Three, especially Chrysler, in financial difficulties, the U.S. government announced the Voluntary Restraint Agreement (VRA). Under this plan, the Japanese government "voluntarily" agreed to prevent Japanese carmakers from increasing exports to the United States. Effectively, American producers believed that they had countered the threat by limiting access of Japanese carmakers to the large and profitable U.S. market.

However, the VRA, combined with increasing demand for higher-quality Japanese cars and continuing stiff competition in their home market, provided push-and-pull pressures on Japanese automakers to begin overseas production. For firms such as Honda with its relatively small domestic market share, insufficient quota allocation, growing demand in the United States, and significant competitive pressure from Japan's "Big Two," Toyota and Nissan, the logic of U.S. production was obvious. For the others, with their quotas under the VRA, exports to the United States could not increase.

In the late 1970s, Japanese carmakers began to explore strategies to increase access to the U.S. market. One strategy was to develop joint ventures with U.S. automotive producers that would allow them to share in the profits from Japanese automotive imports and thus buy off potential opposition. While such joint ventures were partially successful, they did little to dissipate growing grassroots opposition to Japanese automotive imports that came from American trade unions and American industry, especially in the hard-hit industrial Midwest. Further, exporting vehicles through U.S. firms did not circumvent the VRAs and placed Japanese carmakers' success at the mercy of their marketing partner, who was also a competitor in the United States. As a short-term strategy, original equipment manufacture (OEM) was satisfactory, but in the long-term sharing the profits generated by the VRAs made little sense.

It became increasingly evident to Japanese automotive companies and Japanese government policymakers that the establishment of U.S. production facilities was necessary to stave off protectionist political forces and continue to ensure access to and growth in the U.S. market. In the 1970s, both Honda and Nissan had investigated the feasibility of establishing automobile assembly plants in North America. Honda was especially keen on establishing a U.S. production base; thus, in 1977, it became the first Japanese automotive company to build a production facility in the United States when it announced the selection of a site in Marysville, Ohio, to assemble motorcycles. Motorcycle production would function as a pilot for the possible manufacture of automobiles, serving as a low-cost experiment for a later venture in automobile production. This was done because internal feasibility studies had predicted financial losses from transplant automobile production.[5]

By 1980, it was clear that Japanese auto assemblers would have to establish a U.S. production base. As a result of worsening U.S.–Japan economic relations, in January 1980, Toyota's president, Sadazo Yamamoto, held a new conference to announce that Toyota was considering building a truck assembly plant in the United States.[6] Just a few days later, Honda announced construction of a $200 million automobile assembly plant adjacent to the Marysville motorcycle plant to produce 100,000 cars a year. MITI officials hailed the plant as a major breakthrough and "a wonderful sign that United States–Japan economic relations are set on a path of cooperation, not confrontation."[7]

In early 1980, United Auto Workers' (UAW) president Douglas Fraser lashed out at the Japanese assemblers, stating that voluntary restrictions "are not enough, we want firm, solid commitments [to establish U.S. production] this time."[8] That month, Fraser visited Japan to engage in negotiations over U.S. production with industry executives and government officials. On February 13, 1980, the *Wall Street Journal* reported:

> The Japanese government is urging auto makers to curb exports to the U.S. and begin American production to ease trade frictions between the two countries. The Ministry of International Trade and Industry said the government message has been conveyed to the heads of the Toyota Motor Co. and Nissan Motor Co., the two largest Japanese auto manufacturers, in recent meetings. The meetings preceded the arrival in Japan of the United Auto Workers' president, Douglas A. Fraser, who has called on Japan to hold down its auto exports. A Japanese government official prefaced these remarks, by stating: "Of course, they [Japanese carmakers] have to think about a lot of things before doing that—whether they can acquire necessary parts in the U.S., the labor situation in the U.S. and Japan as well as distribution systems. This is the kind of thing that takes a lot of time to do, and money, too."[9]

Japanese automakers quickly set in motion plans for U.S. production. Both Nissan and Toyota announced their intentions to consider U.S. plant sites in early 1980. Just a few days after the Japanese government's announcement, Nissan announced plans to establish a U.S. assembly plant. In April, Toyota hired three consulting firms, SRI International, Arthur D. Little, and Nomura Research Institute in Japan, to study the feasibility of U.S. production and to identify potential production sites.[10] That same month, Nissan's president, Takashi Ishihara, announced that the company would build a $300 million assembly plant somewhere in the Great Lakes region or in the Southeast.[11] In May, Mitsubishi announced a possible joint venture with Chrysler to produce cars in the United States.[12] And in July 1980, Toyota began discussing a possible joint venture with Ford to assemble small cars in the United States at one of Ford's "idle" assembly plants.[13] Toyota's plans stalled when negotiations with Ford bogged down and the joint venture was abandoned.[14]

In October 1980, Nissan became the second Japanese automaker to select a site for U.S. production, announcing that it would build a truck assembly plant in Smyrna, Tennessee, and, shortly thereafter, that former Ford executive Marvin Runyon would head up its new U.S. venture. In 1982, Toyota started talking to GM about a joint venture to produce small cars.[15] This proposed alliance generated serious domestic opposition from Chrysler and Ford, who claimed that the joint venture violated antitrust laws.[16] Nonetheless, in February 1983, Toyota and GM formalized their agreement to establish a joint venture, New United Motor Manufacturing, Inc. (NUMMI), to produce cars on the site of an old GM assembly plant in Fremont, California.[17] Toyota's purpose in agreeing to the joint venture was to test the feasibility of transferring the Toyota system to the United States.[18] By July 1985, Toyota announced plans for two additional North American plants—one in Kentucky to produce Camrys and the other in Ontario, Canada, to produce Corollas.[19]

Between late 1984 and 1986, a second wave of Japanese automakers announced their plans to begin U.S. production. In December 1984, Mazda said it would build a $450 million automobile assembly plant adjacent to Ford's abandoned Michigan Casting Center in Flat Rock, outside Detroit.[20] In April 1985, Mitsubishi announced a $500 million joint venture assembly plant with Chrysler, called Diamond-Star Motors; by October it had selected a site in Normal, Illinois.[21] In 1986, Fuji Heavy Industries and Isuzu Motors together announced plans to build a $475 million assembly plant in Lafayette, Indiana.[22] In September 1988, Nissan and Ford said they would rebuild and equip a Ford plant in Avon Lake, Ohio, to produce Nissan-designed minivans.[23]

The next stage of investment involved the addition of engine and transmission casting plants. Honda added the first such foreign-owned plant in Anna, Ohio, in 1986, then a second assembly plant in 1988, and, most recently, a major R&D facility, bringing its total U.S. investment to more than $2 billion (see Table 4.1). Honda now has the capacity to produce more than 510,000 cars in the United States annually and is poised to overtake Chrysler as the third largest automaker in the United States.[24] Toyota also added an engine and transmission plant in 1987, and in September 1990 the company announced plans for a second assembly plant on its Georgetown, Kentucky, site, bringing its total investment to more than $2 billion as well.[25] Meanwhile, NUMMI is installing a second line to assemble pickup trucks.[26] In 1990, Nissan added a $500 million expansion to its assembly facility and began construction of a $600 million engine and transmission plant approximately 60 miles north of its Smyrna, Tennessee, assembly plant, bringing its total investment to $1.7 billion and expanding its total U.S. production capability to

450,000 cars and light trucks.[27] In early 1991, Mazda, Subaru-Isuzu America (SIA), and Diamond-Star were considering building engine and transmission plants near their existing assembly complexes.[28]

Still other reports have suggested that Honda will invest in a fourth assembly plant, perhaps to manufacture down-market subcompacts, or, alternatively, may design and produce a luxury automobile in North America in the mid 1990s.[29] In November 1990, Mitsubishi and Chrysler announced plans to establish a joint venture in Canada to produce medium-sized cars.[30] Japanese automakers have also opened major R&D, engineering, and design facilities in the United States (see R&D section later in chapter).

The Transplant Corridor

With the exception of the NUMMI plant in California, the automotive transplants are located in a "transplant corridor" that stretches from southwest Ontario and southeast Michigan on the north, in an almost straight line along Interstate 75 south through Ohio, Kentucky, and Tennessee, and west to Indiana and Illinois. Figure 4.1 shows the location of the automobile assembly transplants. Mazda, Honda, Diamond-Star, and SIA are located in the traditional midwestern automobile-producing states of Michigan, Ohio, Illinois, and Indiana, respectively. However, most of these plants have located outside traditional blue-collar cities, on rural "green-field" sites.[31] Nissan and Toyota are located in the upper South just outside the

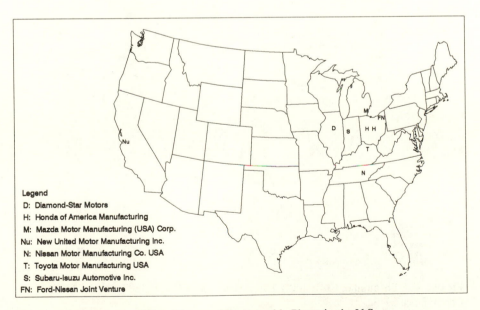

Legend
D: Diamond-Star Motors
H: Honda of America Manufacturing
M: Mazda Motor Manufacturing (USA) Corp.
Nu: New United Motor Manufacturing Inc.
N: Nissan Motor Manufacturing Co. USA
T: Toyota Motor Manufacturing USA
S: Subaru-Isuzu Automotive Inc.
FN: Ford-Nissan Joint Venture

FIGURE 4.1. Japanese-Affiliated Automobile Assembly Plants in the U.S.
Source: Adapted from authors' database.

industrial Midwest, but still close enough to benefit from the existing industrial infrastructure and to minimize transportation costs.

Generally speaking, the transplants are located slightly south of the traditional midwestern automotive assembly belt. However, the concentration of Japanese investment in the lower Midwest and adjacent southern states of Kentucky and Tennessee stands in contrast to the recent decentralized location pattern of the Big Three carmakers. Figure 4.2 shows the location of the Big Three automobile assembly plants in 1990, indicating both the traditional concentration in the industrial Midwest and the more recent southern drift.

All of the large automobile-producing states are home to one transplant assembler, and only Ohio, which will soon have the Ford-Nissan joint venture, has more than one Japanese company's assembly operations. One explanation of this is that it allows Japanese carmakers to maximize their political capital by spreading investments across a series of different states. According to a city planner who has served as a consultant to Toyota: "Japanese carmakers recognize that every state means two votes in the U.S. Senate."[32] However, an equally plausible explanation is that each Japanese firm is seeking privileged access to state and local governments; therefore, when one firm locates in a state, other firms are more likely to seek another location. This theory provides a rationale for locational choice that alleviates the need for conspiracy—whether or not there was a conspiracy in any particular case.

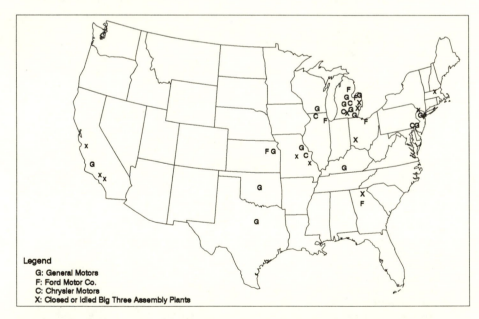

FIGURE 4.2. Location of Current Big Three Automotive Assembly Plants and Those Closed Since 1979.
Note: This map refers only to automobiles and excludes trucks and sport utility vehicles.
Source: Adapted from various industry sources.

Location: Where and Why?

Japanese automakers have demonstrated a preference for rural greenfield locations in exurban areas; that is, locations with rural labor forces that are proximate to mid-sized cities with airports and other urban amenities. Thus, Honda, Toyota, Diamond-Star, and SIA are located in newly constructed plants in small towns in rural or fringe metropolitan areas.

Rural midwestern locations enable Japanese carmakers to gain the benefits of an existing transportation and supplier infrastructure while avoiding areas with high levels of unionized labor, long histories of industrial conflict, or legacies of fordism. Nissan considered sites in Illinois and Ohio, in the heart of the indigenous automobile supplier infrastructure, but it eventually selected Tennessee, where labor union organizing is hampered by right-to-work statutes. This decision was largely an effort to minimize the likelihood of labor representation by the United Auto Workers. Paradoxically, although the UAW lost a representation election at Nissan, it has been more successful in gaining support there than at Honda or Toyota despite the fact that these plants are in more highly unionized states. This may be due to the more "Americanized" nature of the Nissan plant. This reinforces the point that it is the nature of the labor-management relationships implemented that determines the state of conflict as opposed to the "nature" or "climate" of the location (see Chapter 9).

Greenfield sites provide access to "fresh recruits"—rural labor with little or no experience in manufacturing, who can be socialized to the requirements of Japanese production methodology. Honda managers indicate that a major factor in the selection of a greenfield site was to avoid experienced manufacturing workers who "have picked up bad habits."[33] Selection of greenfield sites is further designed to enable firms to control their work force. Rural workers are viewed as having low levels of occupational and geographical mobility, thus reducing the likelihood that training investments and on-the-job-training skills would be lost because of employee turnover. The counties that are home to the Diamond-Star, Honda, Nissan, Toyota, and SIA plants had pretransplant manufacturing employment of 4,400, 2,700, 8,200, 10,500, and 24,700, respectively.[34] Toyota's Georgetown plant currently accounts for more than two-thirds of total manufacturing employment (3,300 of 4,900 manufacturing workers) in Scott County, Kentucky.[35]

Rural labor forces are often characterized as having low rates of absenteeism and high attendance—a must for the Japanese production system, which is predicated upon keeping costs down and ensuring continuity in the labor force to facilitate just-in-time production. This allows the firm to capture fully its "human capital" investments. As an example of this concern, a vice president of one automotive assembly transplant indicated that the company looked closely at high school attendance data and information on employee attendance and turnover supplied by local employers in selecting its site.[36]

In addition, selection of rural greenfield sites provides the open space needed to develop broader just-in-time supplier complexes in the immediate vicinity of assembly plants. The selection of rural sites reflects a desire of Japanese automobile producers to transfer the Japanese production system to North America. Manufacturing locations were selected expressly to ease adoption of just-in-time supply practices. This explains the concentration of most assembly transplants within the Midwest and the international migration of nearly 300 Japanese supplier firms to North America. While they certainly recognized that transferring just-in-time techniques to North America did not rest solely on geography, the Japanese firms saw locational decisions as among the crucial determinants of success in this regard.

There are two exceptions to the rural bias in transplant location. Toyota selected an urban location at Fremont, near San Francisco, for its initial North American production site, the joint venture with GM (NUMMI). The assembly plant that NUMMI occupies had previously been under GM management. NUMMI is in Fremont, California, a city of more than 130,000 people in a county with more than 1.1 million residents and a 30 percent minority population; NUMMI's work force is nearly half minority—19 percent African-American and 28 percent Hispanic.[37]

Mazda is located in Flat Rock, Michigan, outside Detroit and in the fourth largest urban county in the nation with a population of 2.3 million and a 37 percent minority population.[38] Mazda's site is a "quasi-greenfield"—located at the outskirts of this urban area and attracting workers from Detroit, its suburbs, and rural areas two or three hours away. Although Mazda is unionized and located close to Detroit where African-Americans are 29 percent of the available labor force, they comprise just 14 percent of Mazda's work force.[39] Thus, location in a highly urbanized area does not necessarily mean that a larger percentage of jobs will go to minority group members. (We return to racial issues in Chapter 9.) The Ford-Nissan site is adjacent to a Ford van plant in suburban Cleveland and will also employ UAW members. Here it is interesting to note that recognition of the union appears to hinge on having a U.S. joint-venture partner—a point we discuss in greater detail later.

Work and Production Organization in the Transplants

The most fundamental issue in the study of industry is work and production organization—the labor process at the point of production—because it is the place where value is generated. At the outset, it is important to stipulate that each plant or firm has its own personality or corporate culture. However, it is also true that Japanese automobile companies resemble each other more than they do U.S. automobile companies. Table 4.2 summarizes the main characteristics of work and production organization at the transplant assemblers.

As Chapters 2 and 3 have shown, the most fundamental building block of the Japanese production system is the team. All of the Japanese automotive assembly transplants have organized the work process at the point of production on the basis of work teams. At Honda, Toyota, and NUMMI, teams meet daily to discuss production improvements and redesign of tasks. At NUMMI, each team has its own team room adjacent to the production line where workers meet; NUMMI workers tend to personalize these rooms with bulletin boards, announcements, and pictures of family and events.[40] At the other transplants, meetings are less frequent but take

TABLE 4.2.   Work and Production Organization at Transplant
Assemblers

	No. of Job Classifications	*Work Teams*	*Rotation*
Honda	3	+	+
Nissan	4	+	+/0
NUMMI	4	+	+
Toyota	3	+	+
Mazda	2	+	+/0
Subaru-Isuzu (SIA)	2	+	+/0
Diamond-Star	3	+	+
Big Three (Avg.)	90	NA	NA

Source: Personal interviews by authors.
Note: + = similar to Japan; 0 = modified; − = different from Japan.

place at least once a week.[41] All the assemblers use just-in-time production internally.

All of the transplants rotate workers. This is done to train them in multiple tasks and to reduce the incidence of repetitive-motion injury. However, the frequency of rotation varies among specific companies—as it does in Japan. Toyota, Honda, and NUMMI rotate workers in the same team quite frequently.[42] Toyota workers in high-stress jobs, such as those requiring the use of a high-impact torque gun or involving constant bending or lifting, will rotate as frequently as once an hour; others will rotate at break times, at lunch, or every other day. Honda and NUMMI also rotate workers quite frequently.[43] A worker we interviewed summed up the rotation process at the NUMMI plant:

> We would be rotating every time we had a break or change. If we had a break in the morning, we rotated. And then lunchtime, we rotated. And if we had a break in the afternoon, we rotated. Every time the line stopped, a break or whatever, we rotated.[44]

Rotation is less frequent at Mazda, Nissan, and SIA.[45] While these companies consider rotation a long-term goal, each has slowed or even stopped the use of rotation during production scale-ups. As one SIA executive put it: "Basically the teams do the rotation. We haven't done a real good job of it. . . . But again, we're still trying to build the basic skills to get the job done."[46] Our interviews with Mazda workers confirm that infrequent rotation has been a major cause of repetitive-motion injury at the Mazda plant.[47]

Rotation between teams is less frequent in the transplants, as in Japan. In Japan, this type of rotation is typically mandated by management; in the United States, it is more likely for workers to apply for job transfers. Honda workers are encouraged to apply for rotation to new teams every year or so, although in some instances management will suggest that a worker rotate to a new job.[48] Both U.S. and Japanese managers at all the transplants we visited, as well as many workers, suggested that it is too early for implementation of a full Japanese-style rotation system, indicating that it may take a few years before workers have enough basic skills and knowledge to be moved regularly from team to team.

In Japan, workers rotate regularly among shifts. In the transplants, shift assignments are based upon seniority—length of service with the company. Senior workers are able to choose which shift they work on—typically the day shift—while junior workers are assigned to the afternoon and night shifts. This contrasts with the view of Japan as a seniority-oriented society. Indeed, the Japanese system of shift rotation appears to be more egalitarian than the U.S. seniority-based one.

Interestingly, according to Japanese managers, American workers appear far more seniority conscious than do Japanese workers. In a Japanese-language interview conducted by our Japanese collaborators at Ritsumeikan University, the manager of a major Japanese automobile assembly facility stated:

> I think the atmosphere or social custom of respecting "seniority" or the length of work experience that a worker has within a company is much stronger in the U.S. . . . I feel that respect for seniority is very deeply rooted in the work ethic in the U.S. So, once they are told that we will ignore seniority, they [U.S. workers] will not be satisfied with that. . . . We Japanese are surprised to be faced with the importance of seniority so often . . . [as] an adjustment method to coordinate all these different claims. How to adjust? Well, the easiest way is like this: "What year were you born?" "I was born in 1942." "I was born in 1952. . . ." What is the worth of being born earlier?[49]

The transplants organize work on the basis of just a few job classifications. There are four job classifications for production workers at Nissan and NUMMI, three at Honda and Toyota, and only two at Mazda and SIA. This is dramatically different from the traditional U.S. production organization where virtually every job has its own job classification, and where these job classifications are seen by workers and unions to provide the basis for wage increases and employment security.[50] In 1986, Thomas Kochan and his colleagues reported that the unionized plants in a multidivisional manufacturing firm had an average of 96 job classifications.[51] The former GM Fremont facility, which is now NUMMI, had between 75 and 80 job classifications.[52] One would expect that the implementation of smaller numbers of job classifications would be especially difficult at a transplant like NUMMI, which has a large percentage of former GM workers. However, our interviews with NUMMI officials and workers indicate few adaptation problems. A number of transplant assemblers indicate that they do feel some pressure from their American workers to institute more levels of job classifications than would be ideal. Japanese managers see this as undesirable but suggest that this would function to keep American workers happy by providing the appearance of an internal career ladder.[53] While the transplant assemblers have thus far resisted such pressures, a number of automobile suppliers and electronics transplants have instituted such internal career ladders (see Chapters 5 and 8).

Team leaders are a key job category at all of the Japanese automotive assembly transplants. Team leaders are members of shop-floor work groups but also have managerial responsibility for immediate production activities. There are no foremen or lower-level managers whose job is to supervise or "boss" shop-floor workers.[54] At Honda, Toyota, NUMMI, Nissan, and SIA, team leaders are the first line of supervision and play crucial roles in organization, design, and allocation of work on a daily basis. At some transplants, team leaders are selected by management, whereas at others, especially the unionized transplants, team leaders are selected by joint labor-management committees. All the transplants consider the input of workers to be an important criteria for the selection of team leaders.

As we have already seen, there is much less of a blue-collar/white-collar divide in Japan than in the United States. In Japanese auto plants, for example, workers and managers eat in the same cafeteria. Managers typically do not have walled-in offices but sit at desks on a large open floor adjacent to the production facility. The automotive assembly transplants conform to this dimension of Japanese production practice and management philosophy. All transplants we visited had single cafeterias. Nissan is the only transplant where status distinctions are more visible, with a separate parking lot for use by top managers and plush American-style offices.[55] This may be explained by the fact that Nissan has a much higher percentage of former Big Three automobile executives than other transplants.

All the automotive assembly transplants provide uniforms; while some make uniforms mandatory, others give workers the option to wear either uniforms or their own street clothes. However, most top executives wear company uniforms, Nissan again being the exception. Interestingly, the transplants tend to have lower levels of visible status equality than in Japan where top executives have chauffeur-driven company automobiles and wear suits and ties as opposed to work uniforms.

In one study, James Lincoln and his collaborators found that management hierarchies are taller in Japan than in the United States.[56] However, our findings suggest that management hierarchies in the automotive transplants are relatively flat. At Honda, there are nine levels in the internal hierarchy: associate, team leader, coordinator, department manager, plant manager, assistant vice president, senior vice president, executive vice president, and president. This kind of structure is typical of the other transplants as well. At Honda, the various vice presidents do not form separate levels in the reporting structure. Rather, they are part of Honda's senior management team, which also includes the plant manager and the president of Honda of America Manufacturing. This senior management team makes decisions as a group and thus functions to some extent as a single reporting level. The president of Honda of America is a member of and reports to the board of directors of Honda's Tokyo headquarters.[57] A number of shop-floor workers have already risen to management ranks at Honda, and the company actively encourages such mobility. Toyota officials indicate that shop-floor workers are being recruited for middle-level management positions in both the factory and the front office.[58]

Form vs. Substance: The Transfer of *Kaizen* Activity

It is important to distinguish between the "form" of Japanese organization, and its "substance"—that is, its effects on actual worker behavior. As earlier chapters have shown, a main objective of the Japanese system of work and production organization is to harness the collective intelligence of workers as a source of continuous product and process improvement. In sharp contrast, American fordist practices are predicated upon formal organizational barriers and norms that inhibit the exercise of worker discretion and intelligence.[59] In Japan, workers actively participate in company suggestion programs and quality-control circles, as well as informal, everyday *"kaizen,"* or continuous-improvement, activities. Japanese automakers (in Japan) emphasize different aspects of *kaizen* activity. Toyota places greater emphasis on team activities (quality circles) whereas Honda emphasizes individual initiative and innovation.

Japanese scholars use the term *"voluntarism"* to explain the extraordinary worker self-initiative in Japan.[60] It should be noted here that Japanese automakers differ significantly in their ability to generate "voluntaristic" behavior—with Toyota being the most effective. A transplant executive who has visited Japan says that suggestion systems in Japan are really ways of formalizing and awarding credit to workers who are continuously providing ideas on a voluntary basis:

> That is a real powerful tool. . . . It seems to be an outgrowth of the *kaizen* effort and almost a documentation of the *kaizen* effort. . . . When I was over there, from what I could understand, the suggestions were made, but a lot of times, by the time they got up to where they were actually being reviewed, the team had already implemented the idea. It just went up and they tried to decide on whether it was a good idea, bad idea, whether this person could be given some form of recognition or not. But usually it had already been implemented.[61]

One way the transplants encourage worker self-initiative is through the delegation of managerial authority and responsibility to shop-floor workers. Workers at the transplants, especially Honda and Toyota, have significant input into the design of their jobs.[62] At Toyota's Georgetown, Kentucky, plant, work teams design, develop, and post standardized task descriptions at their work stations.[63] The plant's *Team Member Handbook* devotes an entire section to *kaizen,* which it defines as the search for a better way:

> *Kaizen* is a Japanese word meaning improvement or search for a better way: it is a process of finding and eliminating waste in machinery, materials, labor or methods of production and office procedures. It is a process by which team members work together to plan their own jobs to make them easier to perform, thus helping the team work more efficiently. To understand how *kaizen* operates, you must understand the concept of "standardized work." It is the sequencing of the tasks that make up a job. . . . Each task will be constantly subjected to the process of *kaizen;* that is, the team members themselves will meet and discuss ways to make the job easier and the way it is performed more efficient.[64]

The assembly transplants use Japanese-style suggestion systems to harness workers' knowledge and ideas. Honda and Toyota have fairly well-developed suggestion systems; Toyota's Georgetown plant averages roughly 88 suggestions per month.[65] Nissan has a mandatory suggestion program in Japan but makes suggestions voluntary in the United States because managers feel U.S. workers tend to compete in terms of numbers rather than quality of suggestions.[66] Mazda has a suggestion system, but Mazda workers have at times boycotted it to voice their dissatisfaction with management policy.[67] SIA does not yet have a suggestion system, although management said that the company will institute one in the future.[68]

Quality circles are an important element of the Japanese system.[69] In Japan, quality circles are comprised of groups of workers who devote effort outside regular work to improve an element of the production process. According to James Lincoln and colleagues, 76 percent of employees in a sample of Japanese plants participated in quality circles compared to just 27 percent of workers U.S. plants.[70] The transplants vary as to the extent and intensiveness with which they employ quality circles. In the United States, Toyota and Honda use quality circles extensively.[71] Mazda and NUMMI make moderate use of them.[72] SIA had not yet implemented quality circles, although it planned to do so in the future. According to a company official: "We're going to try to implement something. I don't know if we are definitely calling it quality control. . . . I guess we consider quality as sort of falling under responsibilities related to *kaizen,* working for improvement all the time."[73]

Participation in quality circles mainly occurs immediately before or after shift work. Transplant assemblers have set up competitions between quality-control circles and use prizes, plaques, and cash awards to provide additional incentives for quality circle participation. Some transplants have sent American quality circles to Japan to participate in annual company quality competitions. All the transplant assemblers we visited indicate that they will devote significant effort to establishing quality-control circles on par with Japan. Here we find ourselves in agreement with Robert Cole's assessment that it is still too early in the transfer process to expect full use of quality-control circles.[74] However, management of the automotive assembly transplants is striving to increase quality-control circle activity over time, as these firms complete the process of implanting organizational forms and move on to more subtle techniques of shaping and motivating worker initiative.

In addition, we asked Japanese managers to tell us how much, in percentage terms, Japanese *kaizen,* or continuous improvement, activity they have been able to replicate in their American work force. Honda executives said they had come close to replicating Japanese practice in their Marysville, Ohio, plant.[75] A Toyota manager, who worked in numerous Toyota plants in Japan as well as at NUMMI, thought the Georgetown, Kentucky, plant is at 60 percent of Japanese practice and NUMMI at 40 percent to 50 percent.[76] Given that Toyota is the leader in such activity in Japan, our assessment is that the Georgetown plant is already on par with many (non-Toyota) automobile plants in Japan. Mazda and Nissan have had more difficulty implementing *kaizen* activity, and they stand at roughly 50 percent of Japanese practice.[77] Executives of SIA, which is the most recent transplant, estimate that their plant is currently at about 30 percent of Japanese practice.[78] Still, the progress of the transplants on this dimension is remarkable, given the time they have had to stabilize the production process sufficiently to implement these activities and to train American workers to the requirements of Japanese production.

One of the biggest barriers to successful *kaizen* activity is management attitudes that discourage worker initiative. Older managers at some transplants, especially those who have worked in a traditional fordist context, often give signals that discourage workers from making suggestions or contributing their ideas. An even bigger problem arises when management fails to listen to or implement worker suggestions. This problem became evident at Mazda when workers made suggestions for fans and water coolers to relieve the extreme heat in summer working conditions. When the company failed to act on those suggestions, the workers reacted angrily and the issue became a source of protracted dissent and conflict (see Chapter 9). An SIA executive suggests that workers may in fact develop *kaizen* capacity faster than the company can respond to implement their ideas.

> Our biggest problem is that our *kaizen* process has not developed as fast as some of the people have. They've given a lot of ideas, but we haven't implemented them. We have to learn how we can better use that information and implement those ideas so we encourage them to continue to give them. Because we already hear some say, "Hey, I've given 10 ideas, and I haven't seen any of them implemented. I feel like I've been ignored." And then you see the faucet being turned off.[79]

Transplants recognize this deficit and are working hard to replicate the self-initiative and the voluntaristic behavior of Japanese firms.

Numerous Japanese executives see the lack of independent initiative on the part of American workers as a product of previous attitudes and socialization, and they suggest that it can indeed be remedied by further education and socialization to Japanese practices. Executives at Japanese transplants indicate that this is an area that they will concentrate on in the next few years. Toyota is working with the local school system to redesign curriculum and other socialization mechanisms to impart group-oriented behavior, problem solving, and self-initiative to students.[80] SIA has also sent local school officials to Japan so that they can learn more about Japanese group-oriented educational practice.

Selecting and Socializing Production Workers

Production systems—whether old or new—cannot be unilaterally imposed on workers. As E.P. Thompson pointed out some time ago, modes of work organization are historically created, as workers are socialized and acclimated to production systems and their norms.[81]

Japanese industry, like all industry, has developed mechanisms to socialize workers to new forms of work organization and production practice. In Japan, as Thomas Rohlen's research has shown, recruitment and socialization are used to select for and to inculcate characteristics such as company loyalty and group orientation in new employees.[82] Prior to start-up, all the assembly transplants sent key employees (e.g., managers and team leaders) to Japanese sister plants for three- to six-month stays where they received both formal training and informal socialization to Japanese practice (e.g., team work and *kaizen*). In Japan, they worked closely with veteran Japanese trainers and also spent time with them during and after work. These same trainers then came to the United States for three-month to two-year periods to work alongside the same U.S. employees and their teams. For example, in June 1984, 240 NUMMI workers travelled to Toyota's Takaoka plant for three weeks of one-on-one training. After this, 120 trainers returned to NUMMI to assist in start-up operations for the remainder of the year. This process not only provides formal training and skill but facilitates the transfer of tacit knowledge of the production process and behavioral aspects of Japanese production practice. The nature of behavioral reinforcement is evident in the interview comments of a NUMMI worker:

> A company that works together plays together. That's what I saw when I went to Japan for my training over there. You worked, but after work my trainers [and I] we were a family. I didn't know these people naturally. And my Japanese isn't that good, but we still communicated. We enjoyed ourselves. We worked very, very hard and we partied kind of hard. It gave you the motivation to keep going. I think that the key to any success is being a team, period. The American worker is spoiled. The American does not live to work. The American worker works to live.[83]

According to a number of workers at different transplants, trainers provide the most substantial and significant exposure to Japanese practice.[84] According to one Nissan worker: "I was sent to Japan and worked side-by-side with Japanese workers in a Nissan plant there. . . . They assigned me a trainer and that guy stayed with me."[85] Trainers thus function as "human carriers" of the less formal, behavioral elements of Japanese production and work organization.

Just as significantly, recruitment of new employees is geared to identify workers who possess initiative, who are dedicated to the corporation, who work well in teams, and who will not miss work.[86] This differs markedly from the typical U.S. practice of hiring "off the street." The transplants subject potential workers to cognitive and psychological tests and other screening procedures to identify workers who "fit" the Japanese model (see Chapter 9). Previous job records or high school records are scrutinized for absenteeism. Prospective employees go through extensive interviews with personnel officials, managers, and at times potential team members to identify their self-initiative and group-oriented characteristics.[87]

Transplants often use state employment services to prescreen and test applicants. They then require interviews with team members and managers. These interviews focus on issues such as work ethic, attendance, and overall attitude toward team-based work."[88] Applicants who make it through this level are often sent to assessment centers where they are judged on their ability to take initiative and to work in groups.

While theorists have generally treated the so-called loyalty of the Japanese work force as a function of Japanese culture, the screening and selection process constitutes organizational mechanisms used to select potentially "loyal" workers from a larger, more diverse population. Clearly, this apparent cultural effect can be, at least in part, duplicated through concrete organizational practice.

The selection process evaluates workers based upon group skills, problem-solving or *kaizen* capability, and individual initiative. Company workers are used in the interview process to make sure that new recruits can fit into a group context.

Recruits are often made to go through exercises, where they are asked to devise solutions to a problem. For example, they may be asked to assemble part of a vehicle, or simply put various pegs into a board. This is frequently done in a group or team context. Such exercises attempt to gauge the individual's capability to solve problems as part of a group. According to one transplant official:

> Basically the problem solving took place in a group discussion. Afterwards . . . we were able to see how well they worked with a group, and also how well they were able to identify a problem and come up with a solution. . . . You may have a person that may be able to identify a problem and come up with a solution but was absolutely terrible in a group situation. Problem solving and problem identification was important, but if a person did not show good team cooperation, that would carry more weight and could be a knock out [a reason for rejection].[89]

The transplants use ongoing training and socialization programs to acclimate workers to Japanese production practices. Most employees begin with a six- to eight-week introductory session that includes an overview of automotive assembly and fairly rigorous socialization in the Japanese model. After this, workers are inserted into teams where they continue to "learn-by-doing" from more senior employees.[90] At Nissan, the average line candidate is given a minimum of 21 hours of training and then up to an additional 20 hours for specific jobs, such as trim work, body or chassis assembly, or working in the stamping plant. This training is used to increase workers' knowledge and skills and to inculcate company norms and values.

At SIA, the entire training sequence is three weeks, full time. This mainly consists of formal training in the assembly process, which is designed to provide some basic skills and to familiarize workers with the various shops. But it also includes two hours a day of aerobic exercise to get workers physically ready for assembly-line work. Further, this training period provides an introduction to group processes and teamwork. According to one training official at the plant,

> A lot of times in the classes I make them [the workers] participate as much as possible: Break them into subgroups, have them do activities in small groups . . . where they actually have to come up with something and present to the rest of the group. Pick a spokesman, come to a consensus, who's going to take it up and present to the rest of the group. . . . Even though they may not work together in the plant, they've built a relationship in three weeks here. So we inter-mix them . . . and we set it up so you have a different spokesman every time, so one person cannot take charge.[91]

SIA workers also receive an introduction to *kaizen* activity as a part of the training process. As a training official put it:

> We say *kaizen* is what you do in your everyday lives. You drive to work; there's three highways [to choose from]; which highway is best for you to come to work? And, it's something you do everyday. When you go out on your job, there's nobody that can do it better than you, and nobody is going to know how to do it safer,

shorter, or more cost-effective than you. Instead of keeping that idea to yourself, present it to your team, present it to the group leader, present it to the manager. Tell them what you think can be done, why it can be done, and go for it. . . . The main thing we say is if you got a way that you think you can do it better and do it cheaper and do it safer, let us know; we'll be more than willing to sit and listen to you. . . . We tell them, that's what *kaizen* is, you're constantly looking for the little things, not the big things, but the little things.[92]

Wages

In any industrial system, the immediate organization of production is embedded in a set of rules, regulations, and norms that create the context in which production activity takes place. This broader production environment includes wage rates, wage determination, the organization and function of the internal labor market, degree of tenure security, type of unionization, and pattern of labor relations. These factors create incentives for work effort, establish a context for labor-management relations, and set up a framework for mobilizing employee demands and mediating disputes. In Michael Burawoy's terminology, they provide the concrete social context for the "manufacture of consent."[93]

To operate in the American environment, Japanese automotive transplants had to match the wage levels paid by the UAW-organized Big Three. This was certainly necessary for the unionized transplants, and for the nonunion transplants it was a way to stave off potential union organizing drives. Thus, the transplants are high-wage employers (Table 4.3). In 1989 NUMMI workers had an average annual salary of about $36,000, just below the industry leader, Ford, at $37,400 but ahead of GM and Chrysler, which averaged just over $35,000. Honda workers earned an average of $33,700, Mazda workers $32,900, Nissan workers $32,600, Toyota-

TABLE 4.3.   Wages at Transplant Assemblers vs. Big Three Carmakers, 1989

Company	Average Annual Earnings	Hourly Wages (production workers)	Hourly Wages (maintenance workers)
Ford	$37,434	$16.47	$18.20
NUMMI	$36,013	$16.81	$19.74
GM	$35,462	$16.24	$17.33
Chrysler	$35,371	$16.27	$16.27
Honda	$33,685	$14.55	$16.75
Mazda	$32,970	$15.13	$15.85
Nissan	$32,579	$13.95	$16.44
Toyota	$29,598	$14.23	$16.28
SIA	$28,995	$13.94	$16.58
Diamond-Star	$28,038	$13.48	$15.58

Source: Kathy Jackson, "Transplant Wages Will Rise to Match Any Gain Made at Big 3," *Automotive News* (2 July 1990), pp. 2, 60–61.

Georgetown Workers $29,600, SIA workers $28,990, and Diamond-Star workers $28,000.[94] A NUMMI team leader who was interviewed said that he earned $47,000 in 1989.

Given such high wages, team leaders may be reluctant to take promotions to management posts, which require them to give up overtime and thus in effect take a pay cut. A NUMMI team leader we interviewed had declined to be promoted because he would lose his overtime pay. This wreaks havoc on plans to promote managers from the shop floor and disrupts the Japanese-style mobility pattern that Japanese firms wish to install in the United States.[95]

The wage levels and wage determination policies of the Japanese automobile assembly transplants are more standard and uniform than in Japan. This is somewhat striking given that both academic studies and the conventional wisdom contrast American "individualism" to Japanese "familism." Transplant assemblers pay uniform wages for each class of workers and increase those rates at regular intervals.[96] Typically, there is a single base wage for production workers and a slightly higher base wage for more skilled maintenance workers. This differential is approximately $2.00 per hour (see Table 4.3). Entering workers are paid a standard base wage, which increases at regular intervals. It takes roughly 18 months for workers to reach the top of the pay scale. Wage increases accrue equally to all workers across the board. Officials at the nonunionized transplants indicate that, although they would prefer an individualized wage system, they are concerned that any attempt to institutionalize such a system might cause workers to organize a union. A manager at SIA put the issue this way:

> I don't see it happening, mainly because of our desire to remain nonunion. A lot of people were trying to put in a performance appraisal for base pay in a factory job. This could cause a lot of problems and could turn out to be an issue that could kill it if the UAW organizers came knocking on our door. We really haven't heard that much in the way of complaints from people on the floor about "I'm paid the same as this guy, and do that all the time and he doesn't do as good a job as I do."[97]

Bonuses are not as important or large in the transplants as they are in Japan, and tend to be across-the-board wage supplements that accrue in equal percentages to all workers. Of the transplants, only Nissan and Honda use actual bonuses. NUMMI's bonus is 3 percent of qualified earnings, while Nissan supplements wages by $1.55 a hour every six months. Honda and Mazda also provide monthly bonuses of $100 for perfect attendance. In addition, the transplants provide small individual bonuses for aspects of individual performance such as suggestions and participation in successful quality-control circles.

The transplants are re-creating aspects of Japan's highly segmented or dual labor markets, which we discussed in Chapter 2. In Japan, for example, a large manufacturing facility will typically have nonunionized temporary workers or lower-paid workers from subcontractors working side-by-side with regular employees. The transplants use part-time or temporary employees to provide flexibility. At both Mazda and Diamond-Star, temporary employees were laid off during a downturn in the automobile market in early 1990.[98] The use of temporaries has been the source of an ongoing labor-management conflict at Mazda where (in distinct contrast to Japan) union leaders see temporary workers as a threat to labor solidarity. This points out a distinction between American and Japanese unions. American unions have the goal that every nonmanagement person on the shop floor should be a union member. The goal of Japanese unions is that every regular company employee should be a union member.

Gender is the most blatant line of work-force segmentation in Japan. Japanese women are prohibited from working in assembly plants by Japanese laws that make it illegal for women to work the night shift. Because of U.S. law, the transplants cannot practice the gender-based segmentation common in Japan.

Unions and Industrial Relations

The transplants have developed two basic strategies to cope with U.S. labor relations and to re-create some elements of the Japanese enterprise, or plant-specific, union system (see Chapter 2). Where possible the transplants have simply chosen to resist unionization. The unionized transplants have devised strategies to align company and union interests and turn the union into a "constructive partner" in the transfer process.

As we have already seen, the four nonunionized transplants—Honda, Toyota, Nissan, and SIA—have chosen rural greenfield sites at least in part to avoid unionization. Nissan went to great lengths to defeat a unionization drive, implementing a powerful anti-union campaign.[99] The nonunionized transplants, notably Nissan and Toyota, use employee "handbooks" that provide plant-level rules and regulations and have formed "employee associations" that assist in aggregating employee input. They have also created institutional channels through which work-related grievances can be addressed. Nissan's handbook clearly outlines the company's position on unions: On page 8 of the handbook, under the heading "Company Policies," is the subheading "Nissan's Position Regarding Unions":

> A question many new employees ask is: "what about unions?" We do not favor a union because we strongly feel that unionism would be detrimental to both the Company and to all employees. We prefer to deal with each other directly rather than through a third party. Our personnel policies and programs are specifically designed to meet the needs of employees in a union-free environment by providing open communication, opportunity for personal growth and competitive wages and benefits. As a result, we are able to work with one another in an atmosphere of mutual cooperation without the hostilities and disruptions that often result from unionism.[100]

We discuss these nonunion practices in greater detail in Chapter 9.

The unionized transplants have forged comprehensive restructuring agreements with their respective union locals that have helped prepare the way for implanting Japanese production organization. Indeed, a number of labor-relations scholars have suggested that the U.S. system of plant-specific union "locals," which aggregate worker demands at the plant level, is similar in some basic respects to the Japanese enterprise union system.[101] The UAW was unopposed at Mazda, NUMMI, and Diamond-Star, and each company reached an independent agreement with its respective union local. The UAW agreed to a smaller number of job classifications, more flexible work rules, and a pay system that differed markedly from the typical U.S. assembly plant in return for jobs and some commitment to employment security. The union essentially agreed to assist in the implementation of Japanese work organization, thus implicating the union in management.

The NUMMI-UAW agreement was the pioneering one and established the blueprint for later agreements between transplants and the union. The old GM plant in Fremont, California, was known for confrontational labor relations between management and the UAW local. Absenteeism averaged over 20 percent, there were problems of alcohol and drug abuse, and when GM closed the plant there was a backlog of 800 labor grievances that had been filed. According to one GM executive, it was "one of the worst plants in the industry."[102] According to the UAW's original representative for NUMMI:

> There were numerous wildcat strikes . . . constant bickering, and infighting. . . . It was not unusual to have a grievance load in that plant on any given day of five to six thousand grievenaces. . . . The employees were treated like cattle. They were not encouraged to come forward with ideas, nor were those ideas wanted. Layoffs took place annually and more frequently than that: a regular roller coaster. . . . When the plant was closed we had all the suffering that went along with it: the families torn apart, the separations, divorces, homes lost, and indeed several suicides.[103]

The plant had been closed two years when NUMMI signed an agreement allowing the UAW to continue to represent the work force. The NUMMI agreement between GM and Toyota stipulated that Toyota personnel would manage the factory, whereas GM personnel would manage sales and marketing.[104] Moreover, NUMMI hired most of its employees from among the same autoworkers who had been laid off when GM halted operations at the plant (the UAW contract stipulated that at least 51% of NUMMI employees should be ex-Fremont workers, and the eventual figure was 85%). The NUMMI agreement basically trades management flexibility over work and production organization for rehiring and greater employment security. As the UAW-NUMMI contract specifies that:

> The parties agree that the Company will utilize a team concept, whereby employees will be organized into teams of approximately 5–10 members. All members share responsibility for the work performed by the team, and for participation in Quality/ Productivity improvement programs such as QC Circles and *kaizen.* Generally, and as practical, team members are expected to rotate jobs within the team.[105]

Mazda openly, if apprehensively, welcomed UAW organizing and representation (which was approved by 89% of its employees).[106] The firm may have been pressured to recognize the UAW by Ford, which owns 25 percent of Mazda, and like other Big Three producers would prefer the Japanese transplants to accept unionization in order to "level the competitive playing field."[107] Given that Mazda expected to be unionized, it is possible that the firm decided it might as well locate in metropolitan Detroit anyway so as to take advantage of proximity to parts suppliers. The Mazda agreement is similar to that of NUMMI.

> Our employee responsibilities are to support the team concept and other team members, set and support team goals, support and achieve a high quality standard, participate in *kaizen* and M.Q. [Mazda Quality]. Circle opportunities, respect the rights of others, promote the MMMC [Mazda Motor Manufacturing Corporation] philosophy and work within reasonable guidelines, support and abide by reasonable rules regarding attendance and conduct, promote and maintain a safe work environment and assist MMMC in meeting its production goals and schedules.[108]

The automotive assembly transplants thus split on the issue of unionization. However, even those that did unionize demanded and secured the ability to reorganize the shop floor according to Japanese work principles. Effectively, American unions faced the dilemma of organizing companies by surrendering hard-won privileges or being excluded from these plants. The decision made was a tactical retreat in order to organize the plants. In the eyes of some observers, these agreements have implicated the UAW in managing and controlling the work force and have thus destroyed its independence.[109] Interestingly, both NUMMI and Mazda have recently seen the rise of new union leadership that is less conciliatory toward management and that seeks increased autonomy.

Job Security at the Transplants

Permanent employment, or more appropriately long-term employment tenure, is a much discussed feature of the Japanese system.[110] The nature of employment security differs between unionized and nonunionized assembly transplants, and between assemblers and suppliers. The unionized transplants, NUMMI, Mazda, and Diamond-Star, all have contracts that stipulate tenure security, "guaranteeing" jobs, except under conditions that jeopardize the financial viability of the company.[111] The NUMMI labor contract spells out job security provisions, specifying that:

> New United Motor Manufacturing Inc. recognizes that job security is essential to an employees' well-being and acknowledges that it has a responsibility, with the cooperation of the Union, to provide stable employment to its workers. . . . Hence, the Company agrees that it will not lay off employees unless compelled to do so by severe economic conditions that threaten the long-term financial viability of the Company. The Company will take affirmative measures before laying off any employees, including such measures as, the reduction of salaries of its officers and management, assigning previously subcontracted work to bargaining unit employees capable of performing this work, seeking voluntary layoffs, and other cost-saving measures. In summary, the Parties to this Agreement recognize that job security for bargaining unit employees will help ensure the Company's growth and that the Company's growth will ensure job security.[112]

Thus far, both NUMMI and Mazda have fulfilled their commitment to no lay-offs. NUMMI has kept full employment in periods of up to 30 percent reduction in output; it has done so by slowing the work pace, offering workers voluntary vacation time, placing workers in special training programs, or transferring them to other jobs. To avoid layoffs, Mazda has even lent workers to local governments during slowdowns.

The nonunionized transplants provide informal assurance of tenure security but this is not reflected in contractual agreements with workers. According to a human resource manager at a non-unionized assembly transplant: "We really don't provide any guarantee employment security; we just make the statement that it's not our intention to lay off." During production slumps, Nissan and Toyota have also redeployed workers to other jobs.[113] It is impossible to tell at this stage if the nonunionized automobile assembly transplants will in fact remain committed to tenure security in the event of a severe economic downturn. And recently, a number of transplants in nonproduction related operations have laid off workers. But as of June 1991, the transplant assemblers had not laid off full-time, regular production workers.

How Workers Are Adapting

Thus far, shop-floor workers in the United States have experienced few problems adapting to the Japanese production system. NUMMI workers we interviewed who previously worked for GM indicate that they prefer the Japanese model to U.S. fordist practice.[114] According to one NUMMI worker,

> I was at GM and the part I didn't like—which I like now—is that we had a lot of drug and alcohol problems. It was getting to the point, even with me, when it got around lunchtime I had to go out and take down two or three beers to just make the afternoon out. They would come in in the morning already spaced out and I had to do their work. And, it kept getting more and more laid on me. And I said, "Enough is enough." . . . I was ready to go out the door, because I really didn't like going to work.[115]

A second NUMMI worker stated:

> I used to stand by the door and I'd watch people come in that were either drunk or smoked dope or whatever. . . . I used to hate to go to work. I'd say, "God, it's time to go to work again? I don't feel like I want to go." There's a lot of times I'd just stay home.[116]

A third NUMMI worker, who indicated that he missed more than a month of work in his first year of employment under the old GM management, adds that NUMMI is

> over and above the GM system, the Ford system, the Chrysler system. This might sound kind of corny, but . . . I have never been treated like this—I have never been

treated like a person. I have always been a number. . . . But now that NUMMI is here, I've been treated like a person. My wife has been able to go to company picnics, PT [Personal Touch, a company program] parties, meet other people, my trainers—everything.[117]

Despite these positive reports, problems exist at the NUMMI plant. In June 1991, a dissident group within the union, the "People's Caucus," won control of the UAW local at NUMMI by running candidates who emphasized the problems inside the plant (see Chapter 9).[118]

A recent book by two business journalists, Joseph and Suzy Fucini, based upon interviews with Mazda workers and union representatives, suggests that Mazda has seen the most significant adaptation problems.[119] Our own interviews and those of our Japanese collaborators suggest that there is indeed significant worker discontent at Mazda. This was reflected in the election in 1990 of a new union local that is less conciliatory toward management.[120] However, Mazda workers indicate that such adaptation problems have largely been caused by management's failure to implement all of the Japanese production methods (e.g., by not rotating workers to prevent repetitive-motion injury; see Chapter 9). Some managers echo these sentiments. A former Ford manager who became plant manager at Nissan characterized the differences between the two companies:

I have about ten times more to say as a plant manager here [at Nissan's Smryna, Tennessee, plant] as I did at Ford. Here I only have to talk to two people to get to the top man. At Ford I had to talk to fifteen or twenty people and I never did get to the top. . . . At Ford I rode around in a golf cart and I wore a tie instead of a company uniform.[121]

However, in general, management has been the source of recurring adaptation problems at the automotive transplants. During site visits and interviews, we were repeatedly told that American middle managers, especially those recruited from U.S. auto companies, have experienced great difficulty in adapting to the Japanese organization, in taking orders from foreign nationals, and in understanding the importance of shop-floor workers. Honda officials indicate that the preformed attitudes and prejudices of U.S. middle managers toward factory workers is a serious problem.[122] White and Trevor document a similar problem in U.K. transplants.[123]

NUMMI workers have complained that old-style GM managers are a major obstacle to implementation of a full-blown Japanese system, which they see as more favorable to workers than the old fordist system. According to a NUMMI worker,

A lot of things have changed. But see, you hear people talk. You hear them saying once in a while: "Oh, we're going back to the GM ways." I hope not. That was rough. . . . I think to completely bring back the Japanese way, Japan would have to take over the plant completely and have nothing to do with General Motors at all.[124]

Another NUMMI worker observed, "I think middle management is fighting it [the Japanese system] because it takes too much power away from them."[125]

In recognition of this problem, Japanese managers have begun promoting shop-floor workers to lower-level supervisory positions and grooming some of them for top-level positions.[126] This solution may be effective in circumventing the great divide in the U.S. work force between blue-collar and white-collar workers. In terms of hierarchy, the Japanese system lowers the barrier between these two groups, prompting some U.S. managers to feel they are suffering a status degradation. Still, blue-collar workers support these changes because their role in the production system is enhanced.

The Transplants and the Big Three

The remarkable success of the transplants stands in sharp contrast to the sagging fortunes of the Big Three automakers. Faced with declining profits and increasing foreign competition, the Big Three embarked on a "Southern" strategy in the 1970s designed to reduce wages and avoid unions through nonunionized Sunbelt plants and with factories in Mexico meant to export to the U.S. Later, U.S. carmakers moved to a "global car" strategy, making vehicles from parts produced by off-shore subsidiaries around the world. The basic idea was to disperse production geographically so as to limit the power of organized labor by closing down unionized U.S. plants and opening new factories in various countries that would produce identical parts. Between 1979 and 1991, U.S. car manufacturers closed 66 plants of all types—30 by GM, 27 by Chrysler, and 9 by Ford, eliminating between 250,000 to 300,000 jobs.[127]

While both business and critical academic commentators believed that the global car strategy would be successful, its true impact has not been so clear-cut.[128] The global car strategy weakened the U.S. automobile industry as a whole, as transportation costs rose, new administrative layers were added, and the entire production process fell victim to serious international bottlenecks. The industrial relations climate also worsened, as workers grew increasingly anxious about their jobs, and so-called docile Third World labor grew increasingly more concerned with improvements in their wages and working conditions.

The combined failure of the global car strategy and the success of the transplants have caused a significant decline and dislocation for Big Three carmakers. During the 1980s, GM's share of the U.S. auto market fell from 47 percent to 35 percent. In 1986, GM announced a $1.23 billion cost for the closing of 11 assembly and components plants. Between 1987 and 1988, it eliminated 40,000 white-collar jobs, 25 percent of total. In November 1990, GM announced another $2.1 billion restructuring charge to close 7 of its remaining 36 assembly plants in the United States and Canada.[129] A year later in November 1991, GM announced a sweeping retrenchment of its North American operations, including plans to close 21 additional manufacturing plants, massively cut-back capital spending, and eliminate 74,000 jobs. In January 1992, Wall Street downgraded the status of the company's debt, stating that "The proposed realignment program will be insufficient to make GM fully cost competitive in the global industry."[130]

In February 1991, Big Three carmakers temporarily closed 21 assembly plants, laying off more than 60,000 employees.[131] Then in the second quarter of 1991, output of Big Three carmakers sank to its lowest point in 33 years, causing temporary closings at eight more assembly plants.[132] Chrysler was hit so badly that it sold back its entire stake in Diamond-Star Motors to Mitsubishi for $99.8 million in cash.[133] At the same time, the transplants geared up for a 7.1 percent production increase in April-June 1991 over the same period in 1990.

The Big Three response to this situation has been to look for more government protection. In the summer of 1990, Lee Iacocca was quoted as saying, "We didn't anticipate that the transplants would cut us off at the knees."[134] In a letter dated March 6, 1991, Iacocca urged President George Bush to install market share limits on Japanese manufacturers, arguing that without immediate production cutbacks Japanese producers would capture 40 percent of the U.S. automotive market. Iacocca concluded that "Chrysler is gone and Ford could be mortally wounded from a competitive standpoint. Even GM is at risk."[135] In October 1991, Iacocca called for federal limitations on the Japanese share of the U.S. auto market. However, the Bush administration has consistently resisted the Big Three on demands for greater protectionism.[136]

Partly as a result, Big Three carmakers are now trying to emulate aspects of the transplants' strategy. This has resulted in some imitation and further diffusion of Japanese practices. The diffusion process has been accelerated by the joint-venture participation, which provide the Big Three with a window through which to observe Japanese practices in action. This adoption is being furthered by pressure for job security provisions for workers in American firms. Each one of the Big Three automakers currently operates plants that use the "team concept," smaller numbers of job classifications, pay-for-performance, and other organizational practices that have been influenced by the Japanese. American automakers are also trying to create production complexes in the U.S. Interestingly, while organizational theorists and industrial sociologists have typically predicted that Japanese organizational forms would converge toward the U.S. model, the exact reverse is occurring as American producers attempt to adopt the Japanese model.

The most all-encompassing attempt by American management to emulate the Japanese model is GM's Saturn plant. However, this project is off to a weak start. As of December 1990, Saturn had produced just 2,162 vehicles and had to delay the opening of 40 dealerships because of output problems. The first group of Saturns suffered from quality-control problems such as inadequate door seals and severe vibrations in vehicles with automatic transmissions.[137] Maryann Keller, a leading automobile industry analyst, noted this about Saturn: "Whatever its impact it won't be worth $3.5 billion, which is how much the project cost."[138] The reason is that Saturn and other American attempts at restructuring have not gone far enough to empower workers and provide the long-term economic security required to unleash their ideas. In fact, Saturn has already experienced growing worker discontent and was forced to renegotiate its labor contract in the fall of 1991. A recent study by Thomas Kochan of MIT suggests that U.S. reforms are essentially "hybrid forms" where workers are grouped in teams but not given decentralized decision-making authority.[139]

Often, such reorganizations amount to little more than a "group fordism" where tasks are rearranged in teams but workers are given little actual decision-making authority. In many plants, such reorganizations have simply been a way to reduce the work force, increase the workload, and speed up the pace of work. The comments of a former GM employee who now works in the NUMMI plant are illustrative:

> When I made supervisor at GM—this was in 1979—they already sent the Japanese engineers over there. . . . Anyway, the company put us through a week's training, 40 hours' training. It was called "Quality of Work Life," which actually talked of "Team Concept." When I returned after these classes, my supervisor stated to me, "Forget that class. You do it my way."[140]

It is not surprising that rank-and-file elements in the UAW oppose such reorganization and movement to this version of the "team concept," especially given the way that Big Three management has tried to use such measures to get workers essentially to eliminate their own jobs.

Perhaps the most telling example of the limits of restructuring by the Big Three automakers comes from Chrysler. In the mid-1980s, Chrysler embarked on a major study of new forms of work and production organization to inform a potential restructuring effort. In 1987, Chrysler's Youth Committee began a study of Honda and other auto transplants. Lee Iacocca agreed to the recommendation that Chrysler reorganize and integrate development, design, engineering, and marketing in terms of the current model of concurrent development. However, when the Youth Committee recommended that Chrysler institute teamwork, create a more egalitarian work environment, and develop new ways to empower workers, Iacocca balked, suggesting that the Youth Committee "got carried away" with Honda. "They [the committee] wanted us [the executives] to eat in the cafeteria and go through the rain to the parking lot like everyone else. We don't go for that." Chrysler vice president, Tom Denomme, added, "The word *teamwork* was used about 5,000 times."[141] The Chrysler response was typified when in March 1990 it reorganized its board of directors, dropping UAW president Owen Bieber from the board—reneging on its commitment of ten years earlier to provide the union with a seat on the board in exchange for concessions.[142] The response of Chrysler's leadership to change will likely be most costly for workers who lack the lucrative "golden parachutes" afforded its top management cadre.

Beyond the "Screwdriver Factory": Transplant R&D in the United States

Many academic commentators and policymakers have argued that the Japanese automobile transplants are little more than "screwdriver" facilities that simply assemble parts imported from Japan. However, Japanese automakers are making major investments in R&D, design, and engineering to supplement and enhance their expanding production capabilities.

The transplants currently operate 22 R&D, product engineering, and/or design facilities in the United States (Table 4.4).[143] Figure 4.3 shows the location of major Japanese automotive R&D facilities in the United States. Here, two patterns are evident. First, most transplants operate an R&D/product development engineering

TABLE 4.4. Automotive Transplant R&D and Design Centers

R&D Center	Location	Date Opened	No. of Employees	Major Function
Honda R&D of North America, Inc.	Torrance, CA	1975	125	Automotive design
	Marysville, OH	1985	175	Develop prototypes and components; qualify suppliers
Honda Engineering of North America	Marysville, OH	1988	180	Design and develop production equipment
Toyota Technical Center USA, Inc.	Gardena, CA	1977	NA	Vehicle development and testing
	Torrance, CA	1977	82	Prototype testing
	Ann Arbor, MI	1984	48	Evaluate prototype parts; emissions testing
	Southfield, MI	1989	50	Design components and production equipment
	San Francisco, CA	1989	50	Support NUMMI plant
	Lexington, KY	1989	6	Support Georgetown plant
Calty Design Research (Toyota)	Newport Beach, CA	1973	45	Automotive design
Nissan Design International	San Diego, CA	1979	45	Automotive design
Nissan Research & Development	Ann Arbor, MI	1978	NA	Engine and power train research; emissions testing
	Plymouth, MI	1983	400	Parts engineering for U.S. vehicles
Mazda Research & Development	Irvine, CA	1972	85	Automotive design
	Ann Arbor, MI	1988	20	Engineering research, emissions testing
	Flat Rock, MI	1988	39	Engineering; local parts sourcing
Mitsubishi Design Studio	Cypress, CA	1973	88	Automotive design & engineering
Mitsubishi Motors of America	Southfield, MI	1984	NA	Joint Chrysler-Mitsubishi development; emissions testing
Isuzu Technical Center	Cerritos, CA	1985	62	Automotive design & testing
	Plymouth, MI	1990	18	Components engineering; emissions testing
Subaru Research and Design	Newport Beach, CA	1986	13	Automotive design
Subaru Technical Center	Garden Grove, CA	1973	65	Develop and test components and vehicles

Source: Lindsay Chappell, "The Japanese–American Car," *Automotive News* (November 26, 1990), pp. 42–43.

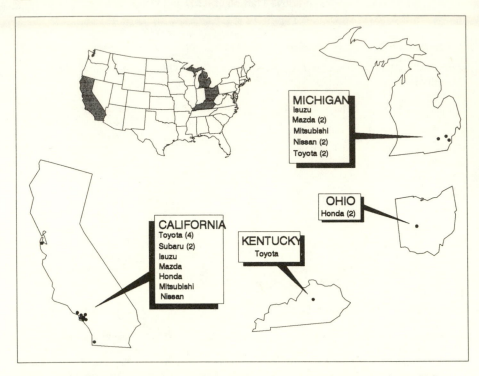

FIGURE 4.3. Japanese Automotive R&D, Engineering, and Design Centers in the U.S.
Source: Lindsay Chappell, "The Japanese-American Car." *Automotive News.* (26
November 1990).

facility near or at their actual assembly plants. This is in keeping with the Japanese
practice of locating R&D close to production facilities to improve interaction and
to integrate suppliers into the product development process. There is an especially
heavy concentration of R&D facilities in Michigan around the traditional center of
automotive R&D.

Honda was the first Japanese auto manufacturer to make a major investment
aimed at developing R&D and engineering expertise in the United States. The cen-
terpiece of the Honda engineering investment was the 1987 purchase of the Ohio
Transportation Center which was located less than ten miles from its assembly
plant.[144] Honda's R&D and engineering operations in Ohio now employ over 350
people. Honda's U.S. R&D units recently engineered the new 1991 Accord station
wagon.[145] Honda's stated goal is to produce new cars from design to production
entirely in the United States.[146] Honda's engineering center also works with suppliers to design, qualify, and test components. Toyota has smaller engineering operations at both its NUMMI and Georgetown, Kentucky, plants, and also operates a
technical support facility in Michigan to develop new production technology and
evaluate parts. In 1990, Toyota announced it was building one of the largest automobile test tracks in the world in Arizona.[147] Nissan operates engineering and testing facilities in Plymouth and Ann Arbor, Michigan, but its largest investment is

an $80 million R&D and engineering center in Farmington, Michigan, which will employ 600 persons by 1992.[148] Mazda has built relatively small technical centers in Michigan (in Flat Rock and Ann Arbor) largely for emissions testing and local parts sourcing.

The second pattern is that each of the transplants has a design facility in southern California to develop new models for introduction in the United States. There are now 11 transplant R&D or design facilities in California. Southern California was chosen by the Japanese for design facilities even before their initial success in exporting to the United States.[149] For example, Mazda opened its design facility in Irvine, California, in 1972; Mitsubishi, Toyota, and Subaru followed in 1973; Honda arrived in 1975, Nissan in 1979, and Isuzu in 1985.[150] The reasons for locating in southern California are interesting and provide insight into the Japanese production system.

Southern California is the most automobile-dependent region in the world. It is also the largest regional market in the world and has over 50 percent import car penetration. The area is highly diverse, as are its vehicles, and it is a design trendsetter. In such an environment, new ideas are generated and the designers can give free rein to their imaginations. For example, the Mazda Miata, the MPV, and MX-6 were largely designed in California as were Nissan's 240SX, Maxima, and Pathfinder, and Toyota's Celica and Previa minivan.[151] The success of these design studios has led Japanese automakers to increase their investments in California. Ironically, Japanese automakers were the first to set up design studios in southern California. American and European manufacturers have only recently followed suit and built design facilities in California.

There can be little doubt that the Japanese "Big Three," Toyota, Nissan, and Honda, are moving in the direction of making their North American transplant operations capable of standing on their own. As the following chapter will show, suppliers who deal with automotive transplants are also developing engineering and R&D capabilities in the United States. Such investments are to be expected given the close linkages between the factory and the lab under the Japanese expression of innovation-mediated production. The recent massive investment in R&D, design, and testing facilities casts considerable doubt upon the argument that Japanese automakers are operating "screwdriver" facilities that simply assemble parts or kits produced overseas or that they are only locating so-called low-wage and unskilled jobs in the United States.[152]

Indicators and Elements of Success

The Japanese transplants have been successful in economic terms. In 1990, the transplants produced 1.49 millions automobiles in the United States. Combining import sales and domestic production, Japanese automobile producers captured 31 percent of the U.S. car market in 1991. Both Honda and Toyota surpassed Chrysler in share of the U.S. market, transforming the Big Three into a "Big Five" comprised of GM, Ford, Honda, Toyota, and Chrysler, in that order.[153] By 1993, transplant production is projected to reach 2.3 million automobiles. The automotive analyst,

Maryann Keller, has predicted that "the Japanese can easily take 50 percent of the North American market in five to ten years."[154]

A number of transplant producers are likely to grow beyond the U.S. market and to compete in global markets as well. Nissan and Honda already reverse-export vehicles to Japan.[155] Honda ships American-made cars to Korea, which excludes Japanese imports but allows cars from the United States, and Toyota has announced plans to ship 5,000 automobiles a year to Taiwan.[156] Honda has announced it will ship the U.S.-designed Accord station wagon to Europe, placing the U.S. government in the awkward position of either protecting the right of U.S.-made autos to be exported to Europe or allowing Europe to exclude U.S. autos. In February 1990, U.S. officials cautioned European Community leaders not to restrict entry of American-built Japanese cars.[157]

Productivity estimates and comparisons done by the MIT International Motor Vehicle Program indicate that the transplants have productivity ratings higher than U.S.-owned automobile assembly plants and comparable to their Japanese sister plants.[158] In 1989, according to the MIT group, productivity (measured as hours per vehicle) was estimated to be 21.2 hours at the transplants, 16.8 for Japanese plants in Japan, and 25.1 for traditional Big Three American plants.[159] Quality, as estimated by J.D. Power Initial Quality Survey, was 65 assembly defects per 100 vehicles at the transplants, 60 defects per 100 vehicles in Japan, and 82 defects per 100 vehicles in Big Three American plants.[160] Some observers suggest that the economic effectiveness of the transplants and of the Japanese model more generally is due to the fast pace of the assembly line, overwork, the internal discipline provided by teams, and a general practice of "management by stress."[161] This, however, is only a partial explanation. Clearly, the transplants operate a fast paced assembly line, effectively filling in the pores of the working day; at most of the transplants the "tack time" is roughly 60 seconds, meaning workers have less than a minute to complete their jobs. However, a number of Big Three assembly plants also run this fast. Workers at NUMMI and Mazda have expressed concern about line speed and work pace, but workers at both plants express a general preference for the Japanese model over the previous U.S. fordist system.[162]

The key to the transplants' success stems from three core elements of the Japanese model of production organization: (1) use of teams and rotation to achieve functional integration of tasks, (2) recruitment, socialization, and remuneration policies designed to motivate work and increase work-force commitment, and (3) a pattern of work organization that harnesses the mental as well as manual capabilities of workers. At Honda, for example, engineers are required to listen to and respect shop-floor workers. In some instances shop-floor workers actually supervise college-educated engineers.[163] This is the result of a conscious policy to harness workers' intelligence and ideas. The effectiveness of the transplants lies in the new model of innovation-mediated production that integrates the intellectual as well as the manual capabilities of labor—the collective intelligence of workers. This mode of production organization represents a more sophisticated way of extracting value and harnesses workers' capabilities more completely and totally than before.[164]

That Japanese corporations have successfully implanted their model system of work and production organization in the U.S. automobile industry is a telling sign given that the American automotive industry is virtually synonymous with fordism. However, the transfer and diffusion of this new model in just one industry is not sufficient proof of its generalizability. Automobile assemblers are just that—they put together component parts supplied from various input industries and suppliers. The next chapter deepens our analysis by examining the source of these components—the suppliers of transplant parts.

5

Building a Just-in-Time Complex: Automotive Parts Suppliers

> We are going to be very dependent on our suppliers and they on us. There has to be close cooperation between us for both parties to stay in business.
>
> MARVIN RUNYON, President of Nissan.[1]

More than 300 Japanese or Japanese–U.S. joint-venture automotive parts suppliers have been established to supply parts to transplant auto assemblers in the United States. These transplant suppliers include a large number of wholly owned Japanese companies along with another, sizable number of joint ventures between Japanese and U.S. automotive parts companies. Thus far, transplant suppliers have invested at least $8 billion in U.S. production, creating a virtual second automobile industry in the United States.

Three types of transplant automotive suppliers have come to America. The first group, representing the majority, are original-equipment manufacturers who supply inputs directly to another stage in the assembly process, such as windshields, stamped metal parts, brake systems, seats, etc. The second group are "after-market" or replacement part suppliers who make parts that are supplied to assemblers and also the replacement market, such as batteries, brake pads, mufflers, etc. For example, the transplant supplier NGK not only supplies spark plugs to auto manufacturers, but also sells them through automotive parts stores. The final group consist of "capital goods" manufacturers who provide manufacturing and assembly-line equipment to the transplant assemblers (these are treated in more depth in Chapter 7).

This chapter focuses on three related issues: First, we continue our analysis of the transfer of Japanese work and production to consider the far greater number of transplant suppliers. Indeed, the transplant suppliers afford an important test of the transfer and diffusion of the Japanese model because of their significant number and more diverse locations. In contrast to the assemblers, who employ thousands of workers and have tremendous power, the suppliers are typically much smaller and cannot so easily dominate both their workers and their labor markets. Further, their sheer geographical dispersion means that they plant far more "seeds" of the Japanese system in the United States.

Second, we extend our analysis to examine the transfer of relationships between firms—that is, the transfer of the Japanese "just-in-time" (JIT) supplier system to the United States. The ability of the transplants to replicate the tightly networked and densely linked JIT supplier system in the United States is a crucial issue. This will provide an understanding of the success of Japanese companies in overcoming the long legacy of adversarial, arm's length supplier relations in the United States.

Third, we explore the more general question of new network forms of industrial organization. This issue has stimulated considerable debate in both the academic and policy-making communities. Alfred Chandler and Oliver Williamson have argued that both vertical integration and the in-house provision of supplies are frequently more efficient methods than external subcontracting.[2] Sociologists have countered that network relations, if properly organized, can capture the advantages of market efficiency and retain some of the control and coordination advantages of integration.[3] Masahiko Aoki suggests that, whereas vertically integrated firms may economize on transactions, networks are able to generate powerful information flows, which more than compensate for these advantages.[4] Others suggest that the Japanese model is a distinctive system centered around large core companies.[5] This chapter examines the transfer of the Japanese production system in the automotive parts transplants in light of these conceptual issues.

Building a Just-in-Time System

Transplant suppliers are building an integrated supplier complex in the United States, providing the broader JIT industrial infrastructure for Japanese automobile production. Figure 5.1 is a map that illustrates this growing industrial infrastructure

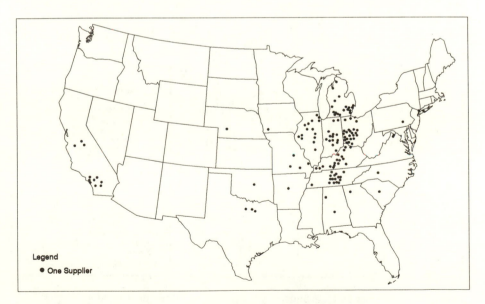

FIGURE 5.1. Japanese-Affiliated Automotive Parts Suppliers in the U.S.
Source: Adapted from Authors' database.

in the United States. Figure 5.2 supplements this with a more detailed map of transplant suppliers in the transplant corridor. As these maps show, transplant automotive suppliers are mainly concentrated in the lower Midwest, in the same states where transplant assembly facilities are located. Most of these plants are in states with transplant assembly plants. According to the most recent estimates from our database on transplant suppliers, Ohio is home to 65 transplant parts companies, Michigan has 44, Kentucky has 42, Indiana has 41, Illinois has 28, and Tennessee has 30. These states account for 250 of 322 total transplant suppliers. The next leading state is California with 9; no other state is home to more than 4 transplant suppliers.

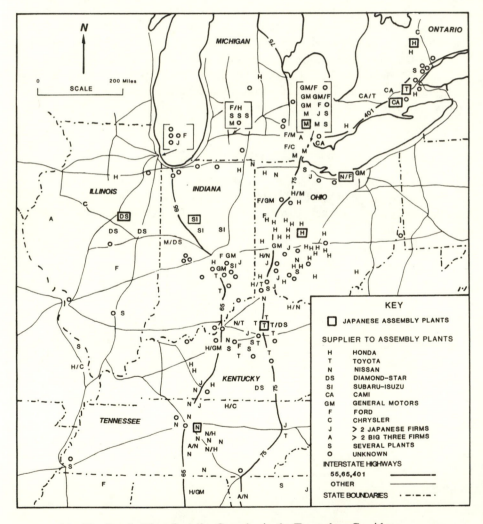

FIGURE 5.2. The Just-in-Time Supplier Complex in the Transplant Corridor.
Source: Andrew Mair, Richard Florida, and Martin Kenney, "The New Geography of Automobile Production: The Japanese Transplants in North America," *Economic Geography* (October 1988), pp. 64, 4.

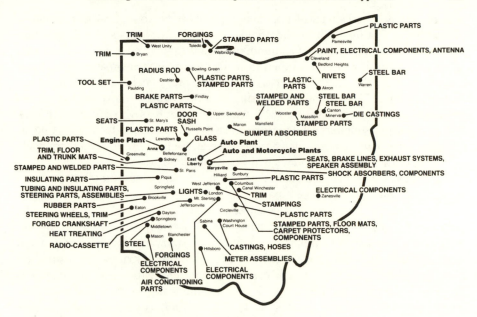

FIGURE 5.3. Honda's Ohio Supplier Complex.
Note: Includes both transplant and U.S. suppliers.
Source: Honda of America Manufacturing, 1991.

Figure 5.3 provides a detailed view of the dense supplier complex surrounding the Honda plant in central Ohio. The core of the Honda complex consists of two automobile assembly plants, a motorcycle assembly plant, an engine and transmission facility, and a major R&D facility. Honda is also beginning to use the indigenous infrastructure for second-tier suppliers, extending the supplier linkages upstream to include local companies. As one example, a very small machine shop in rural Ohio has capitalized upon previous expertise in rebuilding tractor engines and farm machinery and now rebuilds robot heads for Honda suppliers.[6] In effect, Honda is using the indigenous manufacturing infrastructure of central Ohio and surrounding areas to build a multi-tier supplier complex.

The development of a transplant automobile supplier complex has proceeded in three stages. Initially, Japanese assemblers built facilities in the Midwest to take advantage of the indigenous infrastructure of parts suppliers.[7] A small number of Japanese automobile suppliers were already in the United States, having established production facilities to supply Big Three carmakers and the after-market for Japanese imports. However, they quickly discovered that American suppliers could not adapt to JIT quality and delivery requirements.[8] Even obtaining basic inputs like high-quality steel or glass proved to be difficult.[9] In 1988, Mazda's Flat Rock plant estimated that the defect rate for the company's U.S.-owned suppliers was anywhere from three to five times higher than its Japanese suppliers. In 1990, Toyota officials estimated that defect rates for components supplied by 75 of the company's major American and European suppliers were 100 times greater than those supplied by 146 Japanese companies.[10]

Unfamiliar with the JIT system and believing Japanese quality demands unreasonable, many American parts suppliers simply chose not to supply the transplants. According to Osamu Nobuto, the original president of Mazda's Flat Rock plant, "What is disturbing and quite astounding to us is that we have actually had suppliers tell us that if we insist on their insuring quality in their process, rather than simply replacing the defective parts as they occur, they may have to abandon their business with us."[11] A Honda purchasing executive adds: "Many people are not willing to make our designs our way."[12] Transplant suppliers who have tried to work with U.S.-owned suppliers echo these concerns. A Nippondenso technician told us: "We get parts that are not dimensionally correct; we have got to send them back. . . . Some of them even tell you it's bad when they send it to you."[13]

The shortage of qualified parts suppliers left Japanese automobile assemblers little choice but to build a new parts industry in the United States. Transplant assemblers thus encouraged their Japanese suppliers to come to America.[14] Honda, for example, provided financial assistance to four of its Japanese suppliers to form KTH Parts, a transplant supplier producing small stampings for fuel tanks, wheel housings, and dashboard parts in Ohio.[15] More recently, Japanese parts suppliers have established facilities on their own initiative in an effort to secure contracts from both the transplants and the Big Three American companies. Many of the most important Japanese suppliers to Honda, Nissan, Toyota, and Mazda have now opened U.S. branches.

The Japanese and American Supplier Systems

The Japanese supplier system differs markedly from the traditional U.S. fordist supplier system with its arm's length relationships and short-term contracts. Big Three American automakers typically have had relationships with thousands of suppliers, with the supplier decision based largely on who can offer the lowest price. An executive of a U.S. supplier firm characterized the nature of traditional U.S. supplier relations this way: "The strategy was line 'em up and beat 'em up until you get 'em to a point where they can't make money anymore. Then you've got the best price."[16]

The Japanese JIT system is quite different. Under this system, which Ronald Dore has called "relational subcontracting," the assemblers contract out approximately 70 percent of the entire value of the finished car.[17] In contrast, the Big Three automakers traditionally relied upon suppliers for only 30 percent to 50 percent of inputs.[18] However, in the last ten years the Big Three have attempted to spin out their in-house parts operations. In Japan there is an asymmetric but nevertheless close relationship between the assembler and the primary or first-tier supplier based on long-term interaction and intense information sharing.[19] To be effective, the JIT system must reflect certain traits: close geographic proximity of producers, long-term relationships, and tight interorganizational linkages characterized by personnel sharing, joint participation in product development, and regular communication and interaction.[20]

As Chapter 2 has shown, the Japanese supplier system is organized in a pyramidal structure. In a fully developed system, there can be up to ten tiers of suppliers.[21]

The assembler, at the apex of the pyramid, plays a key role in this system by helping to structure linkages and coordinate flows within the network of producers.[22] First-tier suppliers are next in importance, playing a role as coordinators and organizing flows of supplies between lower-level suppliers and the final assembler. The power of this method of organizing suppliers is that the companies at each tier are responsible for organizing the next tier. Consequently, no firm is overwhelmed with huge numbers of suppliers requiring the assembler to have a vast purchasing bureaucracy or be unable to monitor its suppliers. Thus, the overhead burden is spread out and simultaneously reduced.

Assemblers often have financial holdings in their suppliers and subcontractors. As mentioned earlier, the Toyota group owns 21 percent of Nippondenso. In the case of Stanley Electric Co., an important supplier of automobile electrical equipment and an important Honda supplier, Honda owns 4 percent of its stock and Mitsubishi Motors owns 3.1 percent, thereby ensuring both automakers a close relationship with Stanley.[23] However, it is a mistake to see these pyramids as monolithic. Nippondenso, for example, in addition to supplying Toyota also supplies most of the other Japanese (and the Big Three) automobile companies and most of the Japanese transplants as well.[24]

Both the conventional wisdom and the academic literature suggest that it should be difficult, if not impossible, to transfer this kind of supplier system to the United States. Mark Granovetter suggests that organizations are strongly influenced by relationships with other organizations with which they interact as well as by the broader social and economic context in which they are embedded.[25] Some argue that organizations with similar structures are more likely to have formalized interorganizational relations than those organizations that are different; others contend that existing relations between organizations tend to make organizations conform to their environment.[26] Even Ronald Dore suggests that the Japanese system is surrounded by a set of supportive social relationships without which it might not function.[27] The implication here is that the Japanese supplier system would be difficult to relocate outside the Japanese context, especially in the United States with its long legacy of adversarial supplier relations.

The data that undergirds our analysis of transplant suppliers derive both from a survey we conducted of transplant suppliers and from numerous site visits and personal interviews conducted with Japanese-owned, Japanese-American joint venture, and American automotive parts suppliers. The survey questionairre obtained information on start-up date, employment, sales, industry, end-users, work organization, number of job classifications, use of teams, rotation, quality-control circles, wages, and employment security as well as just-in-time delivery practices. (For further discussion see Appendix A.)

Diffusion of Japanese Work and Production Organization

Table 5.1 outlines the major characteristics of work organization at the transplant suppliers. As this table indicates, transplant suppliers have successfully transferred many features of Japanese work organization. According to the supplier survey, 68

TABLE 5.1. Characteristics of Transplant Parts Suppliers*

Characteristic	Number	Percent Share	Total Number of Suppliers Surveyed (n)
JIT system in use	50	68.5	73
Work Teams	56	76.7	73
Rotation within teams	60	87.0	69
Rotation between teams	45	66.2	68
Production workers maintain their own machines	58	79.5	73
Production workers do routine quality control	72	94.7	76
Production workers help design their own jobs	42	60.9	69
Number of job classifications			
one	23	34.3	67
two	10	14.9	67
three	11	16.4	67
four	10	14.9	67
five	4	6.0	67
Subtotal (five or fewer)	58	86.6	67
Starting hourly wage	$7.21	–	68
Hourly wage after 12 months	$8.01	–	60
Average annual compensation	$21,268	–	65

Source: Transplant Supplier Survey, by authors (June 1988).
*Includes Japanese-owned and Japanese–U.S. joint-venture automobile parts suppliers.

percent (50, n = 73) of the suppliers are using a JIT system internally, although 64 percent said the system had been modified from the one used in Japan. The reasons for this are in large part due to forces outside the plant, such as the difficulty in securing parts on a JIT basis from subcontractors.[28]

More than three-quarters of respondents (76.7 percent, n = 73) indicate that work is organized on the basis of teams. Roughly 87 percent (60, n = 69) of transplant suppliers rotate workers within teams. However, only 66.2 percent (45, n = 68) rotate between teams, a fact that may be explained by the relative newness of these plants, which means that workers are probably not yet well trained within teams. The use of teams and work rotation is also confirmed by our site visits to and interviews with managers of transplant supplier facilities.[29] At Nippondenso, which is a Toyota group company and the largest transplant supplier in the United States, workers are rotated as frequently as every hour or two hours, depending upon the type of job they perform. According a Nippondenso executive, rotation is used to increase flexibility, minimize repetitive-motion injury, and keep workers interested in their jobs:

> One reason is the flexibility it gives you. If a person can do every job in the team, that gives you the greatest flexibility in case someone's sick or there are two people out. But the second purpose is safety, ergonomics. So if you've got a job that's highly repetitive, if I job-rotate I'm not going to injure anybody on a carpal tunnel. The third is just sheer boredom. People get tired doing the same job. If they get into that rut, they can make mistakes.[30]

Workers at transplant suppliers have significant responsibility over and discretion in the performance of multiple shop-floor tasks. More than 60 percent (42, n = 69) of the respondents indicate that workers are involved in the design of their tasks, an activity which in U.S. companies is entirely controlled by management and engineers. Close to 80 percent of respondents surveyed indicate that workers perform routine maintenance on their machines. In contrast, U.S. management has tried to prevent workers from being knowledgeable about their machines.[31]

At Nippondenso, work teams develop and design their own jobs. At every station, teams post a "working manual"—essentially a set of drawings or photographs, either handwritten or typed, with an explanation of how to perform the various jobs for that team. These working manuals instruct the operators on the exact procedure to make a certain part. This standardizes tasks so as to simplify rotation and ensure uniformity among the various shifts. These manuals are changed every time there is a change in the process. In this way, after every improvement, the team essentially rebalances the line.

In response to the survey question "How similar is your manufacturing process to one that might be found in Japan?," 86 percent of suppliers (66, n = 73) said that their U.S. operations were either exactly the same or very similar to one that might be found in Japan. Only one supplier said that it was not similar at all.

Job Classifications

Like the assemblers, transplant suppliers use a small number of job classifications. More than 85 percent (n = 58) indicate that they use between one and five job classifications for production workers and 23 use only one job classification. Nippondenso, for example, has two broad job classifications, skilled and unskilled. According to the company's vice president of human resources: "We don't really get hung up on titles; matter-of-fact we discourage titles within the firm. We don't have a title called assembler, we don't have a title called a tube-bending machine operator; there's none of that. You're an associate."[32] Nippondenso has three pay and promotion groups within its job classification scheme. Associates can be promoted from entry or "qualified" level to "proficient" and then "advanced." Each promotion takes two years, three or four training classes, and a good performance appraisal.

The results of our supplier survey indicated that only eight suppliers had more than five job classifications for production workers. (Three was the median, four was the average, and one was the mode.) In actual numbers, 23 suppliers use 1 job classification for production workers, 10 use 2, 11 use 3, 10 use 4, and 4 use 5. Most startling was the fact that one company had 53 job classifications. A number of transplant suppliers indicated that they instituted more job classifications than would be ideal (as many as ten) in response to American workers' wishes to have an internal career ladder—this is especially important to workers who wish to have interfirm mobility.[33]

TABLE 5.2.   Tasks Performed by Team Leaders

Tasks	Rank	Number	Percent	Total Respondents
Assign workers to jobs	(1)	55	88.7	62
Fill in for absent employees (e.g., five minutes)	(2)	45	72.5	62
Quality-control paperwork	(3)	42	67.7	62
Take worker suggestions to management	(4)	31	50.0	62
Organize safety meetings	(5)	29	46.8	62
Organize team member vacation time	(6)	26	41.9	62
Fill in for absent employees for whole shifts	(7)	25	40.3	62
Prepare work standards and task descriptions	(8)	24	38.7	62

Source: Transplant Supplier Survey, by authors (June 1988).

As in the automotive assemblers, team leaders play a vital role in organizing the actual production process. As Table 5.2 indicates, team leaders perform a variety of tasks necessary to keep production functioning smoothly. The most important of these tasks is to assign workers to jobs, fill in for absent employees, and do quality-control paperwork. Other tasks vary by firm. As in the automobile assemblers, team leaders act as intermediaries between shop-floor workers and management. At Nippondenso

> The team leader is first level. He or she is a working member of the team. So they actually work on the line with the people. They cover for breaks in hot weather. We have Gatorade breaks in hot weather. The team leader will let people take some time off to get some Gatorade. Take the job. Fill in for absentees.[34]

The organizational structure of transplant suppliers varies greatly, but basically it is similar to the flat hierarchies found in transplant assemblers. At Nippondenso, there are basically seven levels: associate, team leader, subsection, manager, department manager, vice president, and president.

Quality Control and *Kaizen* Activity

As the previous chapter has shown, quality-control and *kaizen* activities are key aspects of Japanese work organization. Slightly less than half (44%, 31, n = 71) of suppliers use quality circles, and 68 percent (28, n = 41) of those who do not yet use quality-control circles plan to do so in the future. In contrast to Japan, where quality-circle activity sometimes occurs without pay, transplant suppliers tend to pay workers for quality-circle activity. Eighty-three percent of suppliers (26, n = 31) who use quality circles pay workers for normal hours spent working on quality circles. In transplant suppliers, participation in quality circles mainly occurs immediately before or after shift work. Suppliers have also set up competitions between quality-control circles and use prizes, plaques, and cash awards to provide additional incentives for quality-circle participation. Some transplants have sent American quality circles to Japan to participate in annual company quality competitions. Thirty percent of transplant suppliers (22, n = 73) provide cash awards for worker suggestions. Two-thirds of these suppliers (48, n = 73) indicate that "willingness to suggest new ideas" is a key criteria for evaluating production workers.

Nippondenso puts heavy emphasis on quality-control (QC) circles and other forms of *kaizen* activity. All Nippondenso workers belong to QC circles, which are usually formed by members of teams or work groups. The workers are allowed to pick the theme or focus of the circle and typically choose a highly personal "funny" name—for example, the "Nuts-kopfs," a QC circle that developed new ways to place the nuts on car air conditioners, or the "Ninjaneers," an engineering group. These QC circles meet an average of 45 minutes a month and make competitive presentations to managers every six months.

Nippondenso has perhaps the most well-developed suggestion system of any Japanese automotive transplant. In 1991, Nippondenso U.S. recorded 5,435 suggestions. The participation rate was 73 percent of the work force and the adoption rate was 98 percent. Nippondenso's suggestion system is modelled on the system used by its Japanese parent and is extremely "Japanese-like" in character, emphasizing continuous incremental improvement through a combination of individual initiative and team effort. As in Japan, individual team members take the initiative to make the initial suggestion directly to their team leaders, who are also shopfloor workers. The suggestion is then presented to the entire team for discussion and further development to see if it is potentially viable. If the team decides that the suggestion is worth trying, it then works to actually implement the idea on the line. Only when the suggestion has been fully proven by the team is it formally presented to management which simply accepts and recognizes the suggestion that has been already implemented by the workers. The company recently instituted a suggestion program, which pays $14 per accepted suggestion. Officials estimate that 1,400 suggestions were received in about nine months. The participation rate is roughly 30 percent, and 97 percent of all suggestions are accepted.

At Nippondenso, teams are seen as the cornerstone of *kaizen* activity. Teams are expected to meet every morning for about three minutes to share ideas, organize jobs, and do production planning. There are 45-minute meetings every Friday, which are devoted to more detailed problem solving and information sharing. Once a quarter, each team meets with the vice presidents of production and sales for about an hour to share information and ideas.

According to Nippondenso officials, there have been few problems in getting workers to contribute ideas, form QC circles, or engage in *kaizen* activities.

> Ninety-five percent of the American work force want to do a good job. And they want to continue idea. So our job is to remove the roadblocks blocking those ideas. Where I've got a team leader, a supervisor, who puts somebody down the first time they bring up an idea, we've got to teach them that they can't do that. So it isn't really that tough. We run a series of meetings, we ask for their input, and they do a good job of it.[35]

Even though Nippondenso has had great success, other suppliers have experienced problems. Yet most of these companies believe that successful integration of their employees into the firm is vital and will require continued efforts.

Recruitment and Selection

The suppliers also use employee recruitment techniques designed to select employees who fit the demands of Japanese production methodology. Workers are typically given a set of written tests and then undergo a rigorous interview and screening procedure. At Nippondenso, applicants for associate are put through the basic GATB, or General Aptitude Test Battery, which tests basic math and reading skills required for statistical process control. Nippondenso originally used the Michigan Job Service to administer the GATB tests but changed to another standardized test when the U.S. Department of Labor decided that GATB testing may be discriminatory. Workers who successfully complete the test are interviewed by two team leaders and a human resource specialist.

Nippondenso's interview was designed to select workers who are assertive in a group context and work well in teams. For example, the interviewers could ask questions to gauge the level of assertiveness, such as, "What do you do if you're standing in line going into the theater, and somebody gets in front of you?" If the candidate answers "I don't do anything," they may be seen to be unassertive, and not what the company is looking for. The interviewers may come back to the issue later, asking, for example, "When you go to a restaurant and you are served a well-done steak when you ordered it medium, how do you handle that?" This information is then combined with other information to determine whether the candidate is assertive and can work well in teams. A Nippondenso executive provides a detailed depiction of a typical question-answer interview process.

> We always start with an open-ended question. After we feel you're comfortable, of course, we go into "Why don't you tell us a little bit about yourself, where you're from, a little about your family and your career and education." . . . We get a chance to see, Does he use inductive or deductive reasoning? Where does he start? Does he talk about now and go backwards or does he start back in high school and go forward? Do they get into mind-sets; are they stuck with one issue? . . . So we just let them talk for a while, get a sense of what kind of reasoning ability they have, what their key interest points are. And from there, then we'll come back into specifics. . . . Sometimes we'll get into hypothetical cases. We'll ask him about a problem and how to solve it. . . . The ideal candidate will say, "Gee, I got a team of people together; I got the guy off the floor that actually runs the machine; I got this team together and this team acted as facilitator; we solved the problem that way." That's an ideal response. . . . "I went out and yeah, boy, I kicked ass." That's no good.[36]

The selection criteria used by transplant suppliers appear to be biased against minority group members and employees who have been members of unions. Only 11 percent of factory workers are minorities, and an even smaller percentage had ever been members of unions. In contrast to the assemblers, automotive suppliers usually require a smaller number of employees and therefore do not overdraw the local labor pool. According to the supplier survey, most factory workers (83 percent) live within 30 miles of the plant in which they work. Surprisingly, on average 67 percent of the production employees had factory experience. However, the responses to a follow-up question on whether factory experience was a major hiring criteria diverged widely. Some suppliers found factory experience essential; for others it was not a factor. The possible explanation for this is that some plants require experienced personnel, whereas others could use inexperienced workers. (see Table 5.3)

Transplant suppliers also use careful screening and selection procedures to pick management employees. Nippondenso uses a series of interviews that are more stringent than its interview procedure for associates. These interviews are designed to screen out traditional American-style managers, who see their role as one of "bossing" workers, and to find those who can manage in a team environment. Management employees are usually white, male, and college educated. Just 9 percent of management employees are members of minority groups. Fully 29 percent of management employees are Japanese, a higher percentage than at the assembly plants. This is likely due to the smaller average employment size of transplant parts suppliers. It also stems from the fact that in 1988 many plants were still in the start-up phase—a period that normally requires more Japanese engineers and manufacturing specialists. Thirty-three percent of American managers have visited Japan,

TABLE 5.3. Characteristics of Management and Production Employees of Transplant Suppliers

Characteristic(s)	Rank	Percent	Total Respondents
Management Employees			
Experience in manufacturing	(1)	81	72
College educated	(2)	65	72
American, but have visited Japan	(3)	33	72
Japanese-born	(4)	29	72
Recruited from outside local area	(5)	28	72
Female	(6)	10	72
Ethnic minority	(7)	9	70
Production Employees			
High school education	(1)	91	69
Live within 30 miles of facility	(2)	83	70
Factory experience	(3)	67	65
Recruited through a government program or private industry council	(4)	39	69
Female	(5)	34	69
Under 25 years old	(6)	28	69
Former union member	(7)	19	55
Ethnic minority	(8)	11	69
Currently belong to labor union	(9)	6	68
Over 50 years old	(10)	5	70

Source: Transplant Supplier Survey, by authors (June 1988).

and 28 percent were recruited from outside the local area. Interestingly, 81 percent of the management employees had experience in manufacturing.

Robert Cole reports that the Toyota-Nippondenso joint venture, Michigan Automotive Compressor, which opened in 1990, contracted with a local junior college to train the 400 initial workers in nine different production technologies. When the junior college official enquired as to how many people were needed in each technology, the Japanese plant manager said that he "wanted all 400 employees trained in all nine of the production technologies." The plant itself was designed to be one of the most automated in the world; however, the Japanese managers felt it was necessary to train workers to understand fully the robots they would be operating. Cole concludes that this company does not merely want machine tenders; "rather . . . Japanese managers aim to create a large cadre of middle-level technicians with broad flexible skills."[37]

Transplant suppliers, especially the large ones, make use of ongoing training and socialization to Japanese production methodology and management practices. For example, Nippondenso sent its managers to Japan for additional training and socialization to the Japanese system and has an in-house video training facility that it uses to train its workers. The supplier survey indicates that 33 percent of American managers were sent to Japan for training.

Wages and Employment Security

Wages paid by transplant suppliers are below those paid by transplant assemblers. Average pay in 1988 for transplant suppliers was $7.21 per hour to start and $8.01 after 12 months. The range was from $5.00 to $14.50. This is below the wage rates paid by unionized U.S.-owned automotive suppliers. Nippondenso pays entry-level workers $9.41 per hour, with 3 percent increases when workers reach the proficient and advanced levels. Overall, the ratio of supplier to assembler wages is approximately 70 percent, which is similar to the ratio in Japan.[38] Total compensation, including wages and benefits, was $21,200 per year. According to our supplier survey, transplant suppliers report that work effort (67, n = 73), absenteeism (66, n = 73), "willingness to work in teams" (65, n = 73), and "willingness to suggest new ideas" (48, n = 73) are the major criteria used to evaluate workers for salary increases and promotions.

Transplant suppliers do not use bonuses as a major mechanism for compensating workers. According to the supplier survey, bonuses comprise an average of less than 1 percent of total compensation for workers employed by transplant suppliers. Few suppliers offer attendance awards. Some, like Nippondenso, simply recognize good attendance. Nippondenso has a formal attendance policy, with workers allowed six absences a year. Most smaller suppliers do not have formal attendance policies.

The transplant suppliers generally do not offer formal guarantees of tenure security, and few even offer informal guarantees of employment. However, the transplant supplier survey asked a question designed to get at the potential for future transfer of employment security: "Do you believe that the Japanese system of long-term employment should be transferred to the U.S. in the future?" The response to this question is quite interesting. Roughly 65 percent (47, n = 73) of transplant suppliers indicate that the Japanese long-term employment and compensation system should be transferred to the United States; and only 19 percent disagreed (14, n = 73). The open-ended responses are especially revealing and indicate a wide spectrum of views. One respondent felt that "if you eliminate the fear of layoff the employees feel more secure and will do a better job." A second believed "the system of motivation through peer pressure will [not] succeed, therefore making long-term employment invalid." A third said, "Let's leave Japanese culture in Japan; it doesn't work here." And a fourth felt that long-term employment was inappropriate for American workers: "The U.S. worker still needs a small hammer over his head—potential termination."[39] Thus, a wide variety of views prevail among transplant parts suppliers on whether to implement something like long-term employment system in their U.S. facilities.

Transplant suppliers are almost entirely nonunionized, and there is little likelihood of unionization. Only 4 of 71 (5.6%) respondents to the supplier survey were represented by unions. In contrast, U.S. parts suppliers have a far higher rate of unionization. Additionally, only 19 percent of the transplant workers had ever been in a union. Most respondents indicated that a nonunion background was not an overwhelming factor in the hiring decision and that it was not a major determinant of their location decision. A Nippondenso executive remarked, "Our position is that we don't want to waste time fighting the union. If we put our time into being good managers, that's going to take care of itself. That's kind of where we concentrate on."[40] The transplant suppliers we studied were opposed to unionization and were prepared to resist union-organizing drives.[41]

After its failures at Honda and Nissan, the UAW adopted a strategy of organizing the transplant suppliers, hoping that these could be used as a springboard to organizing the assemblers. In early 1991 there were three straight representation elections at Indiana transplant suppliers and the UAW lost all three, although one was close with a vote of 37 to 29 against unionization.[42] However in May 1991, the UAW scored a victory by organizing the Delta USA Corporation, a Japanese-owned parts supplier in Monroe, Michigan, by a vote of 68–58. Delta is in the same UAW district as the Mazda assembly plant, which has experienced the greatest level of tension between labor and management. The Mazda local played a crucial role in the Delta unionization drive.

Transfer of Japanese Just-in-Time Supplier Relations

The supplier survey also provided a range of information and data on the transfer of Japanese-style supplier relations to the United States. The questions were designed to obtain detailed information on the linkage and subcontracting patterns used by transplant automotive parts suppliers. Table 5.4 summarizes the main characteristics of Japanese supplier relations.

In keeping with the general features of the Japanese supplier system, transplant suppliers are located in close geographic proximity to the firm they supply. Of the

TABLE 5.4.   Transfer of Just-in-time Supplier Relations

Characteristics	No. of Suppliers	Percent	Number Responding
Delivery			
Deliver according to JIT schedule	56	80.0	70
Transit time			
<30 minutes	5	6.9	72
30 minutes–2 hours	24	33.3	72
2–8 hours	28	38.9	72
8–24 hours	7	9.7	72
Production Interaction			
Immediate feedback on defective part	70	97.2	72
Customers' engineers visit plant site			
For quality control problems	60	96.8	62
For production problems	46	74.2	62
Design Interaction			
Close interaction between supplier and customer	36	50.0	72
Supplier bids on customer design	23	31.9	72
Supplier can alter customer design	16	22.2	72
Supplier designs subject to customer approval	11	15.3	72
Supplier designs but customer can alter	5	6.9	72

Source: Transplant Supplier Survey, by authors (June 1988).

suppliers, 27.9 percent are located within a 50-mile radius, 12.5 percent within a 50- to 100-mile radius, 21.2 percent within a 100–200-mile radius, 25 percent within a 200–400-mile radius, and just 13.5 percent beyond a 400-mile radius. The distances separating them are greater than in Japan, but the superior American highway system mitigates the actual delivery times. In temporal terms, about 40 percent of suppliers are located inside a 2-hour shipping radius of end-users, another 40 percent are located within an 8-hour radius, and the remainder between 8 and 24 hours. Roughly 80 percent of the respondents indicate that their deliveries to transplant assemblers conform to just-in-time delivery requirements. This was corroborated in site visits and interviews conducted by the research team.

Transplant complexes are, in many respects, stretched out versions of Japan's spatially concentrated just-in-time system. An example of some of the changes undertaken in the United States is that one of Toyota's main U.S. suppliers, Nippondenso's Battle Creek, Michigan, plant is a 7-hour drive from Toyota's Georgetown Kentucky assembly plant. Still, orders from Toyota's Georgetown plant are received by Nippondenso's computer every hour and Nippondenso trucks deliver parts to Toyota's Georgetown plant once an hour. Nippondenso seldom fills a whole truck—it typically ships a quarter to a half truck. This is in part due to the greater availability of land, better highway systems, larger trucks, and greater storage capacity available in the United States.

The transplants also keep greater inventories on hand in the United States than in Japan. Toyota's Georgetown plant, for example, keeps a one-and-a-half-day supply of American parts (and three-day supply of imported parts) compared to a four-hour supply at its Japanese plants.[43] An SIA purchasing official explains that buffer stocks are kept even for the most important of its synchronized components.

> Even when it's synchronized, we normally have some stock within the company. Instrument panels vary, different radios, different colors—so we cannot cover everything. But fortunately we are producing only the Subaru Legacy here, so there are not too many. I believe we have about 15 pieces of instrument panels in our "backstore" so whenever they find a defect, . . . our production people . . . go to the backstore and find what they want. After that, we call the supplier. . . . That's our normal procedure.[44]

While JIT supply is a defining feature of Japanese automobile production, synchronized delivery is more crucial for some parts than for others. For example, it is typically necessary for seat and dashboard assemblies to be delivered according to JIT principles. However, materials such as steel, glass, or paint can be stored in larger inventories. Then there is equipment used to produce parts and assemble cars and typically purchased in intervals. The purchasing manager at an assembly transplant provides some background on the way transplant assemblers differentiate among types of supplies:

> Basically what we purchase at the auto plant are the parts and materials used in production and also some other things like office material. We distinguish direct material and indirect material. When we say direct materials, the definition is anything which will be fitted into a vehicle, including steel, paint, and parts. And when we say indirect material that includes equipment and machinery and also any materials or equipment or tooling. A good example is petrol and gas. When we pour it in the vehicle it would be defined as a direct material, but if we put in a forklift, we can say indirect material. Within direct material, there are three categories. The first one is parts: parts and the components such as steering wheels, glass, tires, wheels. The second category is steel. This is the steel coil which we stamp in the stamping shop. The third category is bulk materials. That means paint or any liquid things or resin materials—that kind of thing. So we say parts, steel, and bulk material.[45]

Transplant suppliers share information and interact frequently with assemblers.[46] As Table 5.4 shows, there is a continuous exchange of information in both production and design. Approximately 97 percent of the transplant suppliers responded that they are contacted immediately by phone when they deliver a defective part. As Table 5.4 reports, 96 percent indicated that engineers from their major customer visit their plant to help with quality-control problems and 74 percent responded that engineers from their major customer visit to help with production problems. The purchasing manager at one of the transplant assemblers stated that:

> When trouble causes a shortage or quality problem, two or three guys visit the supplier. The main purpose of that visit is not just to help, but to see what was the problem. Sometimes they may not have enough information from us. If so, we provide the information. And sometimes we help to solve the problem. . . . We try to think together to solve the arising problem.[47]

Honda communicates with its suppliers on a daily basis and often several times during the day regarding their performance, their production, and developments within their facility. Honda even sends vanloads of employees including engineers and shop-floor personnel to work with U.S. suppliers.[48] According to a company executive,

> We want to know if they're having any problems or if they're anticipating any problems. We're checking to see if they have enough raw material and adequate parts from their suppliers. We check when they're scheduled to put in a mold or die to make our parts. We just try to head off any problem before it develops.[49]

Transplant suppliers work alongside assemblers to design new components.[50] Design is an important indicator of the intimacy of interfirm relationships, because design directly affects manufacture and production costs. While production mistakes can easily be corrected, a bad design is a far more serious problem. Interorganizational participation in design accelerates the design process and reduces probability of serious design flaws. Fifty percent of the suppliers participated closely with assemblers in the development of new products (Table 5.4). These engineers help with troubleshooting even before production begins. Honda engineers, for example, developed new production techniques for a small Ohio plastics firms that became a Honda supplier.[51] Honda intends to use its Marysville R&D center to integrate both transplant and U.S. suppliers into the design of future cars. These findings lead to the conclusion that elements of Japanese supplier relations and interorganizational linkages (e.g., high levels of interaction, joint development, long-term contracts) that have typically been seen to be a function of Japan's sociocultural environment are actually a transferable element of the organizational relationship itself.

Transplant assemblers also work closely with equipment suppliers to ensure that both assembly-line machinery and processing equipment are tailored to their needs. In U.S. automotive companies, such decisions are frequently left to the purchasing department, but in the transplants, manufacturing engineers and production experts from the factory are directly involved in purchases of equipment. According to the head of equipment purchasing at one of the assembly transplants,

> The engineers will do that [purchase equipment]. Obviously, a purchasing agent doesn't know machinery like an engineer, so we work together on it. They go after what they want as far as the performance of the piece of machinery, the specs for it; and then I help pick out people that can supply that particular item. Once they pick out the three or four companies that have what they want, then it's my job to get it for the best price. . . . It's a team effort.[52]

In Japan, first-tier suppliers play a critical role organizing broader supply patterns, especially the coordination of supply flows. This function is, if anything, more evident among the U.S. transplants. For example, the glass for windshields for Honda's American-made vehicles originates at PPG, an American producer. PPG supplies windshields to AP Technoglass (until recently a joint venture between Asahi Glass and PPG) twice a week. AP Technoglass then cuts and grinds the windshields and in the process winnows the defects in PPG glass to less than 1 per 100. These are then delivered to a Honda subsidiary, Bellemar Parts, twice a day.[53] Bellemar, which is located one mile from the Honda plant, applies rubber seals to the windshield and makes JIT deliveries to Honda every two hours. Bellemar once again screens out defects so that Honda receives higher-quality windshields than if it had taken the PPG glass directly.[54] In effect, first-tier suppliers simultaneously connect and distance assemblers from the U.S. environment, thereby performing a buffer function.

Table 5.5 sheds additional light on the pyramidal nature of supplier relations among the transplants, providing information on relationships between first-tier suppliers and their second-tier suppliers. Some first-tier suppliers interact frequently with their suppliers. For example, Nippondenso works very closely with a group of local suppliers including Koyo and Asmo, which are located in the same industrial park, but most do not. As Table 5.5 shows, most second-tier suppliers have little interaction in design or development of new products. Roughly one-third of first-tier suppliers integrate second-tier suppliers in new product development. Distances separating first- and second-tier suppliers are also longer than those between assemblers and first-tier suppliers. Slightly more than 40 percent of second-tier suppliers are within a six-hour driving radius of their major customer; an additional 18 percent are located within a six- to ten-hour radius, but more than 40 percent are located more than ten hours away from their main customer. Just 43 percent of the (first-tier) suppliers in the survey receive JIT deliveries from their (second-tier) suppliers. This contrasts with Japan where tight supplier relations also include second- and third-tier suppliers. However, this may be stem from the fact that the transplant complex is still in the process of formation so such interactive linkages are at an early stage of development. As the next two chapters will show,

TABLE 5.5.   Just-In-Time Linkages Between First-Tier Transplant Suppliers and Their Second-Tier Suppliers

Characteristics	No. of Suppliers	Percent	Number Responding
Delivery			
Deliver according to JIT schedule	31	43.0	72
Production Interaction			
Immediate feedback on defective part	70	97.2	72
Customers' engineers visit plant site			
For quality-control problems	63	96.9	65
For production problems	54	83.1	65
Design Interaction			
Close interaction between supplier and customer	24	33.8	71
Supplier bids on customer design	44	62.0	71
Supplier can alter customer design	8	11.3	71
Supplier designs subject to customer approval	8	11.3	71
Supplier designs but customer can alter	6	8.5	71

Source: Transplant Supplier Survey, by authors (June 1988).

such linkages are being forged with producers of basic inputs such as steel and auto-motive plastics.

The emergence of a JIT supplier complex contrasts sharply with the previous practices of U.S.-owned automotive parts suppliers, which has followed the same globalization pattern of Big Three carmakers. The U.S. automobile parts industry includes "captive" parts subsidiaries of Big Three automobile firms that produce 40 percent of all automotive parts, large diversified auto parts producers (e.g., Borg-Warner, TRW, Rockwell, Fruehauf Corp., and the Budd Company), and roughly 15,000 small- and medium-sized firms. Although the American automobile parts industry was historically concentrated in the Midwest,[55] since the 1970s U.S. parts producers have begun to relocate manufacturing to off-shore plants. Trico, for example, recently moved most of its windshield-wiper manufacturing from Buf-falo, New York, to Mexico.[56] Between 1982 and 1986, American auto parts sup-pliers tripled their foreign capital investment and increased direct foreign investment from $3.1 billion to $4.9 billion.[57] This is a recent phenomenon. According to Glasmeier and McCluskey, approximately three-quarters of all auto-motive components were made in the Midwest as late as 1976. Overall, capital investment in off-shore plants increased from 17 percent of total investment in 1982 to roughly one-quarter of total investment by 1986. This occurred during a period when domestic capital expenditures increased by a modest 13 percent. For-eign branches of U.S. auto parts producers currently supply engines, transmissions, wire harnesses, seat belts, radiators, brake pads, and electrical components to Big Three assemblers.

Such geographic dispersal has gone hand-in-hand with the arm's length char-acter of fordist supplier relations, which emphasized low cost and disregarded prox-imity. This has resulted in a dramatic decline in U.S. employment in the industry. Between 1963 and 1987, total employment in the U.S. auto parts and accessories industry declined by more than 250,000 jobs, from roughly 650,000 to 389,000; manufacturing employment fell by more than 220,000, from 536,000 to 309,000 jobs over the same period.[58]

The transplant complex that is emerging is an adaptation of Japan's dense JIT complexes to U.S. conditions. While the transplant assemblers are successfully putting together a first-tier supplier ring, second and third tiers of suppliers have not yet appeared. However, a number of first-tier suppliers are forging links to U.S. pro-ducers, extending the supplier complex backward to include local companies.

The Japanese JIT supplier system is certainly being successfully transferred to the United States. This provides additional evidence that the Japanese system is not culture-bound, but that it can indeed be transferred to foreign environments. The Japanese transplants show little evidence of conformity to the prevailing U.S. model as organization theory would predict. Instead, the transplants have acted on the environment to create the resources and conditions necessary for their success. Further, transplants replicate the long-term relations, high levels of interaction, and joint problem-solving characteristics of their internal relations in their external rela-tionships with suppliers and subcontractors in terms of long-term contracts, fre-quent interaction, and participation in design and development. In this case, features such as mutual dependence, shared problem solving, and continuous interaction, which have been commonly thought to be a function of Japan's sociocultural environment, turn out to be a critical component in the relationship between an assembler and a parts supplier.[59]

Role of Transplant Assemblers

Transplant assemblers have played an active role in the transfer and creation of this new production system by financing and helping to set up U.S. branches for their key suppliers. Dodwell Marketing Consultants publishes a report detailing all of the major Japanese automobile assemblers and their major parts suppliers.[60] Nearly half of Honda's main suppliers listed in the Dodwell report operate U.S. branches. For example, Honda encouraged two of its Japanese suppliers to form Bellemar Parts to supply it with seat subassemblies. As mentioned earlier, in another instance Honda provided technical and financial assistance to a group of Japanese suppliers to form KTH Parts Industries Inc., a company that took over U.S. production of chassis parts that were once produced in-house at Marysville, Ohio.[61] NUMMI established a joint venture between one of Toyota's major Japanese suppliers, Sumitomo Denso, and the U.S.-owned company Packard Electric to design and construct a new plant to produce wire harnesses for the NUMMI assembly plant.[62] In fact, 12 of 73 suppliers that answered our supplier survey are partly owned by the assemblers they supply.

Table 5.6 summarizes the major factors that influenced the decision of suppliers to come to the United States, and Table 5.7 outlines the reasons for their choice of particular locations in the United States. These data indicate that assemblers have played a key role in both decisions. More than 75 percent of suppliers said that they relocated to maintain close ties to a major Japanese customer. In addition, 90 percent of respondents said that they chose their specific location to be close to a major customer. Interestingly, traditional location factors such as local labor market or local labor costs had a much smaller effect on supplier location. Only 55 percent of automotive suppliers said that the local labor market was an important determi-

TABLE 5.6.   Relocation Factors for Transplant Supplies

Rank	*Why Did Your Firm Choose to Come to the United States?* Factor	Score
1	Maintain relationship with Japanese customer	3.4
2	Request from firm we supply	3.1
3	Need to find new markets	3.0
4	Foreign currency fluctuations	2.8
5	Trade restrictions	2.6
6	Cheaper to produce in U.S. than in Japan	2.1
7	Government trade delegations	1.9
8	Other	1.4

Source: Transplant Supplier Survey, by authors (June 1988).
Note: Based on a 5-point scale where 5 = essential factor, 1 = not a factor.

TABLE 5.7.   Site Selection Factors for Transplant
Suppliers

Why Did You Select a Particular Location in the United States?		
Rank	*Factor*	*Score*
1	It is close to our customers	4.1
2	Proximity to major transport routes	3.5
3	Local business attitudes	3.4
4	State and Local government attitudes	3.3
4	A nonunion environment	3.3
6	A strong work ethic	3.2
7	Government assistance and incentives	2.9
8	An experienced labor force	2.7
8	Labor costs	2.7
8	Labor force with mechanical aptitude	2.7
11	Cultural amenities	2.2
12	Proximity to sources of parts and materials	2.0
13	No other suppliers located within ten miles	1.6
14	Purchase of existing firm	1.5
15	Other	1.2

Source: Transplant Supplier Survey, by authors (June 1988).
Note: Based on a 5-point scale where 5 = essential factor, 1 = not a factor.

nant of location, whereas 58 percent said that labor costs were a significant factor. More recently, a subgroup of Japanese parts suppliers have begun to relocate on their own to tap the growing market for their products.

Transplant assemblers have tried to cultivate long-term relationships with and high levels of dependency among their suppliers. A Honda executive said of the long-term nature of relationship with the company's suppliers: "Once a supplier becomes a supplier for an item, he is from then on *always* the supplier for that item."[63] Honda also likes to cultivate dependency in its suppliers. It prefers to dominate output and, as such, to have some degree of control over its suppliers. The company likes its purchases to comprise at least one-third of a supplier's total volume and even up to 100 percent. "We want . . . Honda to be dependent on the supplier and the supplier to be dependent upon us. We feel it is only then—when you really have dependency—that the very best comes out in both sides."[64] Of course, in actuality, it is the assemblers who have the real power.

Transplants vs. U.S. Suppliers

A growing number of U.S. suppliers complain that the emerging transplant supply complex is hurting their business. Some American firms contend that Japanese transplants will not give them business, preferring to "keep it within the family." Others charge that transplants push them too hard, driving them close to financial ruin. Still others suggest the Japanese companies exert too much control over their suppliers.[65] According to one American critic of Japanese supplier relations, the

Japanese "have a manufacturing complex that organizes everything the way they want it organized. Toyota is a model of absolute control. The pressure is on small companies that are fed business by the big colossus Toyota."[66]

In 1990, the *Wall Street Journal* featured a front-page story on the relationship between Honda and an American supplier, Variety, which resulted in bankruptcy for the U.S. company.[67] This was later featured in a Frontline television documentary in October 1991. According to both reports, the Variety-Honda relationship began to sour soon after it was forged. Japanese equipment arrived weeks late; much of it was defective and did not work. Honda then sent in a team of its own people to help get Variety back on track, virtually running the company. The company lost its business with General Motors, and in early 1989 it filed for bankruptcy. The *Wall Street Journal* quoted a Variety official as saying: "The pressure was unbelievable. . . . You had mass confusion, and it seemed like you got nowhere."[68] The Frontline documentary strongly implied that Honda was responsible for the company's bankruptcy.

Honda has challenged these analyses in a detailed memorandum.[69] According to this memo, the Japanese (Honda) equipment supplied to Variety was not defective, but suffered from lack of proper maintenance. In addition, the memo claims that Variety produced unacceptably low quality parts, stating that Variety accounted for 51 percent of all parts rejected by all Honda suppliers in March 1988. It reports that when Variety stopped being a Honda supplier, the parts it had been producing were then produced to Honda standards by five U.S. domestic suppliers, one Japanese transplant supplier, and one Canadian supplier. The memo further states that Honda has had continuously good relations since 1988 with the five other domestically-owned stamping suppliers.

A reporter who covered the Variety-Honda relationship for *Crain's Business Journal* in Cleveland provides a third perspective. His view suggests that Honda did not cause the bankruptcy. According to his analysis, Variety was unable to perform to Honda's standards and could not deliver parts on a just-in-time basis. He adds that the company then fell behind in paying its bills, causing three of its own small suppliers to sue for bankruptcy. Interestingly, Variety's president failed to show up at a hearing to defend against the bankruptcy suit, thus sending the company into "involuntary bankruptcy."[70] While no unambiguous conclusions can be drawn from any single example, this one highlights the extreme ambiguity and contradictory perspectives which frequently emerge around high salience political-economic issues.

In March 1991, an American supplier scored a minor legal victory over Nissan.[71] Earlier, in 1987, the supplier, Automotive Moulding Co. of Warren, Michigan, signed a contract with Nissan to supply door moldings and rain guards for all two-door and most four-door Sentras made in the United States through 1990. The contract called for Nissan to pay $9.52 for each rear-door rain guard and $4.02 for each front-door rain guard. However, the material needed to make these parts—a specialized form of black resin—was only produced in Japan and unavailable to American manufacturers. Under a contract amendment signed in 1988, Automotive Moulding agreed to act as a conduit for "pass-through" parts produced by one of Nissan's Japanese suppliers until it developed the capability to produce the parts itself. In 1989, the company filed suit against Nissan, claiming $1.6 million in damages on the grounds that Nissan was paying less to Automotive Mouldings than it would have if it bought the parts directly from its Japanese supplier. Nissan filed a counter-claim charging breach of contract when Automotive Mouldings stopped shipping parts in early 1989. In March 1991, Automotive Mouldings won a small arbitration award as settlement of the suit.

Some critics believe that the influx of Japanese transplant suppliers may threaten the long-term viability of the American auto parts supplier industry. Both the U.S. automobile supplier trade associations and congressional representatives from impacted areas of the Midwest, such as Rep. Marcy Kaptur of Ohio, have argued that the Japanese are predatory in the way they target certain markets. Lee Kaldrich of the Automotive Parts and Accessories Association outlines this position: "If there's no change in the discriminatory buying patterns . . . there is only going to be further erosion in U.S. parts sales. The market isn't growing. When these new plants come over here, they are displacing, not adding, to production."[72] T. Boone Pickens, as part of a stock raid organized by a Japanese speculator on Koito Manufacturing Co., a Toyota supplier, has voiced concern in congressional hearings and in the press about the emergence of "closed" Japanese *keiretsu* groups in the United States. The UAW shares these sentiments, contending that transplant assemblers

> have shunned traditional U.S. parts makers, including those that meet or exceed their quality and cost standards, preferring to import key components from Japan or buy them from an estimated 250 Japan-based suppliers that have also migrated here. The practice of buying parts "within the family" is destroying a major U.S. manufacturing infrastructure at a cost of tens of thousands of jobs and threatens to turn the U.S. into a "branch plant" economy in which we supply basic materials and relatively unskilled labor while many of the most important technologies and higher-order skills remain in Japan.[73]

The UAW also sees the Japanese model of out-sourcing and its emulation by Big Three American carmakers as a broader strategy to keep down wages and to replace unionized jobs in Big Three plants and organized suppliers with nonunionized jobs in transplant suppliers. According to UAW vice president Stan Marshall, "The Big Three are putting more and more pressure on the independent parts plants by forcing them to ask for so many [contract] cuts that they are actually breaking our union and other unions out there."[74]

To some extent, the problems encountered by U.S. parts suppliers are of their own making. Brought up in an environment of an arm's length just-in-case relationship, American suppliers do not know how to deal with Japanese assemblers. According to one expert on U.S.-Japanese supplier relations

> An American supplier wants to sell to a Japanese company. They want a reasonable answer in a reasonable length of time. Reasonable, by American standards, is a week to maybe a month. By Japanese standards, it may be six months to a year. The American company may not hear anything for a month and figure they lost the deal. . . . The perspective of the American company is: Let's make the deal, and

then let's work out the details. Let's agree to do business; let's set some pricing, some quality outlines. We'll iron out the details down the road. The Japanese say give us all the technical details first. The American company sends off some information and they don't hear anything for a month or two and they say, "What the hell; we must have lost it." They drop the whole thing.[75]

Working with U.S. Suppliers

Despite these problems, a growing number of traditional U.S. automotive parts suppliers are becoming integrated into the transplant supplier complex. According to a survey done by a leading automobile industry trade journal, roughly 57 percent of all automotive suppliers are involved in joint ventures, and 85 percent of these are involved in at least one joint venture with a foreign company.[76] Recent research indicates that 45 percent of U.S. auto parts companies supply at least one product to the transplants.[77] According to a recent report, more than half of Mazda's U.S. suppliers are U.S.-owned firms. Of 96 total Mazda suppliers, 43 (45%) are independent U.S.-owned firms, another 10 (10.5%) are divisions of the Ford Motor Co., and 43 (45%) are Japanese or Japanese-U.S. joint ventures.[78] According to a report on the transplants published in *Ward's Auto World* in February 1991, 75 percent of the 174 domestic suppliers to Toyota's Georgetown, Kentucky, plant are long-standing U.S. companies. Of NUMMI's 123 North American suppliers, 87 (70%) are American-owned, 24 (20%) are Japanese transplants, and 12 (10%) are joint ventures.[79] Purchasing executives indicate that roughly half of Subaru's suppliers are U.S.-owned:

Subaru has 64 parts suppliers [in the United States]. . . . Out of these 64 parts suppliers, 31 are pure U.S. suppliers and 33 are transplants. When we say transplants it includes 100 percent Japanese-owned or Japan-U.S. joint ventures.[80]

Transplant assemblers are increasing their efforts to establish links to U.S. parts suppliers, especially given increasing political pressure from American industry and government bodies. Many have formed teams to increase business from local suppliers. These teams visit suppliers; examine their production process, ability to produce quality products, and meet JIT delivery schedules. The potential suppliers are asked to build prototypes, which are then tested at the assembler's plant. Advanced test equipment is used to analyze and test parts and compare them to blueprint specifications. Meeting these standards is difficult for U.S. suppliers, who are used to the far less stringent specifications of the Big Three (also see Chapter 6 on steel). A purchasing executive at one of the transplant assemblers describes the process by which his company locates and qualifies potential U.S. suppliers:

There are mainly two ways to get to know the suppliers. Say we are importing a part from Japan—this is very costly because transportation costs are very high. So we decide: let's purchase this part locally here. In that case, we would gather a lot of information on what kind of supplier can make [this part]. Then we may call them, we visit them. Also, we get a lot of sales offers; suppliers visit us and leave their brochures. After we have found potential suppliers, normally purchasing, manufacturing, and engineering visit those suppliers to see what is the process capability or what kind of quality assurance and administration and get an appraisal. If we find good candidates then we will get a [price] quotation and evaluate the cost and also whether they can comply with the specifications, provide good quality, and have a capability to make this part. This is a very rough process . . .[81]

Honda has an extensive program to develop its U.S. supplier base. The vice president of purchasing has two full-time people who are responsible for helping suppliers develop employee-involvement programs. There are some 40 engineers in the purchasing department who work full-time helping suppliers improve quality and productivity. In addition, another 120 engineers in the quality-control department deal with incoming supplier parts. Special teams are established to assist suppliers. Honda has a "guest engineer" program in which engineers from suppliers are sent to Japan for one to four months to work with Honda engineers on the design of parts that will be produced for Honda of America. Honda also has a "Quality Up" program that is used to help improve the performance of suppliers whose quality is lower than Honda would like. Honda personnel visits suppliers, talks to their employees, and helps review financial and business plans. As part of the company's "loaned executive" program, Honda executives work in supplier companies at the executive vice president level to help overcome difficulties and integrate the suppliers into the Honda system.[82] Nonetheless, as we have already seen, not every Honda supplier is successful, and failure can be costly.

When Nissan opened its American plant it established a Local Sourcing Task Force to identify U.S. suppliers and assist with improving their quality and production.[83] SIA has created several teams, composed of engineers, buyers, inspectors or manufacturing people, who visit suppliers and consult with them in an effort to improve quality.[84] NUMMI, which is supplied by a larger number of U.S.-owned parts suppliers than are the other automobile transplants, organized a supplier council (similar to the one Toyota has in Japan) of 70 mostly U.S.-owned suppliers to facilitate information sharing and product improvement.[85] In April 1990, members of Toyota's engineering and purchasing departments met in Las Vegas with 35 U.S. suppliers and came to agreement on 36 components; the company was said to be considering sourcing another 33 parts from this group of suppliers.[86] In the fall of 1990, Toyota brought its top executives, procurement representatives, and engineers to a meeting in Las Vegas with potential U.S. suppliers; at about that same time the company brought 200 executives of U.S. parts makers for a three-day visit to Nagoya, Japan, in an effort to teach them about the Japanese system and to develop "long-term stable relationships."[87] A similar meeting was held in the fall of 1991.

First-tier suppliers are also trying to secure capable U.S.-owned suppliers, especially as Japanese assemblers feel mounting pressure to increase domestic content. Nippondenso, for example, indicates that in one or two years it must increase to more than 75 percent the domestic content of the heaters and radiators and other parts it manufactures. The company has formed a "Localization Group," whose job is to work closely with domestic suppliers to increase local content. In the words of one Nippondenso employee,

> If we can find somebody from Battle Creek it's ideal, because then they can meet you just in time for deliveries. But to do this you have to certify the part, which means you go through quality levels, meet delivery schedules, be big enough to supply us. We build a million radiators per year. That means it must be a pretty good-sized factory to be able to supply us. We're looking for a million parts.[88]

The Bluegrass Automotive Manufacturers Association

The Bluegrass Automotive Manufacturers Association, or BAMA, is perhaps the most ambitious attempt to create a Japanese-style supplier federation in the United States. BAMA was formed by Toyota in 1990 to help create a state-of-the-art JIT supplier structure for the company's Georgetown, Kentucky, assembly operation.[89] The company has "strongly encouraged" all of its suppliers to become members. BAMA is made up of approximately 60 of Toyota's suppliers in and around Kentucky. For Toyota, BAMA is a vehicle for instilling cooperation and interaction among its suppliers to improve its domestic supply base and diffusing JIT practices to U.S.-based suppliers. Toyota has placed a number of its top suppliers at the head of BAMA. Their role is to work with other members to help them improve productivity, quality, and delivery practices. Toyota has frequently worked hard to show U.S. suppliers the value of cooperative product development. In a number of instances, the company has used the carrot of potential business to get American suppliers to share confidential data on internal production in order to improve production operations and product quality. This has been difficult for U.S. suppliers, who are long accustomed to competition and rivalry and hesitant about sharing their internal production data.

The point of all this is rather basic. It has taken a large, powerful company to develop a domestic JIT complex and to begin to overcome a long legacy of competitive, indeed, adversarial, relations among companies. This has not occurred organically, but was the systematic result of Toyota's efforts to organize relationships and force its suppliers to work together. Simply put, Toyota is the glue that holds the supplier complex together.

JIT Takes Hold

Linkages to U.S. suppliers are encouraging the diffusion of Japanese JIT supplier practices in the United States. Overall, 79 percent of American suppliers surveyed by *Ward's Auto World* indicate that they are in favor of supplier joint ventures that enhance R&D capabilities and lower costs.[90] There is evidence that U.S. suppliers are adopting Japanese practices and, in this sense, converging toward the Japanese model.[91] Moreover, the development of this new Japanese-style supplier system in the United States is exerting a sizable demonstration effect on American automobile assemblers and their suppliers and encouraging diffusion of Japanese practices in the United States. In this way, Japanese transplant suppliers are transforming American supplier relations and the immediate environment of automobile production in the United States.

This convergence toward state-of-the-art JIT practices is occurring in two ways. On the one hand, U.S. suppliers who wish to tap the growing transplant market are bringing their practices into line with Japanese standards. On the other hand, in order to narrow sizable Japanese competitive advantages in production, Big Three automobile assemblers are reforming their procurement standards to conform to JIT principles. While it remains to be seen how effective such reforms will be, there is anecdotal evidence that U.S. assemblers are attempting to impose these new relations on their suppliers without providing the mutually supportive socioeconomic context (e.g., long-term supply contracts and joint cost-sharing in development) that is necessary for such a system to succeed.[92] A recent report quotes a Japanese parts supplier to General Motors as saying: "The finance boys are in total control [at GM]. It's a money grab and they are foaming at the mouth. They've got a lot and they want more." Another parts supplier went further: "U.S. vehicle manufacturers are interested in price/cost reductions—everything else is a distant tenth.[93]

R&D Investments by Parts Suppliers

Like the automotive assemblers, transplant parts suppliers are beginning to develop R&D facilities in the United States. Currently, no data are collected on R&D investments by transplant suppliers. Thus, in September 1990, we sent a survey to all of the transplant parts suppliers inquiring as to whether they had R&D operations in the United States. Some 181 surveys were originally sent out; of these, 81 responded for a response rate of 44.7 percent. Generally speaking, the results of this survey indicate that while most transplant suppliers still do not have R&D operations in the United States, the number that do is increasing. According to the survey results, 27 parts suppliers already established or plan to establish R&D facilities in the United States.

Most of these supplier R&D units are rather small (fewer than 30 employees). However, two suppliers have more than 90 R&D employees. Similarly, only two of the respondents had invested more than $1 million in their facility. One company claimed to have invested more than $28 million in R&D—a figure that seems high. Generally speaking, the supplier R&D facilities are involved in product development and the qualification of U.S. produced inputs. Still others are involved in customizing Japanese products for the U.S. market—basically making sure that production inputs are of sufficiently high quality. Few are involved in scientifically oriented applied R&D and none are involved in basic research.

Figure 5.4 shows the location of these R&D facilities. As the map indicates, the vast majority of these facilities are in the Midwest and, of course, many are located on or near the plant site. Our survey asked transplant suppliers to rank the factors that influenced their location decision on a 1–5 scale (1 = least important, 5 = most important). The two most important location factors were proximity to the company's own manufacturing facility and proximity to customers, which both

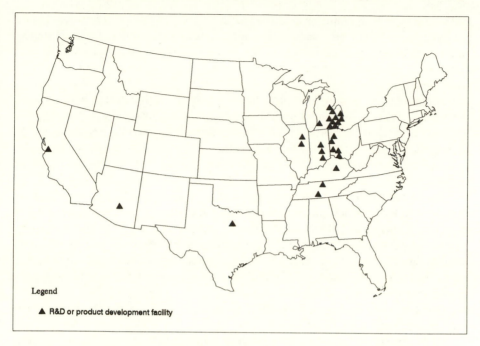

FIGURE 5.4. Transplant Automotive Supplier R&D and Product Development Facilities in the U.S.
Source: Authors' database.

scored 3.93. These results are fully in keeping with the Japanese model. Access to good engineers was next, scoring 3.87, followed by proximity to a customer's R&D at 3.57, and proximity to a major university at 3.40. Other factors such as state and local government incentives (3.07) and local amenities (3.13), proximity to other R&D facilities in the same industry (2.77), inexpensive land (2.83), and proximity to its own suppliers were much less important.

While automotive parts suppliers have thus far been relatively slow in investing in American R&D, it would be a mistake to assume that this situation is static, especially as Japanese assemblers begin to design and engineer cars entirely in the United States. As this occurs, suppliers that wish to have their parts "designed in" these new vehicles will be pressured to initiate R&D in the U.S. to provide the innovative capability so crucial to supplier–end-user relationships in the Japanese automotive industry.

Global Localization

As GM and Ford were important vehicles for transferring fordist techniques to Europe in the immediate postwar period, the transplant supplier complexes are proving to be important vehicles for the transfer and implantation of the Japanese model in the United States. But the mode of transfer contrasts with that of U.S. fordism. With the exception of Europe, most of the fordist producers established independent branch plants around the world to take advantage of low-cost labor markets. Even if there happened to be a large concentration of these branch plants in a single geographic region (e.g., U.S.-operated factories in Northern Mexico), these plants created little growth dynamic in their region and thus did not transform their host region.

The transplant supplier complex that is emerging in the United States, combines the transfer of work and production organization inside the plant with the simultaneous transfer of broader interorganizational relations between plants and their parts suppliers. This is having a powerful effect on the broader environment and is creating a whole new and supportive environment for the Japanese system of production.

The creation of an integrated just-in-time supplier complex in the United States may well represent a new mode of organizing the corporate division of labor. This can be thought of as "global localization." Instead of the decentralized branch plants of fordist industry, Japanese firms transplant an entire level of the division of labor, grouping production activities and necessary inputs at specific sites to promote functional integration. They are now complementing this with localized product development and R&D.

One can envision a scenario wherein Japanese corporations develop localized and semiautonomous innovation-production centers that are responsible for design and production of cars for a specific regional market (e.g., Japan, United States, or Europe). These regional systems would then be linked together in a corporate hierarchy with Tokyo at its center. Some standardized and smaller parts would flow throughout the corporate network, but many would be produced locally. The most advanced R&D might be done in a central, typically Japanese facility; however, product development related to production would be carried out by the local complex. Of course, important innovations would diffuse internationally throughout the complex.

The Japanese system of automobile production that has been transferred to the United States remains a system organized around large companies: Honda, Toyota, Mazda, Nissan, etc. These large automakers have actively used their resources and power to construct JIT complexes and continue to play the pivotal role in these complexes, bringing a source of discipline and a structure for interaction to the network of producers. The Japanese model represents a distinct path, one that is perhaps better suited to the demands of advanced industrial production than either the earlier model of fordist mass production or the utopian formulation of flexible specialization. In other words, the transplant supplier complex in the United States is the most advanced regional manifestation of the new global reach being instituted by Japanese corporations.

The automobile supplier complex that is emerging in the American industrial heartland provides striking evidence of the transfer and generalizability of the Japanese model of production both inside and outside the corporation. In Japan, automobile and steel producers are closely linked and steel remains one of the core industries of advanced economies. The next chapter turns to current developments in the steel industry, exploring growing Japanese investment in American steel production.

6

The "New Iron Age" Comes to America: Japanese Investment in Steel

It's a living lab, with bright, capable people . . . We are empowering people. That, in itself, takes time.[1]

Executive at I/N-Tek, Inland Steel and Nippon Steel joint venture.

The most important basic input for producing an automobile is steel and iron. In 1986 the average American automobile weighed 3,175 pounds; of this, 2,160 pounds were steel and iron.[2] In 1986, steel accounted for 76 percent of the total materials content by weight of the average Japanese car. The U.S. International Trade Commission concluded that "the U.S. iron and steel industry's status is closely tied to health of the domestic auto industry."[3] The importance of steel to successful automobile production cannot be overestimated—quality problems in the steel will certainly be reflected in the final product.

As the first part of this book has shown, the steel industry in Japan is moving into a "new iron age"—from a traditional heavy industry to a technology-intensive, highly automated, continuous-process industry. Nippon Steel's 1987 Annual Report highlights this transformation: "Steelmaking is now and will remain at the company's core. . . . Nippon's Steel's entry into the dynamic fields of electronic equipment, information and communications systems, and telecommunications is backed by a long history of computer applications and software development to meet the company's own needs."[4] Along with its steelmaking operations with Inland Steel in Indiana, the company established a branch in Silicon Valley to gain access to U.S.-developed software. In 1988, NKK released its "New Future Vision" plan for the twenty-first century.

> Our New Future Vision begins with the need to strengthen our current operations especially in steelmaking. At the same time, it calls for development of new possibilities and expansion into the new technologies that will serve social and economic needs in the years ahead. The plan repositions NKK as a creative manufacturer, one that has the most advanced technology and that is keyed to new trends.[5]

Japanese investments in steel are bringing this new iron age to America, as Japan's leading steel corporations establish U.S. manufacturing operations to supply this critical input to the expanding transplant automotive production complex.

155

Table 6.1 shows the major Japanese investments in the U.S. steel industry. The major Japanese investments have been as joint ventures undertaken with American firms. The entire investment in these joint ventures totals roughly $8 billion in steel producing and steel related facilities. The pace of this growth will probably continue even in the current recessionary period as Japanese firms may be forced to acquire the remainder of their floundering partners, especially since U.S. steel makers continue to want to abandon steel-making activities. Japanese steel producers in the United States currently employ more than 30,000 workers in their joint ventures. These ventures are crucial to the expanding transplant complex.

In 1984, Japan's second largest steelmaker, NKK, purchased 50 percent ownership in National Steel for $300 million.[6] NKK recently increased its ownership of National to 70 percent.[7] NKK had been interested in entering the U.S. steel industry for some years, especially after two of NKK's Japanese customers, Honda and Nissan, opened American plants. NKK initially considered purchasing Ford's River Rouge steel works, but reconsidered due to labor relations difficulties at the mill.[8] Since obtaining an ownership stake in National Steel, the company has undertaken a $1.8 billion investment program and established an extensive organizational restructuring program to improve both quality control and yield.[9] National and NKK also have joined Marubeni Trading Company in establishing a new steel-processing facility, ProCoil, in Canton, Michigan.[10] NKK-National has also made significant investments in National's Technical Research Center.

Japan's largest steelmaker, Nippon Steel, is involved in a $1 billion joint venture with Inland Steel. This includes I/N Tek, a $520 million new cold-rolled steel plant, and I/N Kote, a $550 million electro-galvanizing line.[11] To safeguard its financial position, Nippon became Inland's largest shareholder by purchasing a further 13 percent of its stock for $186 million in December 1989.[12]

In another major joint venture, Kawasaki purchased a $350 million, 40 percent stake in Armco Steel's Eastern Division in late 1988 to form Armco Steel Co. LP.[13] In 1989, Kawasaki invested another $350 million in Armco, increasing its stake to 50 percent ownership.[14] Kawasaki also holds a 50 percent stake in California Steel in Fontana, California. This steel complex outside Los Angeles was formerly owned by Kaiser Steel Corp. The Kaiser plant was once the largest steel plant in the western United States, a fully integrated facility employing more than 8,000 workers, before being closed by Kaiser in 1983.[15] California Steel now employs approximately 725 workers.[16]

Sumitomo Metal has built two modern steel galvanizing lines with LTV.[17] The company also operates a mini-mill with Auburn Steel, a steel pipe plant with Baker-Hughes, and small steel processing facilities. In March 1989, Sumitomo Metal of Japan formed a new subsidiary, Sumitomo Metal USA Corp., to coordinate its U.S. ventures.[18] In 1985, Nisshin Steel entered into a joint venture with Wheeling-Pittsburgh to build a new steel-coating plant in Follansbee, West Virginia, on the site of an old Wheeling-Pittsburgh steel plant under the name Wheeling-Nisshin.[19]

In 1989, Kobe Steel purchased a 50 percent ownership stake in the old U.S. Steel Lorain Works to produce bar and tube steel for the automotive transplants and other markets.[20] Kobe has also opened a $25 million steel powder plant in Indiana to serve the transplants.[21] Earlier, in 1983, Kobe purchased Midrex Corp., a subsidiary of Korf Industries.[22]

TABLE 6.1. Major Japanese Investments in the U.S. Steel Industry*

Japanese Company	U.S. Partner	Joint Venture Name	Type of Operation	Location	Date	Employment	Investment ($)	Japanese Share (%)
Nippon Steel	Inland Steel	I/N Tek	Cold rolling mill	New Carlisle, IN	1990	280	520 million	40
Nippon Steel	Inland Steel	I/N Kote	Galvanizing line	New Carlisle, IN	1991	250	550 million	50
Nippon Steel	Inland Steel		Integrated steel mill	Indiana Harbor, IN	1989	11,500	186 million	14†
NKK	National Intergroup	National Steel	Integrated steel mills	Ecorse, MI; Granite, IL; Portage, IN	1984	12,000	2.2 billion‡	70
Kawasaki Steel	Armco	Armco Steel Co. Ltd.	Integrated steel mill	Middletown, OH	1989	9,500	1.6 billion§	45
Kawasaki Steel	Armco	Armco Steel Co. Ltd.	Galvanizing line	Middletown, OH	1991	100	150 million	50
Kawasaki Steel	CVRD (Brazil)	California Steel	Rolling mill	Fontana, CA	1984	725	275 million	50
Kobe Steel	USX Corp	USS-Kobe Steel	Integrated bar and pipe mill	Lorain, OH	1989	3,000	300 million	50
Kobe Steel	USX Corp.	Protec Coating Co.	Galvanizing line	Leipsic, OH	1992	100	200 million	50
Sumitomo Metal	LTV Corp.	LSE I	Galvanizing line	Cleveland, OH	1986	83	100 million	40
Sumitomo Metal	LTV Corp.	LSE II	Galvanizing line	Columbus, OH	1991	100	180 million	50
Nisshin Steel	Wheeling-Pittsburgh		Integrated steel mill	Steubenville, OH	1988	5,500	15 million	10‖
Nisshin Steel	Wheeling-Pittsburgh	Wheeling-Nisshin	Galvanizing and coating line	Follansbee, WV	1988	100	96 million	67
Nisshin Steel	Wheeling-Pittsburgh	Wheeling-Nisshin	Galvanizing line	Follansbee, WV	1993	100	120 million	100
Yamato Kogyo	Nucor	Nucor-Yamato	Mini-mill	Blytheville, AR	1988	320	210 million*	50
Kyoei/Sumitomo Corp.		Auburn Steel	Mini-mill	Auburn, NY	1975	315	300 million	100

*This table does not include numerous Japanese investments in steel service centers and smaller steel-processing facilities
†Purchase of 13% of Inland Steel Industries stock, which includes steel service centers.
‡$439 million original investment plus $1.8 billion in planned capital improvements.
§$525 million original investment plus $1.1 billion in planned capital improvements.
‖Purchase of 10% Wheeling-Pittsburgh common stock.
Source: Authors' database.

On a smaller but still significant scale, Yamato Kogyo is involved in a $210 mini-mill joint venture with Nucor, named Nucor-Yamato, in Blytheville, Arkansas, to produce structural steel beams.[23] Yamato Kogyo and Sumitomo purchased ownership of Auburn Steel in Auburn, New York. Daido has reopened an old Copperweld steel mill in Warren, Ohio, in a joint venture with CSC-Copperweld, a French company that purchased former U.S. steel producer, Copperweld.

Growing Japanese investment in U.S. steel production contrasts with the long legacy of decline, disinvestment, and plant closures of U.S. steel corporations. Between 1960 and 1970, American steel corporations—USX, Bethlehem Steel, Armco Steel, National Steel, LTV, Inland Steel, Wheeling-Pittsburgh, Republic Steel, and Allegheny Ludlum Industries—closed more than 100 plants.[24] The result was the decline of the traditional steel region of western Pennsylvania, Ohio, West Virginia, Indiana, Illinois, and Michigan.[25] In the 20-year period between 1967 and 1987, total steel industry employment declined by nearly 345,000 jobs (65%) from 533,100 to 189,900, while the number of production workers fell by 286,400 (66%) from 434,000 to 147,600.[26] Indeed, it has been decades since a U.S. corporation has built an "integrated" steel mill (i.e., one that turns raw iron into steel). The last two were U.S. Steel's Fairless mill, built in the 1950s, and Bethlehem's Burns Harbor Works in the 1960s. A substantial share of new U.S. investment has been confined to mini-mills, smaller plants that make steel products from scrap metal.[27] In 1988, the seriousness of the decline was captured by the president of Inland Steel who admitted that Nippon Steel—Japan's leading steelmaker as well as Inland's joint-venture partner—possessed the technological capability of the entire U.S. steel industry put together.

This chapter examines the transfer of the Japanese system of work and production organization to the U.S. steel industry—and the simultaneous acquisition of that industry. The steel industry is important for three reasons: First, steel is essentially a pre-fordist industry. In fact, it was the industry where Taylor conducted his initial time-and-motion studies. Arising in the mid-nineteenth century, it precedes the automobile industry and the rise of the mass-production assembly line associated with Henry Ford. In fact, steel in the United States has long been a batch industry, although one that saw sweeping rationalization of production under the Taylorist model of scientific management and time-and-motion study in the late nineteenth and early twentieth centuries.[28]

Second, steel has played a central role in the economic development and growth of both the United States and Japan. The emergence of huge integrated steel mills in the Pittsburgh, Chicago, northern Indiana, and northern Ohio regions catalyzed America's rise to industrial preeminence in the late nineteenth and early twentieth centuries. Similarly, in Japan, steel has been a focal point of economic development throughout the twentieth century. Steel was the cornerstone of Japan's postwar economic development strategy, and early technological and industrial successes in steel helped pave the way for Japan's postwar economic miracle.[29]

Third, as we have already mentioned, the U.S. steel industry has undergone a 30-year period of decay and decline characterized by disinvestment and plant closures. Partly in response to the decline of the U.S. steel industry, a general product cycle model of economic development by shifting into new sectors has come to be accepted as the conventional wisdom in the United States.[30] According to this model, advanced industrial nations continue to grow and retain competitive advantage by moving upstream into high-technology, high value-added areas, leaving older and traditional industries like steel to newly developing countries. The ability of Japanese corporations to remain globally competitive in steel, and moreover to transfer Japanese technology and production organization in ways that can help rebuild U.S. steel capability, questions this widely accepted model of development. And it would lend additional support to the claim that underlying changes in production organization underpin both national- and regional-level development, making once abandoned regions and even industries competitive again.

The Japanese Move into American Steel Production

In the mid-1980s, Japan's steel industry saw domestic profits fall because of declining domestic demand and increasing competition from low-cost steel producers in Brazil, Korea, and elsewhere in basic steelmaking operations.[31] Japanese steel companies have invested in the United States in order to supply the U.S. market and bolster sagging profits. The strengthening of the yen relative to the dollar in the 1980s threatened Japan's export sales to the United States and also made U.S. assets appear less expensive. According to the 1987 report of the Japan Iron and Steel Foundation:

> The year 1986 was an extremely difficult one for the Japanese steel industry. The sharp decline in the yen . . . brought about significant decrease in both direct and indirect exports of steel. This development, coupled with steel demand stagnation both at home and abroad and increasing steel imports into the Japanese market, accelerated the slump in steel production. Consequently, crude steel production dropped by 6.7 percent in 1986. . . . The steel companies thus ran into the red. To cope with their difficult situation they began to implement several measures including partially paid leaves, . . . consolidating production facilities, and reorganizing steel mills. Under these circumstances, the steel makers are compelled to urgently address a number of issues: practicing thorough rationalization in every area of activity, pushing technological innovation, expanding operations in new fields of business, improving financial bases, and *promoting tie-ups with overseas steel companies.*[32]

Further, as with the automotive transplants, direct investment in the United States was also seen as a strategic investment to provide a political wedge against U.S. protectionism. In 1984, for example, the U.S. government imposed quotas on Japanese steel coming into the country. The use of joint ventures as a mode of entry into the United States enabled Japanese steel corporations to gain access to the American market without adding major new steel production capacity to an already saturated North American and worldwide steel market. These joint ventures often have a long history. After World War II technological partnerships were forged between U.S. and Japanese steelmakers with a number of U.S. firms transferring technology to their Japanese partners. By the 1970s U.S. producers were turning to Japanese steelmakers for state-of-the-art technology, and a number of technology sharing and technology assistance agreements were established.

Joint ventures have the additional feature of "buying" access to U.S. markets while "buying-off" opposition from U.S. steelmakers who receive significant cash inflows from the sale of domestic steel mills and are able to derive a share of the profits of the investments. Joint ventures also enabled Japanese steelmakers to mute the opposition of trade union officials by ensuring that American workers would remain employed. Japanese direct investment in existing U.S. facilities thus provided a way to serve the growing transplant market while reducing the political risk of having these markets suddenly cut off.

But the overriding reason Japanese steel companies have come to the United States is to serve their most important customers—the automotive transplants—who have had significant difficulty getting high-quality steel from American producers. In November 1988, the Japanese publication *Asahi Shimbun* reported: "The investment by the large Japanese steel companies in the U.S. is to respond to the request for steel supply by Japanese manufacturers. They have also accepted the invitation by American steel companies which needed capital to renovate and rationalize their old production facilities."[33] An American steel executive who is now involved in a joint-venture partnership with a Japanese steelmaker noted that the transplant automotive companies basically told their Japanese steel suppliers:

We want domestic content. At some point there's going to be a backlash; before that gets here we want to have clearly established that our autos being produced in the United States are United States products; and we want to get as close to 100% as we can. We want it as fast as we can. So Japanese steel companies had no choice but to get something established here to satisfy all of their customers.[34]

For U.S. steel producers, joint ventures served a variety of functions. After nearly two decades of technological neglect and underinvestment, by the early 1980s, it became clear that American steelmakers needed state-of-the-art Japanese technology and capital to implement those technologies.[35] According to Hans Mueller, a steel economist, two-thirds of all U.S. investment made in the U.S. steel industry between 1950 and 1979 occurred in the 1950s.[36] Further, much of that investment was very inefficient. Given pressure for short-term returns and top management's conservative investment strategy, U.S. steel investment was concentrated in existing plants. American steelmakers basically grew by "rounding-out"—that is, by adding to existing mills and plant sites. As early as 1952, an analysis of the U.S. steel industry noted the following:

Capacity [by rounding out] is increased by adding to existing facilities—to the point where most mills are so hopelessly cluttered that any attempt at efficient operations in the charging-room floor is hopeless. Rounding-out is popular because it costs only about $100 a ton of capacity, but is obviously no long-term solution to the production of steel. Eventually, in those steel plants something has to give.[37]

However, since the 1950s, little effort has been made to channel investment into plants that held promise to become truly "world class" mills or to install current technology. Only last year did the first U.S. producer become 100 percent continuous cast—and that was National Steel, which is now 70 percent Japanese-owned.

In contrast, in Japan steelmakers have invested heavily in plant, technology, and equipment, making important advances in steel-production technology, plant layout, and design. From 1950 to 1979, Japanese steelmakers built 11 integrated steel mills, incorporating modern layout, very large terminal size, new technology, and in many cases direct access to deep-channel harbors. As a result, capacity increased from 4 million to 116 million tons per year.[38] In addition, newer Japanese steel mills and facilities were designed with state-of-the-art computer systems. In these plants, capacity, process, equipment, and layout decisions were integrated with the computer system from the outset instead of needing to be retrofitted. Although the U.S. strategy may have appeared to be cost-effective in the short run, in the long run it is actually more expensive—and far less effective—to retrofit antiquated plant and technology. By the 1980s, the U.S. steel industry was far behind its Japanese and European competitors.[39] As late as 1980, for example, there were no computerized control-feedback systems in use at U.S. basic oxygen furnace plants.[40]

In the late 1970s and early 1980s, major U.S. steel corporations embarked on a strategy of diversification designed to exit the steel business. This is illustrated by National Steel's name change to National Intergroup. But the most publicized effort was U.S. Steel's purchase of Marathon Oil, the seventh largest oil company in the United States in 1982. In 1986 the company changed its name to USX, but in late 1990 moved to formally separate its oil and steelmaking subsidiaries by partitioning its stock.

In most American steel companies, existing steel businesses were used as "cash cows" to finance diversification efforts. The final step in these efforts was taken in the early 1980s when top American steel executives began making annual trips to Japan to find buyers for their company's steel units. In the words of a high-ranking National Intergroup official, the NKK joint venture "represents the final leg in our exit from the steel business."[41] The joint-venture route was and is being used by some U.S. steel companies to achieve their ultimate goal, which is to leave the steel business entirely.

Ironically, but understandably, given the neglect by top U.S. steel executives, securing Japanese capital and technology came to be considered a "survival strategy" for the managers of U.S. steel units. For years these managers had complained about technological neglect and the use of their divisions as cash cows for corporate diversification efforts. In this environment, Japanese investment became the only way for these middle-level managers to save existing steel units and their livelihoods. For example, executives at the former US Steel (USS) bar and tube mill in Lorain, Ohio, now USS-Kobe, reported that USX management prohibited them from making any major investments in the facility and simply drained off capital for years. For these managers, Japanese capital meant survival and succor from the raiders and dismantlers that prowled the steel industry.[42] Japanese investment would provide the benefits supposed to be gained by a leveraged buyout without the overwhelming debt burden that resulted in the crushing of viable firms in other industries. In steel, Japanese joint-venture participation meant that facilities were liberated from the constraints imposed by finance-oriented top executives and their constant quest for greater cash flow.

The quintessential example is National Steel where American managers lobbied against a proposed merger with U.S. Steel because they believed the merger would result in the milking of National Steel's plant and facility.[43] Yet these same managers welcomed NKK's investment as a way to rebuild their steel units. The United Steelworkers union also understood that Japanese investment was necessary to ensure the survival of a domestic steel industry. Although the steel union opposed the earlier U.S. Steel takeover of National Steel (citing U.S. Steel's legacy of strained, adversarial labor relations), it decided to support the new NKK-National Steel joint venture.

Steel and the Transplant Industrial Complex

Japanese investment in the steel industry is a crucial component of the Japanese investment that is rebuilding America's rustbelt economy. Figure 6.1 is a map of the location of Japanese-owned and Japanese–U.S. joint-venture steel plants. As the map indicates, most of the activities are clustered in the Midwest and upper South. Two general location patterns are indicated here—one for large joint ventures in integrated steel production and galvanizing lines, most of which are located in the industrial Midwest, and another for the smaller steel service centers that have operations in both the upper South and the industrial Midwest. Most of these plants are ideally situated to provide steel to the automotive transplants on a just-in-time basis. Japanese-owned and joint-venture steel producers in the United States provide a critical input to the blossoming of heavy industrial transplants in the United States.

Figures 6.2 and 6.3 compare the location of Japanese steel investments to U.S. steel firms. Figure 6.2 shows the location of major integrated U.S. steel mills; Figure 6.3 shows the location of U.S. steel plant closures between 1951 and 1971. Here it is obvious that Japanese investment in steel has occurred in the same general region, in many cases on the same sites, that U.S. corporations had abandoned.[44] This lends additional support to the argument that the decline of the U.S. steel industry had little to do with high wages, unruly workers, or a poor business climate. The failings of the U.S. steel industry were a combination of outmoded production organization and a lack of investment. Armed with a different way of organizing production, Japanese corporations are able to produce high-quality steel in the heart of the American rustbelt.

Producing Coated Steel for the Automotive Transplants

A significant share of Japanese investment has been aimed at building modern plants for coating and preparing steel coils for use by transplant carmakers. This coated steel is used for body parts, frames, and mufflers. Japanese carmakers

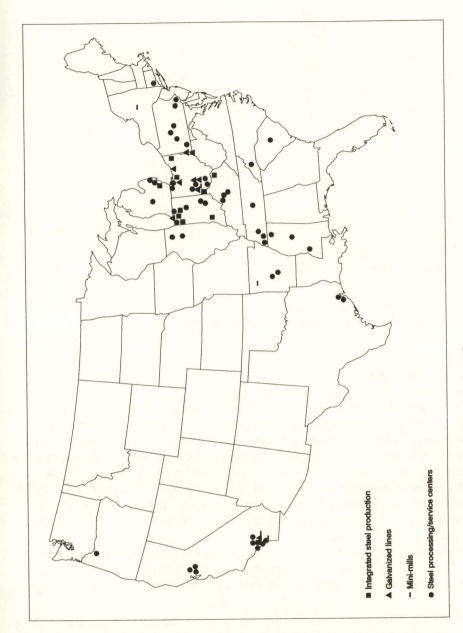

FIGURE 6.1. Japanese-Affiliated Steel Plants in the U.S.
Source: Authors' database.

Legend:
- ■ Integrated steel production
- ▲ Galvanized lines
- – Mini-mills
- ● Steel processing/service centers

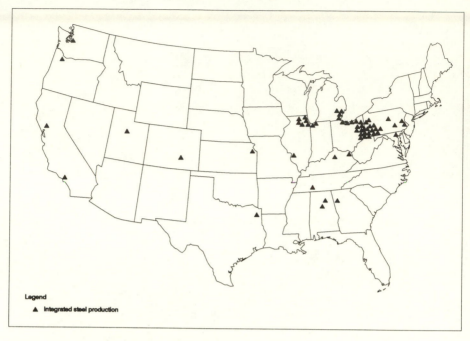

FIGURE 6.2. Major Integrated U.S. Steel Mills.
Source: Adapted from *1990 Directory of Iron and Steel Plants.*

require galvanized steel in their vehicles because it is rust and corrosion resistant.[45]
Such steel is produced by a process called "galvanizing."

According to Wharton Econometric Forecasting Associates (WEFA) data, in
1990 coated steel comprised roughly half (48.5%) of all steel used in automotive
applications. Typically, steel coating plants use either "hot-dip" or electro-galvanizing to coat steel with zinc or nickel and thus make it more corrosion resistant.
Electro-galvanized steels make up 16.5 percent of all automotive steel, while hot-
dipped products comprise 26.5 percent of the automotive steel market.[46] Hot-dip
products are typically used in inner body panels and underbody applications,
whereas electro-galvanized products are used for outer body parts because it results
in a higher-quality paint finish.

Each automotive assembler has its own unique specification for coating materials. These coatings can be quite sophisticated and difficult to apply. In an interview one steel executive referred to Toyota's new coating blend as "unusual":

> When you take steel and you put zinc on it to prevent rust, and then right after that
> you put iron on top of the zinc. The iron coating is for compatibility with the paint;
> they get a better luster out of the paint.[47]

In contrast to U.S. steel producers who simply provide consumers with a standardized product, Japanese steelmakers make the specific product each customer wants.

There has been much cooperation between the automotive transplants, who are the end-users of galvanized steel, and the steel producers. They have established long-term agreements and have worked with steel producers to ensure a high-quality product. This is different from the relationship between the U.S. automobile and steel industries. According to one steel industry official

> American customers—they're generally more into beating on you, and saying fix the problem and if you don't then you'll lose participation. . . . So it's more of a club with them . . . where with the Japanese transplants it's more of a helping hand. . . . If your raw materials have escalated or something has changed materially in your cost structure, they have an interest in keeping you profitable. Not as profitable as they are, but they want to keep you solvent. . . . It's not the same intensity that takes place with American customers, who sometimes we felt that they would like to take us into a loss position if they could.[48]

Because American producers have inferior technology and production skills in general, Japanese transplant auto assemblers initially imported these products from

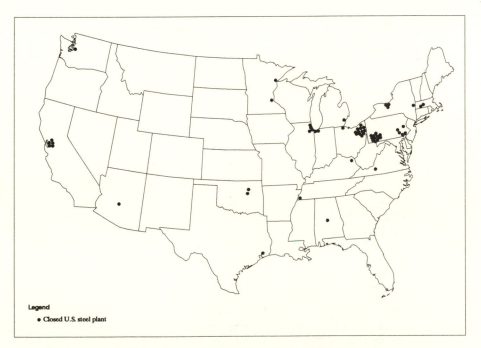

FIGURE 6.3. U.S. Steel Plant Closures, 1951–71.
Source: Adapted from Gordon Clark, "Corporate Restructuring in the Steel Industry: Adjustment Strategies and Local Labor Relations," in George Sternlieb and James Hughes (eds.), *America's New Market Geography* (New Brunswick, NJ: Center for Urban Policy Research, 1988) pp. 192–95.

home.[49] By the mid-1980s the success of the automotive transplants and their continued growth became apparent. In response, Japanese steelmakers began to make investments in U.S. production.

Table 6.2 provides a list of galvanizing lines in the United States. Sumitomo Metal was the first Japanese company to make major investments in U.S. galvanizing capability. In 1986 it opened LS Electro-Galvanizing Company, in a $150 million joint-venture electro-galvanizing plant with the now bankrupt LTV. LS Electro-Galvanizing is located on the site of LTV's huge Cleveland steel complex and has an annual capacity of 400,000 tons.[50] In 1991 the two companies opened a second, $200 million electro-galvanizing line, LS Electro-Galvanizing II, in Columbus, Ohio, to produce 400,000 tons of zinc-nickel coated sheet steel per year for the automotive transplants.[51] The Wheeling-Nisshin facility in West Virginia makes hot-dip steel for various automotive applications. NKK has made major improvements to National Steel's older galvanizing facilities as part of the two firms' broader joint-venture agreement. Kawasaki has made major improvements to the existing Armco galvanizing line in Middletown, Ohio, as part of its joint-venture with Armco.[52]

Additional Japanese-owned or joint-venture galvanizing lines are expected to be completed in the near future. The largest of these is I/N Kote, a $550 million

TABLE 6.2.   Major Steel Galvanizing Lines in the United States

Company	Annual Capacity (tons)	Date Opened	Country
Electro-Galvanizing			
USX (Gary)	425,000	1977	U.S.
USS-Rouge	700,000	1986	U.S.
National-NKK	400,000	1986	U.S.-Japan
LSE I (LTV-Sumitomo)	400,000	1986	U.S.-Japan
Bethlehem-Inland	400,000	1986	U.S.
Armco-Kawasaki	250,000	1986	U.S.-Japan
LSE II (LTV-Sumitomo)	400,000	1991	U.S.-Japan
I/N Kote (Inland-Nippon)	400,000	1991	U.S.-Japan
Armco-Kawasaki	290,000	1991	U.S.-Japan
Hot-Dip Galvanizing			
Wheeling-Nisshin	360,000	1988	U.S.-Japan
Metaltech	100,000	1990	U.S.
I/N Kote (Inland-Nippon)	500,000	1991	U.S.-Japan
NKK-Dofasco	400,000	1992	Japan-Canada
Bethlehem	450,000	1992	U.S.
USS-Kobe	600,000	1992	U.S.-Japan
Wheeling-Nisshin	240,000	1993	U.S.-Japan
Bethlehem (Sparrows Point)	260,000	1993	U.S.
Bethlehem (Burns Harbor)	450,000	1993	U.S.
Bethlehem (Southwest)	260,000	1993	
Mitsubishi-Stelco	NA	1992–93	Japan-Canada
California Steel	240,000	1994	Japan

Source: Wharton Econometric Forecasting Associates, Steel Division (December 1991).

joint venture between Nippon Steel and Inland Steel located in New Carlisle, Indiana, adjacent to the existing I/N Tek joint venture. I/N Kote will process cold-rolled steel produced at I/N Tek on two parallel coating lines, a hot-dip and an electrogalvanizing line. Its total capacity will be 900,000 tons per year, 400,000 of electrogalvanized steel and 500,000 of hot-dip galvanized steel. Kawasaki had planned to build a second, $200 million electro-galvanizing line at the Middletown site; however, construction of that line was temporarily postponed in June 1991 because of the sluggish U.S. steel market. USS-Kobe will build a $200 million, 600,000-ton-per-year, hot-dip galvanizing line under the name Aztec Coating in Leipsic, Ohio, near Toledo.[53] Wheeling-Nisshin plans to add a second coating line in Follansbee, West Virginia.

According to data provided by WEFA, Japanese steel companies are involved in four of seven major expansions of hot-dip galvanizing lines, and all but one of eight expansions of electro-galvanizing lines. Bethlehem Steel is the only U.S. producer not involved in a major galvanizing joint venture with a Japanese company. Bethlehem, however, is expanding its existing galvanizing facilities in Burns Harbor, Indiana, and Sparrows Point, Maryland, and is purchasing most of Inland Steel's portion of a jointly held Bethlehem-Inland galvanizing line, Walbridge Coatings, in Walbridge, Ohio, as soon as the Inland-Nippon venture, I/N Kote, comes on line.[54] There is some fear among steel-industry executives, consultants, and experts that the recent surge in galvanizing investments will lead to significant overcapacity in this segment of the industry, which could lead to competition and perhaps a costly shakeout.

Integrated Steel Production

The Japanese steel industry began by investing in galvanizing operations for automobile body parts. However, companies soon discovered that the problems of the U.S. steel industry were even deeper than they thought and were forced to move downstream to eliminate those problems from earlier phases of the steel-production chain. Thus the increasing Japanese financial control of the U.S. Steel industry has come in tandem with and been driven by the underlying production control that Japanese steelmakers believe is required to ensure the production of high-quality steel.

Japanese companies have made major investments in integrated steel production to ensure high-quality steel inputs from the mill. Unfortunately, traditional U.S. steel mills produce steel that is not the type of steel needed to satisfy the demands of Japanese coating lines and their automotive customers. The American steel industry, protected by quotas and the difficulties of truly massive import penetration, had become used to producing the various grades of steel that satisfied their most important customers, the Big Three automakers. The steel was of highly inconsistent quality—that is, one batch might be good quality and within specifications, still others fair, and some unacceptably poor requiring internal rejections at the steel plant. As we pointed out earlier, the Japanese production system is built around zero defects. The concept essentially means that all surprises are eliminated and that everything must be exact—averaging is not acceptable. A former American steel industry executive reported that his former employer could not have met the demands of Japanese coating lines for continuous high-quality steel. It was his estimate that of 2,000 tons his company produced, 1,900 tons would be good enough for a traditional customer, of this 1,900 tons only 100 would satisfy a highly selective Japanese transplant—100 tons would have been unacceptable to everyone.[55] Indeed, even Big Three auto makers eventually became dissatisfied with the low quality steel produced by American steelmakers. However they did not switch completely to foreign steel since they did not want to destroy the American steel industry. In this regard joint ventures between American and Japanese steelmakers were a solution to the problems facing the Big Three as well as those of the transplants.

Product delivery is another major difference between U.S. and Japanese steel producers. These differences are explained by the very different supply relationships between automobile and steel companies in the two countries. To minimize inventory and reduce cost, Japanese steel mills are operated upon a just-in-time basis. This production pattern is reinforced by Japanese automobile companies who demand that steel be delivered as needed. In contrast, U.S. steel companies produced in enormous batches, which were then stored in huge inventories. This production pattern was required by Big Three automotive companies whose swings in demand meant that steel companies must retain large inventories "just-in-case" it was needed to meet an upswing in production.

An American steel executive, in charge of production at a major U.S. producer, provided an illustration of the relationships between American steel producers and American automakers. Although Big Three customers ordered steel on an annual basis, they actually utilized the steel at a highly variable weekly rate, which was predicated on how many cars they would build that week. This variable "withdrawal rate" forced the steel company to keep large inventories "just-in-case" a Big Three customer wanted to withdraw its full quota on a given week. In an attempt to reduce costs for both the steelmaker and the customer, this American steel company devised a system for tracking variability in the "withdrawal rate" and producing steel to meet that rate. The company then proposed to a Big Three customer that it provide updated monthly orders for steel based on its withdrawal rate, in return for which that customer would receive a discount based upon inventory savings. Ultimately, according to the steel executive,

> We made a proposal for a $10 discount, if they would give us four-week firm schedules. . . . We gave them the discount, and they gave us the four-week firm schedule. And they went right back to the same thing but now we got $10 a ton less.[56]

In contrast, another Big Three company did comply with the new plan, but, the executive continued, with a transplant customer there was never any problem because "they withdrew their steel on a straight line."

Japanese investments in integrated steel production mainly involve existing U.S. plants in the industrial Midwest. While it might have been easier for Japanese steel companies to build new integrated steel plants, the timing and immediate needs of automotive transplants provided insufficient time. According to one steel industry executive, "If the timing was different, I would say sure. But they don't have that kind of time; these customers are very impatient. . . . Timing doesn't allow them to build, . . . they've got to fix."[57] Of course, it remains questionable if Japanese steelmakers could ever build a new integrated mill in the United States both because it is very expensive and because the return from such an investment might never be realized.

Japanese corporations have worked hard to upgrade technology at these American steel mills. U.S. steel production has been organized as a "batch process" with separate and discrete steps in production such as steel casting, rolling, and coating. In contrast, Japanese firms have developed new technology to make steel production a highly automated, fully integrated, and continuous process, thus ushering in the "new iron age." A former American CEO of National Steel has suggested that the continuous-process capabilities were an important reason for the company's joint venture with NKK. In his words, "We want our steelmaking process to be less of a batch process and more of a materials process."[58]

Since purchasing an equity stake in National Steel, NKK has implemented an extensive organizational and management restructuring to turn National Steel into a modern "integrated" steel producer.[59] This effort has involved the wholesale introduction of state-of-the-art Japanese steel technology. NKK has added new equipment, including a continuous caster and a $70 million vacuum degasser to National Steel's Great Lakes Works. Degassing is an additional refining step after steel leaves the basic oxygen furnace: Japanese technological leadership in degassing has allowed carbon in steel to be reduced to very low levels, thus making steel easier to bend and form. The degassing process also allows finer adjustments in steel chemistry and the development of alloys with far greater precision than a traditional steelmaking furnace.[60] The steel produced using the degassing process is required by Japanese automakers for body parts. The company also installed a state-of-the-art ladle metallurgy facility at the Great Lake works which allows further refinement in steel chemistry. NKK added a second continuous caster at National Steel's Granite City Division in Granite City, Illinois. In November 1990, National Steel announced that it would build a major new coke processing complex on the site of its Great Lakes works.[61] The company is also upgrading existing hot-strip and cold-reduction mills at Great Lakes. At Granite City, National Steel plans to spend approximately $1 billion to rebuild two blast furnaces, add a new continuous caster and pickling line, and upgrade the existing hot-strip mill. In addition, National Steel has expended significant time and resources to simply tearing down and clearing old, dilapidated facilities which littered its mill sites. This according to company officials has significantly increased safety and reduced the injury rate.[62]

A crucial part of NKK's efforts at National Steel has been predicated on identifying and addressing the myriad technological and organizational factors effecting output and quality and now is working to improve them. NKK dispatched a team of 60 engineers and technicians to analyze and study National's production process and recommend improvements. The NKK team identified more than 300 technical improvements to improve output and another 400 to improve quality.[63] NKK also established an extensive maintenance program for National's steel units, which had suffered from neglect and decay. According to the Japanese chairman of National Steel: "We are changing from breakdown maintenance to preventive maintenance."[64] He might have easily added—from the U.S. system to the Japanese system.

National Steel's massive investment and technological upgrading program has resulted in significant improvements in quality and yield. Between 1986 and 1988, the proportion of liquid steel to steel shipped increased from 75 percent to more than 85 percent, and the percentage of hot-band steel to shipped steel at Great Lakes rose from 88 percent to more than 92 percent over the same period. In other words, the Japanese drastically increased yield by eliminating waste, often through simple housekeeping and maintenance activities.

Kawasaki and Armco have established a $1.3 billion investment program to modernize both Armco steel plants.[65] New continuous casters and vacuum degassers will be installed at Middletown, Ohio, and Ashland, Kentucky, cold-rolling mills will be converted to fully continuous operations, and hot-strip mills will be upgraded. At Middletown, slab furnaces on the hot-strip mill will be converted to walking-beam units, and the finishing stands and the pickling line will be upgraded. A new thin-slab caster may be installed at Ashland.[66] Kawasaki has also made significant improvements to the old Kaiser Steel facilities in Fontana, California, as part of its joint venture with the Brazilian firm Rio Doce. These include improvements to the hot-strip mill, cold-rolling mill, plate mill, and coating lines.[67]

Kobe Steel has made major investments in a former U.S. Steel bar and tube mill in Lorain, Ohio. This is the first major Japanese foray into U.S. production of steel pipes and bars, which are used in automobile axles and chassis parts.[68] While the U.S. Steel Lorain mill was fairly modern by American standards, it had suffered from a lack of reinvestment and creeping technological obsolescence. As noted earlier, U.S. Steel's management had used the Lorain division as a cash cow, and had not reinvested in the plant, which would have improved production technology. One of the stipulations of the USS-Kobe joint venture was that the Lorain management could reinvest its earnings in the operation. USS-Kobe is investing $400 million, including $120 million to rebuild the blast furnaces and construct a new metallurgical technology center; the remainder will be spent on a new continuous "bloom" caster for the production of steel bars and modernization of the seamless pipe mill.[69]

Interestingly, Kobe's efforts to transfer Japanese work and production organization to the Lorain mill were enhanced by U.S. Steel's past financial mismanagement. Operating under extreme financial stringency, the Lorain plant was unable to hire a full complement of managers and was forced to move toward work teams and worker self-management. Indeed, the success of these early efforts to move toward worker self-management is part of what convinced Kobe to purchase an ownership stake in the plant in the first place.[70]

I/N Tek, the joint venture between Nippon Steel and Inland Steel, is a brand-new facility. While this is not a fully integrated mill, it involves a critical step in steel production: cold-rolling. Cold-rolling is the third or fourth step in the steel production process, coming after the steel is cast into slabs and then processed in a "hot-strip" mill to produce large steel coils. Cold-rolling basically processes the thick steel coils into much thinner sheet steel for application in automobiles, office furniture, refrigerators, washing machines, and other home appliances. It is the step which comes immediately before steel is coated or galvanized. High-quality cold-rolled steel is of critical importance in producing high quality galvanized roduct.

Restructuring Work and Production

Achieving such a reversal in the operations of the U.S. steel industry cannot be attributed solely to technological improvements. Massive changes in work and production organization have been crucial. This has meant transforming a long legacy of ingrained fordist and even pre-fordist organizational practices. These organizational factors have been a major obstacle to the transfer of Japanese production methodology since many of the Japanese entries into U.S. steel production involve existing steel plants and most involve workforces organized by the United Steelworkers union.

Traditionally organized steel mills are characterized by literally hundreds of job classifications which were explicitly written into employment contracts hammered out over the past 55 years of often bitter labor-management contract disputes. These classifications reflect an employment system with an internal job ladder which ensures that the most senior workers receive the highest paying and most secure jobs. We asked the human resources manager of a major U.S. integrated steel mill to tell us how many job classifications were used in the steel complex he managed. He said he did not know exactly, but estimated somewhere in the range of 300 to 400. He then pointed to a line of a dozen or so file cabinets which he said contained the relevant information, and said that perhaps the industrial engineering department could provide an answer with a few days of research.[71]

Most U.S. steel mills have an additional system, referred to as "lines of progression," which are basically informally negotiated patterns of pay and promotion by which both union and management abide. This system is extraordinarily complicated. The same human resources manager showed us file cabinets filled with hand-drawn diagrams on which "lines of progression" for various units were outlined. Figure 6.4 provides an example of one of these pay and progression diagram used in a major steel company.

Restructuring of the work organization has been complicated by the fact that work organization is a fundamental fact of labor-management relations. In steel, much more so than in the automobile industry, work organization reflects a combination of pre-fordist craft positions and fordist work organization. In steel, elements of work organization such as high number job classifications and very restrictive work rules define the essence of labor-management relations. According to a high-ranking executive at a U.S. steel company

> The rank and file . . . they just don't trust the company, at all—in any way, shape, or form. There's a lot of resentment toward anything that's changed; anything, [any] job classification that might lead to reduction of jobs[72]

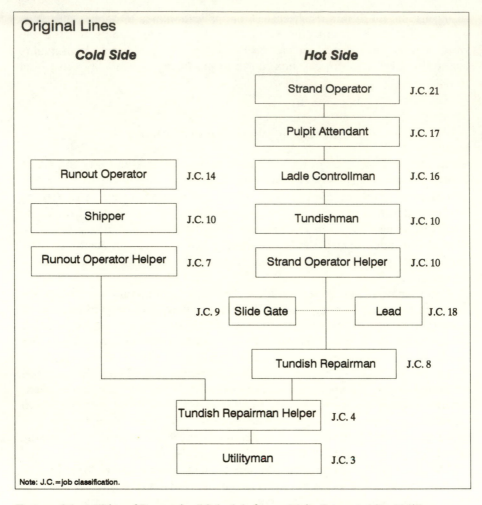

FIGURE 6.4. A "Line of Progression" Schedule from a Major Integrated Steel Mill.
Source: Personnel manager at a U.S. Steel plant.

These rules and organizational practices are a virtual imprint of past class struggles and compromises—as such, they are extraordinarily difficult to alter. In many steel companies, the context of labor-management relations is highly adversarial. This leaves little room for the more cooperative team efforts required for Japanese production organization. According to a top steel-industry executive, his company "has got a union relationship that management worked hard at establishing for about 40 years. . . . It's pretty deep, very adversarial."[73]

It is these arcane, almost Kafkaesque rules that frame the environment in which workers and managers "manufacture consent" and ensure that steel is produced and the power relations of the workplace are reproduced.[74] Under normal conditions, disruption of these relations means that all or, at least, some of the players may lose. Thus, resistance can be stubborn and can come from any number of sources including shop-floor workers, union representatives, and entrenched managers—who are all comfortable with the system they know. However, the decline of the American steel industry created a crisis situation, placing everyone's job in jeopardy and convincing all parties of the inevitability of a major restructuring.

Japanese steel makers have worked closely with both their U.S. joint-venture partners and the United Steelworkers union to restructure this existing framework of labor-management relations to facilitate the transfer of Japanese work and production organization. As with the automotive assemblers, "restructuring" agreements between the union and management have been used to open the door for the transfer of Japanese work organization. In steel, however, the agreements have differed depending upon the preexisting relations at the specific plant.

The LTV-Sumitomo Metal joint venture, LS Electro-Galvanizing (LSE), is often cited as the model for restructuring agreements in the steel industry. The company has reduced the number of job classifications from 100 to just 3—"entry-level," "intermediate," and "advanced"—and has instituted self-managing work teams. LSE does not pay hourly wages; rather, it has put all workers on a salary.[75] This salary system is highly individualized, with workers paid a wage based upon the various skills they possess and/or learn. The use of this individualized salary system of remuneration bears even greater similarity to the Japanese system of wage determination than the uniform hourly wages paid by the automotive transplants and most other steel ventures. Base pay is supplemented by a "gain-sharing plan." A "pay and progression" committee comprised of workers as well as managers determines the rate and progression of workers through this "pay-for-knowledge" system. The training committee has responsibility for determining the rate at which workers are trained in new skills. While LSE is a new facility, it is located within LTV's existing Cleveland steel production complex and employs workers recruited from LTV's present and laid-off work force.[76]

LSE has gone further than most other Japanese or Japanese-U.S. ventures, extending worker self-management to oversee much of the management of the plant. The vehicle for accomplishing this is the worker-run committees for hiring, pay and progression, training, profit-sharing, safety, process control, scheduling, and many others. In effect, workers are responsible not only for shop-floor production activities but also for various higher-level management and administrative responsibilities that have typically been "management only" activities in the steel industry.[77] For example, at the beginning of each shift or "turn," workers meet to learn what happened on the previous shift. Both management and labor indicate that the plant runs smoothly, and there have been no major complaints from workers.[78]

I/N Tek has also implemented a knowledge/skill based compensation program.[79] There are only four classes of skilled workers: operator attendant, electrical craftsman, mechanical craftsman, and instrumentation craftsman; and there is one semiskilled class: material handler. The skilled classes are paid $14.50 an hour base wage; material handlers are paid $8.00, which increases to $10.00 per hour at the end of one year. The average base pay for skilled workers is roughly $32,000 annually, and workers have the opportunity to earn considerable bonuses, adding up to as much as an additional 45 percent to 50 percent of their regular salary. The company uses a "pay-for knowledge" system to encourage workers to learn additional skills. According to one I/N Tek executive:

> It's not our plan that everybody will learn everything because that would be just asking for every football player to play so many games in every position. In baseball they might do that, but in football it's damn tough. But you want to become expert at a number of positions in order to get cross-training and relief. Again, that adds to *kaizen* capability, because you have a better understanding of what's happening over here and you broaden your horizon in your thought process of what the impacts are.[80]

I/N Tek is located in New Carlisle, Indiana, near South Bend, approximately 60 miles east of Inland's main steel production facility at Indiana Harbor, Indiana, near Chicago. Inland Steel officials initially debated whether to locate the I/N Tek facility on Inland's huge Indiana Harbor steel complex. The decision to locate I/N Tek on a new greenfield site was influenced by market-related factors, transportation costs, construction costs, and quality-of-life factors. It also aimed from the beginning to secure a blank slate in an effort to avoid the existing organization, culture, and behaviors associated with both workers and managers at the old Inland Steel complex.

Wheeling-Nisshin has implemented a Japanese-style system of work and production organization in a plant that is on the site of an old Wheeling-Pittsburgh coating line in Follansbee, West Virginia. As a result of the restructuring effort, there are seven classifications of production workers: utility, warehouse, entry, exit, center, lab, and leader; and there are four skilled classifications: electrical technician, mechanical technician, electrical leader, and mechanical leader.[81] This is in contrast to the dozens of job classifications at the old Wheeling-Pitt coating line. Hourly wages range from $10.50 to $13.78 for production workers to between $12.68 and $14.80 for skilled positions.[82] Work is organized in self-directed teams. Workers have considerable latitude in the design and performance of their jobs. Workers are trained for and can perform many different jobs. According to the general manager of human resources at Wheeling-Nisshin,

> Our mechanics and our electricians actually assist the line personnel whenever there is any type of a problem. And our mechanic may be asked to be a pipe fitter or a welder or a machinist of some kind in the course of one turn. Our electricians are also electronic people, as well as computer people, as well as people who run conduit or change light bulbs.[83]

Many of the restructured Japanese-U.S. steel ventures have replaced front-line supervisors and foremen with team leaders. At Wheeling-Nisshin, for example, the center operator also functions as team leader. I/N Tek has a position referred to as coordinator. The coordinator is not tied to a specific job and can move around to help with problem-solving efforts. During shift changes, coordinators participate in "face meetings" where they provide information on problems and glitches to the

next shift. They also have responsibility for monitoring equipment and for conducting equipment checks.[84]

Restructuring the Integrated Mills

National steel has experienced greater difficulty in its efforts to transfer Japanese-
style work and production organization. The reason is simply that its steelmaking
operations are huge complexes with their long legacy of fordist, even pre-fordist,
production arrangements. Still, numerous changes have been made. In its 1986
agreement with the union, National Steel compressed the number of job classifications for craft workers at its Great Lakes mill from 86 to 16 by combining a broad
range of existing classifications, and established a "flexible assignment policy" to
eliminate barriers to job assignment and reassignment in the mill. In return for this,
management agreed to greater job security, higher wages, and a no-layoff policy.[85]
According to the American vice president of National's steelmaking operation:
"We guaranteed job security to all National employees in exchange for a promise
by the United Steelworkers that they would work with us to improve our steelmaking."[86] However, the mill has retained traditional classifications for operating positions. According to both management and union officials, attempts to implement
organizational restructuring have been received differently at the company's mill
sites which have multiple union locals. While National's Great Lakes Works has
seen little difficulty, the Granite City plant has been the site of greater conflict.[87]

National Steel has experienced resistance to its attempts to reduce the number
of job classifications. An industry consultant who visited NKK in Japan reports
that Japanese officials believe that a large part of the problem is American management, which has miscommunicated the Japanese concept of employment security
to workers as meaning "job-based" security.[88] This is compounded because workers
understand that removing these job classification barriers will mean that there is
less idle time so they will have to work more minutes of the workday. The alternative in the short term is to fight to retain the old system, even though it is steadily
becoming less competitive. In response to these obstacles Japanese management is
increasing the number of Japanese engineers and managers at its mills in hope of
remedying these problems. As of summer 1991, National Steel was contemplating
a major company-wide effort to socialize and train middle-managers according to
Japanese principles.

These efforts, while difficult, have resulted in productivity improvements at
National Steel. Figure 6.5 shows the trend in productivity measured as man-hours
per steel ton shipped between 1985 and 1991 for National's Great Lakes Works.
Over this period, productivity almost doubled, as man-hours per shipped ton
declined from 4.2 in 1985–87 to 2.8 by 1991.

Kawasaki Steel has experienced greater difficulty in its attempts to implement
restructuring at Armco's mills in Ohio and Kentucky. The problems have been
especially acute at its Ashland, Kentucky, mill which is organized by a federation
of craft unions. The combination of pre-fordist production organization and well-
entrenched craft union elements comprise a substantial obstacle to restructuring.

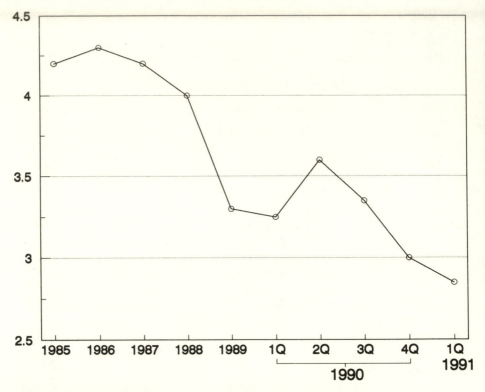

FIGURE 6.5. Productivity Improvement at National Steel's Great Lakes Works, 1985–91.
Note: Productivity measured as man-hours per ton of steel shipped.
Source: National Steel, June 1991.

In response to these difficulties, Armco hired a new American CEO known for his cost-cutting strategies and hard-line position with labor. In summer 1992, Armco eliminated 700 jobs and in September announced a plan to eliminate large numbers of both hourly and salaried workers. While such strategies may increase short-term earnings, they are likely to impede efforts to restructure work and production organization along the lines of the Japanese model.

Employment Security

National Steel is the only one of the Japanese-U.S. steel ventures to offer workers a formal guarantee of employment security. According to a representative of the United Steelworkers union, it is the only steel company that provides a serious commitment to long-term employment security.[89] At the other Japanese-U.S. ventures only informal commitments to job security have been offered. An I/N Tek human resource manager claims that, "barring catastrophic circumstances, which I cannot conceive of, we will not lay off the people who are other than material handlers.

They [not including material handlers] are protected from layoffs."[90] At Wheeling-Nisshin, employment security is a "goodwill commitment" that is not codified in the formal labor-management contract and applies only to the original 65 workers hired by the company. According to a local union official:

> What they say is that they won't lay off those 65 people for the length of the contract. But again it's a "trust me" thing. Any company in either the United States or Japan, if there's a downturn in the economy [they will lay-off]. I don't think by rights you can hold them to something like that. I don't really think that you'd want to. . . .[91] Wheeling-Nisshin's labor-management contract does however expressly state that the company will not lay-off workers as a result of "contracting out." In May 1991, the company had a one-week period when it could not operate due to lack of orders. Instead of being temporarily laid off, workers performed general plant maintenance and even worked on tree-cutting jobs and the like.

In response to the deepening steel recession of 1991–92, Armco steel announced lay-offs of hundreds of workers.[92] It appears to have accepted the basic U.S. "roller-coaster" approach for responding to downturns, as it is simple though brutal. Still, workers in the unionized ventures would like to see greater guarantees of job security along the lines of the system in Japan. As one worker put it, "That I think is the name of the game. You can work for a little less money if you know that you have total job security."[93]

Attempts to Avoid the Union

While all of the large Japanese investments in the U.S. steel industry involve unionized workers, a number originally entertained the possibility of implementing Japanese production and work organization in a nonunion environment. The Wheeling-Nisshin joint venture saw significant internal conflict on whether to recognize the union or to try to operate a nonunionized facility. This was complicated since the Wheeling-Nisshin complex is located on the site of an old Wheeling-Pittsburgh plant that operated as a unionized plant and was covered by a plant-closing agreement requiring that any new ventures on the site be unionized. Wheeling-Nisshin originally signed a pre-employment labor agreement with the union, in effect establishing a preliminary labor contract. However, owing to internal disagreements the company reevaluated its position and during construction of the plant decided not to recognize the union. With the assistance of outside legal counsel, the company was able to have the preemployment agreement deemed illegal and void. This led to a struggle between the company and the union over unionization. The company's position was that workers should decide whether or not they wanted union representation. According to one company official:

> When they returned from training in Japan, our workers basically told us that they really didn't feel that it was necessary to be represented by the Steelworkers, or for that matter any collective bargaining group. Obviously we didn't argue with them or attempt to change their minds.[94]

Wheeling-Nisshin then established an Employee Council to deal with employee relations issues such as working conditions, overtime, scheduling, holidays, etc.

The United Steelworkers (USW) responded by launching a campaign to organize the plant. The basic issue was wages. Wheeling-Nisshin's wage rates were lower than traditional steel mills. In recompense, the company held out its profit-sharing plan which might pay as much as 50 percent of an employee's salary in a once a year bonus. But first year bonuses for the start-up company were rather small, averaging $300 dollars. The company then initiated a "union-defense" campaign, countering that profits were much lower than anticipated and that employees did not need "third party" representation. The president of the company sent letters to the workers and wrote opinion pieces in the local papers on the advantages of not having a union. According to a company official, "So we ran, I don't want to say an anti-union campaign, but we sent out letters and explained the advantages of not having a union and so forth."[95] Both company and union officials insist that this was a "mild" campaign, and it certainly did not resemble the aggressive anti-union campaign at Nissan. Eventually, Wheeling-Nisshin workers voted by a 2-to-1 margin to join the union. According to a company official:

> It was a fairly strong mandate for the union. . . . We made a strong point not to lose
> a lot of sleep over it because we worked with everyone before when we expected
> that they would be Steelworkers, we worked with them when they told us they
> didn't want to be Steelworkers, and we knew that we could work with them once
> they were represented again. So we eventually sat down and negotiated a labor
> agreement.[96]

The president of the Wheeling-Nisshin union local confirmed this in an interview, indicating that the anti-union drive was not especially bitter, and that the company and the union work well together. He believes that the new environment is significantly better than the environment of the old Wheeling-Pittsburgh plant where he also served as union president. "We have yet to file a grievance at Wheeling-Nisshin. At Wheeling-Pitt, in probably five years' time, I filed 100 grievances."[97] He added that the company's struggle against the union should be taken in context, indicating that they hired him for a top shop-floor position even though they knew he was the president of the union local for the previous Wheeling-Pittsburgh plant, and would actively work to organize the plant.

Inland Steel also had internal debates over whether to locate I/N Tek in a "non-union" region of the United States such as the Sunbelt to provide an environment where it might be easier to implement Japanese-style work and production organization. However, after internal debate the company decided to locate in New Carlisle, Indiana just 60 miles from their main steel plant and in a strong union area. This made unionization virtually inevitable. Moreover, a number of Inland Steel officials argued that unionization would provide labor-force stability, while not materially affecting costs because steelmaking has become so technology- and capital-intensive. An official involved in the site-selection process characterized the relationship between capital-intensive steel production and the need for a highly skilled and reliable work force in this way:

You've got an engineering system here that basically has taken all of the labor out of it. If you can convert the labor structure such that it's a win-win when the company wins, and lose-lose when it loses, you got everything aligned so that you have congruence in what your mission is and how you measure success. . . . We think we have a labor-cost advantage. You talk to people and they'll say, "You pay too much for your people." In the long run I don't think we're paying too much for our people. We expect to get much more value out of them. They become an asset and become the reason you're able to constantly improve your enterprise and stay in business longer.[98]

The relationship between management and labor in Japanese-U.S. joint ventures can operate in such a way as to weaken the national union's bargaining position. For example, the USS-Kobe joint venture in Lorain, Ohio, has a separate agreement from that between the USW and USX. When there was the possibility of a strike against USX's U.S.-managed operations, the USS-Kobe local considered working through the strike without a new contract. The *Wall Street Journal* reported that the USS-Kobe local's president sent a letter to his members "seeking permission to request a contract extension."[99] The restructuring process that Kobe Steel is nurturing ties workers to the operations of the plant in a way that the confrontational style of USX never could.

Selecting and Training Workers

Some steel ventures use selection procedures like the automotive transplants to find workers who fit into Japanese production methodology. LSE employees were selected from a large pool of 10,000 workers consisting of both laid-off and current LTV employees and were submitted to rigorous evaluation procedures designed to pick workers who would "fit into" the new system.

I/N Tek used a very stringent screening process to select employees from the existing pool of 12,500 workers at Inland Steel's Indiana Harbor Works. To select employees from the joint venture from the 1250 Inland workers who applied, the company used a combination of written tests, simulations, and interviews. The State of Indiana Department of Employment and Training Services conducted the initial aptitude, technical, and psychological screening tests. According to a company official, these tests provided insight on the type of "environment in which one liked to work and whether one was an independent contributor to a team kind of environment or required lots of supervision."[100]

Applicants who made it through the initial tests were sent to an assessment center at a community college near Inland's Indiana Harbor Works where they were subjected to detailed evaluations using work-like simulations in an effort to determine applicants' interpersonal characteristics, judgment, decisiveness, initiative, analytical abilities, safety awareness, work standards, and ability to work in a group context. A human resources official involved in the screening and selection process summarized its objectives: "We were looking for people who had an ability to analyze for themselves, diagnose problems, develop their solutions, to take action, be a self-starter, go beyond the norm, not need to be directed, not want to be directed, but also capable of working with a group of people who are very much like them so they would not be antagonistic toward one another in this kind of environment."[101] Those who made it through the assessment center were subjected to a series of interviews with managers and workers. Of the roughly 1,250 workers who originally applied, 950 actually took the tests, 345 were successful in the tests and went to the assessment center, and 220 were successful at the assessment center. All of these candidates were interviewed to select the final 120 hirees.

Wheeling-Nisshin recruited from the pool of laid-off workers at the old Wheeling-Pittsburgh Follansbee plant as well as the broader labor market. The company sent out letters to laid-off workers, but most of these workers had already passed retirement age. Only a handful of former Wheeling-Pitt workers applied for jobs, and out of that group just two were hired. The company used the state employment office to test and screen workers initially. Potential candidates were then subjected to rigorous interviews with technical people, other workers, and American and Japanese executives. According to the company's human resources manager,

> The [initial] interview was myself, the manager of operations, an American, and a Japanese electrical technical person. . . . After we put the people through the initial screening we then selected . . . candidates to come back for our second interview. That second interview consisted of the president of the company and the vice president, as well as the initial group of people involved in the screening. . . . Every person that was hired for our plant was seen by at least the president of the company and the majority of the management people that were employed and were interviewed by the chairman of the company. . . . And we would run reference checks, background checks, to the extent that we could do it.[102]

The screening and selection of managers is a great concern for Japanese-U.S. steel ventures. Potential managers are subjected to a battery of written tests, assessment centers, and multiple interviews with managers and workers—the objective being to identify managers who fit into a Japanese team environment and who will not fall back on the old steel industry's authoritarian practices. A top manager at a major Japan-U.S. joint venture highlighted the dimensions of this process and the internal conflicts it can generate.

> I've got a classic story. Our managers of operations were just licking their chops at this young man that had shown good skills at getting things accomplished in our existing steel plant. We put him through our three-tier selection process and one of them was an interview so I interviewed him. I asked him what he liked to do: "I really like to make decisions." So I turned him down and I got hell. Finally, the manager of operations made him an offer against my advice. He called back and said that he really needed more money. The manager that hired him wasn't there so I got the call. He was talking to me and I said I'll get right back to him. I went to the president and said I would like to withdraw the offer to this young man. He just likes the old traditional way of doing things. He can't be anything but a John Wayne, and they need John Waynes where he is. Why bring him over here, where he'll fail. It's not fair to him, it's not fair to us. I said I want to withdraw the offer. So I called him back and said, "I understand, I think you'll be successful where you are, so I'm withdrawing the offer, good luck." . . . We saw it as a signal of the fact

that we had an individualistic guy that was paramount to the way he values himself, and it would be hard for him to bring himself to empowering the team.[103]

Training is further used to inculcate workers to Japanese production methodology and ensure that they are able to fit into the new system; it also gives them the new skills that they need to operate in the high-technology environment of Japanese-style steel production where computers and electronic systems are extensively used. The original group of I/N Tek workers were sent to Japan for two to six weeks of training. Roughly 25 Japanese trainers then returned to provide additional instruction in the United States. I/N Tek officials estimate that roughly $10 million, or $80,000–$100,000 per worker, was spent in this initial training effort.

Wheeling-Nisshin's original work force was also sent to its Japanese sister plant. Managers and key shop-floor workers such as team leaders were sent to Japan for nine months; a small group of shop-floor workers were sent for six months to get electronics training, and a large group of 18 to 20 workers were sent for three months. In Japan, workers were exposed to Japanese production methodology and behavioral norms. They learned both the "hard" skills of operating production equipment and the "soft" skills of working in a team environment. Technology transfer was accomplished by watching and learning about the production process and by working closely with Japanese trainers. A Wheeling-Nisshin worker recounts how this process works between two workers who speak different languages:

> We were given manuals that were translated. Have you ever tried to read Japanese/ English manuals? They're very difficult. . . . We had interpreters, but they had no basic steel background. . . . If we spoke the same language, what I learned in three months I probably could learn in a month. But it was a lot of question-asking. They would take their leaders who would be responsible for training maybe three or four employees and they would bring people in from different sections, maybe somebody from their computer department, to explain this and explain that. There was a lot of learning, but there was good bit lost in the translation.[104]

The groups of American workers also had to operate a quality-control circle and present their results to Japanese workers and managers. According to a worker who participated in one of these circles,

> We had a QC to do. It was on air knives. . . . They're computer controlled and everything like that and there's a million variables. . . . There's four of us, and we have these manuals out and half of them we can't even read. . . . Mostly we were studying; we would go in-plant . . . and spend a couple of hours just watching the action as they worked, taking notes on it, talking to the operators, why did you do this? Why did you make this change? What does it do? And they were very helpful; they spoke more English than we speak Japanese. . . . A lot of times we'd get together at night and compare notes, work like that because I might see something that maybe somebody else missed and they might pick up something that I had no idea even existed. We'd just get together and compare notes like that, jot down and recheck it the next day.[105]

At most Japanese steel ventures in the United States, training is ongoing and continuous. It becomes a way to bolster and improve human resources capabilities as workers receive classroom and on-the-job training in computers, electronics, and advanced automation. According to one American executive at a Japanese-U.S. joint venture steel facility,

> Training is like R&D. It's your commitment to improve your people. It's an investment in R&D—training your people. Those are your resources, your scientists, your lab technicians, but they are on the operating floor.[106]

In practical language, this executive has captured the essence of innovation-mediated production—the interpenetration of the laboratory and the shop-floor.

Harnessing Workers' Intelligence

Japanese-U.S. steel ventures have sought to implement Japanese-style *kaizen* activity, to harness the intelligence of factory workers, but this effort has met with mixed success. Most American workers were used to the "get the metal out the door" mentality of U.S. managers. As an example, the operations manager at I/N Tek describes the way traditional steel operations worked:

> Many times people were afraid to stop the operations if they had a quality problem because they would have to answer many questions as to why they did that. There was always the fear that if they had not made the decision properly that they would be in trouble and there was always the fear of reprisal.[107]

This way of dealing with production meant that the output was of low quality and led directly to the high wastage described earlier.

At I/N Tek, workers are responsible for the quality of the operation and are able to stop the line to remedy quality problems. While I/N Tek encourages workers to be involved in individual *kaizen* activities and to contribute suggestions, it does not yet have an organized QC circle program. A top Japanese executive at I/N Tek indicated that Nippon would push to implement "JK circles," its own version of voluntary quality-control circles, over the next few months. He stressed that because I/N Tek had only been operating for less than a year (when the interview took place) it was "too early" to expect full transfer of Japanese *kaizen* and quality-control activities.[108]

A number of joint ventures have experienced worker opposition to QC activity. Wheeling-Nisshin originally initiated a QC program, which was disbanded after it generated opposition from workers. But, strikingly, both company and union representatives thought that the nonresponsiveness of management was the critical feature that led to the failure of the original program. Workers were initially enthusiastic about the program but became discouraged when management failed to act on their suggestions. The company is currently trying to reintroduce QC circles and has begun to provide small cash payments for successful groups, although it no longer refers to them as "quality control circles." As an example, according to a

Wheeling-Nisshin worker, "The warehouse right now is doing nothing more than a QC and they have been doing a QC for the past two months. But they're calling it a problem-solving group and they're not looking at it as a QC. It's just an ongoing committee that's solving problems and moving on to another problem.[109]

In fact, Wheeling-Nisshin's union local is working with management to reintroduce QCs. They are doing so because they are convinced that effective quality circle activity can be used to improve elements of the production process that cause injuries, thereby making work less stressful and promoting safety. In doing so, successful quality circles reduce the grievance load faced by the union. According to a union official, "Every time we solve the problem for us, we generally solve the problem for management. We have begun to cooperate on a lot of things . . . to the benefit of both parties."[110]

Worker and Management Adaptation

At the moment, indications are that workers are not actively resisting the revamping of the U.S. steel industry to one that has greater resemblence to the Japanese production system. Indeed, there appear to be fewer adaptation problems in steel than in the automobile industry. Part of this has to do with the very nature of work and the labor process in steel. Steel-industry jobs are fairly highly skilled, often individualized, and nonrepetitive—it is not an assembly-line-type of work process. Workers we interviewed do not appear to resent or be fearful or even concerned with what Parker and Slaughter refer to as "management by stress." Although a number of workers we interviewed were fully cognizant that their own *kaizen* and improvement activities sometimes result in a faster work pace, this did not appear to them as highly problematic. A number of workers indicated that such activities represented their own "long-term job security," seeing such activity as "working to protect their jobs." Workers in companies that had performance bonuses and profit sharing saw such activities as a way to increase their income. One worker put it this way: "We sped up our line. We sped it up six months into production. But we have a very lucrative profit-sharing plan, so I'm making probably $12,000 a year more here than I was before" [at a traditional steel mill].[111] It is interesting to note the workers agreed collectively to speed up production; in effect, the firm had effectively tied the workers' interests to its own.

Union-management relations also appear to be much improved over traditional steel-industry relations. LSE's worker committee structure has been able to reduce drastically the number of grievances handled by the union. Many of the smaller galvanizing facilities—as opposed to the large integrated mills—were also able to eliminate or significantly lower the number of grievances handled. According to the union president of the union local for one of the steel joint ventures: "Being a union president is like being a father. You mainly have to iron out little details. [At this plant] two guys were arguing today—it's like running a family. Honestly, it's not so much like being a union president per se."[112]

The most serious and recurrent problem highlighted by both workers and managers revolves around the problematic adaptation of middle managers. Many of the

Japanese-U.S. joint ventures started out with a fairly large group of front-line factory supervisors steeped in fordist managerial philosophy and practice. As production commenced and work teams have become more and more self-managing, these managers became redundant and, at times, a source of resistance to Japanese production methodology. Top managers we interviewed indicated that their biggest problem was giving these front-line and middle-level managers "something to do." A number of workers as well as senior officials suggested that at times these managers fall back upon "old ways" and try to "boss" workers—with very detrimental effects. Interestingly, the head of one of the union locals reports that his counterpart in the Japanese union offered him a strategy for coping with this problem: "The president of our sister plant's labor union in Japan . . . suggested that I try to communicate more with the Japanese managers, because he said they would be a lot more sympathetic to what you want than your American managers."[113]

Steel Processors and Service Centers: Linking Steel to Autos

In addition to major Japanese investments in integrated steel production and galvanizing lines, Japanese corporations and especially trading companies have invested heavily in steel service centers and processing centers that warehouse steel coils and do some cutting and forming. These service centers serve a bridge function between steel-coating lines, which produce steel coils, and either transplant assemblers or suppliers who form that steel into actual body parts. Table 6.3 provides a list of major Japanese steel service centers in the United States.

Most of the Japanese steel service and processing centers differ from traditional American steel service centers, which simply serve as warehousers of steel products. Japanese steel service centers are intermediary processors who perform a variety of blanking, slitting, and cutting operations for their automotive customers. Nearly all

TABLE 6.3.   Major Japanese Steel Service and Processing Centers in the United States

Company	Location	Principal Ownership	Annual Production Capacity (tons)
Nisco Steel Services	Memphis, TN	Nissho-Iwai	120,000
Toledo Distribution Inc.	Toledo, OH	Sumitomo Corporation	160,000
Michigan Steel Processing	Flat Rock, OH	Sumitomo Corporation	120,000
Mi-tech Steel Inc.	Murfreesboro, TN	Mitsui/Steel Technologies Inc.	120,000
Tennessee Metals Corp.	Nashville, TN	Sumitomo Corporation	70,000
C. Itoh Steel Inc.	Winchester, KY	C. Itoh	120,000
Bleim Steel	Toledo, OH	Marubeni	120,000
Berwick Steel Co.	Columbus, OH	Nissho-Iwai	180,000
Nova Steel Processing	Tipp City, OH	C. Itoh/Armco	200,000
ProCoil Corp.	Canton, MI	Marubeni/National Steel	220,000
Coilplus Inc.	Athens, AL	Mitsubishi	120,000
Coilplus Illinois Inc.	Bloomington, IL	Mitsubishi	120,000
Coilplus Ohio Inc.	Springfield, OH	Mitsubishi	120,000

Source: Japan Steel Information Center, New York, April 1989.

of these facilities are owned by Japanese trading companies, although at times they also have a steel company as a partner. In fact, nearly every major Japanese trading company operates service centers in the United States. For example, the best-known Japanese steel processor is ProCoil, a three-way joint venture among National Steel, NKK, and Marubeni. ProCoil is a $20 million steel blanking and slitting facility located 15 minutes from the NKK-National Great Lakes Works.[114] Among the other trading companies, Sumitomo, Mitsubishi, and Toyo Menka operate three steel service and processing centers; Nissho-Iwai operates two, and Mitsui operates one.[115]

Steel service and processing centers are usually located in rural greenfield sites in the Midwest and South. Steel service centers are located in close proximity to automotive assembly transplants so they can provide steel on a just-in-time basis.[116] The service centers supply both American Big Three and Japanese transplant auto assemblers. For example, ProCoil supplies both the transplants and the Big Three automakers.[117] Coilplus Inc., a Mitsubishi Corporation joint venture, supplies Diamond-Star.[118] These centers pay wages of between $7.50 and $12.50 per hour. The wages are comparable to the transplant automotive suppliers, but considerably lower than either the unionized steel or auto firms.

Operation of a service center can lead to other opportunities for the trading companies. For example, C. Itoh operates a $7 million joint-venture processing facility with Armco, called Nova Steel Processing, in Tipp City, Ohio, and a wholly owned steel service center under its own name in Winchester, Kentucky.[119] But building on this relationship with Armco, C. Itoh also financed and served as general contractor for Armco's new cold-rolling mill in Butler, Pennsylvania.[120] Not surprisingly, Kawasaki Steel, which eventually purchased a 50 percent share of Armco's steel operations, is also in the Dai-ichi Kangyo group with C. Itoh.

Although rapidly increasing in numbers, the few dozen Japanese steel service centers are a small fraction of the more than 5,000 U.S.-owned steel service centers. Still, the pronounced concentration of transplant steel service facilities in the lower Midwest and upper South contrasts markedly with the highly decentralized pattern of U.S.-owned steel processing centers. According to one report, in 1982 the top ten locations for U.S. steel service centers were ranked as follows: Chicago, New York City, Los Angeles, Houston, Detroit, Philadelphia, Cleveland, Dallas, St. Louis, and Atlanta.[121]

Backward Integration into Steel Refractory Products

Japanese corporations, which provide inputs and other supplies to the major steel-makers, have also begun to establish American branches. A good example of this type of backward integration is TYK Refractories, the U.S. branch of Japan's TYK Corporation, whose largest shareholders are NKK and Daido Steel.[122] TYK was established in the immediate postwar period as a spin-off of Daido Steel's Tajimi plant. It is now the largest Japanese producer of high-technology ceramic refractory products for use in steel furnaces, electric arc furnaces, continuous casters, and in modern steel ladles. In the United States, TYK supplies high-tech refractory products to National, USS-Kobe, Daido-Copperweld, Bethlehem, and Allegheny Ludlum.

TYK Refractories entered the American market by purchasing Swank Refractories, a U.S. company. Swank was one of the original U.S. refractories. The company was formed in 1856 to supply the Cambria Iron Works with refractory bricks and pottery devices for pouring molten iron.[123] Later it became a major supplier of refractory bricks used in steel furnaces and pouring devices (e.g., sleeves, stopper rods, nozzles, and ladle bricks) for major U.S. steelmakers. At its peak, Swank operated four refractories in Pennsylvania and Ohio and employed some 350 workers. The decline of the American steel industry had a devastating impact on Swank. In 1974, the company was purchased by an investment firm and used as a cash cow. By 1979, Swank had closed all but one of its plants in Pennsylvania and one in Ohio.

In 1982, TYK purchased both of Swank's Pennsylvania plants. It began by modernizing the one Swank plant that remained open, in Irvona, Pennsylvania, to shift from clay refractory products to new high-performance materials used in continuous-casters. It then reopened Swank's plant in Large, Pennsylvania, an old steel town along the Monongahela River outside Pittsburgh, adding new equipment and constructing two new buildings on the site. TYK later added a new plant at Irvona to make high-performance alumina graphite used in continuous casters. As with larger Japanese investments in galvanizing and integrated steel production, the company has coupled technological upgrading with organizational restructuring. This includes reducing the number of job classifications and implementing work teams, quality circles, and suggestion systems. This restructuring effort has proceeded much more smoothly at the Large plant than at Irvona. The Large plant currently has done away with most job classifications; workers are more or less multifunctional and move between jobs. According to a TYK official,

> Oh Lord! I would have to say that there were at least 40 to 50 job classifications
> before. If you swept the floor in the boiler room, you had one classification; if you
> swept it in the plant you had another. It was ridiculous. Plus that little plant with
> maybe 120 employees, it was actually split into three separate departments. Now
> you got one department and eight or nine job classifications.[124]

In addition, workers are involved in QC activities, and they have been sent to Japan to participate in companywide QC competitions. The suggestion program at the Large plant averages 85 suggestions per worker annually. According to managers, the Large plant has been able to replicate 20 percent to 30 percent of Japanese *kaizen* activity in roughly three years time, a figure that they expect to improve.

Restructuring has not gone as smoothly at the Irvona plant. In 1987, the plant was struck over wages and the reduction of job classifications, which effectively halted the restructuring effort there. Irvona is organized by the traditional refractories union, the International Brotherhood of Aluminum, Brick and Glass Workers Union, whereas the Large facility is organized by the United Steelworkers. The difficulties in implementing restructuring may be due to the fact that the former union has a stronger craft tradition than does the steel union and also because the USW is experienced in dealing with various Japanese restructuring efforts in steel.

The steel-production-equipment industry is not very large in comparison to the automotive parts industry. However, high-quality inputs are as significant to steel production as they are to any other production process. As the commitment of the Japanese steel industry to the U.S. market grows, there is little doubt that more of these smaller input firms will relocate to the United States and set up operations. In November 1991, Kurosaki Refractories Co. Ltd announced a joint venture with North American Refractories to produce alumina-graphite tubes used in continuous casters.[125] The success of these companies is likely to have an important impact on the broader success of the Japanese steel industry in the transplant process.

Future Trends

Japanese steel producers are becoming deeply involved in U.S. steel production as they backward integrate to ensure high-quality products. In fact, the current joint-venture strategy of Japanese producers is operating more like a gradual takeover as profit-driven top executives of U.S. "steel" companies diversify in an effort to maximize their short-term return. Japanese steelmakers have paid between $300 million to $500 million on average to participate in joint ventures. A number of companies have already invested or plan to invest more than $1 billion in U.S. steel production. Such investment might deepen should Japanese steelmakers decide to develop new or upgraded primary steel-making capability in the United States either with current joint-venture partners or as a consortium effort.

In the meantime, we can expect serious efforts by Japanese firms to restructure their U.S. joint-venture partners so that they can provide high-quality steel to the automotive transplants. According to a former Inland Steel executive who is now a top executive at I/N Kote, Nippon Steel is helping to rebuild Inland's huge integrated steel production facility at Indiana Harbor. As he puts it:

> They have 40 engineers working at Inland to help improve things. But they're going to send a high-level team to do an assessment of capability relative to these customers' requirements. These guys that have been there have been working to improve quality and cost, but not to some standard, just to improve it. But now they're going to do an assessment relative to the requirements as they know them of Toyota, Nissan, and Mazda, and based on that they'll sit down with top management and make a recommendation for how to get that big jump in quality.[126]

How such efforts turn out over this decade will largely determine whether or not Japanese steel companies continue to work with U.S. steelmakers or whether they scale back their investments in integrated production and focus instead on high value-added steel finishing.

As in the automobile industry, the success of Japanese steel ventures has pro-

vided the impetus for reform and restructuring of traditional U.S.-owned producers. American steel producers involved with Japanese partners—Inland, LTV, and
Armco—are attempting to implement aspects of Japanese production organization, such as reduced numbers of job classifications and work teams, in their traditional American steel units. Both top managers and union officials indicate that
they are committed to accomplishing this restructuring effort. However, such
efforts face considerable opposition from both middle-level managers and shop-
floor workers (especially senior workers in high-paying positions) who see the existing set of organizational practices as an integral part of their own existence. It will
be very hard to accomplish the kinds of organizational and labor-process restructuring needed to implement Japanese production organization at U.S. mills
because of entrenched practices such as an extraordinary number of job classifications and the long legacy of harshly adversarial labor-management relations. Thus,
it will be difficult not only to bring about changes in management organization and
attitudes necessary to implement Japanese production organization but also to con-
vince union workers that they should trust American management in a move to
new work rules and more cooperative policies.

Japanese involvement in the American steel industry is likely to expand especially as Japanese automotive investments and U.S. steel producers continue to
move out of the steel business and sell off their remaining steel assets. USX has put
its steel business up for sale. Sumitomo Metal has considered purchasing its joint-
venture partner, LTV Steel, which continues to operate under Chapter 11 bankruptcy and provided $200 million in assistance to save LTV from bankruptcy. In
addition, British Steel and Usinor have also considered purchasing U.S. steel companies.[127]

Japanese investment in the North American steel industry continues to grow.
Japanese steelmakers have begun to invest in galvanizing and coating ventures in
southern Canada to serve the growing transplant automotive assembly complex
there. In October 1989, NKK, National Steel, and Dofasco of Canada announced
the construction of a $300 million, 400,000-ton-per-year hot-dip galvanizing line
in Hamilton, Ontario.[128] In May 1990, the Mitsubishi Corporation announced a
joint venture with Stelco of Canada to build a $170 million hot-dip galvanizing steel
coating line in Ontario.[129] Japanese investment is also moving into Mexico. In February 1990, Mitsui established a $100 million joint venture with Mexican steel-
maker Altos Hornos de Mexico.[130]

The "New Iron Age" Comes to America

The power of the Japanese system to transform the American steel industry has
been astonishing. Major strides have been made in an industry with a legacy of disinvestment probably unparalleled in the U.S. economy. To accomplish this, Japanese steel corporations have combined capital investment with a broad-based
strategy of organizational restructuring. At the root of this has been an effort to
transfer and implant the Japanese system of work and production organization in
the steel sector—in the face of a debilitating legacy of institutional forms, organi-

zations, and historical behavioral practices on the part of both management and labor. Japanese corporations have taken an active role in restructuring the workplaces in which they have invested. Basically, there has been a massive effort to replace the Gramscian capital-labor battle lines with a new set of relations. While these efforts have met with considerable achievements the process is not complete or assured of final success.

At bottom, the success of the Japanese steel companies lies in the new model of innovation-mediated production they have implemented. This new model harnesses a worker's intelligence and ideas as a source of continuous-process improvement, which in turn generates increased productivity and new sources of economic value. This is a major advance over the traditional Taylor-Ford model, which views innovation as a discrete activity taking place in laboratories and then simply implemented with little regard for those who will actually undertake and oversee production.

In steel, the new model is most powerfully illustrated by I/N Tek,[131] which has revolutionized the production of cold-rolled steel in the United States. In both America and Europe, cold-rolling traditionally has been a batch process. Steel coils would be transported from one process to another. First, they would go to a machine that cracks the rust and oxidation on the surface, then onward to be soaked in a chemical solution referred to as "pickling" to chemically remove the surface oxides. The next step was for the cleaned hot rolled steel coils to be squeezed to the desired thickness, and ultimately they went to the final cutting and preparation stage. According to a former Inland Steel executive:

> If you go to Inland you'll see the pickle line is one process and then there's a stack of inventory. Then there's the tandem mill and then there's a huge inventory for the anneal and then we have the annealing process. And then there's another inventory where it cools for six or seven days and then there's the temper-rolling operation, then there's another inventory for finishing and inspection and then there's the final shipping. So the plant has inventories everywhere. And everything is discrete.[132]

At Inland Steel the work cycle was typically more than a week and the product quality was variable. Costs were high because these batch steps boosted inventory costs.

I/N Tek has adopted Nippon Steel technology to turn this procedure into a highly automated and completely continuous operation that takes less than an hour to complete. As Chapter 3 has shown, Nippon Steel transformed all the formerly discrete steps—breaking oxides, pickling, tandem, and temper mill—into a single continuous operation that resembles the production of rolls of paper. While this may appear to be a miraculous breakthrough in steelmaking technology, Nippon Steel accomplished this by combining a series of small, incremental process innovations in an evolutionary fashion. According to an Inland Steel executive,

> They started in one place and they put the pickle lines and tandem mill together, and another place they put the tandem mill and the anneal together; another place they put the anneal and finishing together and different combinations. And they saw what worked and finally they could put them all together.[133]

This was accomplished by massive investment *and* the harnessing of shop-floor workers' intellectual capabilities. The company mobilized both factory workers and R&D workers to combine the various batch processes. With the help of computer specialists, computer controls were added. The end result was a continuous production process.

These innovations were not achieved in an isolated R&D center far from the factory. Rather, as the discussion in Chapter 3 has shown, the factory became a laboratory constantly experimenting to develop continuous improvements and methods of linking the separate steps in the production process. The role and importance of regular shop-floor operators is crucial—they work the machines and program the computers that control the entire production process. At I/N Tek there are screens and computer monitors on the shop floor where workers watch the product and adjust the process. There are actual laboratory facilities beneath the steel production line where workers continuously conduct tests and simulations to monitor both the product and the process to ensure quality and efficiency.

As this example indicates, the modern Japanese steel mill has been transformed into an arena in which workers' intelligence is the source of continuous manufacturing process improvements that are crucial for corporate success. In steel, as in so many other industries, the production process is becoming increasingly like a laboratory with experiments and a constant effort to eliminate impurities and "noise" to increase predictability. For Japan of the 1950s, steel was to the economy what semiconductors are today—the critical input. And, as this chapter and Chapter 3 have demonstrated, the Japan of the 1990s is applying many of the advances generated in electronics to steel. This is especially striking in the way that Japanese investment is transforming American steel from a nineteenth-century basic industry to a twenty-first-century high-technology industry as part of the move into the "new iron age."

While steel is the single most important input to automobile production, it is not the only one. In the next chapter we turn to some of the other major inputs and industrial sectors related to automobile production. These other industries are the ones that round out the transplant industrial complex and provide the additional impetus for its further growth.

7

Rounding Out the Industrial Infrastructure

The deal would be the biggest test yet of whether Japanese management techniques are transferable to the United States. Judging from the turnaround of the LaVergne factory, Japanese money and management skills can make a big difference.

The *New York Times* on Japanese tiremaker, Bridgestone's acquisition of Firestone's
LaVergne, Tennessee, plant.

It was like going from hell to heaven.

Mark Ayers, safety engineer, on the transition from Firestone to Bridgestone at
the LaVergne plant.[1]

Japanese investment in American basic industry is not limited to automobiles and steel. Indeed, it extends into a series of related input and supplier industries—rubber and tires, automotive glass, industrial chemicals, machine tools, industrial robotics, and others. Today, four of Japan's five major rubber and tire companies, Bridgestone Tire, Sumitomo Rubber, Yokohama Rubber, and Toyo Tire operate U.S. factories (see Table 7.1). Japan's major glass producer, Asahi Glass, has established U.S. plants to supply the automotive assembly transplants. Large Japanese producers of automotive plastics and chemicals have also opened U.S. production facilities. A growing number of Japanese companies supply the assembly-line equipment, production equipment, robots, stamping presses, and machine tools used by the automobile transplants. Yamazaki Mazak, a major Japanese machine tool company, produces numerically-controlled lathes and machining centers in Kentucky and is opening a major R&D center in Ohio. Hitachi Zosen makes large stamping presses for automotive assembly plants in Illinois.

Clearly, each of these industries has developed and will continue to develop along its own, particular developmental trajectory. Still, all were crucial components of the older fordist industrial complex and victims of its demise; and all are becoming important elements of the burgeoning transplant industrial complex that is emerging in and around the industrial heartland of America.

This chapter begins by exploring Japanese investment in the rubber and tire industry and other industries related to both automotive production and the transplant industrial complex. After this, we turn to a more general discussion of the logic and dynamics of the heavy industrial complex as a whole and to a variety of questions that are bound up with the shift from fordist deindustrialization to reindustrialization that has been spurred by Japanese investment and the transfer of innovation-mediated production.

Japanese Investment in Rubber and Tires

The rubber and tire industry is a large industry and an important component of the transplant heavy industrial complex. Today, Japan's leading tire and rubber companies operate 20 U.S. factories (Table 7.1) Japanese involvement reflects the broader globalization of the rubber and tire industry and has come mainly through acquisitions of American companies.

Bridgestone was the first Japanese tire company to establish U.S. production. In 1983, it purchased a Firestone tire plant in LaVergne, Tennessee. In 1988, Bridgestone purchased Firestone, then the second largest U.S. producer, for $2.6 billion, thereby becoming the second largest tiremaker in both America and the world.[2] Bridgestone then opened a new $350 million radial truck tire plant in Warren County, Tennessee. In April 1989, Bridgestone purchased four companies in the forest-equipment tire business: Webco Corp., Webco Tire, Webco Southern, and Southern Wheel and Rim.[3] In total, during the 1980s and early 1990s, Bridgestone invested over $3 billion in U.S. rubber and tire operations.

TABLE 7.1. Japanese Tire and Rubber Companies in the United States

Japanese Company	U.S. Operations	Date	Manufacturing Employment	Investment (millions of dollars)
Bridgestone	Purchase of Firestone plant, LaVergne, TN	1983	1,300	122*
Sumitomo	Purchase of Dunlop's U.S. operations (3 plants)	1986	2,700	460†
Bridgestone	Buy-out of Firestone (13 U.S. plants)	1988	15,000	4,100‡
Yokohama Rubber and Toyo Tire	GTY Tire Corp., Joint venture with Continental Tire	1988	500	200
Yokohama	Purchase of Mohawk	1989	1,150	150
Bridgestone	New plant in Warren County, TN (start-up in 1991)	1989	750	350
Totals			21,400	5,382

Source: Compiled by authors based on data from Japan Economic Institute, JETRO, U.S. International Trade Commission, and trade journal articles.
*$52 million purchase plus $70 million in additional investment.
†$240 million purchase plus $220 million in additional investment.
‡$2.6 billion purchase plus $1.5 billion in additional investment; includes an additional 40,000 managerial, clerical and service workers.

In 1986, Sumitomo Rubber bought Dunlop's U.S. tire operations for $350 million.[4] The company had previously acquired Dunlop's European operations.[5] Sumitomo has spent $100 million each to modernize two Dunlop plants and is building a $7 million tire test track near its Huntsville Alabama plant.[6] Yokohama Rubber recently purchased Mohawk Rubber, a small after-market producer.[7] Toyo Tire is involved in GTY Tire Corp., a $200 million joint venture with Yokohama and General Tire which is owned by the German rubber and tire company, Continental.

Japanese investment in the rubber and tire industry has been prompted by a number of factors. The first and most important was the internationalization and consolidation of the tire industry as the major firms began to acquire or merge with smaller competitors. Second, the growth of the automotive transplants created a new market for their tires. Third, the attractiveness of acquisitions was heightened by the increasing value of the yen relative to the dollar. As the United States experienced declining competitiveness during the late 1980s, the response was to decrease the value of the dollar thus effectively increasing the cost of Japanese-made products in U.S. markets. It also essentially devalued the immense number of dollars held by Japanese firms and investors. Japanese companies which were already cost-effective producers, responded in three ways. They began drastic cost-cutting efforts as a way to hold the line on prices in the U.S. and swallowed smaller profit margins. Perhaps most significantly, they began to purchase newly inexpensive U.S. assets. Ultimately, if a firm or industry cannot compete economically, neither exchange rate machinations nor government protectionism will be sufficient to reverse its economic slide, as U.S. firms and industries would discover. Purchase of U.S. firms also provided Japanese companies with the dealer networks required to sell not only tires built in the U.S., but also those imported from Japan.

Further, Japanese investment in the U.S. rubber and tire industry has been actively facilitated by U.S. producers who have attempted to bolster profits and dividends through diversification and disinvestment, and finally by selling their rubber and tire operations. In the mid-1980s, General Tire transformed itself into GenCorp, and then sold its General Tire unit to a West German tire company, Continental AG.[8] In 1986, Uniroyal and B.F. Goodrich merged; and in 1989 Uniroyal-Goodrich was acquired by Michelin.[9] With the purchase of Firestone and Dunlop by Japanese companies, Goodyear became the only remaining major U.S.-owned tire company.

Remaking the Factories

The U.S. rubber and tire industry was a quintessential fordist mass-production industry and its decline is in large part due to the slavish adherence to fordism even in the face of global change.[10] The industry was virtually defined by autocratic management, restrictive work rules, and a long legacy of extraordinarily adversarial labor-management relations. The union itself was literally borne from strikes during the 1930s, and this adversarial tradition continued into the early 1970s when nearly every major contract negotiation was punctuated by a major strike. The organization of work was highly specialized functionally, defined by an extensive and rigid system of job classifications that averaged between 100–150 per manu-facturing plant. Fordist organization permeated the very core of production orga-nization—the organization of technology and machines. A long-time Firestone executive explains:

> In the old days, when tire building was a manual operation, various machines would run better than others. People would want to have seniority rights on a par-ticular machine. There were arrangements whereby people could actually select jobs within a classification. So, if you had 125 classifications in a plant, essentially you might have double that many since some of the classifications in the tire assem-bly room have numerous tire machines. People essentially had seniority rights to each of those machines.[11]

Under Firestone's last CEO, John Nevin, the company moved from being pri-marily a tire manufacturer to being an operator of service centers, with little empha-sis on manufacturing tires.[12] In the process of manufacturing disinvestment, morale at the factories suffered, and little effort was put into maintaining production facil-ities. An American executive at Bridgestone-Firestone, who has spent most of his career with Firestone, explained it this way:

> In the period between the late sixties and the late seventies, Firestone fell on some very hard times. We had a company that was faced with converting from bias tires to radial tires during that decade. We saw our stock go from $40 some dollars a share down to $6 dollars a share—a company that was quite possibly on its way out. In 1979, John Nevin was brought in from the outside, from Zenith, to head up the company, and during the period from 1978 through 1988 we closed 14 of 19 North American tire plants. We bargained concessions at most other locations. We sold off a lot of the business, some very profitable pieces of business, in order to use the money as a cash cow to keep the rest of the company going. And in 1988, scarcely 10 years after he arrived on the scene, John Nevin sold the company that was worth six bucks a share for eighty bucks a share. So he in fact accomplished his objective of trying to turn the company around and attend to the interests of the stockholders. But you can imagine all of the discouragement and disenchantment that brings to everyone in the company, selling off assets, bargaining concessions with our unions. By the time the latter part of the eighties got here, everybody was pretty much in the dump. What's going on, how long can this last, and where will we go from here?[13]

As with the automobile and steel transplants, Japanese rubber and tire trans-plants have worked to implement the Japanese model of work and production orga-nization. Since most of the major Japanese tire and rubber investments are in existing U.S. plants and involve existing work forces, the implementation of Japa-nese work and production organization has involved significant restructuring. To accomplish this, both Bridgestone-Firestone and Dunlop have secured contracts with the union to facilitate such organizational restructuring.[14]

Bridgestone-Firestone has experienced the most significant restructuring in the rubber and tire industry. In fact, the organizational restructuring effort at Bridge-stone-Firestone is perhaps the most sweeping of the Japanese investments in heavy industry, involving existing Firestone plants with a long legacy of traditional labor-management relations and a new greenfield facility.

The starting point for this restructuring effort was Firestone's LaVergne Tennessee plant which Bridgestone acquired in 1983. At the time of the acquisition, morale, quality, and productivity at the plant were quite low. Labor relations were among the most strained in the industry. The LaVergne plant was opened in 1972 as a new greenfield facility. At the time, it was one of Firestone's most technogically advanced plants and its only radial tire production facility in the United States. The choice of a location in Tennessee was tied to Firestone's broader corporate strategy to avoid the union and reduce wages by locating new plants in the South. The management of the plant was extremely anti-union and autocratic and saw its mission as keeping the union out. The strategy ultimately backfired, as workers became increasingly angered at autocratic management practices; and the plant was ultimately unionized after a bitterly contested organizing drive.[15] According to both union and management officials the plant was among the worst in the industry, beset by a level of social conflict and disorganization that in the words of union officials "made it difficult to believe that tires could actually be produced there."[16] A former Firestone employee who went through the transition to Bridgestone ownership described the atmosphere at the plant before the Bridgestone acquisition:

> The management went through several campaigns to break the union. There were hard feelings. The management would hold meetings telling people they'd lose their jobs. Every two, three months there would be warnings here about money lost and threats about the plant closing. You didn't know if you would have a job in a couple months. We got a plant closure notice when Bridgestone was already in the picture. Morale was very bad.[17]

During the 1970s and early 1980s, the LaVergne plant experienced chronic disinvestment and was extremely under-maintained. The factory was dirty, grimy, and cluttered. Workers were not responsible for cleaning up their work environment—this was the responsibility of a separate janitorial staff—and the factory environment suffered. This general state of disrepair not only had negative effects on morale, but it also directly contributed to inferior product quality and high defect rates. For example, foreign materials, such as paper cups, nails, and cigarette butts would become embedded in tires. By February 1982, Firestone announced that it would either close or sell the LaVergne plant—less than ten years after it had opened. Two-third of the production workforce was laid off in March; and, by June, production was shut down two weeks of every month. By late 1982, daily production was down to 820 tires a day and the production workforce fell to just 235 workers with 441 workers on the layoff recall list.[18]

Upon acquiring the plant, Bridgestone management implemented a comprehensive technological and organizational restructuring program.[19] It set a goal of increasing production from 700 low-quality tires to 2,800 high-quality tires per day within four years. An initial basic step was for the workers to sweep the floors, remove the trash, and paint the walls. This resulted in an immediate increase in quality as there were fewer impurities to contaminate tire production; and it also improved worker morale. Next, new equipment was brought into the plant and a new preventive maintenance system was established. Roughly $70 million dollars was invested in new equipment. Some of this equipment was used to automate tire production and release operators to perform multiple tasks and monitor the production environment.

A new system of work organization was implemented and a new cooperative relationship forged with the union. Team-based work organization was introduced; job classifications were broadened and their numbers reduced; and greater flexibility in task assignment was introduced. Workers were involved in a new "total quality program" and in broader *kaizen* activities. An extensive training program was established covering quality control, group problem-solving, job skills and basic mathematical literacy. Between 1984 and 1987, more than 67,000 hours of training were provided, the great bulk devoted to training shop-floor workers. In addition, the plant initiated a series of special recognition awards, and bonuses were established to provide incentives for workers to participate in such activities (e.g. teamwork awards, suggestion awards, safety awards, and attendance bonuses). By 1987, 15 quality circles were in operation at the plant.

Management—especially middle and front line management—was the focus of sweeping changes to facilitate the shift from fordist to Japanese work and production organization. Eight managerial and supervisory levels were collapsed down to five. The ratio of indirect to direct labor fell from two-thirds (.64) in 1983 to less than half (.48) in 1987.[20] Managers and engineers were moved out of private offices and onto the factory floor. Other traditional management status symbols, such as reserved parking places, were also eliminated. Managers and supervisors were strongly encouraged not to wear ties on the production floor. Managers were put through a rigorous (re)training program in quality control, leadership, job instruction and development, industrial engineering, and basic mathematics. In 1983 alone, 256 managers received 4,910 hours of training. Perhaps most significantly, the management style was changed to include workers in decision-making and to harness their knowledge of the plant and production processes. Japanese executives and managers held detailed discussions with workers on changes in production and quality improvements. American managers were directed to obtain information about problems firsthand and to talk directly with the workers involved.[21] The role of workers was recast to consider them as part of the solution not the cause of the problems. In the words of a veteran Firestone engineer:

> Firestone only cared about numbers and money. . . . Even if you had a suggestion that could improve the operation, they wouldn't pay attention to you. You were workers and they were the bosses.[22]

The company then forged new relationships with its suppliers and established a supplier qualification program. Under this program, only materials that were thoroughly tested at the LaVergne facility and then sent to Bridgestone's testing center in Japan could qualify for use in actual production. The new management visited suppliers, conducted inspections, and issued guidelines for materials quality and inspection procedures.

The cumulative result of these changes was a dramatic turnaround in output, productivity, and quality. Output increased from a low of 16,400 tires per month under Firestone management in 1982 to 82,175 tires per month in 1987. Productivity increased by 74 percent over the same period. Productivity also increased significantly relative to the industry average. During the last year of Firestone's management, productivity at the LaVergne plant was 35 percentage points below the industry average; by 1986, it exceeded the industry average by 27.6 percent.[23] However, this was still only half the productivity rate of comparable Bridgestone plants in Japan. Productivity has increased since then, and Bridgestone-Firestone officials indicate that continued improvements in productivity are expected.[24]

Quality was another area of considerable improvement. Within a year, the quality of the tires produced increased by 30 percent.[25] Between 1983 and 1987, the plant experienced a 70 percent reduction in tires scrapped, from 5.1 percent to 1.86 percent. Production of tires with blemishes declined by 86 percent from 2.8 percent of all tires produced to 0.04 percent in 1986. The injury rate fell from 9.8 lost-time accidents per 100 workers in 1983 to just 2.2 per 100 in 1986.[26] As the plant went from operating in the red to turning a profit, all of the union employees that had been laid off before the acquisition were rehired; the last worker on the recall list was rehired in 1985. Between 1983 and 1987, the hourly work-force nearly tripled, increasing from 215 to 622 hourly workers. Average hourly wages increased from $11.30 in 1983 to $13.17 in 1987, and are currently just slightly below those paid by transplant automotive assembly plants.

As mentioned earlier, Bridgestone opened a new, $350 million tire plant at a nearby site in Warren County, Tennessee. In contrast to the general trend in the rubber and tire industry toward union-avoidance, Bridgestone recognized the union from the outset and negotiated an agreement which facilitated the transfer of Japanese style work and production organization.[27] Together, management and the union then participated in work-force recruitment and selection.

The Warren plant has just two job classifications and work is organized entirely on the basis of self-managing teams. Bridgestone management sees the Warren plant as a model to demonstrate and prove the feasibility of Japanese work organization—a vehicle to facilitate further transfer to the dozen or so traditional plants obtained in its purchase of Firestone. According to a Bridgestone-Firestone human resources executive:

> Our goal at Warren is to find the ways that we can grow the Warren process in a way that makes the Warren plant successful, makes the management of the company successful, makes the management of the union successful, and makes everybody happy.[28]

Bridgestone-Firestone is now actively working to transform production organization and labor-management relations at its remaining plants. It has forged a new cooperative relationship with the union, manifested in a new company-wide "Partnership for Involvement." The union is cooperating with such efforts because it sees both its own future and the future of its members tied to development of state-of-the-art, restructured, competitive plants. The union's cooperation in these restructuring efforts is also the result of Bridgestone's efforts to recognize the union, retain factory jobs, and rehire union workers. A high ranking union official contrasted Bridgestone's recent efforts to Firestone's traditional anti-union attitude:

> If you go back to 1976, Firestone was the lead company in our industry-wide negotiations, and that was our record for a strike on a major contract—144 days. With Bridgestone, we were able to get the contract just prior to the deadline. Bridgestone has been doing some things right. In the process, they have gotten the union's attention. We have felt for a long time that these companies have been overloaded on management, that the worker is carrying too much of a burden on his back. I know they are making adjustments and that management is concerned.[29]

Union officials also contrasted Bridgestone's cooperative efforts with French tiremaker Micheln's pursuit of a virulent anti-union policy in its U.S. factories.[30]

Still, there are obstacles to the restructuring of the remaining Firestone plants. A number of these plants have outmoded technology and are characterized by fordist organization and its concomitant highly adversarial labor relations between local management and local unions. However, both management and the union are working hard to overcome these obstacles and move toward the gradual restructuring of work and production organization along the lines of innovation-mediated production.

Sumitomo Rubber has also made an effort to restructure Dunlop's U.S. rubber and tire facilities. However, these efforts have not gone as far nor been as effective as those of Bridgestone-Firestone. To escape from the entrenched traditional job classifications and rigid work rules that characterized U.S. producers, Sumitomo instituted new, less restrictive work rules in return for job security provisions and a pledge to upgrade plant technology.[31] A similar restructuring process has occurred in the Dunlop facilities Sumitomo purchased in the United Kingdom. As part of the restructuring agreement, Dunlop's U.K. workers received lifetime employment commitments and profit-sharing. Eventually, production was increased by 40 percent with 30 percent less employees.[32]

However, the restructuring effort at Sumitomo's U.S. plants has been complicated by problems in labor-management relations. Sumitomo has not been as effective as Bridgestone-Firestone in forging a new cooperative relationship with the union, and this has to some extent stymied the restructuring effort. Sumitomo pressed the union for wage concessions during the 1990–91 downturn in the rubber and tire industry and, as a consequence, experienced a short strike at its Buffalo area plant in fall 1991.[33] The strike was resolved quickly and wages are now comparable to other plants organized by the United Rubber Workers union.

In contrast to both Sumitomo and Bridgestone-Firestone, GTY Corp.,—the joint venture between General Tire, Toyo Tire, and Yokohama Rubber—has thus far sent out the signal that it will not recognize the United Rubber Workers Union.[34] Since the plant opened in 1991, only time will tell how this will affect the immediate environment of work and production.

Inherited Locations

The Japanese rubber and tire transplants are far more dispersed geographically than are the Japanese automobile and steel producers in the United States. Figure 7.1 provides a national map of their location. In brief, only seven of the rubber and tire transplants are located in states which house assembly transplants: two in Ohio, two in Illinois, two in Tennessee, and one in Indiana. Three more are located in or close to the Midwest, two in western New York, and one in Iowa. The remainder are located in the Sunbelt, a significant share in states that are close to the automotive assembly transplants.

Bridgestone operates three plants in Midwestern locations: Decatur, Illinois (radial tires for cars and light trucks); Des Moines, Iowa (farm tractor and truck tires); and Noblesville, Indiana (air-spring suspensions for trucks); and 10 Sunbelt plants: Warren County (radial truck and bus tires) and LaVergne, Tennessee (radial car, truck and bus tires); Wilson (radial car tires) and Gastonia (industrial textiles), North Carolina; Russellville (inner tubes) and Prescott (rubber roofing materials), Arkansas; Oklahoma City, Oklahoma (radial tires for cars and light trucks), Lake Charles, Louisiana (synthetic rubber); Hopewell, Virginia (synthetic fibers); Orange, Texas (plastics and synthetic rubber); and Williamsburgh, Kentucky (air-spring suspensions for automobiles). It also operates two plants in Canada: Joliette, Quebec (radial tires for cars and light trucks) and Woodstock, Ontario (industrial

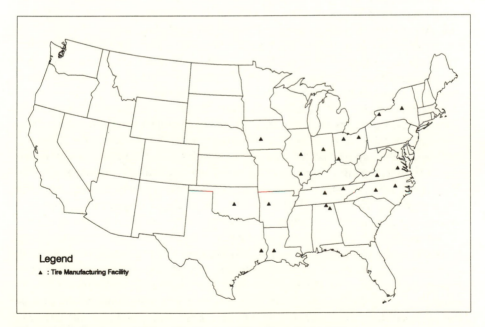

FIGURE 7.1. Japanese-Affiliated Rubber and Tire Plants in the U.S.
Source: Adapted from authors' database.

textiles and synthetic fibers). Sumitomo operates a former Dunlop cord plant in Utica, New York, a belted tire plant in Buffalo, and a radial tire plant in Huntsville, Alabama. Yokohama owns Mohawk's main plant in Salem, Virginia; Mohawk's Tread Rubber subsidiary in Guntersville, Alabama; and the SAS Rubber subsidiary in Plainsville, Ohio.[35]

The reason for this dispersed location pattern is that the Japanese inherited the dispersed geography of the U.S. companies they purchased. In the 1960s and 1970s, U.S. producers had embarked upon a strategy of closing unionized midwestern plants and opening new plants in the Sunbelt to disperse manufacturing, move to "better labor climates," and "union free" environments.[36] Interestingly, the strategy failed as the unions were able to organize the southern plants. Since 1973, American rubber companies have closed more than 30 plants, the large majority of them in Ohio and the Midwest, and expanded radial tire production in new factories in the Sunbelt and the Third World. In 1980 alone, Firestone closed long-standing plants in Akron, Dayton, and Barberton, Ohio; Pottstown, Pennsylvania; and Los Angeles and Salinas, California.[37] In the ten year period between 1977 and 1987, the rubber and tire industry lost 48,600 jobs (42.6%) from 114,000 to 65,400; manufacturing employment declined by 35,700 jobs (40.4%) from 88,300 to 52,600.[38] From 1967 to 1984, 17 new plants were built in the United States and all but one were in the South.[39] By 1982, there was not a single tire plant operating in Akron, Ohio—once the self-proclaimed "tire capital of the world."[40] By 1986, roughly three-quarters of U.S. tire capacity was in the South.

The location of Japanese tire producers is a product of the broader entry strategy of Japanese firms. The rubber and tire industry differs from other basic input industries, such as steel, in that the market includes both original equipment and a large after-market. While proximity is a merit for supplying automotive assemblers, tire producers require access to long-standing dealer networks to tap the after-market fully. Bridgestone's purchase of Firestone, for example, gave Bridgestone-Firestone the ability to sell tires through Firestone's 1,550 auto-care stores.

The major factor in Bridgestone's decision to move to the United States was the "need to find new markets."[41] The major factor in site selection was purchase of an existing firm, followed by proximity to transportation, high-quality labor, a strong local work ethic, labor costs, and government subsidies of which industrial development bonds, road links, and tax abatements were seen to be most important. For Bridgestone a nonunion environment was not important to its locational calculus. The company makes just-in-time deliveries to its major customers and has worked closely with its suppliers to institute just-in-time relations.[42]

Although the dispersed location of tire plants is not ideally suited to just-in-time production, plant concentrations in Illinois, Indiana, and western New York as well as the upper South provide sufficient proximity to the automotive transplants. For example, Bridgestone's LaVergne plant is located less than 10 miles from Nissan's assembly facility in Smyrna, Tennessee.[43] Both Sumitomo-Dunlop and Bridgestone-Firestone supply the automotive transplants.[44] Interestingly, while only two transplants use tires with the Bridgestone label, four transplants use Firestone tires.[45] Moreover, tires are a relatively standard product that can be transported over longer distances and stored in larger inventory lots than other production inputs. Also, Bridgestone is beefing up Firestone's R&D capacity in Akron. However, in keeping with the tendency of Japanese firms to locate their headquarters close to production facilities, Bridgestone announced in June 1991 that it would move its headquarters to Nashville.[46] The new GTY joint venture has located its new plant in the industrial heartland community of Mount Vernon, Illinois.

By 1991, the global tire industry was mired in recession and most companies were either losing money or barely breaking even. The tire transplants faced serious problems—perhaps the most serious of any of the heavy industrial transplants. In March 1991, Bridgestone's losses in the United States led to layoffs of over 425 employees at two plants—165 blue-collar and 20 white-collar workers at its Decatur, Illinois, plant, which employs 1,800 people, and 160 blue-collar, 25 white-collar, and 55 contractor employees at its Oklahoma City plant, which employs over 1,500.[47] However, by May 1991, Bridgestone announced that it would invest another $1.4 billion to secure U.S. operations by both upgrading plant and production technology and reducing interest payments on existing debt.[48] Japanese tire producers appear willing to make major investments to bolster their market presence in the United States, even in the face of an economic downturn.

Industrial Machines, Capital Goods, and Other Major Inputs

Massive Japanese investment in the heavy manufacturing industries of automobile, steel, and rubber has created demand for an incredible number of inputs. These sectors include important input industries such as glass, and producer goods such as machine tools, industrial robotics, and assembly-line equipment and machinery.

In 1985, Japan's leading glassmaker, Asahi Glass, in a joint venture with PPG, established AP Technoglass. In October 1990, PPG withdrew from the joint venture and sold its stake to Asahi Glass.[36] AP Technoglass has plants in Ohio and Kentucky, which cut and prepare glass supplied by PPG for Honda and Toyota.[37] The AP Technoglass plant in Ohio delivers automotive glass to a Honda subsidiary, Bellemar Parts, twice a day. Bellemar, which is located one mile from the Honda plant, applies a rubber gasket to the windshield and makes just-in-time deliveries to Honda every two hours. In March 1989, Nippon Sheet Glass, Japan's second largest producer of automobile glass, purchased a 20 percent share of Libbey-Owens-Ford for $235 million from its British owner Pilkington.[51] Finally, in November 1989 Japan's Central Glass Company announced a $100 million joint venture with Ford Motor Company to construct a glass fabrication facility in the United States.[52] Whether a Japanese company will build a major glassmaking facility in the United States remains an open question. However, in an interview in 1988, AP Technoglass managers expressed concern over the low quality glass provided by an American supplier and the company's lack of familiarity with just-in-time delivery.

Increasingly, Japanese producers of automotive-related plastics are relocating to, or acquiring automobile plastic firms in, the United States, especially the Midwest. Sumitomo Chemical has formed a joint venture with an Ohio firm to produce automotive plastics.[53] Japanese companies are also investing heavily in automotive-related chemicals. In 1989, B.F. Goodrich sold its elastomer business (which employed 300 workers) to Zeon Chemicals Inc., a subsidiary of Nippon Zeon.[54]

Japanese capital goods and equipment producers have opened plants to supply the assembly-line equipment, production equipment, and machine tools used by the transplants. A major Japanese conveyor belt company, Tsubakimoto, has opened plants in Ohio, Illinois, Tennessee, and Vermont. Two Japanese manufacturers of automotive paint systems have opened American plants, one in Ohio and the other in Kentucky virtually next to the site of Toyota's Georgetown plant.[55] One of these, TKS Industrial Co. USA, has installed nearly $45 million in paint equipment in Nissan's Smyrna, Tennessee, plant.[56] Komatsu, the Japanese forklift manufacturer, has opened a U.S. plant to supply the growing base of transplant manufacturers. Toyota Industrial Equipment Mfg., Inc., operates a factory in Columbus, Indiana, which will produce 10,000 forklifts a year for the U.S. market.[57] Hitachi Zosen makes metal stamping presses in Chicago and Houston.

In total, there are now 16 Japanese machine tool companies in the United States: five in Illinois, three in Michigan, two in New York, two in Texas, and one each in Ohio, Kentucky, and North Carolina. The GM-Fanuc plant in Michigan is the largest robotics producer in the United States and one of the largest in the world. This plant is an extremely software-intensive operation. GM-Fanuc imports most of its hardware from Japan and develops the applications software at its Michigan factory.[58] Fanuc Ltd. has a 40 percent stake in Moore Special Tool of Bridgeport, Connecticut, and is focusing on developing new robotic paint systems for the Japanese automotive transplants. The recent sale of Cincinnati Milacron's robot business to the Swiss-Swedish multinational Asea Brown Boveri AG leaves the great bulk of U.S. robot production in the hands of foreign, mainly Japanese, companies.[59] As mentioned earlier, Yamazaki Mazak, a major Japanese machine tool company, produces numerically controlled lathes and machining centers in Florence, Kentucky, and is opening a major R&D center in Cincinnati. Toyoda Machinery has plants in Arlington Heights, Illinois; and Howell and Wixon, Michigan (outside Detroit). Hitachi Seiki produces numerically controlled lathes and machining centers in Congers, New York, and Huntsville, Alabama. Nippon Sanso, an important Japanese industrial gas supplier, recently acquired a U.S. firm, K.N. Aronson, of Arcade, New York, which makes welding positioners.[60]

Capital goods and heavy equipment manufacturers are generally located in close proximity to their main customers—the automobile assemblers and their suppliers—to facilitate close interaction in the development, installation, and maintenance of sophisticated machine tools. Although the base of Japanese capital goods producers and machine tool manufacturers in the United States is growing, it is not yet sufficiently established to supply all of the equipment needs of transplant manufacturers.

The final cogs in the transplant heavy industrial complex are the Japanese industrial construction companies that have opened U.S. subsidiaries to construct transplant facilities.[61] Thus far the Kajima Corporation's U.S. subsidiary has built the Mazda plant in Flat Rock, Michigan, and the Diamond-Star and Subaru-Isuzu plants as well as a number of supplier facilities such as Ogihara in Michigan.[62] Kajima recently acquired a $22 million, 30 percent stake in the second-ranked U.S. architectural design and engineering firm, Helmuth Obata and Kassabaum.[63] Other Japanese industrial construction firms, Kumagai, Shimizu, Takenaka, Shuwa, Hazama, and Haseco, have also established American branches.[64] Shimizu, which specializes in high-technology production facilities, was the main contractor for one of IBM's new state-of-the-art semiconductor production facilities (see Chapter 8).

Rebuilding the Rustbelt

Japanese investment in the automobile, steel, rubber, and related industries is resulting in a highly integrated heavy industrial complex in the United States. This is, in effect, rebuilding the rustbelt industries and rustbelt region that had been abandoned by American producers. At the regional level, Japanese investments are highly concentrated in the rustbelt region. Slightly more than half (51.3%, 218 of 425) of these transplants are in the Midwest: Ohio (80), Michigan (51), Indiana (53), and Illinois (34). Another 20 percent are in the adjacent states of Kentucky (48) and Tennessee (39), which have long been centers of industrial production. Taken together, the six states that are home to major Japanese automobile assembly transplants account for nearly three-quarters (71.8%, 305 of 425) of the automobile, steel, and rubber transplants. Some differences do exist among sectors with steel in the industrial Midwest, automobile assembly in the lower Midwest and upper South, and rubber and tire production in the Sunbelt.

There is a tendency for transplants to concentrate in greenfield locations— either in rural, exurban locations or in small communities at the fringes of metropolitan centers, although a significant number are located in urban locations as well. The pattern here also differs by sector, with those sectors that have high levels of new plant construction (e.g., automobile assembly, automobile parts supplirs, and steel service centers) most concentrated in greenfield locations. While greenfield locations provide a blank slate from which to implement Japanese production organization, the urban transplants have implemented restructuring strategies to bring their environments into line with the requirements of Japanese production organization.

Differences of opinion exist regarding the overall employment impact of the Japanese transplants. A significant debate has arisen regarding the number of jobs gained versus the number of American jobs lost from the transplants. Various estimates have been advanced. In 1988, the U.S. General Accounting Office (GAO) estimated that the automotive transplants would create 112,000 new jobs and displace 156,000 jobs between 1985 and 1990, resulting in a net loss of roughly 44,000 jobs.[65] In a follow-up study for 1989, the GAO estimated that Japanese automobile-related production in the United States provided 66,000 jobs but displaced 77,000 others, resulting in a net loss of 11,000 jobs.[66] A UAW study estimated a net loss of between 74,000 and 194,000 jobs over the same period.[67]

The numbers generated in these assessments—as with all assessments—depend upon a set of underlying assumptions and premises. These assessments, for example, do not take into account that a number of transplants have invested in existing U.S. plant sites and thus continue to employ workers already in the existing pool of American production workers. In other instances, Japanese investment provides U.S. producers access to the state-of-the-art production technology and organizational innovations and thus prevent job loss that would have likely occurred in the absence of Japanese participation. Of course, in many cases, U.S. firms suffering from their own internal, organizational weaknesses are incapable of transforming themselves sufficiently to take advantage of such access.

Moreover, the entire issue of "displacement" is open to question. Perhaps a more appropriate way to frame the question is as a choice between domestic job loss as a consequence of increased import penetration (and continued U.S. manufacturing firms' investments off-shore) versus job gain/retention from domestic transplant production. Transplant production has clearly offset import penetration and in so doing had a significant positive impact on job creation/retention. A February 1991 report in *Ward's Auto World* indicated that in 1986, imports (Japanese and European) accounted for 28.3 percent of the total U.S. vehicle sales, and foreign-owned production in the U.S. was only 4.7 percent of total sales. By 1990, imports had decreased to 25.8 percent, while the transplant production accounted for 15.2 percent. Japanese carmakers are currently holding back exports to protect their U.S. production facilities.[68] This is certainly retaining jobs in the United States.

Our own estimate is that the transplants have created or preserved roughly 110,000 direct jobs, excluding any indirect multiplier effects (Table 7.2). While this is certainly not sufficient to compensate for the hundreds of thousands of jobs lost through U.S. plant closures, it has at a minimum mitigated the decline of the industrial Midwest and may in fact be a net positive development in terms of job generation and retention. By almost any standard, the transplants have pumped much-needed investment into U.S. manufacturing. In addition, the transplants appear to have a neutral to slightly positive effect on wages, offering wages and salaries that are similar to those offered by U.S. producers.[69]

Indeed, transplant investment and the state-of-the-art manufacturing capacity it has put in place appears to be at least partly responsible for the more general rebound in U.S. manufacturing productivity identified by a growing number of

TABLE 7.2.   Japanese Investment and Employment in U.S. Heavy
Industry

Industry	Employment	Investment (millions of dollars)
Automobile assembly	30,080	8,950
Automobile parts	31,860	5,380
Steel	27,418	6,910
Rubber and tires	21,400	5,382
Total	110,758	26,622

Source: Compiled by authors from various sources.

studies.[70] A number of economists interpret rising U.S. productivity as contradicting the "deindustrialization thesis." However, the manufacturing productivity turnaround may well be the result of a combination of the closing of older plant and equipment, which resulted from deindustrialization, and Japanese investment in the creation of new, highly productive plant and equipment—a process of Japanese-led reindustrialization in the face of American deindustrialization. Still, given the limits of the available aggregate data, it is impossible to gauge precisely the exact contribution of transplant production to the more general manufacturing revival.

The Myth of the Screwdriver Factory

It is frequently argued that the automotive transplants are branch operations that assemble cars from "knocked-down" kits imported from Japan and thus have a minimal impact on local and regional economic development. One line of argument, referred to as the "screwdriver" hypothesis, is that Japanese plants have only moved standard, low–value-added operations to the United States, keeping higher value-added and more sophisticated activities in Japan. The available evidence contradicts the screwdriver hypothesis. As we have already seen, the automotive assemblers—Honda, Nissan, Toyota, and Mazda—already produce high value-added components like engines and transmissions in the United States, and both Diamond-Star and SIA plan to do so in the future according to a recent report, Nissan estimated its spending on U.S. parts and materials in 1991 to be $1.5 billion; and Toyota estimated its 1991 purchase of U.S.-made parts to be $2.83 billion.[71] Finally, as we showed in Chapters 4 and 5, both assemblers and major suppliers are moving R&D activities to this country.

A related issue revolves around the "domestic content" of the transplants. It is commonly asserted that the transplants import more than half of their parts from Japan. The domestic content debate has now become a major political debate. A recent University of Michigan study paid for by the U.S. auto parts industry claims that only 62 percent of Honda Accord made in Ohio is U.S. content, but only 16 percent is purchased from U.S. parts suppliers. As Table 7.3 shows, the 1990 data indicate that domestic content has risen to between 65 percent and 75 percent for most transplant auto assembly plants. These content estimates have been challenged on the grounds that they are unsubstantiated estimates provided by the companies. This, however, is the same procedure used by Big Three automakers. Our supplier survey indicates that, as of 1988, domestic content for transplant suppliers was 64 percent. The rise in domestic procurement is attributable to three factors: (1) the movement of engine and transmission facilities to the United States, (2) the influx of Japanese automotive component suppliers, steel companies, and rubber plants, and (3) recent efforts by the transplants to integrate U.S. suppliers.

The UAW estimates lower domestic content using the alternative measure of foreign merchandise imports. It finds foreign merchandise imports in 1988 to comprise 61 percent of total merchandise at Mazda and 39 percent at Honda.[72] However, foreign merchandise imports and domestic content are not the same thing.

TABLE 7.3. Domestic Content for Major Japanese Vehicles Produced in the United
States, 1990

Vehicle	Company	Transplant Facility	Domestic Content (%)
Accord	Honda	Marysville, OH	75.0
Civic	Honda	East Liberty, OH	72.0
Corolla	Toyota	NUMMI, Fremont, CA	75.0
Camry	Toyota	Georgetown, KY	65.0
Sentra	Nissan	Smyrna, TN	74.6
Nissan pickup	Nissan	Smyrna, TN	57.0
626	Mazda	Flat Rock, MI	65–70
MX-6	Mazda	Flat Rock, MI	65–70
Probe	Mazda (Ford)	Flat Rock, MI	65–70
Eclipse	Mitsubishi	Diamond-Star, Normal, IL	60.0
Mirage	Mitsubishi	Diamond-Star, Normal, IL	60.0
Rodeo	Isuzu	SIA, Lafayette, IN	73.0
Isuzu pickup	Isuzu	SIA, Lafayette, IN	65.0
Legacy	Subaru	SIA, Lafayette, IN	53.0

Source: *Automotive News* (4 March, 1991), p. 19.

Domestic content refers to the direct material inputs such as steel, rubber, automotive parts, engines, and transmissions that are used in the manufacture and
assembly of automobiles. Foreign merchandise imports include expensive capital
equipment in the form of heavy machinery, machine tools, conveyor belts, and the
assembly line itself. Mazda's 61 percent foreign merchandise imports (reported in
the UAW study) thus reflects the value of Japanese equipment imported during the
plant's construction and start-up in 1987–88. Although the transplants obtain a
large share of dedicated capital equipment from Japan, the source of the bulk of in-
process materials is the United States. Purchasing officials at the one automotive
assembly transplant explained the difference this way:

> Most of the equipment that we purchased in Japan was presses and things of that
> sort. Basically, when we purchased this equipment, the building wasn't even here.
> The main start-up pieces were purchased in Japan to be shipped over here, because
> they had to be made way before the plant started up. Now once the plant is up and
> going, all the conveyers and all the other machines, the robots, and all that stuff are
> bought right here.[73]

Foreign merchandise imports should begin to decline as transplant producers complete initial start-up and makers of capital equipment open more U.S. factories.

Understanding the Transplant Complex

How do we understand the new Japanese industrial complex in and around the
rustbelt, especially in light of the deindustrialization by American corporations?
Traditional approaches to location theory and regional development provide inad-

equate explanations for the transplant complex since they neglect the connection between production organization and spatial outcomes.[74] Location theory suggests that firms make location decisions to maximize profits. According to most location theory models, firms maximize profits by minimizing labor costs, by lowering costs of transportation and materials, and/or by avoiding unions. Indeed, traditional location theory would have predicted the dispersal of Japanese manufacturing investments in the United States, following the pattern set by American manufacturers.

The spatial division of labor approach suggests that businesses locate different aspects of their production activity (e.g., simple manufacturing, complex manufacturing, assembly, R&D, and administration) according to the availability and cost of labor.[75] Under both this approach and traditional location theory, companies essentially scan the environment and choose the most efficient or low-cost location. Interestingly, this entire genre of geographic theory shares the same strong environmental determinism that permeates the organization theory and industrial sociology literatures discussed earlier. Japanese direct manufacturing investment in U.S. heavy industry contradicts the spatial division of labor view because both simple and complex manufacturing and assembly have been co-located, resulting in the creation of an integrated transplant production complex.

The rise of the transplant production complex suggests that changes in the organization of production alter spatial outcomes and geographic organization in fundamental respects. This can be explained in two ways. On the one hand, it suggests that the failure of existing models of location and regional development to predict and/or explain the transplant complex may not lie with those models themselves, but with the way they have been employed. In other words, the problem lies in attempts to generalize from the behavior of fordist firms under those models. According to this logic, it might be possible to use the same models to explain the locational behavior of the transplants. Looked at in these terms, the locational choices of the transplants could be understood as the profit-maximizing behavior of individual firms, which, given their underlying organization of production, orient their location decisions around high-quality and stable labor pools, and the creation of external agglomeration economies of supply and production.

On the other hand, this very fact highlights the limits of those models. The first and most basic problem revolves around the fact that these models treat changes in production organization as exogenous factors that can simply be inserted into prevailing locational models. The second problem lies in the emphasis on individual location decisions, as opposed to the underlying structural factors that channel and orient those decisions. The third flaw is the assumption that companies passively select locations and then adapt to the environment. This neglects the crucial fact that economic organizations may have the resources and ability to alter and change their locational environments in significant ways.

A more powerful and dynamic theory of spatial organization and regional development begins with the notion that production organization is *endogenous* to the process of regional and spatial change, not an exogenous factor operating outside the system. Framed as such, production organization becomes an underlying dynamic force driving spatial organization and regional development—one that structures and channels the locational decisions of individual firms. Underlying and orienting the individual decisions of the transplants is the locational logic supplied by the Japanese model of production organization itself. The Japanese production system is characterized by tight functional integration both outside and inside the plant—among R&D, manufacturing, and suppliers. At Honda's Sayama, Japan, plant, for example, suppliers literally drive their trucks inside the plant to deliver parts directly to work stations on the assembly line.[76] The glue that holds the complex together is more than the sum of the parts—the spatial and functional integration required for innovation-mediated production.

Moreover, such an approach recognizes the ability of large, economic organizations (e.g., corporations) to act on and effectively alter their environment in light of their needs. This is similar to what Richard Walker refers to as "geographic industrialization" whereby firms create the conditions required for their existence.[77] As we have seen, the transplant production complex did not just happen; rather, it was actively constructed by large economic organizations acting on their immediate environment to bring it into conformance with their needs.[78] In this sense, the actions of transplant companies, especially automobile assemblers, are part of an ongoing and dynamic process of industrial complex formation and "region building." The underlying organization of production thus provides a set of rather firm, but constantly evolving, parameters within which economic organizations act to construct and/or transform their spatial environment. This, in turn, creates a tension that, in large measure, drives the process of regional development.

Basically, Japanese manufacturing investment is creating a Japanese-style production complex in the United States by establishing a new landscape of steel-rubber-automobile production. This complex is integrated across the entire production chain, providing the steel, automotive parts, tires, glass, and even some of the machines used to manufacture automobiles. The complex itself is the source of powerful production efficiencies and competitive advantage.

The high degree of functional and spatial integration within the transplant complex can be illustrated by way of an example. Mazda's Flat Rock, Michigan, assembly plant receives automobile fenders, roofs, and doors on a just-in-time basis from a transplant automotive supplier about an hour west of Detroit. These parts are stamped by two large stamping presses made by a Michigan branch of Hitachi Zosen. The steel blanks come from ProCoil, the Marubeni-National Steel joint venture, located just outside Detroit. ProCoil in turn gets its steel from the National Steel-NKK Great Lakes Works in nearby Ecorse, Michigan.[66] The company also supplies the Canadian transplants—the CAMI plant in Ontario, Diamond-Star in Illinois, and Honda in Ohio, and has recently begun supplying Ford and Lincoln plants in the immediate area.

Battle Creek, Michigan: Reindustrialization of a Rustbelt Town

Battle Creek, Michigan, provides a striking illustration of the role of Japanese manufacturing investment in rustbelt reindustrialization.[67] The initial industrialization and growth of Battle Creek occurred in the early twentieth century. The city developed an extensive agglomeration of companies in the cereal, food processing, and early "health-food" industries, with corporations such as Kellogg, Quaker Oats, C.W. Post, and it rapidly became the nation's center for cereal production. At one time, Battle Creek was home to 33 cereal companies, a number that has shrunk via consolidation to three. The cereal and food-processing industry in turn attracted food-processing-equipment manufacturers such as Johnson Automatic Sealer Co., which developed filling, weighing, and carton lining machinery for the food industry. Battle Creek also developed a significant farm machinery sector during the same period to serve outlying agricultural producers and a number of medical and hospital equipment manufacturers to serve the Battle Creek Sanitarium. The rise of Michigan as a center for automotive production helped to stimulate the growth of a local automotive parts industry. Local industrialization and economic development was given a push during World War I when the federal government established a major military base, Camp Custer, and the subsequent expansion of the base during World War II. During the immediate postwar years, Battle Creek enjoyed a strong and diversified local economic base. Companies often moved between various activities, contributing to the local economy's vitality. One local company, Eaton, for example, shifted much of its production from agricultural equipment in the early twentieth century to defense equipment during the war years and postwar period and to automotive valves later on.

During the 1960s, 1970s, and early 1980s, Battle Creek was hit by a series of economic shocks. In 1963, the government closed the since renamed Fort Custer, eliminating thousands of jobs and causing the closing of a host of defense-related businesses. Moreover, the manufacturing shakeout and deindustrialization crisis of the mid-1970s through early 1980s had a calamitous effect on the local economy. Automobile parts and farm machinery factories closed down, and by the early 1980s, unemployment was over 20 percent. Eaton, for example, which initially survived by shifting from defense production to automotive supply, ultimately closed its Battle Creek factory during the 1983–84 recession.

Virtually at the same time that American producers were closing plants and abandoning the city, Japanese producers began constructing facilities in Battle Creek. Racked by plant closures and skyrocketing unemployment in the late 1970s and early 1980s, Battle Creek is currently home to roughly a dozen Japanese automotive parts companies and other manufacturing firms that employ approximately 2,000 workers. In fact, it now has the single largest concentration of transplant automotive parts producers in the United States. Somewhat ironically, this investment is completely concentrated on the site of the old military base, which has been converted into the Fort Custer Industrial Park. Figure 7.2 is a map of the industrial park, which shows the close proximity of these transplant companies.

Anchoring this Japanese manufacturing complex is a $400 million Nippondenso factory that produces air conditioners, heaters, condensers, and electrical parts for Toyota, Mazda, Honda, Mitsubishi, SIA, and the American Big Three. In close proximity are three related suppliers that supply Nippondenso on a just-in-time basis. Koyo Metals is a Nippondenso supplier of specialty metals. The company is Japan's largest broker of specialty metals, but is still a very small manufacturer in Nagoya, with very little experience in the United States. Tokai Rika makes

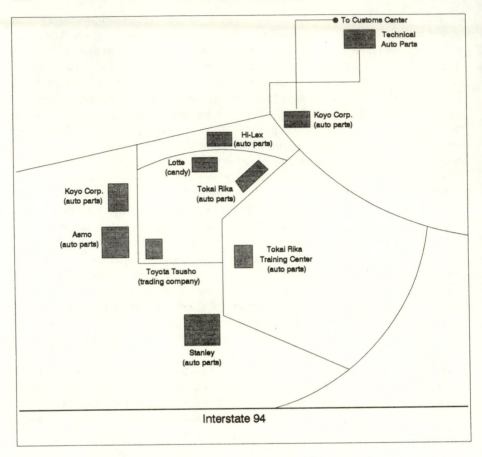

FIGURE 7.2. Battle Creek's Japanese Production Complex
Note: Japanese-Affiliated Firms Located in the Fort Custer Industrial Park.
Source: Authors' compilation.

electronic switches for Nippondenso, is a fellow member of the Toyota group, and is a fairly large Japanese company in its own right. In fact, Nippondenso recommended Battle Creek as a site for Tokai Rika. Toyota Tsusho, the Toyota-related trading company, has a warehousing distribution operation in Battle Creek to supply Nippondenso.

Rounding out the complex are a number of other Japanese firms. Hi-Lex (the former Nippon Cable Company) was the first Japanese company to establish a branch in Battle Creek. It opened its plant in 1978 to supply cables for International Harvester, and currently produces control cables for cars (Honda), boats, and motorcycles. I.I. Stanley is a joint venture of two Honda group companies that supply automotive lighting equipment to Honda. Technical Auto Parts makes suspension systems for Honda and Ford.

Battle Creek's rise as a center for transplant manufacturing can be attributed to a number of factors. The city has a unique "labor pocket," different in a number of important respects from traditional Michigan automotive industry communities.[81] Unlike downstate Michigan communities, Battle Creek has retained a strong agricultural base alongside heavy industry. According to a local official,

> During the early part of the twentieth century, Battle Creek remained heavily dependent upon agriculture with people farming during the day and repairing their farm equipment at night. What you had was kind of a work ethic growing up with an ability to handle equipment machinery, work around it. One hundred years later you have people working around machinery and equipment during the day and farming at night.[82]

As we have already seen, a number of Japanese transplants view a "farm work ethic" as a locational advantage. In addition, the labor relations climate of Battle Creek has traditionally been distinguished by a high degree of corporate "paternalism" and labor accommodation, especially in the food-processing sector, and it differs significantly from the adversarial nature of labor relations in the automobile-producing areas of Michigan (e.g., Detroit and its environs).

Further, the city developed an aggressive set of policies and programs designed to attract foreign, especially Japanese, manufacturing investment. In the early 1970s, Battle Creek began by converting the abandoned Camp Custer military base into an industrial park so as to attract foreign manufacturers. It acquired the rights to the land, created a new nonprofit agency—Battle Creek Unlimited—to manage it, established a foreign trade zone and inland port, and became one of the first American cities to market itself in Japan working through the state of Michigan's office in Tokyo. James Hettinger, a community leader and executive director of Battle Creek Unlimited, summarized the important elements of this process:

> You look back at it and you'd think it was just a stroke of brilliance. But the city acquired 1,800 acres in 1968 and 1,200 acres in 1972 with a 20-year land contract. . . . Mayor Bridges said instead of selling those bargain basement rates and inviting in one foundry after another, backing them all up against one another, let's carefully plan this thing. So he went out and raised money from a number of local foundations and, interestingly enough, from the area building trades. The city raised about three-quarters of a million dollars to bring in a nationally known planning firm to look at the whole thing and lay it out for a 20-year period. One of the recommendations was that the development of this park is going to require an organization off on its own, free of the political thicket and all of these other complications that come up when a city tries to do something. So they said create an independent, nonprofit, private corporation, give it the resources it needs to do the job, and then leave it alone. The second thing they said was that many of the companies created in postwar Europe and Asia were reaching a level of maturity where they would begin to seek overseas markets and start to go international. . . . Battle Creek became the first Michigan city to venture overseas. And the first trip occurred in 1974. . . . Another recommendation was that the availability of port facilities tends to act as a magnet for foreign investment. So an act of Congress designated Battle Creek as an inland U.S. customs port of entry. They also said create a duty-free area, a foreign trade zone. There are reasons why companies do things off-shore, why they're induced to do things off-shore. A duty-free designation would

remove some of those reasons and entice them to do things in the United States.
So in 1978, we became a foreign trade zone area.[70]

Generally speaking, Battle Creek has developed a successful strategy of providing support services and infrastructure that enhance the potential for economic and
industrial development instead of industrial subsidies and incentives. Recently, for
example, the Battle Creek public school system created a Japanese-language school.
The city also formed the Council for Employment Needs and Training, or CENT,
to recruit, screen, and train workers for local businesses. The State of Michigan and
the Kellogg Foundation provided $1 million each to build a new training center for
the industrial park. Nippondenso's location was used to attract a $6.5 million
Urban Development Action Grant to extend infrastructure of the industrial park
out to contiguous, undeveloped land.

A key element of this strategy has been ongoing, nonfinancial support. Battle
Creek Unlimited plays a very important role here by providing a single point of
contact for Japanese firms and simplifying the coordination and provision of economic development services. At times, the organization has actively assisted Japanese manufacturers become acclimated to the American environment and
overcome start-up problems. According to James Hettinger, Battle Creek Unlimited made a "name for itself" with Japanese corporations when it helped Hi-Lex,
the original Japanese company in Battle Creek, locate and recruit a key executive.

> They had taken a very distinguished Japanese executive from their ranks and
> brought him over here. He really had very little knowledge, little exposure to the
> American market, and the results of that were fairly predictable. They didn't do
> well at all. They even contemplated closing, after several unionization attempts,
> which they did manage to win. They came very close to abandoning their opera-
> tion. In a last-ditch strategy, our State Senator at the time, he and I, visited them in
> Japan. We said, "Before you really give it up, you got this major customer that
> wants to buy from you. You now got Honda settling in Ohio and you're part of
> their group. Do one last thing. Give it about three more years. Find a top-notch
> American executive to command. Somebody who has knowledge of the market."
> International Harvester, National Bank of Detroit, and Battle Creek Unlimited
> began to look for an individual. National Bank of Detroit found him in Detroit. He
> came out, and it was amazing; within 14 months they began to show a profit. First
> thing he did was cut out most of the administrative bureaucracy, which had gotten
> very fat. Basically they were shielding this Japanese executive from the truth of
> things. In the process of making themselves look good, they did not tell him about
> problems. So the American got rid of all these guys and pretty much assumed per-
> sonal control of just about everything for a while, purchasing, personnel.[84]

City government also provides various types of support for Japanese manufacturers. For example, during Nippondenso's construction phase, the company temporarily transferred more than 100 Japanese engineers to Battle Creek. The city
government handed out ID cards to each one of the engineers, and set up a central
phone number to reach a Japanese-English interpreter to help with emergencies.

Most of the engineers were housed with Battle Creek families in order to provide an American living experience.

Japanese investment has set in motion a dramatic economic turnaround in Battle Creek. The city in turn has attracted a high degree of Japanese investment without resorting to the huge industrial incentives that have been used to lure large assembly plants like Toyota in Kentucky or Subaru-Isuzu in Indiana (see Chapter 9). In this regard, the Battle Creek strategy is a far better guide for economic development policy because it focuses on creating and strengthening assets. These assets have a public goods character that can be used to attract more firms or even provide incentives to local corporations and entrepreneurs.

Maximizing Local and Regional Benefits

Policymakers and economic development planners can use a variety of initiatives to enhance the benefits of transplant investment. An obvious one is to encourage more U.S.-owned firms to tap into the transplant market. American-owned companies can supply the transplants, but only if they are willing to improve radically their quality standards and delivery practices and bring their production methodology into line with the Japanese model. To do so, American corporations will also have to rearrange drastically their underlying production organization and labor-management relations. A growing number of U.S.-owned suppliers are successfully making this transition.

As an example, Johnson Controls Inc., a leading U.S. automotive supplier, has plants in Kentucky, Ohio, Indiana, Tennessee, and California that supply the Japanese transplants. Its Georgetown, Kentucky, operation is the sole source supplier of auto seats to Toyota's assembly plant. The Johnson Controls plant in Kentucky initially adopted a "quasi-Japanese" system in the early 1980s and started working closely with Toyota to implement a full-blown version of the "Toyota Production System," including work teams, worker quality control, and just-in-time production in 1986. The plant receives seat covers and foam from other Johnson plants in Harrodsburg, Kentucky, and Greenfield, Ohio, three times a day and delivers complete seat subassemblies to Toyota every hour. Toyota in turn supplies the plastic parts for these seats, acting as both supplier and customer to Johnson Controls.[85] According to a Johnson Controls executive,

> We are now a true just-in-time facility. We receive a broadcast from Toyota's mainframe to our plant computer and kanban cards are printed out here [on the shop floor] for each seat in each car. Four hours later the seat gets to Toyota. . . . Right now we are making gray and brown seats for gray and brown Camrys that are going down Toyota's assembly line.[86]

Government programs can be used to help local producers gain access to the transplant market. Policymakers and planners, especially in states with large Japanese facilities, should establish outreach and modernization programs for local suppliers. The state of Ohio, for example, successfully used $2.5 million in funds from its Steel Futures Fund and Thomas Edison program to help Armco upgrade its steel production and add a new electro-galvanizing line, which resulted in Armco becoming an important supplier to Honda and other auto transplants.[87]

Another vehicle for this is the industrial extension programs that a number of states have launched. The Pennsylvania Industrial Resource Center works with Pennsylvania companies to upgrade manufacturing processes and tap new markets. However, to be effective, state industrial extension programs must go beyond the identification of new markets and consultation on new technology. Indeed, these programs may have something to learn from transplant assemblers who have had great success in working with both their transplant and U.S.-owned suppliers to accomplish internal organizational restructuring by introducing worker participation in quality control and shop-floor activities to accomplish major improvements in quality and productivity. Planners could conceivably work with Japanese manufacturers to develop lists of potential suppliers and then work with those firms to upgrade their production processes.

There are indications that Japanese manufacturers would welcome such efforts especially since there is increased political pressure to integrate U.S.-owned suppliers. As Chapter 5 has shown, several transplant assemblers have already established teams of engineers, manufacturing experts, and purchasing representatives to assist potential suppliers. MITI's "Global Business Partnership," announced in November 1991, expressly encourages Japanese companies to increase local procurement, purchase more U.S.-made parts for use in Japan, and work with local suppliers to help them restructure and become more competitive. This kind of integrative approach might also help to temper the deal-mania that encourages many state governments to offer huge subsidies to secure Japanese investments (see Chapter 9). States might offer Japanese companies the option of establishing targeted funds to develop local supplier capabilities in lieu of traditional industrial incentives.

There is a highly charged trade policy debate over whether to limit or eliminate foreign direct investment in the United States. Those in favor of limits see direct investment as a threat to U.S.-owned firms, reducing the pool of American jobs and creating new sources of foreign influence in the United States, whereas those opposed to limitations see foreign investment as creating productive activity and employment.[88] However, the real issue here involves differences in the organization of production, differences that are the source of Japanese firms' competitive advantage over American firms. Eliminating foreign direct investment will not change the nature of that advantage; it will simply shift the geographic locus of competition off-shore, exchanging jobs in foreign-owned companies for jobs abroad. Simply put, a ban or significant limit on foreign manufacturing investment, in the absence of other measures, is likely to be ineffectual, and will not encourage U.S. manufacturers to make the internal changes necessary to become economically viable.

A growing number of academics, labor union officials, and business executives argue that the federal government should develop an industrial policy to rebuild decaying manufacturing industries. However, simply pumping public funds into American steel, rubber, and automobile companies will do little either to improve their performance or to generate broader social and economic benefits. Here again, the real problem lies in the outmoded fordist organization of U.S. manufacturing industry and casino-like activities of financiers, which public funds alone cannot solve. An illustration of the hopelessness of government subsidies to badly operated firms can be found in the protection and other incentives the federal government has provided to the steel industry ever since the 1960s. As Chapter 6 indicated, the steel industry's response has been continued disinvestment, neglect for either technological or organizational upgrading, and the use of steel production as a cash cow for corporate diversification and financial speculation. The American automobile industry has received protection and government bailouts for over ten years, and it is still not competitive. Other sectors such as rubber and machine tools have also been subject to a management strategy, which has emphasized disinvestment, asset stripping, and sell-offs.[89] It is little wonder that economic development planners were so often stymied in their efforts to work with these short-term-oriented fordist firms.

A new approach to redeveloping American manufacturing infrastructure is required to address the underlying organizational and managerial failures of American industry and achieve a fundamental organizational transformation of U.S. manufacturing practice. Such an approach must recognize the new realities of innovation-mediated production organization.

At the core of such a strategy to rebuild manufacturing infrastructure must be a combination of reinvestment and organizational restructuring. As we have already seen, managers and workers in former American plants that are now wholly or partly under Japanese management report that the keys to success have revolved around having the capital to upgrade and modernize their facilities and then learning how to restructure their internal organization. This has required infusions of new capital but simply investing more capital is not sufficient. Many of these plants had been operated as cash cows with earnings siphoned off to finance diversification and high-risk speculative endeavors. Both management and union representatives agree that reinvesting earnings is a necessary component of upgrading and modernizing their facilities and making them competitive. Where existing plant ownership or management is reluctant to undertake needed organizational restructuring, policymakers and planners could conceivably work with labor unions or workers' groups to get these issues on the table. One possible avenue is to use government funds to enable workers to buy out failing plants, reinvest earnings, and implement comprehensive organizational restructuring. These restructured plants might then become models for further imitation and diffusion.

Putting It All Together

The rise of an extensive Japanese automobile-steel-rubber production complex in the United States demonstrates the transferability of the Japanese model of production organization. Geographically, the complex is concentrated in the old fordist industrial heartland of the lower Midwest and upper South. It is characterized by spatial proximity, agglomeration, tight production linkages, and functional integration among Japanese producers—all cornerstones of innovation-mediated production. Basically, Japanese corporation are re-creating a spatially concentrated just-in-time production system in the United States. In general, the transplants have been successful in new greenfield plants and on existing U.S. plant sites, with unionized and nonunionized labor, while paying wages comparable to traditional unionized labor.

The success of the transplants exposes once and for all the myths that high-salaried workers, unions, and/or a poor business climate are responsible for the decline of American manufacturing. This success refocuses attention on the real, underlying causes of America's manufacturing decline: short-term, myopic investment horizons; a lack of reinvestment in manufacturing plant, equipment, and technology; and most significantly an outmoded fordist production organization that sees workers as a necessary nuisance incapable of thought.[90] Indeed, the transplants stand in sharp contrast to the long legacy of disinvestment, relocation, outward investment, and deindustrailization characteristic of U.S. fordist companies. It is in this sense—by establishing a viable new model of manufacturing organization in America—that the transplants are contributing to the "reindustrialization" of U.S. manufacturing industry.

Other attempts to transfer other models of production organization to the United States, such as the German model, have frequently met with serious obstacles and problems. At least part of the reason for Volkswagen's failure in Pennsylvania stemmed from high levels of worker discontent, industrial unrest, and strikes over the high degree of specialization and management control over the production process.[91] Moreover, Volkswagen never even attempted to develop a domestic supplier infrastructure and continued to import its components from Germany. The plant was ultimately closed after less than ten years of operation. The Battle Creek, Michigan, branch of the German seat manufacturer Keiper-Recaro met with a similar fate; after 14 years of "bad experiences" the company sold out to the U.S.-owned Atwood Automotive in Rockford, Illinois. An official who monitored the company's operations reports that Keiper-Recaro

> could write the most extensive guide on how not to do business in the United States of any company I've ever seen. They made every mistake in the book and a few others I didn't think ever existed. They had a bad history of labor relations here. It was primarily the Prussian approach to doing things. Instead of communicating with your workers, they'd say, "Do this, do it this way." And a worker would say, "Why should we do it this way?" And they would say, "Because this is the way we've been doing it in Germany for the past 70 years." End of conversation.[92]

Successful transfer of production systems is neither natural nor automatic; it hinges upon the strategic actions of the company or companies to shape the work force and the environment in ways that can support the new organizational forms. Interestingly, American workers have experienced more difficulty adapting to the German model. This reinforces our hypothesis that the Japanese expression of innovation-mediated production is the international best-practice standard for work and production organization and will likely continue to diffuse and spread throughout the advanced industrial countries and potentially to the developing nations as well.

The last four chapters have demonstrated the transfer of the innovation-mediated production in heavy industry. The next chapter examines the extent to which Japanese electronics companies have transferred innovation-mediated production to their transplant facilities.

8

Consumer and High-Technology Electronics

Frankly speaking, the United States has failed to manufacture. In the new product design or research and development area, the United States is still the top country. But, manufacturing procedure could be better. Japan is better than the U.S. now. So some Japanese manufacturing managers think that we have no more to learn from the United States about manufacturing.[1]

More than steel or automobile or other heavy industrial sectors, electronics—and their crucial microelectronic components—are at the heart of the new industrial revolution in Japan. As Chapter 3 has shown, the largest share of employment and of value-added of any industrial sector in Japan is electronics. It provides a crucial source of technological dynamism for the Japanese economy as a whole and is a focal point for innovation and economic expansion. Tapping the global technological trend toward digitization, new developments in electronics in Japan open up new markets for consumer electronic products, are increasingly used in industrial products like automobiles and office equipment, and are perhaps the defining feature of new automated and computer-assisted industrial processes.

As with automobiles and steel, Japanese producers have become major players in the international electronics market and have caught up with—and in many cases surpassed—American and European producers. This is most evident in the area of consumer electronics, most notably audiovisual equipment where Japanese firms perfected high-quality mass production and rapidly expanded their global market share, while U.S. producers virtually abandoned the field. Japanese electronics corporations already have a sizable advantage in mass-produced semiconductors such as dynamic random access memories (DRAMs) and laptop computers and are closing in on long established American leads across the virtual gamut of high-technology electronics.

In this chapter we explore the transfer of the system of innovation-mediated production by the Japanese electronics transplants in the United States. The evidence, findings, and arguments we present here are drawn from extensive site visits and personal interviews at Japanese facilities in the United States. We conducted multiple interviews in ten electronics transplants: three computer/business machine or telecommunications plants, one computer company headquarters facility, one semiconductor headquarter facility, one semiconductor plant, two

218

television factories and one semiconductor equipment supplier, and one *maqui-ladora* factory in Tijuana. All of these are large, important facilities employing hundreds of workers. Each plant had different internal organizational structures and different levels of Japanese participation in its operations. As a condition of entry we agreed to corporate anonymity. In return, we believe that the discussions were especially frank.

Japanese Electronic Investments in America

All of Japan's major electronic corporations currently operate U.S. production facilities. According to a recent report by the U.S. International Trade Administration of the U.S. Department of Commerce, there are 225 transplants in virtually all segments of electronics production, from televisions and consumer electronics to semiconductor fabrication, semiconductor equipment, personal computers, computer disc drives, and telecommunications equipment (Table 8.1). The electronic transplants employ more than 80,000 American workers.[2]

TABLE 8.1. Japanese Electronic Transplants by Sector

Technology Sector	Number of Plants	Employment (1989)
Computer Equipment		
Computers	11	16,285
Printers	9	2,031
Disk drives	4	1,165
Motors, fans, blowers	3	556
Floppy disks	10	2,843
Semiconductors		
Semiconductors	18	6,110
Printed circuit boards	10	4,475
Semiconductor materials and equipment	24	5,800
Telecommunications		
Telephone apparatus	6	2,000
Communications equipment	13	3,581
Fiber optics	2	300
Television and Radio		
Color TV, audio, radio	25	8,813
Color TV tubes	7	4,375
Glass for TV tubes	1	900
Copiers and Photographic Equipment	15	3,847
Electronic Components	25	8,257
Medical Equipment	11	1,191
Robotics	3	471
Numerical Controls	5	1,427
CDs, Tapes, and Records	18	6,212
Total	225*	81,484*

Source: U.S. Department of Commerce, International Trade Administration, *Japanese Direct Investment in U.S. Manufacturing*, Washington, D.C., October 1990.
*Totals include other electronics-related firms.

The initial investments came in the 1970s when Sony, Sanyo, Mitsubishi, Matsushita, Toshiba, and others built or acquired American television plants. Sony initiated U.S. production in 1972 by building a large plant in San Diego. Matsushita (Panasonic) followed in 1974 by purchasing Motorola's TV operations. Sanyo bought Warwick's TV operations in 1977. As Table 8.2 indicates, every major Japanese consumer electronics producer operates a U.S. color TV plant. These plants in turn attracted a small but significant contingent of approximately 20 Japanese component suppliers.

Investments in American production were driven by the combination of rising U.S. protectionism and the desire to escape the extremely competitive consumer electronics market in Japan.[3] It should also be added that these investments came at the same time that U.S. producers were closing factories and abandoning television production. Today, the only remaining American-owned manufacturer of television sets, Zenith, assembles most of its sets outside the United States.

In this respect, Japanese penetration of the U.S. consumer electronics industry mirrors the more general pattern of Japanese investment in the wake of U.S. deindustrialization, which we have already chronicled in the automobile, steel, and related heavy manufacturing industries. In fact, some of the initial Japanese investments in consumer electronics were in plants that were abandoned or sold off by U.S. producers. Matsushita operates a former Motorola factory near Chicago, Sanyo operates a former Warwick (Sears, Roebuck) TV plant in Arkansas, and Toshiba produces picture tubes in a former Westinghouse facility near Elmira, New York, and will produce 35-inch large-screen color televisions at its Tennessee factory. Currently, Sony is building a state-of-the-art color TV plant on the site of the former Volkswagen assembly plant outside Pittsburgh. The company expects the plant to be the most integrated color television production facility in the United States and to eventually produce high-definition television (HDTV) sets for the U.S. market. In February 1991, Matsushita announced that it would produce high-technology "fuzzy logic" vacuum cleaners in Danville, Kentucky.[4] These firms also invested in low-wage *maquiladora* production facilities near the Mexico-U.S. border.

The late 1970s and 1980s saw a massive wave of Japanese investments in high-technology electronics manufacturing in the United States. Mitsubishi, NEC, Hitachi, Fujitsu, and Toshiba operate American plants that produce everything from semiconductors to personal computers and telecommunications equipment. Both Hitachi and NEC operate large U.S. factories producing current-generation 4-megabit DRAMs. Kyocera, at its San Diego plant, makes semiconductor packages that are used by most of the U.S. semiconductor industry. Sharp turns out color televisions and is building in Washington state the only U.S. factory capable of mass producing flat-panel LCD displays used for laptop computers. Here, too, Japanese producers have responded to increasing U.S. protectionist pressure. The establishment of U.S. production also was aided by the declining dollar relative to the yen, which made purchase of American assets increasingly attractive.

Most of the high-technology electronic transplants were built as greenfield

TABLE 8.2. Japanese Color TV Production in the United States

Manufacturer	U.S. Production Site	Employees in Factory	Products (size)	Annual Output (units)	Production	Notes
Hitachi	Anaheim, CA	250+	Color TV (19-26″) Projection TV (40-50″)	140,000 60,000	1979	*
Mitsubishi	Braselton, GA Santa Ana, CA	300 600	Color TV (14-35″) Projection TV (36-45″)	600,000 (color)	1977	†
NEC	Atlanta, GA	270	Color TV (20, 26, 27″) Projection TV (46″)	240,000 24,000	1985	‡
Matsushita	Chicago, IL Vancouver, WA Troy, OH	1,100	Color TV	600,000	1974 1986 1991	§
JVC	Elmwood Park, NJ	100+	Color TV (13-26″)	200,000	1982	‖
Sharp	Memphis, TN	880	Color TV (larger than 19″) Projection TV (40″)	1,000,000	1979	#
Sanyo	Forrest City, AR	2,000+	Color TV	1,000,000	1977	**
Sony	San Diego, CA	1,700	Color TV (larger than 19″) Projection TV	850,000	1972	††
Sony	New Stanton, PA	1000+	Color TV	N/A	1992	**
Toshiba	Lebanon, TN	630	Color TV (9, 13, 14, 19, 20, 26, 30″)	850,000	1978	‡‡
Pioneer	Chino, CA	170	Projection TV (40, 45, 50″)	40,000	1988	§§
Orion Electric	Princeton, IN	225	Color TV	N/A	1987	‖‖

Source: Dempa Publications, Inc., *Japan Electronics Almanac 1990,* (Tokyo: Dempa Publications, Inc., 1991).
*Discontinued in 1992 and moved production to Mexico.
†Producing VCRs.
‡Planning an integrated production system beginning with chassis.
§Producing 400,000 color TVs in Mexico.
‖Planning to add 35″ color TVs.
#Producing 800,000 microwave ovens.
**Producing microwave ovens.
††Annual production reaching 1 million units.
‡‡Producing VCRs and microwave ovens.
§§Another production line in Pomona, Calif., for stereo speakers and racks employs 280 persons.
‖‖Otake Trading Co. Ltd. is the Japanese minority shareholder.
**Under construction.

plants. However, Japanese corporations have also purchased U.S. facilities as a strategy for rapidly establishing American production. For example, in 1989 Sony purchased an AMD wafer fabrication facility in San Antonio, Texas, and in 1990 Matsushita Electronics Corporation bought National Semiconductor's Puyallup, Washington, wafer fabrication facility for $86 million. The Washington facility sale is particularly interesting because it would have been sold to Fujitsu in 1987 had its proposed purchase of Fairchild been approved.[5] When the Fairchild-Fujitsu merger was blocked for putative national security concerns, National Semiconductor acquired Fairchild, laid off hundreds of employees, and began selling the assets. The final result turned out to be little different from what it would have been had the original sale gone through, except that hundreds of workers were dismissed in the interim.[6]

As the scale of Japanese investments has grown, a number of Japanese semiconductor equipment and component suppliers have also opened or acquired U.S. manufacturing facilities to supply the growing complex of Japanese high-technology manufacturers. As we shall see, many Japanese supplier firms have opened factories in the Portland, Oregon, area to supply semiconductor production-related inputs. In another case, Sony purchased Materials Research Corporation, a semiconductor production equipment and materials company.[7] Japanese suppliers have aggressively penetrated the American market, as they see market opportunities that cannot be served from Japan.

The incredible diversity of electronic products and the variety of corporations involved in this complex industry have led to a far more dispersed siting of facilities than in autos and steel. Some locations have attracted a larger number of firms and thus there are agglomerations of some significance. Perhaps the single largest agglomeration is the transplant consumer electronics and business machines complex of Southern California, including Los Angeles and San Diego, but especially in Orange County in the vicinity of John Wayne Airport. These firms include Canon, Fujitsu, Hitachi, NEC, Oki, Ricoh, Sanyo, Sony, and Toshiba among others. They are often linked with *maquiladoras* in the Tijuana, Mexico, area. Another budding agglomeration is the high-technology electronics, corporate sales, and design operations in California's Silicon Valley. Some of the major firms here are Fujitsu, NEC, Oki, and Toshiba. The Portland, Oregon, area has received an unusually large amount of Japanese electronics investment and is the largest producer of silicon wafers for semiconductor production in the United States owing to Japanese and German investment. Finally, at least 28 electronics and related firms have opened factories in Georgia. Despite these budding clusters, the electronic transplants do not exhibit the pronounced spatial concentration evident in the heavy industrial transplants.

Japanese activities in electronics mirror the sector itself. They are highly diverse, and over the last 20 years the total investment has been quite substantial. Still, with the exception of semiconductor fabrication facilities, individual investments are not as great as in automobile assembly or steel production. Perhaps the single largest electronics investment thus far is the NEC 4-megabyte DRAM facility in Roseville, California, completed November 1991 at a cost in excess of $500 million.

U.S. Transplants and the Globalization of Japanese Electronics

It is important to understand the Japanese electronic transplants in America in the context of the broader globalization of Japanese electronics production. For some time, Japanese electronic corporations have maintained an extensive and far-flung network of off-shore, mainly Asian, factories. This is quite different from the automobile, steel, and rubber sectors where foreign direct investment and the globalization of production are more recent developments.

In 1989, Japanese electronic corporations, according to the best available but admittedly partial count, operated 696 off-shore plants employing approximately 400,000 workers.[8] Japanese electronic corporations employ more than 250,000 Asian workers in 413 plants. The majority of the plants are located in Thailand, Malaysia, and the Philippines and are low-wage, labor-intensive manufacturing and assembly branch plants. Employment in the United States exceeds 80,000 and includes roughly 225 plants (Table 8.1). Investment in Europe is far less extensive and has occurred more recently; however, it is increasing at a rapid rate.

The off-shore investments in Asia have had considerable influence on the management styles, types of activities, and technology transfer pattern adopted for the United States. For the most part, Japanese electronic corporations have transferred relatively standard production activities to the United States. Often, the alternative location to the United States has been Southeast Asia. The general pattern is to develop new technologies, products, and production processes in Japan; standardize these processes in Japanese factories; and when routinized sufficiently, transfer them abroad by building production facilities with very similar layouts in the United States. Sharp, for example, recently started construction of a passive matrix LCD production facility in the United States—a production technology that is well-established in Japan. Simultaneously, it has invested nearly $700 million in a new active matrix LCD production facility in Japan.

Likely, the reason for this is not technological protectionism. The real reason is embedded in the technology development process itself. Japanese companies develop new technology and products in Japan because that is where the R&D and manufacturing capability are. Japanese electronics companies use their Japanese factories to move the new product down the learning curve, and only after most of these economies are achieved is the production process relocated to an off-shore plant.

Work and Production Organization

In Japan, similar production organization and methods operate in electronic corporations as in the automobile, steel, and other heavy industrial firms. As Chapter 3 has shown, the Japanese model of work and production organization is present in both traditional and high-technology industrial sectors. Japanese consumer and high-technology electronic companies organize work on the basis of teams, use few job classifications, and rotate workers to different jobs. The organization of production in the Japanese electronics industry is thus characterized by high levels of functional integration, the synthesis of intellectual and physical labor, emphasis on continuous process improvement, and tight integration of R&D and production both within companies and between end-users and their suppliers. In addition, the Japanese electronics industry is organized around a series of large firms integrated across a number of what in the United States are separate industrial branches. These range from consumer electronics to semiconductors and computers, office equipment, industrial equipment, and electric power and transmission systems. This broad range of activities makes it possible to capture powerful production synergies and to contain more of the ripple effects of technological innovation within the firm.

Still, the production process in electronics is quite different from those used in traditional assembly-line industries such as automobiles. The basic difference is that each product requires fewer parts and fewer workers; hence, the plant-level coordination and control problems associated with a complicated product such as an automobile are less severe. Electronic products themselves are smaller and have fewer components. Often, production runs are small. The manufacturing process is less energy-intensive and assembly lines have fewer workers per line. In addition, electronic products are characterized by extremely short and rapidly changing product life cycles as new features are constantly introduced. Whereas automobile models change roughly every four years, electronic products change every year or even more frequently than that. They are the quintessential product in the perpetual innovation economy.[9]

As a result, electronic products require greater adaptability on the part of the work force. Japanese electronic firms tend to have a high ratio of engineers, or white-collar workers, because of the R&D intensity and the ability to standardize and automate production processes. The Japanese computer maker, Fujitsu Ltd., for example, is now 50 percent white-collar and 50 percent blue-collar.[10] These factors have a strong influence on the organization of production and the labor process.

Very few English-language studies are available on the organization of work and production in Japanese electronic corporations in Japan and even fewer on the Japanese electronic corporations operating in the United States. A recent study by a group of social scientists at the University of Tokyo examined the organization of work and production at six Japanese consumer electronic firms and three semiconductor fabrication facilities in the United States.[11] This study compared the organization of work and production at these plants to a small group of automotive transplants. The basic finding was that the electronic firms tended to transfer much less of the Japanese system and to show a much higher level of adaptation to the American environment than the automotive transplants. The study found that consumer electronic companies had transferred the least of the Japanese system of work and production organization. The semiconductor producers occupied a middle ground. Similarly, the Japanese computer and communications manufacturing facilities in America have received little scholarly attention even though transplant investment in these two areas is growing.

The University of Tokyo study reported that Japanese electronic firms tended to have extensive job classifications or labor grades, did not use work teams very extensively, and did not practice job rotation. Our own analyses, interviews, and site visits suggest that the use of work teams and job rotation is mixed, and that it varies both within and between plants. Much of the reason has to do with the nature of the production process itself and the division of labor it entails. As we have already seen, often production is standardized so as to facilitate off-shoring of low-end, labor-intensive tasks. For example, in Japanese transplants it is relatively common to find groups of up to 30 workers doing exactly the same thing, such as soldering. Each worker will undertake a set of activities alone, such as inserting a number of components into a circuit board. In the consumer electronics segment especially, it appears that many of the production processes transferred to the United States are similar to those that have been transferred to the Third World. However, teams may be used for other, more complicated tasks and processes that are organized on the basis of a more complex division of labor. A number of electronics transplants practice task rotation, though not to the extent found in the automotive transplants. In one consumer electronics firm, which claimed to be run in a "U.S.-style," we found the most organized set of rotation practices of any of the electronic companies we visited. Yet the Japanese president of this transplant said that the rotation arose without his interference.[12]

All of the electronic transplants we visited use significantly higher numbers of job classifications than either comparable plants in Japan or the automotive transplants. Most of the electronic transplants have developed relatively extensive classification systems and internal career ladders for their American employees, both blue collar and white collar. Table 8.3 provides the 11 job classifications as of 1985 at a unionized Japanese-owned TV plant in Arkansas. It is interesting to note that the wage differential in starting pay of the various job classifications is not great (just

TABLE 8.3.   Job Classifications and Wages at a Unionized Color TV Plant

Labor Grade	Job Title	Starting Wage Rate*
1	General Operator	$7.17
2	General Operator; Chassis Handler	$7.23
3	General Operator; Custodian	$7.32
4	Handler, Stock; Handler, CRT Insp.; Strap. Mach. Operator	$7.44
5	Truck Driver; Machine Set-up Operator; Set-up Repair; Mech/Elect. Insp. Repair; Mech. Set-up Repair	$7.54
6	Cabinet Patcher	$7.70
7	Painter/Sprayer Operator	$7.84
8	Tool Crib Attendant; Cabinet Refinisher Box Make up Machine Operator	$8.04
9	No titles listed	
10	Analyzer	$8.83
11	General Maintenance	$9.14

*Wage rates in 1985, in U.S. dollars.
Source: University of Tokyo, *Local Production of Japanese Automobile and Electronics Firms in the United States.* (University of Tokyo: Institute of Social Science, Research Report No. 23, 1990) p. 103.

under $2.00 an hour from lowest to highest). Thus, these classifications provide lit-
tle financial benefit either to the company or shop-floor workers, but they do provide workers with traditional labor union protections and drastically limit
management's ability to shift workers. The larger number of job classifications is
one of the main areas where the electronic transplants diverge from Japanese auto
assembly transplants.

The main reason for this appears to be fitting in with traditional American
employment and production practices. The Japanese computer plants we visited
used a relatively large number of job classifications—certainly for a Japanese facility. According to both Japanese and American executives at these plants, this was
done to fit in with local employment practices. The personnel manager at one of
these plants, who was recruited from the dominant American firm in the region,
indicated that their system was expressly designed to be similar to others in the
region:

> [I]n order to gain data from your other brothers and sisters in the industry you have
> to be scrutinized, your structure, your salary. . . . You have to be graded and tested
> and you have to have enough structure. . . . You have to have job matches. . . . You
> have to have a structure and everything, submit it for review. They will call you and
> say, "OK, you look like you have some semblance of civilization; we'll allow you
> [in]."[13]

Another company found it necessary to increase the number of job classifications and to create an internal career ladder to cope with dissatisfaction on the part
of American workers and with increasing labor turnover. According to the top-level
American manager at the plant, the company is

> evaluating the positions by a point basis and the point basis establishes a level and
> then that level has a salary range attached to it. And then beyond each level or each
> category you may have the next category. It would be based on some additional
> experience or some additional training or some additional skill level. . . . We are in
> the process of creating that more from a wage and salary standpoint than from a
> category of production worker one, production worker two, production worker
> three, although that may be what evolves from this. . . . This is a way of differenti-
> ating between somebody who's been here only doing their time and is an average
> guy and somebody who has been here for a while but is doing a little bit better
> work.[14]

However, Japanese managers have actively resisted this move toward greater
"Americanization." Japanese managers said that they found it difficult to understand the need for such a complicated job hierarchy, and some actively resisted its
implementation. The Japanese executive vice president of manufacturing said that
he basically ignored the system on the shop floor.[15] This was echoed by an American
human resources manager at this plant:

> In the beginning it was very difficult for me to explain why we had to set out the job
> structure, why we had to do this, because I remember the very beginning when the

company was founded, and it was a lot of work to set up what I thought were operating procedures. . . . In the beginning I remember having a lot of discussion about
why, why, why, why, why do we have to do that [write job descriptions, rules and
procedures]. . . . The Japanese would want to glance through this stuff. . . . I felt
that I needed to be sort of a purist . . . and stay with the group [the American electronic firms in the area], and not muddle our job descriptions or pay too much.[16]

While most plants had instituted job classifications and an internal career ladder, they did not consider the medium- to long-term effects of this kind of system
on flexibility or plant-level productivity. Indeed, given past American experience,
it is likely that the impact of this type of plant-level system will be negative and,
moreover, that once implemented will be difficult to reverse or change.

Even though the electronic transplants use a relatively large number of job classifications, the management hierarchy remains "thinner" than in comparable
American plants. Japanese electronic firms in the United States typically make use
of team leaders, production workers who oversee production activities. The lines of
authority extend from work groups to team leaders to supervisor. In all of these
companies, leaders tend to be recruited from the shop floor, as are many supervisors. Sony encourages upward mobility from the shop floor to the lower-level supervisory positions.[17] Every company we visited indicated that promotion from the
shop floor to managerial levels was encouraged and supported. As we shall see
below, this is at least partially done to cope with high levels of turnover for engineers
and managers.

Most transplant electronic facilities have not implemented quality-control,
kaizen, or other worker-improvement initiatives. Only one plant we visited tried to
implement QC circles; however, this attempt failed. The executive vice president
for manufacturing attributed failure to a "lack of understanding by the managerial
class." He added that, at present, the company is still busy boosting production, but
when this is complete he intends to bring a quality assurance manager from Japan
and try again.[18] Others believe that the problem lies more generally with American
workers who lack initiative and motivation. A Japanese manager at a consumer
electronics plant stated that American workers refused to take the initiative
required to correct their mistakes or to help others.

> They feel it is wrong to say that a fellow worker has made an error, or even to correct
> the errors they see. But surely this is essential if the company is to turn out good
> products. If we make defective products, who will buy them? And where will these
> people work if nobody buys them?[19]

Generally speaking, the Japanese electronic transplants have not implemented
the Japanese system of work and production organization. At best, the system they
have implemented can be considered a hybrid of Japanese and American characteristics. The actual level of transfer varies by firm and is influenced by when the
company entered into U.S. production, whether the company purchased a U.S.
facility or built a new greenfield factory, the company's own management style, and
the rigors of the market. A number of Japanese consumer electronic companies

who entered into U.S. production early believed they would best fit into the American context by imitating U.S. labor-management and work-organization practices. Still others such as Matsushita and Sanyo entered the United States by purchasing existing American companies. In doing so, they inherited the legacy of American work and production organization and the attendant labor-management relations in which those production systems were embedded.

Unrest at Sanyo: The American Labor-Management Legacy

Sanyo's Forrest City, Arkansas, consumer electronics plant illustrates how some Japanese transplants have become trapped by the existing context of U.S. labor-management relations and thus have been unable to transfer Japanese work and production organization. In 1977, Sanyo acquired Warwick's television plant in Forrest City from Sears. The plant was unionized and had a history of combative labor-management relations. After reaching peak production in the 1960s, the plant started to decline in the early 1970s mainly under the pressure of foreign competition. Quality suffered, and Warwick found it difficult to produce TV sets for Sears that worked reliably. According to one manager at the plant,

> The infant mortality on those sets was awesome. We would consider it a triumph if, by the time a completed set arrived at the end of the assembly line, it simply lit up when we pressed the ON button. Sears was frantic. We kept shipping them sets that either wouldn't work in their showrooms, or worse, in their customers' living rooms.[20]

Sears then began purchasing TV sets from Sanyo in the 1970s for sale under the Sears name, thus reducing its need for output from Warwick. In 1976, Warwick discontinued production of its color TV sets and closed down four of five assembly lines at its Forrest City plant. Employment fell from a high of 2,500 workers to about 500.

Sanyo took over the plant in January 1977. It brought in new technology and quickly began producing a variety of Sanyo color televisions at the plant. The plant experienced an extraordinary turnaround and production boomed. By 1981, employment had increased to more than 2,400 workers.

Sanyo initially wanted to implement Japanese-style management. It developed plans for reorganization and tried to implement a Japanese-style quality-control system. However, union resistance led the company to drop these plans. In 1979, production was interrupted by an eight-week strike during negotiations over a new three-year contract with the International Union of Electrical Workers (IUEW). Sanyo essentially found itself trapped in traditional U.S. labor relations and was unable to restructure production organization along Japanese lines. In 1981, a top Japanese executive at the plant was quoted as saying:

> Given different American conditions, we haven't been able to transplant the Japanese way to America. . . . American workers maintain a much looser relationship

to the company compared with Japanese. However, we learned some lessons from the strike and are now trying to improve the situation. In Japan the union lives with the company and never pulls the trigger unless it finds itself in an extremely serious situation. It tries as much as is possible to work with us on the same ground, because its members' future and prosperity are directly linked with ours. The important question for us right now is how to instill this concept in our American workers. . . . The key element is teamwork, with the responsibility resting squarely on management to motivate the workers. The reason there are workmanship problems in the U.S., I believe, is the different concept of teamwork. In a Japanese plant there is much more dialogue between blue-collar and white-collar workers; in fact, the rapport is so natural we take it for granted. Such, however, is not the case in the U.S.[21]

In 1985, the company again moved to implement Japanese production organization. This provoked a second, even more violent, strike. The key issues in the strike were "seniority system changes and the right to shift workers from job to job" as well as medical insurance cuts and the earlier firing of the union leaders.[22]

The case of Sanyo underscores the fact that the existing labor-management relations created a context that constrained the transfer of Japanese work and production organization. Once Sanyo had allowed the original U.S. fordist system to continue and to solidify, it found it almost impossible to change. It essentially became trapped by the American system of production and work organization, which made it increasingly difficult to implement Japanese production. Attempts to force change led to serious labor-management conflict. By 1990, Sanyo had decreased its employment at the Forrest City plant to 800 and had shifted production to its San Diego factory and its Tijuana, Mexico, *maquiladora,* where employment increased to over 2,400.[23]

However, other Japanese electronic corporations in the United States—especially later entrants—are surmounting these problems faced by Sanyo and implementing a Japanese system. Sony plans to transfer and develop a full-blown Japanese-style production system at its new plant in Westmoreland County, Pennsylvania. Sony, it should be added, is known for high quality, which the company believes stems directly from Japanese work and production organization. In addition, later entrants have learned from early mistakes and are trying to implement full-blown Japanese work and production organization at the outset. Indeed, it appears that the strategy of the transplant automakers to begin with Japanese-style work organization and labor-management relations was shaped in light of the difficulties faced by consumer electronic companies in this earlier period.

Manufacturing Consent: Unionization, Wages, and Long-term Employment

In Japan, electronic manufacturers comprise an important part of the core of the Japanese industrial structure. Workers are unionized, receive high wages, have long-term tenure guarantees, and are not subject to layoffs. In the United States, workers in the American electronics industry have far less power and security. Most consumer electronic firms have abandoned U.S. production, and companies such as IBM, Unisys, DEC, and Hewlett-Packard are nonunion. Labor unions are strongest in government-supported, tightly regulated sectors, and/or defense-related segments of the industry, in companies such as AT&T, General Electric, and Westinghouse.

Wages at the Japanese electronic transplants are relatively low. The wage for operators in all the electronic transplants were comparable and averaged $6.00 an hour to start with a high of $10.00 an hour. A smaller semiconductor equipment factory in the Portland, Oregon, area paid starting wages of $5.50 an hour, which increased to $6.50 after a year. This is far lower than the wages at the heavy industrial transplants. The University of Tokyo study concluded that "practices characteristic of Japanese companies in Japan, such as bonuses or some kind of relation between wages and ability or long-term seniority, were not discovered."[24]

The wage system at the electronic transplants reflects the weakness of organized labor in this sector. Wages follow prevailing U.S. wage rates and are typically set in light of the local job market. The wage structure in the plants we studied was essentially the same as that of the dominant U.S. electronic firms in the area. The great majority of electronic transplants are nonunion. The only unionized electronic transplants are those that were previously unionized under American ownership.

The Japanese electronic transplants do not deploy the elaborate recruitment and socialization strategies used by the automobile, steel, and heavy industrial transplants. The majority recruit workers themselves. A common practice is to secure workers from temporary agencies and then select the best for permanent status. There are two reasons for this. First, workers can be thoroughly evaluated before the company makes any commitment to hire them permanently; and second, as such, the large number of temporary workers can be used as a buffer to changes in the market and demand for products.

Absenteeism, tardiness, and policies regarding absence from work are areas where electronic transplants have tended to follow Japanese practices. All have strict policies regarding absence from work and tardiness similar to those of the automotive transplants. According to a manager of one transplant,

> We consider failure to report to work on time and absenteeism a serious matter. Whenever somebody comes to work late, we give a warning. When this happens four times a year we ask the person to take a day off and consider if he can improve himself. If he doesn't improve himself after that, we fire him.[25]

The transplants do not provide formal guarantees of tenure security. Four of the six firms examined in the University of Tokyo group had laid off employees; these companies displayed little commitment to a long-term employment system. Our interviews and site visits indicate that, whereas Japanese managers are committed to long-term employment as a goal, they will lay off employees in response to crises and reorganizations. Still, they seem less likely to do so than traditional American companies. Sony, which has produced television tubes in San Diego since 1972, has never had a layoff. As an alternative during downturns, workers were reassigned to maintenance and housekeeping or increased training.

One of the computer transplants we visited has a standard assembly operation that requires a large number of operators. In traditional American plants, these operators have always had insecure positions and been vulnerable to layoffs. While this plant does not guarantee long-term employment, during a downturn in 1986 the Japanese executive vice president for manufacturing decided to redeploy regular production line employees rather than lay them off. As he put it: "Layoffs are dangerous, like suicide. Working people will lose belief in the company."[26] Workers were redeployed throughout the plant and to accounting, personnel, and other staff jobs. The cleaning contract with an outside vendor was canceled and taken over by the plant's employees. This was done over the objections of the American managers. With these measures and the reassignment of work from Japan, the plant escaped the need for a layoff. The initiative to preserve the jobs came entirely from the Japanese vice president of manufacturing. In six months, the market recovered and business resumed as usual.

A Japanese executive with another major electronics firm said that "there was no guarantee [of worker employment], though we would like to keep them [employees] because we have invested in them."[27] The president of the same company stated that layoffs were dangerous because the plant would lose employees that had learned the ins and outs of the production process. However, the firm was in the process of reorganization and unnecessary employees were being let go.

Every Japanese manager we interviewed claimed to be committed to doing everything possible to limit layoffs of full-time employees in periods of economic downturns. This was true even in the highly cyclical semiconductor industry. Their argument was that after investing in the training of personnel, it would be a great loss to simply fire them.

The White-Collar/Blue-Collar Divide

There is a much greater gulf between blue-collar and white-collar workers in the Japanese electronic transplants than in Japanese electronic firms in Japan or in the automotive transplants. Japanese electronic transplants did not as actively resist the traditional blue-collar/white-collar divide, and in the process they created a management style far closer to the old American-style environment where power is concentrated in the hands of management.[28] The power of management is thus much greater in the electronic transplants than in Japan. In the words of one Japanese official:

> I used to be an engineering manager in Japan, but my power or right to do things for my subordinates was very small. . . . I could not do anything about personnel. . . . But here [in the U.S.] I have very big power; that is a big difference from Japan. A manager can decide his subordinate's salary or can even fire them. We do not have such power in Japan.[29]

This was reinforced by another Japanese manager at the plant.

> The responsibilities of a manager is completely different [in the U.S. system] from the Japanese system. American managers have a lot of responsibility for manufacturing itself and also human resource activities like salary increases or hiring or improving relations. In the Japanese system the manufacturing manager never does human resource activities such as hiring. . . . The manufacturing manager does not have any power regarding salary definition or salary determination for his subordinates. The operator does not work for him. . . . In the Japanese system it is a balance. Japanese managers have the power to rate the performance of each of the personnel, but he never decides the salary for each operator. . . . Human resources decides the salary for each operator.[30]

Thus, control is far more diffuse than in the United States. However, the lack of power of the individual may be the very strength of the system.

Reporting hierarchies are both taller and stricter in the electronic transplants than in Japan or in the heavy industrial transplants. In the electronic transplants, factory-level "operators" (they are not called "associates" as in the automobile transplants) are expected to report only to their supervisors, who in turn transmit information up the heirarchy.[31] A team leader we interviewed indicated that she must always report to her supervisor before going to anyone else.[32] Again, this differs from both Japan and from the automotive transplants where shop-floor workers are encouraged to report to other managers in addition to their immediate supervisor if required. The Japanese president of one electronic transplant complained that in the United States there is a strict hierarchy through which information must flow sequentially from level to level.

> In the United States, a manager will keep to his own area and never see another area. But, in Japan, every manager will see more than their area. That is one of the big differences. Also, in the United States, the manager will report to the person who is his direct boss only. But, in Japan, of course, they report to another person if necessary, flexibly, case-by-case.[33]

He believed that such strictly defined channels of communication restrict information flow and contribute to narrow perspectives. He thought that American employees were too concerned about who they are supposed to report to, not where the information is most needed.

One electronic transplant has gone to some length to break down the labor/management divide. Factory-level operators are encouraged to communicate with engineers and work with them to solve problems. According to the president of this plant, operators are told that the "engineer is not your supervisor; he is your helper. If we tell [the operator] the engineer is your supervisor then he will bring any problem to him."[34] The objective was to place more responsibility on the worker to handle routine problems and not always report them to the engineers.

The open-style office characteristic of Japanese firms in Japan and many of the automobile transplants was far less prevalent in the electronic transplants. High-level executives are provided regular offices, while middle-level managers have high partitions at all except two of the companies we visited. One exception was a semiconductor facility where the newly appointed Japanese plant manager, over the vehement objections of the American staff, had "cut down" all the partitions to waist-level.[35] Another company had a seemingly schizophrenic attitude regarding office layout: high partitions and private offices in the "headquarters area" and an open layout in accounting and production. However, our interviews indicated that the headquarters area was controlled by American managers, whereas Japanese managers controlled production and accounting.[36] Another firm had an open-office policy in its continuous-process chemical production area. A European emigre manager was proud of this open system and felt that it was necessary for efficient operation:

> [The open office] is very beneficial for . . . easy communication and daily communication. This [production] process cannot be done by individuals. We have similar production lines in [a European country] and Japan. We exceeded the yield in Japan and [the European] factory yield was much lower. And what was the problem [in Europe]? The problem was everybody had his own job. But this cannot be. This is a team effort. . . . Here everybody has to take care of everything. Of course, everyone is assigned a task. . . . We do everything to promote teamwork and daily communications. So everyday we have morning meetings and we include at least one or two of the workers.[37]

In most of the electronic transplants, the outward trappings of status equality so prevalent in the automobile transplants, such as uniforms, were not evident. With regard to parking, the evidence was more mixed. Two headquarters facilities in Silicon Valley had reserved parking (probably a necessity for recruiting American managers). At another semiconductor manufacturing facility, only the managers had reserved parking. At another transplant there was reserved parking for the executives, while other employees were provided open parking. A computer/communications firm initially provided reserved parking for all of its employees; but when faced with a shortage of space due to expansion, the company instituted a new system based upon seniority. The other facilities had open parking policies.

The University of Tokyo study identified only one firm that required employees to wear uniforms. None of the plants we visited used companywide uniforms for workers or managers. With the exception of one plant, all employees wore street clothes. In one transplant, all of the operators were required to wear blue smocks, but lower-level managers wore shirts and ties. A Japanese executive said this was a historical decision that he did not participate in nor agree with, implying that American managers had made the decision and Japanese were reluctant to change it.[38] A computer plant intends to require that employees wear antistatic uniform jackets to help protect the product from static electricity. The Japanese executive vice president of manufacturing seemed pleased that this would be implemented, although he was careful to point out that this was done for "rational" rather than "spiritual" purposes.[39] In factories making integrated circuits, workers were required to wear "bunny suits" and "booties," but even this met some resistance. In several plants, Japanese shop-floor managers wore uniforms while American managers did not.

Our interviews and site visits suggest that there is a fundamental division of opinion between Japanese and American managers on the blue-collar/white-collar divide: American managers work to preserve the traditional divide, whereas Japanese managers would like to see a greater blurring of these distinctions. Moreover, it may well be that American managers are enforcing the traditional U.S. managerial system without the consent or perhaps even the knowledge of the Japanese managers. In other words, American-style management may be reasserting itself, even though most Japanese managers are opposed to it.

An interesting illustration can be gained from contrasting two plants operated by the same company. In one factory, manufacturing operations were organized and managed by Japanese expatriates; in the other, manufacturing was controlled by American managers. According to company officials, American managers were far less familiar with the manufacturing process than were Japanese managers at the other factory. We were able to observe that the plant managed by Americans was somewhat messier and more disorganized and that labor discipline was not as strict as at the Japanese-managed plant.[40] Top Japanese officials at the company's headquarters were dissatisfied with the performance of the American-managed plant and were considering plans to bring in Japanese production managers to take control of manufacturing.[41]

Managers and engineers who are distant from or uninterested in the shop floor lack the knowledge and connection to the actual production process to make informed decisions. According to Japanese executives in the electronic transplants, American managers do not understand the activities that the workers are undertaking, and they are in great measure incapable of effective supervision. A Japanese manager added, "When I talk with U.S. engineers in my section about learning from the [assembly] line, they have not been interested."[42] Shop-floor workers react to this by hoarding and protecting their own knowledge. They do not offer suggestions for fear they will be turned down, ignored, or even disciplined. Such a divide stymies crucial information-sharing, communication, and learning, making it difficult—if not impossible—to achieve the crucial continuous process improvements on the shop floor that are the hallmark of innovation-mediated production.

The situation is complicated by the fact that many Japanese managers are not only unfamiliar with the U.S. environment and the American management system, but they are only tacitly familiar with the Japanese system. A Japanese human resources manager suggested that many Japanese manufacturing personnel who are sent to the United States to manage production facilities have a only limited understanding of the way the Japanese system differs from the American one. In Japan, they receive some general training, but this is often insufficient to prepare them for their new responsibilities. These managers can be very successful in Japan where their actions are reinforced by a supportive organizational system and environment. However, they tend to take their own environment for granted. The system seems "natural" to them; thus they understand the system tacitly, but are unaware of its concrete organizational dimensions. When they come to the United States, they find it difficult to manage in a nonsupportive environment and/or articulate the kinds of organizational changes required in that environment. This can lead to misunderstandings and problems that would not occur had they a better understanding of the concrete organizational dimensions of the Japanese system.[43]

The Japanese model is not simply a set of concrete organizational structures; rather, it is a series of tacitly understood roles, norms, and behaviors that are not simply picked up and transferred abroad. The transfer process involves the transfer of social relationships, which are frequently understood only tacitly. Thus, the transfer process must be calculated and planned—it will not occur automatically. A system that grew almost unconsciously in Japan requires conscious "transplantation" to be effective in the new environment. This is the reason that compromises with the American method of management can be so dangerous to effective transplantation and can have long-term negative effects such as those suffered by Sanyo in Arkansas.

Turnover: A Crucial Dilemma

A central problem faced by the electronic transplants is labor turnover. In Japan, labor turnover is low; both management and shop-floor employees stay with one company for their corporate career. The electronic transplants have experienced turnover rates that are higher than those in Japan but somewhat lower than those of comparable firms in the area. This complicates efforts to develop the long-term socialization to the norms, behaviors, and management styles of innovation-mediated production. The University of Tokyo study found that the annual turnover rates for Japanese electronic firms in the United States in 1984 ranged between 10 percent and 50 percent depending upon the company, sector, region, and year. This is comparable to our findings for 1990–91.

Labor turnover was considered a serious problem in all of the electronic transplants we studied. High worker turnover makes it hard to develop a base from which to build, and it limits the possibility for generating company-specific knowledge or learning-by-doing. A small semiconductor equipment company in the Portland, Oregon, area had a turnover rate of over 50 percent in its first 18 months. This was attributed to wages slightly lower than the area's average and a low ceiling (between $5.50 and $6.50 per hour). Also, initially the company hired the chronically unemployed who had been referred from the state employment service. However, the American manager stated that the new foreign immigrants seemed to be more motivated and therefore made better employees than the chronically unemployed.[44] Finally, a number of other plants reported that their turnover rates were settling down especially as the recession was leading to layoffs at U.S. firms.

Turnover of managers and engineers has been a serious problem. This was especially problematic in California where labor turnover is accepted. A Japanese electronics parts manufacturer in the United States was reported saying:

> There is a serious shortage of semiconductor designers. You employ someone and teach him for three and four years, and soon as he learns the art, some other company will offer a better salary and take him away.[45]

Interestingly, there is a bidding war going on between Japanese firms for American managers. Therefore, the electronic transplants are actually exacerbating turnover among themselves by raids on others.

Japanese companies located in and around Silicon Valley experience the same high turnover of engineers as do other companies in the area.[46] As a response, Japanese firms are increasingly locating new plants in the Midwest or Southeast to escape this problem. A number of Japanese managers indicated that if they were to choose their location over again, they would not locate in California because of high worker turnover, high labor costs, and problematic local suppliers.[47] In the Los Angeles and Dallas areas during the 1980s, the transplants lost engineers to higher-paying positions with defense contractors.[48] The American manager of a major Japanese telecommunications plant in the United States indicated that turnover of American managers is the "single biggest problem" facing the plant. He added that when he sees more Japanese managers and engineers coming to the United States he is relieved because "these are the guys I can depend on."[49]

Japanese electronics manufacturers in the United States are devising methods to cope with high turnover. One strategy is simply to bring in more engineers from Japan. According to the president of Japanese semiconductor subsidiary,

> We must bring engineers from Japan. How can we train U.S. engineers in [our] method of producing semiconductors? How do we keep them at [our firm], because they must stay at least five years to become a first-rate semiconductor production engineer; if they leave in two or three years they lose out.[50]

A common pattern in a number of the plants we visited was that they initially had hired American managers for production. However, the American managers had problems in handling their responsibilities. The companies have been gradually replacing American managers with Japanese managers.

According to a Japanese production manager, his company's "original intention had been to control manufacturing from the engineering and planning departments."[51] By using plant layout and controlling the pace of the production line, the Japanese managers believed they could manage production. This strategy was unsuccessful because the American managers were unable to manage the plant efficiently and eventually Japanese managers were sent in to take over. Interestingly, the Japanese manager interviewed claimed that this replacement and a simultaneous reorganization led to a rapid improvement in product quality and turnaround time. This is not an isolated event. Increasingly, managers of Japanese electronic plants are becoming confident that they can deal with American workers; it is dealing with American managers that is problematic.

Another strategy that these companies are using is to recruit young engineers directly out of college, who are not "polluted" by American management ideology and techniques. Two firms had explicit programs for hiring American engineers directly from college campuses and transferring them to Japan for two to three years. After that, the recruits can either return to the United States or stay in Japan. The goal is to develop a cadre of American engineers and managers to return to America with a more comprehensive understanding of the Japanese system.[52] Of course, the weakness of this program is that these engineers often quit and join another firm.

The other response has been to recruit production supervisors from the shop floor. Japanese electronics executives believe shop-floor workers are both more reliable and stable than American managers. According to an American executive at one of our computer transplants, his company is finding it necessary to "recruit managers from a different social status group"—that is, from among the ranks of shop-floor workers.[53] The University of Tokyo study quoted the president of an electronics firm as saying that to circumvent the problem of turnover "we would like to establish a system whereby competent persons emerge from lower strata one after another no matter how many engineers decide to leave." Every company we visited said that it intended to increase the number of promotions of shop-floor operators to supervisory positions, because they were both more reliable and knew what was really going on in production. This is roughly in line with Japanese practice where shop-floor workers are routinely promoted to production management positions. The president of a Japanese semiconductor subsidiary in the United States said that in Japan his firm recruits 50 percent of its production managers from the shop floor.

Turnover, especially in the white-collar segment of the work force, is considered a serious problem. The most important response to this is to increase internal promotions. The hope is that these employees will be more loyal and understand the actual workings of production better. Whether or not these "homegrown" managers will be less likely to leave is still an open question.

Global Coordination: A Growing Problem

The rapid growth and geographic dispersal of Japanese electronic transplants in the United States is causing serious communication and coordination problems. In Japan, electronic manufacturers are distinguished by excellent information-sharing and coordination not only between R&D and manufacturing but also between manufacturing divisions. These various divisions typically supply one another and often collaborate in new product development. The semiconductor unit of a integrated Japanese electronics firm will, for example, supply both its computer and consumer electronic units. While these units may indeed be rivals within the corporation for investment, there is typically excellent interaction and communication between them.[54] This constant liaison facilitates the development of new products and new hybrid innovations that come from combining two or more technologies, such as opto-electronics or mechatronics.

Japanese electronic companies operating in the United States are experiencing significant communication and liaison problems that more generally mirror those of multinational corporations.[55] One dimension of the problem is that these plants are geographically dispersed and spatially segregated. For example, Table 8.4 provides the legal name, location, and activity of each NEC facility in the United States, highlighting the spatial dispersion of its facilities. As Figure 8.1 shows, Toshiba's U.S. R&D and production facilities are similarly dispersed. This dispersion is

TABLE 8.4.   NEC's Corporate Organization in the United States

Subsidiaries	Activity	Location	Business Area
NEC America	management	Melville, NY	headquarters
	production	Dallas, TX	telecommunications
	production	Hillsboro, OR	telecommunications
NEC America	management	Boxboro, MA	headquarters
	management	Wood Dale, IL	administrative
	production	Boxboro, MA	personal computers & peripherals
	production	McDonough, GA	laptops & TVs
NEC Electronics	management	Mountain View, CA	headquarters & semiconductor design
	production	Roseville, CA	semiconductors
NEC Systems	R&D	Boxboro, MA	market research
NEC Industries	management	New York, NY	finance, leasing
NEC Research	R&D	Princeton, NJ	basic R&D
NEC Logistics	management	Los Angeles, CA	distribution
HNSX Supercomputers	joint venture	Burlington, MA	supercomputers
Bull HN Info.	joint venture	Billerica, MA	mainframes

Source: Adapted from personal communications with NEC America, 1991.

emphasized by the fact that the various factories are legally constituted as separate wholly owned subsidiaries. These plants typically have their own engineering support and their own sales force. In contrast to Japan where there is continuous personnel rotation between the branches, in the United States the various branches share few personnel and often do not communicate with the other U.S. subsidiaries or supply one another.

These coordination problems derive in part from the complex nature of the electronics industry where different products (e.g., integrated circuits, cathode ray tubes, matrix displays) require different production skills, are sold into very different markets, and have different supplier relationships. This problem is far less likely to crop up in industries like steel or automobiles, which have a more clearly delimited end-product. For example, U.S. Honda's assembly plant and its engine and transmission casting facility are tightly coupled and must work well together.

But the main problem lies in the way they are linked back to Japan. With one exception, the electronic transplants are linked to a Japanese sister plant and a corporate division. Thus, even if a plant was supposed to report to a common U.S. headquarters, its real affinity would be to its Japanese sister plant. Given this situation, coordination among the U.S. branches can become difficult and may itself depend upon the Japanese sister plants. According to the American executive vice president and plant manager of a large electronic transplant: "[There] is no direction from [U.S. corporate headquarters]. It all comes from various parties in Tokyo."[56] The vice president at the corporate headquarters of the same firm added that "very few meaningful decisions are made here. There are stacks of requests

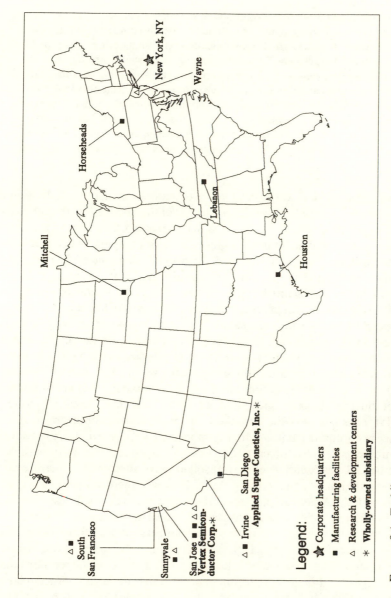

FIGURE 8.1. Toshiba America's Manufacturing and R&D Facilities.
Source: Toshiba America, Inc., 1991.

waiting for answers from Tokyo."[57] The Japanese president of a U.S. subsidiary of a large Japanese electronics firm that has a number of other American subsidiaries put it this way:

> That [coordination between the various U.S. subsidiaries] is the very critical issue which we are now starting to discuss with our . . . family companies in the United States. So, we try to make a good communication between the other . . . companies in the United States, even as far as the manufacturing standpoint is concerned. Whether making television sets and numerical controls, or other consumer electronics or communication equipment or automotive components, they have a very common production operation. They have common items like human resources or labor control or union control. . . . So, from that point of view I think we have to help each other and exchange information with each other. I think we can do that to strengthen the power of [our company], as far as the operation in the United States.[58]

In most cases, the decision to establish production was made by a division in Tokyo, and the U.S. subsidiary was linked to one of the division's plant. Site selection usually was typically made by the division in Japan. So, for example, the American director of sites and facilities planning of a major computer transplant's U.S. headquarters said that his group was hardly consulted when one of the company's divisions decided to build a new plant.[59] As a result, locations are chosen that optimize for each individual facility but not the company's manufacturing system as a whole. This ad hoc locational process sacrifices the benefits of locational clustering, interaction, and synergy achieved by Japan's electronic production complexes.

Most of the subsidiaries are closely supervised and controlled by their sister plants, and this can lead to serious problems in responding to changing conditions in the United States. An opposite problem can arise when a U.S. factory manufactures products (e.g., color televisions and personal computers) that are linked to a number of different divisions and plants in Japan.[60] In these cases, no group is responsible for the success of the transplant, making it difficult for the transplant to have a voice in corporate planning. Jointly sponsored corporate image, joint advertising, combined sales task forces, and/or research teams are often not feasible.[61] Recently, the U.S. headquarters of the transplants have attempted to increase their control over individual manufacturing plants. However, these initiatives have been blocked by both the American plants and their Japanese sister facilities.

The sister-plant relationship also has technological ramifications. The benefit is simply that the U.S. plant can secure needed technical assistance from its Japanese sister plant. The cost is that the U.S. plant frequently becomes technologically dependent upon its Japanese sister facility. As a result, American operations may perennially lag behind their more technologically dynamic Japanese sister plants. It becomes very difficult to develop a capacity to accomplish state-of-the-art innovations in the United States. American employees are unable to gain a full understanding of the dimensions of the firm's activities or to contribute innovations that will improve the company's operations. This is even true in the case of the plant managers who should play a crucial role in forging corporate alliances and projects.

If this continues, U.S. plants may be locked in a position of chronic dependence and never rise above their current status as assembly plants.

Suppliers and Domestic Content

In Japan, electronics corporations use a supplier structure similar to that of the automobile industry (see Chapter 5). Companies are dependent upon outside suppliers for approximately 70 percent of the value of the final product. As in the automobile industry, over time the electronic firms have organized well-articulated, multi-tier supplier systems.

The electronic transplants have for the most part failed to replicate a large-scale just-in-time (JIT) supplier structure in United States. When we asked the president of a major Japanese consumer electronics facility about his ability to develop a JIT system in this country he said,

> Just-in-time—that sounds very good. The just-in-time system works very well, very much the ideal situation for a manufacturing company. But we have a very important issue for that system—that is, the supplier can always supply the material just-in-time. It is very simple, but it is very difficult. . . . So, the just-in-time system needs many parts suppliers, which are located close to the main assembly plan. . . . But first of all, in this area we do not have such electronics components suppliers. Currently, we have to buy the components from Japan or Southeast Asia, which takes a very long lead time and also there are problems with the accuracy of delivery times. If the delivery situation with the local vendors is OK, then we can do that. But, still we have some delivery problems from local vendors.[62]

In areas with larger concentrations of electronic transplants, some larger electronic parts suppliers are establishing facilities. For example, in the business parks surrounding the Orange County airport a number of suppliers have located warehouses and manufacturing facilities. However, these suppliers are not exclusive and serve a number of Japanese companies. Still, some companies such as Sony and Matsushita have developed small supplier networks. For example, Sony's San Diego plant has developed a small concentration of local suppliers, and the company intends to develop a similar supplier structure around its new television assembly plant outside Pittsburgh. These supplier systems remain small and underdeveloped both by the standards of the Japanese electronics industry and in comparison to the just-in-time complexes that have been developed by transplant auto assemblers.

The consumer electronic transplants continue to rely upon a relatively high percentage of parts imported from Japan. This is especially true of complex, sophisticated parts such as very large television picture tubes, production equipment, and advanced microelectronics. However, the United States has a 15 percent duty on TV picture tubes, and this has put pressure on a number of Japanese companies to move picture tube manufacturing to the United States. So, for example, Toshiba produces color picture tubes in a facility it purchased from Westinghouse in New

York. For many firms, the decision to localize picture tube manufacture is a complicated trade-off. Picture tube production facilities are expensive to build, and the production process is a complicated one and requires significant engineering and manufacturing skills to ensure high yield and high quality. It is difficult to build up the required capabilities in transplant facilities. And yet, TV picture tubes are fragile and bulky components that are expensive to ship from Japan. A major television manufacturer is considering localization of picture tube production because it either has to import or purchase the tubes from a non-Japanese manufacturer whose quality is inadequate. This problem was reinforced on a plant tour in a company that used both Japanese-made and U.S.-made television picture tubes. In the "burn-in" test room there were a number of rejected television sets, all of which were marked with the name of the non Japanese supplier.[63]

In addition, most of the specialized production equipment used by the consumer electronic transplants is imported from Japan. This is not surprising since the deterioration of the U.S. television industry and the "off-shoring" of large parts of the electronics industry in the 1970s resulted in the decline of the equipment sector of the U.S. consumer electronics industry. One firm indicated that it is difficult to secure electronic parts from the United States because most of the parts suppliers have gone offshore. This plant has 60 percent non-Japanese content, but only 45 percent is U.S. content.[64]

The local content in the Japanese computer/communications transplants is also relatively low. It was in the range of 30 percent to 50 percent at the plants we visited. These factories tend to purchase low-value, nonelectronic components such as sheet metal containers and plastic injection molded parts locally; to import the most complex components and technologies from Japan; to secure other parts from branch plants in Southeast Asia; and to locate the bulky, labor-intensive activities such as printed circuit board-stuffing in Mexican *maquiladoras.*

Semiconductor transplants have moved the furthest toward developing supplier networks. But here again they have not developed anything like the dense supplier networks typical of semiconductor production in Japan. And, as importantly, the numerous back-end facilities connected to Japanese semiconductor fabrication facilities do not exist. A procurement specialist at a major Japanese semiconductor facility said that at his plant local (domestic) content has risen to 70 percent— roughly one-half of this procurement came from Japanese transplant suppliers in the United States. Each of the major inputs such as the silicon, silicon wafers, photomasks, plastic and ceramics for encasement, gold wire for bonding, and ultrapure gases necessary for semiconductor fabrication came from a Japanese transplant supplier.[65] As in the automobile transplants, Japanese semiconductor plants in the United States have opted to deal with the same suppliers that they use in Japan. When it is uneconomical for these suppliers to build facilities and begin production for relatively small American demand, these companies purchase the item in bulk in Japan and ship it to the United States. This also permits global standardization of inputs, which makes engineering simpler.

Semiconductor production requires more rigorously controlled production environments than do other forms of electronics production. There are few standard inputs to be contracted through the arm's length bidding so favored by American companies. Indeed, semiconductor production is not merely science; it is also an art. Yield improvement is absolutely crucial to success, and it depends upon cleanliness, lack of contamination, experience, and process improvement. Suppliers of industrial gases, silicon wafers, and chemicals thus play a crucial role in forming the infrastructure so necessary in operating a successful production facility. This is complicated by the fact that each Japanese semiconductor company has its own idiosyncratic process for semiconductor fabrication. Each firm's specific production recipe evolves over time through learning-by-doing and cooperation with suppliers. At the end of this process each semiconductor manufacturer will have evolved its own slightly different production process. So, for example, a wafer supplier such as Shin-Etsu Handotai (or in this country SEH America) will provide a different crystal grown according to a specific formula to each firm (i.e., NEC, Oki, Fujitsu etc).

To cope with these problems, a growing number of Japanese companies have acquired or purchased large shares in American semiconductor equipment manufacturers. These firms provide a wide range of semiconductor equipment used by transplant and domestic producers alike. Table 8.5 shows the major U.S. semiconductor equipment manufacturers and input suppliers that have been purchased by Japanese companies.

Nippon Sanso's acquisition of Matheson Gas, a leading domestic producer of gas used in semiconductor production, illustrates the now familiar story of American disinvestment, diversification and asset sell-offs to bolster corporate earnings. In the mid-1980s, Matheson Gas was acquired by Searle Corporation. Searle used the company as a "cash cow" and eventually sold a 50 percent stake of the business to Nippon Sanso, Japan's largest industrial gas producer. The Japanese partner brought much needed capital and state-of-the-art manufacturing technology to the company but tensions grew over the need for reinvestment. Searle consistently refused to put in the capital required for upgrading on the grounds that it was unnecessary and would damage short-term earnings. However, it offered to sell its remaining shares in the business to the Japanese partner. Nippon Sanso was left with no other choice than to acquire the entire company in order to make the investments needed to keep it competitive.[66]

As Japanese semiconductor production in the United States continues to grow, it is likely that more Japanese semiconductor materials and equipment firms will open American plants. For example, in late 1990, Japan Synthetic Rubber Co. Ltd. announced that it would build a factory to produce photoresists for Japanese DRAM facilities in the United States.[67]

The Japanese electronic transplants have experienced difficulties dealing with American suppliers. As with the automobile transplants, the major difficulties revolve around unacceptable quality, failure to meet delivery schedules, and the short horizons of American suppliers and the attendant inability to forge a long-term customer-supplier relationship. The Japanese president of a major consumer electronics manufacturer described his initial experience in the United States as follows:

> I was shocked. Not only by the delivery situation but by the quality level. Because when we make a consumer electronics product, quality is crucial. When I came here [over ten years ago] the quality control manager of a supplier said we have a

TABLE 8.5. Japanese Investment in U.S. Semiconductor Equipment Companies

Japanese Corporation	U.S. Company	Technology	Location	Date	Share Acquired (%)
Sony Corp.	Materials Research Corp.	Etching equipment	NY	1989	100
Mitsubishi	Siltec Corp.	Water production	CA	1986	100
Nippon Sanso	Semi-Gas Systems Inc.	Gas handling	CA	1991	100
Nippon Sanso	Matheson Gas Products Inc.	Gas handling	NJ	1989	100
Japan Metals & Chemicals Co.	U.S. Chrome Corp.	Chrome/metals	CT	1990	100
Komatsu Electronics Metals	Advanced Silicon Materials (Union Carbide)	Polysilicon	VA	1990	100
Toppan Printing Co.	Toppan Printronics (Texas Instruments)	Photomasks	CA	1989	85
Hoya Corp.	Micro Mask Inc.	Photomasks	NJ	1989	100
Tokuyama Soda Co.	General Ceramics Inc.	Ceramic packages	NY	1989	100
Osaka Titanium Co.	Semiconductor Materials Inc. (Cincinnati Milacron)	Epitaxial wafers	OH	1989	100
Osaka Titanium Co.	U.S. Semiconductor Corp.	Epitaxial wafers	CA	1988	100
Tosoh Corp.	Varian Associates (specialty metals)	Sputtering targets	OH	1988	100
Kawasaki Steel Corp.	NBK Corp.	Epitaxial wafers	CA	1985	100
Asahi Glass Co.	Aegis Inc.	Metal IC packages	MA	1987	49
Nippon Mining Co.	Koltran Corp.	LC lead frames	CA	1985	37
Shin-Etsu Handotai Company/Mitsubishi	Hemlock Semiconductor Corp.	Polysilicon	MI	1984	37
Marubeni Hytech Corp.	Mattson Technology	Photoresist equipment	CA	1991	20
Sumitomo Metal	LTX Corp.	Digital test equipment	CA	1990	15
Canon	AG Associates	Thermal processing equipment	CA	1989	30
Canon	Lepton Inc.	Electron beam lithography	NJ	1990	10
Sumitomo Metal	Lam Research Corp.	Plasma etching	CA	1989	4.5
Sumitomo Corp.	Prometrix Corp.	Metallurgy equipment	CA	1990	3
Seiki & Co.	Novellus Systems Inc.	Deposition equipment	CA	1988	N/A

Source: Japan Economic Institute, "U.S.-Japan Competition in Semiconductor Manufacturing Equipment: The Consequences of Shifting Positions," *JEI REPORT* 21a (7 June 1991) pp. 9, 10.

40 percent reject rate, but he said, "You can fix that on your own line." Yes, physically we can do that; we need some labor to do so; that is why I asked him to please give us high-quality material. He said he did not have the professional competence as far as manufacturing.[68]

Most surprising for the Japanese was that often the American suppliers had no intention of improving. A recent JETRO report quoted the manager of an electronics parts transplant as follows:

When we decided to place an order, we went to the supplier's plant and asked to see the production line. The company was a supplier for a large U.S. manufacturer and the production line shown to us looked reliable. We placed an order on the condition that they would use the same line for us. We thought that by stipulating the use of the same line we would secure the same experienced workers producing parts for the big manufacturer. When the delivered goods began to arrive, we found so many defective products in the batches that we went to the supplier's plant once again. We found that the parts for us were manufactured on a brand-new line with newly employed workers. Their explanation was that the line they had agreed to use for us was needed full time for that big American manufacturer, so they had no choice. We immediately canceled our order.[69]

In other cases, American suppliers have managed to improve their quality. In the late 1970s and early 1980s, Sanyo's Arkansas plant worked extensively with its suppliers to improve both quality and delivery. The quality of supplies was poor, even for standard products such as the corrugated boxes used to package the TVs. According to the American supervisor in charge of inspecting incoming supplies:

The Japanese managers were shocked by the quality of those . . .boxes. There were imperfections. . . . The letters printed on them were often uneven and the color wasn't uniform. . . . I went to the company and said, "I want perfect boxes—no flaws in the corrugation, perfect letters, and uniform color." They said, "You've got to be kidding. You don't need perfect boxes; we can't produce them, and even if we could produce them it would cost more than it's worth."[70]

After a year of work the supplier eventually turned around and won business from both Sharp and Toshiba as well as Sanyo.

Japanese electronic transplants have tried to cope with American suppliers by devoting more time and effort in managing these relationships, but with only partial success. According to a Japanese telecommunications manufacturer:

We buy components that require only simple processing from American suppliers, but often find them defective and inferior to what we get in Japan. Also, our local suppliers are quite lax on delivery. To cope with this problem we have made our inspection process very thorough. At the same time, whenever defective parts are identified, we try to discuss possible improvements with the supplier. To cope with irregularities in delivery we make frequent telephone calls to assure on-time delivery. These measures are time-consuming and sometimes annoying, but we think they are worth the effort.[71]

The use of American managers in the purchasing departments of some electronic transplants has at times made it even more difficult to move toward Japanese supply organization. At one plant we visited the Japanese manager in the purchasing department said that it was very difficult to get American purchasing managers to accept Japanese purchasing practices. A problem arose when one of the plant's major customers drastically reduced an order. In response to this, the American managers simply canceled their purchase order with one of the company's Japanese transplant suppliers but offered no explanation. Two days later the company got a large new order and the American managers simply contacted the supplier and asked them to start up again. The supplier's management then complained to its Japanese headquarters, which in turn contacted the assembler's superiors in Tokyo. Tokyo then called the U.S. facility and demanded an explanation. The Japanese manager had been unaware of this situation and was forced to intervene. In Japan, such a scenario would not have occurred; the purchasing agents would have provided the supplier with a complete explanation before any cancellation to preserve future cooperation.[72] The American managers were dealing with the supplier in the traditional arm's length manner, but the Japanese supplier expected the closer cooperation characteristic of Japan.

Such supplier problems can seriously impact on transplant operations. A Japanese executive we interviewed indicated that one of the largest Japanese semiconductor production facilities in the United States was having difficulties because of its inability to adapt to local materials and personnel.[73] When we related this to the firm in question, the company did not deny it, but said that other companies had similar problems. Securing adequate suppliers is likely to remain an important problem for Japanese electronic transplants for some time to come.

Portland, Oregon: An Emerging Electronics Complex

An interesting and growing complex of Japanese electronic manufacturers is forming in the Portland, Oregon/Vancouver, Washington, metropolitan area (see Table 8.6).[74] Since 1983, the Portland area has received over $500 million in investment from Japanese electronic manufacturers. In 1990, these firms employed approximately 5,500 people, and employment was projected to increase to at least 15,000 as the facilities already located there continue to expand.

The first major Japanese investment came in 1984 when NEC America announced that it was building a factory in Hillsboro, Oregon. Almost simultaneously, Shin-Etsu Handotai Co., a silicon wafer producer, began construction of a silicon crystal factory in Vancouver, Washington, which is directly across the Columbia River from Portland, Oregon. In October 1984, Epson announced that it would build a plant in Portland. In 1985, Fujitsu America said that it would also build factories in the area. That same year, Matsushita Electric Industries Co. and Kyocera announced their move to Vancouver. Later a consortium of Mitsubishi firms purchased Siltec Corporation, a Salem, Oregon, producer of silicon crystals.[75]

Portland's rise as a center for semiconductor crystal production has attracted additional investment from Japanese electronic firms. Semiconductor suppliers and input firms have begun to locate in the Portland area. Toshiba Ceramics, for example, recently opened a facility to produce the quartz crucibles from which the silicon crystal for integrated circuit wafers is pulled. This was followed by Shinetsu announcing plans to open a quartz crucible manufacturing facility in a joint venture with Hereaus, a German company, to make crucibles. (These crucibles are used in conjunction with TT America Inc., another Portland transplant whose graphite products go into the crystal-pulling process.) In February 1991, Sharp announced that it would build a factory to assemble passive matrix flat panel displays (which also use silicon as their base material) in Camas, Washington.[76]

Several reasons lie behind Portland's emergence as a center for Japanese electronics investment. While Portland is relatively close to Silicon Valley, it benefits from significantly lower land prices and labor costs. In addition, the Portland area has high-quality, abundant water resources and low-cost electricity—both important inputs in many electronic production activities. Portland is also relatively close to Japan and offers direct flights to both Tokyo and Nagoya.

The Portland area has also made a conscientious effort to recruit Japanese producers. In the early 1980s, Oregon's lumber and natural resource-based economy went into a severe recession. Both the city of Portland and the state government developed an aggressive industrial recruiting effort to diversify the area's industrial base. Public officials saw only limited opportunity to recruit American firms and turned their attention to foreign, especially Japanese, companies.[77]

The first effort to attract a Japanese firm was unsuccessful. In 1983, the state of Oregon lost out in the competition for a Mitsubishi Electric semiconductor plant, which ultimately located in North Carolina's Research Triangle. The reasons for choosing North Carolina were the abundance of high-quality engineers and Oregon's unitary tax system.[78] However, Japanese firms continued to show interest in the Portland area as a potential site for manufacturing. In 1984, a delegation from Keidanren (the Japanese Federation of Employers) visited Oregon and indicated the interest of Japanese manufacturers. However, the delegation conveyed the message that they would only be willing to do so if Oregon repealed its unitary tax.[79]

The state of Oregon quickly set in motion an effort to repeal the tax. The governor called a special session of the Oregon legislature to consider the issue. In hearings before the Special House Revenue Committee, the chairman of a committee of prominent citizens stated:

> The global marketplace is changing quickly—new markets are opening up, others are closing rapidly. Oregon must move away from its dependency on East Coast and California wood products markets and look at the global economy to find its own niche. . . . Since talk of the special session began, the staff of the Keidanren, the most influential organization of Japanese business people, has called me every day to find out the possibilities of modifying Oregon's unitary tax method. In addition, our Ambassador network has been working with several other Japanese firms who are quite interested in Oregon, but will not even consider locating here if the unitary system is maintained. Many of these firms already have California operations, but are looking elsewhere to expand, because of California's unitary method. Accordingly, whether one finds the unitary tax fair or unfair, good or bad, the fact remains it has become a barrier, and Oregon will not share the available economic

TABLE 8.6. Japanese Electronics Investments in the Portland, Oregon, Region

American Name	Parent Firm (Japanese)	Start-up Date	Initial Investment (in millions of dollars)	Investment (in millions of dollars)	Current Employment	Product
SEH America Inc.	Shin-Etsu Handotai Co., Ltd.	June 1984	45	45	960	Silicon wafers
NEC America Inc.	NEC Corp.	October 1985	50	80	650	Fiber-optic systems for modems, transmitters, etc.
Kyocera Northwest Inc.	Kyocera Corp.	November 1985	10	10	430	Ceramic capacitors
Fujitsu America Inc.	Fujitsu Ltd.	Spring 1986	25	55	900	Information processing, disk drive, and telecommunications equipment
Epson Portland Inc.	Suwa Seikosha & Epson Group	July 1986	10	20	890	Computer printers
America Kotobuki	Matsushita Electric Industries Co., Ltd.	September 1986	20	20	200	Large-screen TVs and video recorders
Siltec	Mitsubishi Metals Group Co.	1986	30	30	403	Polished silicon wafers
TTAmerica Inc.	Toyo Tanso Co., Ltd.	September 1987	6	6	45	Graphite products for machining and processing

248

Company	Japanese parent	Date			Product
Ushio, Inc.	Ushio, Inc.	Late 1987	3	80	Halogen lamps
Dynic USA Corp.	Dynic Corp.	April 1988	2	60	Photoresists
Fujitsu Microelectronics	Fujitsu Ltd.	Fall 1988	100	450	Semiconductors
Technology Electronics of America	Tozuka Denki Inc.	November 1988	1	35	Wire harnesses
Fujimi	Fujimi Abrasives Company, Ltd.	January 1989	unknown	8	Polishing compounds for the silicon wafer industry
Toshiba Ceramics	Toshiba Corporation	Early 1989	9	44	Quartz glass crucibles used for growing silicon crystals
JAE Oregon	Japan Aviation Electronics Co.	December 1989	10	50	High-volume electronic connectors
Oki Semiconductor	Oki Electric Co.	Spring 1990	25	120	Semiconductors
Tok International, Inc.	Toyo Ohka Kogyo Co.	1991–92	70	60	Photoresists
Sharp Microelectronics*	Sharp Corp.	1992	35	150	R&D for semiconductors
Toshiba Microelectronics	Toshiba Corp.	1992	100	—	Semiconductor fabrication
Heraeus Shin-Etsu America, Inc.†	Shin Etsu Quartz Products Co., Ltd.	Mid-1992	10	—	Quartz glass crucibles used for growing silicon crystals
Matsushita	Matsushita Electric Works Ltd.	—	—	—	Printed Circuit Boards

*Originally an R&D facility; company is building a factory to produce laptop display screens.
†Joint venture with a German firm.
Source: Authors' compilation from Portland Development Commission data, 1991.

growth opportunities if we do not repeal it. Japan's concern over this method is not just bluster, not just bluff. There is a serious interest in investment in Oregon that can be carried out if Oregon opens the door.[80]

On July 30, 1984, the Oregon State Legislature repealed the unitary tax and the governor signed the bill. With this decision, Oregon set itself up to compete with California for large corporate investment. Furthermore, an innovative "Semiconductor Training Program" was established at Clackamas Community College and sponsored by United States, Japanese and German semiconductor firms. This exerted an additional positive influence on the Japanese firms which were looking to develop U.S. production facilities.

It is difficult to assess the impact of Japanese investment on the Portland area economy with any real precision. Still, it is quite clear that Japanese investment has provided a major source of new manufacturing growth and is one of the biggest sources of economic development overall. According to Mark Clemons, business development manager for the Portland Development Commission:

> Japanese [firms] have been our major new recruitment successes. U.S. firms have been relatively minor in terms of job creation. Ninety percent of the new jobs have been from Japanese firms.[81]

This growth has been especially important since one of Portland's largest American employers, Tektronix, has laid off nearly 3,500 workers in the Portland area since the mid-1980s. Many of these employees have been hired by Japanese firms.[82]

It is even more difficult to calculate the multiplier effect of Japanese investment in the Portland area. A large number of the inputs used by these Japanese factories are imported from Japan. At one plant we visited, domestic content still had not reached 50 percent. Local inputs tended to be low-technology items such as metal cabinets, connectors, and other more general items. However, there is evidence that a number of transplant firms are developing links to Portland-area manufacturers. NEC's Hillsboro plant, for example, has sent its technicians to Tektronix Inc. "to help the vendor produce circuit boards more efficiently for NEC.[83] Here again, it appears as though the Japanese companies are trying to develop closer ties to suppliers and make the transition from traditional American arm's length relations toward a more Japanese-style system.

Japanese electronic investment in the Portland area is just beginning and is likely to expand. Toshiba Corporation has announced plans to build a major semiconductor fabrication facility in Hillsboro, Oregon, and Matsushita Electric Works, Ltd. has announced that it will build a new plant in Forest Grove to manufacture printed circuit boards. A number of smaller Japanese silicon wafer production equipment firms are also said to be planning to build facilities in the Portland area.

Japanese *Maquiladoras*

Japanese electronic firms have extended their reach to the Mexican border where they have established a large and growing number of *maquiladora* production facil-

TABLE 8.7.   Japanese *Maquiladoras* in Consumer Electronics

U.S. Subsidiary	Mexican Site	Number of Employees
Assemblers		
Sony	Tijuana	1,700
Sanyo	Tijuana	2,400
Matsushita/Panasonic	Tijuana	1,400
Hitachi	Tijuana	500
Toshiba	Ciudad Juarez	750
Suppliers*		
Pioneer	Tijuana	500
Nishiba Metal	Tijuana	170
Tabuchi Electric	Tijuana	300
Tocabi America	Tijuana	300
O&S California	Tijuana	200
Kyowa America	Tijuana	110
Mutsutech	Tijuana	100
Tomita Electric	Tijuana	300
Taisho	Ciudad Juarez	175
Murata	Ciudad Juarez	400

Source: Author's compilation 1991.
*Also, may supply inputs to other industries.

ities. The *maquiladora* plants perform labor-intensive operations such as TV assembly and chassis production.[84] Table 8.7 provides information on the most important maquiladoras that serve Japanese consumer electronic transplants and consumer electronic suppliers. All except one of the Japanese consumer electronic transplants operate *maquiladora* facilities. Other Japanese electronic firms such as Canon, which also have *maquiladora* facilities, are omitted from the listing. The only major consumer electronics firm without a *maquiladora* is Mitsubishi Consumer Electronics, the leader in the expensive big-screen and projection television field.

The primary incentive for undertaking *maquiladora* operations is to reduce labor costs by taking advantage of low-wage Mexican labor. In 1991, the average wage paid by Japanese *maquiladoras* was $1.10 per hour compared to a $6.00 starting wage at U.S. plants. Here, Japanese corporations have followed the traditional pattern set in Asia where labor-intensive manufacturing and assembly functions are performed in low-wage, off-shore plants. Essentially, *maquiladoras* are factories where labor-intensive work is undertaken before products are shipped back north for final assembly and for additional activities that require higher skills.

Part of the reason for the large-scale Japanese operation in Mexico lies in the nature of the consumer electronics industry, which has elements of what can be termed "simple" assembly. Many operations are labor-intensive; that is, wages represent a much larger share of the costs of production in the electronics industry than in steel or automobiles. This is exacerbated by the highly competitive conditions in the low-price end of the market and thus has made labor costs a salient factor in profitability. Competition from Korean manufacturers and other low-cost producers has placed significant pressure on Japanese manufacturers to reduce their labor costs. In fact, the competitive struggle in standard consumer electronics products is so intense that there is little profit to be made in color televisions with screens under 25 inches, in standard microwave ovens or small refrigerators. Companies—especially those aiming at less expensive market niches—are under constant pressure from Third World producers, and their response has been to build *maquiladoras*.

However, the competitive situation in Mexico is becoming more difficult, as wages, especially for skilled labor, and managers are bid up and turnover is increasing. Companies are responding in various ways. A personnel official at the *maquiladora* of a major Japanese consumer electronics firm indicated that "the big companies are integrating everything from robots and part production to final assembly because the [transplant] parts suppliers [in Mexico] are finding it difficult to keep quality up."[85] Others are moving into higher-value market niches, in effect ceding the low end of the market to Korean and other low-cost producers. These firms are improving quality and moving into production of stereo television and large-screen projection television. These Mexican plants use very few inputs from Mexico. For example one firm's domestic content in the United States was reported as 20 percent, the Mexican content at its *maquiladora* facility was less than 2 percent.[86] The *maquiladoras* are an important aspect of the Japanese consumer electronics activities in the United States because they allow Japanese firms to use low labor costs to compete against low-cost Asian producers such as the Koreans, while still increasing their North American content and providing a base to supply the emerging, integrated North American market.

Japanese Electronics R&D in the United States

Japanese electronic transplants in the United States originally started out as lower-level assembly and branch plants. This has changed in recent years as Japanese transplants have increased product development activities at their facilities. And, more recently, a number of Japanese electronic corporations have begun establishing basic R&D laboratories in the United States. As the Japanese electronics industry moves increasingly to the cutting-edge of global technology and operations become global in scope, it has become necessary to tap experienced engineers and researchers throughout the world. Fujitsu now operates six product development and R&D facilities in the United States; Toshiba operates seven; Matsushita has eight.

Fujitsu, the world's second largest computer company, has R&D operations throughout the United States. With the exception of a Northlake, Illinois, facility, these R&D operations are located either at a manufacturing facility or at the company's San Jose, California, headquarters.[87] As of this writing, Fujitsu is constructing a large telecommunications research facility on the site of its Richardson, Texas, telecommunications plant. The new R&D facility is designed to assist the factory in developing new products and customizing Japanese products for major accounts in the Dallas area. The company is trying to develop a product development capability comparable to its plants in Japan and is gradually building up the number of product development engineers at its Texas plant.[88]

Toshiba is also increasing its American R&D substantially. Returning to Figure 8.1, it is evident that Toshiba's R&D and product development facilities are located in close proximity to its manufacturing plants. In late 1990, Toshiba opened a design center for ASICs in Beaverton, Oregon, close to both Silicon Valley and the emerging Portland production complex. The company wants to preserve the close interaction between production and engineering that has been so successful in Japan.

Canon Inc. has established a number of different types of R&D facilities in the United States. The first is a product development facility located on the site of Canon's business machines manufacturing plant in Costa Mesa, California. Recently, Canon decided to relocate all of its electric typewriter development to the Costa Mesa site. In 1990, Canon opened Canon Information Systems in Costa Mesa to develop hardware for computers and office products, as well as systems and application software for computers and peripherals. The objective is to increase the company's sensitivity to the American market. Also in 1990, Canon opened its Canon Research Center America as a "think tank for fundamental research in computer technologies . . . in areas such as optical recognition, image data compression algorithms, and network management and architecture."[89] Canon, which is the largest producer of laser printer engines in the world, a global leader in copiers, and an important name in the office automation field, has for all intents and purposes set up a facility meant to mimic and if possible reproduce the success that the Xerox Palo Alto Research Center experienced but upon which Xerox was unable to capitalize. Sony too has numerous R&D facilities in the Silicon Valley area conducting research on various aspects of high-technology electronics.

The movement of electronics R&D to the United States is a very important trend and is in keeping with practices in Japan. As we discussed in Chapter 3, nearly all Japanese electronics firms have substantial engineering and product development staffs at production facilities. However, at important manufacturing facilities they go further and also place an applied research facility on the site. Co-location of product development and manufacturing activity is seen to promote cross-fertilization and innovation. As discussed earlier, in Japan factory workers focus their activity on moving down the learning curve of process improvement. Plant-level product development units in turn work on moving to a new and more efficient manufacturing process frontier. In Japan, electronics corporations also support extensive basic research activities at central R&D laboratories. These labs develop innovative new products that are then brought into actual factories for process implementation.

Japanese electronics corporations have opened product development units in the United States to bolster the technological capability of American plants, establish an indigenous innovation and product/process improvement capability, and provide technical support to manufacturing facilities.[90] In late 1990, for example, Matsushita Electric Corp. of America began construction of a new Factory Automation Technology Center on the site of its Franklin Park, Illinois, production complex to bolster its efforts to develop new manufacturing automation technologies for its North American plants.[91] Clearly, in electronics, R&D has become crucial to competitive success. Strong linkages between manufacturing and R&D are recognized as vital by Japanese firms. It is not surprising that Japanese companies are complementing their manufacturing investments with new investments in the United States. This is in keeping with the pattern set by Japanese automobile transplants, which are making major R&D investments in the United States.[92]

The Japanese electronic transplants are also moving into high-end basic R&D. In 1989, NEC became the first Japanese electronics firm to establish a basic R&D institute in the United States. This facility is located in Princeton, New Jersey, and is expected to grow to 60 scientists and basic researchers and 40 support staff by 1993.[93] Hitachi is also establishing a new HDTV (high-definition television) lab in Princeton. Sony, Toshiba, and Matsushita also operate HDTV labs in the United States.[94] In late 1990, Matsushita announced that it would also set up an Information Technology Laboratory in Princeton to conduct basic research on computer graphics, document processing, and system software. This is its eighth R&D or product development facility in the United States.[95] In early 1991, Mitsubishi Electric announced that it would establish a 50- to 100-person basic R&D laboratory in Cambridge, Massachusetts, to do research on next-generation parallel processing and super computers.[96] Fujitsu and Ricoh are also considering establishing basic research institutes in the United States.

These R&D facilities focus on basic science and are located near major American universities.[97] These new labs are aimed at recruiting top-flight American scientists from both universities and corporations. The idea is to locate close to the available pool of top-quality R&D scientists in the United States and to create the environment necessary to attract these researchers. Most of these labs are designed to conduct research in areas where Japanese industry remains behind the United States (e.g., parallel computing, software development, and artificial intelligence).

Transplant R&D investments will surely increase as investments in manufacturing facilities in the United States grow. On the one hand, the number of product development facilities will expand at factory sites as these operations become increasingly complex. On the other hand, Japanese electronic firms (and Japanese firms in other industries as well) will increasingly open more basic research facilities in an effort to tap into important sources of new ideas. The basic research facilities will likely be located in existing innovation centers—Silicon Valley, Boston-Route 128, and the northern New Jersey area. These R&D centers probably will not be linked with transplant manufacturing facilities, but rather with central R&D laboratories in Japan. Similarly, the funding for the laboratories will not be allocated by the American subsidiary's corporate headquarters, but by the Japanese R&D division.

Japanese Equity and Venture Capital Investments in U.S. Start-ups

The last significant area of electronics investment by Japanese firms is venture and equity investments in U.S. high-technology start-ups. Many Japanese companies have taken on the role of venture capitalists and are now bankrolling small firms in exchange for access to technology and the opportunity to manufacture the new products that are being developed. As Table 8.8 shows, such investments have increased dramatically over the course of the 1980s. By 1989, Japanese corporations and financiers invested an estimated $320 million in 60 U.S. start-up com-

TABLE 8.8. Japanese Investment in U.S. Start-up
Companies and Venture Capital Funds

	Investments in Companies			Investments in Venture Capital Funds	
Year	No.	Investment (millions of dollars)	Average Size	No.	Dollars Invested (millions of dollars)
1983	11	7	6	4	18
1984	15	44	2.9	14	28
1985	15	42	2.8	24	31
1986	20	142	7.1	9	33
1987	49	151	3.1	8	14
1988	47	176	3.7	22	46
1989	60	320*	5.3	16	54
1990	48	230	4.8	—	—
1991	18	97	5.1	—	—

Sources: Venture Economics Inc., *Corporate Venturing News* 4 (4 May 1990);
William Bulkeley and Udayam Gupta, "Japanese Find U.S. High Tech A
Risky Venture," *Wall Street Journal* (8 November 1991): B1, B2.
*Includes a $100 million investment by Canon Inc. in NeXT Inc. Excluding
the $100 million investment, average investment size for 1989 was $3.7 mil-
lion.

panies. Japanese investors also placed an estimated $54 million for investment by
U.S. venture capital funds.[98] Such investments provide Japanese companies with a
window on new technologies, possible capital gains, and a foothold in newly developing technologies.

A substantial share of this investment has come through Japanese electronic
companies and their U.S. transplants. In spring 1991, NEC's U.S. semiconductor
unit formed a broad agreement with one of the top U.S. semiconductor design software firms, Cadence Design Systems, to develop software development tools.
Toshiba purchased a 10 percent stake in Synergy Semiconductor Corp. of Silicon
Valley, which specializes in process technology for high-speed ASIC (application
specific integrated circuits) chips.

But, such investments are by no means confined to electronic companies. They
extend to a wide range of Japanese firms in so-called traditional industries.[99] Among
Japanese steelmakers who are striving to enter the new industries, Nippon Steel
recently purchased a 10 percent, $200 million share of Oracle, a leading database
software company,[100] and has partnerships with Concurrent Computer Corp., Synergy Computer Graphics Corp., GTX Corp., and Sun Microsystems. NKK recently
acquired equity stakes in Paradigm Technology Inc., a producer of high-speed static
RAMs and Silicon Graphics and has manufacturing and distribution agreements
with Artel Communications Corp., Convex Computer Corp., and Raster Graphics.
Kubota Ltd., the agricultural equipment and building materials company, has
made major investments in MIPS (a company which makes reduced instruction set
chips), Maxtor (disc drives), Ardent Computer (graphics supercomputers), Synthesis Software (MIPS-based software), C-Cube (image compression software), Rasna

Corp. (CAE software), Exabyte (tape drives), and Akashic Memories (thin-films). Nippon Sheet Glass has taken an equity position in Arreal Technology Inc., which produces 2.5-inch glass-based hard drives.

Japanese venture capitalists are also becoming somewhat more active in U.S. electronics. In 1984, Japan's largest venture capital fund, Japan Associated Finance Co. Ltd. (JAFCO), opened a Silicon Valley branch.[101] In 1988, Nippon Steel joined with the Boston-based Advent Capital to form a $15 million venture capital fund targeting the biotechnology, electronics, and advanced materials industries.[102] In spring 1991, a consortium of Japanese investors led by Nikko Capital Corp. Ltd. provided $7 million in venture capital funding for DSP Group, Inc., a Silicon Valley start-up that supplies digital signal processing chip-sets.[103]

Japanese Electronic Transplants in Europe

Japan's leading electronic corporations have also expanded into Europe. Most of the major Japanese television makers now operate manufacturing plants in England. As in the United States, these consist of both acquired and greenfield facilities. Japanese investment in Europe is spreading into semiconductor and computer production. The most important Japanese computer operation in Europe is ICL, which is 80 percent owned by Fujitsu, and in early 1991 ICL agreed to purchase the computer operations of a Finnish firm, Nokia.[103] Also, the French computer manufacturer, Bull, is becoming increasingly dependent upon NEC for technology. Similarly, in semiconductors most of the major Japanese producers have built semiconductor fabrication facilities in Europe.[104] In economic terms, Japanese electronic investment in Europe is becoming nearly as important as investment in the United States.

This section briefly examines the available record on the transfer of the Japanese industrial system to Europe.[105] Evidence of the transfer of Japanese relations to Europe would be an important indicator of the strength of the Japanese system on a global scale. On the other hand, the failure of the Japanese system in Europe would argue for Japanese and American exceptionalism (or vice versa). As we shall see, there is some reason to believe that important elements of the Japanese system have been transferred to England. And, in fact, in electronics, the European environment may be more congenial to the Japanese system than is the United States.

In contrast to the United States, most of the major Japanese electronics companies in England have accepted unions. However, they have managed to insist that the operations remain an open shop and that there be only one union in the factory, thereby circumventing the problems traditionally organized English factories have of multiple unions and the concomitant inability to shift workers freely from one job to another.[107] This also ensures that the union remains relatively weak vis-à-vis management. All sources report that workers are responsible for routine maintenance of their machines and for keeping their workplaces tidy.

The most exhaustive study of the operations of a Japanese consumer electronics firm in England is Malcolm Trevor's study of Toshiba. Trevor's main finding was that Toshiba's British plant is a "hybrid" that shares characteristics of Japanese and traditional British organization and management. According to Trevor, the

Toshiba plant has four job grades. However, these do not really define the jobs, but rather simply reflect different pay levels. The company has attempted to institute a "single-status" approach—essentially dining facilities that are open to all employees without discrimination on the basis of rank. It requires employees from the managing director down to wear a company coat or uniform. But uniform requirements vary at other companies. Matsushita has a uniform requirement similar to Toshiba's. Hitachi, which acquired a factory operated by a British firm, has been unsuccessful at implementing a uniform requirement. Toshiba places great emphasis on training and has devoted significant resources to provide both on-the-job and off-the-job training. Trevor also reports that Japanese engineers have kept control of production management at Toshiba.[108]

Most of the Japanese transplants in England report that they offer "high job security for blue-collar workers."[109] As in the United States, Japanese electronics operations in England have very strict rules regarding absence and tardiness. Japanese engineers and managers play an extremely hands-on role in British facilities. A study by Makoto Takamiya reports that every staff employee at one particular Japanese electronics firm "visits various departments and works for a few days at each before he formally starts working in the department he or she is assigned to."[110] Another Japanese company requires that "each newly recruited engineer spend at least his first six months at every section of the shop floor as a repairman," though these jobs are "more routine and less prestigious."[111] Interestingly, none of the Japanese electronic companies we visited (nor studies by other scholars) indicated that such a "to the shop floor" policy has been implemented in the United States.

Japanese electronic firms in England have tried to develop Japanese-style relationships with their suppliers. In 1982, Toshiba began inviting personnel from the suppliers to visit its factory. According to Malcolm Trevor, the purpose "was to talk to the shop-floor people who worked with the suppliers' products and could explain what was needed and what problems would be caused by any shortcomings."[112] Toshiba also offered to send its own engineers to its suppliers to provide technical assistance. Further, according to Trevor, Toshiba was said to be having trouble operating on a JIT system because of problems with its Asian sources and was trying to increase local sourcing.[113] However, thus far, only two Japanese electronic suppliers, Tabuchi and Alps Electric Co., had relocated to England.[114]

Japanese electronic manufacturers have found it difficult to get English suppliers to provide quality parts. According to a study by John Dunning, Sony found it necessary to bring much of its production in-house when it found it difficult to secure quality parts locally.[115] Still, Japanese electronic companies operating in England appear to have more local content than those in the United States. Sony's color television operation in Britain, for example, has approximately 80 percent to 85 percent local content level.[116]

In sum, the available evidence indicates that the Japanese electronic transplants in Europe have been more effective at transferring the Japanese model of innovation-mediated production than their counterparts in America. There are two possible reasons for this. First, the level of class formation and class consciousness is much higher in Europe and unions are also much stronger than in the American electronics industry. This is likely to have acted as a constraint on Japanese electronic producers who, in the United States, have benefitted from labor's extreme weakness in electronics and the existing "hire and fire" mentality. This hypothesis is supported by the fact that transfer of the Japanese model has gone much more smoothly in the U.S. automobile industry where the legacy of unionization and union strength is much stronger. Second, Europe is much more protectionist than the United States and has stricter regulations regarding domestic content. According to a recent study by the American Electronics Association, 70 percent of the semiconductor chips in Japanese televisions assembled in Europe came from European suppliers, whereas in the United States the domestic chip content is less than 1 percent.[117] Thus, Japanese electronic firms have been forced to transfer more of their suppliers and, as a result, more of their production system to Europe.

Limited Transfer

Japanese electronic corporations in the United States have not gone nearly as far as the transplant heavy industries in transferring the Japanese model of work and production organization in the United States. There is a tendency to have far more job classifications, to use fewer work teams and job rotation, to have more rigid reporting hierarchies, and to reproduce the traditional gulf between blue- and white-collar workers that still exists in American business. The transfer process also appears to vary more widely from firm to firm as well as between the various U.S. divisions of the same firm. The Japanese electronic transplants in the United States have an organizational structure and character that more resembles their American counterparts than their Japanese sister plants. They seem to have chosen the easier path by accepting the U.S. system as given, rather than attempting to transplant their Japanese operations.

Much of the reason for this is embedded in the structure and organization of the electronics industry itself. As we indicated at the outset, the electronics industry is not one industry or one product. The activities of a semiconductor fabrication facility, a consumer or business electronics assembly operation, and a communications equipment operation are remarkably different—though in Japan they all share a basic underlying model of production organization. Operations in the United States are complicated by coordination and reporting problems, which have thus far made it difficult for the various operations of even one company to work together and learn from one another.

Further, Japanese electronic manufacturers have had a long history of off-shore production activities in Asia and probably modelled their original strategy for U.S. production after their low-wage Asian branch plants. That is, they began by transferring low-end, highly standardized and routinized production processes that did not require innovation-mediated production. Usually, it has been stabilized processes, products, and technologies that were developed and perfected in Japan which have been transferred in toto to American production facilities.

Moreover, a number of the electronic transplants have been trapped by the existing context of work organization and/or labor-management relations. Some purchased U.S. facilities that they did not immediately attempt to restructure. Still others hired a large number of American managers and let them set up a U.S.-style operation. They unconsciously or consciously copied American practices in order to fit into local labor markets. Managers at one plant openly acknowledged that one of the leading U.S. firms in the area served as a model for much of their production and work organization. Japanese electronics firms have tended to adapt rather than to alter their environment. Simply put, electronics is a case of uneven transfer and limited transplantation of the Japanese production system.

In the area of supplier relations, the electronic transplants have found it difficult to recreate Japanese-style just-in-time production complexes. Perhaps the various U.S. subsidiaries will become somewhat better knit over time and allow the giant firms such as Toshiba, Matsushita, and Sony to use domestic suppliers. Investments by Japanese electronic suppliers are growing and thus local content will increase. Still, it is unlikely that regional transplant complexes and true just-in-time relations such as those in the automotive-related transplants will develop soon. The single exception may be the dense and rapidly growing concentration of transplants in the Portland area.

There is evidence to suggest that Japanese electronic manufacturers in the United States are disappointed with the current situation and are attempting to implement elements of innovation-mediated production. Many of them are seeking to institute work teams, to reduce job classifications, and to develop a capacity for continuous improvement in their work forces. Some are replacing American managers with Japanese managers as they endeavor to do this, and they are sending more and more of their workers to Japan for training. In addition, companies appear to be working harder to establish something approximating Japanese-style relations with their U.S. suppliers, and virtually all are increasing investment in plant-level product development and new high-end R&D laboratories. Japanese electronic companies may well become more Japanese in organization as time progresses.

III

FURTHER EVOLUTION

9

Tensions and Contradictions of the Transplants

Hegemony here is born in the factory and requires for its exercise only a minute quantity of professional and political intermediaries.

Antonio Gramsci[1]

Japanese corporations, their transplant factories and American work forces have faced numerous obstacles in the transfer of the Japanese industrial system to the United States. As we have already seen it has been hard for some workers and managers to move beyond the outmoded fordist organizational structure and behaviors to the innovation-mediated production model. The strategies and actions of some Japanese corporations and their transplant factories have at times complicated the transfer process.

This chapter moves our analysis in a new direction. It focuses on the obstacles and adaptation problems faced by the transplants, their work forces, and American communities. First, we consider the problematic impacts of this new mode of production organization on workers, including the fast pace of work, physical and mental stress, and injury. Second, we explore the use of both traditional and new forms of corporate control to orient, discipline, and control the work force. Third, we explore how the transplants have adapted to the racial, ethnic, and economic divisions of American society. Fourth, we consider the relationship of the transplants to the communities in which they are located by exploring a range of issues from government incentives and tax breaks to new forms of community control.

The transplant factories are not paradises. There is indeed an underside to the transfer and diffusion of Japanese work and production organization to the United States. Transplants in various industries impose strict rules on their workers; some even use methods of intimidation and surveillance to enforce company loyalty. A few transplants that have tried to get to full production very quickly have experienced high rates of injury among their workers. Some transplants are hostile to unions, which they see as constituting a major obstacle to their success, even though there are numerous instances of success with unionized plants. Others have pursued location, screening, and work-force selection policies that, in practice, operate to discriminate against minority groups.

This chapter also explores an underlying tension or contradiction of the model of innovation-mediated production more generally. This is a tension between the model's powerful ability to unleash human creative and intellectual capabilities and the use of forms of corporate control which differ from those used by U.S. corporations. These forms of corporate control function to align the individual interests of workers to broader corporate interests. This is especially crucial given the high degree of power and authority allocated to workers under this model so that they can contribute both their intellectual faculties and physical labor as a source of economic value and productivity growth. Such corporate control does not occur in a top-down fashion; rather, the relationships among the transplants, workers, and communities are part of an evolutionary process that evolves and changes in response to worker and community demands and often resistance to corporate prerogatives. In this sense, we emphasize again a main theme that has run throughout this book: the importance of ongoing, continuous, and frequently behind-the-scene tensions between labor and management in shaping the organization of work and production on the factory floor and the growth and effectiveness of new models of production organization.

Pumping Work Out of Workers

The transfer and diffusion of the new model of work and production organization to the United States has meant that American workers are required to adapt to a new, faster-paced, and more intensive labor process. Where highly functionally specialized fordist labor process was characterized by considerable redundancy and significant periods of downtime, the Japanese just-in-time system of work and production organization is premised upon eliminating downtime and waste—at filling in the pores of the working day.

Long work hours are a defining feature of Japanese manufacturing. In Japan, manufacturing workers average 2,088 working hours per year compared to 1,989 in Britain, 1,957 in the United States, 1,646 in France, and 1,638 in Germany. Japanese workers take an average of 7.9 holidays per year compared to 9.2 in the United States, 25 in Britain, 29 in France, and 27.9 in Germany.[2] Working hours are even longer for Japanese automobile workers who average more than 2,100 hours annually, hundreds of hours more than their counterparts in the United States and Europe but less than Korea where manufacturing workers average 2,400 plus hours per year. This represents on-the-job hours only and does not include the large number of hours devoted to after-work socializing. In addition, overtime is mandatory in Japan. A 1986 survey by the All Toyota Union found that approximately 124,000 of its total members suffer from chronic fatigue.[3]

In Japan an issue of increasing concern is *karoshi,* the Japanese word for death from overwork.[4] Japan's National Defense Council for Victims of Karoshi reports that a telephone hot-line in major Japanese cities registered 1,806 cases of overwork between June 1988 and June 1990, with 55 percent of the reports coming from wives who lost their husbands because of stroke or heart disease. According to the National Defense Council, the underlying causes of *karoshi* are unsound work practices, including heavy physical labor, long overtime, working without days off,

and excessive stress resulting from intense work responsibility, solitary job transfers, and forced job assignments. An official of Japan's National Institute of Public
Health defines *karoshi* as

> a condition in which psychologically unsound work practices are allowed to con-
> tinue in such a way that disrupts the worker's normal work and life rhythms, lead-
> ing to a buildup of fatigue in the body and a chronic condition of overwork
> accompanied by a worsening of preexisting high blood pressure and finally result-
> ing in a fatal breakdown.[5]

While overwork and *karoshi* are found in the blue-collar labor force, both are even
more prevalent among white-collar management workers, or the "salary-men."

The transplants appear to be creating some elements of overwork, although not
nearly to the extent as in Japan. To our knowledge, there have not been any cases
of *karoshi* among workers employed by the transplants. Still, employees in transplants in various industries work more time on average than do workers in fordist
factories. For example, employees at a major electronics firm we visited were
required to work up to 60 hours a week. Moreover, the pace of work is often faster
in the transplants than in traditional fordist factories. For example, a female
employee in a unionized automotive assembly transplant said that the pace of work
was so fast that she would at times be lifted dangerously off her feet and carried
down the assembly line as she worked to keep up with the line.

> There were times where you are so busy, you're working, you're bent over, you're
> kind of like lying on your back, you almost go with the car. . . . You just automat-
> ically go up, and you don't realize you're going up, then you slip and you fall down.[6]

Under the philosophy of Japanese production organization, workers are able to
stop the assembly line if they cannot immediately remedy production or quality
problems. Under fordist production methodology, stopping the line was an exclusive management right, and workers would simply continue producing defective
parts. Of course, the aim of the Japanese policy is not to slacken the pace. Rather,
the intended result is that when problems occur, workers and supervisors will work
frantically to remedy production or quality problems, even as the line is running.
Workers are supposed to notify team leaders who will then get the entire team working to overcome these problems, increasing the intensity of work for the group as a
whole. Workers at two of the unionized transplants indicated that they were pressured by management not to stop the line, while simultaneously they must keep
quality high.[7] As in the fordist factory, transplant management uses direct mechanisms to keep up the work pace. For example, workers may feel social pressure not
to take unscheduled breaks.

The crucial mechanism for maintaining the work pace is the team itself. The
team uses social pressure to push workers to work as hard and as fast as possible.
Since workers are part of an integrated production unit, when one worker slows
down, other workers must work harder to compensate. These pressure techniques
are most effective with fresh recruits who have not been socialized to relations in

fordist factories. These new workers do not have manufacturing work experience and want to make a good impression on management.

Repetitive-Motion Injury

Physical injuries are an obvious consequence of the fast work pace—and perhaps the most notable drawback of the transplants. Repetitive-motion injuries are common in automobile assembly and other forms of labor that place continuous stress on workers' wrists, hands, arms, shoulders, backs, etc. However, the number of injuries has apparently been unusual at some automobile assembly transplants. There have been reports of a high rate of repetitive-motion injury cases, in particular wrist and hand injuries such as carpal tunnel syndrome, at least two automotive assembly transplants. According to the *Detroit Free Press*—using Michigan Labor Department data—Mazda had more than three times as many injuries per hundred workers (4.1 per hundred) than the average for Big Three plants (1.2 per hundred) in 1988.[8] A female Mazda worker we interviewed said she left the company for fear of permanent injury.

> The reason I left was because I didn't want to be old at 40. A lot of my friends were getting hurt. . . . It's probably a man's job. Maybe that seems kind of sexist. My hand got hurt because the job I was on was using a big torque gun. I was putting lights on Probes. They weren't switching us around a lot so my hand got hurt, and every time I got put back on that job my hand would go numb again. And I would see the other women in my team were just looking old beyond their time and I didn't want that to happen to me and that's why I left. . . . It was the gun that you had to use. You always used it in one hand, and once in a while we'd switch to the other side. But it always seemed to be my right hand, because I'm right handed, so I ended up using the right hand, and it was kind of like the torque gun—it was hurting your nerves. But I saw a lot of girls and women, older women, really getting hurt—carpal tunnel. And I haven't had a problem since. There was one lady in my group that ended up having surgery. And I just didn't know if it was worth it.[9]

During the struggle to unionize Nissan, a UAW health and safety officer reported that one in five Nissan workers was injured in 1988, a rate it claimed was higher than at most automobile assembly plants. According to the Tennessee Department of Labor, 151 injuries at Nissan (59% of the total) were so serious that they caused the injured workers to miss more than a week of work.[10] A Nissan worker was quoted in the *New York Times* as saying:

> In my work area, I had back surgery and another guy had back surgery. . . . I can name four people who had back surgery, two people who had surgery on the elbows, another who had surgery from tendonitis and another guy who was out a long time with back trouble. That's out of 20 people.[11]

It is difficult to obtain reliable injury data for transplants and other industrial manufacturers, since injuries are often under-reported. Nissan refused to provide a list of the number and extent of individual injuries to state regulatory agencies.

Prior to the union representation vote, Nissan refused to allow workers to inspect the plant's injury logs. These logs are meant to be open to all employees by law, but Nissan charged that the workers were agents of the UAW and refused them access. The company was then fined $5,000 by the Tennessee Office of Occupational Safety and Health for not complying with state law.[12]

In extreme cases, workers have been fired as a result of being injured on the job. *Wards' Auto World* reported that a Mazda worker was terminated after injuring her shoulder, arm, and elbow. When she was initially injured, company doctors took this worker off the job and placed her on medical leave. Eventually the company told her to report back to work, even though she continued to experience pain and provided evidence that she was suffering from chronic carpal tunnel syndrome. When she refused to report to work, Mazda sent her a letter and fired her. According to one of her former co-workers at Mazda, "When she phoned and said, 'I'm on medical; how can you fire me?,' Mazda replied, 'Bring in your stuff; you're fired.' She is currently working at McDonald's."[13]

Repetitive-motion injury has been made worse in a number of the automotive assembly transplants that have recruited "fresh" workers with little or no manufacturing experience, and in other instances when large numbers of women have been placed in high-stress production jobs. This was due to the fact that in trying to reach full production quickly, a number of transplants were faced with shortages of sufficiently skilled and rotatable workers. These transplants forced workers to remain in high-stress jobs for extraordinarily long periods without rotation, thus increasing both the risk and the actual incidence of repetitive-motion injury.

A team leader at one automotive assembly transplant recounted a distressing cycle of injuries on his team, which does stressful, repetitive, but highly skilled work requiring significant training and experience. He said that every time he loses a worker it places additional pressure on the remaining workers and increases their stress levels, causing more injuries.

> At the present time I have got four people out on medical transfer or medical leave. . . . It takes anywhere from three to four months to become real proficient, depending on how quickly the person picks up the knowledge and what needs to be done and the right kind of quality. . . . We may get a temporary and not even have enough time to train them. We originally had eight people allotted for masking. Now I've got five people here and the team leader is masking daily, all day long. Those people were the stronger ones; they were able to adjust to all the movements, all different types of things that are involved. They were strong enough to hold out and not have medical problems. The other ones saw early on that they had medical problems even before we got into half of what our full production was then. So now I have five people that are doing the work that eight people should be doing. Now they're starting to develop the same medical problems that the other ones have.[14]

Management Failure

Management's failure to implement the Japanese system of work and production organization—not the system itself—may be at least partly to blame for the high rate of injury at a number of the automotive transplants. Contrary to what some critics have implied, such a high level of repetitive-motion injury is not a necessary result of Japanese production organization.[15] Rather, the large number of injuries experienced at some transplants appears to result from a failure to implement the Japanese system properly. Indeed, the Japanese system of team-based production and worker rotation is designed in such a way that it should minimize repetitive-motion injury through rotating workers in high-impact jobs. At Japanese automobile assembly plants in Japan, workers in high-stress jobs rotate as often as once an hour to reduce the risk of repetitive-motion injury. Workers also do morning exercises to reduce risk of injury even further. However, the automotive transplants are not always managed in the same way as in Japan. The team leader quoted above on the cycle of injuries to his team members indicated that the injury rate for the same work group is much lower at his company's sister plant in Japan.

> The people that they employ in their masking area are continually turning over. And the people that they bring in are very young, so they are a lot more agile, capable of bending and the stooping moves; I think their bodies are still toned from athletics in high school to be able to do the job and not bother them. I was there in January and February of 1989 and I just went back September of 1990; they had already turned over the whole masking area. Here, we don't discriminate by age. . . . A lot of people I got have degrees; they were working at a desk. Now they're thrown into something that their body has to get used to. A lot of the ones right off the bat who didn't get used to it or felt like they couldn't get used to it had problems. It presents a real big problem. I feel for the people who are still working because they're having to pick up the extra because we don't have anybody else to do it. And I'm afraid that I'm eventually going to lose all of those new people, and our turnover rate is probably going to be equal to that of Japan's. But ours is going to be very different.[16]

Mazda workers we interviewed indicated that the high initial rate of injury appears to be caused at least in part by the American management's failure to implement fully the Japanese system of rotating workers to different jobs daily. This forced workers to remain in jobs for lengthy periods of time (i.e., one to four weeks), thus contributing to repetitive-motion injuries. According to one Mazda worker:

> That was one of the biggest problems. . . . I don't think it would have hurt your hand if you moved around using it doing different things, but it was always the same type of equipment for a long period of time. It could have been a month. We always would complain and they'd say that they were so short-handed that the team leaders had to be on line too, which was true. But it was at least a month sometimes. . . . People started getting hurt when they got stuck on a job too long.[17]

A recent UAW-sponsored survey of over 2,400 Mazda workers sheds additional light on management failure in the Mazda plant. Fifty percent of workers answered no to the question "In my team, do we rotate jobs fairly?" Eighty-six percent of workers thought that their "unit leaders" or first-level supervisors could not "be trusted to implement the Mazda philosophy." And only 26 percent believed they could "stay healthy and make it to retirement" at the "present work intensity."[18] Over the past several years, Mazda has tried to cope with its work force by moving so-called hard-liners into top human resources posts in order to cope with the union. This strategy only appears to have made matters worse. Here, it is worth pointing out that Mazda recruited one of its top human resource officials from Volkswagen's defunct New Stanton, Pennsylvania, plant—a plant which was characterized by sorely adversarial labor-management relations and was thought by many to have among the worst labor relations climates in the automobile industry.

Nissan has experienced similar problems. Its American assembly plant hired large numbers of American managers and tried to implement a hybrid system of work and production organization. Management officials we interviewed plainly stated that the company stopped job rotation completely during recent production buildups.

It is worth highlighting that Nissan and Mazda are somewhat unique among the automotive transplants—both have faced pressure to accelerate production quickly, and this has led to the use of traditional American techniques—for example, training workers in one task and keeping them in that one job during the entire accelerated period. Part of the reason for this at Nissan appears to have been its large contingent of former Big Three managers who were initially recruited to staff upper-level management positions and apparently attempted to implement a Japanese work pace by using some traditional fordist techniques. Mazda faced even greater pressure from its U.S. partner, Ford, to initiate high-volume production of the new Ford Probe. In Japan, acceleration of production proceeds much more slowly and allows workers to be cross-trained and rotated. Moreover, new Japanese plants have the advantage of being able to draw a significant portion of the work force from existing, highly experienced workers. The partial polluting of the transfer process by the injection of fordist practices by American managers appears to be a general problem faced by many transplants.

At times, such problems have been compounded because workers have not been allowed to exert control over important elements of production such as job rotation and work design. According to a union official for the Mazda plant, "Mazda has complete control of job design, how many people work at a station, how fast they work, how long they work, are you rotated, are you not rotated, complete control."[19] A number of transplants such as Toyota, Honda, and Nippondenso have avoided these problems by rotating workers frequently and implementing a much more complete version of Japanese production methodology from the start. In these transplants, work teams have much greater control over crucial aspects of shop-floor production such as when and where to rotate.

Some transplants, facing acute shortages of trained or acclimated employees have forced production workers to work while injured. Most of the automobile transplants have on-site medical clinics that evaluate and treat injured workers. This can cause problems as a number of workers and union officials reported instances where employees were sent to a company doctor, examined, given cursory therapy, and returned to their jobs. At times, the number of injured workers can be so large that they exceed the capacity of company clinics; as a result, many employees are forced to continue working without receiving necessary treatment.

In other instances, the work pace may be so demanding that supervisors and team leaders do not allow workers to go to scheduled doctors' appointments. A female worker at a unionized automotive assembly transplant recalled her experience with the company doctor:

> Sometimes the clinic was so backed up that it would take you an hour and a half [to be seen]. . . . They would give you an ultrasound or something like that, and wrap your hand. Then if the doctor didn't say no you couldn't do the work, then you would go back to work. If the doctor said no you can't go to work, then they would put you on another job; it just depended. What happened with me is that my hand would numb. It was tingling, and without any tests or anything he said you're using the hand too much so they did change my job, but I was still doing the same type of job only with a smaller gun.[20]

It is important to point out that such injury problems are much less pronounced in the steel, rubber and tire, and electronics transplants.

Corporate Control

There is a fairly extensive literature on corporate control. Richard Edwards has differentiated among "direct," "technical," and "bureaucratic" forms of corporate control, the latter involving a combination of technological and administrative control.[21] Michael Burawoy suggests that a crucial aspect of factory organization lies in the organizational elements, norms, and practices used to "manufacture consent," suggesting that factories and factory regimes differ in the ways they organize corporate control.[22] He refers to corporate control in the Japanese factory as encompassing a form of "hegemonic despotism" involving a high degree of direct and indirect control over workers' lives. Another perspective suggested by Ronald Dore argues that the nexus of corporate control in Japan lies in the Japanese form of "welfare corporatism," a unique synthesis of bureaucracy and paternalism where corporate institutions ensure that workers' needs are met by the company.[23] A number of Japanese scholars view long-term employment as a central element of corporate control—one designed to foster employee loyalty and dedication, and more importantly to align worker and company interests.[24] These perspectives offer important insight into the exercise of corporate control.

However, we believe that Antonio Gramsci formulated the question of corporate control in a unique way that provides an important insight in understanding Japan. What he focused upon was the power and influence of hegemony in the workplace. For Gramsci, corporate hegemony could be indirect as well as direct; in fact, hegemony was more effective when it evolved and operated behind the backs of workers. According to Gramsci, "Adaptation to new methods of production and work cannot take place simply through social compulsion. . . . Coercion has therefore to be ingeniously combined with persuasion and consent."[25]

The core of the new model of innovation-mediated production lies in its ability to get workers to contribute ideas, offer suggestions, and make continuous improvements in products, quality, and manufacturing processes. These ideas are used to generate productivity improvements—in effect, workers are called upon to increase their own rate and pace of work. While the transplants certainly push workers hard, operate at a fast pace, and in some cases have injury problems, this is not the core of their difference from fordist plants. In contrast to critics of the Japanese labor process, who focus exclusively on the fast pace and physical stress brought about by the process, the real key to understanding the Japanese model of production organization lies in the way it extends its reach to the workers' intellectual capabilities and uses group social processes to increase the total work accomplished.

Clearly, it is difficult to get workers simply to hand over their intellectual abilities to management. This, however, is the real key to the new model of innovation-mediated production. To harness workers' intellectual capabilities effectively, Japanese corporations utilize various motivational mechanisms and forms of corporate control. Such control mechanisms are required to align the interests of the workers with that of the company and create a context within which workers will "voluntarily" contribute their ideas, suggestions, and improvements in production. A key element of this form of corporate control involves establishing an identity between workers and the corporation—creating what might be termed a "corporatist hegemony" over work life. Such identification makes workers feel as though they are a part of an over-arching corporate entity. As such, it creates implicit and subtle forms of coercion and motivation, spurring workers to work hard, think for the company, and assist in motivating fellow workers.

Some Japanese labor sociologists refer to this phenomenon as "voluntarism"— a concept they use to describe the process of workers readily supplying their ideas, suggestions, and intellectual capabilities to management.[26] Japanese corporations establish extensive means of social control and, indeed, socialization to ensure that workers identify with the company. These include company activities, corporate socializing, company-sponsored sports events, and even company towns like Toyota City. Corporations became "total institutions" exerting influence over many aspects of social life. In this sense, they bear some resemblance to other forms of total institutions such as religious orders or the military.

While most Japanese scholars tend to take a top-down view of voluntarism, seeing it as imposed by the company, a more dialectical view of voluntarism can be developed by building upon the pioneering work of Andrew Gordon, who suggests that the framework of Japanese labor relations and work organization has evolved in the process of resistance and accommodation between capital and labor, which sometimes assumes explicit forms like strikes, but more frequently goes on behind the scenes. This perspective of the labor process suggests that corporate control is not simply forced upon workers in a top-down fashion; rather, it evolves and changes in a dynamic way as a result of ongoing struggles and negotiations at the point of production.[27]

Given this perspective, it is possible to outline a general or model theory of corporate control as a dynamic and adaptive process comprised of four related elements: socialization, daily routines, discipline, and resistance. First, socialization consists of direct inculcation into the rules, regulations, norms, and values of the corporation. In Japanese firms, socialization occurs and is reinforced continuously through various formal and informal mechanisms such as initial training, ongoing counseling, and reinforcement of company norms and practices.[28] Second, daily routines are a key aspect of corporate control in both Japanese corporations and in the transplants. Through individual workers' routines, and more importantly through the overall structure of daily routines, workers learn their role in the company—what is acceptable and unacceptable behavior. Daily routines reinforce and go beyond formal and informal socialization.

Third, as theorists such as Michel Foucault have shown,[29] discipline is a crucial component of control in social institutions and nations. Discipline is an integral part of control in the factory. However, Japanese firms differ from American firms in the way they organize and utilize discipline to control their work forces. In the American factory, there is a clear and codified distinction between "right" and "wrong," with wrong or improper behavior subject to punishment via suspension, imposed layoff, or dismissal. Often such punishments are given purely for punishment's sake, rather than to help remediate what is seen to be improper behavior. For example, workers who are chronically late in American companies are typically given mandatory time off as their punishment. In Japan there is a less formalized distinction between right and wrong, and workers are rarely punished. Instead, discipline under normal conditions takes the form of ongoing "counseling" by peers as well as superiors. Such counseling typically consists of pointing out the improper behavior, discussing its likely causes, and reinforcement of the correct or company way. Of course, if the behavior does not change, termination could be used.

Fourth, corporate control is not simply organized and implemented from above. Rather, corporate control in the Japanese factory evolves in response to worker demand, labor-management struggle, and active resistance on the shop floor. Workers' resistance and struggles create a constant and continuous process of change in the organization of control on the factory floor. For example, as Chapter 2 has shown, suggestion systems and *kaizen* were originally implemented in response to the militant strikes and industrial unrest of the postwar period as a way to obtain information on sources of worker dissatisfaction.[30] Only later did *kaizen,* Q.C., and suggestion systems evolve into the current system, which is designed to improve productivity. Evolving continuously and almost imperceptibly, such control mechanisms are far more effective than ones imposed upon workers from above.

The Japanese transplants employ various forms of corporate control to ensure the successful transfer of Japanese production and work organization to the United States. Like their parent firms in Japan, the transplants exert direct and indirect control over their work forces to motivate them and encourage them to identify with the company. Workers are urged to dedicate their efforts to the goals of the company. Criticism often voiced by workers must be understood as resembling the "voice" option because "exit" is difficult.[31] But prior to exploring the various forms of corporate control we have found in the transplants, it is useful to outline briefly the nature of corporate control in the fordist factory.

Corporate Control in the Fordist Factory

In the U.S. fordist system, redundancy was built into both the organization and actual functioning of the labor process. As numerous students of the fordist labor process such as Harry Braverman, David Noble, and William Lazonick have shown, fordist production methodology involved the de-skilling of shop-floor labor.[32] Under fordism, factory workers were (incorrectly) looked upon as easily replaceable cogs in the machine. While management tried to push and coerce employees to work harder, gradually workers and their unions developed an entire apparatus of rules, job descriptions, and social norms against management encroachments. These can be conceptualized as a series of fordist "trench lines" that protected workers against managers, but also provided managers with a stable framework within which to deal with workers. The most important and salient of these was the extensive system of job classifications, which expressly limited the activities of specific workers. This system of job classifications created formal rules over the allocation of work within the division of labor. Formal rules developed that delineated management and worker rights, production standards, layoff proce- dures, and rules of behavior on the shop floor covering everything from absences to eating at a work station to fighting with fellow workers.[33]

Under these formal and informal systems of shop-floor control, workers grad- ually won a significant degree of control over work timing. Automobile workers were able to take breaks and even eat lunch or have a snack while performing line operations. These systems conferred differential benefits to the various strata of workers. In the automotive industry, for example, the labor aristocracy of skilled trades was able to take advantage of significant idle time in the factory, while the masses of regular production employees were forced to labor more continuously and work significantly harder.

In steel, an even greater amount of time was spent not working as employees developed elaborate systems to resist management's efforts to make them work harder. Ultimately, workers in fordist factories were able to spend a considerable amount of their time not working. In his account of the decline of the American steel industry, John Hoerr recounts his own experiences as a steelworker in the late 1940s and 1950s:

> No one in the plant seemed to care that an enormous amount of time was spent not working. I'm not referring here to furnace operators or to production crews that operated blooming mills and pipe mills. Working on incentive pay, these crews worked steadily, if not at breakneck speed, to meet an output standard that would give them sufficient return for a day's labor. Some mills had larger crews than were actually needed; the least skilled crew members could double up on duties and spell one another for extended breaks. . . . Maintenance workers, laborers, and people assigned to other miscellaneous jobs, however, had neither the economic or psy- chological incentive to do any more work than the foreman required them to do. . . . In the dark recesses of a mill building it was easy to find a place to hole out for a few hours to read or sleep. . . . Most employees carried a dog-eared Bantam novel in their hip pockets, to read a chapter at a time, behind a stack of pipe, when the foreman wasn't around. . . . Barney Joy, a foreman at National Tube from 1954 until he retired in 1976, remembered the time especially well. "It was difficult to break them of those Bantam books," he said. "We had set up rules that anybody who was caught reading would get time off. If they'd sit and read while you broke down, you wouldn't mind. But trying to read and operate, that created hazards."[34]

This limited form of workers' control also extended into other areas. Workers and their unions also fought vigorously for and eventually won the right to have an important measure of control over the choice of days when they would come to work. Unions developed an elaborate contractual structure and grievance mechanism to protect employees from management's attempts to exert social control by limiting absences or days off. Labor contracts devoted extensive portions of the agreement to the rights of workers to have sick days and vacation days and to have significant discretion in the use of the days they wished to take off. Thus, control of the disposition of a worker's time was constantly disputed. Employees could take days off whenever they chose, read magazines on the shop floor, take unauthorized breaks (i.e., without the direct permission of management), and so forth. The response of American managers was to hire large reserves of utility workers whose role was to fill in for absent regular workers. There was always a surplus of workers to perform given tasks.

However, by the 1970s and early 1980s, the entire fabric of control and indeed of organization broke down in many fordist factories. Workers had achieved a significant ability to thwart management initiatives. Within the context of the fordist factory and the alienating conditions of its labor processes, this power was expressed in negative ways. Workers were absent frequently, some whenever possible. For many who did come to work, drugs and alcohol became necessary crutches for coping with the conditions inside the plant. This created a worsening downward spiral of decay and disorganization.

Socializing American Workers

The Japanese expression of innovation-mediated production aims to have workers identify as closely and completely with the company as possible. This form of social control and socialization is embedded in the recruitment, selection, and initial training of workers. As we have already seen, most Japanese transplants employ elaborate recruitment procedures, using a combination of intelligence and psychological tests, physical examinations, drug and alcohol tests, personal interviews, and two- or three-day visits to specialized recruitment facilities designed to select workers who are group-oriented, who identify with their employer, and who generally fit Japanese production methodology.[35] Workers may be sent to Japanese sister plants where they experience intensive immersion in Japanese production methodology and more directed socialization to the company's particular behavioral norms. Nearly all transplants use temporary employment and/or probationary periods to screen workers more thoroughly. According to a dissident union official at a transplant assembly facility, temporary workers provide the company with "a very good way to screen out . . . any worker who complains." He then went on to characterize the company's decision-making process as follows:

> We will hire this man; he told on two workers, . . . he plays golf with the union leader; yes, we will hire him. This person, he asks too many questions, no. Wife died; he missed two days work, no. This person . . . caused trouble; no. This person took vacation; no.[36]

Socialization is an ongoing and continuous process with constant training and counseling. Trips to Japan for team leaders and supervisors are both an incentive and a reinforcement mechanism. Ensuring workers' consent is considered crucial for successful operations. Behavior is reinforced through group meetings and more targeted counselling sessions for employees who have trouble fitting in. These counseling sessions are aimed at pointing out problematic behavior in a nonthreatening way, thereby reinforcing corporate norms and explaining methods of correcting problematic behavior. The transplants go to great lengths to minimize and limit dissent and morale problems while avoiding the drawing of clear lines of conflict.

A variety of mechanisms are used to limit dissent and identify potential "troublemakers." A former employee of a nonunionized transplant assembler indicated that workers are afraid to speak out against the company for fear of being branded "difficult" or "troublemakers." There are reports that some managers at other transplants sometimes use threats and intimidations to motivate employees to work harder. According to the dissident union president at one automotive transplant, the company has "threatened people with their jobs."[37] Not surprisingly, transplants that have the most confrontational relations appear to be experiencing the least success transferring aspects of the Japanese system, which requires worker initiatives such as *kaizen* and quality-control activities.

Creating a Corporate Family

As in Japan, the transplants endeavor to blur the distinction between work and home life, creating an extended corporate family to encourage workers to identify themselves closely with the company. Managers and team leaders are encouraged to build social relationships with workers inside and outside of the plant. As in Japan, team leaders at some transplants are expected to organize parties and sporting events for their teams. At others, managers are required to know a whole range of personal information about workers and their families: birth dates, anniversaries, names of spouse, children, etc. This is done to reinforce the identity between worker and company. The importance of such an alignment is highlighted by a Japanese executive coordinator for human resources who has been integrally involved in the transfer of the Japanese manufacturing management model at his company's U.S. facilities:

> The individual versus the organization: we always emphasize that you work for the *company* [emphasis added]—what is best for the company organization. We recognize effort as group performance. Although we have to recognize individual contribution, this development must produce group performance. When you go into many organizations in the United States you will find that the individual is working for himself or for the boss, not for the company. Maybe they are a very capable person, but their direction is not necessarily [that] of the company. Particularly when you start a new plant, you must develop a corporate culture which is common for all employees. We emphasize problem-solving skills and that helps us *kaizen* out many problems. Americans don't understand that. So we need a common language, a common company goal. It doesn't mean that you sacrifice individual

development. We want to keep both—company and individual development—
hand in hand.[38]

A number of transplants use various mechanisms such as company days, sporting events and recreational activities to create this alignment. Toyota, for example,
has an extensive program called "Personal Touch" at both NUMMI (in Fremont,
California) and its Georgetown plant, which finances group activities such as picnics that are meant to infuse corporate spirit. Toyota also has a similarly named
though much more extensive program in Japan. Many transplants have regular
company picnics. Others have family days in which workers can invite their families to visit their plant. These activities have an impact. For example, a worker at
the NUMMI plant said:

> We just had our family day at NUMMI. I took my whole family. They get to see us
> build cars. It's another good feeling. This guy [the worker's young son] hasn't
> missed one since I've been working there. He gets to look at all the robots.[39]

The ultimate purpose is to build a set of social relationships that are supportive of
the company and that create a close alignment between work and home life. The
corporation shows that it cares and establishes a much firmer bond with the
employee. In return, workers are expected to sacrifice themselves and, owing to at
times extreme overtime demands, some of their family life as well for the enterprise.

Communication and Corporate Control

The transplants employ various mechanisms to communicate company messages
to their employees. A number of automotive transplants use signs and other forms
of "visual management" to urge workers to work harder, faster, and smarter, to
improve quality, and devote themselves to the company.[40] Two nonunionized
assembly transplants have installed internal television systems to communicate
company messages to workers and specifically to combat union organizing drives.[41]
Nearly all transplants of significant size use a company-sponsored newspaper to
communicate with workers. Others communicate through personalized letters to
employees. The dissident union president at one automotive assembly transplant
stated in an interview that the company has used letters to urge workers to work
harder and more selflessly for the company, and that these letters create a clear distinction between "good" and "bad" workers and encourage recipients to work
harder for the good of "all."

> Japanese company letters always start very nice. Thank you for your hard work.
> Next paragraph. Are you a terrible worker? Quality is terrible; we're not profitable.
> Very interesting. All Japanese letters start out nice, happy family . . . very good,
> aren't we lucky. Next paragraph: going down the tubes, it's your fault, terrible work-
> ers, we made no money. But I don't mean to insult Japanese; it's the same thing
> with the American manufacturers.[42]

Uniforms are another, seemingly benign mechanism of social control. The wearing of uniforms by all workers helps create the perception of equality in contrast to the blue-collar/white-collar distinction that is so glaring in the fordist environmment. Uniforms also have the technical advantage of being designed with the work process in mind and thus may be safer and offer less possibility of scratching or damaging the work in process.

On the other hand, uniforms can be seen as an element of social control. Uniforms are used to make all workers look the same and identify with company managers who wear the same uniforms (i.e., they create the image of an egalitarian corporate family). They also make it difficult for workers to wear personalized clothes or symbols. At nonunionized transplants this can be an effective way to combat the union, which uses caps, badges, and other artifacts to communicate its message and build solidarity. At least one nonunionized transplant assembler prohibited its workers from wearing UAW caps to work on the grounds they might promote injury. Another nonunionized transplant has made uniforms mandatory to prevent workers from wearing any kind of UAW emblem or paraphernalia. According to an American human resources manager at a nonunionized assembly transplant:

> That's why we do some of the things we do. Like with the uniforms. For example, another transplant has a uniform that the people are not required to use, so when they had their campaign down there, people were wearing UAW T-shirts, people were wearing anti-UAW T-shirts, and they had a lot of friction between the work force. Now our workers are required to wear a uniform. You can't wear the UAW stuff and make that friction visible to everybody. "Oh, he's a supporter, and I'm not."[43]

Another contradictory feature of the Japanese system is the emphasis on warmup exercises. Stretching exercises are an excellent idea for any person preparing to do strenuous physical activity, but there is simultaneously an aspect of regimentation and coercion in them.[44]

Information gathering can also serve as an element of social control. The transplants go to great lengths to encourage communication with workers and urge them to express their feelings about things that bother them. Many transplants have information sessions between workers and managers; others use an open door policy to encourage workers to come forward with their problems. While many of these practices can be seen as positive, they also provide crucial sources of information on worker attitudes and potential sources of discontent. They can also be used to identify potential troublemakers. Workers at some transplants are encouraged to tell managers about others who are experiencing problems adapting or fitting in. A former engineer at an automotive assembly transplant recounted being called in for mandatory counseling after complaining to a secretary about working conditions and management procedures.[45]

There can also be problems in the unionized transplants with the cooperation between union and management. At two of the unionized automotive assembly transplants, union representatives shared the same office with company labor relations staff and some workers apparently could not distinguish between them. At one of these transplants, a number of workers unwittingly complained to managers, thinking they were union representatives, and it is reported that some of these workers were fired. According to the union president:

> Our union representatives shared the same office with labor relations. There are no doors, walls. Whoever comes in has a problem with their supervisor. But the supervisor's boss is right here. . . . Originally, our members did not even understand the difference between someone from labor relations and someone from the UAW; it's all one in the same. Many times members would cut their own throats speaking to a labor relations person, thinking it was the UAW, saying my supervisor he did this. "Oh, is that right?" and he would be fired.[46]

The union representatives at this plant now wear identification badges.

Absence and Attendance Policies

In contrast to the fordist factory, both union and nonunion transplants have very few or no replacement workers, thus attendance rules are very tight. Excellent attendance is critical to the Japanese production system, and the companies do everything in their power to achieve it. Most transplants use positive sanctions such as monthly bonuses to reward workers with perfect attendance records. But attendance is mandatory and workers are counseled and/or disciplined for as little as one absence in a month. They can be fired if they are absent four or five times in a year. Unexcused or frequent absence is seen as a serious breach of company policy and will lead to rapid termination.

Many transplants use what are referred to as "no-fault" absence policies. In these systems, all absences are counted on the record—even documented illnesses. A three-day absence counts as three absences—only a documented doctor's note can have it reduced to one. In contrast, unionized fordist plants provide a large number of rotating sick days for workers. Even the strictest fordist plants allow workers 15 to 20 unaccounted absences before any sort of discipline is invoked. A typical absenteeism policy, such as that at NUMMI allows worker's three absences over a 90-day period before being counselled or disciplined; four absences in a year can result in dismissal.[47] And this is a unionized transplant where workers' protections are more formalized.

Management in the nonunionized transplants has even greater latitude in disciplining and firing workers who are absent. At Toyota's Georgetown, Kentucky, plant, the absence policy does not specify any sick days. Workers intending to be absent are required to call their team leader at least one-half hour before work begins. Toyota managers indicated that an employee with more than three absences within a year is considered dubious; five absences is seen as a problem. Toyota's attendance policy has one exception: Workers are allowed three consecutive days off with pay "up to and including the day of the funeral" for a death in the immediate family. The "Team Member Handbook" for Toyota workers devotes an entire section to the company's attendance policy under the title "Good Attendance Is Critical to Our Success," which reads as follows:

> We cannot emphasize enough the importance of good attendance to the success of the Toyota production system. . . . TMM's expectation in the area of team member attendance is that people come to work each day—on time. . . . When a team member develops problems with respect to their attendance, these problems will be addressed . . . through the TMM "Corrective Action Program." It is important to note, however, that if team members demonstrate that they cannot or are not willing to come to work on a regular basis, then they will be subject to discharge from employment. . . . If you are absent from work for three (3) consecutive workdays and fail to contact TMM, the Company will assume that you have resigned your employment effective on the third day of absence.[48]

The Japanese transplants are adamant that employees work the entire working day. This is in contrast to the fordist plants, where labor had greater discretion regarding punctuality. Workers were simply paid for the time they worked, but were not usually disciplined if they choose to come in late or leave work early. At the transplants, coming to work late or leaving early are typically seen as serious breaches of company policy, as serious as absence. NUMMI workers receive a warning after being late or leaving early just three times in a 45-day period; as with absenteeism, four offenses can result in dismissal.[49] The transplants also firmly control the other elements of shop-floor behavior with strict policies prohibiting workers from eating or drinking at their workstations.

Mazda's attendance and absence policy has been a bitter point of contention between management and the union. In October 1989, after much pressure from the union, Mazda management agreed to institute a "no-fault" absentee policy allowing up to 15 unexcused absences a year before dismissal and providing financial bonuses for good attendance. Mazda's top Japanese executives opposed this new policy citing Mazda's already high absenteeism rate. According to reports in *Automotive News,* Mazda's American vice president of operations and manufacturing and American vice president of personnel resigned under pressure from Japanese top management immediately after the new program was instituted.[50]

Peer Discipline

Peer discipline is perhaps the most important element of social control in the Japanese transplants because it does not involve a direct confrontation between management and labor. The work teams and peer review committees become the first line of discipline. Team members are expected to counsel workers who miss work or experience other problems, and if problems persist to transmit that information to management. At many transplants, it is the responsibility of team members to talk to workers who are having problems, offer support, and through this process reinforce company policies. Managers at Toyota, Nissan, and numerous transplant suppliers suggested that teams provide the peer pressure required to keep most workers in line. The Toyota "Team Member Handbook" clearly states that, "Problems are resolved through team effort. When a team member feels overburdened, it is considered to be a problem and through a team effort we strive hard to resolve it."[51]

Peer pressure is intense because there are no extra workers in the Japanese transplants. The absent worker's load falls on fellow team members. When a worker is
out, the team leader is usually required to substitute. This burdens the entire team
since the team leader is no longer free to help other workers with direct production
or quality problems. If two workers are absent, the team must redesign its tasks to
fulfill the production demands, creating additional pressure on the remaining team
members. Thus pressure on workers not to be absent is engineered into the system.

In a similar way, other types of disciplinary activities are mediated through
peers and team members. The team leader is expected to discuss absences with a
worker. Frequently, team members are encouraged to help counsel workers who
are absent and transmit information to team leaders or to management. Workers
who are absent a few times are typically placed in mandatory counseling where
team leaders or management representatives probe the cause of absence and suggest
ways to remedy the problem. They reiterate the importance of good attendance to
both the worker's team and to the company. At some transplants, workers who
exceed the absenteeism policy have their cases reviewed by "peer review" committees made up of other workers.

Peer committees also review other cases and can actually implement discipline.
This places much of the burden of work discipline on the workers and deflects attention from what usually is an important area of labor-management conflict. A
NUMMI worker put it quite succinctly: "In the past there was a foreman, so we
could file a grievance. But now it's a union member bossing people around, and the
line between union and management is so confused it's hard to know how to fight
back."[52] The power of the peer discipline is that it effectively obfuscates the antagonistic aspects of the employment relation.

Temporary Workers

Nearly all Japanese transplants use large numbers of temporary workers. This
divides the work force and undermines shop-floor solidarity. Temporary workers
provide a class of relatively cheap labor that can be hired and fired virtually at will.
This is most evident in the unionized transplants where permanent workers have
some measure of job security. At one automotive assembly transplant, the use of
large numbers of temporary workers has become a central issue in ongoing labor-
management controversies. According to the president of the union local:

> Temporary workers pay union dues but have no rights to union representation.
> The company can hire and fire, no seniority, no rights, no nothing. . . . It's a very
> vicious system. [These workers] are very intimidated; they work very fast, disregard
> injuries, have no rights, and they know they have no rights. If they go to medical,
> complain that their hand does not work, they're out. So they work injured; they
> work very fast; they're afraid to ask questions to complain, afraid to demand proper
> safety and training, etc.[63]

By the very nature of their insecure position, temporary employees are forced
to work very hard in the hope of obtaining a permanent employment slot. Tem-

porary workers can be used to show permanent employees "how good they have it" and further heighten their commitment to the company. Regular workers may perceive themselves as better than or more privileged than temporaries, thereby weakening their workplace solidarity. A temporary worker at one automotive transplant was quoted in the *New York Times* as saying:

> It doesn't give us much of a life, working on the edge as a temporary employee. They think of us as throwaway people.[54]

Similarly, Japanese electronics operations in this country use temporary employment as a way of evaluating employees before hiring them permanently.

The temporary-worker phenomenon is the direct transfer of a feature of the Japanese system. This category of workers is essentially powerless and vulnerable. This contradiction, though visible in Japan (and certainly visible in the U.S. in the form of companies such as Kelly Girl and Manpower), has been resisted by unions in American factories. Still, in the nonunionized plants the use of temporary employees is likely to continue unabated.

The Myth and Reality of Long-Term Employment

Long-term employment is a key feature of the Japanese model. Long-term employment extends to workers in core production facilities in the automobile, steel, rubber, and electronic industries in Japan. According to the best available estimates, roughly one-third of the Japanese production labor force is covered by long-term employment.

In Japan long-term employment is not formally guaranteed but is a practice that has become the norm in large firms. At most of the large transplant facilities, managers wish to have long-term employment. However, they do not want this written into contracts as it limits flexibility. Thus, in the United States, where the same expectations and commitment do not exist, Japanese transplants have not made contractual commitments to long-term employment. Hence the ability to hire and fire freely is one area where the transplants appear to have adapted to prevailing American practice. Only a small number of unionized automotive assemblers and only one of the steel transplants, National Steel, provides formal guarantees of long-term employment. The automotive parts suppliers do not provide guarantees of employment security, and neither the unionized nor the nonunionized electronic transplants provide any tenure security at all. In electronics and a number of other industries, long-term employment is far more tenuous; often, long-term employment is not even mentioned to employees. While a number of Japanese firms have made efforts to retain employees during a downturn, the commitment to employment security is not nearly as strong as it is in Japan. In contrast to American practice, however, the transplants see white-collar workers as more expendable than blue-collar workers, who are directly involved in production activity. In recent years a number of Japanese transplants have actually laid off American workers. In January 1991, the *Wall Street Journal* reported:

282 FURTHER EVOLUTION

At many American facilities, Japanese employers are furloughing workers. When Japanese companies operate overseas they operate under the customs of the countries they work in. . . . NEC making several downsizing moves says it has no guaranteed employment policy, despite some people's assumptions. Matsushita Electric of America, Sanyo and Toshiba all have laid off American employees.[55]

And, in February 1991, the Japanese publication *Nihon Keizai Shimbun* reported that a number of Japanese companies were laying off U.S. workers in response to the recession, including layoffs of 500 by Bridgestone-Firestone, 500 at Armco Steel's Middletown and Ashland works, and 200 more by Komatsu-Dresser.[56] Only time will tell how committed the other transplants are to tenure security as well. The phenomenon of layoffs is especially interesting, since the employment relationship forms the bedrock of Japanese labor relations, with security seen as key to having "smart workers" who are committed and involved. If, as we hypothesized, long-term employment is an important factor in the successful retention of employee commitment and active participation in innovation-mediated production, it follows that the absence of security may make it difficult to maintain the work-force commitment required for successful *kaizen* and continuous process improvement in the United States.

Race and the Transplants

Perhaps the most hotly debated underside of the transplants involves the question of race. In a widely debated article published in 1988, Robert Cole and Donald Deskins reported data suggesting that the siting decisions of automotive transplants had a discriminatory impact on African-Americans and other minorities.[57] They conclude that "Japanese firms can stay within Equal Employment Opportunity Commission (EEOC) guidelines and still hire very few blacks. By placing their plants in areas with very low black populations, they in effect exclude blacks from potential employment."[58] From the data that Cole, Deskins, and others have provided, and from our own interviews, it is reasonably clear that some Japanese companies have had and continue to have a bias against hiring certain racial and ethnic minorities. However, it must be pointed out that there is significant variation in minority hiring by company.

Rural greenfield sites also allow Japanese companies to avoid hiring large numbers of African-Americans or members of other minority groups. Honda and SIA are located in counties with less than 3 percent minority populations; the minority percentages for the counties where Diamond-Star, Toyota-Georgetown, and Nissan are located are 4.8, 7.6, and 11 percent, respectively.[59] In 1988, Honda settled a 1984 EEOC suit and agreed to increase its hiring of minority applicants.[60] An executive of one assembly transplant was more blunt, stating that his company selected its location to "avoid unions and blacks."[61]

Recent data indicate that the transplants have significantly improved minority hiring, perhaps as a result of increased political, public relations, and legal pressure in Japan and the United States. Honda increased its minority work force from 2.8

percent in 1987 to 10.6 percent in 1990. Toyota's Georgetown, Kentucky, plant has increased its percentage of African-American workers to 15 percent—in a county that is less than 3 percent minority.[62] Toyota's Georgetown plant was recently honored by the Lexington, Kentucky, branch of the National Conference of Christians and Jews for its minority hiring record. The president of the Lexington-Fayette NAACP was quoted as saying: "Some companies have been around here a long time and don't have numbers like that."[63] At Honda, less senior minority workers are mainly concentrated on the second shift, and there are reports of racial tension between first- and second-shift workers.[64]

At Honda, the recent hiring of minorities in accordance with the EEOC ruling and burgeoning political pressure appears to have generated escalating racial tension in the work force. According to one of our interviewees, a problem with this late hiring is that, owing to seniority, minority workers are concentrated on the night shift, whereas the day shift has more white workers. Because the early hires were mainly rural whites who may have had negative racial stereotypes, the influx of black workers has led to racial tensions. These tensions have led to racially motivated comments that management finds difficult to control.[65] Here, a poor initial decision, which excluded minorities, has led to a situation in which management must deal with the racial division within the plant.

The racial and ethnic divisions of American society have not been created by the transplants. Indeed, the transplants have tried to implement Japanese production organization in the midst of a society rent by deep racial and ethnic division. In industry, these divisions were used and at times exacerbated by U.S. industry in its efforts to divide and control the work force and keep down wages. For Japanese companies in the United States, it has been, and continues to be, necessary to develop a strategy to deal with these divisions in American life.

A number of transplants have successfully dealt with the racial issue and have tried to develop an integrated work force. For example, the NUMMI plant in California is nearly 50 percent Hispanic and African-American and thus far has proven quite successful and does not appear riven with conflict. Similarly, the experiences at NUMMI led Toyota to employ 15 percent minority workers at its Georgetown, Kentucky, facility.[65] It is noteworthy that Toyota, which is oriented toward stringent control of its work force and surrounding community, has a positive record on minority hiring.

At a deeper and more fundamental level, there is no reason to believe that the Japanese model of innovation-mediated production is premised upon racial and/ or ethnic division or that it should be *a priori* biased against minorities. In fact, it is likely that racial and ethnic divisions in the labor force, if transferred into the workplace, will impede the transfer and effective functioning of the Japanese model of innovation-mediated production. Such divisions are problematic since they divide workers and decrease information transfer and cooperation.[67] Generally speaking, the hiring practices of transplant manufacturers have been shaped by their initial acceptance of the long history of discrimination, segregation, and outright racism in American labor markets in particular and American society in general. However, it does seem likely that the transplants will respond to public and legal pressure on this issue and work to overcome discrimination in hiring—interpersonal discrimination on the shop-floor may be more difficult to overcome.

Anti-unionism

The nonunionized transplants couch their opposition to unions in the euphemisms favored by American anti-union companies. Many assert that there is no need for workers to be represented by "third parties." In the words of an American vice president in a nonunionized assembly transplant: "We have an open communications system between our workers and managers with no need for what we refer to as *third party intervention*."[68] The very phrase "third party" is telling. For the nonunionized transplants, American unions are seen as a recalcitrant obstacle to the transfer of new team-based forms of production organization. Unions are organizations that would break the identity and asymmetric relationship between worker and company, which currently exists.

A large number of Japanese transplants in the automobile and electronic sectors have vigorously opposed unions, and some have mobilized aggressive anti-union campaigns. As an example, in 1981, the National Labor Relations Board (NLRB) ruled that Honda violated federal labor law by prohibiting the wearing of UAW caps and other pro-union symbols and insignia at its motorcycle plant in Marysville, Ohio.[69] In 1982, Nissan was found guilty by the NLRB of unfair labor practices at a small distribution center. Nissan was found to have interrogated and threatened union sympathizers and then to have withheld raises from employees after they voted to recognize the union.[70]

The classic battle to organize a plant was waged by the UAW in 1989 at Nissan's Smyrna, Tennessee, assembly plant. The outcome was a company campaign that handily defeated the UAW organizing drive.[71] A company official outlined the "union-defense" strategy.

> If the employees choose to join the union at any time we will, of course, abide by that choice. But we believe that they should make that decision knowingly. So when the union came in here and decided to organize we said all right, we'll participate in this campaign. But when a union tells you something we believe not to be true, we're going to tell you that. And then you can make your decision having seen both sides of the issue. For example, during the course of the campaign we would receive reports or people would tell us that they're being told by union organizers that the union no longer strikes. . . . At the same time that our employees were being told that, Owen Bieber, who is the president of the International UAW, was making speeches in Los Angeles at his convention saying we absolutely will use the strike as a weapon if we need to use it. So people here were telling our folks one thing but the leadership of the union was saying something different. And we came in and told them. We said you decide, but I understand you are being told two different things.[72]

In July 1989, during the height of the union organizing campaign, *Business Week* reported, "To beat the UAW the company is carrying on a fierce anti-union battle through in-plant TV presentations that focus on scenes of strike violence. Such propaganda works in a region with an anti-union culture."[73] The company made extensive use of its in-plant video system to counter the union drive. Interestingly, there have been reports in the Japanese business press criticizing the extreme anti-union position taken by Nissan and other Japanese manufacturers in the United States.

Electronics transplants have experienced great difficulty working with American unions and are resisting unionization. As Chapter 8 showed, Sanyo has had a series of bitter strikes in its Arkansas plant, which may have shaped its decision to relocate production to its Mexican plant. Other Japanese electronic companies have actively resisted unionization. A number have sought to decertify existing unions. For example, according to the *Wall Street Journal,* unions have been defeated in decertification votes at Sony plants in Illinois and Hawaii.[74]

It is important to understand the underlying causes and motivations for such anti-unionism and to get away from oversimplified accounts that simply claim that Japanese companies dislike unions, a claim that is questionable because nearly all of the transplants' parents are unionized in Japan and since some transplants recognize unions. A more sophisticated and accurate interpretation is that the transplants, and the Japanese production system in general, require a close alignment of worker and company interests. They therefore are opposed to any organizational forms that complicate or impede such an alignment. However, this does not mean that they are opposed to unions per se. Rather, Japanese companies appear to be opposed to American unions, which create a separate and relatively autonomous source of identification and hegemony for workers.

In Japan, these same companies work closely with Japanese enterprise unions to create a greater alignment between worker and company interests. In England, where unions are far more powerful and are a part of doing business, transplants are largely unionized. But the Japanese have succeeded in limiting the number of unions in any given plant to one.[75] The transplants are opposed to forms of alternative worker identification, including traditional American unions, which create a separate sphere of identity for workers and disrupt the alignment between worker and company.

The Union as Partner

As we have already seen, not all the transplants are nonunion or anti-union. In fact, a fairly large number of Japanese steel, rubber and tire, and automobile assembly transplants have effectively implemented innovation-mediated production in a unionized environment. These corporations have developed a variety of strategies to transform the union into a partner in the implementation of the new production system. The primary strategy has been to involve the union directly in the restructuring effort. The union thus becomes at least partially aligned with the corporate planning and administration apparatus.

The other strategies are similar to those used by U.S. employers to control the union. One such strategy is to threaten to "go nonunion" to force the union to moderate its demands. This has caused a number of unions to accept major restructuring agreements. The fundamental position of the dissident union president at one automotive transplant, was as follows:

The union strategy has been to quite honestly give up everything in order to get the plant to accept the union. I disagree with that. And although the labor/management relationship should not be combative there are definitely two distinct sides. . . . We are not all one in the same; two sides must be separate to a degree.[76]

Another management strategy has been to blame the union for problems. According to this same union president, the company has been

very effective at exploiting anger to discredit our union. They are treating our membership badly; they turn it around and blame us. The company refuses to put in fans, but somehow it's turned around and it's my fault that we do not have fans. They own the plant. They have the money. I cannot afford to buy industrial fans. Water coolers—it's my fault. [They say] "Go see your union if you want water coolers." They are very effective at making all our problems seem like the fault of the union.[77]

Another strategy is to work with moderate factions of the unions who are supportive of the company and against dissidents who more actively pressure the company. At NUMMI, there have been reports that the leadership of the UAW has worked with management against a more radical "People's Caucus."[78] According to the President of Mazda's local union, the leadership of the UAW orchestrated an unsuccessful campaign to defeat him, supporting a more moderate "pro-company" union faction. In his words:

Our international leadership and regional leadership were very powerful and very intimidating. They sent very strong signals to our leadership that if you want to disagree with us or if you don't agree and go with the program we will make life very hard for you. . . . I don't know that anyone has ever won an election when most of the leadership was against him. . . . I was called a drunkard, a child-abuser, a communist, an atheist.[79]

Even with this opposition, this group won the election and now controls the Mazda union local. The new union local has taken a less conciliatory stance toward management. Here, it must be added that Mazda has by far the most adversarial and embattled labor-management relations climate of any automotive transplant.

Unions are a fundamental fact of production in advanced industrial societies. Japanese capital and labor have developed a certain set of rules within which their struggles are contained and channelled. American capital and labor had another set of rules. The transplants have decided that they will not accept the American rules and are in a position to demand a new set of rules. As we have shown, American unions have responded differently to this challenge of the major industrial unions. The United Auto Workers have been the most resistant to change. The United Steelworkers and United Rubber Workers have proven much more capable of adapting to and working effectively to represent the members within this new set of rules. Remember: virtually all the major steel and rubber transplants are represented by unions. Surely the current situation in the automotive sector will change, and it is likely that eventually all of the transplant automobile assemblers will be unionized. However, the local union organization and goals will likely be markedly different from the current UAW structure.

Unreconstructed American Management

The U.S. corporate world is organized in a caste system of salaried managers and blue-collar workers who toil on the factory floor. The clear distinction between white-collar and blue-collar workers is codified in a legal system that separates employees by categories such as exempt and nonexempt. The hallmarks of American management are centralization and a command system of authority.

American managers who have been trained to protect their own power and authority have trouble understanding the Japanese system, which operates on the basis of securing workers' participation—not the unilateral exercise of managerial power. Under this system, workers have a great deal of discretion and even authority. In Japan, shop-floor workers often move into lower managerial tasks. More importantly, their "stake" in the firm is similar to that of the managers.

American managers find it difficult—and sometimes impossible—to manage in the Japanese production system. They are used to taking orders from superiors and telling their subordinates what to do. Japanese executives complain that American managers often revert to authoritarianism toward workers. In the words of the human resources vice president at a major transplant supplier, who is an American,

> I think they [managers hired from U.S. firms] have been trained that way. They have always done it. . . . When they get under pressure, they want to revert back to what they are familiar with . . . which is hollering and yelling at people. I do not know. I believe you can train people the way you want them to be, but it's a long-term process to train an autocratic manager into a different style.[80]

This creates sizable obstacles to *kaizen* and quality-circle activities, which depend crucially upon worker self-initiative. In a 1981 interview the president of the Sanyo Electric Co. U.S. subsidiary summarized some of the problems that stem from the strict blue-collar/white-collar divide in the United States:

> The reason there are workmanship problems in the U.S. . . . is the different concept of teamwork. In a Japanese plant there is much more dialogue between blue-collar and white-collar workers; in fact, the rapport is so natural, we take it for granted. Such, however, is not the case in the U.S. In this respect we may even be more advanced in the concept of democracy than Americans.[81]

It is interesting to note that by 1990 and after significant labor strife, Sanyo laid off a significant number of workers at its Arkansas plant and moved much of its operations to a *maquiladora* factory in Mexico.

Interestingly, Japanese managers see unreconstructed American managers as an important obstacle to effective transfer of the Japanese system. In nearly every plant we visited, Japanese managers voiced concern about the manner by which American managers operate. An executive at Honda of America Manufacturing told us that his greatest problem was teaching American managers the Honda way.[82] There are two dimensions upon which Japanese discontent with U.S. management is most prevalent: commitment and the exercise of power. These two dimensions are handled very differently in Japan from the way they are handled in the United States, and they form two key elements of the Japanese management system.

American managers have experienced serious problems adapting to the Japanese rotation system. American managers consider themselves specialists in specific areas such as personnel management, accounting, finance, production management, purchasing, etc. In effect, their loyalty is to the profession and not the firm. This also means that these individuals cannot be easily redeployed to different areas. Further, a "that's not my department" attitude is prevalent, frustrating the close interaction and mutual reinforcement so characteristic of innovation-mediated production.

As we have already seen, the nature of fordist labor relations promoted status divisions not only between white- and blue-collar workers but within the group of shop-floor workers. In the fordist factory, there was a hierarchy of production jobs, with "skilled trades"—essentially holdovers from the older craft system of manufacturing—afforded the most exalted positions. In the automobile industries, the skilled trades comprised a significant "labor aristocracy" vis-à-vis the mass of relatively unskilled assembly-line workers. This intraclass divide has reappeared in unionized transplants, which retain a sizable group of workers in the skilled trades who have simply been reclassified under the category of "maintenance." According to a former GM worker now employed at the NUMMI plant:

> Our maintenance people . . . like to sit in team rooms and drink coffee, read books, and go to sleep. They are called "skilled trades." I guess in America once you become a maintainance man in the auto industry you are labelled a "skilled tradesman." I guess they feel they don't have to work. In the meantime, the team members, team leaders, and group leaders have the desire to make the system work by doing their job, while they are sitting out their going, "Oh, that's nice." This is a really bad attitude. This came over from General Motors—Ford, Chrysler, they all had the same problems.[83]

Securing commitment is the key to Japanese success. The Japanese system is management-intensive, and it is important for the company to retain its managers because of the large investment in training them, and because of their knowledge of the firm. Managers stay with the company for life.[84] Less capable managers are not fired, but are shunted into relatively unimportant positions as "window gazers," so named because they supposedly spend their time staring out the window. However, in the United States managers are extremely mobile and have a tendency to switch jobs and companies often.

American managers both see themselves and are seen as agents of the owners or stockholders of the firm, whereas in Japan the manager is far more a representative of the employees of the firm (i.e., those who constitute the value-producing members of the company). For American managers, the commitment to the company is conditional and subject to renegotiation or termination. The response by Japanese managers has been to refuse to extend long-term employment to American managers. In effect, they have accepted that American managers will change jobs and thus have decided to treat them as expendable. Still, Japanese managers are shocked when their American managers leave and join competitors. In interviews, Japanese executives complain that American managers demand high wages and do not consider themselves as tied to the company but rather expect to move from company to company. Japanese managers are surprised that such moves are made strictly for salary increases.

Because of the relatively unrestricted information flow inside a Japanese firm, a defecting manager can take valuable information to a competitor. In the fluid U.S. environment, the trust and free flow of information is called into question owing to the risks of leakage. This lack of loyalty is a significant problem since job-hopping means that training and other investments in managers are lost.

American managers have trouble working within the diffuse hierarchy of a Japanese firm. In most Japanese corporations, the real locus of power is not at the top but rather more widely diffused throughout the firm. Similarly, through techniques such as *nemawashi, ringi,* and a generalized pattern of far greater discussion of activities, responsibility is far less clear. This lack of a clear distinction in terms of wages, benefits and more fundamentally, power makes the managerial task more one of persuasion than of giving direct orders. American managers have great difficulty with the Japanese consultative approach to decision making, especially when that involves consulting with junior employees or involving shop-floor workers. These managers like to work individually and have difficulty adapting to the consultation and team effort characteristic of the Japanese system. The executive vice president of a Japanese electronics firm in the United States explained it this way:

> In Japan, when I want a difficult project done I must discuss it extensively with my managers to convince them to undertake it. On the other hand, if I ask my American managers to undertake a difficult project they will assent immediately and undertake the project. However, they may not complete the assignment successfully. However, the Japanese managers once they have agreed to the project will complete it.[85]

Japanese executives frequently complain that American managers find it hard to take initiative and would rather wait to execute orders that come down from above. This is a significant problem since the Japanese system requires middle-level managers, after consultation with other managers, to initiate activity and get things done without direct orders from the top.[86]

In a growing number of Japanese transplant companies open tension exists between Japanese and American managers. It is not uncommon for American managers to resent their Japanese superiors and their Japanese corporate parents.

Such resentment is particularly acute in American companies that have been acquired by Japanese firms. There are reports from Japanese executives, American shop-floor workers, and clerical staff of American managers who refer to their Japanese counterparts in derogatory, even racist, terms.

Recently lawsuits have been instituted by white American managers charging that they were discriminated against in corporate promotions.[87] In cases against two Japanese trading companies, C. Itoh and Company and Sumitomo Shoji Trading Co., American employees charged that the companies discriminated against them by favoring Japanese employees. The argument by plaintiffs was that no employee should be discriminated against because of ethnic background. This can be even more complicated if, as some have charged, Japanese-Americans are preferred over white Americans. High-level American managers are using antidiscrimination laws to combat dismissals. For example, Fujitsu America was recently sued by an American manager who was laid off in 1989 from his position that earned $210,000 per year, allegedly because Fujitsu wished to replace American chief financial officers with Japanese personnel.[88] In another case, Sumitomo Corp. was charged with rotating Japanese managers into senior positions in the United States instead of promoting American managers. In November 1990, a federal court in New York City ruled against Sumitomo and required the company to make "good faith efforts" to add more American managers to its senior- and middle-management groups, to develop a career development program for non-Japanese employees, to raise the base pay for American managers, and pay at least $1,500 in back pay to employees with two years or more of service.[89]

However, a U.S. Federal Appeals Court ruling in December 1991 upheld the right of Japanese companies in America to basically discriminate in favor of Japanese nationals. The court ruled that Matsushita Electric did not violate American civil rights law when it fired three American executives at a Quasar facility in Illinois.[90] The three executives originally charged that they experienced "national-origin discrimination" when they were fired, in part because Japanese executives were given "preferential treatment." A Federal District Court initially ruled in favor of the Americans. But the Appeals Court overturned this stating that "there is no evidence of discrimination here save what is implicit in wanting your own citizens to run your foreign subsidiary." The Appeals Court based its decision on a treaty between the United States and Japan which permits such discrimination on the basis of "citizenship"—a treaty that in effect legitimates what U.S. companies do abroad. The court added that "if this conclusion seems callous toward the Americans who lost their jobs at Quasar, we remind that the rights granted by the treaty are reciprocal [and that there are] Americans employed by foreign subsidiaries of U.S. companies who, but for the treaty, would lose their jobs to foreign nationals." It seems likely that this decision will stand both because of the court's inability and/or reluctance to overturn a treaty legitimately entered into by the United States and the fact that any reversal might have untenable consequences for U.S. multinationals operating abroad.

Thus, curiously, the most serious problem in transferring the Japanese system to the United States appears to be the development of management and the retention of managers. The strength of the Japanese system is the organic linkage between managers and workers; this is very difficult to reproduce in the United States with traditional American managers. As a result of their problems with unreconstructed American managers, some major Japanese companies such as Honda, Toyota, Mitsubishi Electric, and Fujitsu are trying to groom young managers right out of school and increasingly to promote workers from plant into management positions.

Community Control

In Japan, some corporations extend their reach far into the community, blurring the usual demarcation of work and home life. Some large Japanese corporations have developed company towns that provide a supportive social and cultural context for the company's activities. At a number of companies, performance evaluations extend beyond job-related performance. Performance at company athletic or social events is a factor in job performance evaluations, which are the major part of the company's complex system for determining wages. In extreme instances, if a worker goes on a Sunday drive with his family and gets into a traffic accident, he can receive a performance demerit from the company. Toyota is the most extreme example of the nexus of corporate and community control. It has gone further than any Japanese corporation in creating a complete social structure and cultural system to motivate its employees and reinforce its production system. Toyota City, the home of most of Toyota's manufacturing operations in Japan, forms a large, residential-commercial-industrial complex that houses the company's production, R&D, and headquarters facilities as well as those of dozens of key suppliers. Toyota has a seemingly all-pervasive presence as Toyota employees work in Toyota factories, live in Toyota houses, shop in Toyota stores, participate in Toyota events, and go on vacations with other Toyota families. When workers need money, they are able to draw funds from the Toyota Family Fund. The social structure and stratification system is intertwined with Toyota. In the process, the distinction between work and home life has been blurred to the point at which Toyota seemingly permeates all activities. Basically, social status within the company is coterminus with status within the community. This is a powerful aspect in the blurring of the Western boundaries between the corporation and civil society.

Some sociologists suggest that Toyota City can be understood as an advanced form of "welfare corporatism" where the class boundaries between capital and labor are much less saliently perceived than the boundaries between membership and nonmembership in the corporate community.[91] However, Toyota's version of "corporatism" extends far beyond the paternalistic welfare capitalism found to varying degrees and at various times in the United States and Europe as well as in Japan.[92] Toyota has created a total and "hegemonic" sociocultural sphere, in the truly Gramscian sense, that envelops a worker's entire existence. In other words, because work and home life are tied so closely together, the worker has little choice except to conform to the standards and norms of the corporate community. This corporate hegemony provides a powerful source of identity, control, and internal motivation for Toyota's work force.

The extension of corporate prerogatives into social institutions and community organization is not new. Corporations have long been involved in local politics and even local schools. And company towns date back to the beginnings of industrial capitalism. Indeed, when posed conceptually, there appears to be a general correspondence or symmetry between new forms of work and production organization and the broader forms of sociocultural organization. The rise and subsequent diffusion of the fordist model, for example, coincided with a sweeping transformation of educational institutions and philosophy (e.g., the rise of vocational education, new engineering schools, and business degree programs to train and acclimate various strata of workers to the needs of fordist production). This occurred first in the United States and later diffused to Europe and to other regions as well. During the 1960s and 1970s, a number of American business schools even set up foreign branches to train foreign managers in the requirements of fordist production and management. Moreover, the rise and diffusion of fordist production organization also coincided with and motivated a unique pattern of social and community organization—characterized by extensive suburbanization and the attendant separation of work and home life.

The diffusion of the new model of innovation-mediated production is setting in motion a new round of change in social and community organization. But this is not to imply a monolithic and uniformly deterministic relationship between production and social organization. Rather, it is more appropriate to conceptualize this process in terms of a "selection mechanism" favoring forms of social organization that map well to particular forms of production organization over those that do not.[93] Corporations and corporate interests in part work to create these supportive contexts and they are able to influence them to some extent; however, the emergence of new patterns of sociocultural organization depends upon many forces in addition to direct corporate influence.

The relationship between corporation and community enters the transfer process in an interesting way. The transfer of organizational forms basically means that such forms are transferred from one social, cultural, and environmental context and implanted into a new one. This raises the question: Where exactly is the line drawn between corporate organizational forms inside the factory, and the social relationships which surround those forms and within which they are embedded? Simply put, how much of the supportive social context is lifted up and transferred alongside the corporate organizational forms and practices we have already explored? This takes us beyond the question addressed by Gramsci in his study of Americanism and Fordism.[94] Gramsci, by posing the question at the level of society, suggested that the two could indeed be separated: fordism—although it was supported by Americanism—could be separated from Americanism and transferred to Europe as a set of organizational forms, or mode of production organization. It is interesting and valuable to explore the way individual firms deal with the relationship between internal organizational forms and their social and cultural embeddedness.

Generally speaking, the large majority of Japanese transplants have focused on transferring only organizational forms that are directly related to work and production organization. In developing a work force and a supportive environment for production, the transplants have found it necessary to change the attitudes and values of workers, and that means inculcating a broader cultural context. While most transplants have selected supportive community contexts, the great majority have not tried to transfer social characteristics or to restructure the communities in which they have located along the line of a "Japanized" model. However, there is a great deal of difference among firms. An interesting subset of transplants has attempted to influence and shape more actively the local community and to recreate a more or less "Japanized" immediate environment. Not surprisingly, the company that has gone the furthest in this regard is Toyota.

Toyota is trying to introduce some of the community features that have developed in Toyota City, Japan, into Georgetown, Kentucky, home of its major U.S. assembly facility.[95] It has done this gradually, and to some extent indirectly. Still, the result is becoming obvious; Toyota is re-creating a number of the conditions associated with its Japanese environment in its American home.[96] The company has sponsored Japanese trips including visits to Toyota City for the mayor, county executive, school superintendent, and other local officials to expose them to Japanese practices, and it has established "sister city" relationships between Georgetown and a Japanese city to make this an ongoing process. In this way, Toyota extends its reach into community life in a way that is similar to although not nearly as extensive as Toyota City in Japan.

Toyota has partially financed a new community center that is used to expose residents to Japanese culture. The company is also involved in local cultural events, which are held at Cardome Center, partially financed by Toyota. The recent Community Day festivities, which featured exhibits and background on Japanese culture and which enabled local residents to interact with Japanese families, were host to more than 5,000 community residents. To reconstruct the environment which it has in Japan, Toyota has helped to establish a new organization representing the local business community, the Scott County Industrial Foundation; its purpose is to bring local industry together and create an outreach vehicle. The Industrial Foundation sponsors expositions that are done in conjunction with the Scott County Fair. Toyota uses such events to interact with the community by showing photographs of the plant and displaying the Camry, which is produced at the Georgetown factory.

Moreover, Toyota is active in the local school system; it hopes to create a more supportive populace and develop potential workers and citizens suited to its needs. The company has established elaborate joint programs with the Scott County schools. Toyota provides adjunct faculty to teach high-tech courses in robotics, automation, and other fields. And the school system takes all eighth and tenth grade students on plant tours where they are exposed to Toyota's production system and its corporate philosophy. Toyota is investing to create a high-quality labor pool in the future. The rural nature of Scott County provides a high probability that these socialized students can then be hired by Toyota.

Toyota has sent most of the local political leadership, including the school superintendent and other school officials, to Japan to expose them to the Japanese system. Based on these experiences, the school system is now implementing new teaching approaches emphasizing group skills over individual effort. The school superintendent indicated that the school system is moving in the direction of group-based education and teamwork. He lamented the traditional emphasis on individualized learning (i.e., the fact that in American schools group activity is labelled "cheating").

Toyota is extremely concerned about its corporate image and actively monitors community attitudes. The company contracts with a private firm to conduct annual telephone surveys of workers and citizens. The survey asks people what are the best and worst things about their community, what they would most like to see done, and how development should proceed. The survey consists of questions on quality of life, satisfaction with public services, feelings regarding Toyota, how it fits into the community, Toyota's economic incentives, and other social concerns. The specific questions regarding Toyota are those such as, "Have you met people who have moved here as a result of Toyota?" and "How do you feel about Toyota?" In this way, Toyota monitors its own image. A knowledgeable local source described one such survey this way:

> There were telephone surveys conducted by the University of Kentucky every year. They accurately reflect the attitudes of people of Georgetown and Scott County. . . . At year one in 1986, most people who were interviewed were asked, "Do you want to work at Toyota?" Oh yes; oh yes. Then they began to see it's very hard, very demanding. Then more people once they learned more about the system said, that's not for me. The percentage of people who wanted to work at Toyota became less and less, the more they knew about the expectations required of Toyota workers.[97]

Such information enables Toyota to monitor community attitudes continuously and if necessary to take action to head off, react to, or alter significant trends.

Toyota and a number of other transplants are able to apply such pressures in part because, as we have already seen, they prefer to settle in rural areas where they can exert a large measure of control over both workers and community—and are able to shape both to their needs. These communities provide a "blank slate" where Japanese production and work organization can be implemented, and where corporations can exert considerable direct and indirect control over their environment as well as their work forces.

The Toyota case is unique in many ways. This has much to do with its own history. Very few Japanese firms have so centralized their facilities in one location. Clearly, any company with large-scale economic activities in a small town will have inordinate power, and Japanese firms with their extreme sensitivity to local prejudices and feelings, pay more attention to local political leaders than comparable U.S. companies.

It is important to emphasize that Toyota has gone much further than most Japanese corporations to control both its work force and the broader community. Other Japanese transplants seem far less interested in community control. Other transplants encourage their its employees to live where they want to and involve themselves constructively in whatever community they choose to live. A Japanese executive of another Japanese automotive transplant provides important insight here:

We don't have company housing and we don't give any instruction to live in a certain place. Even in Japan, [our] employees try not to live together to form a community, because we would like to live as a local citizen rather than a member of the [company's] community. However, in Toyota's case—this is not to blame them—they usually form a Toyota community; all the employees live together within the same community. Whether this style is good or bad, I don't know. But the first priority for [our] employees is to live as local citizens.[98]

Government Giveaways

Some Japanese transplants have been the recipients of generous government incentives. Large transplant facilities, especially automotive assembly plants, have been granted hundreds of millions of dollars in direct and indirect assistance. Today, 39 states and a large and growing number of American cities have development offices in Japan. Recent years have witnessed a rapid escalation of state industrial incentives to Japanese transplants. As Table 9.1 shows, the direct cash costs of incentives have climbed from $2,500 per job created at Honda to nearly $100,000 at SIA. These figures are for direct costs only and exclude interest paid on bonds and forgone tax revenues.[99]

When Toyota moved into Georgetown, Kentucky, it was given a generous incentive package negotiated by the state and company representatives. Kentucky provided the company with an incentive package totalling more than $350 million, including $12 million in land acquisition; $15 million in site preparation; $47 million to build a new road around the plant; $10 million for an on-site training center; and $33 million in training-related expenses. Toyota also received $800 million in industrial revenue bond financing for its original assembly plant and another $100 million in industrial revenue bond financing for its new engine and transmission plant, making the plant completely exempt from property taxation.

Proponents suggest that such incentives attract investment and jobs, whereas opponents argue that such programs are giveaways to foreign competitors who are taking profits and jobs away from U.S.-owned firms. As mentioned earlier Port-

TABLE 9.1.   Industrial Incentives to Automotive Transplants

Japanese Company	Start Date	Total Direct Incentives (in millions of dollars)	Projected Jobs	Assistance per Job
Honda	1982	20.0	8,000	$ 2,500
Nissan	1983	33.0	5,100	6,470
Mazda	1987	48.5	3,400	14,263
Toyota	1988	149.7	5,000	18,713
Diamond-Star	1988	83.3	2,900	28,724
SIA	1989	166.7	1,700	98,059

Source: Incentive data from Carole Davies and John Lowell, "Incentives Survive but Live Quiet Lives," *Ward's Auto World* (April 1990): 39–49, except for Ohio which is from Andrew Mair, Richard Florida, and Martin Kenney, "The New Geography of Automobile Production: Japanese Transplants in North America," *Economic Geography* 64 (October 1988): 352–73.

land, Oregon, has targetted Japanese firms for recruitment.[100] The use of industrial incentives is a highly political process, frequently driven by political actors and their designated "deal-makers" whose sole concern is to "land the company" and thus win votes. Industrial incentives to Japanese automakers became the key issue in 1990 gubernatorial elections in Kentucky and Indiana, with opponents arguing that the state had given away too much. In both cases the party that gave the incentives lost. In Kentucky there was concern that one part of the state had been favored over another, and that the cost of landing Toyota was too high. As one local government official put it, "In the end it was very much of a bidding war between states. And there was concern that we had simply paid too much."[101]

There is an extensive literature on industrial incentives, and its conclusions are fairly clear: Incentives have at best a marginal impact on influencing the site the company chooses.[102] Some go further and suggest that firms essentially make their location decision and then create a fictitious competition to maximize state subsidies and incentives.[103] Moreover, industrial incentives drain resources away from other important public uses. Transplants are large profitable corporations that do not need such incentives; and some transplants do not even want them.

Transplant officials have frequently said that incentives play only a minor role in their locational calculus. According to Roger Lambert of Honda: "Incentives were never part of what has drawn us to this area [Marysville, Ohio] or caused us to expand."[104] Former Ohio governor James Rhodes was quoted as saying on the negotiations between Honda and the state government, "They could have had near anything they wanted, but they didn't choose to do business that way."[105] Our interviews with other transplants and the very low ranking given government incentives in our survey of supplier location (see Chapter 5) further suggest that incentives play at best a very minor role in the location decisions of transplant companies. A number of large Japanese firms, such as the I/N Tek and I/N Kote plants near South Bend, Indiana, received little in locational assistance. Battle Creek, Michigan, has been able to attract a large Nippondenso plant and a dozen or so of Japanese parts suppliers while offering little in industrial incentives (see Chapter 5).

Incentives have only a marginal effect on location. Such incentive packages typically have little effect on the location of transplant firms since spatial proximity to suppliers and customers is the absolute first priority. In addition, transplant companies are becoming sensitive to the political controversy surrounding incentives to foreign firms, which may cause them to seek smaller incentive packages. In the words of a Nissan executive, "The company does not want to get too much in taxpayers' money. We are careful not to ask for or accept too many incentives. The company is being as conservative as possible."[106]

Policymakers and planners often find themselves facing the following dilemma: how to generate economic development and jobs yet avoid the zero-sum consequences of interjurisdictional competition, especially since states and localities continue to compete fiercely for new plants and jobs, firms expect subsidies, and politicians are likely to use incentives to ensure that their jurisdiction comes out the "winner." The only control mechanism for the drive to grant incentives is for the federal government to forbid these incentives for all corporations, foreign or domestic. Policymakers and planners should press for strict limits and/or complete elimination of industrial incentives to Japanese transplants and, for that matter, all industrial transplants.

Capital vs. Community

At times a contradiction exists between capital and communities. This is true of any industrial system. It should not be surprising that a number of the transplants bring us face-to-face with that contradiction. Some transplants overlook community needs in the zeal to transfer Japanese production organization and maximize profits. A number have located on land outside existing municipal boundaries to avoid taxation. Others have received industrial revenue bonds or other state provisions that allow them to avoid local property taxes. This is compounded by high-level state officials who overlook the needs of communities in their quest to "do the deal," or worse yet, make promises that communities cannot deliver. Frequently the result is that community interests get left behind. Large corporations always have a sizable economic and political effect on the communities in which they locate. This effect is muted in large cities, but it can be quite significant in small towns.

The basic problem here is that different levels of political power operate with different incentives and goals and that small communities do not have the resources to make themselves effectively heard. So, for example, state governments may wish to attract a firm and certainly local elites are often happy to have the new firm locate in their jurisdiction. But a new plant places major demands on services, most of which are provided by the local jurisdiction. If the plant is outside the town limits, the town can easily get the added costs of providing services without tax benefits. This is compounded when the incentive package includes a tax holiday as an incentive.

When Toyota moved into Georgetown, Kentucky, it was given a generous incentive package negotiated by the state and company representatives. However, both the town and county governments were left out of this process. Even the mayor of Georgetown, and a big supporter of Toyota, was critical of the process:

> The original negotiations that brought Toyota to Kentucky were conducted entirely between the state of Kentucky and the corporation. . . . The local community's needs were not really addressed. . . . The incentive package focused entirely on the company's needs.[107]

The company located outside the borders of Georgetown in Scott County to minimize its tax liability. However, the city and county remained responsible for providing services to the plant. As a result, both the town and the county found themselves facing rather acute fiscal stress.

To remedy this situation the city and county were forced to negotiate with Toyota to seek relief. The mayor of Georgetown describes negotiations as follows:

Shortly after I became mayor in the fall of 1986 I sat down with company officials and explained to them that we had to have a revenue source from their plant, that this city faced the possibility of terrible financial difficulty without some way to tax that location. I wanted to discuss annexation . . . to make that a part of Georgetown. We began a series of weekly breakfast meetings. Top management of the plant and I and the city attorney sat down once a week for breakfast. We would begin at 7:00 or 7:30 and work until 10:00 or 10:30 in the morning. What we were attempting to do during those meetings was reach a better understanding of the ways in which the plant was going to impact on the city financially and get a better understanding of what the company's needs were.[108]

Although Toyota was reluctant at first, when faced with the possibility of negative publicity it ultimately agreed to have its plant site annexed by the county and to provide a special "in lieu of tax payment" of $8 million to compensate for lost property taxes and to avert a severe local budgetary crisis. The company also agreed to be annexed and thereby come under the tax assessment jurisdiction of both the city and county with their 1 percent payroll tax and 1 percent profit tax. With Toyota's annual payroll in excess of $100 million that means over $1 million per annum in revenue for both jurisdictions. The profit tax is less certain because Toyota as a large multinational can move its profits around so it might never "show a profit" in Georgetown. Still, $1 million per annum in new tax revenues is significant.

Toyota did not make this deal entirely out of a sense of altruism and goodwill. Georgetown's indigenous base of local industries, tobacco farms, and horse breeders had already begun to build a coalition to force Toyota to pay taxes. Before the agreement, the city council was considering a measure to forcibly annex Toyota to become part of Georgetown. According to a knowledgeable local official who wished to remain anonymous:

The fact of the matter was that city council representatives were going to introduce the resolution to annex Toyota. They would have been put into a reactionary position that was going to be very difficult. . . . I told the mayor this is what you need to do. You need to get with a senior Toyota executive, meet with him on a regular basis, and tell him the problem of what is going to happen when a member of the council introduces annexation in public. Explain to them the problems that we all would have and particularly what Toyota would have. So then where are we? Well, then we have a problem. We've got an industrial giant here that's not paying its fair share. So Toyota could be criticized for bringing an impact in the community and not paying its share. Instead, Toyota says we want to be a full corporate citizen of Georgetown and Scott County. All problems are solved.[109]

The problems of handling growth and increased demand for government services are not unique to either Toyota or other Japanese firms. However, it is more noticeable at the moment with Japanese companies because they are making large manufacturing investments. Richard Hill and his collaborators report that Flat Rock, Michigan, the home of Mazda has also experienced problems.[110] This pattern is not unique to automobile manufacturing; however, the sheer size of such facilities and their enormous demand for utilities, for transportation facilities, and for other heavy industrial services mean that they will have an extraordinary impact.[111]

Still, Japanese transplants appear to be more willing than their American counterparts to work with local communities. This is not surprising given their preference for stability and the highly charged political climate surrounding Japanese investment. Japanese companies generally try to cultivate a good image within the community. At the local government offices we visited expensive Japanese gifts were prominently displayed. Japanese firms are very conscious about maintaining excellent relations with local jurisdictions. Toyota did in fact work out an arrangement with the local community, something virtually unheard of among American firms. A planning consultant who has worked for Toyota, Nissan, and the Big Three American automakers suggests that his American clients would never have renegotiated with the community in the way that Toyota did. Furthermore, Toyota has been subjected to stinging criticism in the Japanese press by corporate leaders and Japanese government officials who see its bargaining tactics as bad politics that cast a poor reflection on Japanese corporate investments in the United States. For these officials, the issue is clear: Access to the American market is far more important than locational subsidies.

Into the Future

The negative aspects of the transplants are more than a laundry list of "bad things"—fast-paced work, repetitive-motion injury, corporate control, anti-unionism, racial tension, and overlooked community needs. These tensions and contradictions are complex. Many problems are tied inextricably to the model itself. Social control is used to align workers' interests to those of the company and to ensure that the delegation of decision-making power to the shop floor and the unleashing of workers' creative capabilities take place within the framework of explicitly capitalist social relations. Other problems such as racial discrimination are not unique to the Japanese factory but are pervasive in the fordist factory and American society as well. Still others stem from the long, ingrained legacy of fordist production organization and labor-management relations. A few problems, such as extravagant incentives, are a product of the particular constellation of the state-business relation in the United States. Some are unique to the transplants but not to Japan. Others occur during the transfer and adaptation processes.

This chapter has explored the other side of the Japanese expression of innovation-mediated production—its tensions and contradictions.[112] Thus, the merits and innovative aspects of the system are embedded within social relations that entail regressive aspects. A system that saves labor and eliminates waste has workers toiling more hours than the old fordist system. Workers are organized into teams—a highly social and intersubjective way of producing; yet the team itself is used to pump more work out of the employee. Workers are given more authority and trained in multiple tasks, yet new forms of corporate hegemony control expressions of individuality.

Underlying the Japanese model of innovation-mediated production is a tension between new forms of work and production organization that unleash powerful new sources of human creativity and economic value, and the need to channel and harness those heightened capacities with new forms of corporate control.

Critics of the Japanese model simply argue for a return to a putative golden era of fordism. Unfortunately, there is no such golden era to return to—its factories are being demolished or transformed and its working class dispersed. Just as fordism developed in new industries and transformed other ones, now a new model of innovation-mediated production is replacing fordism. This new model is overwhelming the outmoded practices of the past.

For the time being, both the transplants and the Japanese model itself appear quite resilient. Japanese manufacturers have shown themselves to be adept at responding to problems and altering their corporate control strategies in line with shop-floor resistance, demands, and struggles. Presently, transplant producers are developing various strategies to cope with their American work forces—to more effectively mobilize and channel workers' intellectual and physical capabilities in a way that leaves them committed to the enterprise. While some of the transplants have been reticent to recognize American labor unions and have found it difficult because of legal restrictions and other factors to provide an employment relation along the lines of the Japanese model, ongoing dynamics may move them increasingly in these directions. A number of transplants speak of creating hybrid forms, which retain basic Japanese organizational forms and characteristics within a framework for manufacturing consent that is more American in character.[113] Only time will tell how successful they can be.

10

Conclusions and Implications

Japan is now in the process of strategically repositioning its entire economy. It is setting in place the base for sustained growth through the 1990s essentially through strategic and structurally driven capital investment. . . . In 1988, for the first time, Japan invested in absolute terms more than the U.S. did. Last year it invested about 10 percent more, and this year it is investing about 25 percent more. . . . The Japanese economy is today three-fifths the size that of the United States. And with current investment and research trends, the momentum continues to move in Japan's favor. Not once in a quarter of a century has the U.S. invested, as a proportion of GNP, as much as Japan. And Japan is also investing much more than any economy in Europe.

KENNETH COURTIS, senior economist for global research, Deutsche Bank Capital
Markets (Asia) Ltd. Tokyo[1]

The late twentieth century will be remembered as an epoch when capitalism again demonstrated its Janus face, as the new technologies and productive forces gestating within burst forth, destroying the established ways and calling forth new ones. Such political and economic upheaval is abrupt, uneven, and at times even pitiless.[2] Countries, industries, corporations, and even human beings that for decades appeared the beneficiaries of the old system now find themselves on its trailing edge—losers. Yet hidden by the decay and destruction, the seeds of a new order are sown. A new system rushes forward to unleash yet a new round of economic and technological development—the further advance of capitalism's powerful productive forces.

This book began with a discussion of the new system of *innovation-mediated production.* We argued that in Japan this system has encompassed both the traditional and high-technology industries. The question we then posed was whether this system would be confined to Japan or whether it could succeed in other political economies. In effect, the question was the same as Antonio Gramsci answered affirmatively in the case of fordism. Or even earlier, when Marx was queried by German friends about why he studied British capitalism, he answered that the fate of British capitalism would also be theirs. Just as Europeans, Japanese, and others made their pilgrimages to Detroit from 1920 to 1960, now those who wish to understand the future of industry and economy must visit and study Japan. Fables based on northern Italy or Silicon Valley are enchanting reading, but are irrelevant for understanding the future development of global capitalism. Not to predicate a discussion of the future on developments in Japan indicates a lack of seriousness.

The second section of the book aimed at answering the questions of the transferability and generalizability of the new model. Here our answer was affirmative but not unequivocal. Clearly the heavy industries grouped around automobile production have actively and, in large measure, successfully transferred the new system to the United States. The record in electronics is more mixed. However, significant evidence suggests that Japanese electronics corporations are becoming more assertive in their attempts to transfer innovation-mediated production. The ultimate outcome of this process remains open, however.

This chapter will build a number of tentative but important arguments necessary to understand both the new model of innovation-mediated production and its global generalizability.

The Model Revisited

As its very name implies, innovation-mediated production is defined by an accelerating pace of innovation. Under this new model, innovation becomes an inherent part of the very process of production. Indeed, innovation constantly mediates and informs the production process. This is a potent advance over the discontinuous nature of innovation under fordism. The future of capitalism is one of accelerating—indeed, continuous—innovation.

The shift to continuous innovation is bound up with the shift to new information-intensive technologies. In semiconductors and computers, product life cycles are being dramatically compressed. Consumer electronics products, from televisions and stereo components to telephones, are now outmoded in a year or less. A similar process is also at work in automobiles, where entirely new models appear every two or three years. The use of new microelectronic and design technologies in traditional industries accelerates this process.

The accelerated pace of technological innovation results in a more or less continuous stream of commodities that make previous generations appear obsolete, create new demand, and generate new streams of value, profit, and accumulation. The short product life cycles and rapid performance increases associated with new technologies make innovation itself an increasingly important source of value. In this new environment, economic success and competitiveness are tied to a company's constant ability to improve products and processes, to revamp the production process itself, and to deploy new products and technologies rapidly—that is, to engage in a process of perpetual innovation continuously geared to creating new sources of value.

In the age of accelerated, continuous innovation, knowledge and intellectual labor replace physical labor as the fundamental source of value, capital accumulation, and profit. Indeed, advanced industrial economies are changing from a system built upon the mere extraction of physical labor to one based on continuous knowledge mobilization and innovation. This is not simply the knowledge and intellectual capabilities of R&D researchers and engineers, but the knowledge and capabilities of all employees—including regular factory workers. Indeed, workers' knowledge is now a fundamental and explicit element of production and of continuous innovation—a source of direct value creation and productivity improvement.

Under fordism, the R&D lab was separated from the factory and its role was conceived of as creating innovations that would be implemented by others. College-trained reseachers and engineers were considered the white-collar or managerial class. There was a fundamental distinction among them, technicians, and factory workers. The factory was not the site for "creative" work, but rather a place where second-rate engineers were sent. The separation of conception and execution outlined by Harry Braverman was accepted as an axiom.[3] The brains, like power, were centralized up the corporate ladder where they could control and be controlled.

At the core of the new model of innovation-mediated production stands a set of fundamental changes in the organization of work at the point of production—a "new shop floor"—which is geared toward harnessing and mobilizing intellectual labor. Both the factory floor and the R&D lab become a source of continuous innovation, productivity improvement, value creation, and capital accumulation. This is predicated upon a reintegration of innovation and production and of intellectual and manual labor.

The Factory as Laboratory

The factory itself is changing from a center of physical labor, grease, muscle, and sweat to a locus of continuous innovation. Indeed, the factory itself is becoming a laboratory—a setting for both product and process innovation. Under fordism, new products and processes would be invented by a few researchers working in a controlled laboratory environment. This made it difficult to transfer the new ideas to manufacturing. It was one thing to invent a new process. It was quite another to implement it in a factory setting.

The factory as laboratory allows new products to move from the controlled setting of the R&D lab to the factory rapidly and with a minimum of problems, and it allows processes to be worked out in a realistic environment. In this new environment, operators and technicians actively participate by using their knowledge to improve products and process—to get the bugs out. The entire process is closely monitored as information is constantly collected, fed back, and used to improve the process.

But there are other aspects to the factory as laboratory. The factory is increasingly assuming the physical characteristics of the laboratory. It is becoming a clean room environment as free as is possible of dust particles and other impurities that can adversely affect the production process. In fact, production takes place in an environment in which direct human intervention is minimized. This is currently most visible in electronics, but it is also occurring in continuous-process steel mills and in aspects of automotive production such as painting. Humans monitor and control the process but do not directly touch the work-in-process; this is accomplished by robotic and other automated tools. Increasingly, workers take on the role of super-technicians who monitor, review data, and adjust and control the process.

These super-technicians have skill levels that are equivalent to electrical engineers of two decades ago. In the factory as laboratory, innovation is an ongoing and collective process.

Production is becoming ever-more social.[4] Employees must work together to produce things. In his early philosophical writings, Marx referred to this as the social or intersubjective nature of production. In fact, capitalism has been marked by increased "socialization" of production over time as capitalist economies have moved from individual craft production, to machine-based manufacturing, or what Marx termed "machinofacture" to large-scale factory production, to fordist mass production, and ultimately to the blurring of the lines between inovation and production, R&D and manufacturing, under innovation-mediated production,[5]

With the synthesis of innovation and production, the mobilization of intellectual (and manual) labor clearly becomes a more social, intersubjective, and collective process than under previous capitalist epochs. Knowledge and intellectual labor are mobilized on a collective basis. As we have seen, the team is the basic organizational mechanism used to harness the collective intelligence of researchers, engineers, and factory workers and turn it into commodities—a new microelectronic product, a new computer, a new piece of software, a new form of genetic material. The self-managing work team devolves a variety of managerial responsibilities to the shop floor. It thus facilitates the functional integration of tasks; this, in turn, overcomes the fine-grained functionally specialized division of labor of fordism.

To critics, the team is merely a vehicle for pumping more labor out of workers by increasing the speed of production. This is only a part of the team concept, not its essence. The team is the mechanism through which workers are mobilized to solve production problems and innovate for management. It becomes the source for overcoming production bottlenecks as workers use their own intelligence and knowledge to devise cooperative strategies to overcome such obstacles. The team is a simultaneous source of motivation, discipline, and social control for team members, driving them to toil harder and more collectively. In this way, workers are encouraged, stimulated, and provided incentives to share their ideas and continuously innovate and improve the production process.

In innovation-mediated production, the intellectual capabilities of a variety of different types of workers are integrated and explicitly harnessed to turn knowledge into commodities. This overcomes artificial divisions and facilitates efficient production. Thus, there is a fusion of researchers who create innovations, engineers who develop them and turn them into commercial products, and shop-floor workers who produce them. Overlapping membership allows R&D workers to work alongside product development engineers and even factory workers, blurring the boundaries among them. This creates an interplay and synthesis of various types of knowledge and intellectual labor in an explicitly social context. Such integration of functions is required so all the relevant actors can interact, exchange thoughts, and create new ideas, as a unified "social brain," and then translate and embody those ideas into new products and production processes.[6]

Of course, production really was social all along. When labor sociologists and anthropologists visited the shop floor, they frequently reported back on the social aspects—such as workers talking together, sharing tasks, or solving problems without telling management.[7] However, these social aspects were typically viewed as aberrations that occurred outside the bounds of legalistic work rules. In fordism, even though tasks were organized on an individual basis, the division of labor in the fordist factory reconstructed these individual actions in a social production process. The social aspect could also be seen in the creation of a huge class of industrial workers, and the growth of the new industrial unions, which came to represent these workers. Innovation-mediated production brings the social explicitly into the immediate organization of production and into the labor process.

From these developments, we expect the eventual rise of new forms of worker organizations that go beyond the conventional mass-production unions—a situation analogous to the earlier shift from the craft-based organization of the AFL unions to the new CIO industrial unions. Indeed, the socialization of production, coupled with the role of intellectual labor, opens up new resources and new avenues of struggle for workers and unions. For one, the new model places increased shop-floor power and control in the hands of the few operators. Innovation-mediated production is extremely vulnerable to the withdrawal or withholding of labor. If they are to be successful in this new era of capitalism, unions will have to devise new strategies that are in line with the new model—for example, organizing researchers, engineers, and shop-floor operators or new tactics based upon the strategic withholding of intelligence. If they continue to be boxed in by the old fordist organizational structures and strategies, labor unions will continue to lose membership and power, undergoing a gradual, irreversible decline.

Innovation-mediated production is bringing about the further socialization of production in the factory and the laboratory.[8] However, it does so only "objectively"—subjectively, as we have seen, extreme corporate control is used to cause the worker to identify more closely with the company. Japanese industry has created a new and more powerful corporate hegemony over everyday life that makes workers align more closely with the company and voluntarily give of themselves in the name of corporate progress.[9]

Transcending Industrial Boundaries

Innovation-mediated production is leading to the redefinition and transcendance of traditional industrial boundaries. This is evident in high-technology industries where the formerly separate industries of semiconductors, computers, software, and consumer electronics are intermingling. It is also evident between traditional and high-tech industries as automobile and steel production undergo new waves of creative destruction and are themselves transformed into high-technology industries. Increasingly, automobile and steel companies must produce software, integrated circuits, programmable logic controllers, advanced robotics and machine tools, and the artificial intelligence and software programs that run those various machines, tools, and pieces of equipment. These companies are developing their own software capabilities, spinning out software subsidiaries, and acquiring high-technology software start-ups in the United States and elsewhere as they endeavor to compete in the new age of technology-intensive, digitally based manufacturing.

The boundaries of the traditional capitalist firm are also being redefined. How-

ever, the current debate over the changing organizational morphology of the capitalist enterprise misses the crucial aspects of this reorganization.[10] This debate
typically contrasts two ideal types: the vertically integrated firm of either the United
States or Japan, and cooperative small-firm networks. But the real issue is not where
the lines of the enterprise are drawn, but how organizational forms produce and
harness value.

As we have seen, a cornerstone of the Japanese production system and of the
new model more generally is the rise of complex interconnected networks of small
companies organized around larger ones. These networks are not simply new
mechanisms for efficient parts supply and procurement. They function as yet
another organizational mechanism for mobilizing knowledge and intellectual labor
on a collective, social basis. The networks provide a powerful dynamic of innovation. Each firm in the network feels economic and social pressure to improve; thus,
the network is constantly stressed. Suppliers respond by improving technology and
speeding up work. In this organizational system, R&D is far more decentralized.
As a supplier's knowledge advances, it becomes expertise-laden and is able to innovate on its own. These improvements are in the interest of the assembler, so they
encourage the process through extension of technical and other assistance. Thus,
the entire network evolves in a way that is similar to constant improvement on the
factory floor. The network becomes another format for continuous innovation and
improvement.

Production and Culture

This book informs an alternative conceptualization of the relationship between
production and culture. This relationship has been the source of considerable
debate in social theory and the social sciences. For many mainstream theorists, culture is either autonomous or is seen to have a determinate effect on industrial and
productive activity. This is clearly reflected in the great bulk of work on the Japanese industrial system, which sees the Japanese model as informed by, and indeed
as derivative of, Japanese society and culture.[11] Recent postmodernist writings
advance the broader proposition that culture is important, autonomous, and in
some cases determinant of economy and society.[12]

At bottom, production systems are comprised of social relationships and organizational forms and practices that are geared toward harnessing human labor as a
source of value. These social relationships and production systems are of course
informed by culture, but they are by no means reducible to it. As this text documents, these social relationships and organizational forms can, with strategic effort,
be removed from their original cultural context, transferred, and implanted in different societies and cultures. This does not mean that culture is unimportant.
Rather, supportive cultural forms and cultural hegemony are crucial for workers to
identify with innovation-mediated production. As Chapter 9 has shown, new penetrating forms of corporate control and hegemony appear to be required for the
model's success.

But production shapes these relationships and informs the cultural context that
surrounds them. It does so by orienting, selecting, and at times actively creating

supportive cultures. This can be clearly seen with the rise and transfer of Japanese production organization to the United States and elsewhere. This is in line with Gramsci's conceptualization of hegemony being born on the factory floor.[13] Indeed, Gramsci is badly misinterpreted by postmodernists who abuse his work to support theories of cultural autonomy or determination.

The Process of Industrial Transformation

Capitalism, as both Marx and Schumpeter explained, is a revolutionary economic system. However, we still lack an adequate theory of capitalism's self-revolutionizing and transformative potentialities. Marx, after all, was mainly concerned with major transhistorical shifts in "modes of production"—for example, feudalism to capitalism.[14] While Schumpeter focused on shifts within capitalism, which he saw as technologically motivated, he did not specify causal mechanisms with any real precision.[15] Underlying the concepts and arguments advanced in this book is a conceptualization of the more general process of how capitalism moves from one phase to the next.

At the root of our thinking lies the notion of realignments in the forces and relations of production. Such realignments shift the parameters in which value is extracted in production, capital is accumulated, profits are made, and economic growth occurs. While existing theories often point to the outcomes of such realignments, they fail to specify causal forces with any real precision. Most, including neo-Schumpeterian theories of technological change, long-wave approaches, flexible specialization, and even regulation theory, are concerned with the forces and structures that create stability and order.[16] Our conceptualization, however, is concerned with the process of dynamic change—in other words, how advanced industrial societies move from one production system to another.

Schumpeter and Marx both saw the impetus for economic, social, and structural change as dynamic—as resting within the relationship between technological change and the organizational-institutional structure of society. Both saw this process as evolutionary but emphasized the discontinuous and abrupt nature of the evolutionary process.

The relationship between technological innovation and the social and organizational structure lies at the heart of the Schumpeterian model.[17] For Schumpeter, technology exists within the organizational and institutional structure of society. In stable or "good" times, technology and the process of technical advance within this institutional shell as existing organizational forms and institutional structures enhance, even hasten, the development, application, and diffusion of new technology. Eventually, technology comes up against the limits and constraints of the institutional structure to further technical advance.

Yet, according to the Schumpeterian model, technological change holds within it the capability to overcome the limits imposed by institutional structure. In more formal terms, in the Schumpeterian schema, "technology effects" are both powerful and determinant. According to Schumpeter, during these periods revolutionary change occurs through sweeping "gales of creative destruction" that overturn the old established institutional structure and usher in a new one.[18] Ultimately, the pressure for technological change comes from the strong dynamic of capitalist competition. In the Schumpeterian model, companies compete with one another through innovation as well as through price competition. Innovation allows companies to revolutionize both production and product markets and in so doing to transform the terms of competition. For the early Schumpeter, the crucial agent of the change process was the "exceptional entrepreneur" who is able to both perceive new technological opportunities and to marshal the resources required to address them.[19] For the later Schumpeter, the exceptional entrepreneur gave way to the modern R&D-intensive corporation, which rationalized and routinized the innovative function and in doing so internalized the "creative destruction" process.[20]

For Marx, the process of technological development and industrial transformation also derives from the tension between technology and social structure.[21] However, according to the Marxian perspective, technology and social structure—the forces and relations of production—are inseparable, existing together in dialectical unity. Technological change is thus a social process, defined by actual organizations, institutions, and social relationships. Innovation, as such, entails both technological and organizational innovation. According to the Marxian view, innovation enhances the process of value creation, basically by reducing the labor time required to produce products—in other words, process innovation lies at the heart of the Marxian model.

Moreover, in the Marxian model, the innovation process is strongly influenced by the existing organizational context at the point of production—the relationship between capital and labor on the shop floor. Technology thus evolves through a constant and continuous process of adaptation and struggle—through an ongoing, implicit, micro-level struggle on the factory floor. Over time, technology runs up against binding organizational constraints.

But, in contrast to Schumpeter, technology effects alone are insufficient to untie this Gordian knot. Neither exceptional entrepreneurs nor the most farsighted corporations can set this process of transformation and change into motion. During these crucial junctures, it is necessary to reset and realign the forces and relations of production, to create a whole new context for mobilizing and harnessing value at the point of production. The motor force here is industrial unrest—or struggle at the macro level—which functions to recast the forces and relations of production.

Our conceptualization attempts to capture the dynamic process of constant change in both technology and, moreover, in the organizational context of both production and innovation. We thus emphasize the tension between technology and social structure and posits change as a process of dynamic mutual adjustment. At the center of our view lies the concept of production systems—the organization of technology, work, and innovation at the point of production. At crucial junctures within capitalism, production systems undergo sweeping change and reorganization. For us, this transformative process within capitalism is mediated by the organizational context of production and by the labor-management relationship evolving out of the ongoing tension between labor and management and the process of continuous dynamic adjustment on the shop floor.

Once established, production systems tend to be relatively stable and to follow an historically informed evolutionary trajectory, and thus exhibit a high degree of what Paul David and Brian Arthur refer to as historical "path dependence."[22] At critical junctures, however, these path-dependent systems break down and new trajectories emerge. This process of growth and change is, in some sense, analogous to the biological concept of mutation, particularly the emerging notion of abrupt, discontinuous mutation as opposed to more gradual evolution.[23] The mutation process of production systems is ongoing and fairly constant; however, it takes major mutations to set a new system in motion—and open up new sources for value generation, productivity improvement, and profit. Thus, new trajectories are formed by major discontinuous mutations.

In our view, mutations in production systems are driven by a process of dynamic mutual adjustment, basically industrial unrest or struggle at both the micro and macro levels. This process sets off internal changes in different capitalist corporations or countries, which in turn shape different "mutations" moving along different trajectories. Most mutations are minor variations on a dominant strain; e.g., various European adaptations to fordism. Some, however, move off in radical new directions; e.g., the Japanese production system. These are typically, though not necessarily, set in motion by major realignments of the forces and relations of production and a deep recasting of the capital-labor relation. Over time, one, two, or several of these significant mutations then emerge to challenge the existing dominant system. The different mutations or models of production organization then compete with one another, until ultimately one proves itself more effective at harnessing value and moves ahead of the others to become a new dominant system. For us, the process of industrial struggle and unrest at the point of production is a vital variable that in large measure motivates the process of innovation and change.

This is not to suggest that exogenous variables, such as competition, are unimportant. However, these forces are relatively constant across companies, nations, and industrial systems. It is the endogenous forces which differ—and which matter—most notably localized labor-management relations, and local institutional adaptation to this. As Chapters 2 and 3 have shown, the roots of the Japanese production system can be found in the intense labor-management conflicts of the immediate postwar era that essentially recast the organizational context of the Japanese factory, setting Japanese capitalism on a new trajectory. The rise of U.S. fordism was similarly shaped by industrial unrest and struggle—the rise of the industrial workers' movement alongside mass production. This provided the force that pushed the system in a direction beyond the previous system of craft manufacture.

Simply put, in our view, the key force driving the transformation process—or movement from one model to another—is the underlying process of adjustment, unrest, and struggle at the point of production. Further, we see the process of change and transformation as ever-changing, dynamic but conditioned by real-world events and actual historical processes. It is neither predictable nor does it follow a preordained teleology of history. Today, for example, new models of production and economic organization are emerging, hidden from view, that may in time challenge the Japanese model.

Looking Ahead

As this book has made clear, a new industrial revolution is sweeping the advanced capitalist world. It is now time to reflect and to speculate on some key implications of that epochal transformation. Different companies and different nations are responding in different ways to the emergence of innovation-mediated production. This is to be expected. However, it should be remembered that various adaptive responses are neither automatic nor governed by a process of natural selection; rather, these relationships are politically mediated—imposed and negotiated by social groups and classes. As we have already seen, such adaptive responses bear the imprint of past history, and they are strongly influenced by existing social structures, organizational forms, management practices, forms of labor organization, political constellations, articulations of struggle, and so on.

In the view of Richard Nelson and Sidney Winter, the past "selection environment" affects and indeed shapes new paths of change; or in the framework of Mancur Olson, institutional rigidities create blockages to industrial progress.[24] Furthermore, many theorists have noted that different forms of production organization (e.g., craft production, simple industrial production, fordist mass production, etc.) frequently coexist within a given political-economic formation and that it is impossible to generalize completely from one form to the organization of all economic activity. Indeed, it is frequently the case that different forms and articulations of production organization can and do exist in a symbiotic, mutually dependent way to constitute an economic system. Still, it is important to discern which forces and trends are dominant and which can function as trendsetters for advanced capitalist economies.

Over the past decade or so, Japanese corporations have positioned themselves to assume a place of global dominance in both traditional heavy industries and high-technology fields. Up until now they have done so by developing new organizational forms that effectively harness and advance these new productive forces. In a telling account of things to come, the Japanese economy registered a phenomenal 11 percent rate of real GNP growth during the first quarter of 1991, a period when the United States and the advanced Western industrial nations were badly mired in serious recession, in some case verging on depression.[25] Japan's advances in both technology and the immediate organization of production—its very expression of innovation-mediated production—will likely set the tenor for the next long wave of capitalist expansion.[26] According to a recent account

> Japan is now experiencing a boom that will be seen as the longest and most powerful cycle of expansion of the last sixty years. As a measure of the momentum, Japan's economy is today one "Canada" larger than it was just thirty months ago. At the average rate of growth of the past four years, the [Japanese] economy, in real terms, is doubling in size every thirteen and a half years. . . . If you look carefully at trends today, it is clear that Japan is becoming the new product laboratory of the world. . . . In the mid-1990s the rest of the world is going to wake up and say, "Where are all these new products coming from?" And it is not just going to be obvious things—palm-sized video cameras, personal computers the size of a legal

pad, wrist-telephones, personalized cars—it will also be advances in services, in how production is organized, and in the management of business itself.[27]

In each of the industries we have explored, the strength of Japanese business is apparent. Whereas ten years ago Japanese companies competed mainly on the basis of price and product quality, in the early 1990s, Japanese firms increasingly define the global state-of-the-art in design and innovation. Innovation-mediated mass production, which originally emerged on the shop floor, is now the leading method for organizing R&D labs. Work teams, job rotation, constant improvement, and overlapping functions now characterize the organization of R&D scientists and engineers.

Most studies of the Japanese production system have focussed upon the automobile[28]—a worthy topic in its own right. However, the automotive industry is no longer the defining feature of technologically advanced capitalism. As with steel before, and textiles before that, the automotive sector is now giving way to a new industrial trendsetter—the digitally based microelectronics sector. The automobile industry was clearly important as a precursor and breeding ground for the organizational changes that underpin innovation-mediated production, but here again its role is analogous to the steel industry of an earlier period where Frederick Taylor's innovations in scientific management set the stage for fordism—the coupling of scientific management with the moving assembly line.

But it is the new information-intensive, digital, high-technology sectors that currently comprise capitalism's leading edge. These industries are important as a source of value, profit, and accumulation in their own right, and, increasingly, the products of these leading industries—the computers, advanced chips, and robotic equipment—are being used to transform older heavy industries.

Fujitsu, Hitachi, Matsushita, NEC, Sony, Toshiba, and others increasingly define the competitive terrain of the high-technology, information-intensive, digital industries of the twenty-first century. These corporations straddle the entire complement of high-technology sectors from semiconductors, the basic building blocks of the microelectronic age, to supercomputers, mainframes, personal computers, laptops, workstations, high-definition TV, information-storage devices from hard drives to CDs, telecommunications and transmission equipment, robotics, computerized manufacturing systems, and home and office automation systems. Once dismissed as imitators, these corporations have increasingly become innovative across the entire spectrum of core electronic technologies.

Japanese companies are now making the strategic investments in state-of-the-art basic research, innovative technology, and industrial infrastructure that will allow Japan to move into a position of unquestioned global leadership in these new sectors and perhaps to begin to pull away from its major competitors, the United States and Germany. Small, medium-sized, and large firms alike are increasing R&D spending at a rapid pace. According to Japanese R&D planning managers, their firms intend to increase R&D expenditures drastically over the next ten years. A number stated that they are currently held back by an inability to hire more suitably qualified graduates.[29] Invariably, Japanese firms that were at 2 percent a decade ago are now spending 5 percent on R&D; those at 5 percent are now spending 10 percent; and all are intent on moving to higher and higher levels of R&D spending. All of these companies recognize the importance of R&D to survival. As these firms grow, their R&D is moving from only being development-oriented toward strengthening their applied research and increasing their basic research. As the manager of a major Japanese optoelectronics firm put it:

> Increasingly, in our industry there are no foreign competitors left. And so, there is no one to purchase technology from except our Japanese competitors. Therefore, we have no choice but to increase our R&D expenditures.[30]

As this pattern continues, Japan's lead over the West in key industries from steel and automobiles to electronics will grow ever wider, and perhaps become insurmountable for some time.

International Restructuring: The United States, Europe, and Beyond

The forecast is not too bright for American and Western European companies. American industry has developed a unique ability to maintain profitability by retreating from one market after another when competition grows. That has basically meant abandoning manufacturing for the huge "paper" (and often illusory) profits in financial speculation, the defense business, and diversification. Businesses, plants, and entire work forces are scuttled in the vain hope of gaining riches from new endeavors. The result is that U.S. firms shrink and lose segment after segment of the market. Employees are then left to fend for themselves in the labor market and increasingly on the unemployment line.

Clearly, the Big Three automakers have come a long way. However, if they are unable to adopt innovation-mediated production, they will doubtless fail. Chrysler already seems destined to cease to exist as an independent automaker. Despite all the hoopla, Saturn appears to be only an experiment or a case of too little, too late. In steel, the shift to innovation-mediated production is occurring apace. Unfortunately, it is being accomplished under increasing Japanese ownership. The future of steel in the United States is likely to see greater and greater segments of the American steel industry sell their operations to Japanese firms. And much the same is true of rubber and tires. The U.S. consumer electronics industry is already largely Japanese-owned. Of the industries examined in this book, that leaves only high-technology" ones—computers, semiconductors, software, etc. These sectors, which were bastions of American competitive strength just five years ago, are also slipping. In a harbinger of the future, IBM has contracted with Japanese firms to build its new state-of-the-art semiconductor fabrication facilities, shifted most of its personal computer development to Japan, and formed a new joint venture with Toshiba in Japan to produce advanced displays for its computers.

The outlook for Europe may, in fact, be worse. Partly due to staunch government protection and the creation of so-called national champions, European companies remain somewhat competitive in the automobile, steel, and consumer electronic sectors—considerably more so than the United States. However, Europe is in dismal shape in high-technology where both Japanese and American firms stand poised to annihilate European producers. While European corporations such as Siemens, Alcatel, and Ericsson are holding their own in telecommunications, Europe is technologically laggard in semiconductors, computers, and software—the key sectors that will drive the digital electronics revolution.

Furthermore, European industrial weakness combined with protectionism has prompted large-scale Japanese direct investment.[31] During the 1980s, Japanese capital penetrated the United States; during the 1990s it will increasingly penetrate Europe. According to the Japanese chairman of Mitsubishi Electric Europe, "In the first part of the 1980s we concentrated our resources on North America; now we have started to look at Europe."[32] Between 1988 and 1990, Japanese direct investment in the European Community more than doubled, increasing from $25 billion to more than $55 billion. According to a JETRO report, Japanese direct manufacturing investment in Europe grew by 62.4 percent in 1989 alone, exceeding the 51.8 percent rate for North America.[33] As Chapter 8 has shown, Japanese corporations such as Sony, Toshiba, Matsushita, Sharp, Alps, and others have already made large investments in consumer electronic facilities in England and has had success transferring the new model of production organization including fledgling supplier complexes.[34] Sony, Hitachi, and Toshiba operate plants in Germany. Matsushita operates a joint venture facility with Bosch in Germany producing VCRs.[35] In France, Sony operates three factories that make compact discs, and audio and videocassettes; Canon Inc. has a photocopier and electronic typewriter plant, and Akai makes stereo equipment and VCRs in French factories.[36] These companies and others are encroaching on long-established markets held by European producers—Philips, Thomson, and Grundig.

Japanese firms are rapidly penetrating the European automotive assembly and automotive-related industries. Leading Japanese automakers—Nissan, Toyota, and Honda—are building just-in-time production complexes in Britain and opening smaller assembly facilities on the Continent.[37] Mitsubishi has formed a joint venture partnership with Volvo, which will operate the Volvo assembly plant in Holland. The European Community recently agreed that there will be no limits on Japanese automotive transplant production in Europe after 1992. In return, Japanese automakers agreed to voluntarily restrict imports to Europe to 1.23 million cars annually. This deal is essentially analogous to the one reached earlier between the U.S. government and Japanese automakers. The European Community also agreed to treat vehicles produced at Japanese transplants in the United States as "U.S.-made cars" rather than as Japanese imports. In rubber and tires, Sumitomo has acquired all of Dunlop's European branches, and Bridgestone has increased access to the European market due to its purchase of Firestone; together these companies hold nearly a 15 percent share of the European tire market. In response to this, Italian tiremaker Pirelli had sought to acquire German tire producer Continental.

In high-technology, Japanese firms are moving into Europe through a combination of acquisitions, joint venture, and direct investment. As mentioned earlier, in 1990, Fujitsu acquired a majority interest in ICL, Britain's largest computer maker, and the Finnish company Nokia Data; at the same time, Mitsubishi took a majority stake in Apricot Computers, a British PC maker.[38] NEC holds a small 5 percent stake in French computer maker Machines Bull. Fujitsu operates a semiconductor facility in northern England that produces 4-megabit DRAMS, erasable programmable read-only memories (EPROMs), and static-RAMs (SRAMs), and NEC has a similar facility in Scotland. In December 1990, the European Community granted Mitsubishi Electric Corp. an $8 million subsidy to build a $350 million DRAM plant near Aachen, a depressed coal-mining region Germany. In 1990, Sharp, Fujitsu, and Hitachi opened major R&D units in England, and NEC invested $18 million in a European Technology Center in Dusseldorf, Germany, to design semiconductors for Europe's automotive, telecommunications, and consumer electronics industries.[39]

In the key sectors of automobiles, consumer electronics, semiconductors, and steel, Japan is developing a considerable technological lead over U.S. and European producers. In this environment, American and European firms must rapidly restructure or face technological extinction. These companies must reinvest in R&D and manufacturing simultaneously. And just as investments compound through time, so too does a widening gap in technological capability. A small differential today may well be insurmountable five to ten years from now. By that time, even massive "crash" projects will not be sufficient to spur a catch-up.

Merely increasing R&D spending is not enough. More important is creating a production system that can capitalize on new innovations and turn them into the continuous stream of products. In today's constantly changing commercial environment, the rapid movement of new products through design and development to the market is absolutely required. Most U.S. and European firms, with their entrenched fordist organization, caste-like hierarchies, and managerial arrogance, find it nearly impossible to achieve such speed.

Future Transfer: Obstacles and Opportunities

How far will the Japanese production system and its transplant factories ultimately diffuse? In this book we have argued that the Japanese production system is a set of organizational forms and practices—a model of innovation, production, and work—that is reproducible throughout the advanced capitalist world. Still, this does not mean that there will not be obstacles and blockages to its further transfer and diffusion.

Clearly, it will neither be easy nor problem-free to expand the Japanese expression of innovation-mediated mass production throughout the globe. The United States has been the first real test and there has been marked success. A bigger test awaits in Europe, where nationalist and protectionist sentiments run high. And in America, too, forces are gathering that may limit Japanese investment and impact on the further transfer of the Japanese production system.

The opposition to further penetration of the Japanese production system comes from various sources. The first is from impacted sectors of domestic capital who see internal Japanese competition as a major threat to their existence. In the United States, this sort of opposition has been and continues to be manifested by a host of firms in traditional and high-technology industries. While Japanese companies have been able to "buy-off" the opposition of large steel companies, basically by involving them in joint ventures, opposition continues to mount from the Big Three and the automotive parts sector and elements of high-technology industries.

Japanese corporations have thus far been quite successful in staving off such opposition. They have done so by making strategic investments that allow them to defuse corporate, political, and regional opposition. They have integrated large corporations into joint ventures and have spread investments around to a variety of key geographic centers. In France recently—in the wake of Prime Minister Cresson's anti-Japanese tirade—NEC acquired almost 5 percent of the French national computer champion Machines Bull. Moreover, in keeping with the notion that capitalism knows no boundaries, many of the most dynamic and profitable firms in the United States and Europe are dependent upon Japanese producers for crucial inputs and supplies. In the United States, recently, leading computer makers IBM, Apple, Compaq, and others provided a powerful lobbying force for their Japanese suppliers of advanced active-matrix display screens, attempting to block an effort by small high-technology American producers to halt the flow of Japanese screens into the United States.[40]

Perhaps the most significant potential barrier to the diffusion of the Japanese production system comes from the indigenous labor movements in America and Europe. In the United States, the major unions have consented to experiments with this new model of production organization. But their cooperation is far from etched in stone. The labor movement has been under significant pressure from elements of their rank and file, especially the very powerful craft elements, to move away from participation. The New Directions faction of the UAW is vehemently opposed to Japanese work and production organization. Similar trends are evident in other unions where factions oppose work teams, worker participation, and the reduction in job classifications.

Still, it is unlikely that union opposition alone can halt the transfer of the Japanese production system. Labor unions are in retreat across the advanced industrial nations; without large-scale support from domestic business, there is little they can do to stop the further encroachment of the Japanese system. Ultimately, it is much more likely that opposition from indigenous labor movements will alter the trajectory of the Japanese production system rather than create an impenetrable obstacle to transfer. These forces and struggles are likely to push the model in new directions, some of which may actually strengthen it, rather than call it into question. Workers' groups at the Mazda plant in Flat Rock, Michigan, and the NUMMI plant in California are developing alternative programs that call for more control over production, shorter work weeks, and better working conditions. It is likely that Japanese firms will find themselves forced to make some concessions here. To the extent that this actually improves workers' conditions, this will perhaps be for the good.

Despite these gathering forces, we are led to conclude that opposition from such quarters will be unable to stop the spread of Japanese capital and the epoch-making new system of innovation-mediated production. Like the opposition to fordism in Gramsci's Europe, opposition to the transfer of the Japanese production system comes from the laggard, indeed backward, segments of society. Except under the most exceptional circumstances, such elements are incapable of inhibiting the further advance of capitalism's powerful productive forces. There can be little doubt that innovation-mediated production will continue to spread throughout the world economy both through the vehicle of Japanese transplant companies and increasingly through imitation by American and European companies and others. Figure 10.1 shows the extent to which this is occurring already, providing a map of the worldwide locations of Japanese automotive assembly plants. Simply put: The future of the advanced capitalist world will be defined in terms of innovation-mediated production.

From Production to Reproduction

Thus far we have focused our attention on production and its organization. However, to build a system that can underpin long-term industrial growth, advances in production organization must interface with a broader structure of demand and consumption. This was exactly the case with fordism, which coupled advances in mass-production technology to new forms of mass consumption that occurred through systematic wage increases, new forms of government involvement in the economy, and the expansion of consumer credit, especially for housing.

We now turn our attention to the possible emergence of a new model of social and economic reproduction that would mesh with innovation-mediated production.[41] Such an emergence would require a stable allocation of economic resources among profit, reinvestment, and consumption and the creation of a stable set of social institutions for organizing demand and establishing the conditions for self-sustaining economic growth. The contours for this balance are set by two basic facets of the Japanese political economy: organization of domestic demand based upon long-term employment and the rise in new forms of consumption.

The Japanese structure differs markedly from the organization of demand under U.S. fordism, which was premised upon productivity-indexed wage increases for core workers, trickle-down effects for others in the labor market, and government-associated social welfare spending for marginal groups.[42] The fordist economy worked well during periods of low inflation and steady growth, but it could not adapt to periods of extreme cyclical volatility and rapid changes in consumer preferences. Basically, slumps in corporate profitability were quickly translated into layoffs and dismissals, causing significant decreases in consumption and demand. Upturns, on the other hand, were characterized by a rapid tightening of labor markets, rising wages, inflationary pressures, and potential squeezes on corporate profit. During the 1970s and 1980s, economic and social reproduction became increasingly difficult and a vicious circle was set into motion.[43]

In contrast, the Japanese economy is characterized by substantial resilience. In an environment of growth, wages and consumer demand slightly lag but track productivity increases and corporate profits. During downturns, however, the Japanese system provides a resilience that can ameliorate decreases in demand. Long-term employment ensures that workers face layoffs only as a condition of last resort. The export orientation of the Japanese economy lends additional cyclical stability. The

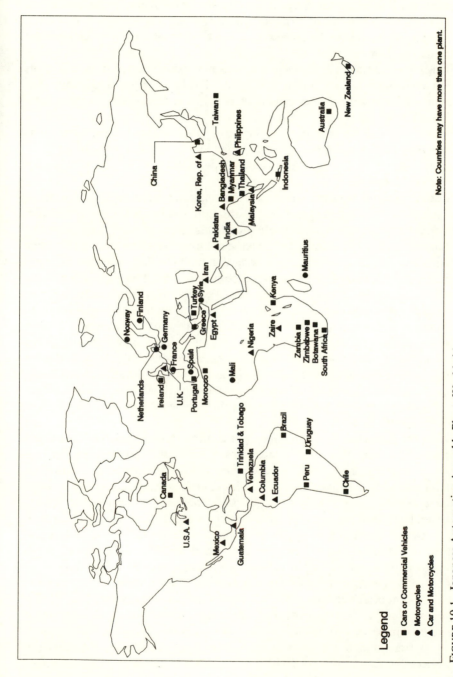

FIGURE 10.1. Japanese Automotive Assembly Plants Worldwide.
Source: Japan Automobile Manufacturing Association, 1989.

317

Japanese system of wage determination allows workers' incomes to fluctuate with corporate performance (especially through the size of the bonus). This is bolstered by enterprise unionism that often forces unions to moderate demands in economic downturns. In this way the Japanese system has been capable of smoothing out the business cycle.

This Japanese system certainly imposes burdens on workers, but these burdens are not as onerous as dismissal (a la fordism). The long-term employment commitment mitigates fear of unemployment as a reason for workers to resist automation. Simultaneously, in Japan automation is not an immediate threat to consumer demand because of the long-term employment commitment. The employment commitment also creates tremendous additional pressure for management to generate new schemes to redeploy workers, to enter new high-growth fields, and to innovate.

Institutional mechanisms to channel consumption are crucial. Japan currently possesses the second largest aggregate consumption base in the advanced industrial countries with over 40 million, largely middle-class, households.[44] Japan has not been merely an export platform, but because of income equality and rapid income growth it has had a vibrant internal market that has provided enormous opportunities for Japanese manufacturers. Yet this consumption differs markedly from the housing/automobile complex of U.S. fordism. Perhaps most significantly, Japanese households devote a much smaller share of disposable income to housing than do U.S. and European households. This is because a large share of Japanese families (more than 60 percent) own their homes and because a large share of the remainder live in company-subsidized or public housing. According to data compiled by Japan's Agency of Management and Coordination in 1989 housing expenditures comprised just 12.9 percent of monthy disposable household income, which is considerably below the 20-30 percent of household income which is devoted for housing in the United States.[45]

With the exception of automobiles, penetration rates in Japan for consumer durables are comparable to the United States. More importantly, demand for consumer durables has increased in parallel with the rise of Japanese incomes. This demand unleashed massive waves of purchases of items such as color televisions, washing machines, air conditioners, VCRs, stereos and compact disc players. Household penetration rates went from zero to 90 plus percent in periods as short as ten years. Such enormous waves of demand encouraged a rapid build up of capacity, which meant large capital investments that further reinforced demand. And as demand slackened, export offensives would then begin.

Currently, Japan is at the center of a number of revolutionary consumption trends. An important element of this is what has been termed the "home information revolution." At one level, this concerns the consumption of personalized entertainment devices or consumer hardware such as televisions, videocassette recorders, stereophonic equipment, compact disc players, and other digital recording devices that can be combined with entertainment software. As of 1990, two out of three Japanese households owned a VCR, and one in five owned a computer word processor. In 1990, the percentage of households owning a VCR increased by 10 percent, while those owning a word processor increased by 6 percent. However, during the same period, the rate of growth in ownership of consumer durables such as washing machines and color televisions levelled off to just 0.3 percent.[46] The largest new looming market is high-definition television (HDTV), which is already in use in Japan. HDTV will be furthered by direct satellite broadcasting to parabolic antennas, which are already in evidence outside many Japanese homes and apartments.

This has been accompanied by increased home automation as Japanese consumer electronic firms add sophisticated integrated circuitry and so-called "fuzzy logic" to old home appliances. Further, these products are becoming ever more design-intensive in terms of both looks and operation. For example, a recent Hitachi floor fan not only has the usual different speeds, but also has controls that allow the choice of two types of wind-flow variability: One increases the speed of the fan at regular intervals; the other oscillates the speed of the fan at irregular intervals, providing the illusion of a natural breeze. Further, the fan is handsomely designed and painted. No longer are Japanese products merely well made and engineered; they must also be aesthetically designed.

The second level is consumption of more sophisticated information-processing and telecommunications devices—including personal computers, word processors, car phones, information storage devices, personal facsimile and copying machines. Here too there is a huge market for software such as computer software proper, database information, and computer communications and computer shopping. In many high-consumption sectors of information electronics, Japanese industry has proven its rapid ability to penetrate growing markets and revolutionize production technologies (especially hardware), making products quickly obsolete and establishing new niches for expansion and profit making. A recent analysis by the Long Term Credit Bank of Japan outlines these trends:

> After the Second World War, the Japanese aspired to an American-type lifestyle complete with home electrical appliances and automobiles. In the 1990s, Japan is at the forefront of semiconductor technology and is starting to blossom into an information oriented society. Perhaps, it is now our turn to convey to the world a new Japanese-type lifestyle. As products become more portable and personal, individuals will commonly carry around information and communication equipment. When that happens, personal computers, facsimile, and portable telephones will become consumer necessities.[47]

Infrastructure is a critical element in the organization of demand and for creating the context of social organization and reproduction. This is witnessed by the important, dynamizing roles played by canals, railroads, and the automobile in previous periods of capitalist expansion. In 1990, Japan announced a major new $2.7 trillion program to develop airports, transportation projects, new communities, an automated underground mail-delivery system, and a technology-intensive infrastructure. Japanese industry and government are currently building the information infrastructure for the twenty-first century.[48] This includes the development of digital fiber optic information highways, wired cities, teletopias, and smart buildings. The ultimate goal is the creation of a societywide telecommunications and information infrastructure.[49]

A huge segment of Japanese consumption is social consumption, most notably education.[50] Japan devotes a relatively high proportion of public expenditures to education. Education accounts for a larger and larger share of household spending—providing a new outlet for consumption. However, the education phenomenon runs much deeper than formal public education. An entire industry has grown up in Japan to prepare students to take the examinations for entrance into the university system. These preparatory schools, called *juku,* have become a big business in Japan. In the mid 1980s, expenditures on *juku* schooling totalled $5 billion. According to one study, families with one child in *juku* spent 2 percent of total income; family expenditures rose to 3.5 percent of income for four *juku* courses.[51] However, this is only the largest sector of an increasing emphasis on education and training. Private schools service a wide array of demographic groups on subjects as diverse as traditional Japanese arts such as *ikebana* and *origami* to foreign languages and aerobics. Private tutoring is extensive, and corporations have constant training and skill-upgrading programs.

The emphasis on education also creates important new markets for information-intensive electronic products—computers, smart video games, and software. But most importantly, massive social investment in education is vitally important since it enables Japan to generate extraordinarily skilled and remarkably adaptable labor across all segments of society. This is likely to confer distinct competitive advantages in a world economy which is increasingly premised upon intellectual labor. Indeed, the emphasis on education dovetails with and reinforces the development of smart workers—a highly skilled and potent work force to man the new information-intensive and innovative industries of the twenty-first century.[52]

Japan is also witnessing the fragmentation of mass consumption in line with the rise of innovation-mediated production. This is not the illusory, democratic fragmentation championed by U.S. marketers, economists, and post-modern theorists, but rather a structured, rational, and almost planned fragmentation which is informed by the productive capabilities of innovation-mediated production. Japanese marketing experts argue that "the Japanese consumer is changing from being primarily interested in having as many things as possible to desiring items that express individuality."[53] This is a result of the desire among consumers to have unique products. As the basic needs of Japanese consumers have been met, demand has begun to evolve from one characterized by a relatively undifferentiated mass consumption to what Wakao Fujita has termed "micromass consumption"—small social groupings with unique but internally consistent purchasing patterns.[54] The emergence of differentiated and rapidly changing markets is facilitated by the flexibility of innovation-mediated manufacturing which can quickly reorganize production, discontinue weak products, and meet expanding market opportunities.

Today, the Japanese market is characterized by constantly changing fashion and fads. One important example of this new genre of consumption has been the rise of Japanese fashion designers who are now globally renowned. Young people are increasingly driving this market. According to a recent account:

> Among the new generation, however, fads are much smaller in scope and shorter in duration. An example of this can be seen in the domestic automobile industry.

One leading automaker introduced a subcompact specifically designed for young people. The car experienced a meteoric rise in popularity; but the craze was short-lived, and sales quickly plunged after reaching a zenith.[55]

While many fads die off, some diffuse and open up truly huge domestic and even international markets. The Sony Walkman rapidly went from a premium-priced product to one that has an extremely broad-based product line available at almost every price.[56] The rapidly changing domestic market constantly presses Japanese manufacturers to apply new technologies to bring down costs and increase the capabilities of current products. Japanese producers must continually develop new products and rapidly boost production of successes and quickly bring out follow-on products to keep up with competitors. Simply put, contemporary Japan has overturned the meaning of "consumer durable," replacing standard mass production goods with goods aimed at a rapidly changing consumer market. These new consumption goods combine the mundane with the truly revolutionary. For example, Japanese companies have developed "fuzzy logic" vacuum cleaners that can sense how dirty the carpet is, and washing machines that can sense the load levels and the dirtiness of the clothes; these machines adjust themselves to optimize their operation.[57] Japanese consumers are now becoming the world's test market for new consumer products,[58] and Japanese industry is becoming the leading developer of design and technology-intensive consumer goods.

The rise of this new form of "micro-mass" consumption extends well beyond national boundaries and is increasingly global in scope. During the past decade or two, stratified consumption groups whose memberships are international have proliferated. The rise of international yuppie groups consuming high-end automobiles, audio and video equipment, new computers, facsimile machines, and telecommunications equipment is perhaps the best exemplar of this. In fact, it is now possible to find the same or similar micro-mass groupings of consumers in Europe, North America, and Japan. This is a major change from fordism, which tended to create homogeneous national markets for its products and only later to extend those relatively homogeneous markets across national borders.

Another example of the rapidity of change being created by innovation-mediated production is automobile production where new models and even types of vehicles are rapidly sent out into the market—sports cars, luxury sedans, economy cars, utility vehicles, sport trucks, minivans, etc. Some of these are hits, but many others are misses. The Mazda Miata, which was designed in the United States, but built in Japan, is an example of a hit. Nissan recently released a series of new models. Its Pao, for example, resembles the old British Mini Countryman except that it has crude-looking hinges that are on the outside of the car and an interior that is deliberately primitive. The name itself was chosen to evoke images of China or Mongolia. In other words, the Pao was designed to resemble a "Third World" car. The vehicle was marketed on a limited-time basis and orders were taken for only six months. The Pao was a standout best-seller. Another example is the Nissan "S-Cargo," which is shaped somewhat like a snail (escargot) and marketed as a utility vehicle for young women. The Japanese automobile industry is moving toward marketing techniques that resemble those of the high-fashion industry, with constantly changing designs and enforced scarcity through artificially limited numbers or limited time periods in which to order the car.

But again, the real power of the emerging system of consumption and continuous innovation is to be found in the new, increasingly digital fields of electronics. Recent years have seen many new audio and video formats, CDs, digital audiotape, laser discs, minidiscs, etc. These new formats open up new markets for new hardware. Moreover, the hardware comes in multiple shapes and sizes for multiple uses and activities—large-screen TVs, small-screen TVs, watchman TVs, advanced video recorders, palmcorders, Walkmans, discmans, watchmans, boom boxes, and high-fidelity audio and video equipment. And, all of this changes in looks and fashion—one year it's wood-grain exteriors, the next it's steel gray or chrome, then black, then white, sometimes day-glo. A similar process is occurring in the computer business where new generations of more portable, sleeker-looking, more fashionable, and more powerful notebook computers are seemingly released every few months. And every time there is a new product, often the same product, it finds a market. Tremendous rounds of value and profit are realized, even though few new human needs have been served.

These electronic devices simultaneously create ever-larger markets for software—videos, CDs, tapes, discs, computer games, television programs, etc.—which the very same companies frequently provide. Here, perhaps more than anywhere else, the new model obliterates national boundaries, penetrating the globe to discover new, salable forms of music, art, literature, film, and culture. Cultural forms that were once the exclusive domain of so-called primitive cultures and perhaps the property of a few leading museums now become commodities themselves or inform the development of new fusion commodities to be bought and sold in international markets. What we are seeing here is nothing less that the further globalization and "commodification" of culture goods and of culture itself.

In this way, innovation-mediated production throws off huge numbers of new products that crystallize new or potential markets by appealing to undefined or only partially defined and rapidly changing groups. This has extended the fashion mentality, once limited to clothing and shoes, to automobiles and advanced electronic products. The operative rule is simple: Those products that succeed in creating a market are quickly manufactured and distributed; those that do not are scuttled.[59]

The emergence of these new forms and patterns of consumption fits nicely with innovation-mediated production, which can quickly reorganize production, discontinue weak products, and meet expanding market opportunities. To address the emerging micro-mass markets, Japanese companies have developed new techniques for connecting market feedback to design, product development, and production. Kenneth Courtis, an analyst for the Deutsche Bank, has termed this revolution in design and production "Just-In-Time Development and Design"—the key to which is continuous product and process innovation.

Innovation always accounted for a high percentage of Japanese capital investment, but now there is a major difference. During Japan's 1975–85 export boom, about three-quarters of industry leaders responding to MITI's investment surveys reported that innovation investment was driven by the need to develop new products and services for penetrating the North American and European markets. Since

1986, however, there has been a complete reversal, with about 80 percent of this innovation investment now targeted to the domestic market. That means that new products and services will be increasingly introduced in Japan first. . . . The country is actually positioning itself to play a role in the world economy similar to that which America played in the 1950s and '60s, when new products were first developed and introduced into the U.S. market, and then, as the international life cycle unfolded, such products were released in sequence around the world. Over the 1990s, we will see Japan moving to play a similar role in the world economy.[60]

Curiously, the growth of these micro-mass markets creates a self-reinforcing cycle that has Japanese firms desperately looking for new and unique products, thus driving the system to ever-greater expenditures on R&D. This has unleashed massive investment in developing new materials that have unique functions or properties; these include advanced ceramics, rare earth metals, organic compounds, and even new synthetic textiles. These are then rapidly developed into products and thrown onto the market. This producer investment then drives the input industries and creates the new jobs that reinforces the entire system. It also threatens to annihilate greater and greater segments of the competition in the United States and Europe.

These developments go far beyond conceptualizations of the "information society."[61] And they stand in stark contrast to the postmodernists' insistence on rising "multiculturalism" and the flourishing of alternative cultures and similar arguments about the democratic breakup and fragmentation of mass markets. Indeed, the postmodernists have it reversed. The cultural trends, patterns, and forces that postmodern theorists identify as driving changes in advanced capitalist societies and economies are, in actuality, motivated by innovation-mediated production. We are seeing the rise of a whole new pattern of capitalist social organization and reproduction oriented around the rapid creation of new product "fashions," attenuated hyper-consumptionism, further globalization of markets, and extensive "commodification" of human needs—a pattern of social organization born from and articulated to the underlying model of innovation-mediated production itself.

At a deeper and more fundamental level, the ascendance of the Japanese system of innovation-mediated production calls into question the very tenets of Western cultural, moral, and indeed "racial" superiority. For approximately 400 years, the Europeans and the European settler states congratulated themselves on their technological and industrial superiority—sure that Judeo-Christian traditions, the Protestant ethic, and the basic cultural tenets of Western civilization provided an edge—perhaps forgetting that it was their system of organizing production and work to harness value that was in truth the key to their advantage. Now as the twentieth century is almost past and the twenty-first century looms on the horizon, it is the West that is beginning to experience economic decline, social disorganization, and the questioning of its long assumed cultural superiority.[22] The rise of Japan, clearly a non-European state, fundamentally questions putative notions of the superiority of the West. If what we argue in this book is correct—if the Japanese expression of innovation-mediated production proves over the long run to be both superior and transferable to the West—then a profound new humility will be required from the Anglo-European nations.

The advanced capitalist world has crossed a historic turning point—one from which there is no return. A new future is unfolding. Out of the chaos and detritus of the old order, a whole new model for organizing technology, production, work and industry has emerged. A revolutionary new system of harnessing value, generating profit, and creating economic wealth is now upon us. Its effects will be felt in the social, cultural, political, and economic organization of global capitalism for decades to come.

Appendix A: Overview of the Research

The research for this book aimed to understand the underlying structure, institutions, and organizational dynamics of the Japanese production system and its transfer to the United States. It is part of a larger, ongoing project exploring the new industrial revolution and the restructuring of production systems as they are occurring across the advanced industrial nations, most notably the United States and Japan.

The research presented here is multidisciplinary in orientation and in scope. In developing the concepts, theories, and arguments forming the core of this text, we rather quickly bumped up against the limits of the individual social science disciplines. Early on, we made a conscious decision to be inclusive and not be confined by disciplinary boundaries of the social sciences. Basically we let our questions be our guide, and we endeavored as much as is possible to incorporate those theories and concepts that were needed to understand the questions we wanted to answer or at the very least to understand. In contrast to typical social science studies, this one spans the boundaries of political economy, organizational studies, sociology, social theory, theories of technological innovation, institutional economics, labor and industrial relations, geography, regional science, and urban planning. This interdisciplinary approach permitted new insights, hypotheses, and ways of framing questions beyond the confines of single disciplines.

Our research effort encompassed a number of social science methodologies. Here, we followed the same sorts of guidelines outlined earlier. We employed research techniques and methodologies that would enable us to answer the questions we posed. Hence, we used a combination of micro- and macro-oriented methodologies: intensive case study, in-depth oral interviews, archival and documentary analysis, large-scale data development, statistical and geographic analysis, and survey research.[1]

Our research was divided into two parts: research conducted on the Japanese production system in Japan, and research on the transfer of this system to the United States through the vehicle of transplant facilities. We provide a brief summary of each.

Research in Japan

The research in Japan was aimed at understanding the origins, historical development, institutional structures, and organizational forms of the Japanese production
system as it exists in Japan. This part of the research included data gathering and
development from both secondary published sources and from primary source documents, interviews, site visits, and survey research. This part of the research was
undertaken in a series of visits and trips during the period 1984–91, including an
extended six-month research visit during 1988–89.

All in all, the Japanese component of the research consisted of roughly 60 site
visits to factories, R&D labs, and corporate headquarters and more than 120 interviews with executives, R&D scientists, engineers, workers, and government officials, and survey research on the organization, location, and interaction between
R&D and manufacturing facilities in Japanese high-technology industry.

Research and development in the Japanese biotechnology industry was the sub-
ject of a research visit made in May-June 1984. Multiple interviews were conducted
with executives, managers, and R&D scientists at a number of the most important
Japanese pharmaceutical and food processing companies: Ajinomoto, Fujisawa
Pharmaceutical, The Green Cross Corporation, Kyowa Hakko Kogyo, Mitsubishi
Chemical, Meiji Milk Products, Otsuka Pharmaceutical, Suntory Limited, Tanabe
Seiyaku, and Takeda Chemical Industries. Also, on this trip, government officials
and university professors were interviewed.

A second trip in November-December 1987 followed up this research on R&D
in the biotechnology industry and also initiated separate research on the Japanese
software industry and automotive industry. Site visits and oral interviews were conducted at the following biotechnology firms: Kirin Brewery, Mitsubishi Chemical,
NEC, Nippon Kokan K.K., Nippon Oil and Fats, Nippon Zeon, Shin-etsu Chemical, Suntory Limited, Taisho Pharmaceutical, Tosoh, and Taito. Dr. Kozo Inoue
of S.T. Research was very helpful in providing introductions and explaining the
development of the Japanese pharmaceutical industry. The software component
included site visits and oral interviews with Fujitsu, Kanrikogaku Kenkyusho,
Microsoft Japan, PCA, Software Consultant, and Tokyo Systems Laboratory. Also,
interviews were conducted with Honda Motor Co. and Japan Automobile Parts
Industries Association.

Another trip in May-June 1988 further explored the organization and process
of research and development in Japanese firms in the electronics and automotive
industries. The companies visited included Canon, Honda Motors, and NEC.
Additional interviews were conducted at Techno-Venture, a Japanese venture capital firm.

Extended research in Japan was carried out between October 1988 and March
1989, while Martin Kenney was a visiting professor at the Institute of Business
Research of Hitotsubashi University. The research focused on the underlying organization of R&D and of production in Japanese firms in both traditional and high-
tech industries. Site visits and personal interviews were conducted at the following
software firms: ASCII, CSK, Enicom, Enix, Exec, Fujitsu FIP, Hudson Soft,
JustSystem, Kanrikogaku Kenkyusho, Koei, Lotus Japan, Mitsubishi Electric

Computer Systems, NEC, NRI&NCC, Shokai Joho Service, Softbank, Softwing, Something Good, Spice of the Spices, and System Approach. The interviews were also conducted at Nihon Sun Microsystems, SRI International (Japan), Toshiba, Japan Information Service Industry Association, the Japan Personal Computer Software Association, and the Information Processing Promotion Division of the Ministry of International Trade and Industry. Separate plant visits were conducted at Hitachi and Konica factories. A plant visit and interviews were conducted at Honda Motor Corporation.

During these research visits, professors at various universities provided insights and opportunities for discussions of the research effort. For all of these interviews, Shoko Tanaka provided vital translation services and discussions of the interviews that assisted in understanding the meanings and implications of the information and interview data. Finally, there was a more informal method of collecting information by simply asking people about their work. These "candid" interviews provided ideas and understanding that often cannot be achieved in the more formal interview setting.

During 1990–91, a mail survey of R&D and manufacturing in Japanese high-technology industry (e.g., electronics and biotechnology) was conducted to provide information on a broader sample population of Japanese firms and also to provide a context to view the findings from the case studies, site visits, and personal interviews. The survey instrument was designed to obtain information on the organization, location, and relationship between R&D laboratories and manufacturing facilities. The survey population was identified as the 115 largest companies in these industries as identified in the *Japan Company Handbook.* A total of 115 surveys were mailed and a follow-up survey was conducted. Ultimately, a total of 54 usable surveys were received, for a response rate of 46.9 percent.

Research on the Transplants

Research on the Japanese transplants in the United States focused on the transfer of the Japanese production system to America and involved multiple data-collection strategies and methodologies. America provides an especially good site from which to examine the transfer of the Japanese production system for three related reasons. First, the United States accounts for a relatively large and growing share of all Japanese foreign direct investment in manufacturing. As such, the United States can be considered a trendsetter for future efforts to transfer the Japanese production system to other advanced industrial countries. Second, the United States is the home of the former dominant model of mass-production—fordism. As such, it could be considered a potentially hostile environment in which to transfer the Japanese production system. Third, American and Japanese culture are often seen as diametrically opposed—the United States as "individualistic" and "market-oriented," Japan as "group-oriented," "paternalistic," and/or "welfare-corporatist." Given these differences, evidence of the successful transfer of Japanese practices to American society would shed important light on the longer-run transfer and diffusion of the Japanese production system and its ability to function as a successor model to mass-production fordism.

Our research on the transfer of the Japanese production system to the United States concentrated on five industrial sectors: automobile assembly; automotive component parts; steel; rubber and tires; and electronics broadly defined (e.g., TVs and consumer electronics, semiconductors, computers, telecommunications equipment and semiconductors). These sectors account for the highest levels of Japanese foreign direct manufacturing investment in the United States. They also represent the sectors of the Japanese industrial system that have the most full-blown expressions of innovation-mediated production. Still, important differences exist among them: Automobile assembly and supply are the quintessential examples of fordist production methodology; steel is a pre-fordist industry; rubber and tires have elements of fordist production methodology and chemical processing; electronics is at the cutting edge of the movement toward high-technology, information-intensive, production.

The research, which was conducted mainly between 1987 and 1991, consisted of more than 50 site visits and 200 interviews with executives, managers, engineers and R&D scientists, workers, union officials, and state and local government officials.

We developed a comprehensive database on Japanese transplant firms in the automotive assembly, automotive parts supply, steel, and rubber and tire industries. We defined "transplants" to include firms that are either wholly Japanese-owned or have significant Japanese participation in joint ventures. The main source for this data was the list of Japanese manufacturing establishments in the United States published by the Japan Economic Institute, supplemented with American and Japanese government sources, and an extensive bibliographic file of trade journal, newspaper, and magazine articles. The database, which is continuously updated, currently includes information on the name, location, corporate parent, investment, and employment of 11 North American transplant automotive assembly complexes, 322 automotive component parts suppliers, 72 steel facilities, and 21 rubber and tire factories.

We conducted site visits, plant tours, and/or personal interviews at six of the seven operating transplant assembly plants in the United States (Honda, Nissan, Toyota, Mazda, NUMMI, and Subaru-Isuzu). The site visits and interviews examined both the organization of production inside the factory and between companies and their suppliers and the strategies employed to transfer the Japanese production system. We were unable to arrange a visit to Diamond-Star, and the Ford-Nissan venture was not yet operational. Part of this research was conducted in conjunction with a team of scholars from Ritsumeikan University in the summer of 1990. Site visits and personal interviews were also conducted at roughly a dozen transplant parts suppliers, including an extended visit to Nippondenso, the largest transplant parts supplier in the United States. More than 100 personal interviews were held at transplant assembly and supplier facilities. Interviews were conducted with both Japanese and American executives, managers, R&D scientists, engineers, personnel managers, and procurement specialists and focused on investment strategies, location, production organization, supplier relations, and industrial incentives. To reduce the potential for bias and increase reliability, the interviewees in assembly plants and among suppliers were asked similar questions. As mentioned above, we visited Honda's main assembly facility in Japan as well as several automotive parts suppliers to provide a comparative context for the analysis.

During 1990–91, we conducted detailed research on Japanese-owned and Japanese-U.S. joint-venture steel mills, galvanizing lines, and steel-processing facilities in the United States. Here again, the research focused on the underlying organization of production and strategies used by various firms to transfer the Japanese production system to the United States. Site visits and personal interviews were conducted at the following facilities: the National Steel Great Lakes Works outside Detroit; I/N Tek; the Inland Steel-Nippon Steel joint-venture cold-rolling mill in New Carlisle, Indiana; LS Electrogalvanizing; the LTV-Sumitomo joint venture on the site of LTV's Cleveland Steel complex; the Wheeling-Nisshin galvanizing line in Follansbee, West Virginia; TYK Refractories, a Japanese-owned company making high-technology refractory products in Clairton, Pennsylvania; and a handful of smaller steel-processing facilities and steel service centers. Interviews were conducted with American and Japanese executives and with officials of the United Steel Workers International union in Pittsburgh, local union leaders at plant sites, and with plant-level workers as well. In addition, site visits and oral interviews were conducted at two traditional American-owned and -operated integrated steel mills to provide a basis of comparison between traditional American-owned and transplant steel facilities. Site visits and interviews were conducted at Nippon Steel and NKK facilities in Japan.

It is important to highlight that interviews were conducted with the various types of people associated with transplant facilities: shop-floor workers, union officials, state and local government officials, and community residents, as well as managers, engineers, and R&D scientists. These were done to provide an additional check against respondent bias and to compile as objective a factual basis as is possible in this type of research. We interviewed union representatives of the United Auto Workers, United Steel Workers, and United Rubber Workers. We interviewed shop-floor personnel about work organization and working conditions. Whenever possible, interviews were conducted with former employees to provide a check against response bias from current employees. We interviewed state and local government officials about the use of industrial incentive programs and the impact of transplant facilities on local development. We also did three detailed community case studies to further explore how transplants affect the communities in which they are located: These included Marysville, Ohio, where the Honda plant is located; Georgetown, Kentucky, site of Toyota's major assembly plant; and Battle Creek, Michigan, where a number of transplant automotive parts suppliers are located.

The research on the transplants included a survey research component. A mail survey was administered to the universe of Japanese-owned or Japanese-U.S. joint-venture automotive component parts suppliers in the United States. Establishments were the unit of analysis (rather than firms) to capture differences among plants owned by the same firm because establishments may make different components and use different management and organizational practices. Moreover, the research required responses from plant management familiar with the actual operations of the plant. The suppliers responding to the survey were relatively evenly distributed by the assemblers they supply, thereby reducing the possibility for the idiosyncratic practices of one or two end-users to affect significantly the survey results.

The survey instrument was designed to obtain information on start-up date, investment, employment, sales, work organization, number of job classifications, wages and wage determination, employment security and work-force characteristics, just-in-time supplier relationships, frequency of interaction, and cooperation in R&D and product development. Addresses were located for 196 of the 229 suppliers in the original database. (Some of the firms for whom addresses were unavailable likely had not yet begun operations.) Each establishment was then contacted by telephone to identify the appropriate person to complete the survey.

The survey was mailed in 1988. A series of follow-up post cards and letters resulted in 73 completed surveys for a response rate of 37.2 percent, which is comparable to the rates in other research of this type.[2] Both response rate and sample size are comparable to similar surveys and acceptable by the standards of previous research. James Lincoln and Arne Kalleberg, for example, obtained a response rate of 35 percent from American manufacturing firms and 40 percent from Japanese manufacturing firms.[3] Further, Japanese-owned firms in the United States may have been reticent to respond because of the highly charged political climate surrounding their activities. We have no reason to believe that there was any bias between respondents and nonrespondents.

A related mail survey using a similar survey instrument was sent to a small subsample of transplant steel and rubber facilities. While the population used in this survey is too small to derive reliable statistical results, the responses nonetheless provide useful information on the organization of representative firms. In addition, during 1990–91, a short mail survey was sent to transplant supplier firms to determine the extent of their R&D activity in the United States.

The research on the electronics transplants was undertaken between June 1990 and June 1991. It was designed to understand the organization of production, organization of R&D, use of just-in-time supplier relations, global coordination strategies, and efforts to transfer the Japanese production system in the consumer electronics, semiconductor, computer, and telecommunication segments of the electronics industry. Site visits and personal interviews were conducted at 9 plants, including one consumer electronics factory, two semiconductor facilities, one semiconductor supplier firm, three computer/telecommunications plants, one *maquiladora* facility, and one U.S. corporate headquarters. These sites were chosen to be representative of the larger population of transplant electronic factories. In geographic terms, four of these plants were in California, two in the Portland, Oregon, area, one in Texas, and one in Mexico. Thirty-five personal interviews were held with American and Japanese executives, R&D scientists, engineers, and state and local government officials. As mentioned above, site visits and personal interviews were conducted at Japanese electronic facilities in Japan to provide a comparative context from which to evaluate findings for the North American research.

Two regionally oriented case studies were also conducted as part of the research on the electronic transplants. The first was a case study of the Japanese electronics production complex in the greater Portland area, which included interviews with firms, government officials, the Portland Development Commission, and Norris, Beggs and Simpson, a commercial real estate development firm. The second was a case study of the electronics' maquiladora complex along the U.S.–Mexico border. To identify the *maquiladora* branches of major Japanese electronic companies, a phone survey of all Chamber of Commerce branches in border cities was conducted. A plant visit to one *maquiladora* facility, and interviews with approximately five managers, executives, and officials familiar with Japanese *maquiladora* activity were conducted.

Throughout the research, we made it an explicit policy to recognize the right of companies, respondents, and interviewees to retain their anonymity in return for providing relevant information. In all cases, we gave companies, respondents, and interviewees the choice to remain anonymous, either entirely or in part. We asked whether they would like us to not attribute responses to especially sensitive questions. Most companies, respondents, and interviewees did not request anonymity; many requested that we not attribute some part of the information they provided; and a significant number requested full anonymity. A number of firms and individual respondents were concerned about being identified by name in a study of this type. In addition, we also promised anonymity to many workers, union officials, government representatives, and American and Japanese executives who were concerned about being identified with certain information and/or extremely candid expressions of their views. In a few cases, where information is of a particularly sensitive nature, we have chosen to protect the identity of our interviewees and sources ourselves. In all cases, we have endeavored to provide as complete citations as possible while protecting the identity of the individual and/or firm in question.

Notes

Chapter 1

1. See Martin Kenney and Richard Florida, "How Japanese Industry Is Rebuilding the Rustbelt," *Technology Review* (February-March 1991), pp. 24–33.

2. See Japan Economic Institute, *Japan's Expanding U.S. Manufacturing Presence, 1990 Update Report,* no. 46A. 13 December (Washington, DC: Japan Economic Institute, 1991).

3. These figures are based on our own database on Japanese investment in the automobile assembly, automobile parts, steel, rubber, and related industries.

4. See Barry Bluestone and Bennett Harrison, *The Deindustrialization of America* (New York: Basic Books, 1982). For a critique of the deindustrialization position, see William Baumol, Sue Anne Batey Blackman, and Edward N. Wolff, *Productivity and American Leadership: The Long View* (Cambridge, MA: MIT Press, 1989).

5. Information provided by public relations personnel at General Motors, Ford, and Chrysler.

6. See Andrew Mair, Richard Florida, and Martin Kenney, "The New Geography of Automobile Production: Japanese Transplants in North America," *Economic Geography* 64 (1988), pp. 352–73.

7. Various Japanese steel executives, personal communication with Richard Florida, April 1991.

8. Data are from Venture Economics Inc., *Corporate Venturing News,* 4 (4 May 1990).

9. See, for example, James Abegglen, *The Japanese Factory* (Cambridge, MA: MIT Press, 1985); Ruth Benedict, *The Chrysanthemum and the Sword* (Boston: Houghton Mifflin, 1946); Chie Nakane, *Japanese Society* (Berkeley: University of California Press, 1970).

10. See Ronald Dore, *Japanese Factory, British Factory* (Berkeley: University of California Press, 1973).

11. This literature is indeed extensive. A good summary of the relevant work can be found in Dexter Dunphy, "Convergence/Divergence: A Temporal Review of the Japanese Enterprise and Its Management," *Academy of Management Review,* 12, 3 (1987), pp. 445–59.

12. See, for example, Michael Burawoy, *Manufacturing Consent* (Chicago: University of Chicago Press, 1979).

13. Mike Parker and Jane Slaughter, "Management by Stress," *Technology Review* (October 1988), pp. 36–46.

14. The concept of systemofacture is an extension of the concept of "machinofacture" advanced by Marx in *Capital, Vol. I.* (orig. 1867) (New York: Vintage Books, 1977); see Kurt Hoffman and Raphael Kaplinsky, *Driving Force: The Global Restructuring of Technology, Labour and Investment in the Automobile and Components Industries* (Boulder, CO: Westview Press, 1988).

333

15. See John Krafcik, "A New Diet for U.S. Manufacturers," *Technology Review* 92 (1989), pp. 28–38; James Womack, Daniel Jones, and Daniel Roos, *The Machine That Changed the World* (New York: Rawson Associates, 1990).

16. See Antonio Gramsci, "Americanism and Fordism," in Quintin Hoare and Geoffrey Nowell Smith (eds. and trans.), *Selections from the Prison Notebooks,* (New York: International Publishers, 1971), pp. 277–320.

17. See Richard Florida and Martin Kenney, "Transplanted Organizations: The Transfer of Japanese Industrial Organization to the U.S.," *American Sociological Review* 56 (June 1990), pp. 381–398.

18. See Knuth Dohse, Ulrich Jurgens, and Thomas Malsch, "From 'Fordism' to 'Toyotism'? The Social Organization of the Labor Process in the Japanese Automobile Industry," *Politics and Society,* 14 (1986), pp. 45–66; Parker and Slaughter, "Management by Stress."

19. David Hounshell, *From the American System to Mass Production, 1800–1932* (Baltimore: Johns Hopkins University Press, 1984).

20. The concept of "post-Fordism" is itself characterized by fuzzy definition. See Andrew Sayer, "Postfordism in Question," *International Journal of Urban and Regional Research,* 13 (1990), pp. 13:666–95.

21. David Halberstam, *The Reckoning* (New York: William Morrow, 1986).

22. For an articulation of the "disorganized" capitalism perspective see Scott Lash and John Urry, *The End of Organized Capitalism* (Madison: University of Wisconsin Press, 1987).

23. As reported in *JEI Report,* No. 12B (29 March 1991), p. 5.

24. See Satoshi Kamata, *Japan in the Passing Lane* (New York: Pantheon, 1982).

25. See Shinji Sakuma and Hideaki Ohnomori, "The Auto Industry," chap. 2 in National Defense Council for Victims of Karoshi, *Karoshi: When the Corporate Warrior Dies* (Tokyo: Mado-sha Publishers, 1990).

26. Ibid.

27. N. Kondratiev, "The Long Waves in Economic Life," *Review of Economics and Statistics* 17 (November 1935), pp. 105–15.

28. Ernst Mandel, *Late Capitalism* (London: New Left Books, 1975).

29. Christopher Freeman, "Prometheus Unbound," *Futures* 16 (October 1984), pp. 494–507; and *Long Waves and the World Economy* (London: Pinter, 1984).

30. David Gordon, "The Global Economy: New Edifice or Crumbling Foundation?" *New Left Review* 168 (1988), pp. 42–65.

31. Carlotta Perez, "Microelectronics, Long Waves and World Structural Change: New Perspectives for Developing Countries," *World Development* 13, no. 3 (March 1985), pp. 441–63.

32. Daniel Bell, *The Coming of Post-Industrial Society* (New York: Basic Books, 1973); Alain Touraine, *The Postindustrial Society* (New York: Random House, 1971). In Japan this perspective was pioneered by Yoneji Masuda, *Social Impact of Computerization: An Application of the Pattern Model for Industrial Society* (Tokyo: Kodansha Publishers, 1970). These views were later popularized in Alvin Toffler, *The Third Wave* (New York: William Morrow, 1980).

33. See Fred Block, *Postindustrial Possibilities: A Critique of Economic Discourse* (Berkeley: University of California Press, 1990).

34. For the quintessential statement, see Larry Hirschhorn, *Beyond Mechanization: Work and Technology in a Postindustrial Age,* (Cambridge, MA: MIT Press, 1984).

35. We are indebted to W. Richard Goe for long and extremely valuable conversations on this topic over the last six years. For an insightful discussion of these issues, see W. Richard Goe, *Information Technology and the Social Restructuring of Food Technology* (Norwood, NJ: Ablex Publishers) forthcoming.

36. See Baumol, Blackman, and Wolff, *Productivity and American Leadership;* and Stephen Cohen and John Zysman, *Manufacturing Matters: The Myth of the Post-Industrial Economy* (New York: Basic Books, 1987).

37. See Michael Cusumano, *Japan's Software Factories* (New York: Oxford University Press, 1990); and Cusumano, "From Auto Factories to Software Factories," (MIT, Sloan School of Management, working paper, 1991).

38. Shoshona Zuboff, *In the Age of the Smart Machine* (New York: Basic Books, 1988); Ramchandran Jaikumar, "Postindustrial Manufacturing," *Harvard Business Review* (November/December 1986), pp. 69–76.

39. This again is not new. Noble's study on the evolution of numerical control shows this quite vividly. See David Noble, *Forces of Production* (New York: Knopf, 1984).

40. See Richard Florida and Martin Kenney, *The Breakthrough Illusion: Corporate America's Failure to Move from Innovation to Mass Production* (New York: Basic Books 1990).

41. See Michael Piore and Charles Sabel, *The Second Industrial Divide: Possibilities for Prosperity* (New York: Basic Books, 1984); Charles Sabel, "Flexible Specialization and the Re-emergence of Regional Economies," in Paul Hirst and Jonathan Zeitlin (eds.), *Reversing Industrial Decline? Industrial Structure and Policies in Britain and Her Competitors* (New York: St. Martin's Press, 1989); and Sabel et al., "How to Keep Mature Industries Innovative," *Technology Review* (April 1987), pp. 27–35.

42. See Meric Gertler, "The Limits to Flexibility: Comments on the Postfordist Vision of Production and Its Geography," *Transactions of the Institute of British Geographers* 13, (1988), pp. 419–32; Richard Florida and Martin Kenney, "Silicon Valley and Route 128 Won't Save Us," *California Management Review* 33 (Fall 1990), pp. 68–88; and "W(h)ither Flexible Specialization?" *California Management Review* 33 (Spring 1991), pp. 143–46.

43. Oliver Williamson, "The Vertical Integration of Production: Market Failure Considerations," *American Economic Review* 61 (May 1971), pp. 112–27; *Markets and Hierarchies* (New York: Free Press, 1975); *The Economic Institutions of Capitalism* (New York: Free Press, 1981); "Organizational Innovation: The Transaction Cost Approach," in Joshua Ronen (ed.), *Enterpreneurship* (Lexington, MA: Lexington Books, 1983), pp. 101–33. For the seminal statement of the transactions cost perspective, see R.H. Coase, "The Nature of the Firm," *Economica* 4 (1937), pp. 386–405.

44. Mark Granovetter, "Economic Action and Social Structure: The Problem of Embeddedness," *American Journal of Sociology* 91, no. 3 (November 1985), pp. 481–510.

45. Charles Sabel, "Studied Trust: New Forms of Cooperation in a Volatile Economy" (Cambridge, MA: MIT, Department of Political Science, unpublished paper, August 1990).

46. The business and organizational literature here is immense. See, for example, Michael Best, *The New Competition Institutions of Industrial Restructuring* (Cambridge, MA: Harvard University Press, 1990).

47. Charles Perrow, "Small Firm Networks." Paper presented at the Harvard University Conference on Networks (Summer 1990).

48. Alfred D. Chandler, Jr., *Strategy and Structure: Chapters in the History of the American Industrial Enterprise* (Cambridge, MA: MIT Press, 1962); *The Visible Hand: The Managerial Revolution in American Business* (Cambridge, MA: Belknap/Harvard University Press, 1977).

49. See Michel Aglietta, *A Theory of Capitalist Regulation: The U.S. Experience* (London: New Left Books, 1979); Alain Lipietz, *Mirages and Miracles: The Crises of Global Fordism* (London: Verso/New Left Books, 1987); Michel De Vroey, "A Regulation Approach Interpretation of Contemporary Crisis," *Capital and Class* 23 (1984), pp. 45–66; Alain Noel, "Accumulation, Regulation, and Social Change: An Essay on French Political Economy," *International Organization* 41, no. 2 (1987). A summation of regulation theory can be found

in Robert Boyer, *The Regulation School: A Critical Introduction* (New York: Columbia University Press, 1990).

50. See Aglietta, *Theory of Capitalist Regulation;* Phil Blackburn, Rod Coombs, and Kenneth Green, *Technology, Economic Growth and the Labour Process* (New York: St. Martin's Press, 1985); and Daniele Leborgne and Alain Lipietz, "New Technologies, New Modes of Regulation: Some Spatial Implications." Paper presented at the International Conference on Technology, Restructuring and Urban-Regional Development, Dubrovnik, Yugoslavia (June 1987).

51. Knuth Dohse, Ulrich Jurgens, and Thomas Malsch, "From 'Fordism' to 'Toyotism'? The Social Organization of the Labor Process in the Japanese Automobile Industry," *Politics and Society* 14, no. 2 (1985), pp. 115–46.

52. For a contrasting perspective, see Martin Kenney and Richard Florida, "Beyond Mass Production: Production and the Labor Process in Japan," *Politics and Society* 16, no. 1 (1988), pp. 121–58.

53. Annemieke Roobeek, "The Crisis in Fordism and the Rise of a New Technological Paradigm," *Futures* 19, no. 2 (April 1987), pp. 129–54.

54. See Benjamin Coriat, *Penser a l'envers: travail et organisation dans l'enterprise japonaise* (Paris: Christian Bourgois Editeur, 1991); and *L'atelier et le robot: Essai sur le fordisme et la production de masse a l'age de l'electronique* (Paris: Christian Bourgois Editeur, 1990).

55. On the role of organizational restructuring at the point of production and the process of value creation, see the insightful discussion in William Lazonick, *Competitive Advantage on the Shopfloor* (Cambridge, MA: Harvard University Press, 1990).

56. On fujitsuism, see Kenney and Florida, "Beyond Mass Production," and the debate in the Japanese journal *Mado,* nos. 1–5 (1989–1990).

57. See, for example, Harry Braverman, *Labor and Monopoly Capital* (New York: Monthly Review Press, 1974); Michael Burawoy, "Between the Labor Process and the State: The Changing Face of Factory Regimes Under Advanced Capitalism," *American Sociological Review* 48 (1983), pp. 587–605; and Burawoy, "Toward a Marxist Theory of the Labor Process: Braverman and Beyond," *Politics and Society* 8 (March-April 1978), pp. 246–312.

58. Tessa Morris-Suzuki, "Robots and Capitalism," *New Left Review* 147 (1984), pp. 109–21; and *Beyond Computopia: Information, Automation and Democracy in Japan* (London: Kegan Paul International, 1988).

59. See Florida and Kenney, *The Breakthrough Illusion.*

60. See Hounshell, *From the American System to Mass Production.*

61. See Taiichi Ohno, "How the Toyota Production System Was Created," *Japanese Economic Studies* 10 (Summer 1982), pp. 83–104.

Chapter 2

1. In Akio Morita (with Edwin Reingold and Mitsuko Shimomura), *Made in Japan* (New York: Dutton, 1986), p. 205.

2. "The Global 1000," *Business Week* (16 July 1990), pp. 111–40.

3. Chalmers Johnson, *MITI and the Japanese Miracle* (Stanford, CA: Stanford University Press, 1982).

4. E. Kaplan, *Japan—The Government-Business Relationship* (Washington, DC: Department of Commerce, 1972).

5. T.J. Pempel, "The Unbundling 'Japan, Inc.': The Changing Dynamics of Japanese Policy Formation," *Journal of Japanese Studies* (December 1986), p. 304.

6. Knuth Dohse, Ulrich Jurgens, and Thomas Malsch, "From 'Fordism' to 'Toyotism'? The Social Organization of the Labor Process in the Japanese Automobile Industry," *Politics and Society,* 14, no. 2 (1985), pp. 115–46.

7. Ibid., p. 141.

8. See Michael Burawoy, *The Politics of Production* (London: Verso, 1985), p. 143.

9. Mike Parker and Jane Slaughter, "Management by Stress," *Technology Review* 91 (October 1988), pp. 36–44.

10. Satoshi Kamata, *Japan in the Passing Lane* (New York: Pantheon, 1982).

11. See especially, Kamata, *Japan in the Passing Lane;* also, Ichiyo Muto, *Class Struggle on the Shopfloor: The Japanese Case, 1945–1984* (Binghamton, NY: SUNY–Department of Sociology, 1984).

12. Stanley Aronowitz, *False Promises: The Shaping of American Working Class Consciousness* (New York: McGraw-Hill, 1973).

13. See James Womack, Daniel Jones, and Daniel Roos, *The Machine That Changed the World* (New York: Rawson Associates, 1990).

14. See James Womack, "A Post-national Automobile Industry by the Year 2000," *JAMA Forum* 8, no. 1 (September 1989), pp. 1–7

15. See Michael Piore and Charles Sabel, *The Second Industrial Divide: Possibilities for Prosperity* (New York: Basic Books, 1984); idem, "Italian Small Business Development: Lessons for U.S. Industrial Policy," in John Zysman and Laura Tyson (eds.), *American Industry in International Competition* (Ithaca, NY: Cornell University Press, 1983); Charles Sabel, *Work and Politics: The Division of Labor in Industry* (New York: Cambridge University Press, 1982); Charles Sabel, Gary Herrigel, Richard Kazis, and Richard Deeg, "How to Keep Mature Industries Innovative," *Technology Review* (April 1987), pp. 27–35.

16. David Friedman, *The Misunderstood Miracle: Industrial Development and Political Change in Japan* (Ithaca, NY: Cornell University Press, 1988); idem, "Beyond the Age of Ford: The Strategic Basis of the Japanese Success in Automobiles," in Zysman and Tyson (eds.), *American Industry in International Competition,* pp. 350–90. For a devastating review of *The Misunderstood Miracle* see Leonard Lynn, *Journal of Japanese Studies* 15, no. 2 (1989), pp. 490–94.

17. Charles Sabel, "Flexible Specialization and the Re-emergence of Regional Economies," in Paul Hirst and Jonathan Zeitlin (eds.), *Reversing Industrial Decline? Industrial Structure and Policies in Britain and Her Competitors* (New York: St. Martin's Press, 1989).

18. The literature here is immense and virtually all of it contradicts the claims of the flexible specialization adherents. See, for example, Banri Asanuma, "The Organization of Parts Purchases in the Japanese Automotive Industry," *Japanese Economic Studies* (Summer 1985), pp. 32–53; Asanuma, "The Contractual Framework for Parts Supply in the Japanese Automobile Industry," *Japanese Economic Studies* (Summer 1985), pp. 54–78; Toshihiro Nishiguchi, "Competing Systems of Automotive Components Supply: An Examination of the Japanese 'Clustered Control' Model and the 'Alps' Structure" (Cambridge, MA: MIT International Motor Vehicle Program, unpublished paper, 1987); Konosuke Odaka, Keinosuke Ono, and Fumihiko Adachi, *The Automobile Industry In Japan: A Study of Ancillary Firm Development* (Tokyo: Kinokuniya, distributed by Oxford University Press, 1988); Mari Sako, "Neither Markets nor Hierarchies: A Comparative Study of the Printed Circuit Board Industry in Britain and Japan" (London: London School of Economics, unpublished manuscript, 1989); Sako, "Competitive Cooperation: How the Japanese Manage Inter-firm Relations" (London: London School of Economics, unpublished manuscript, 1989); Sako, "Partnership Between Large and Small Firms: The Case of Japan," in Directorate for Enterprise of the Commission of the European Economic Communities, *Partnership Between Large and Small Firms* (London: Graham and Trotman, 1988), pp. 66–79;

Paul Sheard, "Auto Production Systems in Japan: Organizational and Locational Features," *Australian Geographical Studies* 21 (April 1983), pp. 49–68.

19. See Florida and Kenney, "W(h)ither Flexible Specialization?" pp. 143–46.

20. See Haruo Shimada, "Japanese Industrial Relations in Transition," Sloan School of Management, MIT Working Paper No. 1854-88 (December 1986); and Haruo Shimada and John Paul MacDuffie, *Industrial Relations and 'Humanware,'* (Cambridge, MA: Sloan School of Management, MIT Working Paper No. 1855-88, 1986).

21. Masahiko Aoki, *Information, Incentives and Bargaining in the Japanese Economy* (Cambridge: Cambridge University Press, 1988); "A New Paradigm of Work Organization and Coordination? Lessons from the Japanese Experience," in Stephen Marglin and Juliet Schor (eds.), *The Golden Age of Capitalism: Reinterpreting the Post-war Experience* (New York: Oxford University Press, 1990), pp. 267–93; "Aspects of the Japanese Firm," in Masahiko Aoki (ed.), *The Economic Analysis of the Japanese Firm* (Amsterdam: North-Holland, 1984); "The Japanese Firm in Transition," in Kozo Yamamura and Yasukichi Yasuba (eds.), *The Political Economy of Japan: Vol. 1, The Domestic Transformation* (Stanford, CA: Stanford University Press, 1987), pp. 263–88; Kazuo Koike, "Human Resource Development and Labor-Management Relations," in *The Political Economy of Japan*, pp. 289–330.

22. Kazuo Koike, *Understanding Industrial Relations in Japan* (New York: St. Martin's Press, 1988); and "Internal Labor Markets: Workers in Large Firms," in Taishiro Shirai (ed.), *Contemporary Industrial Relations In Japan* (Madison: University of Wisconsin Press, 1983), pp. 29–62.

23. See, for example, Ken-ichi Imai, Ikujiro Nonaka, and Hirotaka Takeuchi, *Managing the New Product Development Process: How Japanese Companies Learn and Unlearn* (Kunitachi, Japan: Institute of Business Research, Hitotsubashi University, 1984; Discussion Paper No. 118).

24. Andrew Sayer, "New Developments in Manufacturing: The Just-in-Time System," *Capital and Class* 30 (1986), pp. 43–72.

25. Benjamin Coriat, *Penser a' l'envers: travail et organisation dans l'enterprise japonaise (Paris: Christian Bourgeois Editeur, 1991).*

26. Stephen Wood, "The Deskilling Debate, New Technology and Work Organization," *Acta Sociologica* 30, no. 1 (1987), pp. 3–24; "The Japanese Management Model: Tacit Skills in Shop Floor Participation," *Work and Occupations* 16, no. 4 (November 1989), pp. 446–60.

27. Alain Lipietz, *Mirages and Miracles* (London: Verso, 1987), p. 137.

28. Kurt Hoffman and Raphael Kaplinsky, *Driving Force: The Global Restructuring of Technology, Labour and Investment in the Automobile and Components Industries* (Boulder, CO: Westview Press, 1988).

29. See Andrew Gordon, *The Evolution of Labor Relations in Japan: Heavy Industry, 1853–1955* (Cambridge, MA: Harvard University Press, 1985).

30. Andrew Gordon, "The Right to Work in Japan: Labor and the State in the Depression," *Social Research* 54, no. 2 (Summer 1987), pp. 246–72.

31. It should be recognized that the working class did not successfully attain state power in either the United States or Western Europe. See Joe Moore, *Japanese Workers and the Struggle for Power, 1945–1947* (Madison: University of Wisconsin Press, 1983). As Moore shows, the Japanese working class embarked on a quite radical class effort before being thrown back. For an excellent discussion of the Japanese labor relations system, see Yasuo Kuwahara, "Industrial Relations System in Japan: A New Interpretation" (Tokyo: Japanese Institute of Labor, 1989).

32. Taishiro Shirai, "A Supplement: Characteristics of Japanese Managements and Their Personnel Policies," in Shirai (ed.), *Contemporary Industrial Relations in Japan*, p. 376.

33. The following historical account draws from Moore, *Japanese Workers and the Struggle for Power, 1945–1947;* and Gordon, *Evolution of Labor Relations in Japan.*

34. Theodore Cohen, in Herbert Passin (ed.), *Remaking Japan: The American Occupation as a New Deal* (New York: Free Press, 1987).

35. An important contribution to the broader discussion of the influence of the post–World War II occupation of Japan is Robert Ward and Yoshikazu Sakamoto, *Democratizing Japan: The Allied Occupation* (Honolulu: University of Hawaii Press, 1987).

36. Moore, *Japanese Workers and the Struggle for Power.* pp. 158–160.

37. See, especially, Kazutoshi Koshiro, "Development of Collective Bargaining in Postwar Japan," in T. Shirai (ed.), *Contemporary Industrial Relations in Japan,* pp. 205–58; Shigeyoshi Tokunaga, "A Marxist Interpretation of Japanese Industrial Relations, with Special Reference to Large Private Enterprises," in T. Shirai (ed.), *Contemporary Industrial Relations in Japan,* pp. 313–30.

38. See Muto, *Class Struggle on the Shopfloor,* p. 5.

39. Gordon, *Evolution of Labor Relations in Japan,* p. 355.

40. T. J. Pempel, *Policy and Politics in Japan* (Philadelphia: Temple University Press, 1982), p. 93.

41. Gordon, *Evolution of Labor Relations in Japan.*

42. Muto, *Class Struggle on the Shopfloor.*

43. Gordon, *Evolution of Labor Relations in Japan.*

44. Ibid.; Hirosuke Kawanishi, "The Reality of Enterprise Unionism," in Gavan McCormack and Yoshio Sugimoto (eds.), *Democracy in Contemporary Japan* (Armonk, NY: M. E. Sharpe, 1986).

45. Nikkeiren (Japanese Federation of Employers' Associations), *Current Labor Economy in Japan,* Tokyo, September 1990.

46. Fordism guaranteed the worker security at a specific job, but not employment security.

47. See Koji Taira, *Economic Development and the Labor Market in Japan* (New York: Columbia University Press, 1970).

48. As we shall see later, this entire discussion refers almost exclusively to *male* workers.

49. The resulting management victory, though apparently complete, is held to have plagued Nissan into the 1980s; see Michael Cusumano, *The Japanese Automobile Industry: Technology and Management at Nissan and Toyota* (Cambridge, MA: Harvard University Press, 1985).

50. Gordon, *Evolution of Labor Relations in Japan,* pp. 386–95.

51. Moore, *Japanese Workers and the Struggle for Power.*

52. As quoted in an interview with Osamu Nobuto, *JAMA Forum* 6, no. 1 (July 1987), pp. 10–13.

53. William B. Gould, *Japan's Reshaping of American Labor Law* (Cambridge, MA: MIT Press, 1984), p. 107.

54. See Masayoshi Kanabayashi, "Labor Disputes Join the List of Problems Western Companies Must Face in Japan," *Wall Street Journal* (24 December 1987), p. 6.

55. Toyohiro Kono, *Strategy and Structure of Japanese Enterprises* (Armonk, NY: M. E. Sharpe, 1984), p. 325.

56. On the U.S. system see, especially, Samuel Bowles and Herbert Gintis, "The Crisis of Liberal Democratic Capitalism," *Politics and Society* 11, no. 3 (1982); Samuel Bowles, David Gordon, and Thomas Weisskopf, "Power and Profits: The Social Structure of Accumulation and the Profitability of the Postwar U.S. Economy," *Review of Radical Political Economics* 18, nos. 1, 2 (Spring and Summer 1986); David Gordon, Richard Edwards, and Michael Reich, *Segmented Work, Divided Workers: The Historical Transformation of Labor in the United States* (New York: Cambridge University Press, 1982); Mike Davis, *Prisoners*

of the Dream: Politics and Economy in the History of the U.S. Working Class (London: Verso, 1986).

57. See Rodney Clark, *The Japanese Company* (New Haven: Yale University Press, 1979), p. 177; Masahiro Okuno, "Corporate Loyalty and Bonus Payments: An Analysis of Work Incentives in Japan," in Masahiko Aoki (ed.), *Economic Analysis of the Japanese Firm* (Amsterdam: North-Holland, 1984), pp. 388–409.

58. Kazutoshi Koshiro, "Development of Collective Bargaining in Postwar Japan," in T. Shirai (ed.), *Contemporary Industrial Relations in Japan,* p. 70.

59. Tsuneo Ono, "The Extent of Union Influence in Japanese Wage Negotiations," *Japan Labor Bulletin* (1 August 1976), p. 6.

60. Ikuo Kume, "Changing Relations Among the Government, Labor, and Business in Japan After the Oil Crisis," *International Organization* 42, no. 4 (Autumn 1988), p. 666.

61. Haruo Shimada, "Wage Determination and Information Sharing: An Alternative Approach to Income Policy?" *The Journal of Industrial Relations* (June 1983), pp. 178–79.

62. The serious environmental polluters were the heavy and chemical industries that had been the key to earlier growth, but now were mature. See Julian Griesser, Koichiro Fujikura, and Akio Morishima, *Environmental Law in Japan* (Cambridge, MA: MIT Press, 1981).

63. Ronald Dore, Jean Bounine-Cabale, and Kari Tapiola, *Japan at Work: Markets, Management and Flexibility* (Paris: OECD, 1989), p. 45.

64. Solomon Levine and Koji Taira, "Interpreting Industrial Conflict: The Case of Japan," in Benjamin Martin and Everett Kassalow (eds.), *Labor Relations in Advanced Industrial Societies: Issues and Problems* (New York: Carnegie Endowment for International Peace, 1980), p. 6.

65. Toshio Kurokawa, "Problems of the Japanese Working Class in Historical Perspective," in T. Morris-Suzuki and T. Seiyama (eds.), *Japanese Capitalism Since 1945: Critical Perspectives* (Armonk, NY: M.E. Sharpe, 1989), p. 156.

66. Executive at a large Japanese electronics firm, name withheld by request. Personal interview by Martin Kenney (October 1990).

67. Most larger firms have switched to 5-day, 40-hour weeks, but smaller firms continue to operate on 6-day weeks. However, most workers still do not take vacations and overtime is common.

68. Nikkeiren (Japan Federation of Employers' Associations), *Current Labor Economy in Japan,* p. 25.

69. Norma Chalmers, *Industrial Relations in Japan* (London: Routledge, 1989), p. 104.

70. See Koike, "Human Resource Development and Labor-Management Relations."

71. Clark, *The Japanese Company,* p. 168; Muto, *Class Struggle on the Shopfloor,* p. 25.

72. Koike, *Understanding Industrial Relations in Japan,* 1988.

73. Ministry of International Trade and Industry, *Census of Manufacturers, 1985* as summarized in "The Changing Nature of Japanese Manufacturing, *JEI Report* (17 June, 1988), no. 23a.

74. Hugh Patrick and Thomas Rohlen, "Small-Scale Family Enterprises," in Kozo Yamamura and Yasukichi Yasuba (eds.) *The Political Economy of Japan: The Domestic Transformation* (Stanford, CA; Stanford University Press, 1987), pp. 331–384.

75. Kuwahara, p. 24.

76. Shigeyoshi Tokunaga, "The Structure of the Japanese Labor Market," in Shigeyoshi Tokunaga and Joachim Bergmann (eds.), *Industrial Relations in Transition: The Cases of Japan and the Federal Republic of Germany* (Tokyo: University of Tokyo, 1984), pp. 25–55.

77. See Chalmers, *Industrial Relations in Japan,* p. 119.

78. See Martin Bronfenbrenner and Yasukichi Yasuba, "Economic Welfare," in Kozo Yamamura and Yasukichi Yasuba (eds.), *The Political Economy of Japan, The Domestic Transformation* (Stanford, CA: Stanford University Press, 1987), pp. 93–136.

79. Dore, Bounine-Cabale, and Tapiola, *Japan at Work: Markets, Management and Flexibility.* Also see Patrick and Rohlen, "Small-Scale Family Enterprises"; Takeshi Inagami, "Changing Japanese-Style Employment Practices," *Japan's Labor Bulletin* 3 (1 October 1986), pp. 4–8; Masanori Hashimoto and John Raisian, "Employment Tenure and Earnings Profiles in Japan and the United States," *American Economic Review* 75, no. 4 (1985), pp. 721–35.

80. For further discussion, see Kazuo Koike, "Workers in Small Firms and Women in Industry," in Toshiro Shirai (ed.), *Contemporary Industrial Relations in Japan* (Madison: University of Wisconsin Press, 1983), pp. 89–116; H. Suzuki, "Age, Seniority and Wages," *International Labor Review* 113, no. 1 (1976), pp. 67–83; see Yoko Kawashima and Toshiaki Tachibanaki, "The Effect of Discrimination and of Industry Segmentation on Japanese Wage Differentials in Relation to Education," *International Journal of Industrial Organization* 4 (1986), pp. 43–68.

81. Kuwahara, "Industrial Relations System in Japan," p. 24.

82. We are indebted to Raymond Jussaume for making this point.

83. Muto, *Class Struggle on the Shopfloor;* Hirosuke Kawanishi, "The Reality of Enterprise Unionism," in Gavan McCormack and Yoshio Sugimoto (eds.), *Democracy in Contemporary Japan* (Armonk, NY: M. E. Sharpe, 1986), pp. 138–56.

84. Koike, "Human Resources Development and Labor-Management Relations."

85. Koike, "Skill Formation in the U.S. and Japan," pp. 63–65.

86. There is an extensive literature on Japanese work organization; see especially Richard J. Schonberger, *Japanese Manufacturing Techniques* (New York: Free Press, 1982); Shimada and MacDuffie, *Industrial Relations and 'Humanware'.*

87. Yasuhiro Monden, *Toyota Production System: A Practical Approach to Production Management* (Atlanta: Industrial Engineering and Management Press, 1983).

88. James Harbour, "Product Engineering: The 'Buck' Stops Here," *Automotive Industries* (1985), p. 32.

89. This citation is taken from Sayer, "New Developments in Manufacturing:

90. As noted earlier, labor in a Japanese factory is extremely demanding; it is not our intention to romanticize work on the Japanese assembly line.

91. The following discussion draws upon Taiichi Ohno, "How the Toyota Production System Was Created," *Japanese Economic Studies* 10 (Summer 1982), pp. 83–104; also see Taiichi Ohno, *Toyota Production System: Beyond Large-Scale Production* (Cambridge, MA: Productivity Press, 1988); Monden, *Toyota Production System.*

92. Ohno, "How the Toyota Production System was Created," p. 97.

93. Ibid., pp. 97, 100.

94. See, for example, Imai, Nonaka, and Takeuchi, *Managing the New Product Development Process* (1984). See also Aoki *Information, Incentives and Bargaining,* 1988; Koike *Understanding Industrial Relations in Japan* (1988).

95. Ministry of Labor, *General Survey of Industrial Relations, 1984* (Tokyo: Ministry of Labor, 1984). Also see Kuwahara, "Industrial Relations System in Japan."

96. For a comprehensive discussion regarding this point see the debate in the Japanese journal (in Japanese only) *Mado,* Nos. 2–4. (1989–1990). Our position here is developed in the debate over our original article "Beyond Mass Production" in *Mado.* For a thoughtful reconceptualization of the underlying features of the Japanese method of production organization, see Hikari Nohara, "Reconsidering the Japanese Production System Model." Paper prepared for the International Conference: Workplace Australia, Designing the Future, Melbourne, Australia (24 February 1991).

97. Masahiko Aoki, "The Japanese Firm in Transition" (Stanford, CA: Center for Economic Policy Research, Technical Report No. 39, 1985).

98. Koike, *Understanding Industrial Relations in Japan,* 1988.

99. Imai, Nonaka, and Takeuchi, *Managing the New Product Development Process,* 1984.

100. Robert Cole, *Strategies for Learning: Small Group Activities in American, Japanese and Swedish Industry* (Berkeley: University of California Press, 1989), pp. 96–98.

101. Takashi Kawashita, "Quality Control Circles in Japan." Unpublished manuscript, School of Industrial and Labor Relations, Cornell University (November 1986), p. 3.

102. Cole, *Strategies for Learning: Small Group Activities in American, Japanese and Swedish Industry.*

103. Monden, *Toyota Production System: A Practical Approach to Production Management.*

104. Ikujiro Nonaka and Seiichiro Yonekura, "Innovation Through Group Dynamics" (Kunitachi, Japan: Hitotsubashi University, Institute of Business Research, unpublished manuscript, 1982).

105. Cusumano, *Japanese Automobile Industry: Technology and Management at Nissan and Toyota,* p. 357.

106. See Kamata, *Japan in the Passing Lane.*

107. We are indebted to Akio Kida for this formulation; personal communication with Richard Florida (October 1990).

108. President, former manager at a chemical plant of a major Japanese electronics firm, personal interview by Martin Kenney (May 1991).

109. Clark, *The Japanese Company.*

110. Kagono, Nonaka, Sakakibara, and Okumura, *Strategic vs. Evolutionary Management: A U.S./Japan Comparison of Strategy and Organization;* Yukio Kitaya, "The Age of Holonic Management," *Japan Echo* 13 (Special issue 1986), pp. 47–53.

111. Kagono et al. *Strategic vs. Evolutionary Management* (1985), pp. 112–13.

112. Ibid., 1985.

113. Jay Galbraith, *Organization Design* (Reading, MA: Addison-Wesley, 1977).

114. Clark, *The Japanese Company,* p. 106.

115. Kagono et al. *Strategic vs. Evolutionary Management,* 1985, p. 116.

116. Teruo Yamanouchi, general manager, corporate technical planning and operation center. Canon Inc. personal interview by Martin Kenney (June 1987).

117. See Harvey Brooks, "Testimony in Hearings before the Subcommittee on Investigations and Oversight and the Subcommittee on Science, Research and Technology of the Committee on Science and Technology, U.S. House of Representatives," in *Japanese Technological Advances and Possible United States Responses Using Research Joint Ventures* (29-30 June 1983).

118. Aoki, "The Japanese Firm in Transition."

119. For more on Japanese banking see Henry C. Wallich and Mable I. Wallich, "Banking and Finance," in Hugh Patrick and Henry Rosovsky (eds.), *Asia's New Giant* (Washington, DC: Brookings Institution, 1976); M. Colyer Crum and David M. Meerschwam, "From Relationship to Price Banking: The Loss of Regulatory Control," in Thomas McCraw (ed.), *America vs. Japan* (Boston: Harvard Business School Press, 1986). On *keiretsu* corporate groupings, see Hirschmeier and Yui, *The Development of Japanese Business 1600–1980,* 2nd ed., p. 355; Yoshio Suzuki, *Money, Finance, and Macroeconomic Performance in Japan* (New Haven: Yale University Press, 1986), p. 39.

120. It is interesting to note that in the United States a similar process goes on in venture capital-financed start-up companies. The lead venture capitalist will replace top-level management in cases of mismanagement.

121. We are indebted to Ronald Dore for making this point.

122. This bears a striking similarity to the argument advanced by Berle and Means that

a type of "managerial capitalism" has developed in the United States. See Adolf Berle and Gardiner Means, *The Modern Corporation and Private Property,* revised ed. (New York: Harcourt Brace & World Inc, 1967). This point is made in Clark, *The Japanese Company,* pp. 85, 86.

123. See Mitsubishi Research Institute, *The Relationship Between Japanese Auto and Auto Parts Makers* (Tokyo: Japanese Automobile Manufacturers Association, Inc., 1987).

124. See U.S. International Trade Commission, *U.S. Global Competitiveness: The U.S. Automotive Parts Industry* (Washington, DC: U.S. International Trade Commission, 1987); and Amy Glasmeier and Richard McCluskey, "U.S. Auto Parts Production: An Analysis of the Organization and Location of a Changing Industry," *Economic Geography* 63, pp. 142–59.

125. See, for example, Sayer "New Development in Manufacturing," 1986; Sheard "Auto Production Systems" (1983) Sako, "Competitive Cooperation" (1989).

126. See Richard Florida and Martin Kenney, "High-Technology Restructuring in the USA and Japan," *Environment and Planning A* 22, no. 1 (1990), pp. 233–52.

127. See Banri Asanuma, "The Organization of Parts Purchases in the Japanese Automotive Industry," *Japanese Economic Studies* (Summer 1985), pp. 32–53; and "The Contractual Framework for Parts Supply in the Japanese Automobile Industry," *Japanese Economic Studies* (Summer 1985), pp. 54–78.

128. Patrick and Rohlen, "Small-Scale Family Enterprises."

129. Cusumano, *The Japanese Automobile Industry,* pp. 250–53.

130. Ibid., p. 192.

131. For further discussion of this phenomenon, see Patrick and Rohlen, "Small-Scale Family Enterprises," pp. 331–84; Banri Asanuma, "Organization of Parts Purchases in the Japanese Automotive Industry."

132. Marco Orru, Mariko Suzuki, and Gary Hamilton, "Domination in Japanese Business Groups." (Research Program in East Asian Culture and Development, University of California–Davis, Working Paper No. 7) Ken-ichi Imai, "The Corporate Network in Japan," *Japanese Economic Studies* (Winter 1987–88), pp. 3–37.

133. See, for example, Sheard (1983) and Asanuma, "Organization of Parts Purchases in the Japanese Automotive Industry" (1985).

134. William Abernathy, Kim Clark, and Alan Kantrow, *Industrial Renaissance: Producing a Competitive Future for America* (New York: Basic Books, 1983).

135. See Stephen Hymer, "The Multinational Corporation and the Law of Uneven Development," in J. Bhagwati (ed.), *Economics and World Order* (New York: Free Press, 1972); Robert Cohen, "The New International Division of Labor, Multinational Corporations and Urban Hierarchy," in Michael Dear and Allen Scott (eds.), *Urbanization and Urban Planning in Capitalist Societies* (New York: Methuen, 1981); Folker Froebel, J. Heinrichs, and J. Kreye, *The New International Division of Labor* (New York: Cambridge University Press, 1981).

136. On dealers, see Kagono et al. *Strategic vs. Evolutionary Management,* pp. 80–82.

137. George Fields, *Gucci on the Ginza* (Tokyo: Kodansha International, 1989).

138. See Oliver Williamson, "The Vertical Integration of Production: Market Failure Considerations," *American Economic Review* 61 (May 1971), pp. 112–27; *Markets and Hierarchies* (New York: Free Press, 1975); *The Economic Institutions of Capitalism* (New York: Free Press, 1981).

139. See Walter Powell, "Hybrid Organizational Arrangements: New Form or Transitional Development?" *California Management Review* (Fall 1987), pp. 47–87.

140. Aoki, *Information, Incentives and Bargaining* (1988).

141. See Armen Alchian and Harold Demetz, "Production, Information Costs, and Economic Organization," *American Economic Review* 62, no. 5 (December 1972), pp. 777–95.

142. Ken-ichi Imai, "Japanese Pattern of Innovation and Its Commercialization Process." Paper prepared for the Economic Growth and Commercialization of New Technologies Conference, Center for Economic Policy Research, Stanford University (11-12 September 1989); Ken-ichi Imai, "The Corporate Network in Japan," *Japanese Economic Studies* (Winter 1987–88), pp. 3–37.

143. Jon Sigurdson, *Industry and State Partnership in Japan: The Very Large Scale Integrated Circuits Project* (Lund, Sweden: Research Policy Institute Discussion Paper No. 168, 1986).

144. See Ronald Dore, "Goodwill and the Spirit of Market Capitalism," *British Journal of Sociology* 34 (1983), pp. 459–82; *Taking Japan Seriously* (Stanford CA: Stanford University Press, 1987).

145. See Mark Granovetter, "Economic Action and Social Structure: The Problem of Embeddedness," *American Journal of Sociology* 91, no. 3 (November 1985), pp. 481–510.

146. Koji Matsuhashi and Koichi Togashi, "Locational Dynamics and Spatial Structures in the Japanese Manufacturing Industries: A Review on the Japanese Industrial Restructuring Process of Leading Sectors," *Geographical Review of Japan* 61, no. 1 (1988), pp. 174–89.

147. An anonymous Japanese subcontractor, as quoted in David Russell, "The Truth About Big Business in Japan," *Business Tokyo* (April 1990), pp. 22–28.

148. In the United States many major suppliers are organized by the UAW and have wages comparable to the Big Three auto assemblers. And, of course, Japanese assemblers have contracted out far more of the value-added costs of an automobile than have American firms. Robert Cole, *Japanese Blue Collar: The Changing Tradition* (Berkeley: University of California Press, 1971), p. 58.

149. Aoki, "The Japanese Firm in Transition," p. 35; Patrick and Rohlen, "Small-Scale Family Enterprises."

150. Ken-ichi Imai, "Network Industrial Organization and Incremental Innovation in Japan" (Kunitachi, Japan: Hitotsubashi University, Institute of Business Research, Discussion Paper No. 122, 1984). See also Yutaka Kosai, "Patterns of Change in Japan's Industrial Society," *Japan Echo* 13 (Special issue, 1986), pp. 32–39.

151. Cusumano, *The Japanese Automobile Industry*, p. 252.

152. Kagono et al., Evolutionary vs. Strategic Management (1985).

153. Cole, *Japanese Blue Collar: The Changing Tradition*, p. 58.

154. Sako, "Partnership Between Large and Small Firms" (1988).

155. This example is taken from Cusumano, *The Japanese Automobile Industry*, p. 363.

Chapter 3

1. National Institute for Research Advancement (NIRA), *Comprehensive Study of Microelectronics* (Tokyo: NIRA, 1985), p. 11.

2. Kiyoshi Kawashima, "Interview," *The JAMA Forum* 1, no. 4 (1983), p. 20.

3. See Nicolai Kondratiev, "The Long Waves in Economic Life," *Review of Economics and Statistics* 17 (November 1935), 105–15; Ernst Mandel, *Late Capitalism* (London: New Left Books, 1975); Christopher Freeman, *Long Waves and the World Economy* (London: Pinter, 1984); Michel Aglietta, *A Theory of Capitalist Regulation: The U.S. Experience* (London: New Left Books, 1979); Alexander Gerschenkron, *Economic Backwardness in Historical Perspective* (Cambridge, MA: Harvard University Press, 1952).

4. See Gerhard Mensch, *Stalemate in Technology: Innovations Overcome Depression*

(Cambridge, MA: Ballinger Press, 1979); Christopher Freeman and Carlotta Perez, "Long Waves and Changes in Employment Patterns," 1988, (unpublished paper); James Kurth, "The Political Consequences of the Product Cycle: Industrial History and Political Outcomes," *International Organization* 33, no. 1 (Winter 1979), pp. 1–34. Also on the concept of the "leading sector" see W.W. Rostow, *The Stages of Economic Growth* (Cambridge: Cambridge University Press, 1960); Robert Gilpin, *U.S. Power and the Multinational Corporation: The Political Economy of Foreign Direct Investment* (New York: Basic Books, 1975).

5. Data compiled by Joseph D'Cruz, University of Toronto, as reported in *Fortune* (Special Issue on "The New American Century," Spring-Summer 1991), pp. 18–19.

6. These data are from 1985 Japanese Census of Manufacturers, as reported in "The Changing Nature of Japanese Manufacturing," *JEI Report*, No. 23A (17 June 1988).

7. See Andrew Grove, "The Future of the Computer Industry," *California Management Review* 35, no. 1 (Fall 1990), pp. 148–60.

8. See, for example, Ernest Braun and Stuart Macdonald, *Revolution in Miniature,* 2nd ed. (Cambridge: Cambridge University Press, 1982).

9. As the United States was driven out of this field, its corporations increasingly concentrated in specialty products and in personal computer microprocessor units where the Intel and Motorola patent positions were used to exclude Japanese competitors. For a discussion of United States vs. Japanese strength in integrated circuits see *Upside Magazine,* "Are We Gaining or Losing Marketshare in Semiconductors?" (February/March 1991), pp. 114–17. See Charles Cohen and William Semich, "Upstart NMB Challenges the Memory Giants," *Electronic Business Asia* (June 1990), pp. 40–45, especially the table on p. 42.

10. Grove, "The Future of the Computer Industry."

11. "Why NEC Has U.S. Companies 'Shaking in Their Boots'," *Business Week* (16 March 1990), pp. 90–92.

12. Japan Economic Institute, *Japan-U.S. Business Report,* no. 253 (October 1990), p. 7.

13. See "Hitachi Developing Neural Computer," *Electronic News* (3 December 1990), p. 11.

14. Most recently, see David Stip, "Concerns Seek U.S. Aid in Race for Technology," *Wall Street Journal* (18 June 1991), p. B3.

15. This, as we have shown elsewhere, contrasts sharply with the highly fragmented U.S. model. See Richard Florida and Martin Kenney, *The Breakthrough Illusion* (New York: Basic Books, 1990).

16. See Martin Kenney and Richard Florida, "Japan's Role in a Postfordist Age" *Futures* 21, no. 2 (1989), pp. 136–51.

17. For a discussion of this see Andrew Collier, "Report Fujitsu Tech Stymied ICL Options," *Electronic News* (6 August 1990), p. 1.

18. Site visit to FANUC by Richard Florida (October 1991). We could as easily have used a term incorporating any of the major Japanese electronic firms (e.g., NEC, Hitachi, or Toshiba). The importance of using an electronic company is that the future growth of the world economy will be undergirded by the application of electronics to all fields of production.

19. See Yoneji Masuda, *Social Impact of Computerization: An Application of the Pattern Model for Industrial Society* (Tokyo: Kodansha Publishers, 1970); Daniel Bell, *The Coming of the Postindustrial Society* (New York: Basic Books, 1973); Fred Block, *Postindustrial Possibilities: A Critique of Economic Discourse* (Berkeley: University of California Press, 1990).

20. Scott Lash and John Urry, *The End of Organized Capitalism* (Madison: University of Wisconsin Press, 1987).

21. Tessa Morris-Suzuki, *Beyond Computopia: Information, Automation and Democracy in Japan* (London: Kegan Paul International, 1988).

22. James Bartholomew, *The Formation of Science in Japan* (New Haven: Yale University Press, 1989), pp. 230–36.

23. Hitachi Corporation, *75 Years and Forward* (Tokyo: Hitachi Corporation, 1985), p. 99.

24. NEC Corporation, *The First Eighty Years* (Tokyo: NEC Corporation, 1984), p. 22.

25. See, for example, Akio Morita, *Made in Japan* (New York: Dutton, 1986).

26. NEC Corporation, *The First Eighty Years,* p. 22.

27. Ministry of International Trade and Industry, *Japanese Industrial Policy and Trade Policy in the High-Growth Era* (Tokyo: Ministry of International Trade and Industry, Background Information Paper, B1–73, 1990), p. 6.

28. National Science Foundation, *International Science and Technology Data Update: 1988* (Washington, DC: NSF, 1989), NSF 89-307, p. 7.

29. Daniel Okimoto and Gary Saxonhouse, "Technology and the Future of the Economy," in Kozo Yamamura and Yasukichi Yasuba (eds.), *The Political Economy of Japan: The Domestic Transformation* (Stanford, CA: Stanford University Press, 1987), p. 415.

30. Ken-ichi Imai, "Japanese Pattern of Innovation and Its Commercialization Process." A paper prepared for the conference on Economic Growth and the Commercialization of New Technologies, Center for Economic Policy Research, Stanford University (11–12 September 1989).

31. William Coates, retired Westinghouse executive, personal interview by Richard Florida (June 1991).

32. As reported in "Research and Development in Japan: 1989 Update," *JEI Reports* no. 24a (23 June 1989).

33. On electronics see, for example, Marie Anchordoguy, *Computers, Inc.: Japan's Challenge to IBM* (Cambridge, MA: Harvard East Asian Monograph, 1989) and Martin Fransman, *The Market and Beyond: Cooperation and Competition in Information Technology in the Japanese System* (Cambridge: Cambridge University Press, 1990). On biotechnology see Malcolm Brock, *Biotechnology in Japan* (London: Routledge, 1989). For a critique of Brock see Martin Kenney, "Book Review of *Biotechnology in Japan,*" *Journal of Japanese Studies* 17, no. 1 (1991), pp. 172–75.

34. See Paula Doe, "Japan Spends Aggressively and Builds for the Future, *Electronic Business* (16 April 1990), pp. 77–79.

35. Interviews were conducted by Martin Kenney in June 1984, December 1987, June 1988, and October 1988 through March 1989. Invariably, interviewees indicated that they thought R&D was the key to corporate survival.

36. Dr. Daizaburo Shinoda, vice president, NEC Corporation. Personal interview by Martin Kenney (June 1988).

37. Our information on Nippon Kokan Kogyo was provided by Ken-ichi Kikuchi, general manager of planning and coordination, engineering, research and development division, NKK. Personal interview by Martin Kenney (June 1988). During this crisis period the *Wall Street Journal* quoted the director of Kawasaki Steel's research laboratory as saying, "We won't cut R&D unless there's absolutely nothing else to cut." Stephen Yoder, "Japan's Troubled Industries Stress R&D," *Wall Street Journal* (27 March 1987), p. 24.

38. Yumiko Ono, "Newly Developed, Pricey Synthetic Fiber Is Becoming Fashion Craze in Japan," *Wall Street Journal* (9 March 1990), p. A2.

39. Authors' survey, 1991. For an example of Japanese biotechnology firms investing in university R&D, see "Advanced Bio Class: That's Over in Hitachi Hall," *Business Week* (7 August 1989), pp. 73, 74. In another case, Shiseido, the leading Japanese cosmetic producer, provided $100 million to fund research at the dermatology department of the Harvard Medical School.

40. Harry Braverman, *Labor and Monopoly Capital* (New York: Monthly Review Press, 1974).

41. See Florida and Kenney, *The Breakthrough Illusion.*

42. Kagono, Nonaka, Sakakibara, and Okumura, *Strategic vs. Evolutionary Management: A U.S./Japan Comparison of Strategy and Organization,* p. 122.

43. See Dennis Hayes, *Behind the Silicon Curtain* (Montreal: Black Rose Books, 1989).

44. *Business Week,* "How Sony Pulled Off Its Spectacular Computer Coup" (15 January 1990), pp. 76, 77.

45. This study tracked the careers of engineering graduates from Japan's Tohoku University and compared them to graduates of Carnegie Mellon University. See Leonard Lynn, Henry Piehler, and Walter Zaharay, *Engineers in the U.S. and Japan: A Comparison of their Numbers and an Empirical Study of their Careers and Methods of Information Transfer* (Pittsburgh: Carnegie Mellon University, 1988).

46. See Florida and Kenney, *The Breakthrough Illusion,* esp. chap. 5.

47. See Hajime Eto, "Research and Development in Japan," in Yasuhiro Monden (ed.), *Innovations in Management: The Japanese Corporation* (Atlanta: Institute of Industrial Engineers, 1985).

48. Kim Clark and Takahiro Fujimoto, *Product Development Performance: Strategy, Organization and Management in the World Auto Industry* (Boston: Harvard Business School Press, 1991), p. 332.

49. Koji Okubayashi, "Values and Attitudes of Japanese Production Engineers Toward Workers Under Microelectronics Innovation," *The Annals of the School of Business Administration* (Kobe University) 32 (1988), p. 59.

50. D. Eleanor Westney and Kiyonori Sakakibara, "Comparative Study of the Training, Careers, and Organization of Engineers in the Computer Industry in Japan and the United States," MIT–Japan Science and Technology Program (September 1985).

51. An excellent overview of Japanese R&D system is presented in Ken-ichi Imai, Ikujiro Nonaka, and Hirotaka Takeuchi, "Managing the New Product Development Process," in K. Clark, R. Hayes, and C. Lorenz (eds.), *The Uneasy Alliance* (Boston: Harvard Business Press, 1985), originally distributed as Hitotsubashi Institute of Business Research, Discussion Paper No. 118, 1984). A very similar argument is made in Masahiko Aoki and Nathan Rosenberg, "The Japanese Firm as an Innovating Institution" (Stanford, CA: Center for Economic Policy Research, Policy Paper No. 106, September 1987). In addition, our discussion of the research process in Japan draws heavily on interviews conducted by Martin Kenney with R&D managers at Japanese electronic, chemical, and biotechnology companies. For a discussion of research in the Japanese biotechnology industry see Martin Kenney, "Some Observations on the Structure of the U.S. and Japanese Biotechnology Industries," *Hitotsubashi Business Review* 34, no. 2 (1986) (in Japanese).

52. See, for example, Ikujiro Nonaka, "Redundant, Overlapping Organization: A Japanese Approach to Managing the Innovation Process," *California Management Review* 32 (Spring 1990), pp. 27–38.

53. See Imai, Nonaka, and Takeuchi, "Managing the New Product Development Process."

54. See Clark and Fujimoto, *Product Development Performance,* 1991. Also Edwin Mansfield, "The Speed and Cost of Industrial Innovation in Japan and the United States: External vs. Internal Technology," *Management Science* 34, no. 10 (October 1988), pp. 1157–68.

55. Westney and Sakakibara, "Comparative Study"; Westney, "Internal and External Linkages in the MNC: The Case of R&D Subsidiaries in Japan," Working Paper No. 1973-88, Sloan School of Management, MIT (June 1987); Westney and Sakakibara, "Designing the Designers," *Technology Review* (April 1986), pp. 25–31.

56. Westney and Sakakibara, ibid., p. 80.

57. Daizaburo Shinoda, vice president, NEC Corporation, personal interview with Martin Kenney (June 1988).

58. Keiichi Miwa, personal interview with Martin Kenney (10 October 1990).

59. Robert Cole, "Issues in Skill Formation and Training in Japanese Manufacturing Approaches to Automation," in Paul Adler (ed.), *Technology and the Future of Work* (London: Oxford University Press, 1992).

60. Yamazaki Mazak Co. *Annual Report* (Tokyo: Yamazaki Mazak, 1989).

61. Name withheld by request, production manager, Canon Inc.; personal interview by Martin Kenney (July 1991).

62. President, former manager at a major chemical plant of a major Japanese electronics firm; personal interview with Martin Kenney, (May 1991).

63. Harvard Business School Case Study 9-686-083, "Yamazaki Mazak" (1986), p. 10.

64. George Landsly, manager, Administration, I/N Tek, personal interview by Richard Florida (November 1990).

65. Karl Marx (translated by Ben Fowkes), *Capital,* Vol. I (New York: Vintage Books, 1977) p. 495.

66. Harry Braverman, *Labor and Monopoly Capital* (New York: Monthly Review Press, 1974).

67. Joseph Schumpeter, *Capitalism, Socialism and Democracy* (orig. 1942) (New York: Harper & Row, 1975).

68. See Herbert Marcuse, "Some Social Implications of Modern Technology," in Andrew Arato and Eike Gebhardt (eds.), *The Essential Frankfurt School Reader* (New York: Urizen Books, 1978), pp. 138–62; David Noble, *America by Design: Science, Technology and the Rise of Corporate Capitalism* (New York: Oxford University Press, 1978).

69. Department manager of assembly and test, Japanese electronics transplant; personal interview by Martin Kenney (May 1991).

70. For an elegant conceptualization of this reconciliation process with reference to the world of science, see Bruno Latour, *The Pasteurization of France* (Cambridge, MA: Harvard University Press, 1990).

71. Gene Gregory, *Japanese Electronics Technology: Enterprise and Innovation* (Tokyo, Japan Times, Inc., 1986); Daniel Okimoto, Takuo Sugano, and Franklin Weinstein, *Competitive Edge: The Semiconductor Industry in the U.S. and Japan* (Stanford, CA: Stanford University Press, 1984).

72. The importance of NTT in the development of the Japanese computer and telecommunications industry can hardly be overestimated, and yet there is little written in English regarding its importance. Curiously, most of the discussions center upon NTT's role in the development of the Japanese computer and electronics industries and not upon its research, development, and procurement of telecommunications equipment. See, for example, Anchordoguy *Computers, Inc., or Fransman, The Market and Beyond.*

73. Christopher Freeman, *Technology Policy and Economic Performance: Lessons from Japan* (London: Pinter Publishers 1987).

74. See the chapter entitled "Mechatronics" in Gamota and Frieman, *Gaining Ground,* pp. 85–106; also James Nevins, "Mechatronics," in Cecil Uyehara (ed.), *U.S.-Japan Science and Technology Exchange: Patterns of Interdependence* (Boulder, CO: Westview Press, 1988), pp. 92–142.

75. "'Photonics': The U.S. is Losing Ground to You-Know-Who," *Business Week* (19 September 1988), p. 88.

76. Personal interview with leading Japanese steel officials, by Richard Florida (April 1991).

77. Henry Ergas, "Does Technology Policy Matter?" in R. Landau and N. Rosenberg (eds.), *The Positive Sum Strategy* (Washington, DC: National Academy Press, 1987).

78. Masao Ito, "Philosophy and Direction of Information Systems at NSC." Unpublished mimeograph, Computer System Division, Nippon Steel Corporation, August 24, 1983.

79. See especially Ramchandran Jaikumar, "Postindustrial Manufacturing," *Harvard Business Review* (November-December 1986), pp. 69–76; Karl Ebel, "Social and Labour Implications of Flexible Manufacturing Systems," *International Labour Review* 124, no. 2 (1985), pp. 133–45; "Factory of the Future," *The Economist* (30 May 1987).

80. Jaikumar, "Postindustrial Manufacturing," p. 75.

81. Koji Okubayashi, "Values and Attitudes of Japanese Production Engineers Toward Workers Under Microelectronics Innovation," *The Annals of the School of Business Administration* (Kobe University) no. 32 (1988), p. 64.

82. Haruo Shimada and John Paul MacDuffie, "Industrial Relations and 'Humanware'," Sloan School of Management, MIT Working Paper No. 1855-88 (December 1986).

83. See Ken-ichi Imai, "Network Industrial Organization and Incremental Innovation in Japan" (Tokyo: Hitotsubashi University, Institute for Business Research, May 1988, Discussion Paper No. 122); and Imai, "Japanese Corporate Strategies Toward International Networking and Product Development" (Tokyo: Hitotsubashi University, Institute for Business Research, October 1988, unpublished paper).

84. For a discussion of the growth of the Japanese semiconductor production equipment industry see, for example, Jay Stowsky, "Weak Links, Strong Bonds: U.S.-Japanese Competition in Semiconductor Production Equipment," in Chalmers Johnson, Laura Tyson, and John Zysman (eds.) *Politics and Productivity: How Japan's Development Strategy Works* (Cambridge, MA: Ballinger, 1989), pp. 241–74.

85. Japan Economic Institute, p. 6.

86. U.S. General Accounting Office, "Sematech's Efforts to Strengthen the U.S. Semiconductor Industry" (Washington, DC: GAO, September 1990).

87. Eric von Hippel, *The Sources of Innovation* (New York: Oxford University Press, 1988).

88. Michiyoshi Hagino, deputy general manager, Tochigi Research Facility, Honda R&D Ltd, Co., personal interview by Martin Kenney (June 1988).

89. Nonaka, "Redundant, Overlapping Organization: A Japanese Approach to Managing the Innovation Process," p. 32.

90. Toyo Keizai Shimposha, *Japan Company Handbook* (Tokyo: Toyo Keizai Shimposha, 1988), p. 697.

91. See Masahiko Aoki, *Information, Incentives and Bargaining in the Japanese Economy* (New York: Cambridge University Press, 1988).

92. Nobuyoshi Miyazawa, general manager of sales administration department, Enicom; personal interview by Martin Kenney (March 1989).

93. See Florida and Kenney, *The Breakthrough Illusion.*

94. Office of Technology Assessment, *International Competition in Services* (Washington, DC: U.S. Government Printing Office, 1987), pp. 160–161.

95. Ibid., pp. 160, 161.

96. See Michael Cusumano, *Japan's Software Factories* (Oxford: Oxford University Press, 1991).

97. For a discussion see Kathleen Hughes, "Japan's Past Ventures in Hollywood Mostly Are Less Than Stellar," *Wall Street Journal* (27 November 1990), pp. A1, A4.

98. Executive, Fujitsu Facom Information Processing Corporation; personal interview by Martin Kenney (December 1988).

99. See Hisao Nishioka and Atsuhiko Takeuchi, "The Development of High-Technology Industry in Japan," in Michael Breheny and Ronald McQuaid (eds.), *The Development of High Technology Industries: An International Survey* (London: Croom Helm, 1987), pp. 262–95).

100. Tadashi Saito, director of planning, Exec Corporation; personal interview by Martin Kenney (November 1989).

101. JETRO (Japanese External Trade Organization), *Your Market in Japan: Computer Software,* no. 36 (March 1985).

102. Robert Poe, "The Era of Packaged Software Dawns in Japan," *Datamation* (15 December 1987), pp. 30–34. See also Andrew Friedman and Joan Greenbaum, "Japanese DP," *Datamation* (1 February 1985), pp. 112–18.

103. Cusumano, *Japan's Software Factories* (1990).

104. Executive, Fujitsu Facom Information Processing Corporation; personal interview by Martin Kenney (December 1988).

105. Yoshihiro Matsumoto, "A Software Factory: An Overall Approach to Software Production," in Peter Freeman (ed.), *Software Reusability* (IEEE Tutorial) (2 December 1986).

106. Yukio Mizuno, "Software Quality Improvement," *Computer* (March 1983), pp. 71–73.

107. U.S. Office of Technology Assessment, *International Competition in Services* (Washington, DC: OTA, 1987), p. 164.

108. Name withheld by request, president and founder of an important independent software firm; personal interview with Martin Kenney (October 1988).

109. Saburo Chatani, president of Mitsubishi Electric Computer Systems Corporation; personal interview by Martin Kenney (March 1989). President and founder of an important independent software firm; name withheld by request; personal interview by Martin Kenney (December 1988).

110. Softic, *1988 Japanese Computer Software Market* (Tokyo: Software Information Center, 1988); Japan Information Processing Development Center, *Informatization White Paper* (Tokyo: Japan Information Development Center, 1988), p. 111.

111. Shuichi Miyazaki, general manager of education and training department, NRI&NCC; personal interview by Martin Kenney (February 1989).

112. In a number of interviews with software managers in smaller firms it was pointed out that it was not merely lower labor costs that made them competitive, but also the fact that they had far less overhead owing to their small size.

113. Michiharu Sakurai and Wallace Growney, "Software Cost Accounting Mechanisms in Japan," unpublished mimeograph (no date).

114. See Andrew Friedman and Joan Greenbaum, "Japanese DP," *Datamation* (2 February 1985), pp. 112–18; Andrew Friedman, "Specialist Labour in Japan: Computer Skilled Staff and the Subcontracting System," *British Journal of Industrial Relations* 25, 3 (November 1987), pp. 353–69.

115. Toshio Hirano "Software Houses," *Japan Economic Almanac 1987* (Tokyo: Japan Economic Almanac, 1987), pp. 100–101. Also, Kazuo Hirono, general manager of the education department, CSK Corporation; personal interview by Martin Kenney (March 1989).

116. Hitachi Corporation, "Hitachi Group Systems Software," (Tokyo: Hitachi Corporation, 1989); Kenjiro Ishihara, deputy manager, Public Communications Office, Toshiba Corporation; personal communication with Martin Kenney (March 1989); NEC, "Corporate Description" (Tokyo: NEC, 1989) (in Japanese).

117. Saburo Chatani, president, Mitsubishi Electric Computer Systems Corporation; personal interview by Martin Kenney (March 1989).

118. Jon Shirley, then president of Microsoft Inc., interview in Ernst and Young, *Electronics 1990: The New Competitive Priorities* (San Francisco: Ernst and Young, 1990), p. 122.

119. Masahiro Kitagawa, manager of product planning and marketing, Justsystem Corporation; personal interview by Martin Kenney (March 1989).

120. Parenthetically, it should be noted that the early IBM PCs were not suited to Japanese-language word processing. IBM Japan developed its own PC for its Japanese customers and lost any opportunity to be an important player in the PC market. The more tragic story is the Apple Macintosh's failure in Japan. The Mac had an excellent operating system for Japanese-language word processing. Yet Apple never invested in developing an excellent word processing system and priced Macs two to three times higher than in the United States, thus ensuring irrelevance in Japan. The size of this error can be appreciated when compared with the much smaller Sun Microsystems, which controls 30 percent of the Japanese workstation market and in 1990 had annual sales of $220 million. Yuichi Murano, product marketing manager, Nihon Sun Microsystems K.K.; personal interview by Martin Kenney (March 1989).

121. For a discussion of this process in the United States, see Paul Freiberger and Michael Swaine, *Fire in the Valley* (Berkeley, CA: Osborne/McGraw-Hill, 1984). Shinichi Ogata, director of information systems consulting program, SRI International; personal interview by Martin Kenney (October 1988).

122. For a comprehensive discussion of the Japanese personal computer market see Japan Personal Computer Software Association/Dataquest, *Emerging Personal Computer Opportunities in Japan* (Tokyo: JPSA/Dataquest, 1988).

123. Hiroyuki Yaginuma, assistant manager of the marketing department, Lotus Development Japan, Ltd.; personal interview by Martin Kenney (November 1988).

124. Nintendo's lock on the family computer market and attendant software has led to lawsuits by U.S. game software firms. See, for example, Richard B. Schmitt, "Atari Is Challenging Antitrust Aspect of Technology in Suit Against Nintendo," *Wall Street Journal* (14 December 1988); p. B8.

125. The first big 8-bit game software boom and bust was in large part due to the issuance of low-quality (full of bugs) software that soured consumers on computer games.

126. Shuichi Miyazaki, general manager, education and training department, NRI&NCC Co., Ltd.; personal interview by Martin Kenney, Nomura Securities (February 1989).

127. For an excellent overview of Nintendo see David Sheff, "Nintendo Isn't Playing Games" *San Francisco Examiner* (2 December 1990), pp. 9–13.

128. Yutaka Takano, managing director, Enix Corporation; personal interview by Martin Kenney (December 1988); Yukihiro Gushi, manager, international marketing, Hudson Soft; personal interview by Martin Kenney (November 1988); Yoichi Erikawa, president, Koei Co., Ltd.; personal interview by Martin Kenney (January 1989).

129. Japan Economic Institute, *Japan-U.S. Business Report*, no. 260, (May 1991), p. 7.

130. Japan Economic Institute, *Japan-U.S. Business Report* (various issues, 1990–91).

Introduction to Part II

1. See, for example, Mira Wilkins, "American-Japanese Foreign Direct Investment Relations, 1930–1952," *Business History Review* 56, no. 4 (Winter 1982), pp. 497–518.

2. See David Edgington, *Japanese Business Down Under: Patterns of Japanese Investment in Australia* (New York: Routledge, 1990).

3. See Michel Aglietta, *A Theory of Capitalist Regulation: The U.S. Experience* (London: New Left Books, 1979).

4. Data in Table 2 are for midyear 1989. This accounts for the difference in totals between Tables 1 and 2. Also, the data in Table 2 are for the following two-digit SIC codes 35, 36, 33, 37, and 30. These figures thus differ from our analysis put forward in the following chapters, which focus on more detailed sectoral groupings. Still, they resonate with and reinforce our own findings and convey the strong concentration of Japanese investment in these sectors.

5. Antonio Gramsci, "Americanism and Fordism," in Quintin Hoare and Geoffrey Nowell Smith (eds. and trans.), *Selections From the Prison Notebooks of Antonio Gramsci,* (New York: International Publishers, 1971), pp. 277–320.

6. Arndt Sorge and Wolfgang Streeck, "Industrial Relations and Technical Change," in Richard Hyman and Wolfgang Streeck (eds.), *New Technology and Industrial Change* (London: Basil Blackwell, 1988), p. 34.

7. James Abegglen, *The Japanese Factory* (Cambridge, MA: MIT Press, 1958).

8. Solomon Levine, *Industrial Relations in Postwar Japan* (Urbana: University of Illinois Press, 1958).

9. R. Marsh and H. Mannari, *Modernization and the Japanese Factory* (Princeton, NJ: Princeton University Press, 1976).

10. Koji Taira, "The Labor Market in Japanese Development," *British Journal of Industrial Relations* 2, no. 2 (July 1964), pp. 209–27; Koji Taira, "The Characteristics of Japanese Labor Markets," *Economic Development and Cultural Change* (January 1962), pp. 150–68; Koji Taira, "Japanese Enterprise Unionism and Inter-firm Wage Structure," *Industrial and Labor Relations Review* 15, no. 1 (October 1961), pp. 33–51.

11. Ronald Dore, *Japanese Factory, British Factory* (Berkeley: University of California Press, 1973).

12. Robert Cole, *Japanese Blue Collar* (Berkeley: University of California Press, 1971).

13. Robert Cole, *Strategies for Learning* (Berkeley: University of California Press, 1989).

14. See, for example, Karel Cool and Cynthia Legnick-Hall, "Second Thoughts on the Transferability of the Japanese Management Style," *Organization Studies* 6 (1985), pp. 1–22.

15. Paul DiMaggio and Walter Powell, "The Iron Cage Revisited: Institutional Isomorphism and Collective Rationality in Organizational Fields," *American Sociological Review* 48 (April 1983), pp. 147–60.

16. See, for example, John Meyer and Brian Rowen, "Institutionalized Organizations: Formal Structure as Myth and Ceremony," *American Journal of Sociology* 83, no. 2 (September 1977), pp. 340–63; and Lynne Zucker, "The Role of Institutionalization in Cultural Persistence," *American Sociological Review* 42 (1977), pp. 726–43.

17. See especially Michael Hannan and John Freeman, "The Population Ecology of Organizations," *American Journal of Sociology* 82, no. 5 (March 1977), pp. 929–64.

18. Mark Granovetter, "Economic Action and Social Structure: The Problem of Embeddedness," *American Journal of Sociology* 91, no. 3 (November 1985), pp. 481–510.

19. The initial formulation of this school of analysis was Michel Aglietta, *A Theory of Capitalist Regulation: The U.S. Experience* (London: New Left Books, 1979).

20. See Alain Lipietz, *Mirages and Miracles* (London: Verso, 1987).

21. Joseph Schumpeter, "The Creative Response in Economic History," *Journal of Economic History* 7, no. 2 (November 1947), pp. 149–59.

22. Jeffery Pfeffer and Gerald Salancik, *The External Control of Organizations: A Resource Dependence Perspective,* (New York: Harper & Row, 1978).

23. Karl Weick, *The Social Psychology of Organizing* (New York: Random House, 1979).

24. Ruth Young, "Is Population Ecology a Useful Paradigm for the Study of Organizations?" *American Journal of Sociology,* 94, no. 1 (1988), p. 16.

25. Dexter Dunphy, "Convergence/Divergence: A Temporal Review of Japanese Enterprise and Its Management," *Academy of Management Review* 12, no. 3 (1987), p. 449.

26. See M. Yoshino, *Japan's Multinational Enterprises* (Cambridge, MA: Harvard University Press, 1976).

27. H. Yoshihara, "The Japanese Multinational," *Long Range Planning* 10, no. 2, (1977), pp. 41–45.

28. Robert Cole, *Work, Mobility and Participation* (Berkeley: University of California Press, 1979), p. 255.

29. Ronald Dore, "More About Late Development," *Journal of Japanese Studies* 5 (1979), pp. 137–51.

30. H. Ishida, "Human Resources Management in Overseas Japanese Firms," *Japanese Economic Studies* 10, no. 1 (1981), pp. 53–81; "Japanese-Style Human Resource Management: CCan It Be Exported?" *Sumitomo Quarterly* 5, no. 6 (1981), pp. 15–18.

31. Michael White and Malcolm Trevor, *Under Japanese Management* (London: Heinemann Educational Books, 1983).

32. Nick Oliver and Barry Wilkinson, "Japanese Manufacturing Techniques and Personnel and Industrial Relations Practice in Britain: Evidence and Implications," *British Journal of Industrial Relations* 27 (1989), pp. 73–91; Jonathan Morris, "The Who, Why and Where of Japanese Manufacturing Investment in the U.K.," *Industrial Relations Journal,* 19, no. 1 (Spring 1988), pp. 31–40.

33. Stuart Crowther and Philip Garrahan, "Invitation to Sunderland: Corporate Power and the Local Economy," *Industrial Relations Journal* 19, no. 1 (Spring 1988), pp. 51–59.

34. R. Pascale, "Communication and Decison-making across Cultures: Japanese and American Comparisons," *Administrative Science Quarterly* 23 (1978), pp. 91–110; M. Macquire and R. Pascale, "Communication, Decision-making and Implementation among Managers in Japanese and American Managed Companies," *Sociology and Social Research* 63 (1978), pp. 1–23; Pascale and Macquire, "Comparison of Selected Work Factors in the U.S. and Japan," *Human Relations* 33 (1980), pp. 433–55.

35. T. Kagono et al., "Mechanistic versus Organic Management Systems: A Comparison of Adaptive Patterns of U.S. and Japanese Firms," *Kobe Annual Reports* (1980), pp. 115–39.

36. See John Krafcik, "Learning from NUMMI" Cambridge, MA: MIT International Motor Vehicle Program unpublished manuscript, 1986); and Clair Brown and Michael Reich, "When Does Union-Management Cooperation Work?: A Look at NUMMI and GM-Van Nuys," *California Management Review* 31, no. 4 (1989), pp. 26–44.

37. Andrew Mair, Richard Florida, and Martin Kenney, "The New Geography of Automobile Production: Japanese Transplants in North America," *Economic Geography* 64 (1988), pp. 352–73.

38. University of Tokyo, Institute of Social Science, "Local Production of Japanese Automobile and Electronic Firms in The United States: The 'Application' and 'Adaptation' of Japanese-Style Management" (1990).

39. Joseph and Suzy Fucini, *Working for the Japanese: Inside Mazda's American Auto Plant* (New York: Free Press, 1990).

Chapter 4

1. Toyota Motor Manufacturing USA, Inc. "Team Member Handbook," First edition, (February 1998), p. 17.

2. Joel Smith and William Childs, "Imported from America: Cooperative Labor Relations at New United Motor Manufacturing, Inc.," *Industrial Relations Law Journal,* 9, no. 1 (1987), p. 78.

3. The reason the Japanese exported small vehicles was that these were the automobiles they produced for the Japanese market.

4. See, for example, Kurt Hoffman and Raphael Kaplinsky, *Driving Force* (Boulder, CO: Westview Press, 1988).

5. Honda of America Manufacturing Company, personal interview by authors (June 1988).

6. "Toyota May Start Auto Output in U.S.," *New York Times* (9 January 1980), p. D4.

7. MITI official as quoted in *New York Times* (12 January 1980), p. 1.

8. As quoted in "Nissan Tells UAW of Plans for U.S. Plant...," *Wall Street Journal* (19 February 1980), p. 4.

9. "Japan Asks Its Car Firms to Limit Exports to U.S. and Start American Production," *Wall Street Journal* (13 February 1980), p. 2; also see "Toyota and Nissan Are Wary of Building in U.S., Fearing Losses, Small Car Glut," *Wall Street Journal* (28 February 1980), p. 23.

10. "Toyota Hires 3 Firms to Make New Surveys on Production in U.S.," *Wall Street Journal* (9 April 1980), p. 4.

11. "Nissan Plans U.S. Truck Plant," *New York Times* (18 April 1980), pp. D1, D2; "Nissan Chooses Tennessee Site for Truck Plant," *Wall Street Journal* (31 October 1980), p. 33.

12. "Joint Production Is Explored," *New York Times* (28 May 1980), p. D7.

13. "Ford-Toyota Venture Is Weighed," *New York Times* (10 July 1980), pp. D1, D7; "Toyota Proposes Venture in U.S. with Ford Motor," *Wall Street Journal* (10 July 1980), p. 2.

14. "Ford Is Likely to Reject Toyota Proposal," *Wall Street Journal* (14 July 1980), p. 3; "Ford-Toyota Officials Resume Talks on Venture in U.S. as Pessimism Grows," *Wall Street Journal* (16 July 1981), p. 14.

15. GM-Toyota Talks on Small Car Venture Put Speculation Mills into High Gear," *Wall Street Journal* (3 August 1982), p. 18.

16. "GM Talks Alarm Competitors," *New York Times* (1 February 1983), pp. D1, D4.

17. "GM and Toyota to Produce Cars in Joint Venture Plant on Coast," *New York Times* (15 February 1983), pp. 1, D5.

18. For an excellent analysis of the operation of NUMMI see John Krafcik, "Learning from NUMMI" (MIT International Motor Vehicle Program Internal Working Paper, 1986).

19. "Toyota to Build Plants in U.S. and Canada," *Wall Street Journal* (24 July 1985), p. 25.

20. "Mazda to Construct Detroit Area Plant," *Automotive News* (3 December 1984), p. 1.

21. "Chrysler and Mitsubishi to Build Small Cars Jointly in the Midwest," *New York Times* (16 April 1985), pp. 1, D13; "Chrysler, Mitsubishi Pick Illinois Site," *New York Times* (8 October 1985), pp. D1, D5.

22. "Fuji and Aces Form U.S. Joint Venture," *Automotive Industry* (June 1986), pp. 25, 32.

23. "Ford Will Join Nissan to Build a Mini Van," *New York Times* (13 September 1988), p. D5.

24. However, when utility vehicles, vans, and other four-wheeled vehicles are included, Chrysler remains ahead of Honda.

25. "Toyota Plans Engine Plant in Kentucky," *Wall Street Journal* (6 November 1987), p. 4; "Toyota to Build Plant in U.S., Reflecting Gains," *Wall Street Journal* (10 September 1990), p. A3.

26. *Wall Street Journal* (6 January 1989).

27. "Nissan Plans to Spend Up to $600 Million on U.S. Engine Plant," *Wall Street Jour-*

nal (21 January 1990); "Nissan Is Expanding Plant in Tennessee," *Wall Street Journal* (29 January 1990).

28. "Mitsubishi-Chrysler Consider Plans to Build Engines for DSM in US," *Metalworking News* (13 November 1989).

29. See *Columbus Dispatch* (25 May 1988); *Ward's Auto World* (January 1988), pp. 29–36.

30. "Mitsubishi-Chrysler Agree on Canadian Joint Venture," *Dow Jones On-Line News Service* (27 November 1990).

31. See Andrew Mair, Richard Florida, and Martin Kenney, "The New Geography of Automobile Production: Japanese Transplants in North America," *Economic Geography* 64, no. 4 (October), pp. 352–73. Also see Michael Storper and Richard Walker, *The Capitalist Imperative* (London: Basil Blackwell, 1989), for a general discussion of the factors that shape the location decisions of capitalist enterprises.

32. Kentucky city planner; personal interview by Richard Florida and the Ritsumeikan University Automotive Research Group (August 1990).

33. Honda of America Manufacturing Company executive; personal interview by authors (June 1988).

34. Data are from *City and County Databook* (1983).

35. Local officials in Georgetown, Kentucky. personal interviews by Richard Florida and the Ritsumeikan University Automotive Research Group (August 1990).

36. Gail Newman; personal interview by Richard Florida and the Ritsumeikan University Automotive Research Group (August 1990).

37. See Robert Cole, "Reflections on Japanese Corporate Citizenship: Company Reactions to a Study of Hiring Practices in the United States," *Chuo Koron,* 10 (October 1989), pp. 122–35.

38. Data are from *City and County Databook* (1983).

39. See Cole, "Reflections on Japanese Corporate Citizenship."

40. NUMMI worker, personal interview by Katsuji Tsuji, James Gordon, and Shoko Tanaka (August 1990).

41. Honda of America Manufacturing executives, personal interviews by authors (June 1988); Toyota, Nissan, Mazda, NUMMI, and SIA officials and workers, personal interviews by Richard Florida and the Ritsumeikan University Automotive Research Group (July-November 1990).

42. Honda of America Manufacturing executives, personal interviews by authors (June 1988); Toyota, Nissan, Mazda, NUMMI, and SIA officials and workers, personal interviews by Richard Florida and Ritsumeikan University Automotive Research Group (July-November 1990).

43. Honda of America Manufacturing executives, personal interviews by authors (June 1988); Honda worker, personal interview by Richard Florida (July 1990); NUMMI officials and workers, personal interviews by Richard Florida and Ritsumeikan University Automotive Research Group (July 1990).

44. NUMMI worker, personal interview by Ritsumeikan University Automotive Research Group (July 1990).

45. Nissan and SIA executives and Mazda workers, personal interviews by Richard Florida and Ritsumeikan University Automotive Research Group (July-November 1990).

46. James Harpool, management associate, Compensation and Benefits, SIA, personal interview by Richard Florida (November 1990).

47. Mazda workers, personal interviews by Richard Florida and Ritsumeikan University Automotive Research Group (August 1990).

48. Honda of America Manufacturing executives, personal interviews by authors (June 1988).

49. Japanese manufacturing automotive assembly transplant, manager, personal interview by Ritsumeikan University Automotive Research Group (August 1991).

50. For a recent discussion see William Lazonick, *Competitive Advantage on the Shopfloor* (Cambridge, MA: Harvard University Press, 1990).

51. See Thomas Kochan, Harry Katz, and Robert McKersie, *The Transformation of American Industrial Relations* (New York: Basic Books, 1986).

52. Smith and Childs, "Imported from America: Cooperative Labor Relations at New United Motor Manufacturing, Inc.," p. 71.

53. Site visits and personal interviews (1987–90).

54. For an enlightening discussion of the difficulties and contradictions inherent in the foreman's role in the Fordist firm, see Lazonick, *Competitive Advantage,* especially pp. 277–80.

55. Site visit by Richard Florida (August 1990).

56. James Lincoln, Mitsuyo Hanada, and Kerry McBride, "Organizational Structures in Japanese and U.S. Manufacturing," *Administrative Science Quarterly* 31 (1986), pp. 338–64. This result seems counter-intuitive and may be because most levels of American management are not located in the plant at all, whereas Japanese corporate headquarters are far smaller in relation to the firm. A potential explanation may be that Lincoln and his colleagues use establishment-level data to study what properly is a company-level phenomenon.

57. Honda of America Manufacturing managers, personal communication with Martin Kenney (June 1990).

58. Toyota managers, personal interviews with Richard Florida (August 1990).

59. Richard Florida and Martin Kenney, *The Breakthrough Illusion: Corporate America's Failure to Move from Innovation to Mass Production* (New York: Basic Books, 1990).

60. We are indebted to Akio Kida for this conceptualization.

61. SIA, human resources manager, personal interview by Richard Florida (November 1990).

62. Honda of America Manufacturing executives, personal interviews by authors (June 1988); Toyota officials, Georgetown, Kentucky, plant, personal interviews by Richard Florida and the Ritsumeikan University Automotive Research Group (August 1990).

63. Site visit to Toyota's Georgetown plant, by Richard Florida and the Ritsumeikan University Automotive Research Group (August 1990).

64. Toyota Motor Manufacturing USA, *Team Member Handbook,* 1st ed. (February 1988).

65. Honda of America Manufacturing executives, personal interviews by authors (June 1988); site visits and personal interview with executives at Toyota's Georgetown plant, by Richard Florida and the Ritsumeikan University Automotive Research Group (August 1990).

66. Japanese executive, Nissan America, personal interview by Richard Florida and the Ritsumeikan University Automotive Research Group (August 1990).

67. Mazda workers and union officials, personal interviews by Richard Florida and the Ritsumeikan University Automotive Research Group (July 1990). Interestingly, even the boycott provides information to management, thus demanding improvement on their part.

68. SIA executives, personal interviews by Richard Florida and Akio Kida, (November 1990).

69. Robert Cole, *Strategies for Learning* (Berkeley: University of California Press, 1989); Paul Lillrank and Noriaki Kano, *Continuous Improvement: Quality Control Circles in Japanese Industry* (Ann Arbor,: Center for Japanese Studies, The University of Michigan, 1989).

70. Lincoln et al., "Organizational Structures," p. 354.

71. Honda of America Manufacturing executives, personal interviews by authors (June

1988); Toyota executives, personal interview by Richard Florida and the Ritsumeikan University Automotive Research Group (August 1990).

72. Personal interviews with management officials and workers (1988–90).

73. American manager, SIA, personal interview by Richard Florida (November 1990).

74. Cole, *Strategies for Learning,* pp. 111–12.

75. Honda of America Manufacturing, personal interviews by authors (June 1988).

76. Japanese production manager, Toyota's Georgetown plant, personal interview by Richard Florida and the Ritsumeikan University Automotive Research Group (August 1990).

77. Site visits and personal interviews with executives and/or workers at the Mazda and Nissan plants, by Richard Florida and the Ritsumeikan University Automotive Research Group (July-August 1990).

78. American and Japanese Managers, SIA, personal interviews, by Richard Florida and Akio Kida (November 1990).

79. American human resources manager, personal interview by Richard Florida and Akio Kida (November 1990).

80. Local school officials, Scott County, Kentucky, and Toyota executives, personal interviews by Richard Florida and the Ritsumeikan University Automotive Research Group (August 1990).

81. For an excellent discussion of this process in a very different historical context see E.P. Thompson, *The Making of the English Working Class* (New York: Vintage, 1966).

82. Rohlen's findings provide powerful support for the view that such practices were the product of organizational design and management strategy rather than an offshoot of Japanese culture. See Thomas Rohlen, *For Harmony and Strength: Japanese White-Collar Organization in Anthropological Perspective* (Berkeley: University of California Press, 1974).

83. NUMMI worker, personal interview by Katsuji Tsuji, James Gordon, and Shoko Tanaka (August 1990).

84. NUMMI, SIA, and Mazda workers, personal interviews by Richard Florida and Ritsumeikan University Automotive Research Group (August-November 1990).

85. Julie Corcoran, a worker who oversees the testing and repair, or "pre-delivery," department at Nissan's Smyrna plant, as quoted in "How the Japanese Run U.S. Subsidiaries," p. 33.

86. This is different from the recruitment policies of Japanese corporations in Japan, but serves a similar function. See James Rosenbaum and Takehiko Kariya, "From High School to Work: Market and Institutional Mechanisms in Japan," *American Journal of Sociology* 94 (1989), pp. 1334–65.

87. Honda of America Manufacturing executives, personal interviews by authors (May 1988); Nissan, Toyota, and SIA managers, and Mazda, Honda, and NUMMI workers, personal interviews by Richard Florida and Ritsumeikan University Automotive Research Group (August-November 1990).

88. James Carpenter, Nissan's director of personnel administration, as quoted in Bruce Vernyi, "Stringent Screening, Training by Nissan," *American Metal Market* (6 June 1983), p. 8.

89. American manager, SIA, personal interview by Richard Florida (November 1990).

90. Honda officials (May 1988), Toyota, Nissan, and SIA officials (August-November 1990) personal interviews.

91. American manager, SIA, personal interview by Richard Florida (November 1990).

92. SIA training group officials, SIA training center, personal interview by Richard Florida and Akio Kida (November 1990).

93. Michael Burawoy, *Manufacturing Consent* (Chicago: University of Chicago, 1979).

94. Wage data are from Kathy Jackson, "Transplant Wages Will Rise to Match Any Gains at Big 3,"*Automotive News,* (2 July, 1990), p. 61.

95. NUMMI worker, personal interview by James Gordon, Shoko Tanaka, and the Ritsumeikan University Automotive Research Group (July 1990).

96. Honda of America Manufacturing executives, personal interviews by authors (May 1988); Toyota, Nissan, and SIA managers, personal interview by Richard Florida and the Ritsumeikan University Automotive Research Group (August-November 1990).

97. American manager, SIA, personal interview by Richard Florida and Akio Kida (November 1990).

98. Melinda Guiles and Krystal Miller, "Mazda and Mitsubishi-Chrysler Venture Cut Output, Following Big Three's Lead," *Wall Street Journal* (12 January 1990), pp. A2, A12.

99. American and Japanese executives at Nissan, personal interviews by Richard Florida and the Ritsumeikan University Automotive Research Group (August 1990).

100. *Nissan Employee Handbook* (revised April 1986).

101. See Solomon Levine, *Industrial Relations in Postwar Japan* (Urbana: University of Illinois Press, 1958).

102. *Newsweek* (31 March 1986).

103. See presentation of Joel Smith in Smith and Childs, "Imported from America: Cooperative Labor Relations at New United Motor Manufacturing, Inc.," p. 71.

104. See Krafcik, "Learning from NUMMI.

105. *Agreement Between NUMMI and the UAW* (July 1 1988), section 14, p. 23.

106. As reported in the *Wall Street Journal* (15 March 1988).

107. *Ward's Auto World* (July 1987).

108. *Collective Bargaining Agreement Between Mazda Motor Manufacturing (USA) Corporation and the UAW* (7 March 1988).

109. See Joseph Fucini and Suzy Fucini, *Working for the Japanese: Inside Mazda's American Auto Plant* (New York: Free Press, 1990).

110. The literature here is enormous. See, for example, Fucini and Fucini, *Working for the Japanese: Inside Mazda's American Auto Plant* (New York: Free Press, 1990). Koji Taira, "The Characteristics of Japanese Labor Markets," *Economic Development and Cultural Change* (January 1962), pp. 150–68; Ronald Dore, *British Factory, Japanese Factory* (Berkeley: University of California Press, 1973); and Robert Cole, *Work, Mobility and Participation* (Berkeley: University of California Press, 1979).

111. NUMMI, Mazda, and Diamond-Star labor-management contracts, various dates.

112. *Agreement Between NUMMI and the UAW* (1988 July 1), section 3, p. 4. The Mazda contract has a similar provision, which reads: "the Company recognizes its basic responsibility, both to its employees and the communities in which it operates, to provide stable and secure employment to the fullest extent possible. For all of these reasons, MMUC agrees that it will not lay off employees unless compelled to do so by economic conditions and financial circumstances so severe that its long-term financial viability is threatened. Even then, the Company will take affirmative measures before instituting any layoffs, including but not limited to such action as: the reduction of salaries of its officers and management and other jointly determined cost-cutting measures; in-sourcing work previously contracted out; the utilization of bargaining unit employees in training programs, quality and customer satisfaction terms; and other non-traditional work assignments. Should layoffs ever be unavoidable, a jointly developed, mutually satisfactory program will be implemented that provides layoffs will be in accordance with seniority and provides the opportunity for voluntary layoffs. *Collective Bargaining Agreement Between Mazda Motor Manufacturing (USA) Corporation and the UAW* (7 March 1988), Article 7, p. 11.

113. Honda of America Manufacturing executives, personal interviews by author (May

1988); Nissan, Toyota, and SIA managers, personal interviews by Richard Florida and the Ritsumeikan University Automotive Research Group (August-November 1990).

114. NUMMI workers, personal interviews by Ritsumeikan University Automotive Research Group (July 1990).

115. NUMMI worker, personal interview by Ritsumeikan University Automotive Research Group (July 1990).

116. NUMMI worker, personal interview by Ritsumeikan University Automotive Research Group (July 1990).

117. NUMMI worker, personal interview by Ritsumeikan University Automotive Research Group (July 1990).

118. Alex Barnum, "Dissidents Win Top Union Posts in NUMMI Vote," *San Jose Mercury News* (7 June 1991), pp. 12D, 19D.

119. Fucini and Fucini, *Working for the Japanese: Inside Mazda's American Auto Plant.*

120. Mazda workers and union officials, personal interviews by Richard Florida and Ritsumeikan University Automotive Research Group (July 1990).

121. Joseph Kieltyka, manager of Nissan's trim and chassis plant, former Ford Motor Co. manager as quoted in Marilyn Wilson and Lynn Adkins, "How the Japanese Run U.S. Subsidiaries," *Dun's Business Month* (October 1983), p. 33.

122. Honda of America Manufacturing executives, personal interviews by authors (May 1988).

123. Michael White and Malcolm Trevor, *Under Japanese Management* (London: Heinemann Educational Books, 1983).

124. NUMMI worker, personal interview by Ritsumeikan University Automotive Research Group (July 1990).

125. NUMMI worker, personal interview by Katsuji Tsuji, James Gordon, and Shoko Tanaka (August 1990).

126. Honda of America Manufacturing, personal interviews by authors (May 1988); Nissan and Toyota managers, personal interviews by Richard Florida and Ritsumeikan University Automotive Research Group (August 1990).

127. *New Directions* (February 1990).

128. See Harley Shaiken, "High-Tech Goes to the Third World," *Technology Review* (January 1988), pp. 39–47; Shaiken and Stephen Herzenberg, *Automation and Global Production: Automobile Engine Production in Mexico, the United States and Canada* (San Diego: University of California, Center for Mexican Studies, 1987).

129. "Smaller Giant: Huge GM Write-off Positions Auto Maker to Show New Growth," *Wall Street Journal* (1 November 1990), p. 1.

130. See Bradley Stertz and Jacqueline Mitchell, "Automakers Hobble into the New Year with Little Hope for a Robust Recovery," *Wall Street Journal* (7 January 1992), pp. B1, B4; Joseph White and Bradley Stertz, "GM's Debt is Downgraded by Moody's," *Wall Street Journal* (8 January 1992), pp. A2, A12.

131. "Ford, Chrysler, GM to Temporarily Shut 21 Assembly Plants," *Wall Street Journal* (8 February 1991), p. B5.

132. "Big Three U.S. Car Output to Sink to a 33-Year Low," *Wall Street Journal* (11 April 1991); "Big Three Car Makers to Curtail Production at Eight More Plants," *Wall Street Journal* (12 April 1991), p. B3.

133. Clay Chandler and Bradley Stertz, "Mitsubishi Buys Chrysler's 50% Stake in Their Diamond-Star Joint Venture," *Wall Street Journal* (30 October 1991).

134. As quoted in John Judis, "Myth vs Man," *Business Month* (July 1990), p. 31.

135. "Chrysler Drive for Limits on Japanese Car Sales Shifts into High Gear," *JEI Report,* no. 13B, (5 April 1991), pp. 8, 9.

136. "U.S. Won't Move to Protect Car Makers From Japanese Competition, Officials Say," *Wall Street Journal* (26 March 1991); Bradley Stertz, "Chrysler's Iacocca Calls for Limitation on Japanese Share of U.S. Auto Market," *Wall Street Journal* (26 October 1991); Christopher Chipello and Clay Chandler, "U.S. Executives Will Seek Protectionist Measures if the Deficit Isn't Cut," *Wall Street Journal* (8 January 1992), p. A2.

137. Neal Templin, "Production Problems Hobbling Introduction of GM'S Saturn Cars," *Wall Street Journal* (4 December 1990).

138. "Big Three Automakers Face Long, Hard Road," *Dow Jones On-Line Business News Service* (14 January 1991).

139. See Thomas Kochan and Joel Cutcher-Gershenfeld, "Institutionalizing and Diffusing Innovation in Industrial Relations," (Washington, DC: U.S. Department of Labor, Bureau of Labor-Management Relations and Cooperative Programs, 1988).

140. NUMMI worker, personal interview by Katsuji Tsuji, James Gordon, and Shoko Tanaka (August 1990).

141. As quoted in Judis, "Myth vs. Man," p. 32.

142. "Chrysler to Cut Board; UAW Chief Is Out," *New York Times* (14 March 1991), pp. C1, C4.

143. Lindsay Chappell, "The Japanese-American Car," *Automotive News* (26 November 1990), pp. 1, 42, 43.

144. Roger Lowe, "Deal 18 Months in the Making," *Columbus Dispatch* (18 September 1987), p. H1.

145. Chappell, "The Japanese-American Car," p. 43.

146. Edward Miller and Drew Winter, "The 'Other Big 3' Are Becoming All-American," *Automotive News* (February 1991), p. 28.

147. Alex Taylor, "Why Toyota Keeps Getting Better and Better," *Fortune* (19 November 1990), p. 79.

148. Miller and Winter, "The 'Other Big 3' Are Becoming All-American," p. 28.

149. It is curious that no one has ever reflected upon the fact that Japanese automotive investment in the United States obviously began with import and distribution facilities but very rapidly developed its design capabilities to meet the needs of the U.S. market. Thus, the history of the Japanese transplants begins far earlier than most commentators believe.

150. Chappell, "The Japanese-American Car," p. 43.

151. Ibid., p. A1.

152. Ibid., pp 1, 42, 43. In large part the "screwdriver" hypothesis was asserted by scholars who did not understand the logic of the Japanese system, which is predicated upon ensuring tight linkages between R&D and manufacturing. For further discussions see Florida and Kenney, *The Breakthrough Illusion* (1990).

153. Transplant production data for 1990 and 1993 projection are from Long Term Credit Bank, *Long Term Credit Bank Research Review* No. 2 (November 1991), p. 26; Japanese market share as calculated from annual U.S. car market data in the *Wall Street Journal* (7 January 991), p. B4.

154. Maryann Keller, as quoted in *Fortune* (12 March 1990), p. 36.

155. *Ward's Auto World* (January 1988); personal interview, Nissan Trading Company official (January 1989).

156. "Toyota to Ship Cars from U.S. to Taiwan, *Asian Wall Street Journal* (22 December 1988).

157. "U.S. Backs Japan in Europe Auto Debate," *New York Times* (23 February 1990), pp. C1, C5. On the Accord station wagon see E. Browning, "Request to Import U.S.-Made Hondas Creates New Trade Dilemma for France," *Wall Street Journal* (June 25, 1991) p. A15.

158. John Krafcik, "A New Diet for U.S. Manufacturers." *Technology Review,* 92, no.

1 (January 1989), pp. 28–38; James Womack, Daniel Jones, and Daniel Roos, *The Machine That Changed the World* (New York: Rawson Associates, 1990).

159. Womack, Jones, and Roos, *Machine That Changed the World,* p. 92.

160. J.D. Power Initial Quality Survey, 1989.

161. See Mike Parker and Jane Slaughter, "Management by Stress," *Technology Review* (October 1988), pp. 36–45; and Knuth Dohse, Ulrich Jurgens, and Thomas Malsch, "From 'Fordism' to 'Toyotism'? The Social Organization of the Labor Process in the Japanese Automobile Industry," *Politics and Society* 14 no. 2 (1985), pp. 115–46.

162. NUMMI and Mazda workers, personal interviews by Richard Florida and the Ritsumeikan University Automotive Research Group (August 1990).

163. Former Honda engineer, personal interview with Richard Florida (August 1990).

164. For a full exposition of our position see the series of issues of the Japanese journal *Mado,* which carried the international debate over our article, "Beyond Mass Production," with articles and comments by Alain Lipietz, Stephen Wood, Benjamin Coriat, Tetsuro Kato, Makoto Itoh, and many others. See *Mado,* nos. 1–5 (1989–90).

Chapter 5

1. As quoted in Steve Lohr, "Nissan Uses Japan's Ways in Tennessee, *New York Times* (4 April 1983), p. D1.

2. See Alfred D. Chandler, *Strategy and Structure* (Cambridge, MA: MIT Press 1962); Chandler, *The Visible Hand* (Cambridge, MA: Harvard University Press 1977); Oliver Williamson, *Markets and Hierarchies*(New York: Free Press, 1981); and "Organizational Innovation: The Transaction Cost Approach," in Joshua Ronen (ed.), *Entrepreneurship* (Lexington, MA: Lexington Books, 1983), pp. 101–33.

3. Mark Granovetter, "Economic Action and Social Structure: The Problem of Embeddedness," *American Journal of Sociology* 91, no. 3 (November 1985), pp. 481–510; Charles Perrow, "Economic Theories of Organization," *Theory and Society* 15 (1986), pp. 11–45; and idem., "Small Firm Networks," paper presented to the Conference on Networks, Harvard University (August 1990); Walter Powell, "Hybrid Organizational Arrangements: New Form or Transitional Development," *California Management Review* (Fall 1987), pp. 47–87; James Robins, "Organizational Networks: Notes on the Use of Transaction Cost Theory in the Study of Organizations," *Administrative Science Quarterly* 32 (March 1987), pp. 68–86.

4. See Masahiko Aoki, *Information, Incentives and Bargaining in the Japanese Economy* (Cambridge: Cambridge University Press, 1988).

5. See Andrew Sayer, "New Developments in Manufacturing: The Just-in-Time System," *Capital and Class* 30 (1986), pp. 43–72; Mari Sako, "Neither Markets nor Hierarchies: A Comparative Study of the Printed Circuit Board Industry in Britain and Japan" (London: London School of Economics, unpublished paper, 1989); Toshihiro Nishiguchi, "Competing Systems of Automotive Components Supply: An Examination of the Japanese Clustered Control Model and the Alps Structure" (Cambridge, MA: MIT International Motor Vehicle Program, unpublished paper, 1987; Richard Florida and Martin Kenney, "High Technology Restructuring in the USA and Japan," *Environment and Planning* V22, pp. 233–252 (1990); Andrew Mair, Richard Florida, and Martin Kenney, "The New Geography of Automobile Production: Japanese Transplants in North America," *Economic Geography* 64, 4 (March 1988), pp. 352–73.

6. Proprietor and machinist, site visit and personal interview by authors (July 1988).

7. Executive vice president, Honda of America Manufacturing, personal interview by authors (May 1988).

8. *Ward's Auto World* (July 1987; January 1988).

9. Japanese executives, Honda parts supplier, personal interview by authors (July 1988).

10. David Sanger, "U.S. Suppliers Get a Toyota Lecture," *New York Times* (1 November 1990).

11. Osamu Nobuto, president of Mazda Motor Manufacturing (USA); in *Automotive Industries* (July 1988), special advertising supplement.

12. Darrell Shown, Honda, purchasing manager, as quoted in *Automotive Industries* (July 1985), p. 29.

13. Nippondenso technician, personal interview by Richard Florida and Akio Kida (November 1990).

14. *Ward's Auto World* (July 1987).

15. Japanese manager, KTH Parts Inc., personal interview by authors (July 1988). For a more general discussion see K. Ishiro, "Internationalization in Japan's Auto Parts Industry," *Digest of Japanese Industry and Technology* 221 (1986), pp. 24–42; Brian Berry,"Honda Goes American," *Iron Age* (16 May 1987).

16. As quoted in John Sheridan, "Suppliers: Partners in Prosperity," *Industry Week* (19 March 1990), p. 12.

17. Mitsubishi Research Institute, *The Relationship Between Japanese Auto and Auto Parts Makers* (Tokyo: Japanese Automobile Manufacturers Association, Inc., 1987).

18. Alan Altshuler et al., *The Future of the Automobile* (Cambridge, MA: MIT Press, 1984); U.S. International Trade Commission, *U.S. Global Competitiveness: The U.S. Automotive Parts Industry* (Washington, DC: U.S. International Trade Commission, 1987); and Amy Glasmeier and Richard McCluskey. "U.S. Auto Parts Production: An Analysis of the Organization and Location of a Changing Industry," *Economic Geography* 63 (1987), pp. 142–59.

19. See Ronald Dore, "Goodwill and the Spirit of Market Capitalism," *British Journal of Sociology* 34 (1983), pp. 459–82: Dore, *Taking Japan Seriously* (Stanford CA: Stanford University Press, 1987); and Dore, *Flexible Rigidities* (Stanford: Stanford University Press, 1986).

20. Banri Asanuma, "The Organization of Parts Purchases in the Japanese Automotive Industry," *Japanese Economic Studies* (Summer 1985), pp. 32–53; and Asanuma, "The Contractual Framework for Parts Supply in the Japanese Automobile Industry," *Japanese Economic Studies* (Summer 1985), pp. 54–78; Konosuke Odaka, Keinosuke Ono, and Fumihiko Adachi, *The Automobile Industry in Japan: A Study of Ancillary Firm Development* (Tokyo: Oxford University Press, Kinokuniya Company, 1988).

21. See Sayer, "New Developments in Manufacturing: The Just-in-Time System." Paul Sheard, "Auto Production Systems in Japan: Organizational and Locational Features," *Australian Geographical Studies* 21 (April 1983), pp. 49–68; Toshiro Nishiguchi, "Competing Systems of Automotive Components Supply: An Examination of the Japanese 'Clustered Control' Model and the 'Alps' Structure" (Cambridge, MA: MIT International Motor Vehicle Program, unpublished paper, 1987); and Mari Sako, "Neither Markets nor Hierarchies: A Comparative Study of the Printed Circuit Board Industry in Britain and Japan"; "Competitive Cooperation: How the Japanese Manage Inter-firm Relations" (London: London School of Economics, unpublished manuscript, 1989); "Partnership Between Large and Small Firms: The Case of Japan," in Directorate for Enterprise of the Commission of the European Economic Communities, *Partnership Between Large and Small Firms* (London: Graham and Trotman, 1988), pp. 66–79.

22. See Florida and Kenney, "High Technology Restructuring in the USA and Japan."

23. Toyo Keizai Shimposha, *Japan Company Handbook* (Tokyo: Toyo Keizai Shimposha 1988), pp. 697, 699.

24. Dodwell Marketing Consultants, *The Structure of the Japanese Auto Parts Industry* (Tokyo: Dodwell Marketing Consultants, 1986).

25. Granovetter, "Economic Action and Social Structure: The Problem of Embeddedness."

26. See Michael Aiken and Gerald Hage, "Organizational Interdependence and Intraorganizational Structure," *American Sociological Review* 33 (December 1968), pp. 912–30; and Paul DiMaggio and Walter Powell, "The Iron Cage Revisited: Institutional Isomorphism and Collective Rationality in Organizational Fields," *American Sociological Review* 48 (April 1983), pp. 147–60.

27. See Ronald Dore, "Goodwill and the Spirit of Market Capitalism," *British Journal of Sociology* 34 (1983), pp. 459–82.

28. Mair, Florida, and Kenney, "The New Geography of Automobile Production: Japanese Transplants in North America."

29. Various transplant suppliers, personal interviews with authors (1988–90).

30. Stan Tooley, vice president, Human Resources and Administration, Nippondenso Manufacturing USA, personal interview by Richard Florida and Akio Kida (November 1990).

31. See Richard Florida and Martin Kenney, *The Breakthrough Illusion: Corporate America's Failure to Move from Innovation to Mass Production* (New York: Basic Books, 1990).

32. Stan Tooley, Nippondenso, personal interview by Richard Florida and Akio Kida (November 1990).

33. Various transplant suppliers, site visits, and personal interviews by authors (1987–90).

34. Nippondenso manager, personal interview by Richard Florida and Akio Kida (November 1990).

35. Stan Tooley, Nippondenso, personal interview by Richard Florida and Akio Kida (November 1990).

36. Ibid.

37. Robert Cole, "Issues in Skill Formation and Training in Japanese Manufacturing Approaches to Automation," in Paul Adler (ed.), *Technology and the Future of Work* (London: Oxford University Press, 1992).

38. See Cusumano, *The Japanese Automobile Industry: Technology and Management at Nissan and Toyota.*

39. Responses to transplant supplier survey, by authors (June 1988).

40. Nippondenso executive, personal interview by Richard Florida and Akio Kida (November 1990).

41. Various transplant suppliers, personal interviuews by authors (1988–90).

42. Lindsay Chappell, "UAW Loses 3rd Attempt to Organize," *Automotive News* (28 January 1991), p. 43.

43. See "Lean, Mean and Through Your Windscreen," *The Economist* (23 February 1991), pp. 68–70.

44. Japanese purchasing manager, SIA, personal interview by Richard Florida (November 1990).

45. Ibid.

46. This is in keeping with the Japanese supplier system; see Aoki, *Information Incentives and Bargaining in the Japanese Economy.*

47. Japanese purchasing manager, SIA, personal interview by Richard Florida (November 1990).

48. Name withheld, personal interview by Richard Florida (July 1990).

49. Darrell Shown, purchasing manager, Honda of America, as quoted in *Automotive Industries* (July 1985), p. 29.

50. See Kim Clark and Takahiro Fujimoto, *Product Development Performance* (Boston: Harvard Business School Press, 1990).

51. Harry Lund, vice president, marketing, The Fabri-Form Company, personal communication with Martin Kenney (September 1988).

52. American purchasing official, transplant assembler, personal interview by Richard Florida (November 1990).

53. Japanese and U.S. managers, AP Technoglass, personal interviews by authors (July 1988).

54. Various personal interviews with Honda and Honda suppliers by authors (1987–88).

55. Glasmeier and McCluskey, "U.S. Auto Parts Production."

56. Robert Kraushaar, State of New York, Department of Development, personal communication with Richard Florida (October 1989).

57. See Glasmeier and McCluskey, "U.S. Auto Parts Production;" U.S. International Trade Commission (1987), pp. 4–27.

58. Data are from the U.S. Census of Manufacturers (SIC 3714, Motor Vehicle Parts and Accessories) for various years.

59. See Richard Florida and Martin Kenney, "Transplanted Organizations: The Transfer of Japanese Industrial Organization to the U.S., *American Sociology Review* 56 (June 1991).

60. Dodwell Marketing Consultants, *The Structure of the Japanese Auto Parts Industry* (Tokyo: Dodwell Marketing Consultants, 1986).

61. KTH Parts Industries Inc., executives, personal interviews by authors (July 1988).

62. See Toshihiro Nishiguchi, "New Trends in American Auto Companies Supply: Is Good Management Always Culturally Bound?" (Cambridge, MA: MIT International Motor Vehicle Program, September 1987).

63. Dave Nelson, vice president of purchasing, Honda of America, former TRW Inc. executive, as quoted in John Sheridan, "Suppliers: Partners in Prosperity," *Industry Week* (19 March 1990), p. 18.

64. Dave Nelson as quoted in Ibid., p. 18.

65. Dana Milbank, "Making Honda Parts, Ohio Company Finds, Can Be Road to Ruin," *Wall Street Journal* (5 October 1990).

66. Rich Nordstrom, a former top executive with Joseph T. Ryerson & Son Inc., Chicago, now an independent consultant, in Andy Collier, "Japanese Auto Interests Stir Midwest,"*Metalworking News* (18 May 1987), p. 14a.

67. Milbank, "Making Honda Parts, Ohio Company Finds, Can Be Road to Ruin."

68. Kim Miller, *Variety*'s former production-coptrol manager, as quoted in Ibid.

69. Scott Whitlock, Executive Vice President, Honda of America, "Memo to Frontline Station Managers" (18 November 1991).

70. Personal communication with David Prizinsky, *Crain's Business Journal* (December 1991). Prizinsky adds that because the claims were rather small, the judge would almost certainly have allowed Variety to continue operating had the company's president appeared at the bankruptcy hearing.

71. See Jean Halliday, "Transplant Supplier Scores Legal Victory," *Automotive News* (18 March 1991), p. 36.

72. As quoted in Al Senia, "Japanese Automaking Lands in America: What It Means to U.S. Suppliers," *Production* (November 1986), p. 48.

73. Owen Bieber, president of UAW, letter to *Newsweek* (5 April 1990).

74. As quoted in Marjorie Sorge, "UAW Angry About Supplier Union-Busting," *Ward's Auto World* (July 1990), pp. 58–59.

75. As quoted in Jon Lowell, "Raising the Stakes in America: Japanese Plants Deal Suppliers a New Hand," *Ward's Auto World* (July 1986), p. 73.

76. Stephen E. Plumb, "Suppliers' Joint Ventures," *Ward's Auto World* (July 1990), p. 30.

77. Susan Helper, "Changing Supplier Relationships in the U.S.: Results of Survey Research" (Cambridge, MA: MIT International Motor Vehicle Project, 1989).

78. Authors' calculations on the basis of an advertisement listing Mazda suppliers. See "Mazda: $1 Billion to Suppliers," *Automotive News* (23 October 1989), p. E29.

79. Edward Drew Miller and Drew Winter, "The 'Other Big 3' Are Becoming All-American," *Ward's Auto World* (February 1991), pp. 24–49.

80. Japanese and American purchasing officials, transplant assembler, personal interview by Richard Florida (November 1990).

81. Japanese purchasing manager, transplant assembler, personal interview by Richard Florida (November 1990).

82. See Sheridan, "Suppliers: Partners in Prosperity," pp. 18, 19.

83. Robert Frinier, Nissan vice president of purchasing and information systems, "Nissan," *Automotive Industries* (July 1985).

84. See Lindsay Chappell, "Increased Capacity and Flexible Production Schedules Are Built into the Design of the Plant," *Automotive News* (7 August 1989), p. 53.

85. John Krafcik, "Learning from NUMMI " (Cambridge, MA: MIT International Motor Vehicle Program, unpublished manuscript, 1986).

86. As reported in *Dow Jones On-Line News Service* (20 April 1990).

87. David Sanger, "U.S. Suppliers Get a Toyota Lecture," *New York Times* (1 November 1990).

88. Nippondenso technician and member of the localization group, personal interview by Richard Florida and Akio Kida (November 1990).

89. Toyota executives and BAMA members, personal interview by Richard Florida and the Ritsumeikan University Automotive Research Group (August 1990).

90. Stephen E. Plumb, "Suppliers Joint Ventures," *Ward's Auto World* (July 1990), p. 30.

91. Susan Helper, "Changing Supplier Relationships in the U.S.: Results of Survey Research" (Cambridge, MA: MIT International Motor Vehicle Project, 1989).

92. See Michael Flynn and Robert Cole, "Automotive Suppliers: Customer Relationships, Technology and Global Competition," in Peter Arnesen (ed.), *Is There Enough Business to Go Around?:Overcapacity in the Auto Industry* (Ann Arbor: University of Michigan Center for Japanese Studies, 1988); David Smith, "Whatever Happened to Teamwork?" *Ward's Auto World* (June 1989) pp. 35–63.

93. Ibid.

Chapter 6

1. Both quotes are by George Landsly, assistant to the President, I/N Tek, personal interview by Richard Florida (November 1990). I/N Tek is a joint venture of Inland Steel and Nippon Steel.

2. United States International Trade Commission, *U.S. Global Competitivness: The U.S. Automotive Parts Industry,* USITC Publication 2037 (Washington, DC: USITC, 1986).

3. Ibid., pp. 4–9.

4. Nippon Steel, *Annual Report, 1987*

5. NKK, *Annual Report* (1989), p. 4.

6. "National Intergroup Agrees to Sell Half of Steel Unit to Japan Firm at $292 Million," *Wall Street Journal* (25 April 1984), p. 3; "New Course Set at National," *American Metal Market* (31 May 1984), p. 1.

7. "NKK Balks at Carrying Full Weight of National," *American Metal Market* (5 Octo-

ber 1989), p. 1; "Control of National May Wind Up in New Hands," *American Metal Market* (4 September 1989), pp. 1, 16. National Steel executives, personal interview by Richard Florida (July 1990).

8. "Nippon Kokan Is in Talks to Purchase Rouge Steel," *Japan Economic Journal* (27 July 1982), p. 1; Leonard Lynn, "The Japanese Steel Industry Moves Into the United States." Paper presented at the American Association for the Advancement of Science (February 1987), pp. 13, 14.

9. "NKK, National Deal Benefits Seen on Both Sides of Pacific," *American Metal Market* (26 April 1984), pp. 1, 16, 24; "New Course Set at National." (31 May 1984), pp. 1, 8; "National Steel's Japanese Ally Nippon Kokan Keeps Close Watch" (30 November 1985), pp. 29–31; Brian Berry, "National Steel Puts Its 'Detroit' Strategy in Gear," *Iron Age* (July 1988), pp. 24–30.

10. "National NKK Eye Processing Venture in Detroit," *American Metal Market* (23 December 1986), pp. 1–16; "National Steel, Marubeni to Build Steel Plant Near Detroit," *American Metal Market* (11 May 1987), pp. 2, 16; "National, Marubeni Open Slit Steel Unit," *American Metal Market* (31 October 1988), pp. 2, 10; "National Steel and Marubeni Open Processing Center," *Iron and Steel Engineer* (June 1989), p. 56.

11. "Inland, Nippon Reported Near Mill Accord," *American Metal Market* (26 September 1985), pp. 1–7; "Nippon-Inland Deal Close to Settlement," *American Metal Market* (13 March 1987), pp. 1, 8; "Nippon-Inland Reported Eyeing Coating Unit," *American Metal Market* (22 June 1988), p. 3; "Inland OKs New Galvanizing Lines," *American Metal Market* (30 June 1989), pp. 2, 8; "Inland Steel Industries, Inc.," *Wall Street Journal* (7 June 1989), p. A26.

12. "Stock Sold by Inland to Nippon," *New York Times* (19 December 1989), p. D4; "Nippon Becomes Top Inland Shareholder," *American Metal Market* (20 December 1989), pp. 1, 16,.

13. Armco Steel executive, phone interview by Richard Florida (September 1989) Kawasaki steel executives, personal interviews by Richard Florida (September, October 1991). Also see "Kawasaki Steel to Buy Stake in Armco Unit," *Wall Street Journal* (22 November 1988), p. C27; "Armco and Kawasaki to Join in Running U.S. Steel Division," *Asian Wall Street Journal* (22 November 1988), p. 2; "Kawasaki Joins Armco Steel," *American Metal Market* (22 November 1988), pp. 1, 8.

14. "Kawasaki Ups Eastern Stake" *American Metal Market* (29 March 1989), pp. 1, 20.

15. For a description of Kaiser and the rise and decline of the West Coast steel industry, see Mike Davis, *City of Quartz* (London: Verso, 1991).

16. "Fontana Sets September Start Up," *American Metal Market* (17 April 1984), pp. 1–16; "Kawasaki's Addition Seen Aiding Pacific Kaiser Unit Reopening," *American Metal Market* (18 May 1984), pp. 2, 8; "California Steel Tie Gives Kawasaki Slab Outlet," *American Metal Market* (19 October 1984), pp. 1–8.

17. "LTV Steel Division Forms Partnership with Japanese Firm," *Wall Street Journal* (8 January 1985), p. 12; "Sumitomo, LTV Finally Reach Galvanizing Ties," *American Metal Market* (29 January 1985), pp. 1, 7; "L-S Formal Opening Set May 13," *American Metal Market* (1 May 1986), p. 3; "LTV, Sumitomo Plan Second Partnership," *American Metal Market* (12 May 1989), p. 2.

18. "Sumitomo Unit to Coordinate U.S. Operations," *American Metal Market* (15 March 1989), pp. 2. 12.

19. "Wheeling-Pittsburgh, Nisshin Joint Venture Is Expected To Roll Soon,"*American Metal Market* (22 January 1985), p. 3; "Wheeling-Pittsburgh Reaffirm Steel Coating Joint Venture," *American Metal Market* (4 November 1985), pp.25–28; "Nisshin Steel Increases Its Share in Wheeling-Pittsburgh Coating Line Venture" (31 December 1985), p. 3.

20. "Kobe to Buy 50% of USX Plant," *New York Times* (15 February 1989), p. 28; "Williams: USX Sold Lorain to Enhance Bar Marketing," *American Metal Market* (23 February 1989), p. 4; "Partnership Pact with Kobe to Buy Operation Is Signed," *Wall Street Journal* (1 June 1989), p. A20.

21. "Kobe Plans Joint Venture for U.S. Iron Powder Plant," *American Metal Market* (13 July 1987), pp. 1–8; "Kobe Steel to Begin Construction of Its 1st U.S. Powder Plant in '88," *American Metal Market* (17 September 1987), p. 12; "Japan's Kobe Steel Plans Steel Powder Plant in U.S.," *Automotive News* (27 July 1987), p. 16.

22. "Kobe Set to Acquire Midrex," *American Metal Market* (10 June 1983), pp. 1, 9.

23. "Nucor Picks Site in Arkansas for Wide-Flange Beam Mill" (11 February 1987), p. 7; George McManus, "Nucor-Yamato Gets on the Beam," *Iron Age* (October 1988), pp. 17–24; W.A. Tony, "Nucor-Yamato Kogyo Join Forces," *Iron and Steel Maker* (July 1987), pp. 15–16.

24. See Gordon Clark, "Corporate Restructuring in the Steel Industry: Adjustment Strategies and Local Labor Relations," in George Sternlieb and James Hughes (eds.), *America's New Market Geography.* (New Brunswick, NJ: Rutgers University, Center for Urban Policy Research, 1988), pp. 179–216.

25. Barry Bluestone and Bennett Harrison, *The Deindustrialization of America* (New York: Basic Books, 1982); Ann Markusen and Virginia Carlson, "Deindustrialization in the American Midwest: Causes and Responses," in Lloyd Rodwin and Hidehiko Sazanami (eds.), *Deindustrialization and Regional Economic Transformation: The Experience of the United States* (Boston: Unwin Hyman, 1989).

26. U.S. Census of Manufacturers, various years.

27. Donald Barnett and Robert Crandall, *Up from the Ashes: The Rise of the Steel Minimill in the United States* (Washington, DC: Brookings Institution, 1986).

28. For a discussion of Taylorism, see, for example, Daniel Nelson, *Frederick W. Taylor and the Rise of Scientific Management* (Madison: University of Wisconsin Press, 1980).

29. For two excellent discussions of the development of the Japanese steel industry see Leonard Lynn, *How Japan Innovates: A Comparison with the U.S. in the Case of Oxygen Steelmaking* (Boulder, CO: Westview Press, 1982), and Seiichiro Yonekura, *The Japanese Iron and Steel Industry: Continuity and Discontinuity, 1850–1970* (unpublished Ph.D. dissertation, Harvard University 1990).

30. For product cycle see Raymond Vernon, *Sovereignty at Bay: The Spread of U.S. Enterprises* (New York: Basic Books, 1971). For a discussion of an innovation cycle see William Abernathy, *The Productivity Dilemma: Roadblock to Innovation in the Automobile Industry* (Baltimore: Johns Hopkins University Press, 1978). For the implications of the product cycle on international politics, see James Kurth, "Political Consequences of the Product Cycle: Industrial History and Political Outcomes," *International Organization* 33 (Winter 1979), pp. 1–34. Finally, for the idea of "shifting versus deepening" see Henry Ergas, "Does Technology Policy Matter?" in R. Landau and N. Rosenberg (eds.), *The Positive Sum Strategy* (Washington, DC: National Academy Press, 1987).

31. See William T. Hogan, *Global Steel in the 1990s: Growth or Decline* (Lexington, MA: Lexington Books, 1991), especially pp. 37–51.

32. Ibid., p. 37.

33. As reported in *Asahi Shimbun* (23 November 1988).

34. American steel executive, personal interview by Richard Florida (1990).

35. See Leonard Lynn, "The Japanese Steel Industry Moves Into the United States." Paper presented to the American Association for the Advancement of Science (February 1987).

36. Hans Mueller, "Capital Productivity Differentials and Steel Trade." (Paper presented to the Steel Market Roundtable Conference, Pittsburgh, March 1991).

37. "Steel: Story of a Shortage" as cited in Paul Tiffany, *The Decline of American Steel: How Management, Labor and Government Went Wrong* (New York: Oxford University Press, 1988), p. 143.

38. See Mueller, "Capital Productivity." Also see MIT Commission on Industrial Productivity, Working Group on the Materials Industry, *The Future of the U.S. Steel Industry in the International Marketplace* (Cambridge, MA: MIT Press, 1989).

39. See Hogan, *Global Steel in the 1990s.*

40. MIT Commission on Industrial Productivity, Working Group on the Materials Industry, *The Future of the U.S. Steel Industry in the International Marketplace.*

41. "National Intergroup to Reduce Holding in Steel Firm with Sale to Nippon Kokan," *Wall Street Journal* (26 April 1990), p. A4.

42. American steel executives at USS, LTV, National, Wheeling-Pittsburgh, and Inland Steel, by Richard Florida (1990–91).

43. "U.S. Steel, Nat'l Merger Aborted," *American Metal Market* (12 March 1984), pp. 1, 18; "Nat'l Steel Future Appears Clouded," *American Metal Market* (14 March 1984), p. 3.

44. On the historical geography of the U.S. steel industry, see Kenneth Warren, *The American Steel Industry, 1850–1970: A Geographical Interpretation* (New York: Oxford University Press, 1973).

45. "Electroplated Steels Seen as Key to Japanese Auto Excellence," *American Metal Market* (27 January 1989), p. 40; "Galvanized Steels Shine Brighter in Detroit," *Iron Age* (July 1990), pp. 19–24.

46. Data from WEFA Group, "Steel Market Quarterly" (Second Quarter 1990).

47. American Steel executive, personal interview by Richard Florida (1990).

48. American Steel executive, personal interview by Richard Florida (1990).

49. "Japan Sees Bonanza in U.S. Market: Electro-galvanized Exports Nearly Doubled, Tech Transfers Underway," *American Metal Market* (21 December 1984), pp. 9, 15.

50. "L-S Electro-Galvanizing Gets Off to a Flying Start," *American Metal Market* (22 May 1986), p. 4.

51. "LTV-Sumitomo Plan Second Partnership," *American Metal Market* (12 May 1989), p. 2; "LTV, Sumitomo Plan Plant," *American Metal Market* (21 October 1988), pp. 1, 18.

52. "Second Electro-galvanizing Line 'Most Likely' Here," *Middletown Journal* (19 May 1989).

53. "USX, Kobe Steel to Form Venture for a New Plant," *Wall Street Journal* (20 October 1989), p. A5; "USX, Kobe Steel Plan Coated Sheet Output," *American Metal Market* (20 October 1989), p. 1, 8. "USS, Kobe to Build Plant in Ohio," *American Metal Market* (16 March 1990), pp.2, 8.

54. Wallace Huskonen, "Demand Galvanizes Capacity Expansion," *Metal Producing* (July 1990), pp. 30–32; *Appliance News* (November 1989), p. 20.

55. Former American steel company official, personal interview by Richard Florida (1990).

56. Ibid.

57. American steel executive, personal interview by Richard Florida (1990).

58. Howard Love, former chairman of National Intergroup, Inc., as quoted in "NII-NKK Deal Gives Stronger Auto Bent," *American Metal Market* (31 May 1984), p.8.,

59. Site visit to National Steel Great Lakes Works and personal interviews with Japanese and American executives, by Richard Florida (August 1991). Also see, Daniel F. Cuff,

"National Steel's Japanese Ally," *New York Times* (30 November 1985), p. 31; and Brian Berry, "National Puts Its 'Detroit' Strategy in Gear," *Iron Age* (July 1988), pp. 25–30.

60. See "Great Lakes Gets a Vacuum De-gasser," *Insight* (Winter 1989), pp. 14–15.

61. "NKK Corp.," *Wall Street Journal* (2 November 1990), p. B2.

62. American safety manager, National Steel Great Lakes Works site visit and personal interview by Richard Florida (August 1991).

63. Personal interviews with Japanese executives of National Steel by Richard Florida (September 1991).

64. As quoted in Berry, "National Puts Its 'Detroit' Strategy in Gear."

65. Japanese executives, Kawasaki Steel, personal interview by Richard Florida (November 1991); "Kawasaki, Armco Overhauling Eastern Division Facility," *American Metal Market* (4 December 1988), p. 5; Norman Samways, "Armco/Kawasaki Partnership: A New World Class Competitor," *Iron and Steel Engineer* (July 1989), pp. 44–45; W. A. Tony, "Armco, Kawasaki Launch Joint Venture," *Iron and Steel Maker* (July 1989), pp. 33–34

66. "Pomp, Optimism Launch Armco LP," *Middletown Journal* (18 May 1989); also Hogan, *Gobal Steel in the 1990s,* p. 18.

67. Norman Samways, "Revival and Survival of California Steel," *Iron and Steel Engineer* (reprint available from California Steel, June 1986).

68. Robert Englebert,"USX and Kobe Announce Joint Venture to Operate Lorain Works," *Iron and Steel Engineer* (September 1989), p. 52; and T. McAloon, "USS/Kobe Now Operating," *Iron and Steel Maker* (July 1989), p. 35.

69. Japan Economic Institute, *Japan-U.S. Business Report,* no. 261 (June 1991), p. 5.

70. Japanese and American managers, USS-Kobe, personal interview by Richard Florida and Akio Kida (December 1990).

71. Human resources manager, major American integrated steel mill, personal interview by Richard Florida and Akio Kida (October 1990).

72. Former executive, major American steel mill, personal interview by Richard Florida (November 1990).

73. Ibid.

74. See Michael Burawoy, *Manufacturing Consent* (Chicago: University of Chicago Press, 1979), and "Between the Labor Process and the State: The Changing Face of Factory Regimes Under Advanced Capitalism," *American Sociological Review,* 48, (1983), pp. 587–605.

75. See "Guaranteed Salaries Key to LTV's Pact," *American Metal Market* (29 January 1985), p. 2.

76. LSE managers, personal interview by Richard Florida (November 1990).

77. The forgoing discussion draws upon interviews with LSE officials, union representatives and workers, and "LS Electro-Galvanizing Company History" (December 1989), made available by LS Electro-Galvanizing.

78. American vice president, LTV Steel Company (April 1990); Union official, United Steelworkers of America (July 1990), personal interview by Richard Florida.

79. Japanese and American executives and managers, I/N Tek, personal interviews by Richard Florida (November 1990).

80. American executive, I/N Tek, personal interview by Richard Florida (November 1990).

81. Japanese and American executives, Wheeling-Nisshin, personal interview by Richard Florida and Akio Kida (September-October 1990).

82. "Agreement Between Wheeling-Nisshin Corporation and the United Steelworkers of America" (1 January 1990).

83. American human resource executive, Wheeling-Nisshin Steel Co., personal interview by Richard Florida and Akio Kida (September 1990).

84. American manager, I/N Tek, personal interview by Richard Florida (November 1990).

85. Japanese and American executives (August-September 1991), and United Steelworkers (July 1990, August 1991), personal interview by Richard Florida.

86. This was reinforced in a personal communication between Howell and Richard Florida (April 1990); quote is from Berry, "National Steel Puts Its 'Detroit' Strategy in Gear."

87. Japanese and American executives (August-September 1991), International Union officials, United Steelworkers (July 1990), personal interviews by Richard Florida.

88. Steel industry analyst, personal communication with Richard Florida (March 1991).

89. International union official, United Steelworkers, presentation to the Steel Market Roundtable Conference, Pittsburgh (March 1991).

90. Human resource manager, I/N Tek, (November 1990), personal interview by Richard Florida.

91. Local union official, Japanese-American steel venture, personal interview by Richard Florida and Akio Kida (November 1990).

92. See "Japanese Companies in the U.S. Are Laying Off Workers One After Another," (translated) *Nihon Keizai Shimburn* (24 February 1991), p. 6. "Armco Steel to cut salaried workers in cost cutting move under new chief," *Wall Street Journal* (23 September 1992).

93. Personal interview by Richard Florida and Akio Kida (December 1990).

94. American manager, Wheeling-Nisshin, personal interview by Richard Florida and Akio Kida (September 1990).

95. Ibid.

96. Ibid.

97. Union official, Japanese-American steel venture, personal interview by Richard Florida and Akio Kida (November 1990).

98. American executive, I/N Tek, personal interview by Richard Florida (November 1990).

99. Clare Ansberry, "USX Union Local May Extend Pact Even if Talks End," *Wall Street Journal* (10 January 1991), p. A2.

100. American human resource manager, I/N Tek, personal interview by Richard Florida (November 1990).

101. Ibid.

102. American human resource manager, Wheeling Nisshin, personal interview by Richard Florida and Akio Kida (September 1990).

103. I/N Tek executive, personal interview by Richard Florida (November 1990).

104. Personal interview by Richard Florida and Akio Kida (December 1990).

105. Ibid.

106. American executive, I/N Tek, personal interview by Richard Florida (November 1990).

107. American operations manager, I/N Tek, personal interview by Richard Florida (November 1990).

108. Japanese executive, I/N Tek, personal interview by Richard Florida (November 1990).

109. Personal interview by Richard Florida and Akio Kida (November 1990).

110. Ibid.

111. Steelworker, U.S.-Japanese joint venture, personal interview by Richard Florida (November 1990).

112. Union official, Japanese-American steel venture, personal interview by Richard Florida and Akio Kida (December 1990).

113. Ibid.

114. "National, NKK Eye Processing Venture in Detroit," *American Metal Market* (23 December 1986), pp. 1–16; "National Steel, Marubeni to Build Steel Plant Near Detroit," *American Metal Market* (11 May 1987), pp. 2, 16; "National, Marubeni Open Slit Steel Unit," *American Metal Market* (31 October 1987), pp. 2, 16; "National, Marubeni Open Slit Steel Unit," *American Metal Market* (31 October 1988), pp. 2, 10; "National Steel and Marubeni Open Processing Center," *Iron and Steel Engineer* (June 1989), p. 56.

115. For more detailed information see "Sumitomo Steel Center to Target Automakers," *American Metal Market* (4 July 1988), pp. 1, 7; "Sumitomo to Build Tenn. Steel Center," *American Metal Market* (12 February 1987), pp. 1, 8. "Memphis-Funded Steel Center Fought," *American Metal Market* (7 March 1984), pp. 2, 9; "Nissho-Iwai Acquires Berwick Steel, Sheet Supplier for Autos, Appliances," *Japan Economic Journal* (21 May 1985),p.11."Joint Venture Sets U.S. Service Center," *American Metal Market* (18 May 1989), p. 1; "Japanese Trading Firm to Put Two Steel Centers on Line in U.S. During May," *American Metal Market* (3 April 1990), p. 4.

116. Mail survey responses, by authors (1988).

117. "National Steel and Marubeni Open Processing Center," *Iron and Steel Engineer* (June 1989), p. 56.

118. "Mitsubishi Picks Illinois as Service Center Site," *American Metal Market* (11 March 1987), pp. 1, 8.

119. "Armco, C. Itoh Select Processing Plant Site" (17 October 1985), p. 4; "Armco, Itoh Centers Link Draws Anger, Resignation," *American Metal Market* (28 June 1985), pp. 1, 16.

120. "C. Itoh to Help Fund $60M Armco Mill," *American Metal Market* (22 December 1987), p. 2.

121. See Wendy Patton and Ann Markusen, "The Development Potential of Distributive Services: A Case Study of Steel Service Centers" (New Brunswick, NJ: Rutgers University, Center for Urban Policy Research, Working Paper No. 18, 1990).

122. Our discussion of TYK is drawn from a site visit and personal interviews with Japanese and American executives, by Richard Florida and Akio Kida (October 1990).

123. See *Refractories: The Hidden Industry* (Pittsburgh: Refractories Institute (no date), p. 12. We would like to thank David Orr of TYK for making this source available to us.

124. TYK official, personal interview by Richard Florida and Akio Kida (October 1990).

125. Japan Economic Institute, *U.S.-Japan Business Report* (November 1991): 7.

126. Personal interview by Richard Florida (November 1990).

127. "Usinor of France, Sumitomo of Japan Consider Bids for Stake in LTV Steel" (16 November 1990), p. A3.

128. *Metal Center News* (October 1989), p. 95.

129. "Stelco Forms Joint Venture with Mitsubishi for Steel Coating Plant," *Wall Street Journal* (21 May 1990).

130. "Mitsui Signed to Revamp Mexican Hot-Rolling Mill," *American Metal Market* (8 February 1990).

131. I/N Tek officials, personal interviews by Richard Florida (November 1990).

132. American executive, I/N Tek, personal interview by Richard Florida (November 1990).

133. Ibid.

Chapter 7

1. Both quotes from Jonathan P. Hicks, "Bridgestone's New U.S. Challenge," *New York Times* (22 February 1988), pp. D1, D4.

2. For a discussion of recent trends in the rubber and tire industry see Diether Plenhe,

"Change and Concentration in the World Rubber Industry" (International Federation of Chemical, Energy and General Workers Union, Brussels, Belgium, 1991). On Bridgestone, see especially "Can Bridgestone Make the Climb?," *Business Week* (27 February 1989), pp. 78–99; "Why Bridgestone's Chairman is Making Tracks to Akron," *Business Week* (20 November 1989), pp. 32–33; S. Wagstyl, "International Expansion Send Out Shock Waves," *Financial Times* (15 December 1988), p. 2; *Modern Tire Dealer* (March 1989).

3. See *Forest Industries* (April 1989), p. 58.

4. *Modern Tire Dealer* (December 1986, March 1989).

5. G. Radford, "How Sumitomo Transformed Dunlop Tyres," *Long Range Planning* 22, 3 (1989), pp. 28–33.

6. K. Zagor, "U.S. Seen as Key to Global Market," *Financial Times* (15 December 1988), p. 3; J. Griffiths, "Reaping the Rewards of Overseas Acquisitions," *Financial Times* (15 December 1988), p. 6; *Modern Tire Dealer* (June 1987, January 1989).

7. Robert Fernandez, "Mohawk Rubber Sale Due." *Akron Beacon Journal* (14 July 1989), pp. A1, A4.

8. Terence Roth, "Uneasy Time for Germany's Continental," *Wall Street Journal* (December 7, 1990) p. A9F.

9. "Michelin: The High Cost of Being a Big Wheel," *Business Week* (5 November 1990) p. 66.

10. Major sections of the following discussion on management-labor relations in the tire industry have been adapted from Michael Matzko's paper "An Overview of Changes in the Tire Industry" (Piitsburgh, PA: Carnegie Mellon University, School of Urban and Public Affairs, unpublished masters paper, May 1990). Also see Michael French, *The U.S. Tire Industry: A History* (Boston: Twayne Publishers, 1991).

11. Personal interview by Richard Florida (September 1991).

12. American executives of Bridgestone-Firestone and United Rubber Workers officials, personal interviews by Richard Florida (summer 1991). Also see Zachary Schiller, "Firestone Peels Out of Tires," *Business Week* (2 February 1988), p. 29.

13. Personal interview by Richard Florida (September 1991).

14. United Rubber Workers union, personal interview by Richard Florida (summer 1991).

15. Ironically, Firestone's strategy of avoiding the union recreated the very problems that characterized its traditional frostbelt plants. Management continuously tried to break the union, creating a vicious cycle of labor-management conflict and declining productivity. Bridgestone-Firestone executives and United Rubber Workers officials, personal interviews by Richard Florida (summer 1991).

16. Management and union officials, personal interviews by Richard Florida (summer 1991).

17. Martin Tolchin and Susan Tolchin, *Buying Into America: How Foreign Money Is Changing the Face of Our Nation* (New York: Times Books, 1988), pp. 82–83.

18. Thomas A. Mahoney, "From American to Japanese Management: The Conversion of a Tire Plant" (Nashville, TN: Owen Graduate School of Management, Vanderbilt University, 1988, Working paper No. 88–14), p. 7.

19. On the transition of the LaVergne plant see Mahoney, "From American to Japanese Management; also see Greg LaBar, "Employee Involvement Yields Improved Safety Record" *Occupational Hazards* (May 1989), pp. 11–14; and Kazuo Ishikure, "Achieving Japanese Productivity and Quality Levels at a U.S. Plant" *Long Range Planning* 21 (October 1988), p. 10.

20. See Mahoney, "From American to Japanese Management" (1988).

21. According to Tolchin and Tolchin, a number of traditional managers were unable to adapt to this new environment and were downgraded to supervisor. Some of them responded by quitting. See Tolchin and Tolchin, *Buying into America*, pp. 81–93. It is interesting to note that the Tolchins' book, which is generally critical of foreign investment in the United States, sees the Bridgestone investment in Firestone as overwhelmingly positive.

22. Larry Pierce as quoted in Jonathan P. Hicks, "Bridgestone's New U.S. Challenge," *New York Times* (28 February 1988), pp. pp. D1,4.

23. Mahoney, "From American to Japanese Management," 1988, pp. 11–12.

24. American executives, Bridgestone-Firestone, Inc., personal interviews by Richard Florida (September 1991).

25. Ishikure, "Achieving Japanese Productivity and Quality Levels at a U.S. Plant," *Long Range Planning* 21 (October 1988), p. 10.

26. See Mahoney, "From American to Japanese Management" (1988).

27. Our discussion of the Bridgestone Warren plant is drawn from personal interviews with Bridgestone-Firestone executives and United Rubber Workers officials, by Richard Florida (summer 1991).

28. Bridgestone-Firestone human resources executive, personal interview by Richard Florida (September 1991).

29. United Rubber Workers, Organizational Director, personal interview by Richard Florida (August 1991).

30. United Rubber Workers officials, personal interview by Richard Florida (summer 1991).

31. *Modern Tire Dealer* (November 1987).

32. G. Radford, "How Sumitomo Transformed Dunlop Tyres," *Long Range Planning* 22 (June 1989), p. 28.

33. Personal communication, United Rubber Workers Research Department, to Richard Florida (December 1991).

34. United Rubber Workers officials, personal interviews by Richard Florida (August 1991).

35. *Modern Tire Dealer* (August 1989).

36. Former Firestone labor relations manager, personal communication with Richard Florida (December 1991). See Charles Jeszeck, "Structural Change in CB: The U.S. Tire Industry, *Industrial Relations* 25, no. 3 (Fall 1986), pp. 229–47; and Jeszeck, *Plant Dispersion and Collective Bargaining in the Rubber and Tire Industry.* (Unpublished Ph.D. dissertation, University of California, Berkeley, 1982).

37. "Shift to Radials Forces Firestone to Close 6 Plants," *New York Times* (20 March 1980), pp. A1, D16.

38. Data are from U.S. Census of Manufacturers (various years).

39. Jeszeck "Structural Change in CB"; "Slow Growth in Tire Sales Forces Consolidation among Suppliers," *Automotive Marketing* (November 1988).

40. Richard Goe and James Shanahan, "Akron, Ohio: Deindustrialization and the Restructuring of the Rubber Capital of the World," in Richard Bingham and Randall Eberts (eds.). *Restructuring the Great Lakes Economy* (Boston: Kluwer, 1990).

41. American Human Resource officials, Bridgestone-Firestone, personal interview by Richard Florida (summer 1991).

42. Ibid.

43. Roger Schreffler, "Tire Tracks to America: Japan's Tiremakers Build a Beachhead," *Automotive Industries* (January 1988), pp. 3–4. This proximity appears to be more related to chance than to planning.

44. "Can Bridgestone Make the Climb?," *Business Week* (27 February 1989), p. 78.

45. Thomas O'Boyle, "Bridgestone Discovers Purchase of U.S. Firm Creates Big Problems," *Wall Street Journal* (1 April 1991), pp. A1, A6.

46. Rich Harris, "Tire Making Is Dying Out in Akron," *San Francisco Chronicle* (5 July 1991), pp. B1, B3.

47. "Bridgestone Plans to Lay-off 425," *New York Times* (12 March 1991).

48. Masayoshi Kanabayashi, "Bridgestone Plans Capital Infusion for U.S. Operation," *Wall Street Journal* (17 May 1991), p. A12.

49. Personal communication with American plant manager, AP Technoglass (January 30, 1991). On the general issue of the internationalization of Asahi Glass, see Kihisa Mushakoji, "The Process of Internationalization at Asahi Glass Co.," *International Management* (March 1986), pp. 73–80.

50. AP Technoglass, personal interviews by authors (1988).

51. *Japan Times* (1989), p. 9

52. "Ford and Japanese Maker of Glass Form $100 Million Venture," *Wall Street Journal,* (9 November 1989), p. A8.

53. "Chemical Venture Is Formed with Japanese Firm's Unit," *Wall Street Journal* (19 October 1988), p. B4.

54. "BF Goodrich Completes Sale of Elastomers Business," BF Goodrich public relations news release (12 October 1989).

55. Toyota officials, personal interviews by Richard Florida and the Ritsumeikan University Automotive Research Group (August 1990).

56. "Smyrna Selects the TKS Paint System," *Automotive News* (25 December 1989), p. 12.

57. Stephen Plumb, "Toyota Knifes New U.S. Niche," *Ward's Auto World* (November 1990), p. 65.

58. Marsha Freeman, personal communication with Richard Florida.

59. "Milacron, Last Big Heavy Robots Maker in U.S. to Sell Line to Asea Brown Unit," *Wall Street Journal* (13 September 1990), p. A3; "How U.S. Robots Lost the Market to Japan in Factory Automation," *Wall Street Journal* (6 November 1990).

60. Interestingly, Nippon Sanso is the same corporation that is the center of a controversy regarding its offer to buy a semiconductor gas supplier, Semi-Gas.

61. See "Kajima to Undertake Construction of Mitsubishi-Chrysler Plant," *Japan Economic Journal* (21 December 1985), p. 13.

62. Hiroshi Yanagi and Kurt Hamlin, SIA Building and Construction Unit, personal interview by Richard Florida (November 1990), Kajima Corp, *Annual Report, 1990.*

63. Japan Economic Institute, *Japan-U.S. Business Report,* no. 261 (June 1991), p. 3.

64. See Kazushi Imamura, "The Japanese Industrial Construction Industry" (Pittsburgh PA: Carnegie Mellon University, School of Urban and Public Affairs, unpublished master's paper, May 1991).

65. U.S. General Accounting Office, *Foreign Investment: Growing Japanese Presence in the U.S. Auto Industry* (Washington DC: GAO, March 1988).

66. U.S. General Accounting Office, *Foreign Investment: Japanese-Affiliated Automakers' 1989 U.S. Production's Impact on Jobs* (Washington DC: GAO, October 1990).

67. UAW, "Transplants and Job Loss: The UAW Response to the General Accounting Office," *UAW Research Bulletin* (May 1988).

68. "Japanese Carmakers Are Coddling Their U.S. Kids," *Business Week,* (4 March 1991), p. 21.

69. These conclusions are in line with recent studies of foreign direct investment, which conclude that foreign manufacturing investment has overall positive effects on domestic employment. Norman Glickman and Douglas Woodward, *The New Competitors* (New

York: Basic Books, 1989); and Edward Graham and Paul Krugman, *Foreign Direct Investment in the United States* (Washington DC: Institute for International Economics, 1989).

70. The most widely cited is William Baumol, Sue Anne Batey Blackman, and Edward N. Wolff, *Productivity and American leadership: The Long View* (Cambridge, MA: MIT Press, 1989). These studies are summarized in a host of newspaper and journal reports; see, for example, Sylvia Nasar, "American Revival in Manufacturing Seen in U.S. Report," *New York Times* (5 February 1991), p. 1; William Schmidt, "Midwest's Heartbeat Still Heard in Steady Hum of Factories," *New York Times* (8 October 1990), p. 1.

71. Jacqueline Mitchell and Neal Templin, "Nissan Will Buy More Parts Made in U.S.", *Wall Street Journal* (8 November 1991). See also Lindsay Chappell, "Fuji Considering Plan for U.S. Engine Plant," *Automotive News* (13 November 1989), p. 2; and Louise Kertesz, "Diamond-Star Execs Consider Engine Plant for 1992–1994," *Automotive News* (31 July 1989), p. 10.

72. *UAW Research Bulletin* (November 1989).

73. American and Japanese officials, transplant assembler, personal interviews by Richard Florida (November 1990).

74. John Blair and Robert Premus, "Major Factors in Industrial Location: A Review," *Economic Development Quarterly* 1, no. 1 (1987), pp. 72–85.

75. See Gordon Clark, "The Employment Relation and the Spatial Division of Labor," *Annals of the Association of American Geographers* 71 (1981), pp. 412–24; Robert Cohen, "The New International Division of Labor, Multinational Corporations and Urban Hierarchy," in Michael Dear and Allen J. Scott (eds.). *Urbanization and Urban Planning in Capitalist Societies* (New York: Methuen, 1981), pp. 287–315; Doreen Massey, *Spatial Divisions of Labor* (London: Macmillan, 1984); Michael Storper and Richard Walker, "The Spatial Division of Labor: Labor and the Location of Industries," in Larry Sawers and William Tabb (eds.). *Sunbelt/Snowbelt: Urban Development and Regional Restructuring* (New York: Oxford University Press, 1984), pp. 19–47; and especially Folker Froebel, Jurgen Heinrichs, and Otto Kreye, *The New International Division of Labor.* (New York: Cambridge University Press, 1980).

76. Site visit by Martin Kenney (November 1988).

77. See Michael Storper and Richard Walker, *The Capitalist Imperative* (London: Basil Blackwell, 1989).

78. See Richard Florida and Martin Kenney, "Transplanted Organizations: The Transfer of Japanese Industrial Organization to the United States," *American Sociological Review,* 65 (June 1991), pp. 381–98.

79. Site visit by Richard Florida and the Ritsumeikan University Automotive Research Group (July 1990).

80. Material in this section is drawn from a site visit to Battle Creek and personal interviews with James F. Hettinger, president and CEO, Battle Creek Unlimited, Battle Creek, Michigan; and corporate officials from Nippondenso, Koyo Metals, Technical Auto Parts by Richard Florida and Akio Kida (October 1990). Also see a case study of Battle Creek Unlimited in Lyke Thomson, "The Politics of Economic Development: A Qualitative Case Study," *Economic Development Review* (Summer 1984), pp. 62–68; Urban Lehner, "Welcome Invasion: Battle Creek, Mich., Owes a Big Debt to Japan, A Big Local Employer," *Wall Street Journal* (10 May 1985), pp. 1, 16; and Janet Braunstein, "Battle Creek's Big Catch," *Detroit Free Press* (9 October 1989), pp. 1, 6.

81. We thank Richard McCluskey of Pennsylvania State University for suggesting this.

82. Personal interview by Richard Florida and Akio Kida (October 1990).

83. James Hettinger, personal interview by Richard Florida and Akio Kida (October 1990).

84. Ibid.

85. Johnson Controls managers, personal interviews by Richard Florida and the Ritsumeikan University Automotive Research Group (August 1990).

86. Larry Hagood, Johnson Controls, personal interview by Richard Florida and the Ritsumeikan University Automotive Research Group (August 1990).

87. Personal communication with Donna Grinstead of the Ohio Department of Development (May 1988) and American officials of Armco Steel (September 1990) by Richard Florida.

88. Good summaries of this debate can be found in Glickman and Wodward, *The New Competitors.* For an update see John Cranford, "Restricting Foreign Investment: Easy to Debate, Hard to Do," *Congressional Quarterly* (31 March 1990), pp. 976–77." Ronald Elving," "Trade Mood Turns Hawkish as Frustration Builds," *Congressional Quarterly* (31 March 1990), pp. 963–71; "The Outlook for U.S.-Japan Trade Relations: An Interview with S. Linn Williams of the USTR," *JEI Report* no. 1A (11 January 1991).

89. For a compelling account of this process in one sector, machine tools, see Max Holland, *When the Machine Stopped* (Boston: Harvard Business School Press, 1989).

90. Richard Florida and Martin Kenney, *The Breakthrough Illusion: Corporate America's Failure to Move from Innovation to Mass Production* (New York: Basic Books, 1990).

91. Personal interviews by Richard Florida (1989–91).

92. Personal interview by Richard Florida and Akio Kida (October 1990).

Chapter 8

1. Japanese staff human resource consultant, major semiconductor transplant, personal interview by Martin Kenney (May 1991).

2. U.S. Department of Commerce, International Trade Administration, *Japanese Direct Investment in U.S. Manufacturing* (Washington, DC: U.S. Government Printing Office, October 1990), pp.15–17.

3. James Abegglen and George Stalk, *Kaisha: The Japanese Corporation* (New York: Basic Books, 1985), pp. 251–53. For a discussion of the anti-dumping debates in the period from 1971 to 1978, see Gene Gregory, *Japanese Electronics Technology: Enterprise and Innovation* (Tokyo: The Japan Times Ltd., 1986), pp. 157–67.

4. Japan Economic Institute, *Japan-U.S. Business Report,* no. 257 (February 1991):3.

5. "National to Sell Puyallup Plant to Matsushita for $86 Million," *Electronic News,* (26 November 1990), p. 4.

6. "Why National Came to the Fairchild Fire Sale," *Business Week* (14 September 1987), pp. 38, 39.

7. Rick Whiting, "Materials Research Gets a New Lease on Life," *Electronic Business* (4 February 1991), pp. 34–36.

8. *Japan Electronics Almanac 1990* (Tokyo: Dempa Publications, 1990), p. 46.

9. Tessa Morris-Suzuki, *Beyond Computopia: Information, Automation and Democracy in Japan* (London: Kegan Paul International, 1988).

10. Dr. Hideo Takahashi, general manager, R&D Planning and Technical Relations, Fujitsu Laboratories Ltd., personal interview by Martin Kenney (June 1986).

11. University of Tokyo, *Local Production of Japanese Automobile and Electronics Firms in the United States* (Tokyo: Institute of Social Science, Research Report No. 23, 1990), p. 103.

12. Japanese president, major consumer electronics transplant, personal interview by Martin Kenney (April 1991).

13. American director of personnel relations, major computer transplant, personal interview by Martin Kenney (November 1990).

14. American director of administration, major computer transplant, personal interview by Martin Kenney (May 1991).

15. Japanese executive vice president of manufacturing, major computer transplant, personal interview by Martin Kenney (November 1990).

16. American director of personnel relations, major Japanese electronics corporation, personal interview by Martin Kenney (November 1990).

17. Thomas Buell, "Life on the Line at Sony," *Pittsburgh Press* (29 April 1990), p. D17.

18. Japanese executive vice president of manufacturing, major computer transplant, personal interview by Martin Kenney (November 1990).

19. As quoted in "Sanyo Manufacturing Corporation—Forrest City, Arkansas," *Harvard Business School Case* no. 9-n682–045 (1981), pp. 9, 10.

20. Ibid.

21. Ibid., pp. 7–9.

22. For more in-depth discussion see J. Ernest Beazley, "In Spite of Mystique, Japanese Plants in U.S. Find Problems Abound," *Wall Street Journal* (22 June 1988), p. A14.

23. For more in-depth discussion of Sanyo's experience in Arkansas see ibid., p. A1, A14; "At Sanyo's Arkansas Plant the Magic Isn't Working," *Business Week* (14 July 1988), pp. 51, 52. For statistics on Sanyo's activities in San Diego and Tijuana see Lisa Thomas, "Japan's Next Wave Is Made of Small and Medium Size Firms," *San Diego Business Journal* (10 September 1990), pp. 20, 21.

24. University of Tokyo, *Local Production of Japanese Automobile and Electronics Firms in the United States* (Tokyo: Institute of Social Science Research Report No. 23, 1990).

25. As quoted in JETRO, *How Japanese Manufacturers Are Coping in the United States* (New York: JETRO, 1990).

26. Executive vice president of manufacturing, major computer transplant, personal interview by Martin Kenney (November 1990).

27. Japanese director of executive support office, major semiconductor transplant, personal interview by Martin Kenney (January 1991).

28. Japanese staff human resources consultant, major semiconductor transplant, personal interview by Martin Kenney (May 1991).

29. Japanese department manager, major semiconductor transplant, personal interview by Martin Kenney (May 1991).

30. Japanese staff human resources consultant, major semiconductor transplant, personal interview by Martin Kenney (May 1991).

31. This was true in two plants we visited that were run by the same major computer firm.

32. U.S. team leader, major computer transplant, personal interview by Martin Kenney (November 1990).

33. Japanese president, major Japanese electronics transplant, personal interview by Martin Kenney (May 1991).

34. Ibid.

35. American staff human resources consultant, major semiconductor transplant, personal interview by Martin Kenney (May 1991).

36. Senior director, president's office, major Japanese electronics firm, personal interview by Martin Kenney (May 1991).

37. American senior director in manufacturing operations of a major Japanese electronics firm, personal interview by Martin Kenney (May 1991).

38. Japanese senior director, major computer transplant, personal interview by Martin Kenney (May 1991).

39. Japanese executive vice president of manufacturing, major computer transplant, personal interview by Martin Kenney (November 1990).

40. Author's observations during plant tour.

41. Japanese director of general affairs, major Japanese electronics transplant, personal interview by Martin Kenney (December 1990).

42. Japanese manager of manufacturing engineering, a major computer transplant, personal interview by Martin Kenney (November 1990).

43. For this understanding we are indebted to a staff human resources consultant at a major microelectronics transplant. Personal interview by Martin Kenney (May 6, 1991).

44. American assistant plant manager, a Japanese semiconductor equipment supplier, personal interview by Martin Kenney (January 1991).

45. As quoted in, JETRO, *How Japanese Manufacturers are Coping in the United States.*

46. For a general discussion of this phenomenon see Richard Florida and Martin Kenney, *The Breakthrough Illusion* (New York: Basic Books, 1990).

47. Various interviews with Japanese managers.

48. University of Tokyo, *Local Production of Japanese Automobile and Electronics Firms in the United States,* p. 131.

49. Steven Miller, director of manufacturing, Richardson, Texas manufacturing facility, Fujitsu, Ltd., personal communication with Richard Florida (April 1991).

50. Japanese president, major semiconductor transplant, personal interview by Martin Kenney (January 1991).

51. Production manager, major semiconductor transplant, personal interview by Martin Kenney (May 1991).

52. However, a recent JETRO report quoted a Japanese electronics parts manufacturer who underscored the problem with this strategy: "We have instituted the system of annually hiring ten to fifteen graduates of the engineering departments of leading universities and sending them to Japan for two years for further training. The problem, of course, is that because of the American job-hopping tradition and the great demand for high-tech engineers, some quit after completing this two-year training program in Japan." JETRO, *How Japanese Manufacturers Are Coping in the United States.*

53. Director of community relations, major computer transplant, personal interview by Martin Kenney (November 1991).

54. For NEC's philosophy of linking computers and communications see Koji Kobayashi, *Rising to the Challenge* (Tokyo: Harcourt Brace Jovanovich, Japan, 1989).

55. William Coates, former Westinghouse executive, personal interview by Richard Florida (June 1991).

56. American plant manager and executive vice president, major Japanese computer transplant, personal interview by Martin Kenney (January 1991).

57. American vice president of human resources, major computer transplant, personal interview by Martin Kenney (June 1990).

58. Japanese president, major consumer electronics transplant, personal interview by Martin Kenney (April 1991).

59. American director of sites and facilities planning, major computer transplant, personal interview by Martin Kenney (June 1990).

60. Japanese director of general affairs, major computer transplant, personal interviews by Martin Kenney (December 1990, February 1991).

61. U.S. manager, public relations, large Japanese computer transplant, telephone inter-

view by Martin Kenney (March 1990); Japanese director of general affairs, large Japanese computer transplant, personal interviews by Martin Kenney (December 1990, March 1991).

62. Japanese president, major consumer electronics transplant, personal interview by Martin Kenney (April 1991).

63. American executive vice president for administration, major consumer electronics transplant, personal interview by Martin Kenney (April 1991).

64. Japanese president, major consumer electronics transplant, personal interview by Martin Kenney (April 1991).

65. Japanese manager of international procurement, major semiconductor transplant, personal interview by Martin Kenney (March 1991).

66. Former American executive of Matheson Gas, personal interview by Richard Florida (August 1991).

67. Japan Economic Institute, *Japan-U.S. Business Report,* no. 255 (December 1990), p. 6.

68. Japanese president, major consumer electronics transplant, personal interview by Martin Kenney (April 1991).

69. As quoted in, JETRO, *How Japanese Manufacturers are Coping in the United States.*

70. As quoted in, "Sanyo Manufacturing Corporation—Forrest City, Arkansas," pp. 5, 6.

71. Japanese telecommunications manufacturer in the western United States, as quoted in JETRO *CITEC Newsletter* 6, no. 2 (September 1989):1.

72. Japanese director and manager of procurement operations, major computer transplant, personal interview by Martin Kenney (January 1991).

73. Japanese president, major semiconductor transplant, personal interview by Martin Kenney (January 1991).

74. For a general discussion of the growth of the electronics industry in the Pacific Northwest, see Dwight Davis, "Electronics Community Flourishes in the Northwest," *Electronic Business* (October 29, 1990), pp. 51–56.

75. In addition to these Japanese investments, Wacker Chemie of Germany purchased Siltronics, an Oregon-based manufacturer of silicon wafers.

76. "Sharp to Make Video Screens in U.S.," *San Francisco Chronicle* (22 February 1991), pp. C1, C3.

77. This effort is similar to that undertaken by Battle Creek a few years earlier. See Chapter 7.

78. "The unitary method is a means for determining the in-state income of a group of interdependent multicorporate businesses [that operate across state and national boundaries]. The net income of the unitary group of corporations is apportioned using wages, property and sales factors. This is considered a good proxy for the income to be reasonably associated with that portion of the unitary business carried on in the state." Cited from State of Oregon, Legislative Revenue Office, "The Unitary Method of Corporate Taxation," Research report No. 2–84 (3 February 1984). The idea behind the unitary tax is to ensure that large multistate corporations do not shift their tax burdens to states or locales with lower tax rates, thereby shortchanging the state in which they do business. For a discussion of the impacts of the unitary tax system on the Mitsubishi Electric Company's decision to go to North Carolina rather than Oregon, see Plantek, Inc., *The Impact of Oregon's Unitary System of Taxation on the Ability to Attract Domestic and International Corporate Investment* (February 1984).

79. A consulting firm prepared a report supporting the repeal of the unitary tax. See Plantek, "The Unitary Tax: An Analysis of the Unitary Tax and its Impact on Jobs, Revenues

and Corporate Investments." Prepared for The Industrial Development Research Council, Atlanta (15 July 1984).

80. Randolph Miller (co-chair, Unitary Tax Committee), "Testimony before the [State of Oregon] House Revenue Committee (25 July 1984), pp. 3, 4.

81. Mark Clemons, business development manager, Portland Development Commission, personal interview by Martin Kenney (January 1991).

82. Jack McConnell, associate vice president, Norris, Beggs and Simpson (a major industrial properties broker), personal interview by Martin Kenney (January 1991). Our discussion of Japanese investment in Portland, Oregon, also benefits from helpful comments by Gil Latz and Wallace Bain, International Trade Institute, Portland State University.

83. Mike Tharp, "Once Insular Oregon Opening Its Arms to Japanese Investors," *Wall Street Journal* (21 July 1987), p. 31.

84. For a broader discussion of Japanese *maquiladoras* in Mexico, see Martin Kenney and Richard Florida, *Japanese Maquiladoras* (Report to the U.S. Congress, Office of Technology Assessment, Washington, D.C., March 1992); Gabriel Szekely (ed.), *Manufacturing Across Borders and Oceans,* (San Diego: Center for Mexican Studies, University of California, San Diego, 1991); Elsie Echeverri-Carroll, *Maquilas: Economic Impacts and Foreign Investment Opportunities: Japanese Maquilas—A Special Case* (Austin: Bureau of Business Research, Graduate School of Business, The University of Texas, 1988).

85. Name withheld by request, Hitachi Electronics Co., Tijuana, California; telephone conversation with Martin Kenney (6 March 1991).

86. Alexander Besher, "New 'Hong Kong' Springing Up South of the Border," *San Francisco Chronicle* (18 January 1988), p. C6.

87. "Fujitsu America at a Glance," (San Jose: Fujitsu America, Inc., 1989).

88. Steven Miller, director of manufacturing, Richardson, Texas manufacturing facility, Fujitsu Ltd., personal communication with Richard Florida (April 1991).

89. *Canon Today 1990/1991* (Lake Success, NY: Canon USA, Inc., 1991).

90. The same general pattern is evident in Europe. See Barbara Berkman, "Japanese Chip Firms Beef Up Design and Research in Europe," *Electronic Business* (17 September 1990), pp. 79, 80.

91. Japan Economic Institute, *U.S.-Japan Business Report,* no. 255, (December 1990), p. 5.

92. See Chapter 3 for discussions of the numerous investments in small U.S. high technology electronics firms in regions such as Silicon Valley and increasing Japanese funding of university research in electronics in the United States.

93. Wataru Noguchi, "NEC's Scenario for Basic Research," *Trigger* (November 1989) (translated from the Japanese).

94. Japan Economic Institute, *Japan-U.S. Business Report,* no. 261 (June 1991), p. 3.

95. Japan Economic Institute, *Japan-U.S. Business Report,* no. 256 (January 1991), p. 6.

96. Japan Economic Institute, *Japan-U.S. Business Report,* no. 258, (March 1991), p. 8.

97. Gina Kolata, "Japanese Computer Labs in U.S. Are Luring America's Top Experts," *New York Times* (11 November 1990).

98. "Venture Economics," *Corporate Venturing News,* 4, no. 7 (4 May 1990). Also see Ray Wise, "Aggressive Japanese Venture Capital Worries Silicon Valley," *Electronic Business* (11 June 1990), pp. 57, 58.

99. See Bruce Rayner, "Japan's Rustbelt Dollars Feed U.S. High-Tech Firms," *Electronic Business* (10 June 1989), pp. 63–65.

100. "Oracle to Get Infusion from Nippon Steel," *Wall Street Journal* (4 June 1991).

101. Alden Hayashi, "Putting Japanese Venture Capital to Work in America," *Electronic Business* (1 July 1988), pp. 69–70.

102. "Venture Economics," *Trends in Venture Capital Activity 1989,* chap. 3, "International Venture Capital Activity" (Wellesley Hills, MA: Venture Economics Inc., 1989), pp. 25, 26.

103. Japan Economic Institute, *Japan-U.S. Business Report,* no. 261 (June 1991), p. 7.

104. Bruce Rayner and Linda Stallman, "In the Throes of Change: Europe's Top Companies," *Electronic Business Asia* (January 1991), p. 69.

105. Berkman, "Japanese Chip Firms Beef Up Design and Research in Europe."

106. The preponderance of available material on Japanese investment in Europe comes from the United Kingdom, which has also received the greatest investment. Thus, for the purposes of this section we will confine our analysis to the U.K. However, it is important to note that the Japanese electronics industry is also rapidly establishing manufacturing facilities in other European countries. As in the case of the United States, the siting decisions for different categories of products came at differing historical moments, and in the late 1980s accelerated with the coming unification of the Common Market in 1992.

107. Nick Oliver and Barry Wilkinson, *The Japanization of British Industry* (London: Basil Blackwell, 1988), pp. 127–30.

108. Malcolm Trevor, *Toshiba's New British Company* (London: Policy Studies Institute, 1988).

109. Oliver and Wilkinson, *The Japanization of British Industry,* p. 123.

110. Makoto Takamiya, "Conclusions and Policy Implications," in Susumu Takamiya and Keith Thurley (eds.), *Japan's Emerging Multinationals* (Tokyo: University of Tokyo Press, 1985), p. 189.

111. Ibid., p. 191.

112. Trevor, *Toshiba's New British Company,* p. 146.

113. Ibid. pp. 153–156.

114. These two suppliers have also located plants in Southern California.

115. John Dunning, *Japanese Participation in British Industry* (London: Croom Helm, 1986), pp. 107–14. See also the short discussion in Oliver and Wilkinson, *The Japanization of British Industry,* pp. 130–132.

116. Oliver and Wilkinson, *The Japanization of British Industry,* pp. 131.

117. John Eckhouse, "How U.S. Could Learn from Europe," *San Francisco Chronicle* (13 November 1991), pp. C1, C6.

Chapter 9

1. "Americanism and Fordism," in Quintin Hoare and Geoffrey Nowell Smith (eds. and Trans.), *Selections from the Prison Notebooks of Antonio Gramsci* (New York: International Publishers, 1971), p. 285.

2. Data are from the Japanese Ministry of Labor and JETRO as cited in *The Economist* (21 December 1991), p. 38.

3. See Shinji Sakuma and Hideaki Ohmori, "The Auto Industry," chap. 2 in *Karoshi: When the Corporate Warrior Dies,* National Defense Council for Victims of Karoshi (Tokyo: Mado-sha Publishers, 1990).

4. See *Karoshi: When the Corporate Warrioer Dies.* National Defense Council for Victims of Karoshi. (Tokyo: Mado-sha Publishers, 1990).

5. Ibid., p. 8.

6. Personal interview by Richard Florida, Terje Gronning, and Akio Kida (August 1990).

7. Personal interviews by authors and the Ritsumeikan University Automotive Research Group (1990–1991).

8. See "Workers at Risk," *Detroit Free Press* (7 July 1990), pp. 1A, 6A–7A. Also see Joseph and Suzy Fucini, *Working for the Japanese: Inside Mazda's American Auto Plant* (New York: Free Press, 1990); John Junkerman, "Nissan, Tennessee: It Ain't What It's Cracked Up to Be," *The Progressive* (June 1987); "The UAW vs. Japan: It's Showdown Time in Tennessee," *Business Week* (24 July 1989), pp. 64, 65; Louise Kertesz, "Injury, Training Woes Hit New Mazda Plant," *Automotive News* (13 February 1989), pp. 1, 52.

9. Personal interview with former Mazda worker (August 1990) by Richard Florida, Terje Gronning, and Akio Kida.

10. Both statistics as reported in "The UAW vs. Japan: It's Showdown Time in Tennessee," p. 65.

11. As quoted in Peter Applebome, "Union and Nissan Near a Showdown," *New York Times* (27 April 1989).

12. According to an American executive at Nissan: "We were fined $5,000. We have appealed that fine; we still haven't paid it. The issue is still before an administrative tribunal and until we are told by that tribunal that we must turn over those logs, until a subpoena is issued for them, we will not turn them over. We see it as a breech of our employees' confidentiality." Personal interview by Richard Florida and the Ritsumeikan University Automotive Research Group (August 1990). See also "The UAW vs. Japan: It's Showdown Time in Tennessee," p. 65.

13. Personal interview by Richard Florida, Terje Gronning, and Akio Kida (August 1990).

14. He continued: "There is no rotation, because there is no place to rotate them to. There's only one sole job and that's to mask bumpers." Personal interview by Richard Florida and Akio Kida (November 1990).

15. See especially Mike Parker and Jane Slaughter, "Management by Stress, *Technology Review* (October 1988):36–46.

16. Personal interview by Richard Florida and Akio Kida (November 1990).

17. Personal interview by Richard Florida, Terje Gronning, and Akio Kida (August 1990).

18. As summarized in Mike Parker, "New Mazda Contract Eases 'Management-by-Stress' System," *Labor Notes* (May 1991), p. 5.

19. Personal interview (August 1990).

20. Personal interview by Richard Florida, Terje Gronning, and Akio Kida (August 1990).

21. Richard Edwards, *Contested Terrain* (New York: Basic Books, 1979).

22. Michael Burawoy, *Manufacturing Consent: Changes in the Labor Process under Monopoly Capitalism* (Chicago: University of Chicago Press, 1979).

23. Ronald Dore, *British Factory-Japanese Factory: The Origins of Diversity in Industrial Relations* (Berkeley: University of California Press, 1973).

24. Haruo Shimada, "Japanese Industrial Relations: A New Model?" in Taishiro Shirai (ed.), *Contemporary Industrial Relations In Japan* (Madison: University of Wisconsin Press, 1983), pp. 3–27; and Kazuo Koike, *Understanding Industrial Relations in Japan* (New York: St. Martin's Press, 1988).

25. Gramsci, "American and Fordism," p. 310.

26. We are indebted to Akio Kida and Katsuji Tsuji of Ritsumeikan University for their discussions of the concept of voluntarism.

27. Andrew Gordon, *The Evolution of Labor Relations in Japan: Heavy Industry, 1853–1955* (Cambridge, MA: Council on East Asian Studies, Harvard University, 1985).

28. For an insightful discussion of this indoctrination process see Thomas Rohlen, *For Harmony and Strength: Japanese White-Collar Organization in Anthropological Perspective* (Berkeley: University of California Press, 1974).

29. See, for example, Michel Foucault, *Discipline and Punishment: The Birth of the Prison* (New York: Vintage Books, 1979).

30. Personal communications with Katsuji Tsuji and Akio Kida (1990–91).

31. See Albert Hirschman, *Exit, Voice and Loyalty* (Cambridge, MA: Harvard University Press, 1970).

32. The seminal formulation is, of course, Harry Braverman, *Labor and Monopoly Capital* (New York: Monthly Review Press, 1974); David Noble, *Forces of Production* (New York: Knopf, 1984); William Lazonick, *Competitive Advantage on the Shop Floor* (Cambridge, MA: Harvard University Press, 1990).

33. See, in Mike Parker and Jane Slaughter, *Choosing Sides: Unions and the Team Concept*, chap. 8, "Work Rules and Classifications: The Balance of Power" (Detroit: Labor Notes, 1988), pp. 74–87.

34. John Hoerr, *And the Wolf Finally Came* (Pittsburgh: University of Pittsburgh Press, 1988), pp. 300–301.

35. For a critical perspective on the recruitment process at Mazda, see "Mazda: Choosing Workers Who Fit," in Parker and Slaughter, *Choosing Sides: Unions and the Team Concept*, pp. 175–185.

36. Personal interview by Richard Florida, Terje Gronning, and Akio Kida (August 1990).

37. Philip Keeling, president, Mazda UAW Local 3000, personal interview by Ritsumeikan University Automotive Research Group (August 1990).

38. Personal interview by Richard Florida and the Ritsumeikan University Automotive Research Group (August 1990).

39. Personal interview by Jim Gordon, Shoko Tanaka, Katsuji Tsuji, and Katsuo Nakagawa (July 1990).

40. These signs were observed in site visits

41. Site visit and personal interviews with company officials by Richard Florida and Akio Kida (November 1990).

42. Philip Keeling, personal interview by the Ritsumeikan University Automotive Research Group (August 1990).

43. Personal interview by Richard Florida (November 1990).

44. Warm-up is rational and beneficial for any person participating in strenuous physical activity. Seeing the refusal to participate in such activities as a benefit seems irrational, at best.

45. Former Honda worker, personal interview by Richard Florida (July 1990).

46. Philip Keeling, personal interview by Ritsumeikan University Automotive Research Group (August 1990).

47. See "NUMMI: A Model of Management-by-Stress," in Parker and Slaughter, *Choosing Sides: Unions and the Team Concept* pp. 106, 107.

48. Toyota Motor Manufacturing USA, Inc., "Team Member Handbook" (February 1998, Edition I), pp. 59–66.

49. See Parker and Slaughter, *Choosing Sides: Unions and the Team Concept* pp. 106, 107.

50. See Timothy Dunne, "Mazda Execs Resign After 'No Fault' Vote," *Automotive News* (16 October 1989; Louis Kertesz and Dutch Mandel, "In Bind over Repairs, Mazda Concedes to Union," *Automotive News* (9 October 1989); John Lippert, "Mazda Exec Chides UAW," *Detroit Free Press* (8 October 1989).

51. "Toyota Team Member Handbook."

52. Eric Mann, "UAW Backs the Wrong Team" *The Nation* (19 February 1987), p. 172.

53. Philip Keeling, personal interview by Ritsumeikan University Automotive Research Group (August 1990). See Fucini and Fucini, *Working for the Japanese;* Paul Judge, "UAW Faces Test at Mazda," *New York Times* (27 March 1990), p. D8; "Mazda-UAW's Michigan Honeymoon Is Over," *Wall Street Journal* (17 April 1990); Jerry Flint, "Constant Improvement or Speedup?" *Forbes* (17 April 1989), pp 92–94.

54. Mazda temporary worker, as quoted in Paul Judge, "UAW Faces Test at Mazda Plant," *New York Times* (27 March 1990), p. D8.

55. "Japanese Companies Often Leave Their Lay-off Policies at Home," *Wall Street Journal* (29 January 1990), p. A1.

56. See "Japanese Companies in the U.S. Are Laying-Off Employees One After Another," *Nihon Keizai Shimbun* (24 February 1991), p. 6 (translated from the Japanese).

57. Robert Cole and Donald Deskins, "Racial Factors in Site Location and Employment Patterns of Japanese Automobile Firms in America," *California Management Review* 31, no. 1 (Fall 1988), pp. 9–23. For an important follow-on article see Robert Cole, "Reflections on Japanese Corporate Citizenship: Company Reactions to a Study of Hiring Practices in the United States," *Chuo Koron,* no. 10 (October 1989), pp. 122–35. See also Jacob Schlesinger, "Shift of Auto Plant to Rural Areas Cuts Hiring of Minorities," *Wall Street Journal* (12 April 1988), pp. A1, A28. For a discussion of Kawasaki Heavy Industries' minority problems see Judis, "Citizen Kawasaki." *The American Prospect* (Spring 1991), pp. 47–60.

58. See Cole and Deskins, "Racial Factors in Site Location and Employment Patterns of Japanese Automobile Firms in America."

59. Data are from *City and County Databook* (1983).

60. See George Embrey, "Honda to Pay Discrimination Penalties," *Columbus Dispatch* (24 March 1988), p. A1

61. Senior Japanese executive, transplant assembler, personal interview by Richard Florida and Akio Kida (November 1990).

62. Executive coordinator of human resources, Toyota Motor Manufacturing USA, personal interview by Richard Florida and the Ritsumeikan University Automotive Research Group (August 1990).

63. As quoted in Lindsay Chappell, "Toyota Praised for Minority Hiring at Kentucky Plant," *Automotive News* (2 April 1990), p. 3.

64. Former Honda worker, personal interview by Richard Florida (July 1990).

65. Former Honda worker, personal interview by Richard Florida (July 1990).

66. As quoted in Lindsay Chappell, "Toyota Praised for Minority Hiring at Kentucky Plant," *Automotive News* (2 April 1990), p. 3.

67. A more serious case of discrimination has been reported at a Yaohan Inc. supermarket in Fresno, California. See, for example, Yumi Iwai and Kimberly Simi, "Conflicts and Concerns in Servicing Minority Communities: A Case Study of Yaohan, a Japanese Multinational Supermarket," Japan Pacific Resource Network Working Paper No. 5 (25 February 1990).

68. American vice president, automotive assembly transplant, personal interview by Richard Florida and the Ritsumeikan University Automotive Research Group (August 1990).

69. "Honda Unit in Dispute Over Plant Organizing Is Charged by NLRB," *Wall Street Journal* (13 October 1980), p. 23; "UAW Wins in Dress-Code Tussle at Ohio Honda Plant," *Wall Street Journal* (5 November 1981), p. 3.

70. Marjorie Sorge, "Nissan Was Unfair, NLRB Says," *Automotive News* (12 April 1982), p. 55.

71. Site visits to and interview with Nissan officials by Richard Florida and the Ritsumeikan University Automotive Research Group (August 1990). Also see Jane Slaughter,

"Behind the UAW's Defeat at Nissan," *Labor Notes* (September 1989), p. 65. "The UAW;'s Chances at Japanese Plants Hinge on Nissan Vote," *Wall Street Journal* (25 July 1989), pp. A1, A2; Gelsanliter, *Jump Start,* pp. 109–21.

72. American executive, personal interview by Richard Florida and the Ritsumeikan University Automotive Research Group (August 1990).

73. "The UAW vs. Japan: It's Showdown Time in Tennessee," *Business Week* (24 July 1989), pp. 64, 65.

74. Ann Hagedorn and Wade Lambert, "Sony Faces Complaint About Union Vote," *Wall Street Journal* (17 August 1991), p. B12.

75. Malcolm Trevor, *Toshiba's New British Company: Competitiveness Through Innovation* (London: Basil Blackwell, 1988). See also Nick Oliver and Barry Wilkinson, *The Japanization of British Industry* (London: Basil Blackwell, 1988).

76. Philip Keeling, personal interview by Ritsumeikan University Automotive Research Group (August 1990).

77. Philip Keeling, personal interview by Ritsumeikan University Automotive Research Group (August 1990).

78. Mann "UAW Backs the Wrong Team," p. 174.

79. Philip Keeling, personal interview by the Ritsumeikan University Automotive Research Group (August 1990).

80. Vice president, human resources and administration, Nippondenso Manufacturing USA, Inc., personal interview by Richard Florida and Akio Kida (November 1990).

81. "How the Japanese Manage in the U.S.," *Fortune* (15 June 1981), p. 98.

82. Executive vice president, Honda of America Manufacturing, personal interview by authors (May 1988).

83. Personal interview by Katsuji Tsuji, James Gordon, and Shoko Tanaka (August 1990).

84. Here we refer to Japanese managers; however, it is important to note that their employment contract and their relationships are no different from those of the blue-collar workers on the shop floor. Thus, we are referring here to all permanent employees of the firm.

85. Name withheld by request, Japanese executive vice president for manufacturing at a transplant electronics production facility; personal interview by Martin Kenney (December 1990).

86. For a discussion of this see, Ikujiro Nonaka, "Toward Middle-Up-Down Management: Accelerating Information Creation," *Sloan Management Review* (Spring 1988), pp. 9–18.

87. For a discussion of this problem see Hiroshi Kashiwagi, "Employment Discrimination at Japanese Firms in America: A Case Study of EEOC Lawsuits," Japan Pacific Resource Network Working Paper No. 4 (no date).

88. "Culture Shock at Home: Working for a Foreign Boss," *Business Week,* (17 December 1990), p. 80.

89. Wade Lambert, "Sumitomo Sets Accord on Job Bias Lawsuit," *Wall Street Journal* (8 November 1990), p. B2.

90. The following discussion and quotations are based upon James Miller, "Matsushita Wins Ruling in Rights Case," *Wall Street Journal* (6 December 1991), pp. A3, A8.

91. Chie Nakane, *Japanese Society* (Berkeley: University of California Press, 1970), first made this argument. Though we do not accept the argument that these relationships are descended from Japanese feudalism, their importance in keeping labor controlled are clear. An interesting discussion of this point can also be found in Hiroshi Ishida, John Goldthorpe, and Robert Erikson, "Intergenerational Class Mobility in Postwar Japan," *American Journal of Sociology* 96 no. 4 (January 1991), pp. 954–92.

92. The classic citation with reference to U.S. attempts to create paternalistic capitalism

is James Weinstein, *The Liberal Ideal in the Corporate State* (Boston: Beacon Press, 1968).

93. For an interesting history and suggestive discussion of the evolution of technology see George Basalla, *The Evolution of Technology* (Cambridge: Cambridge University Press, 1988).

94. Gramsci, "Americanism and Fordism."

95. Even as Toyota is introducing these features into the United States it is in the process of moving its headquarters from Toyota City to Tokyo and has also set up an R&D facility in Tokyo. The NUMMI plant was the first Toyota facility outside the Toyota City area. The Georgetown plant was the second; the new plant in England was the third. As of this writing, Toyota is building assembly plants in Hokkaido and Kyushu in Japan.

96. This section is based both on an extended site visit to Georgetown, Kentucky, and its environs and personal interviews with Toyota officials, government and community leaders, and community residents, by Richard Florida and the Ritsumeikan University Automotive Research Group (August 1990).

97. Georgetown official, personal interview by Richard Florida and the Ritsumeikan University Automotive Research Group (August 1990).

98. Senior Japanese executive, automotive assembly transplant, personal interview by Ritsumeikan University Automotive Research Group (August 1990); translated by Atsushi and Yoshimi Chitose.

99. See Carole Davies and Jon Lowell, "Incentives Survive But Live Quiet Lives," *Ward's Auto World* (April 1990), pp. 39–49; Takeo Miyauchi, "The Man Who Lured Toyota to Kentucky," *Economic Eye* (March 1987), pp. 23–27; H. Brinton Milward and Heidi Newman, "State Incentive Packages and the Industrial Location Decision" (Lexington University of Kentucky, Center for Business and Economic Research Working Paper, 1987); Bill Stack, "Toyota in Bluegrass Country," *Industry Week* (5 June 1989), pp. 30–33.

100. Mark Clemons, Portland Development Commission, personal interview by Martin Kenney (January 1991).

101. Tom Prather, Mayor of Georgetown, Kentucky, personal interview by Richard Florida and the Ritsumeikan University Automotive Research Group (August 1990).

102. For a good overview see John Blair and Robert Premus, "Major Factors in Industrial Location: A Review," *Economic Development Quarterly* 1, no. 1 (1987), pp. 72–85.

103. See Bennett Harrison and Sandra Kanter, "The Political Economy of States' Job Creation Business Incentives," *Journal of the American Institute of Planners* 44 (1978), pp. 424–35.

104. As quoted in Davies and Lowell, "Incentives Survive But Live Quiet Lives," p. 43.

105. As quoted in Gelsanliter, *Jump Start,* p. 15.

106. American vice president, Nissan, personal interview by Richard Florida and the Ritsumeikan University Automotive Research Group (August 1990).

107. Mayor Tom Prather, personal interview by Richard Florida and the Ritsumeikan University Automotive Research Group (August 1990). See also "The Town that Toyota Took From 0 to 60," *Business Week* (11 July 1988), pp. 87, 88.

108. Mayor Tom Prather, personal interview by Richard Florida and the Ritsumeikan University Automotive Research Group (August 1990).

109. Name withheld, personal interview by Richard Florida and the Ritsumeikan University Automotive Research Group (August 1990).

110. Richard Child Hill, Michael Indergaard, and Kuniko Fujita, "Flat Rock, Home of Mazda: The Social Impact of a Japanese Company on an American Community." Paper presented at the Eighth Annual International Automotive Conference, University of Michigan, Ann Arbor (March 1988).

111. For a case study of electronics see Margaret Deane, "Sony Westmoreland: Indus-

trial Incentives and Economic Development" (Pittsburgh: Carnegie Mellon, School of Urban and Public Affairs, unpublished master's paper, January 1991).

112. The contradictory, or two-sided, nature of the Japanese model is also being debated in Japan. See, Hikari Nohara, "Reconsidering the Japanese Production System Model." Paper presented at the International Conference on Workplace Australia: Designing the Future, Melbourne, Australia: World Congress Centre (February 1991).

113. The rise of powerful fordist forms also helped to forge the modern industrial working class and to inform new, more powerful means for organizing and advancing workers' interests. Within the union movement, the mass-production unions such as the UAW and USW and the new CIO emerged to move workers' interests forward, while the AFL became a relic of the past. See David Montgomery, *The Fall of the House of Labor: The Workplace the State and Labor Activism, 1865–1925* (Cambridge: Cambridge University Press, 1987); Mike Davis, *Prisoners of the Dream* (London, Verso, 1986).

Chapter 10

1. Kenneth Courtis, as quoted in an interview published in *The JAMA Forum* 9, no. 1 (November 1990), pp. 18–23.

2. See Karl Marx, *Capital,* Vol. I (orig. 1867) (New York: Vintage Books, 1977); Marx, *Grundrisse: Introduction to the Critique of Political Economy* (orig. 1858) (New York: Vintage Books, 1973); Joseph Schumpeter, *Capitalism, Socialism and Democracy* (orig. 1942) (New York: Harper & Row, 1975); Schumpeter, "The Creative Response in Economic History," *The Journal of Economic History* 7, no. 2 (November 1947), pp. 149–159.

3. Harry Braverman, *Labor and Monopoly Capital* (New York: Monthly Review Press, 1974).

4. See Karl Marx (trans. by T. B. Bottomore), *Karl Marx: Early Writings* (New York: McGraw-Hill, 1964); Marx (trans. by Martin Nicolaus), *Grundrisse.* Also see William Lazonick, *Competitive Advantage on the Shop Floor* (Cambridge, MA: Harvard University Press, 1990).

5. Marx, *Capital,* Vol. 1.

6. This is a major advance over both the functional specialization of fordism and the model of flexible specialization advanced by Michael Piore and Charles Sabel. Simply put, the nature of the advance lies in the explicit recognition of the social nature of production, functional integration, and the role of intellectual labor. See Michael Piore and Charles Sabel, *The Second Industrial Divide* (New York: Basic Books, 1984).

7. See Michael Burawoy, *Manufacturing Consent* (Chicago: University of Chicago Press) or a myriad of other books. A very suggestive analysis in this direction that has not gotten the attention it deserves is Larry Hirschhorn, *Beyond Mechanization* (Cambridge: MIT Press, 1984). A more recent reflection upon this fact is Shoshona Zuboff, *In the Age of the New Machine* (New York: Basic Books, 1988). In a limited sense, Charles Sabel begins to grapple with this social aspect of production in his thought-provoking *Work and Politics* (Cambridge: Cambridge University Press, 1982). This insight is then lost in Piore and Sabel, *The Second Industrial Divide* as they focus on the small firm as a panacea, thus blurring the insight that it is the way production is organized that is important—a case of losing an understanding of the trees in the rush to create a mythical forest.

8. See Karl Marx and Friedrich Engels, *The Communist Manifesto* (New York: Washington Square Press, 1964); Gerald Cohen, *Marx's Theory of History* (Princeton, NJ: Princeton University Press, 1980).

9. See Georg Lukacs, *History and Class Consciousness* (Cambridge, MA: MIT Press, 1971). For a more contemporary exposition of this notion, which draws from rational choice

theory, see Adam Przeworski, *Capitalism and Social Democracy* (Cambridge: Cambridge University Press, 1985).

10. See, for example, Piore and Sabel, *The Second Industrial Divide;* Oliver Williamson, *Markets and Hierarchies* (New York: Free Press, 1975).

11. The classic formulation is Chie Nakane, *Japanese Society* (Berkeley: University of California Press, 1970).

12. Perhaps the classic articulation of the postmodern position is Jean-Francois Lyotard, *The Postmodern Condition* (Minneapolis: University of Minnesota Press, 1984). Also see Jacques Derrida, *Of Grammatology* (Baltimore: Johns Hopkins University Press, 1976); Jean Baudrillard, *Simulations* (New York: Semiotexte, 1983); *In the Shadow of Silent Majorities* (New York: Semiotexte, 1983). From a Marxist perspective, see Frederic Jameson, "Postmodernism, or the Cultural Logic of Late Capitalism," *New Left Review* 146 (1984), pp. 53–93; David Harvey, *The Condition of Postmodernity* (London: Basil Blackwell, 1989). An interesting overview of postmodern theory can be found in Douglas Kellner, "Postmodernism as Social Theory: Some Challenge and Problems," *Theory, Culture and Society,* 5, nos. 2, 3, (June 1988), pp. 239–70.

13. Antonio Gramsci, "Americanism and Fordism," in Quintin Hoare and Geoffrey Nowell Smith (eds. and trans.), *Selections from the Prison Notebooks* (New York: International Publishers, 1971), pp. 277–320.

14. See Marx and Engels, *The Communist Manifesto;* G Cohen, *Marx's Theory of History*

15. See Joseph Schumpeter, *The Theory of Economic Development* (New York: Oxford University Press, 1961); and *Capitalism, Socialism and Democracy.*

16. These theories are summarized in Chapter 1.

17. See Schumpeter, *Theory of Economic Development; Capitalism, Socialism and Democracy.*

18. See Schumpeter, "The Creative Response in Economic History."

19. Schumpeter, *Theory of Economic Development.*

20. Schumpeter, *Capitalism, Socialism and Democracy.*

21. In addition see Nathan Rosenberg, "Marx as a Student of Technology," in Nathan Rosenberg, *Inside the Black Box: Technology and Economics* (Cambridge: Cambridge University Press, 1982); W. Brian Arthur, "Competing Technologies, Increasing Returns, and Location by Historical Events," *Economic Journal* (March 1989), pp. 116–31; Arthur, "Self-Reinforcing Mechanisms in Economics," in P. W. Anderson and K. J. Arrow (eds.), *The Economy as a Complex Evolving System* (New York: Addison-Wesley, 1988), pp. 9–31; Arthur, "Urban Systems and Historical Path Dependence," in Jesse Ausubel and Robert Herman (eds.). *Cities and Their Vital Systems* (Washington, DC: Natural Academy Press, 1988), pp. 85–97.

22. Paul David, "CLIO and the Economics of QWERTY," *American Economic Review* 75 (1985), pp. 332–37; Paul David, "Path Dependence; Putting the Past Into the Future" (unpublished paper, Stanford University, 1988).

23. See, for example, George Basalla, *The Evolution of Technology* (Cambridge: Cambridge University Press, 1988); Joel Mokyr, "Punctuated Equilibria and Technological Progress," *American Economic Review,* 80, 2 (May 1989), pp. 350–54; Joel Mokyr, *The Levers of Riches: Technological Creativity and Economic Progress.* (New York: Oxford University Press, 1990); and Stephen Jay Gould, *The Panda's Thumb: More Reflections in Natural History* (New York: W.W. Norton 1980).

24. See Richard Nelson and Sidney Winter, *An Evolutionary Theory of Economic Change* (Cambridge, MA: Harvard University Press, 1982); Mancur Olson, *The Rise and Decline of Nations* (New Haven: Yale University Press, 1982).

25. See "Japan's GNP Jumps in 1991's First Quarter," *JEI Report,* no. 24B, (28 June 1991), pp. 1–4.

26. On long waves, see the discussion in Chapter 1.

27. Kenneth Courtis, as quoted in an interview published in *The JAMA Forum* 9, no. 1 (November 1990), pp. 18–23.

28. James Womack, Daniel Jones, and Daniel Roos *The Machine That Changed the World* (New York: Rawson Associates, 1990).

29. Personal interviews by Martin Kenney with R&D Planning Section managers in major Japanese corporations.

30. R&D planning section manager, major Japanese precision machinery company personal interview by Martin Kenney (July 1991).

31. See Jonathan Morris, "Japanese Manufacturing Investment in the European Economic Community: The Effects of Integration." Paper prepared for the EEC (no date). Also see the special issue of the *Industrial Relations Journal* on "The Japanization of British Industry," 19, no. 1 (Spring 1988).

32. The Battle for Europe," *Business Week* (3 June 1991), p. 45.

33. Findings of JETRO's annual "White Paper on Foreign Direct Investment," as summarized in JETRO, *CITEC Newsletter,* 8, no. 1 (June 1991), p. 1.

34. On Matsushita's U.K. supplier complex, see Jonathan Morris, "Japanese Inward Investment and the 'Importation' of Sub-contracting Complexes: Three Case Studies," University of Wales College, Cardiff, Cardiff Business School, no date.

35. The Matsushita-Bosch joint venture is described in some detail in Toshihiko Yamashita, *The Panasonic Way: From a Chief Executive's Desk* (Tokyo: Kodansha International, 1989), pp. 106–8.

36. Jack Gee, "Europe's Love-Hate Affair with Japan," *Electronic Business* (1 February 1987), pp. 52–55.

37. See Philip Jones and John North, "Japanese Motor Industry Transplants: The West European Dimension," unpublished paper, University of Hull, England, 1990; Jonathan Morris, Nick Oliver, and Barry Wilkinson, "The Implications of Toyota's Derbyshire Investment for Land Requirements." Report prepared for the Derby County Council (August 1989).

38. "A Japanese Beachhead in European High Tech?" *Business Week* (30 July 1990), p. 36; "Japan-EC Relations: More Ups and Downs," *JEI Report,* no. 41B (26 October 1990), pp. 6–7.

39. Barbara Berkman, "Japanese Chip Firms Beef Up Design and Research in Europe," *Electronic Business* (17 September 1990), pp. 79–80.

40. See Richard Florida and David Browdy, "The Invention That Got Away," *Technology Review* (August-September 1991), pp. 42–54; "Mixed Dumping Verdict on Flat Panel Displays," *JEI Reports,* no. 27B (19 July 1991), pp. 11, 12.

41. The following discussion is modified from Martin Kenney and Richard Florida, "Japan's Role in a Postfordist Age," *Futures* 21, no. 2 (1989), pp. 136–51.

42. See especially Samuel Bowles, David Gordon, and Thomas Weisskopf, "Power and Profits: The Social Structure of Accumulation and the Profitability of the Postwar U.S. Economy," *Review of Radical Political Economics,* 18, Nos. 1 and 2 (Spring and Summer 1986); Michele Naples, "The Unraveling of the Union-Capital Truce and the U.S. Productivity Crisis," *Review of Radical Political Economics,* 18, nos. 1, 2 (1986), pp. 110–31.

43. See, for example, Mike Davis, *Prisoners of the American Dream* (London: Verso, 1986); Stephen Marglin and Juliet Schor (eds.), *The Golden Age of Capitalism: Reinterpreting the Post-War Experience* (New York: Clarendon Press, 1990).

44. Yet surprisingly little has been written in English about this market and how it oper-

ates. Perhaps the best single source is George Shields, *Gucci on the Ginza* (Tokyo: Kodansha International, 1989). Also see Japan External Trade Research Organization, *The Japanese Consumer* (Tokyo: JETRO Marketing Cenes, 1991). For a discussion of the Japanese distribution system see United States International Trade Commission, "Phase I: Japan's Distribution System and Options for Improving U.S. Access," Publication No. 2291 (Washington, DC: U.S.I.T.C., 1990). Also see Martin Bronfenbrenner and Yasukichi Yasuba, "Economic Welfare," in Kozo Yamamura and Yasukichi Yasuba (eds.), *The Political Economy of Japan: Vol. 1. The Domestic Transformation* (Stanford, CA: Stanford University Press, 1987), pp. 93–136.

45. These data on Japanese consuption are adapted from Japan Institute of Social and Economic Affairs, *Japan 1991: An International Comparison* (Tokyo: Keizai Koho Center, 1990).

46. Nobuo Tanaka, "Expenditures on Home Information and Communications Equipment: supporting Brisk Consumption," *Long Term Credit Bank Research Review* (April 1991), pp. 14–15.

47. Ibid.

48. As reported in "Japan to Spend Trillions on Infrastructure," *Economic Development Abroad* 5, no. 1 (November 1990), pp. A1–A2. Also see Akinobu Terasaka, Yoshiki Wakabayashi, Itsuki Nakabayashi, and Kazutoshi Abe, "The Transformation of Regional Systems in an Information-oriented Society," *Geographical Review of Japan,* 61 (1988), pp. 159–71, which discusses a series of new corporate and state-led efforts to develop "new media," "teletopia" projects, and high-speed fiber optic transmission systems in Japan. Interestingly, the authors conclude that in contrast to the prevailing idea that such information infrastructure will bring about decentralization of industrial and commercial functions, the actual result has been further concentration of such activity in the Tokyo area.

49. See, for example, National Institute for Research Advancement (NIRA), *Comprehensive Study of Microelectronics* (Tokyo: NIRA, 1985); N. Gross, "Why Japan Wants Its Buildings to Be So Smart," *Business Week* (28 September 1987), p. 70. Also see M. Moritani, "Information Out of Formation," *Journal of Japanese Trade and Industry* 3 (1987), pp. 10–24; Tadahiko Moriguchi, "INS Services, Application and Impact on Local Administration." (Unpublished mimeo, Commercial Bureau, NTT, 1987).

50. On Japanese education, see Thomas Rohlen, "Why Japanese Education Works," *Harvard Business Review* (September-October 1987), pp. 42–47; Merry White, *The Japanese Educational Challenge: A Commitment to Children* (New York: Free Press, 1987); U.S. Department of Education, *Japanese Education Today* (Washington, DC: U.S. Government Printing Office, 1987).

51. U.S. Department of Education, *Japanese Education Today,* p. 13.

52. Establishing whether the high-quality labor force requires what Arndt Sorge and Wolfgang Streeck term "diversified quality production" for its reproduction or whether there has always been a latent demand for such products is difficult to answer definitively. In other words, did the demand drive the production system toward diversification as the neoclassical economists would argue? Or did the capabilities of the production system and advertising create the market? At this point, it probably is impossible adequately to answer this question. See Sorge and Streeck, "Industrial Relations and Technical Change: The Case for and Extended Perspective," in Richard Hyman and Wolfgang Streeck (eds.), *New Technology and Industrial Relations* (London: Basil Blackwell, 1988), pp. 19–47.

53. "The Rise and Rise of the Japanese Yuppie," *Business Week* (16 February 1987), p. 54.

54. Wakao Fujioka, "The Rise of the Micromasses," *Japan Echo* 13, no. 1, (1986), pp. 31–38.

55. "The New Generation," *Japan Update* (Spring 1986), pp. 6–10.

56. Amy Borrus, "How Sony Keeps Copycats Scampering," *Business Week* (1 June 1987), p. 69.

57. "A Big Bundle of Hot New Exports," *Business Week* (1 July 1991), pp. 40–42.

58. Jacob Schlesinger, "Japanese Get First Crack at New Gadgets as Firms Use Local Stores to Test Demand," *Wall Street Journal* (3 December 1990), pp. B1, B4.

59. While these consumption patterns bear some resemblance to tendencies in the United States, Japan has proceeded far further in this direction. Education, culture goods, and information creation provide a seemingly inexhaustible "space" for demand and employment growth. In Japan, this new "demand space" is discussed under the rubric of "softonomics," which encompasses more than traditional Western conceptions of the "information society." This, in effect, suggests both a partial solution to the shrinkage in employment that may characterize innovation-mediated production and a way to reproduce a new labor force of better educated workers, creating at least the potential for the parallel development of production and consumption. For further discussion see Japanese External Trade Organization, "Softonomics: The Service-Oriented Economy of Japan," *Now in Japan* 35, (1984), pp. 1–39.

60. Kenneth Courtis, "Interview: Strategic Challenge," *The JAMA Forum* 9, no. 1 (November 1990), pp. 18–23.

61. Daniel Bell, *The Coming of Post-Industrial Society* (New York: Basic Books, 1973).

Appendix A

1. Our strategy of employing multiple, complementary methodologies had an additional and very important benefit. Most, if not all, social science research methodologies are beset by weaknesses as well as strengths. As much as possible, we wanted to avoid, or at least temper, the biases and limits inherent in those various methodologies. Interviews and case studies, for example, provide rich detail and insight but are limited to only a few cases from which it is hard to generalize. Survey research provides information on a broader sample of the population but lacks the depth and flexibility of a detailed case study. Analysis of aggregate statistical data (e.g., data on the population of Japanese transplants) can provide a good picture of the broad contours of an issue but provides little real depth. Statistical analysis identifies certain over-arching patterns but can easily overlook, and at times even obfuscate, important underlying trends and deviations within those broader patterns. By using a combination of social science methodologies and data-collection strategies, we were able to minimize or at the very least to temper the biases inherent in any one method.

2. Here we followed the "total design method" of survey design. See Don Dillman, *Mail and Telephone Surveys: The Total Design Method,* (New York: John Wiley & Sons, 1978).

3. James Lincoln and Arne Kalleberg, "Work Organization and Workforce Commitment: A Study of Plants and Employment in the U.S. and Japan," *American Sociological Review* 50 (1985), pp. 738–60.

Index

393